THE BRITISH SCHOOL AT ATHENS

ΜΑΡΚΙΑΝΗ ΑΜΟΡΓΟΥ

MARKIANI, AMORGOS

ΜΑΡΚΙΑΝΗ ΑΜΟΡΓΟΥ

MARKIANI, AMORGOS

AN EARLY BRONZE AGE FORTIFIED SETTLEMENT

OVERVIEW OF THE 1985–1991 INVESTIGATIONS

by

LILA MARANGOU, COLIN RENFREW, CHRISTOS DOUMAS
AND GIORGOS GAVALAS

with contributions by

ANASTASIA ANGELOPOULOU, KIKI BIRTACHA,
PANTELIS ESKITZIOGLOU, EFI KARANTZALI, CHRIS SCARRE,
SARAH VAUGHAN AND TODD WHITELAW

with further contributions by

NEIL BRODIE, CHARLY FRENCH, RUPERT HOUSLEY, LILIAN KARALI-GIANAKOPOULOU,
STURT MANNING, CHRISTINE MORRIS, JANE M. RENFREW, KATERINA TRANTALIDOU
AND HELENI ANDREOPOULOU-MANGOU

SUPPLEMENTARY VOLUME NO. 40
Published by
THE BRITISH SCHOOL AT ATHENS

2006

Published and distributed by
The British School at Athens

Senate House, Malet Street,
London WC1E 7HU

Series Editor: Olga Krzyszkowska

ISBN 0 904887 52 9 / 978 0 904887 52 5

Designed and computer typeset by Rayna Andrew

Printed at Alden Press Limited,
Oxford and Northampton, Great Britain

Στόν Πάνο Renfrew

οι αμοργιανοί φίλοι του

Λίλα, Γιώργος, Σίμος

Contents

Contributors

Anastasia Angelopoulou
Agathoupoleos 38, Athens

Heleni Andreopoulou-Mangou
Chemical Laboratory, National Museum of Athens

Kiki Birtacha
Lesvou 37, Athens

Neil Brodie
Illicit Antiquities Research Centre, McDonald
Institute for Archaeological Research

Christos Doumas
Department of Archaeology, University of Athens

Pantelis Eskitzioglou
Arapaki 120, Athens

Charly French
Department of Archaeology, University of
Cambridge

Giorgos Gavalas
Troupaki 12–14, Athens

Rupert Housley
Department of Archaeology, University of Glasgow

Sturt Manning
Department of Archaeology, University of Reading

Lila Marangou
Department of Archaeology, University of Ioannina

Christine Morris
Trinity College, Dublin

Lilian Karali-Giannakopoulou
Department of Archaeology, University of
Athens

Efi Karantzali
14th Ephorate of Prehistoric and Classical
Antiquities, Lamia

Colin Renfrew
Department of Archaeology, University of
Cambridge

Jane M. Renfrew
Lucy Cavendish College, University of Cambridge

Chris Scarre
McDonald Institute for Archaeological Research,
University of Cambridge

Katerina Trantalidou
Ephorate of Spelaeology and Palaeoanthropology,
Athens

Sarah Vaughan
Institute of Theoretical Physics, University of
California, Santa Barbara

Todd Whitelaw
Institute of Archaeology, University College
London

List of Figures

List of Tables

List of Plates

Abbreviations

EB / EBA	Early Bronze / Early Bronze Age
EC	Early Cycladic
EH	Early Helladic
EM	Early Minoan
MBA	Middle Bronze Age
MC	Middle Cycladic
MH	Middle Helladic
LBA	Late Bronze Age
LH	Late Helladic
Δ	Sample number
EE	Special find catalogue number
K	pottery catalogue number
Ma	Markiani (phase I–IV)
O	Obsidian catalogue number
c.	circa
cm	centimetre
D.	diameter
d.	distal
g	gram
H.	height
ha	hectare
L.	length
max.	maximum
m	metre
p.	proximal
Th.	thickness
W.	width
Wt.	weight
NAM	National Archaeological Museum (Athens)
NM	Naxos Museum

Acknowledgements

The excavators wish first to thank the Greek Archaeological Service, and in particular Dr Ioannis Papachristodoulou, Ephor of the 22nd Ephorate for Prehistoric and Classical Antiquities for permission to work at Markiani. Our profound thanks go also to Mr Simos Giannakos and Mr Manolis Despotidis, representative *phylakes* of the Archaeological Service in Amorgos, for much valued co-operation and assistance during the entire course of the project and indeed over a much longer time period.

Secondly we owe a debt of gratitude for financial support to sponsoring institutions: the Department of Archaeology of the Faculty of Philosophy, of the University of Ioannina, the University of Athens, and the University of Cambridge and to the British Academy, the McDonald Institute for Archaeological Research, and the Ministry of the Aegean.

In addition we wish to thank the Managing Committee of the British School at Athens and Dr David Blackman, the then Director, for their encouragement, and the Editor of the British School monographs, Dr William Cavanagh, for his invitation to publish this account in a Supplementary Volume of the Annual. We also thank his successor, Dr Olga Krzyszkowska for seeing this volume to press (and for her helpful comments and additions on the seal, sealings and bone artefacts). We are grateful to Rayna Andrew for her skill in matters of production.

Third, we owe thanks to those who took part in the excavation and the study of the finds. In addition to the co-authors on the title page the following archaeologists participated in the excavations and site survey:

Surface survey 1985: Aris Blanas, Dimitris Kokkonis, Photini Kolovou, Angelos Palekidis, Peggy Pantou and Vasso Pappa.

Surface survey 1987: Maria Leventopoulou, Prokopis Michailidis, Lisa Nevett, Pavlos Triantafyllidis, Stavros Vlizos and Anna Zaouri.

Excavation 1988–1990: Robin Conigham, Lucy Elkin, Paula Geake, William Johnston, Nikos Kontogiannis, Hilary Meyrick, Tim Pestel, Kalliopi Photiadi, Alex Roberts, Panagiota Sotirakopoulou, Maria Zamanou and the late Anna Gregoriadou.

The workmen from Amorgos whose co-operation added greatly to the progress on the site were: Georgios D. Gavalas, Andreas Giannakos, Georgios Giannakos, Ioannis Giannakos, Ioannis Kovaios, Nektarios Markos Kovaios, Ioannis Oikonomidis, Ioannis Roussos, Simos Giannakos, Athanasios Theologitis, Ioannis Theologitis, Ioannis Zaranis and the late Markos Nomikos.

Special thanks are due to Christine Morris and Neil Brodie for their great help in the preparation of this work at an earlier stage and grateful acknowledgement is made to Alex Doumas for translating part of the text and to Katie Boyle for her help with the editing.

We are very grateful to the following for the illustrations for this report: Chris Scarre, Todd Whitelaw (FIGS. 2.1, 3.1–3.14, and 4.1), Michalis Chalkoutsakis for the topographical plan (FIG. 4.1), Clairi Palyvou for the general plan (FIGS. 4.2, 6.3 and 6.4), Giorgos Antoniou for the plan of the fortifications (FIGS. 6.1 and 6.2) and for the watercolour view of the site on the dust jacket, and Maria-Christina Georgali and Manolis Zacharioudakis for their drawings during the excavation and Jenny Doole for her help in the final stage.

The pottery and the small finds were drawn by Anna Cuss, Jo Lawson, Bruce Tukey and Jenny Doole.

The photographs are by Ioannis Despotidis and the principal excavators.

Chapter 1

Introduction

Markiani is an EBA settlement site on the Cycladic island of Amorgos. As noted below, Amorgos has an important place in the history of research into the EC period by virtue of the early researches undertaken into the EC cemeteries of the island by Dümmler[1] and by Tsountas.[2] Since that time, however, there have been no systematic, public excavations of EC cemeteries in Amorgos, although there have been numerous stray or accidental finds and an undocumented number of illicit excavations by *archaiokapiloi*.[3]

The discovery in 1985 by Professor Lila Marangou of a substantial EC settlement within the Notina region, the lands overlooking the southern coast of Amorgos, as recounted in Chapter 2, therefore offered the possibility of casting new light upon this important period. Her invitation, following a joint site visit in 1986, to Christos Doumas and Colin Renfrew formed the first step towards the institution of the Joint University Research Project on Amorgos and Keros, with the participation of the Universities of Ioannina, Athens and Cambridge.

The project undertook fieldwork at Markiani from 1987 to 1989, with study seasons in 1990 and 1991.[4] It also undertook excavation and survey at Dhaskalio–Kavos on Keros in the years 1987 and 1988, and these will be reported in detail elsewhere.

The excavation work on the site took place on a relatively small scale, directed towards the elucidation of a number of preliminary questions. In particular, we sought to establish a secure relative chronology, as well as the general nature of both the settlement and its occupation, and of the finds which it yielded. It was hoped that radiocarbon dating would permit the establishment of a secure absolute chronology (see Chapter 5), so that the place of Amorgos within the cultures of the EBA Cyclades could be more securely established.

The purpose of the present work is to present the principal results of the Markiani project, including an account of the excavations and a systematic review of the pottery recovered, and of the other finds. The survey project directed by Todd Whitelaw is discussed here in brief in Chapter 3; we hope that the full account of his systematic work will be presented in detail elsewhere. It should be noted that not all the pottery recovered has been studied in detail, although it has been possible to offer a representative sample, which should form the basis for later studies of the EBA of Amorgos. Scope remains for further study, notably of the pottery recovered from Trench 3.

It should be noted that many of the individual contributions here were written by 1993 and have subsequently been revised by the editors.

The intention here is to give a clear account of the pottery recovered from each of the four phases, which we were able to define for the site, and to offer some account of the principal fabrics. An account of the various categories of small finds can also be provided.

[1] Dümmler 1876.
[2] Tsountas 1898.
[3] Marangou 1990, 164, nn. 22–23 and 32a–35, with the earlier bibliography.

[4] Catling 1987, 32; 1988, 28; 1989, 23; French 1980, 19. See also French 1990, 60; Pariente 1992, 930; Renfrew 1991, 44, 45, 96; Davis 1992, 752–3.

Chapter 2

The discovery of the settlement and
the investigations in 1985

Lila Marangou

The prehistoric settlement at Markiani (FIG. 2.1) was discovered during the course of the systematic investigation of the ancient sites and remains of Amorgos,[1] begun in the 1970s.[2] Between 1972 and 1982, a substantial body of material was collected from 18 newly-discovered EC sites in the framework of surface exploration of sites of the historical period. Since 1983, in parallel with the excavation of the ancient Greek city of Minoa,[3] this survey work has continued, yielding further information on the island's prehistory and leading to the identification of other EC sites.[4]

In 1985, while searching for an ancient Greek inscription[5] reported in the nineteenth century at a place interestingly known as 'Sta Grammata',[6] Mr Markos N. Mendrinos, who was at that time living all year round in a farmstead (*katoikia*)[7] at Stavros, led us to the southernmost terraces of a rocky hill. There, as we ascertained, the rock surface was covered with incisions — carvings of various periods.[8]

Although we know that the cemetery sites of Notina and Stavros, excavated by Dümmler[9] and Tsountas[10] respectively, existed hereabouts, we have been unable to determine their precise location. Research at the Archaeological Society at Athens and the National Archaeological Museum in Athens, in the hope of finding Tsountas's excavation notebooks, which would surely contain information about the location, landowners and so on, proved fruitless.

However, there are local accounts of *vresimata* (the dialect term for fortuitous finds, usually of coins but also of other objects potentially profitable to the finder) in this part of Amorgos, as well as an oral tradition about the 'Angelina's Battle', a dispute over a piece of land near Markiani and Stavros, between locals and 'foreign robbers' — obviously illicit diggers (*archaiokapeloi*) — which no doubt reflects an incident that took place just after the Second World War. These probably allude to the chance discovery of grave goods and to deliberate looting in the area. Certainly *tsoukalikia* (pot sherds), *kouklakia* (marble figurines) and some *broutzina* (bronze artefacts) have turned up in the course of cultivation over the years. According to reliable sources, two bronze daggers known in the N. P. Goulandris Foundation Museum of Cycladic Art,[11] originate from graves at Stavros.

As we made our way through the thick, thorny vegetation on the abandoned terraces, in our search for 'Sta Grammata', we observed a few EC sherds and obsidian fragments. Mendrinos, bemused by our interest in the *paliokatakola* (worthless sherds), offered to take us to a small tract of land near the sheepfolds of Nikolaos Synodinos known as Sintas, on the nearby hilltop, variously known as

---

[1] Marangou 1995, 195–8 (with earlier bibliography); 2002.

[2] Marangou 1983, 121; 1990, 159–76; 1994, 467–88; 1996, 307–32; 1999, 20–9.

[3] Preliminary reports by Lila Marangou of the excavations conducted at Minoa have thus far been published in *Ergon* in successive years from 1981–2001 and in *PAE* (1981–99): excavations are still in progress; see also Marangou 1990, 159, n. 1; 2002, 10 n. 36, 15 figs. 18–20, 16 figs. 21–2.

[4] Marangou 1984, 99ff; 2002.

[5] Weil 1876, 333; Bent 1884, 44; Meliarakes 1928, 51, n. 1; Delamarre 1908, 281.

[6] Meliarakes 1928, 51, "πέραν τοῦ Βαλσαμίτου πρὸς τὴν Ἀρκεσίνην, ἀφοῦ διέλθη τὶς τὴν θέσιν 'Στὸν Σταυρὸ', ὑπάρχει θέσις καλουμένη 'Στὰ Γράμματα' διότι ἐπὶ βράχου τινὸς εἶναι κεχαραγμένα γράμματα ἀρχαϊκὰ σημαίνοντα «Ὅρον», ὧν σῆμα καὶ ἐξήγησιν ἐδημοσίευσεν ο Weil : 'Beyond Varsamitis and after the place called "Sto Stavro", there is a place called "Sta

Grammata" because incised on the rock are archaic letters signifying the boundary (*horos*), the shape and meaning of which were published by Weil'. This probably marks the border between the territory (*chora*) of Minoa and of Arkesine. Weil 1876, 333; Delamarre 1908, 281. The inscription was located in 1988, northeast of Markiani.

[7] Marangou 1994, 469, n. 13; see also below.

[8] Ships, spirals etc., of indeterminate date, as yet unpublished.

[9] Dümmler 1886, 15f, Notina. This gives the first map of EC sites on Amorgos (Beil. 1) and was not superseded until 1983 (see also Marangou 1984, fig. 1). Tsountas 1898, 133, note 1; Marangou 1994; Marangou 2001.

[10] Tsountas 1898, 139 '... isolated graves have been located ... five or six at the site called Stavros'. Ibid. 153–4, pls 12.5 and 12.6 (grave 12).

[11] Doumas 1984, cat. nos. 196–197; Doumas 2000, cat. nos. 350–351.

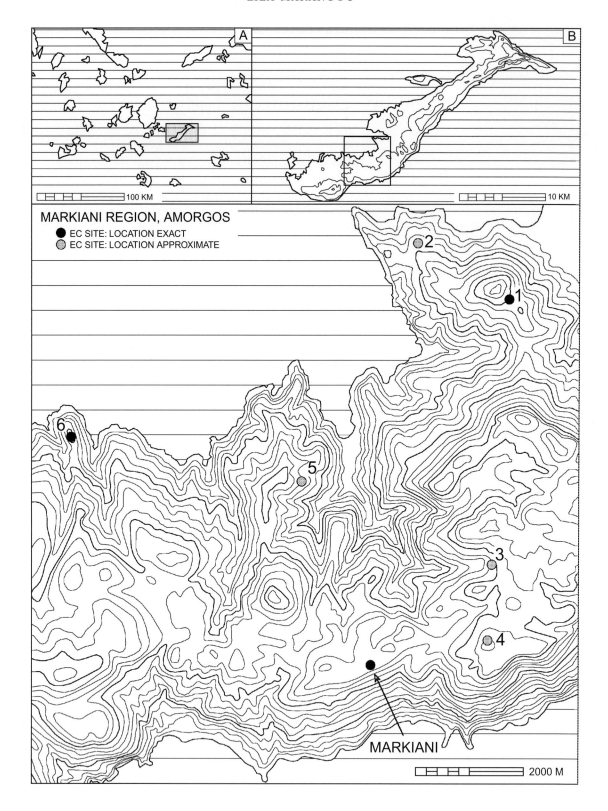

FIG. 2.1. The location of Markiani with prehistoric sites on Amorgos (1 = Minoa, 2 = Kato Akrotiri, 3 = Stavros, 4 = Notina, 5 = Dhokathismata, 6 = Arkesine).

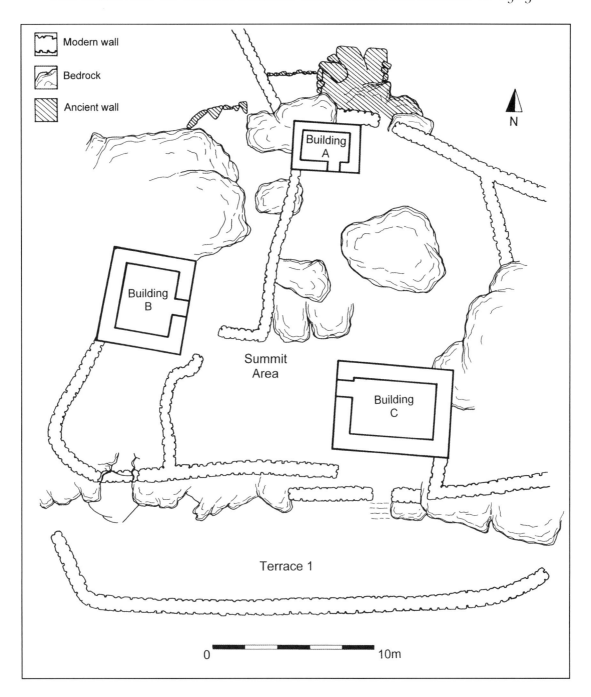

FIG. 2.2. Sketch of the summit area at Markiani showing location of the modern Buildings A, B, and C and modern dry-stone walls of the animal pen.

Martsanadhes or *Markianadhes* or *Markiani*,[12] which he assured us was full of large '*katakola*' (pot sherds) and ancient stones. This was indeed the case and even, on first impression, it was clear that this was an EC settlement site.

The hill of Markiani (FIG. 2.2, PLATE 1 *a–b*) is clearly visible from the road linking Chora, the island's capital, with the villages of Kato Meria, about 1500 m south-west of the chapel of Stavros (the

---

[12] The site name does not appear in Meliarakes' list of toponyms (Meliarakes 1928, 93–6; Vogiatzides 1918, 85–105). The *Hellenodidaskalos*, Emmanuel Ioannides, a native of Amorgos and Headmaster of the Secondary School there, notes in his manuscripts, now in the Archaeological Society at Athens 'Μαρκιανή, παρόδιον χωρίον' 'Markiani, a roadside village' (Marangou 1985, 253; Marangou 1999, 10ff; Marangou 2002, 10, 15, 16 figs. 18–22).

Holy Cross). It rises to a height of 265 m above sea level, on the south coast of 'Notina' (i.e. the southern part of the island), where steep cliffs plunge into the open sea.

The main cultivated land at Markiani is on the lower terraces of the southern slopes, which are sheltered from the north wind and arranged as a series of terraces (FIG. 4.1, PLATES 1 *b* and 2) forming narrow strips of land with dry-stone retaining walls, interspersed with expanses of bare rock and dense scrub. Up until the 1990s many of these flat terraces formed fertile fields which were farmed on a seasonal basis: the first of them (FIG. 2.2, PLATE 3 *a*) is known popularly as *skonovolos* and produced excellent onions. The southern slopes are not exposed to the strong northerly winds and are visible only from the sea. The terraces, supported by dry-stone walling (PLATE 3 *b*), are narrow strips of land, interspersed by expanses of bare rock and dense vegetation. Many of these flat terraces are still exploited today as small arable fields.

On the summit of the hill stands a small, one-roomed house (Building A) (see FIG. 2.2 and PLATES 2 and 8 *a*), now abandoned — but still adequate as a shelter for the needs of our excavation team — along with two roofed stables for livestock (Buildings B and C) (see PLATES 2 and 7 *a*). All three structures are of dry-stone masonry, incorporating ancient material (*spolia*), and are founded either directly on the uneven bedrock (Building A and the west end of Building B) or upon the remains of earlier buildings (the east part of Building C).

Terrace 1,[13] i.e. *skonovolos* is approximately 40 m long and 7.50–8 m wide (FIG. 2.3, PLATE 3 *a*), and lies below the flattish rock of the summit, on which stand Buildings A and B. The terrace is separated from the summit by a rocky escarpment, above and below which is a high dry-stone wall (*traphos*) (PLATE 3 *b*), founded on the bedrock and constructed not only of stones, some re-used, but also of pithos sherds and other large fragments of pots. This terrace is entered from the summit, through the *embassa* (PLATE 7 *a*), an opening in the upper retaining wall that leads down several rock-cut steps to the level surface of the soil. On our first visit evidence of prehistoric habitation was clearly visible — sherds, obsidian blades, fragments of querns and stone rubbers — in and amongst the modern débris — broken *stamnia, laenes* (clay water pitchers, *lagynoi* in ancient Greek) and *armeoi* (clay milking vessels), glass bottles and bits of plastic.

Closer examination of the surface material revealed spindle-whorls, sherds of bowls, clay vase handles with incised decoration, fragments of vase bases with mat impressions and an abundance of obsidian artefacts, all datable without hesitation to the EC period. Much of this material lay at the edges of the terrace, at the foot of the dry-stone walls. The discovery was reported to the 22nd Ephorate of Prehistoric and Classical Antiquities, and with their permission we returned to the site for further investigations.

It was only with the assistance of the Custodian of Antiquities, Mr Simos Giannakos, that we were able to negotiate our way down to the lowest terraces, with their wide sweep of arable land descending to the rocky shore. Here too there were numerous sherds comparable to those on the Terrace 1. And here too most of the material lay at the edges of the terraces, with the greatest concentration on the narrow upper ones, which are least suitable for cultivation.

In late August (24–26 and 30) 1985, surface survey and cleaning works were undertaken, focused mainly on Terrace 1, and specifically on the area at the foot of the rock escarpment with its dry-stone wall, which delimits the north side of the terrace and separates it from the summit.

Several cuttings were noted in this scarp, which were numbered from west to east, 1 to 4 (FIG. 2.3, PLATES 4 *a* and 5 *a*). Sherds were visible around the roots of the large bushes growing out of the clefts in the rocks that define the cuttings. Since we had no tools for clearing the vegetation, we concentrated on Rock Cutting 2 (PLATE 5 *a–b*), where most sherds could be seen.

Cleaning to a depth of 0.05–0.08 m was carried out in front of Rock Cuttings 2 and 3, and the surface material collected. This enabled us to confirm our initial impression that the sherds were indeed *in situ* and had not been deposited accidentally, brought with manure from elsewhere.

Specifically, after the removal of the loose top-soil mixed with dung and rotten leaves from the bushes, it was noted that the two sizeable slabs of schist visible on the surface in the north section were *in situ* and belonged to a built structure. South of Rock Cutting 2, more stones were uncovered *in situ,* part of a curvilinear construction, as well as a 'ceramic level' (PLATES 4 *a* and 5 *a*).

---

[13] To facilitate communication with our collaborators, from the very first visit to the site the terraces were numbered according to their natural sequence, starting from the highest (no. 1) and proceeding to the lowest (no. 14). The numbering of the 'units' of the surface survey in 1987 does not follow the same logic, and is arbitrary, for which reason Terrace 1 has Unit no. 218 (see Chapter 3A).

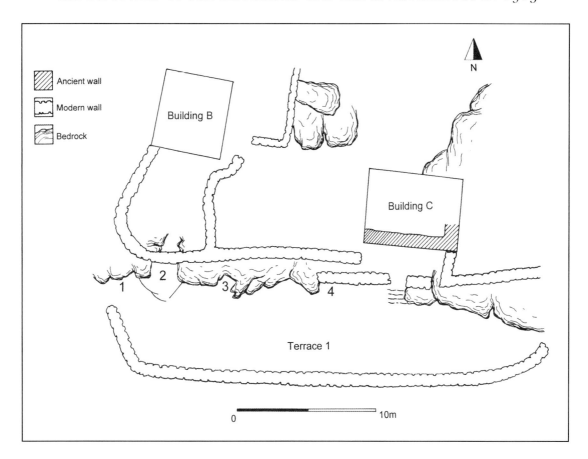

FIG. 2.3. Sketch of Terrace 1 showing location of the Rock Cuttings (1–4), with modern dry-stone walls and Building C (modern) beneath which indications of ancient walls are visible.

A large number of sherds, some of which were later conjoined with others found during the 1988 excavation season, were recovered from the 'ceramic level'. We note indicatively the fragments of an open vessel.[14] Of a type hitherto unknown in the Cyclades, this wide-mouthed vase is dated stratigraphically to the final phase of the settlement.

In this brief season, a considerable quantity of surface material was recovered, including potsherds, spindle-whorls, metal fragments, obsidian, stone rubbers and seashells. Unfortunately it is not possible in the present volume to examine the numerous moveable finds collected from cleaning the cuttings; a few have been selected and are presented as special finds.

This assemblage was sufficient to confirm both the domestic character and the EC date of the site. Architectural features could be recognised on Terrace 1 and it was obvious that undisturbed archaeological deposits lay beneath the surface. A photographic record was made of this surface inspection and a report[15] sent to the 22nd Ephorate of Antiquities, pointing out the significance of the site.

It was clear that this was the first prehistoric settlement to be discovered on Amorgos since Christos Tsountas's investigations in 1894, when he had found clusters of graves and isolated graves of EC date. Moreover, this was a hilltop settlement with indications of deliberate fortification of a naturally defensive site. It obviously called for systematic surface survey and excavation.

It was at this point that I decided to invite the collaboration of two specialists in the EC period, Professor Colin Renfrew (University of Cambridge) and Professor Christos Doumas (University of Athens), who visited the site in 1986. The outcome was the initiation of the Joint University Project on Amorgos and Keros, supported by the universities of Ioannina, Athens and Cambridge. Dr Todd

---

[14] Amorgos Archaeological Collection No. Ma 85/84 with indication '26/08/85: Terrace 1, S of Cutting 2, vase level', and Ma 85/268, with indication '26/08.85: S of Cutting 3, vase level', which were joined to sherds from Trench 1,1, levels 23, 25, 26 = cat. no. **K 1426** (FIG. 7.21: 5).

[15] Dated 1/10/85.

Whitelaw, then at the University of Cambridge, who also participated in the site visit, agreed to organise the surface survey of Markiani, within the framework of the project.

The quantitative results of the systematic surface survey conducted in 1987 corroborated our views on the nature of the site, namely that it is an EC hilltop settlement in a naturally fortified site, the defensibility of which has been reinforced by the addition of fortification walls in places (FIGS. 4.1 and 6.1, PLATE 8 *a–b*).

However, other issues, such as the extent, form and precise date of the settlement and its fortifications, could only be resolved by excavation and careful stratigraphic control, particularly in view of the difficulties presented by the modern dry-stone walls and dense vegetation.

When excavations commenced in 1988 it soon became evident that the finds spanned almost the entire EBA, from EC I to EC III, and that the site had been occupied continuously throughout this long period. Moreover, sherds from the first terrace at least indicate use of the site in the Geometric, Hellenistic and Roman periods, as well as, to a lesser extent, in Byzantine times.

As the first EC settlement site to be excavated on Amorgos, Markiani offers the prospect of understanding the material culture of the island during the EBA. In particular, detailed publication of the rich sequence of pottery will help to clarify its character and to define its relationship with contemporary pottery groups known from other islands. The pottery from Markiani, and indeed all the material recovered, has the advantage of coming from a settlement site, when so much of what we know about the material culture of the early Cyclades is based on evidence from cemetery sites.

The project inevitably encountered a number of practical difficulties, some arising from the geographical position of Amorgos, not least the inadequacies of sea transport, the lack of technical equipment and the shortcomings in technical infrastructure in general. The site of Markiani itself presents a number of conservation problems, and we subscribe to the principle that the island's ancient remains require conservation as well as study.

The Joint University Project did, as this publication documents, produce important results: apart from the new finds that have augmented the rather limited body of EC material in the Amorgos Archaeological Collection,[16] a new archaeological site has been brought to light, which is being conserved through the funding support of foreign colleagues, and, especially, the Ministry of the Aegean, which financially supported preservation work on the site from 1990 until 2004.

---

[16] Marangou 1999, 13.

Chapter 3

The surface survey of 1987

Todd Whitelaw

THE AIMS OF THE SURFACE SURVEY

The 1985 investigations and preliminary reconnaissance in 1986 indicated that archaeological materials principally of EC date were scattered over a considerable area around the central hilltop at Markiani (PLATE 2), particularly spreading down the steep terraces to the south. While it could be assumed that much of this material had eroded from above, it was not possible to determine the original extent of the site, and a detailed surface collection across the site was undertaken in 1987 to identify areas of potentially *in situ* deposit, as opposed to material eroded from above. The first aim of this investigation was to define the areas of the site likely to be the most productive for excavation, based on the nature and distribution of surface materials. The second aim was to define, if possible, the nature and extent of occupation at the site in the different phases of occupation, to provide a broader context for the more detailed information on particular parts of the site which would be obtained through excavation.

THE METHODOLOGY OF THE SURFACE SURVEY

Systematic surface collections were made during two weeks in 1987, across the entire area covered by archaeological materials. Collection stopped when the density of surface material dropped to the level of the background scatter of artefacts in adjacent areas. To the east and west, the collection area was further defined by the direction of the slope; all of the area where material could have washed down from the concentration on the Markiani hilltop was investigated. To the south, collection stopped at a series of broad, relatively flat terraces halfway to the sea, acting as a sediment trap for the material washing from above; very few sherds were identified on the slopes below.

Approximately 14 ha of terrace were investigated, scattered over roughly 20 ha of slope (FIG. 3.1). At the upper and lower ends of the site, shallow slopes permitted continuous coverage, but on the steepest slope only individual scattered terraces were accessible between outcrops of rock and dense vegetation. On these slopes, individual terraces or small groups of interconnecting terraces were defined as collection units. These were analytically coherent units, since collection areas within them shared characteristics such as vegetation cover and soil visibility, and were likely to have had a similar history of cultivation and modification of any archaeological materials present. In the areas of larger terraces and particularly in the level fields at the north of the site, artificial divisions were defined of approximately the same area as the terraces elsewhere; small units allowed monitoring of any localised variations in the distribution of archaeological materials.

In each collection unit, between one and four systematic sample circles of 1 m radius were collected; the number was determined by the size of the unit, the variability in vegetation, soil visibility, or apparent sherd density, the amount of material collected in the initial circles and, in areas of particularly low density, whether any further circles would be likely to increase the reliability of the sample. Circles were placed within the unit so as to be representative of that unit. Within the 1 m radius, all artefacts, and all sherds 1 cm or larger were collected. The remainder of the terrace which was accessible was searched for potentially diagnostic pieces, which were collected as a grab sample. In addition, each collection team recorded a variety of background information (time, date, team members, time taken for collections, etc.), and other details about the collection unit (the vegetation, the visibility of the soil in the collection circles, any archaeologically relevant features), and sketched the unit, indicating its boundaries, relations with adjacent units, and the location of each circular sample collection (see PLATE 4.2).

Following this procedure, 715 circles were collected from 275 different terraces or analytical units, representing 1.6% of the total surface area investigated. The sample circles produced 7088 EBA sherds, which with several thousand more from the grab samples, and 906 later or generally undiagnostic sherds, were counted, weighed, washed and retained for study and analysis.

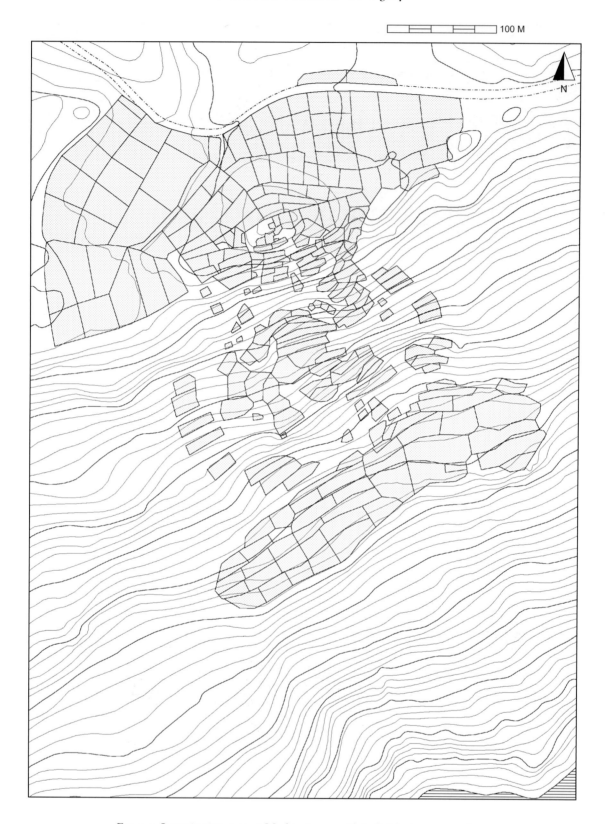

FIG. 3.1. Investigation area at Markiani area with individual survey units.

BASIC DISTRIBUTIONAL RESULTS

In the broadest outlines, the results of the surface collection can be seen in FIGS. 3.2 to 3.7. FIG. 3.2 presents the raw density (sherds/sq. m) of EBA sherds recovered through the systematic samples, for each collection unit across the centre of the study area. While sherds were recovered over the entire area investigated, they are distributed in some density over only about 0.30 ha. A rapid fall-off in

FIG. 3.2. Density of EC ceramics.

FIG. 3.3. Average sherd weight of EC ceramics.

SHERDS/M²
0.1–4.9
5.0–9.9
10.0–14.9
15.0–19.9
≥20.0

WEIGHTED
DENSITY
OF EC
CERAMICS
50 M

FIG. 3.4. Weighted density of EC ceramics.

SHERDS/M²
0.01–0.49
0.50–0.99
1.00–1.99
2.00–2.99
≥3.00

WEIGHTED
DENSITY OF
POST-EC
CERAMICS
50 M

FIG. 3.5. Weighted density of post-Bronze Age pottery.

density away from the summit of the hilltop can readily be seen. While one might initially expect that sherds would tend to be smaller and more worn further away from the centre of the hill because of attrition through downslope erosion, in fact, studies of scree slopes indicate that larger stones tend to move downslope more easily. This latter can be seen particularly clearly in a map of average sherd weight (FIG. 3.3). This pattern will have been exaggerated by the fact that the animal shelters are situated on the summit of the hill, such that the destructive action of animal hooves on eroding sherds is concentrated at the core of the site.

Data recovery will have been affected by a variety of factors, though one of the most crucial is soil visibility, which varies principally with vegetation cover. Weighting of EC sherd densities to account for differences in visibility between collection units produces the distribution mapped in FIG. 3.4.

The post-Bronze Age (principally Hellenistic) material suggests a similar focus on the summit of the hill, with a wider distribution onto the lower slopes (FIG. 3.5). The latter may reflect the more robust character of the more highly-fired later material, which can survive downslope erosion more effectively, as well as the possibility of some cultivation (with manuring?) of the areas of gentle slope at the base of the investigated area.

Other materials, swamped numerically by the sherd counts, are less informative about the nature or extent of EBA occupation on the site.

Experience on various surveys indicates that there are significant differences in the ability of individuals to identify chipped stone. During the fieldwork, it was apparent that some individuals were particularly effective at noting obsidian, whereas the majority were not. Because of the difficulty of moving across the slope, individual collectors generally worked in spatial blocks of units, creating a patchy distribution of obsidian as a result of collection bias. Subsequent spot collections by the field director documented obsidian everywhere on the slope. The documented distribution of obsidian is not, therefore, representative of the actual distribution of obsidian across the site (FIG. 3.6).

The distribution of shell and bone is also problematic (FIG. 3.7). There is no guarantee that the material recovered was introduced to the site during the prehistoric occupation, rather than during the later re-use of the site. Given its susceptibility to weathering and erosion on the surface, its distribution will be strongly conditioned by factors of erosion and survival. At the same time, the limited distribution on the upper slopes is consistent with the density and sherd weight data in indicating that the focus of the site in all periods was on the summit of the hill and upper southern slopes.

POST-DEPOSITIONAL PROCESSES AND THE NATURE OF THE SURFACE ASSEMBLAGE

Artefact densities, however, are not a definite indication of original site size or of the original or present location of *in situ* archaeological deposits, since the site has been subject to significant erosion over a considerable period of time, leading to the dispersion of sherds, probably in all directions — an initial assumption supported by the general decrease in sherd density with distance from the hilltop (FIG. 3.3). It is necessary to understand the processes of post-depositional site modification, before the documented surface distributions can be interpreted in terms of past behavioural patterns. This has been pursued both through the study of sherd condition, and through soil deposition and sediment analysis. The latter have been published independently,[1] and need only be summarised here.

Examination of numerous terrace exposures across the slope and micromorphological analysis of selected sediment samples document several phases of slope modification, which can be correlated with the archaeological evidence for the occupation of the site and utilisation of the slopes around it.

This analysis suggests that, rather than suffering 4000–5000 years of continuous erosion, the cultural deposits at Markiani have only been exposed to relatively brief phases of disruption, during the EBA occupation itself, during the Hellenistic re-occupation of the site and, more recently, with the construction of the now-disused agricultural terraces. This does not, in itself, provide us with an understanding of the surface distribution of archaeological materials, nor allow us to identify which parts of the site still preserve *in situ* deposits or represent areas of original occupation. For this we need to analyse in more detail specific evidence for the nature of the surface assemblage and the erosion of deposits.

All sherds from the systematic samples were documented in terms of size and edge abrasion, to assess the degree to which they had eroded downslope, away from their original depositional context. These indices correspond well with the pattern of surface sherd density, and help to define the original area over which archaeological materials were deposited and which still contains *in situ* material (FIG. 3.9).

[1] French and Whitelaw 1999; Whitelaw 2000.

FIG. 3.6. Density of obsidian fragments.

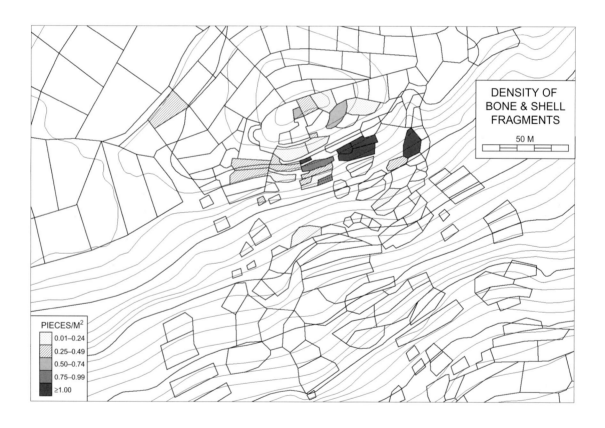

FIG. 3.7. Density of shell/bone material.

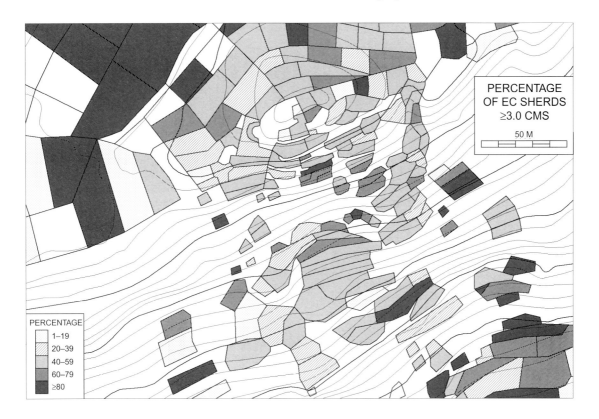

FIG. 3.8. Percentage of EC sherds larger than 3.0 cm

FIG. 3.9. Percentage of abraded EC sherds.

To provide some control on the surface material, and to test areas of the site for additional occupation deposits, three small (1 × 1 m) test trenches were opened to the north and to the west of the summit of the hill (FIG. 3.10). Each of these tests revealed only shallow sediments, without clear evidence for *in situ* EC deposits. The sherds recovered from each were eroded, probably representing wash from further upslope. None of the tests provide any evidence for occupation beyond the area defined by the dense sherd scatter.

The convergent conclusions from these different approaches are that the roughly 20 ha spread of material presently visible on the hilltop and slopes at Markiani has derived, through erosion, from an area of deposition which is unlikely to have exceeded 0.30 ha during the EC period. This is likely to be larger than the occupation area of the site at any single point in time for two reasons: 1) this distribution will also include any areas of substantial refuse dumping, at or beyond the periphery of the habitation area; and 2) this is an aggregate figure for the entire sample of EC material, and makes no allowance for changes in the size of the site, nor drift in its location during different phases of occupation. However, the hilltop itself is likely to have been the focus for activity throughout the EC occupation, particularly once that situation was given a more concrete as well as symbolic focus by the erection of the fortification wall.

OCCUPATIONAL HISTORY AT MARKIANI

In order to provide an overall view of the pottery of each phase, and to define the phases chronologically, a number of deposits were selected for detailed study and are presented in Chapter 7. In an attempt to phase the small and abraded surface ceramics, stratified samples from the excavated deposits were analysed by fabric, and seven principal fabrics identified. While not all fabrics are restricted to a single phase of the occupation, each phase is characterised by some distinctive fabrics, which allows a distinction between pure deposits of each phase, and mixed deposits. Excavated deposits of phases III and IV are distinguishable because a narrower range of fabrics is in use in the earlier phase. Unfortunately, the excavated deposits which can be assigned stratigraphically to this phase are limited, so it is not certain whether this narrower range is an accurate reflection of the full range of fabrics in use during that phase, or results from the smaller sample available for analysis. Obviously, distinctions based on the relative representation of different fabrics are not relevant to dating individual sherds, so it is not possible to distinguish between material of phases III and IV in the surface assemblage. However, as a result of the fabric analysis, it has been possible to phase the less well preserved deposits, even where few diagnostic shapes have been preserved. Together with the spatially more comprehensive sample represented by the surface assemblage, this assessment allows an overview of the occupation history of the site.

The relative chronology of the excavated deposits, in terms of other Aegean assemblages, and the absolute C-14 determinations from the site itself (Chapter 5), suggest that the site was occupied over a span of approximately ten centuries: perhaps two for phase I, two for phase II, three and a half for phase III, and two and a half for phase IV.

Consideration of the spatial distribution of deposits by phase (FIGS. 3.12–3.13), suggests changes in the extent of occupation and deposition areas between the different phases, which correspond with changes in the amount of material deposited during each phase.

The earliest occupation was probably late in the Grotta-Pelos phase, and is represented by a shallow deposit on the northern side of the hill, behind what may be a fortification wall bridging gaps between bedrock outcrops (FIG. 3.12 *a*). The second phase, characterised by material with features of the Kampos Group, is found more widely, associated with a bastion in the north (FIG. 3.12 *b*). Other deposits, without associated walls, were found on the southern summit and small quantities of comparable material were recovered from the first terrace of the southern slope. These may represent wash from above, rather than occupation on the terrace in this phase. While the fortification wall and Bastion were associated with shallow deposits of material of Phase I and II respectively, this material was extremely abraded, which may indicate that the structures were cut at a later date into these shallow deposits which had previously been exposed on the surface and weathered for some time.

The third phase of occupation saw a significant expansion, both across the uppermost southern terrace, and downslope to the south-east (FIG. 3.13 *a*). It is not entirely certain whether all of the house walls on the top terrace were constructed in this period and continued in use into the next, or date primarily to phase IV. Unstratified ceramics in the trenches north of the summit suggest some activity on the summit of the hill, now completely lost through erosion.

In the fourth and final phase, characterised by Kastri Group type-fossils, occupation was also widespread, although the absence of distinctively Kastri forms from the south-eastern trench (Trench 3) leaves it uncertain whether occupation continued in that part of the site or not (FIG. 3.13 *b*).

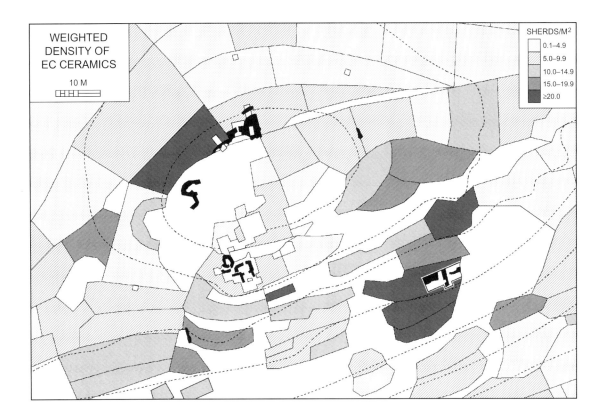

FIG. 3.10. Weighted densities of EC ceramics (summit area).

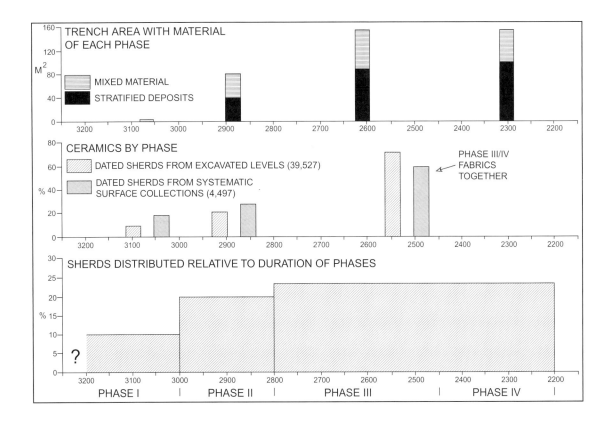

FIG. 3.11. Estimating the occupation span at Markiani, by phase.

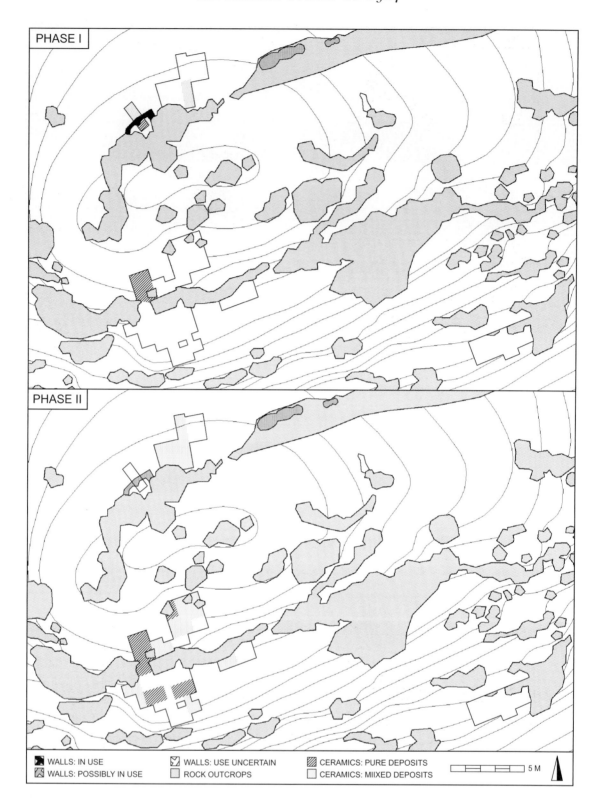

FIG. 3.12. Markiani phases I and II.

If occupied continuously from the late Grotta-Pelos through Kastri phases, Markiani would be an exceptionally long-lived EC community. However, compared to other multi-phase sites in the Aegean, Markiani has anomalously shallow deposits. This might be a function of its extreme exposure, although this is also shared by stratified sites excavated elsewhere in the Aegean.[2]

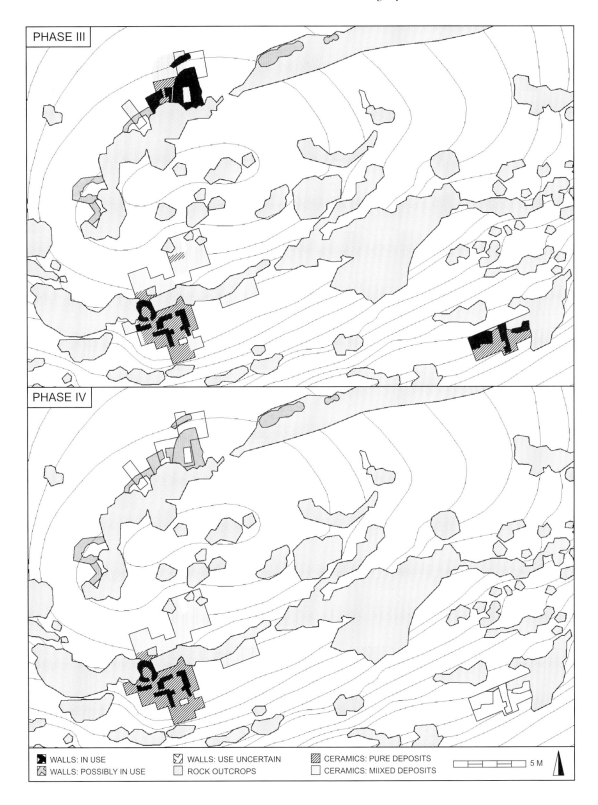

FIG. 3.13. Markiani phases III and IV.

Comparing potential indices of the scale of occupation in the different phases, it is hardly surprising that the quantity of ceramics from the excavated trenches and the area of deposit identified for each phase are in broad agreement (FIG. 3.11). However, the same diachronic pattern is also seen in the surface assemblage, which is not subject to the same preservation and sampling biases as the excavated deposits. All three indices suggest a very small community in phases I and II, expanding significantly in phases III and IV. If occupation had been continuous, one would have to assume that the phase

III/IV material would have been deposited over a significantly shorter period of time, or would represent a much smaller site in the later phases (or a drastically reduced rate of ceramic breakage and deposition), than the spatial evidence suggests. This suggests that the occupation at Markiani was episodic rather than continuous, consistent with the evidence we have from most other EC sites for relatively short occupation spans.[3]

THE EARLY CYCLADIC COMMUNITY AT MARKIANI

The excavated structures on the site, particularly those on Terrace 1 (FIGS. 4.1 and 4.21), represent a dense agglomeration of structures, at least in this confined terrace on the site, paralleled at the few other EC sites which have been excavated to any extent, such as Kastri at Chalandriani on Syros, Panormos on Naxos, Mount Kynthos on Delos, and Skarkos on Ios. Studies of the distribution of material within the excavated rooms at Markiani have not yet produced functional interpretations for the use of particular spaces, so that it is not feasible to speak in terms of individual houses or households. However, based on domestic units defined for the contemporary site of Myrtos–*Fournou Korifi* on Crete,[4] and patterns of interconnection and possible room use at the site of Kastri at Chalandriani on Syros, we may suggest something like an area of 40–80 m² for a household, here presumed to be that of a nuclear family; larger households can be expected to have required larger areas or compounds.[5] It is not the intention, through this series of assumptions, to make any concrete inferences about the nature of EC family structure or domestic units, but rather to define a reasonable occupation density figure for the site — more relevant than trying to apply a general cross-cultural equation.[6]

Extrapolating from this figure, the overall area of deposition at Markiani, as inferred for the different periods on the basis of the excavated and surface data, would suggest a maximum of perhaps 12–15 households, or a population for the site in phases III and IV of *c.* 60–75 individuals, with significantly smaller populations in the earlier phases. It is likely that these figures should be reduced drastically for adjacent areas of extra-mural dumping, which are likely to be included in the area of *in situ* deposits, and for lower occupation densities on parts of the site with major rock outcrops, which would have been less suitable for agglomerated occupation than the area excavated on Terrace 1.

On Amorgos, a preference for low-slope land is consistent with the known distribution of EC sites. Markiani itself, situated at the edge of the upland plateau, near springs feeding the north-draining valleys, was in an ideal location for an agriculturally self-sufficient community. A notional agricultural catchment around Markiani, based on a maximum population of 60 to 75 individuals does not seem unreasonable, given what we presently know of the locations of the nearest EC sites (FIG. 3.14).

Overall for Amorgos, only one-quarter of the surface area of the island would have been available at most for EC settlement, since there is no evidence for the use of agricultural terracing in the EBA Aegean.[7] Applying estimates of settlement density from intensively surveyed Melos would suggest only some four or five sites on Amorgos at any one point during the EBA, and an overall island population of less than 300 individuals.

The analysis of soil profiles[8] on the slope below the site at Markiani, indicates that the area was originally more heavily vegetated than at present, and that significant soil erosion took place, probably associated with the EC occupation of the site. On neighbouring Naxos, pollen analysis has documented deforestation during the EBA.[9] Together, the evidence for vegetation changes, significant soil erosion, and the locations of sites, suggest that EBA farmers throughout the southern Aegean were significantly altering their environments, but did not practice soil conservation measures, leading to dramatic, in some cases catastrophic, soil erosion.[10] Systematic degradation of the local environment around sites may provide some perspective on the short duration and instability of most EC sites, and would be consistent with the suggestion of episodic occupation at Markiani. The cumulative effects of such practices through the colonisation and expansion of population on most of the Cycladic islands may also be a significant element in the increasing inter-community competition and conflict which appears to be implied by the proliferation of fortified sites in the Kastri phase, to which Markiani's fortifications may also belong.[11]

[3] Whitelaw 2000.
[4] Whitelaw 1983.
[5] Whitelaw 2001.
[6] Whitelaw 2001.
[7] Whitelaw 2000.

[8] French and Whitelaw 1998.
[9] Dalongeville and Renault-Miskovsky 1993.
[10] Whitelaw 2000.
[11] Whitelaw 2000.

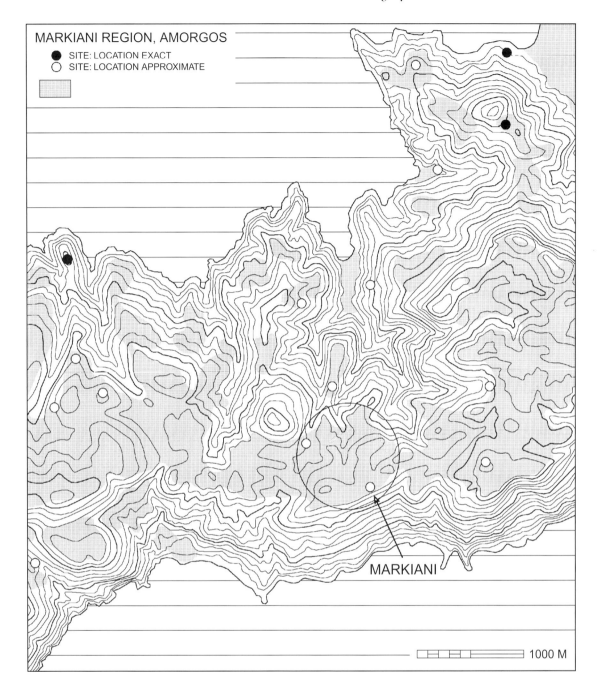

MARKIANI REGION, AMORGOS
● SITE: LOCATION EXACT
○ SITE: LOCATION APPROXIMATE

MARKIANI

1000 M

FIG. 3.14. Markiani area with neighbouring sites and low-slope land.

Geographically, Amorgos is relatively isolated, providing a weak link to the east and south-east.[12] However, with an estimated EC population of under 300, it would have been demographically marginal, and will have had to have been integrated into wider networks for demographic survival. Keros and the other islands of the Erimonisia would have been an essential gateway to a wider population pool in the central Cyclades. Connections between Amorgos and Keros have been well documented by Broodbank's study of the Dhaskalio ceramics,[13] but the non-reciprocal nature of those relationships is as yet less clear. For example, while Amorgian Blue-Schist tempered ceramics make up a significant component of the ceramic assemblage from Dhaskalio–Kavos (some 7.5%, as opposed to 14.5% at Markiani), relatively few ceramics at Markiani appear to have been imported from beyond

---

[12] Broodbank 2000.

[13] Broodbank 2000a; 2000b.

Amorgos. Markiani's relative isolation is also clear through assessing the degree of incorporation of both sites into wider exchange systems: distinctive Talc Ware, probably produced in the western Cyclades, is 30 times more frequent at Dhaskalio; only five fragments have been identified among nearly 50,000 EC sherds recovered from Markiani. Melian obsidian was used at both sites, but at Dhaskalio the ratio of obsidian to ceramics is about 1 to 12, whereas at Markiani the rate of consumption is one-half of that, 1 to 24. In these respects, Markiani can be seen in context as a medium-sized, relatively self-sufficient, community on the periphery on the EC world.

APPENDIX: THE STUDY OF SOIL EROSION AND AGRICULTURAL TERRACING AT MARKIANI USING MICROMORPHOLOGICAL TECHNIQUES

by Charly A. I. French and Todd Whitelaw

During surface investigations at Markiani it had become apparent that downslope erosion had drastically modified the surface distribution of artefactual remains. This process has itself clearly been affected by the extensive construction of agricultural terraces across the site. Three sets of samples were examined micromorphologically. The deposits forming representative terraces were examined, as was the post-depositional sequence overlying the site, and a palaeosol preserved beneath terrace retaining walls at the break of slope. It was determined that the buried, pre-terrace system 'red soil' was a re-worked red palaeosol, much affected by downslope erosion processes, which probably commenced with clearance associated with the EBA occupation of the site. Examination of this soil suggested that there were at least two pre-modern phases of use of the hillside.

An account of this work has been given elsewhere,[14] and the broad results are summarised here.

SUMMARY OF RESULTS

There is little doubt that a reworked *terra rossa*-like soil is preserved in places beneath the terraces on the slope below the site at Markiani. The analysis of this buried soil suggests a sequence of landscape development involving:

1. *terra rossa* soil formation;
2. an initial phase of illuviation and colluviation, associated with increasing leaching and oxidation over time, probably associated with agricultural/pastoral use of the hillslope, leading to the formation of a re-worked red soil;
3. a period of relative slope stability and soil formation processes within the re-worked red soil, which involved the illuviation of fine material;
4. a further period of erosion leading to the deposition of illuvial fines (silt and clay), probably resulting from rainsplash erosion and mass movement of soil washing off a bare ground surface uphill; and
5. burial by the agricultural terrace system.

While the initial period of erosion of this red soil cannot be determined directly, and no archaeological materials have been noted incorporated within it, the most likely period for the onset of such erosion would appear to be the first occupation of the site, fairly early in the EBA, when activity on the hilltop and cultivation and grazing in the immediate vicinity of the site would almost certainly have had an impact on the stability of the slope soils. Alternatively, this period of erosion might highlight an intensification of activity in the second half of the EBA, when the population of the community increased and occupation expanded onto the upper southern slope of the hilltop.

No physical or sedimentological evidence survives to indicate that there was any agricultural terracing on the slope during the EBA. While any such evidence might have been completely removed during later erosion or terrace construction, the illuviation phases indicate that the lower slope deposits were affected by erosion from above, such that the slopes were not, at that time, effectively stabilised by terraces.

Potentially up to 800 years after the initial occupation of the site and the probable start of landscape modification in its vicinity, the site was abandoned. The profile studied in the excavation trenches at

---

[14] French and Whitelaw 1999.

the top of the slope provides clear documentation of the disuse, collapse and silting of the ruins, and subsequent stabilisation of the slope. These deposits were capped and preserved beneath a deflation level consisting of stones and sherds, representing a stable slope surface. This deposit, however, cannot be taken as representative of the entire site area, since the bedrock outcrops which surround this terrace have obviously helped to stabilise and preserve the archaeological levels. Elsewhere on the summit of the hill, the archaeological deposits have been severely eroded, and little survives *in situ* except in pockets in the bedrock. That the later (predominantly Hellenistic) activities on the site did not disturb the underlying EBA deposits in the area sampled probably related to the depth of post-EBA sediment accumulation on that specific shelf, and cannot be extrapolated to the entire site. We can therefore anticipate that there was erosion associated with the post-EBA use of the site, in large part responsible for the deposition of the sediments later reworked into terrace fills on all parts of the slope. Because of the mixing of these deposits in the construction of the terraces, the period of deposition of these sediments cannot be dated on the basis of the sherds incorporated in them. Depositionally, we can only say that they should significantly post-date the abandonment of the EBA community and pre-date the construction of the terraces. However, given the quantity of sherd material down the entire slope, it would be surprising if the Hellenistic phase of activity on the site did not have a detectable effect on slope stability and sediments.

The final period of significant human alteration of the slope deposits is represented by the construction of agricultural terraces. These cannot be dated directly, though the absence of structural evidence for rebuilding suggests that they are of no great antiquity, a conclusion supported by the absence of significant soil structure development in the sediments behind them.

IMPLICATIONS FOR THE SURFACE ARCHAEOLOGICAL RECORD

The detection of periods of stable soil formation and distinct erosion episodes suggests that erosion, and therefore sherd movement on the slope, has been a very discontinuous process, with three potentially major episodes at roughly 2000-year intervals: the later EBA (*c.* 2800–2200 BC), the Hellenistic period (*c.* 300–0 BC), and the recent past (*c.* AD 1850–1990).

The argument for episodic erosion is based in the first instance on the stratigraphic evidence for the formation of a lag deposit on top of the abandoned EBA occupation area. While this may have stabilised particularly deep deposits on the protected rock shelf where the samples were taken, an identical deposit was also found in an archaeological trench downslope 50 m to the south-east. It is equally likely that similar stable deposits would have formed across the rest of the slope, protecting pockets of slope soils. Corroboration for the episodic nature of slope erosion comes from the formation processes of the pre-terrace soil, which document a considerable period of slope stability before subsequent further deposition of sediments.

Sherds and sediments are likely to have been dumped and to have eroded downslope from the settlement on the summit of the hill throughout the life of the community, probably exacerbated during the expansion of population in the later phases of occupation. Erosion is also likely to have increased as exploitation of the surrounding slopes intensified and vegetation was reduced by grazing. Thus, there may have been a period of up to *c.* 500 years during which EBA ceramics moved downslope, with new material constantly being added. After abandonment by the community, a considerable amount of erosion, particularly on the exposed summit of the hill, is documented by the fills inside the collapsing structures on the shelf immediately to the south. Elsewhere, where such natural terraces did not capture sediments, they would have eroded further downslope, until vegetation and deflation stabilised the surface.

The second major phase of erosion may be attributed to the historical use of the site, represented primarily by quantities of Hellenistic sherds on the site and slopes. While some of the better-preserved sherds on the gentle terraces at the base of the slope may have been deposited during cultivation of this section of the slope, some of this material, and all of that on the upper slopes, probably derives from occupation on the summit of the hill. Soil eroding with these sherds probably accounts for the sediments which were later reworked as the fills for the terraces constructed across the entire slope. While the underlying EBA deposits in the excavated trenches just below the summit of the site had not been significantly cut into during this phase of use of the site, this need not apply to other areas, particularly shallower deposits on the summit or slope, and this may have been a period in which previously stable sediments containing EBA sherds were destabilised, and new material added to the surface assemblage subject to erosion. The duration of this phase of use of the site and the erosion which almost certainly accompanied it remains unclear: ceramics (primarily coarse wares) ranging from Geometric to Late Roman in date are present on the slope, although the vast majority appear to be most consistent with a Hellenistic date. Therefore, the serious impact on slope stability may have been confined to a fairly limited period of several generations.

Finally, we can anticipate some additional erosion in the recent past. This may have been severe if there were any significant utilisation of the site or slope before the construction of the existing terrace system, but this seems unlikely. There are very few recent ceramics either on the surface of the slope or in the superficial excavated levels on the site. Furthermore, if serious soil erosion had been instigated on an un-terraced slope, there would have been little sediment with which to construct the existing terraces. Overall, while terrace construction will have mixed and shifted sediments locally, it is unlikely to have induced large-scale erosion, in that the slope would have been disturbed only to be immediately re-stabilised by the terrace walls. While there has been some terrace collapse since the abandonment of cultivation on the slope, exacerbated by the breakdown of some terrace walls by sheep and goats, this appears, so far, to have been fairly limited and localised.

Combining the archaeological and sedimentological observations, it appears that the extensive surface sherd distribution at Markiani, relating to two principal periods of use of the site, results from two periods of disturbance and serious erosion, during the deposition of each ceramic assemblage and the period of time after each occupation until the slope had stabilised. Recent observations suggest that stabilisation through colonisation by vegetation might have been accomplished on the order of decades, rather than centuries.

Chapter 4

Outline of excavations 1988–1990

Colin Renfrew, Lila Marangou and Christos Doumas

The excavations at Markiani were preceded by site surveys in 1985 and 1987, as described in Chapters 2 and 3. These surveys clearly indicated the preponderance of material of EC date. As noted in Chapters 2 and 3, the richest surface concentration was found on Terrace 1, the wide terrace (W. *c.* 5–7 m) running E–W for a length of some 30 m immediately to the south of the summit of the site. As noted in Chapter 2, the summit of the site, on which the modern huts (Buildings A, B, and C) stand was much eroded (see FIG. 4.1).

The site falls away steeply to the south as the contours on FIG. 4.1 indicate, so that the main reasonably level areas are the summit itself and Terrace 1 immediately to the south. To the north of the site there is an extensive level area, now arable land, but this did not form part of the original settlement which was located on the more easily-defensible summit area. The character of the site is clearly revealed in the profile XY (FIG. 4.2) seen from the west where modern huts A and B are seen, and the rock escarpment which goes down to Terrace 1. The profile CD (FIG. 4.2) is likewise seen from the west at a larger scale although at a slightly different orientation (see FIG. 6.3) and clearly shows the summit area on the north, the excavations within Rock Cutting 2, and those of Terrace 1 (i.e. Trench 1,3 and 1,2).

The concentration of later material was highest on the very summit of the site, including the units designated 218 to 222 for the purpose of surface collection (FIGS. 2.2 and 3.5), and on the terraces immediately below, to the south (Terraces 1 and 2) (PLATES 2 and 3 *a*). In addition to a few MC sherds (including Minyan ware) the later material includes a few Geometric sherds, more abundant Archaic material through to the Hellenistic period, with occasional Roman, Byzantine and additional later sherds. The rich finds from the 1985 survey on Terrace 1, and notably at the foot of two of the three rock clefts (PLATES 4 *a* and 5 *a*) along its length, Rock Cuttings 2 and 3, firmly suggested that this was one area on which attention should be concentrated.[1] At the same time it would be logical to investigate also the flat summit of the hill immediately above, to the north, on which there stood three stone-built structures of recent date (PLATE 2), occupied by the shepherd who used the summit of the site as a pen for his goats. The most prominent of the rock cuttings, Rock Cutting 2 (*Engopi* 2) was closed by a well-built stone construction (PLATE 5 *a–b*), while to east and west the summit was surmounted by walling of recent date. This Rock Cutting, from top (on the summit) to bottom (on Terrace 1) was selected for excavation as part of Trench 1.

An area to the east of Trench 1 on Terrace 1, at the foot of Rock Cutting 3, was designated Trench 2. Later a further area some 5 m to the east beneath Rock Cutting 4 was opened and designated Trench 5 (FIG. 4.1). For Trench designations see FIGS. 4.1 and 4.3.

It also seemed desirable to investigate an area on the summit itself, although there were indications that the depth of soil there would not be great. An area within the modern walling was marked out as Trench 4. The modern wall here at its south side (FIG. 2.2–3, PLATES 3 *a* and 7 *a*), surmounting the escarpment sloping down to Terrace 1, was later removed. As noted below Trenches 7 and 9, at the top of Rock Cutting 2 (and above Trench 1,1), are also on the summit. Since the surface survey indicated settlement on the terraces well down the steep slope of the hill to the south of the summit, it seemed appropriate to open an area there, and Trench 3 was defined some 25 m south-east of the summit area (FIG. 4.1).

The other area which evidently required investigation was the system of fortifications which could be recognised at the northern edge of the summit, exploiting there the slight escarpment as the land falls away to the north (PLATES 1 *a* and 8 *a*). As described in Chapter 6, no visible line of fortifications

---

[1] See also Chapter 2.

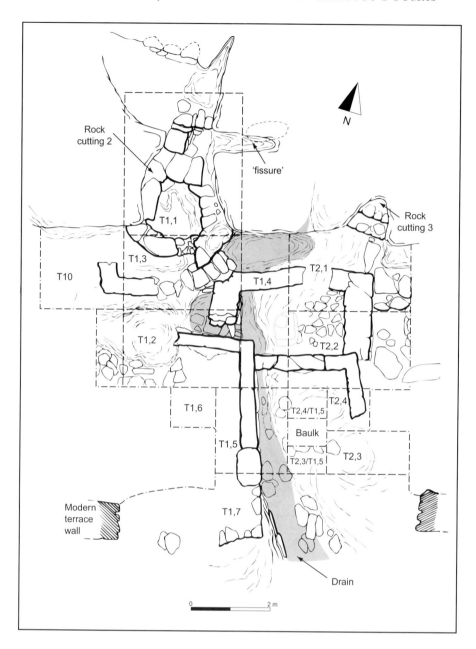

FIG. 4.3. Schematic plan of excavations at the south of the summit area (the drain shaded).

was evident at the south side of the site, where there is a very steep slope down towards the sea. At the north side, however, short stretches of walling constructed of large stones could be recognised, completing the natural rock face of the escarpment. One short stretch was selected for investigation as Trench 8 (FIGS. 10.1–3 and 11.1) and a narrow trench, Trench 6, was cut across the line of the wall further west. The locations of the excavation trenches are indicated on FIG. 4.1.

The areas on the summit overlooking Rock Cutting 2 (*Engopi* 2) and Trench 1 were subsequently opened and designated Trenches 7 and 9. Meanwhile on Terrace 1 the area at the foot of this cutting, Rock Cutting 2 and designated Trench 1, was extended to the west, and this new trench designated Trench 10. It should be noted that the excavation of the material within this cutting was a complex process (see PLATE 5 *a–c*). The levels within the cutting itself (see FIG. 4.13) fell within Trench 1,1. Most of those at the foot of the cutting were within Trenches 1,2 and 1,3. (Note also that levels 43 and 44 along with Trench 9,1, number 5 fall within the small 'fissure' which extends east within Rock Cutting 2). In addition, three very small trial trenches were opened at points further from the central area (FIG. 4.1) to test the depth of soil, and to recover sub-surface material for comparison with finds from the surface collection.

The general topography of the site and the location of the test pits opened in conjunction with the site survey (see Chapter 3) are seen in the general plan, FIG. 4.1. The N–S profile across the site (FIG. 4.2, PLATE 1 a) indicates the steepness of the slope to the south. The scarp to the north of Terrace 1, surmounted by the summit area, is seen in elevation in FIG. 6.3 (PLATES 3 a, 4 a and 5 a).

Thus, as noted below, the excavation trenches opened on Terrace 1 were numbered Trenches 1, 2, 5 and 10, (FIG. 4.3) while Trenches 4, 7, and 9 (FIGS. 4.12 and 4.15) were opened on the summit area. To the north of the summit area Trenches 6 and 8 (FIGS. 4.6 and 4.8) were opened to investigate the indications of fortifications found there. A further area some 30 m to the south-east was investigated by Trench 3 (FIGS. 4.1 and 4.24). The survey units relevant to the areas subsequently excavated are seen in TABLE 4.1 (see also Chapter 3A).

TABLE 4.1. The excavated trenches and the corresponding survey units.

Areas	Excavated trenches	Survey Units
Fortification Wall	Trench 6,1	Not collected (obscured by the vegetation)
	Trench 6,2	315
Bastion	Trench 8,1	Not collected (obscured by the vegetation)
	Trench 8,2–8,6	216
Summit area	Trench 4,1–4,10	218
	Trench 7 and Trench 1,1 summit	222
	Trench 9	Dry-stone wall between 222 and 218 and parts of 222 and 218
Terrace 1, west part	Trench 1,1	Rock Cutting 2/1985
	Trench 1,3	South of Rock Cutting 2/85 and 1W/ 1987
	Trench 1,2, 1,4–1,6	1W/ 1987
	Trench 1,7	Not collected (obscured by the vegetation)
	Trench 10	South of Rock Cutting 1/1985 and Unit 1W/ 1987
	Trench 2,1	Rock Cutting 3/1985
	Trench 2,2–2,4	South of Rock Cutting 3/85 and 1W/1987
Terrace 1, east part	Trench 5,1, and 5, 2	Rock Cutting 3, 1 and 4/1985 and between Units 1W and 1E/1987
South-east of Terrace 1	Trench 3	508
	Test Trench 1	701
	Test Trench 2	702
	Test Trench 3	301

PRELIMINARY REVIEW OF THE SEQUENCE OF OCCUPATION

As indicated above, it was already clear from the investigations of 1985 that the site of Markiani was predominantly of EC construction and occupation. During the 1985 work investigations, mainly on Terrace 1, yielded a considerable quantity of ceramic material and other finds which could be placed chronologically in a later phase of the EBA. Before setting out to discuss the excavations in greater detail, it will be useful to survey briefly the stratigraphic and chronological conclusions which were arrived at, since the description which follows draws in part upon some of the conclusions reached.

It should be noted that there were no direct stratigraphic relations between the area to the north of the site, which includes the fortification wall discovered there, and the areas to the south. Likewise there was only limited stratigraphic linkage between the materials on the summit, at its southern edge, and the structures on the terrace below and to the south, Terrace 1. This does not present a problem, since the early pottery associated with the fortification wall is of a character well known in the Cyclades and undoubtedly belonging to the earlier part of the EC, comparable to material, for instance, from the early levels (Pre-City, level A1) at Phylakopi on Melos. Moreover, it was clear that the material on the upper levels of that terrace, Terrace 1, represented the last phase in the intensive occupation of the site. This has clear affinities with material from other islands including Syros, Delos and Kea, generally assigned to a late phase of the EBA, namely the so-called Kastri Group. This assemblage would therefore represent the concluding phase of EBA occupation at the site, which was subsequently designated Markiani phase IV: Ma IV.

At the north side of the site, north of the summit, the fortification wall runs approximately E–W. In Trench 6 there was, at the western side, a fairly homogeneous deposit of the earliest material found at the site, representing a phase which we therefore described as Markiani phase I (Ma I). Layers 2–10 of Trench 6 are considered typical of Markiani phase I.

Material of phase Ma I character is also found at the top of Trench 1,1 and in the adjoining Trench 7 in the levels in the summit area overlying the rock escarpment; here it was found in the lower part of the stratigraphic sequence. There, in the overlying levels, some finds are accompanied by material with ceramic affinities with the Kampos Group, generally assigned to the transitional period between the Grotta-Pelos and Keros-Syros cultures (the transitional EC I/II phase). This assemblage in these areas containing material of the Kampos Group defines Markiani phase II (Ma II). The following layers are considered typical of Ma II: Trench 7 layers 1–4, layers 6–10, layers 12–13 and layers 16–19, Trench 1,1 layers 2–7 and layers 17–20.

The fact that at Markiani material of Ma I is not generally found in direct stratigraphic relationship beneath material of phase Ma IV is no cause for concern, since the chronological relationship between material of Ma I and Ma IV is already abundantly clear from our knowledge of Cycladic prehistory. We did not require superposition at Markiani in order to verify a chronological relationship that is already well known; the assemblages which represent these phases at the site are closed deposits with good, diagnostic ceramic material.

Materials assigned to what we have termed Markiani phase III came from two sources. The first was a small well-associated assemblage in a cleft in the rock at the east side of Trench 1,1 (specifically between Trench 1,1 layers 43–44 and Trench 9,1 layer 5). Secondly there were various finds on Terrace 1 in Trenches 1 and 2 in levels preceding those of phase Ma IV. However no major assemblage of Ma III was available for study.

As discussed further in Chapter 7D below, materials of Ma III are of a character which is clearly later than those of Ma II (which has affinities with the Kampos Group), and the assemblage in Trench 1,1 is in a position which agrees with that view. Furthermore, in Trenches 1 and 2 material of phase III lies stratigraphically below material of Ma IV (which has Kastri Group affinities). It would, therefore, seem logical to assign Ma III, which lies chronologically between the Kampos and Kastri groups, to what on other islands has been referred to as the Keros-Syros culture (or EC II, or in some terminologies EC IIA). It should be stressed however that the paucity or absence at Markiani of the fine painted and stamped-and-incised sherds establishes the equivalence with Keros-Syros material more on the basis of chronological logic than of direct observation.

It is possible that much of the material from Trench 3 should be assigned to Ma III, since characteristic forms of Ma IV were not seen in Trench 3, where there was a lack of the tankard and the two-handled (depas) cups of phase IV. But certainly the general character of the pottery in Trench 3 was typical of the later part of the EBA (Ma III and IV) rather than the earlier (Ma I and II).

The ceramic finds of Ma IV represent the latest occupation of the site during the EBA. Particularly characteristic are the one-handled tankards and two-handled cups, which are among the defining features of the Kastri Group. Such material was most abundant in the upper levels of Terrace 1. The following layers exemplify the ceramic material of the phase Ma IV from Terrace 1:

– Layers 21 to 30 and 34 to 36 of Trench 1,1 from the interior of the circular feature of Space 7.
– Layers 20, 22 to 31 of Trench 2, layers 3, 4, 5 and 7 of Trench 1,3; layers 3, 17 and 27 to 31 of Trench 1,4 from the area south of and between the two Rock Cuttings 2 and 3 in Space 6; and
– Layers 4, 6, 9, 12 and 22 of Trench 1,4 above floor 'a' of Space 3.

The relative chronology of the various trenches and levels at Markiani are summarised Chapter 7A (TABLE 7.2). The chronology of the various phases is further discussed below, and in Chapter 7C to E by our ceramic specialists, on the basis of the various well-associated assemblages studied. The stratigraphic circumstances of those assemblages are discussed on the pages to follow. Together this information allows us to date the principal architectural features of the site to the appropriate Markiani phases. Then, on the basis of ceramic parallels the phases can be set in their wider Cycladic context, but in our view there is no merit in discussing wider chronological questions until the finds from the successive periods at Markiani have been systematically discussed. However, it is now clear that the so-called 'Amorgos

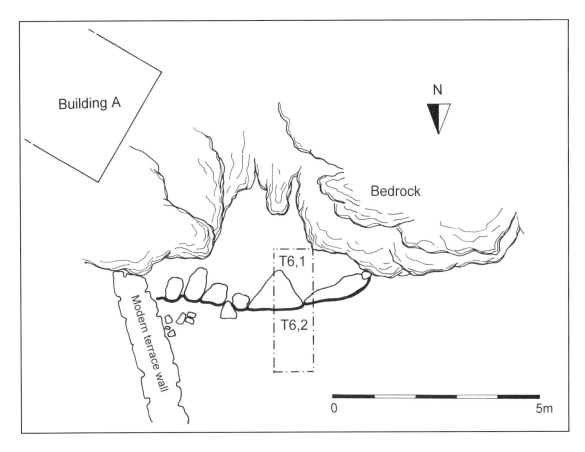

FIG. 4.4. Plan of Trench 6.

Group',[2] first proposed some 30 years ago, is a concept that is no longer useful. The radiocarbon determinations given in Chapter 5 permit the establishment of an outline absolute chronology for the site.

FORTIFICATION WALL

The fortification wall lies at the north (landward) side of the site, and overlaps in places with modern walling on the sheepfold complex. Today, the summit area is entered by an opening in this recent walling adjoining Building A (see FIGS. 2.1, 4.1 and 6.1). The line of the fortification wall is, in places, north of the modern walling (PLATE 4 *d*). The general plan of the fortifications is seen in FIGS. 6.1 and 6.2 and PLATE 8.1 and 2.

TRENCHES 6,1 AND 6,2

A short stretch of walling comprising just five stones in line, the largest more than 1 m long, was investigated by placing across it a trench 3 m long (N–S) by 1 m wide (E–W). The southern part of this trench, inside the stones of the wall, was designated Trench 6,1 (PLATE 9.1) located on Unit 315 of the surface survey. The outside (northern) part is Trench 6,2 (FIGS. 4.4 and 4.6, PLATE 9 *a–b*).

The deposit inside the wall (in Trench 6,1) contained compacted brown soil and stones, and attained a depth of some 80 cm, where bedrock was reached throughout (FIG. 4.5). The uppermost level (Trench 6,1 layer 1) may be regarded as unstratified (humus). Layers 2 to 8 belong to a unified layer or deposit, containing many stones both large and small many sherds, shells, and animal bones and relatively little soil. The larger stones lay mainly against the bedrock at the south-west corner of the trench. This fill should in principle be considered contemporary with the wall, and the latest material in it should date the wall securely (FIGS. 4.5 and 4.7).

Layers 9 and 10 contained few stones, hard clayey soil and few sherds. This deposit was some 20 cm in thickness, and lay directly on the bedrock. Even if there is a small difference in texture (layers 2–8 and layers 9–10) both belong to the same deposit, which constitutes the foundation filling of the fortification wall.

---

[2] Doumas 1977, 23; Renfrew 1972.

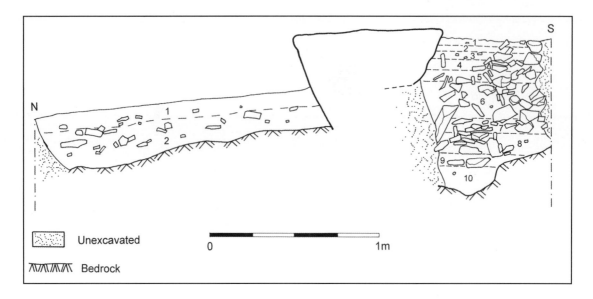

Unexcavated

Bedrock

0   1m

FIG. 4.5. East section of Trench 6,1 and Trench 6,2.

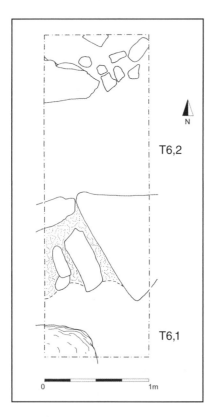

T6,2

N

T6,1

0   1m

FIG. 4.6. Sketch of fortification wall in Trench 6.

TRENCH 6

T6,1   T6,2

1   1
|
2
|
3
|
4   2
|
5
|
6
|
7
|
8
|
9
|
10

FIG. 4.7. Trench 6 layer diagram.

    The pottery from Trench 6,1 was a homogeneous, if fragmentary, assemblage. It is described in Chapter 7C. On excavation it was clear that this was the earliest ceramic material from the site, and this body of material was therefore taken as the defining assemblage for phase I (Ma I).

    The possibility has been raised that the formation of the deposits containing this ceramic material, found against the lowest levels of the wall, post-dates its construction and represents subsequent downwash from earlier deposits of Ma I material nearby. It is also conceivable that this ceramic material, which is as eroded as any sherds from the surface on the site, was already present at the time of construction of the fortification wall, which would have been cut down into these earlier deposits. This possibility cannot be entirely excluded and it is the case that the sherds found were fragmentary and did not fit together to form restorable vessel shapes. Based on this argument the construction of

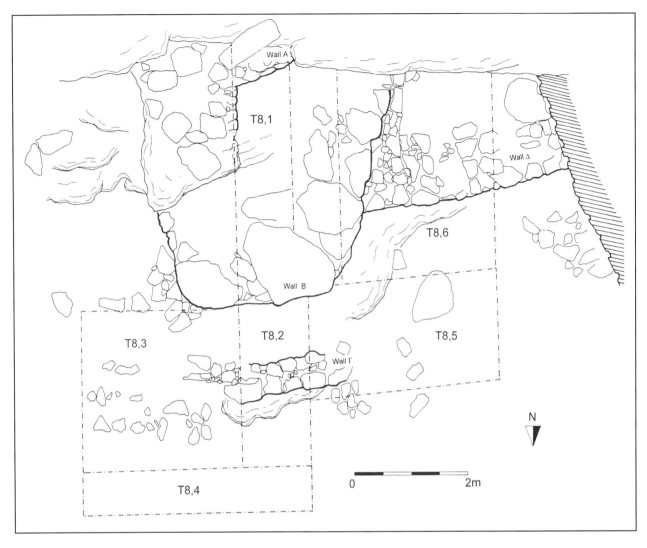

FIG. 4.8. Plan of Trench 8.

the wall could be assigned to a later phase, possibly Ma III or IV. At the same time however, no sherds of the Blue Schist Fabric, characteristic of Ma III and IV, were found here (apart from a single fragment from the superficial layer Trench 6,1, layer 1). It seems safest to follow the principle that archaeological strata are to be dated by the most recent material found in them and to assign these to Ma I along with the pottery found there. At the same time, however, the limited scale of the trench and the relatively small quantities of material recovered mean that this must be a provisional conclusion.

As indicated in Chapter 7C, this pottery belongs securely to an early phase of the EC period. As noted above, the assemblage, the earliest recovered from the site, defines the first phase of occupation at Markiani, Ma I.

The deposit outside the fortification wall (Trench 6,2) slopes down markedly from the south to the north, and consists of dark hard soil, with some stones, sherds, animal bones, seashells, a stone rubber (**EE 603**) and obsidian débitage. Layers 1, Trench 6,2 layer 1 (depth 10 cm) and Trench 6,2 layer 2 (depth 15 cm) which comprise the deposit in this area did not yield large quantities of sherds and lack diagnostic material. Meanwhile, natural bedrock is seen at a depth of 25 cm from the surface.

The stratigraphic context of catalogued finds of Ma I from Trench 6,1 is set out in TABLE 4.2 (p. 56).

BASTION AREA: TRENCHES 8,1; 8,2; 8,3; 8,4; 8,5; 8,6

The Bastion of Trench 8, or rather its foundations, forms a prominent feature of the defences, being situated on the north side of the site immediately to the west of the modern and indeed the ancient entrance, and belongs to Unit 216 of the surface survey (FIG. 4.8, PLATE 10 *a–c*). At its south side, where it abuts the rock outcrop which forms the main line of defence at this point, there is a length (*c.* 1.50 m) of dry-stone walling, designated Wall A. The large stones of the bastion itself constitute Wall

B. The final plan of the Bastion Area is seen in FIG. 6.1 and the elevation of the main fortification wall, Wall A (FIG. 4.10), seen from the north in the Bastion within Trench 8 in FIG. 6.2.

THE INTERIOR OF THE BASTION: TRENCH 8,1

Trench 8,1 was opened inside the Bastion, running between Wall A and Wall B. It was 1 m wide (E–W) and reached a length of 2.74 m. Trench 8,2 continued the same line northwards on its east side, but was 1.20 m wide. It ran 3.80 m north from Wall B, the northernmost portion of the Bastion.

Trench 8,1 (PLATE 8 c) was excavated in a series of arbitrary levels or spits. Wheel-made sherds of Hellenistic date were found in superficial layers 1 and 2, indicating some later activity in this area. After the completion of layer 5, the trench was sub-divided, layer 6 lying in the northern part, layer 7 in the south. The west section of the trench is seen in FIG. 4.9 and the levels diagram in FIG. 4.11.

Bedrock was soon reached in both these sub-areas, the maximum depth of soil in Trench 8,1 being 65 cm. The latest pottery within the lowest well-stratified levels within Trench 8,1 should securely date the Bastion. As reported in Chapter 7C, the character of the pottery is similar in some respects to that of Trench 6, but several sherds show distinctly more developed features which may relate it rather to the pottery of Trench 7 and thus to phase II. The pottery from this area is discussed specifically in Chapter 7C. As noted there the majority of the sherds from inside the Bastion was assignable to Ma I and II. However particular attention must be focused on the well-stratified layers deeper in the sequence, notably Trench 8,1 layers 6, 9 and 10 just inside the Bastion and Trench 8,1 layers 7, 8 and 11 slightly to the south. Two rim sherds of deep bowls (chytrae) of Blue Schist Ware and seven body sherds of the same ware, were found in Trench 8,1 layers 6 and 9. Since this fabric is clearly diagnostic of phases III and IV at Markiani (see Chapter 7A), due weight must given to their presence here. No sherds specifically characteristic of phase IV (as opposed to phase III) were found here and the greater part of the pottery is typical of phases I and II. It would seem then that the early use of the Bastion should be assigned to Ma III, and the same is probably the case for its construction. While it might be possible to argue that the Bastion was built in late phase II and that these sherds represent subsequent use, it seems wiser to follow the principle that the date of construction is determined by the latest well-associated sherds, and thus to Markiani phase III. It should be noted that the radiocarbon samples discussed in Chapter 5 support this conclusion.

The conclusion is that the Bastion represents an addition to the defences belonging to a subsequent phase of occupation. The original defences (Trench 6) are here assigned to Ma I. The Bastion is to be assigned to a subsequent phase: Ma II or more probably phase III.

OUTSIDE THE BASTION: TRENCH 8,2; 8,3; 8,4; 8,5

In Trench 8,2 the removal of a superficial spread of stone revealed a line of stone of relatively small size (c. 25 cm) constituting the lowest course of a wall, designated Wall Γ. It lies about 1.90 m north of the bastion (Wall B). Material from the north side of Wall Γ was kept separate from material between Walls B and Γ. Wall Γ was built at the same time as or after the construction of the bastion. The material in Trench 8,2 dates the use of the bastion rather than its construction. Wall Γ (PLATE 10 b) is of a flimsy character and may not have formed a significant part of the defensive works but, as noted in Chapter 6, it may have the role of an outer defensive wall, albeit of rather slight construction.

Subsequent investigation in the area of Wall Γ, to east and west, did not reveal any considerable extent beyond the 1.20 m length revealed in Trench 8,2. Immediately to the west (and hence just outside Trench 8,2) outside wall Γ the lower part of a jar (stamnos) (K 1524, FIG. 7.12: 1, PLATE 33 a) of Blue Schist Ware was recovered, containing carbonised seeds (see Chapter 9C). A conical cup (K 1523, FIG. 7.11: 18, PLATE 33 b) of Marble Ware was found inside it and a rounded pebble of marble (EE 822-Ma099, FIG. 8.4) and nearby a footed jar (K 1525, FIG. 7.11: 17) of Blue Schist Ware. These may be assigned to the Ma III or IV and thus to a late period in use of the area (see Chapter 7C).

To the west of Trench 8,2 surface cleaning was undertaken with the designation Trench 8,3. Comparable cleaning was undertaken to the north (Trench 8,4) and to the east (Trench 8,5).

AREA WEST OF THE BASTION: TRENCH 8,6

In 1990, the excavation of the Bastion area was completed by the investigation of Trench 8,6, the area lying immediately to the west of the Bastion (FIG. 4.8, PLATE 11 b). Within this trench lies a wall, designated Wall Δ, running westward from the Bastion, along a line some 2.0 m north of the line of Wall A and of the rock face from which the Bastion projects. Wall Δ is of robust construction and should certainly be considered part of the fortification system, abutting as it does against the Bastion itself.

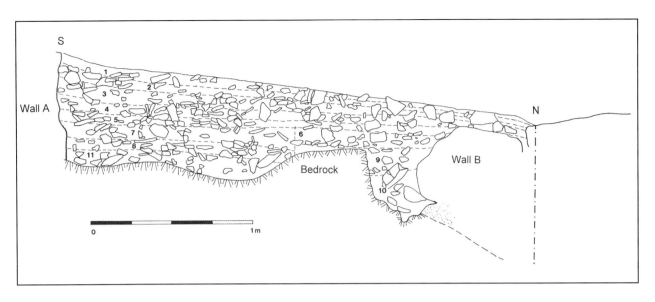

FIG. 4.9. West section of Trench 8,1.

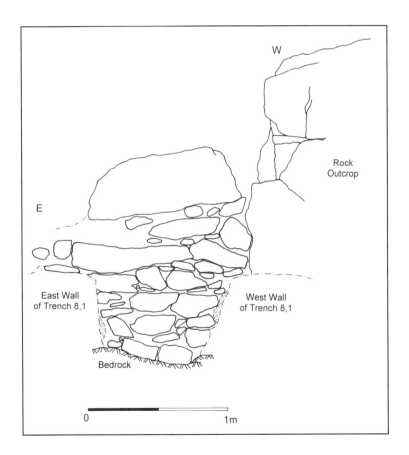

FIG. 4.10. Elevation of Wall A seen from the north from Trench 8, from the Bastion (cf. elevation
of the fortifications in FIG. 6.2 which shows the outside of the Bastion).

During a brief subsequent investigation of the area in 1999 by Giorgos Gavalas, under the supervision
of Professor Marangou, the dry-stone field wall covering the western end of Wall Δ was removed and
the full structure clarified (see FIG. 6.1). It clearly constitutes a small room exterior to the Bastion and
its construction appears to be subsequent to that of the Bastion itself.

Against the west wall of the Bastion, within Trench 8,6, is a well-laid line of stones, 20 cm in
thickness running from the rock face at the south in a northerly direction for some 90 cm (FIG. 4.8).

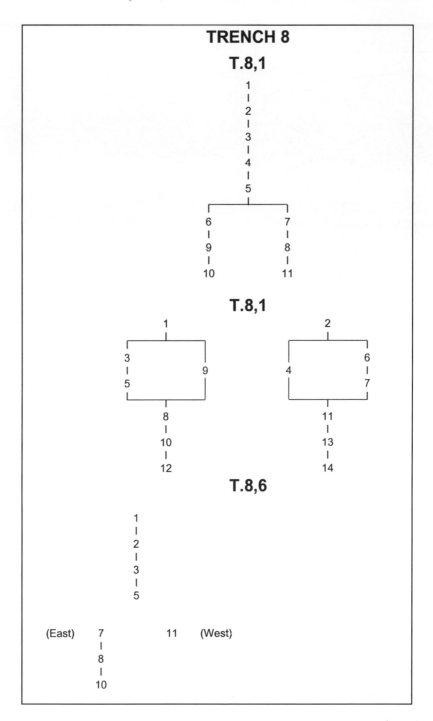

FIG. 4.11. Trench 8 layer diagram.

Against both this and the Bastion is the stonework of Wall Δ which has a well-defined north face, backed by a fill of stones extending back (south) about 1.20 m from the north face. Behind this is a fill of both earth and stones.

The material from the north of Wall Δ was collected separately (Trench 8,6 layer 4 etc.: see FIG. 4.11). That from level 3 downwards, and particularly from layers 7, 8, and 10 should date the construction of Wall Δ, which is later in constructional terms than the bastion. Pottery typical of phase II was found in this area as well as sherds of Grey Schist Ware assignable to phase III. In the upper layers (mainly layer 2) of Trench 8,6 (the area to the west of the bastion) sherds of large coarse storage vessels were found made of Blue Schist Ware, which may be of phase III or IV and certainly represent late occupation of the area.

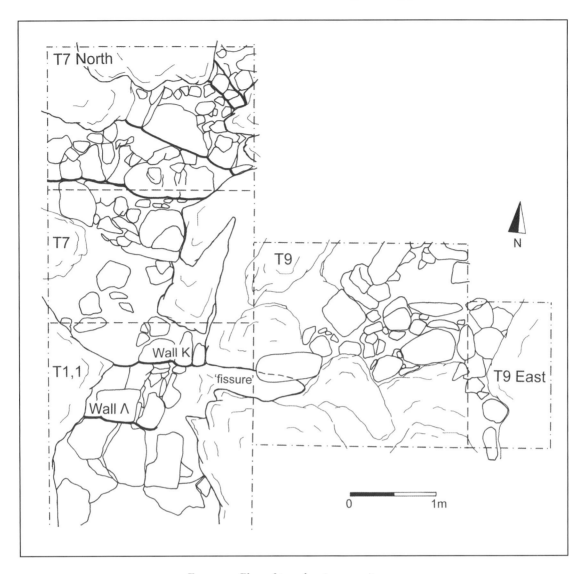

FIG. 4.12. Plan of trenches in summit area.

THE SUMMIT AREA: TRENCHES 1,1 SUMMIT, 7, 9 AND 4

Work on the summit of the site, north of Terrace 1, was initiated within survey Unit 222, which was in fact a small enclosure of stone used mainly as a pen for animals. The area initially selected for excavation lies at the western end of the Unit, immediately above Rock Cutting 2 of the 1985 season. The modern wall at the southern edge of the summit area was dismantled over a length of some 3 m to free the top of the Rock Cutting 2 for excavation (see PLATE 5.1 and PLATE 13 *a–b*).

TRENCH 1,1 SUMMIT

Trench 1,1 was laid out, 3 m wide, extending from the summit down the face of the scarp (a height of 3.20 m) and so down to Terrace 1. It is seen in elevation in FIG. 4.2 and prior to the removal of the modern dry-stone wall (built mainly of ancient material) in PLATE 7 *a*. It is seen after the removal of the modern wall in PLATE 5 *b*. The procedure of digging downwards, down the face of a rocky scarp, naturally produced stratigraphic complexities. It proved possible to resolve these as the work progressed.

The trench runs 4 m N–S, including an extent of some 80 cm in the summit area at the top of Rock Cutting 2. This limited area, Trench 1,1 of the summit, yielded a clear stratigraphy in a series of layers, 1 to 7, at which point natural bedrock was reached. These are all well-stratified layers (see FIG. 4.13), associated layers 17 through 20 representing a small extension to the north of Trench 1,1 measuring 1 m by 1 m (layers 17 to 20, FIG. 4.14).

Cleaning procedures down to the face of the scarp in Rock Cutting 2 revealed Wall Λ, and behind it Wall K (see FIGS. 4.18, 6.3 and 6.4, PLATES 5 *c* and 16 *a*). Layers 8 through 14 were removed during

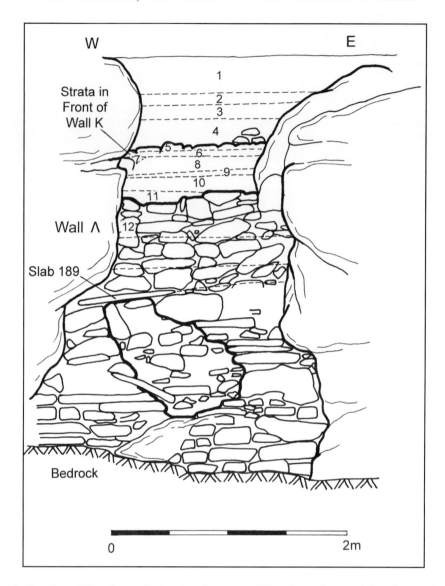

FIG. 4.13. Sketch elevation of Trench 1,1 designating the strata of Trench 1,1 (summit) (levels 1 to 7) against which Wall K was subsequently constructed. Note that the subsequently explored strata from stratum 8 onwards are numbered in the order of the excavation. They lie in the southern part of Trench 1,1 and are later in context and date than strata 1 to 7 of the summit area.

this process. Excavation at the foot of Wall Λ began with layer 21. Excavation of these levels is discussed below along with the discussion of Terrace 1.

It should be noted that there was no stratigraphic connection between the top of the Wall K and the levels at the summit in Trench 1,1 (Layers 1 to 7).

No clear indications of structures were found in the area of Trench 1,1 at the summit, but the investigation was useful in revealing well-stratified deposits of relatively early material. As discussed in Chapter 7C, this was related to the material from Trench 6 (including Heavy Burnished Ware of a fabric with marble filler, forms including bowls with rolled rims and horizontal tubular lug handles); the material here, however, has some more developed features. Moreover, Trench 1,1 layer 7 produced fragments of two 'frying pans' of Kampos type (**K 1071**, FIG. 7.3: 5 and **K 1073**, FIG. 7.3: 2, PLATE 30 *a*).

The stratigraphic context of finds from Trench 1,1 Summit and Trench 7 is set out in TABLE 4.3 (p. 57).

TRENCH 7

During the 1989 season the area excavated at the top of Rock Cutting 2 was enlarged by extending Trench 1,1 northwards in an area designated Trench 7, measuring 2.50 m E–W by 2 m N–S (see plan, FIG. 4.12, and section, FIG. 4.2).

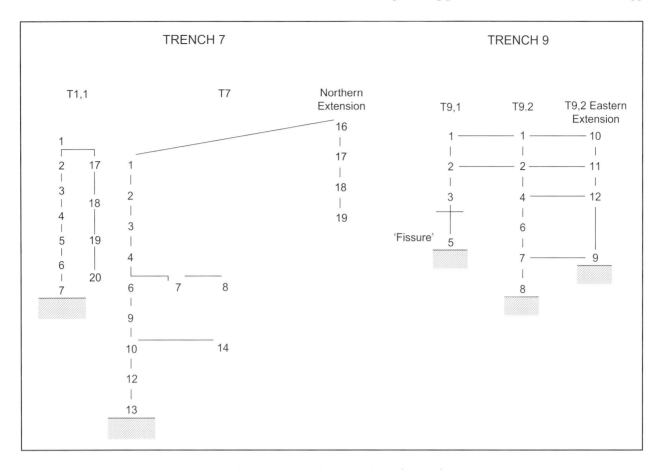

FIG. 4.14. Layer diagram of Trench 7, Trench 1,1 (summit) and Trench 9.

The bedrock slopes down southwards in this area, with many cavities, and there were numerous large stones (of length up to 25 cm) which suggested a deliberate fill, (PLATE 14 *a–b*), perhaps levelling the area in order to sustain structures of which no trace remains today. Amongst these stones were numerous potsherds. This area again proved important, yielding a closed deposit of a more developed phase of material first clearly identified and characterised in Trench 6.

Amongst the pottery were some pieces of interest which merit separate mention:

Part of a jar of Kampos type (**EE 718**, FIG. 7.3: 6, PLATE 30 *b*, Trench 7 layer 10); sherds of two frying pans or related vessels, broadly of Kampos type (**K 1597-EE 705**, FIG. 7.3: 4, PLATE 30 *a*. Trench 7 layer 4; **EE 040**, FIG. 7.3: 1, PLATE 30 *a*, Trench 7 layer 10). There were also two very characteristic Urfinis sherds (**K 1121**, Trench 7 layer 6; **K 1122**, Trench 7 layer 4, FIG. 7.10: 8 and 9) and two clay spoons (**K 1612** and **1613**, FIG. 7.8: 10 and 12, PLATE 32 *a*, Trench 7 layer 9).

A significant number of special finds was made in the deposit represented by Trench 7 layers 6 to 13. The finds included many sherds and fragments of animal bone, various seashells (mainly *Patella*), obsidian flakes, fragments of blades and débitage, stone rubbers (**EE 706**, **EE 707**, **EE 708**, **EE 713**, **EE 721**, **EE 725**, **EE 726**), a clay bead (**EE 714**), clay spoons (**K 1612** and **K 1613**), spindle-whorls (263-**EE 716**, 264-**EE 719**, 266-**EE 723**, FIG. 8.20, PLATE 50 *d*, 265-**EE 724**, 267-**EE 727**), a millstone (**EE 717**), the miniature vase **EE 718**, pottery bases with leaf impressions (**EE 720** etc.). Close to the bedrock in the north-east part of the trench a sherd of a lid and of a Kampos Group frying pan (**K 1597-EE 705**, FIG. 7.3: 4, level 4) were found. At the south part of Trench 7 in level 6 close to the Rock Cutting 2 and the structures (Wall K) three spindle-whorls (259-**EE 710**, 260-**EE 711**, and 261-**EE 712**) were also found. The stones revealed in Trench 7 do not seem to be parts of particular structures but were probably placed so as to level the ground with the highest level of the bedrock, thereby creating a terrace wall up to Rock Cutting 2.

Trench 7 was extended a further 1.60 m to the north in 1990 to bring the excavated area right up against the outcrop of bedrock to the north (layers 16 to 19). Large stones in rows between the higher parts of the natural rock were encountered, suggesting a possible levelling-up operation (see FIG. 4.12, PLATES 14 *b* and 15 *a*).

Although this area was not rich in structural features, the material recovered was well stratified and useful in documenting a more developed phase of the EBA than is seen in Trench 6. As noted earlier the ceramic assemblage of Trench 6 was used to define occupation phase I at Markiani. Similarly the relevant strata of Trench 1,1 (layers 5 to 7) and of Trench 7 (layers 6 to 13) were used to define Markiani phase II.

TRENCH 9

Trench 9, measuring 2 m N-S by 2.70 m E-W, is located to the east of Trenches 1 and 7. It was opened immediately adjacent to these to allow the further investigation of the opening in Rock Cutting 2 in the east side of Trench 1,1 mentioned below and the area between Trench 7 and Trench 4 for the possible relation between Rock Cuttings 2 and 3. Trench 9 was divided into a southern half, Trench 9,1, and a northern half, Trench 9,2, and later also extended to the east. In Trench 9,2, foundations of a wall running from NE–SW were observed, probably belonging to a later (? Geometric) phase. Only in the lowest level, near bedrock of the summit area (Trench 9,2 layer 8) was an undisturbed EC deposit found, similar in character to that of Trench 7. A further spread of stones, indicative of a wall structure, is seen in Trench 9,1, extending north and eastwards from the already noted in Trench 7. To the south the opening in the east of Trench 1,1, 'the fissure', was investigated from above as Trench 9,1 layer 5.

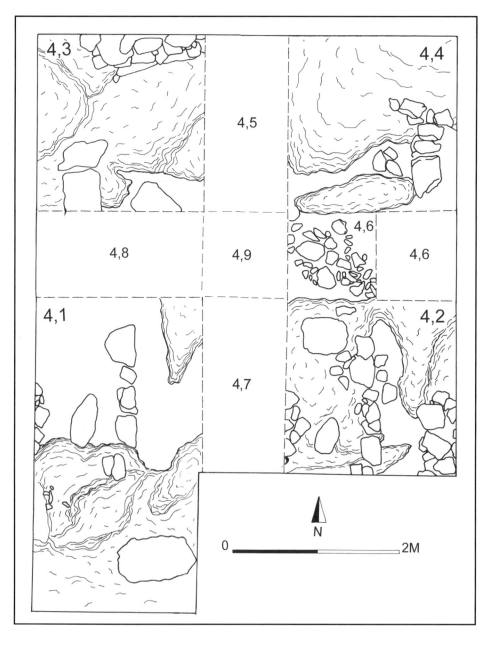

FIG. 4.15. Plan of Trench 4.

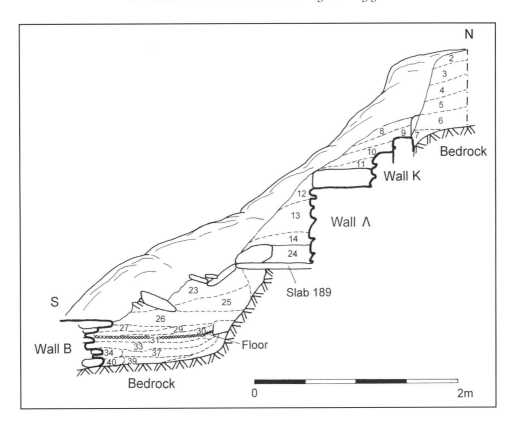

FIG. 4.19. Sketch section of Trench 1,1 (scarp area) illustrating the cleaning and excavation sequence.
Note strata 1 to 7 over the bedrock in the summit area: Wall K was subsequently built against the scarp face
(cf. FIG. 4.18 and also FIG. 6.4 at the end of the excavation process the levels below slab 189 were well stratified).
The levels from Wall K down to slab 189 represent mainly cleaning activities.

noted that layers 8 to 14 of Trench 1,1 were not stratigraphically below layer Trench 1,1, layer 7, which lies above bedrock in the summit area. They are simply material removed during the investigation of Wall Λ, and are not well stratified. The area after removal of Trench 1,1, layers 8 to 14 is seen in PLATE 16.

The area was further investigated in 1989, when the space below and to the south of Wall Λ was excavated. It proved to be an almost circular walled area whose southern side is designated Wall 1,3 B (see FIGS. 4.18 and 4.2, PLATE 5 c). Within this circular space was a series of deposits (FIG. 4.19) which, from layer 21 to the floor (layer 29) yielded an important and homogeneous collection of material. As described in Chapter 7E it included many sherds characteristic of the so-called Kastri Group. Prominent among these was a well-preserved 'depas ampikypellon' (albeit lacking one of the handles) (**K 1723**, FIG. 7.19: 8, PLATES 15 b and 35 a), found stratified in layer T1,1 25, immediately in front of the flat slab (slab 189 and its two neighbours) on which Wall Λ rests. Slab 189 beneath the lower courses of Wall Λ is seen in PLATE 16 a and the depas of Trench 1,1 layer 25 is seen in PLATE 15 b. As already observed in the surface survey of 1985 (see Chapter 2), this material also included a large number of spindle-whorls, some 28 in well-stratified levels. A characteristic sherd of Urfirnis Ware was found in these levels (**EE 047** from Trench 1,1 layer 25), and a painted sherd (**K 1722**, FIG. 7.21: 9, PLATE 38 g) and a sherd with an incision of a fish (**K 1244**, FIG. 7.26: 18, PLATE 38 a) come from Trench 1,1 layer 24.

This important deposit (layers 21 to 30, and 34 to 36 of Trench 1,1), which, as we shall see, is contemporary with other deposits further to the east in Terrace 1, is clearly later than the construction of the circular walling which contains it (Wall B and Wall v) and the vertical walling (Wall Λ) which rests upon that circular walling (Wall ξ) (see FIG. 4.18). It represents a relatively late phase within this local sequence. It represents one of the richest assemblages of the period designated by us Ma IV, the last phase of intensive occupation of the site at the end of the EBA.

Investigation below the floor constituting layers 29 and 30 revealed a sequence of earlier deposits down to layer 40 (see section, FIG. 4.19 and levels diagram FIG. 4.20) This material showed typological as well as stratigraphic indications that it was earlier in date than the deposit just described. Its nature

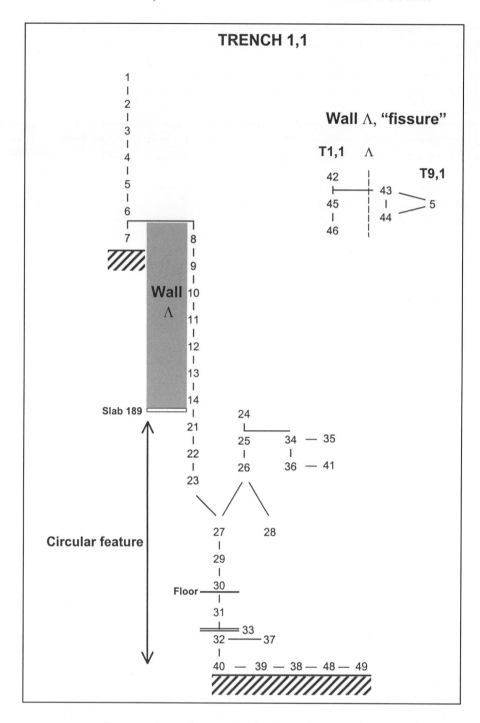

FIG. 4.20. Layer diagram for Trench 1,1 (scarp area).

is discussed in Chapter 7D where its similarity with the finds in Trench 3 is noted. It should be noted that a sauceboat sherd (**K 1213**) came from Trench 1,1 layer 33. Spindle-whorls were also frequent in these levels. The possibility of stratigraphic confusion here, or of mixing, was considered carefully and rejected. Both the stratigraphy and the consistent nature of the associated pottery indicate that spindle-whorls occur with notable frequency in this area in two distinct phases (i.e. during phase Ma IV, and in this earlier phase). This seems a clear indication of continuity in use.

Immediately on the bedrock in this area (Trench 1,1 layers 38, 39, 48 and 49) pottery was found which may be of a slightly earlier aspect.

The subsequent investigation of Wall Λ in 1989, by the removal of its eastern half, revealed an earlier phase of walling behind it, Wall K (PLATES 5 *c* and 16 *a*). Wall Λ is a well-built dry-stone wall, constructed of slabs of up to 40 cm in length in courses of 10 to 15 cm. It fills the 1.50 m width of Rock Cutting 2. It is preserved to a height of some 90 cm, resting on slabs (including slab 189 and its neighbours) which in turn rest on the rear (north) part of the circular installation, Wall B of Trench 1,3. We judged, after much discussion, that in both its phases Wall Λ was simply a retaining wall within the Rock Cutting (which is itself a natural feature).

The circular structure in Trench 1,1 (FIG. 4.18) was built within the cutting at an earlier stage and with it the earlier version of Wall Λ. This is clearly seen in PLATE 5 c and FIG. 4.18. A hollow in the bedrock was delimited on its southern side by the fine dry-stone walling which constitutes Wall B and of which three courses (each of c. 15 cm) are preserved. One prominent slab measures 75 × 50 cm, and this width of 50 cm establishes the width of the wall. Most of the other slabs here are less than 50 cm in length. The west end of Wall B abuts the vertical face of the bedrock to the west of the Rock Cutting. Wall B thus runs east from this face, turns north along the east face of the Rock Cutting, and then turns west following the north edge of the rock hollow. In the north it consists of large slabs (65 × 55 cm). The lower course of Wall L rests on these.

At this point it is convenient to mention Structure Z (FIG. 4.18, PLATE 16 c), immediately to the south, lying against the southern side of the circular wall, Wall B. Structure Z was followed westwards when Trench 10 was opened west of Trench 1,3. Trench 10 measures 2.50 m E–W to 1.50 m N–S. This structure, as we have noted, runs westward and then turns north some 50 cm west of the west side of the Cutting (and of the west end of Wall B). It then turns north and ends after 35 cm (FIG. 4.18, PLATE 16 c). At its east end Structure Z consists, as preserved, of a series of long slabs (length 45 to 60 cm; width 25 to 35 cm) set approximately north–south, lying in part against Wall B. The sherd material found to the west of Structure Z, like that in the lower layers of Terrace 1 (Trench 10, layer 3), clearly pre-dates the materials of Ma IV, and in general sense may be assigned to Ma III. In layer 4 of Trench 10 a clay sealing was discovered (**EE 1802**, FIG. 8.25: 4, PLATE 53 b).

THE 'FISSURE', TRENCH 1,1 AND TRENCH 9

At the east end of Wall Λ a substantial opening (a natural cave?) was found running eastwards in the rock, the 'fissure' (FIG. 4.18, PLATE 16 a–b), which had been formed simply by the splitting of the rock face. It had been surmounted originally by a large stone slab, forming a roofed recess or cupboard. The covering slab had subsequently fallen some way into it.

The investigation of this fissure (Trench 1,1 layers 43 to 44 along with Trench 9,1 layer 5) produced pottery which resembles that beneath the floor (Trench 1,1, layers 30 to 40) of the circular feature already discussed. This opening, it was soon recognised, was a natural fissure in the rock, exploited by the use of covering slabs to form an enclosed space or cupboard.

The construction of the final phase of Wall Λ involved the placing of a stone slab within this opening. Pottery (see Chapter 7D) and other finds, including 25 spindle-whorls were found in the levels above this slab (layers 44 and Trench 9,1 layer 5). Pottery and spindle-whorls were again recovered beneath the equivalent slabs of Wall Λ (layer 46).

A find of particular interest from this area, from layer 44, was the impression of what appears to be a rectangular seal impression on a piece of pottery (**EE 197** FIG. 8.10). The form of the pot is uncertain, but the impression of the stamp with a spiral relief surmounting a triangle relief, is very clear.

The earlier phase of Wall Λ, and behind it Wall K, is not closely dated stratigraphically. There was no stratigraphic linkage with the summit levels of Trench 1,1. However the late phase of Wall Λ which closed the 'fissure' must fall chronologically between the contents of the 'fissure' (assigned to Markiani phase III) and the material which subsequently filled the circular area with pottery characteristic of phase IV. The later phase of Wall Λ is possibly contemporary with that of the circular feature. Wall K of course pre-dates Wall Λ.

The stratigraphic context of catalogued finds from Ma III from the 'Fissure', Trench 1,1 and Trench 9 is set out in TABLE 4.4 (p. 61).

TERRACE 1: TRENCHES 1,2, 1,3 ETC. AND TRENCH 2 AND 5

Terrace 1 is today seen as a level terrace, extending some 30 m E–W, lying immediately below (i.e. to the south of) the 3.50 m scarp which separates it from the relatively flat area at the summit (Surface survey Units 218–222) (FIGS. 2.2 and 2.3, PLATES 4 a, 5 a, 6 b). It should be noted that the nomenclature of the terraces and trenches developed in the course of the excavation of this rather complex terrain. The original nomenclature has been retained despite its apparent complexity

The width of the terrace (from N–S) is some 7 m towards its western end. The terrace is retained on its southern side by a field wall, which is built up to a height of about 1 m above the level of the terrace, enclosing it on the south side (PLATE 3 a–b).

The principal area of excavation undertaken was at the western end of Terrace 1 (see FIG. 4.3). There the area already briefly discussed, Trench 1,1, was extended to the south by some 4 m. The trenches Trench 1,2 (to the south) and Trench 1,3 (to the north) are each 3 m wide (E–W), as is Trench 1,1. Each measures approximately 2 m N-S.

A baulk (width 1 m) to the east separates Trench 1 from Trench 2, which again measures 3 m E–W (PLATE 18 a). It is divided into a southern portion, Trench 2,2, east of Trench 1,2, and a north, namely Trench 2,1, east of Trench 1,3. The baulk between these two was later excavated as Trench 1,4.

Once the walls and other features now to be described had emerged, it proved necessary to extend the trenches by various small additional areas. Thus Trench 2,3 lay to the south of Trench 2,2, separated from it by a 1 m baulk. The east side of Trench 2,3 corresponded to (i.e. lies due south of) the east side of Trench 2,1 and 2, 2. Trench 2,3 measures 2 m E–W. The western half of the intervening baulk (1 m × 1 m) was later removed as Trench 2,5.

Trench 1,5 and 1,6 and two small areas in addition were also opened as indicated on the plan (FIG. 4.21). Trench 10 was also, in a late phase of the work, opened to the west of Trench 1.

These indications, although inevitably somewhat cumbersome, were necessary to give strict stratigraphic control within this rather complex area. The numeration system is thus a conventional one, which is to be read in conjunction with the Level Diagram (FIG. 4.23) for this area, which indicates the stratigraphic relations of the excavated levels.

During the 1988 and 1989 excavation seasons, work proceeded in Trenches 1,2; 1,3; 2, 1 and 2,2 (and indeed also in Trench 1,1) producing the structural configuration seen in FIG. 4.3 and FIG. 4.21. Walls were here designated by the letters[3] assigned by individual trench supervisors.

At the north side of Terrace 1, the bedrock is visible without removing soil, and this bedrock slopes down to the south, so that at the southern side there is a depth of soil of some 1.30 m between the present surface of the terrace and the bedrock.

The terrace has been re-shaped in relatively recent times, and then worked (reportedly for the cultivation of onions, see Chapter 2) so that there is a mixed superficial layer of humus, stones and sherds of various dates. It is of note that some painted sherds, possibly of EC date, were found in these levels (**EE 208**, Trench 2,2 layer 3; **EE 052**, Trench 2,2 layer 10; **EE 051**, Trench 1,2 layer 2). From more deeply stratified levels comes a sherd with the incised outline of a fish, which joined with many others found in the area (**K 1212** FIG. 7.26: 17 and FIG. 7.17: 1, PLATE 36 e, Trench 1,4 layer 6). This rather superficial humus layer is only some 15 to 20 cm deep on the north side, but as much as 60 cm on the south.

The situation on the deeper, southern side is well illustrated by the south section of Trench 1,2 where the depth of superficial humus in 50 cm (layers 1 to 3). Below layer 5 the material may be considered well stratified (FIG. 4.22).

It was not until 1990 that the area was completed by the opening of the various southern extensions, which serve rather to complicate the nomenclature. This revealed the complex seen in the final plan (FIGS. 6.3, 4.21, PLATES 18–25).

To the south-west (in T1, 2 and T1, 5, FIG. 4.3) are the north and east walls of a room designated Space 1 (PLATE 19 a). Abutting its eastern wall is a further wall which runs east into Trench 2,2 and then turns south, thus enclosing another room, Space 2 (PLATES 18 a–b and 19 b). To the north of this, further enclosed by walls, this time on four sides, is an area designated Space 3 (PLATE 18 a–b). East of the east wall of Space 3 and south of Rock cutting 3, is Space 5 where lots of seashells over a layer of schist slabs revealed.

A very striking feature of this complex is the drainage system (FIG. 4.21). A drain runs down immediately against the east side of the east wall of Room 1 (PLATES 19 a and 22 a). Following this drain north (uphill) we can trace it under the north wall of Space 2 and so into Space 3 (PLATES 18 b and 20 a–b), and again north beneath the north wall of Space 3, and so into the area lying between that wall and the vertical scarp to the north of Terrace 1: this area is designated *Space 6*. It is clear that the scarp north of Terrace 1 was worked, in order to channel the run-off water from the summit area. This was then conducted into the drainage system as described.

In addition, the N–S length of the drain in Space 3 (PLATE 22 a–b) is joined from the west by a drain from the space lying immediately to the west (Space 4). This drain again runs between the relevant wall, namely the west wall of Space 3. This second drain runs immediately against the north face of

---

[3] For orthographic convenience the terminology of the walls here differs from that employed during the excavation. Thus, Walls P, Q, R and S in Trench 2 correspond to Walls β, γ, δ and ε.

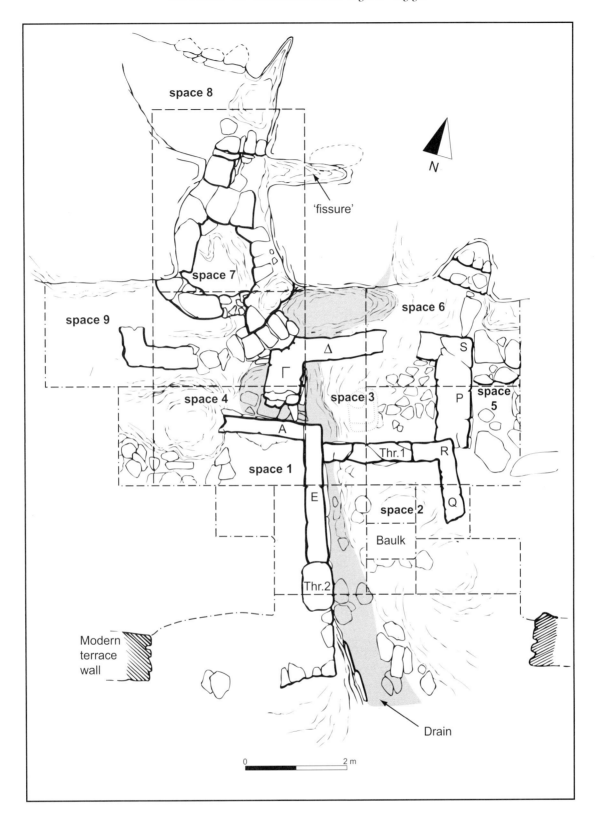

FIG. 4.21. Sketch plan of Terrace 1 showing walls, spaces and other features.

the north wall of Room 1 (PLATE 19 *a*). Against this northern face runs a row of thin, upright slabs, no doubt placed with the intention of controlling the run-off and protecting this wall from erosion (PLATES 21 *b* and 22 *a*).

Before further discussing the process of excavation of this area, it is convenient to mention its relationship to the structures already briefly discussed in Trench 1,1. It will be recalled that south of

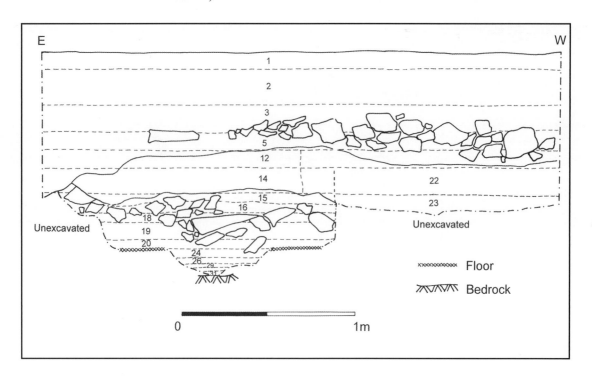

FIG. 4.22. Section of south face of T 1,2 looking south.

the vertical walling at the north of Trench 1,1 (Wall Λ) lies the circular feature whose south side is constituted by Wall B of Trench 1,3. Lying against this, to the south, partly supporting it, and certainly following its line is Structure Z (PLATE 16 c). This was later followed west into Trench 10, Space 9. Even without considering the stratigraphy in detail, it is evident that the outer north-west corner of Space 3 does not make a clear right angle, but follows the curved line of the outer (southern) side of Structure Z (PLATES 18 a–b and 19 a).

These observations could only be made, of course, as the excavation process proceeded. But as far as possible we shall avoid the rather cumbersome nomenclature of walls assigned during excavation and refer instead to the rooms and spaces which it was possible to designate above.

As excavation proceeded, very few features were observed until the principal structures already briefly noted were revealed. An exception was offered by Wall 'a' (of Trench 2, PLATE 17 a–b) running in an E–W direction in the south-east corner of Trench 2,2. It was of broadly 'Classical', possibly late Hellenistic date.

In Trench 2, and mainly in Trench 2,1, near the mouth of Cutting 3, a series of levels north of Wall Γ, and thus within Space 6 (PLATES 18 b and 19 b), contained material including sherds of tankards and other material characteristic of the Kastri Group.

This deposit, mainly in Trench 1,3, layers 3, 4, 5, 7, and layers 17, 27 to 31 of Trench 1,4, and Trench 2, layers 20 and 22 to 31 (FIG. 4.23) is analogous to that in Trench 1,1, layers 21 to 29 and may be used to define the ceramic characteristics of the phase designated Ma IV. As noted in Chapter 7E, this is related to the Kastri Group, but the finds at Markiani are of course to be associated in their own right.

Within Space 3, large flat stone slabs were found lying horizontally in a yellow clayey material with broken pottery in some cases lying above them (PLATE 24 a). One possibility suggested was that this represents the fallen material from a roof, the yellow material resembling the yellow clay used today for sealing roofs. But the very uniformly horizontal position of these stones, and the existence of broken potsherds above them may be taken to suggest, rather, that this is a floor with successive renewals utilising this clay material (Floors 'a' and 'b'). (On the other hand, flat stones and analogous clay material were found overlying a pottery deposit in Space 1, and had obviously fallen from above.) The clay with pottery in Trench 1,4 layer 4, at a higher level than the flat stones to the east, is seen in PLATE 24 a–b.

A significant deposit of pottery was found (Trench 2 layer 44) at about the same level in absolute terms, but to the south of the south wall of Space 3 (Wall δ-δ'-R). It was therefore in the north-east corner of Space 2. It included one of those hitherto enigmatic 'mask-like' objects (**EE 257**, FIG. 7.25: 1, PLATES 19 c and 37 a–e) which may now be considered a small brazier.

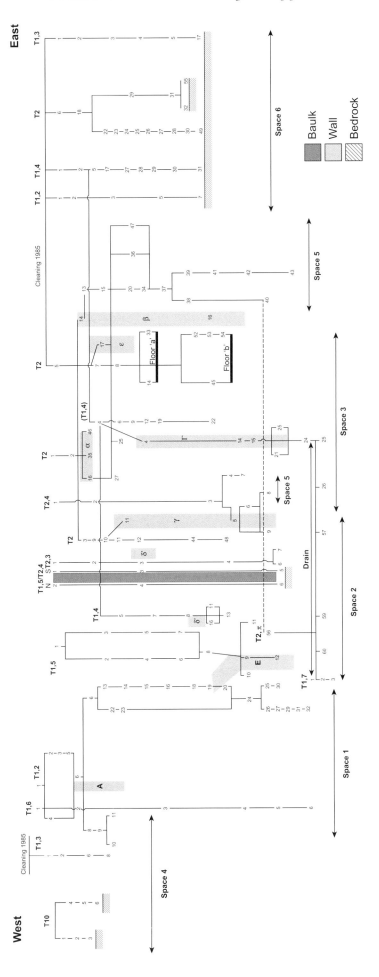

FIG. 4.23. Terrace 1 layer diagram.

Another significant ceramic deposit was found in Space 1 (Trench 1,6 layer 6) under the fallen slabs of the roof briefly mentioned earlier. These were conspicuous in the section (PLATE 19 *b*), and although lying fairly flat were not in a regular horizontal position. The finds here included a narrow-mouthed jug (**EE 098**) and a fine stone pestle (**EE 1612**, FIG. 8.4, PLATE 40 *b*). This deposit is the same as that previously excavated at the very south of Trench 1,2, south of the north wall of Room 1 (Wall A of Trench 1,2). In the north-east corner of this room was found the large coarse stone vessel (**EE 174**, FIG. 8.13, PLATES 19 *b* and 43 *e*, Trench 1,2 layer 27). A Keros-Syros painted sherd was found at a somewhat higher level in this area (**K 1711-EE 161**, PLATE 38 *f*, Trench 1,2 layer 15). The sequence of excavations in this particular area is very well illustrated by the series of plates, from layer 16 to layer 23, where the roof slabs lie over the stone vessel, and so on PLATE 19 *b*.

No indications were found to link the major rectilinear structure (Spaces 1, 2 and 3) with the pottery seen to accompany the earlier use of the site, whether in the very early (Ma I) or the more advanced phase (Ma II). Instead the character of the pottery was very close to that of Trench 3, itself related to the material designated Ma III.

In general pottery of Ma IV (including Kastri-type tankards) is found in the late phase of most of the excavated areas of Terrace 1, with the exception of that from Space 1, which may have gone out of use at an earlier stage. The pottery from Space 6, near the scarp, is presented in Chapter 7E. As noted earlier, this last contains shapes characteristic of the Kastri Group. It is significant therefore that fragments of tankards, a diagnostic form of this group, are found in Trench 1,1 (notably in layers 21, 24 and 29 as already noted) and in Trench 2 (layers 20, 23, 24, 26 and 27), along with Trench 1,4 layer 27 nearby (FIG. 4.23).

Tankard sherds also occur south of the main area of Trench 2, in Trench 2, layer 56 (**K 1197**) and in Trench 2, layer 59. Both of these locations are in Space 2, the latter piece being found actually within the drain at this point. A painted sherd (**K 1710-EE 095**, FIG. 7.26: 19, PLATE 38 *e*) was likewise found in this drain in Trench 1,5 layer 60. The implication here may be that the final use of these rooms is contemporary with the material with Kastri forms found in abundance in Space 6 to the north. The construction of these buildings, however, may be earlier, possibly not long after the construction of the circular features in Trench 1,1.

The stratigraphic context of catalogued finds of Ma phase IV from Terrace 1, Space 7, Trench 1,1; Space 3, Trenches 2 and 1,4; Space 6, Trenches 1,3; 1,4; 2 is outlined in TABLE 4.5 (below p. 63).

Having outlined the process of excavation in this area, it is appropriate to turn again to the main constructional complex itself. Its principal features were outlined above.

The structural and stratigraphic evidence both indicate that the installation with the circular Wall B (of Trench 1,3), to the north-west of the main complex, is earlier. The outer north-west corner of Room 3, as noted above, is of a shape indicating that it is of subsequent construction to Structure Z, which itself was built against pre-existing Wall B.

Space 1 has a north wall 35 to 40 cm in width, faced on both sides. To the west it runs up against the bedrock. At a distance of 1.85 m to the east it reaches the north-east corner of the room. This north wall of Room 1 is designated Wall A. At its north side, thin (5 cm) upright slabs protected it from the waters of the drain which lies immediately north of it.

This wall is joined by the east wall of room 1 (Wall E), which is also 40 cm in width and runs south to a preserved length of 3.40 m. The lowest foundation course is wider than the 40 cm of the wall: it is formed of large flat slabs some 55 cm wide. The southernmost in this line of slabs is no longer surmounted by any further masonry. It measures 1.00 m by 60 cm, and has the appearance of a sill (*katophli*, threshold 2, FIG. 4.21). However, it may simply be a foundation stone for the wall above, which is no longer preserved.

Against the east wall of Room 1, and 45 cm south of the external north-east corner of the room, abuts the north wall of Room 2 (i.e. Wall δ-R of Trench 1,3 and of Trench 2,1). At its west end it crosses the drain so that in that position lower courses are absent. This wall is 35 cm wide, and runs east for 2.80 m across to the north-east corner of Space 2. There is no doubt that it was constructed *after* the east wall of Room 1. In the middle of the length of this wall is a large slab, threshold 1 (FIG. 4.3), dimensions 1.12 m × 40 cm. This may well be the sill giving access from Space 2 into Room 3. The wall turns south, as Wall γ-Q, and is preserved there for a length of 1.60 m. Once again it is here 40 cm thick. The walls of Rooms 1 and 2 have a regular appearance: they are well built (PLATE 23 *a*).

Abutting the north-east corner of Room 2 and in part built around this corner (see FIG. 4.3) is the east wall of Room 3 (Wall β-P of Trench 2, PLATE 23 *b*). It runs 2.10 m N–S, and is 70–75 cm thick.

The north-east corner is very well preserved (PLATE 25 *a*). The north wall here (Wall ε-S, of Trench 2) forms a structural unit with this, but is only 50 cm thick. Part of this wall is missing where the bedrock rises, but the wall was probably not originally interrupted at this point. This wall is again well preserved along the western part of its length. To the west it runs over the drain, so that at this point its lower courses are missing.

The north-west corner of Room 3, as we have noted, is adjusted to meet Structure Z. The west wall of Room 3 (Wall Δ of Trench 1) again forms one construction with the north wall, and is 60 to 70 cm thick. Originally it abutted against the north wall of Space 1, over-sailing the E–W drain.

The E–W drain north of the north wall of Space 1 thus runs underneath this wall and joins the N–S drainage channel, which runs along the east side of the west wall of Room 3 and again along the east side of the west wall of Space 2.

It seems clear that this drain ran *under the floor* of Space 3. The slab at the north-west corner of Room 3 (PLATE 18 *a–b*) very clearly runs over the drain, as does the slab in the south-west corner which is clearly seen on the plan. This may explain the slab construction of the floor of Room 3 which, it should be noted, had clear traces of burning in the centre Meanwhile we obtained no evidence that the drain was roofed in either Space 2 or Space 4.

Rooms 1 and 3 would appear to have been in regular use. Whether Room 2 was roofed, or was simply an open space, is not at present clear.

From the standpoint of our understanding of Cycladic settlement, this complex of rooms makes an important contribution, not least with the drainage system discussed in Chapter 6B. The seeming continuity from an advanced phase of the EBA, Ma III to a late phase Ma IV (with Kastri Group material) is of considerable interest. This continuity may be suggested for the central complex, and can clearly be demonstrated for Trench 1,1, as we have seen.

TRENCH 5

At a distance of 3.85 m east of the east side of Trench 2, a further trench, Trench 5 (FIG. 4.1, PLATE 25.2), was opened at the foot of Rock Cutting 4. Measuring some 3.60 m E–W, and 2 m N–S, it offered the hope of finding EC structures further east along the terrace. Work was delayed here by the discovery of a large part of a pithos of Hellenistic date, clearly *in situ*. Time did not permit further work in this area.

THE SOUTHERN AREA: TRENCH 3

In order to investigate aspects of the settlement beyond the central area, a terrace some 25 m south-east of Terrace 1 was selected lying some 10 m below the level of Terrace 1. This was Terrace Unit 508, and within it Trench 3 was laid out (FIG. 4.1, PLATE 26 *a*).

A straight line running E–W served as a baseline, located some 2 m north of the retaining wall of the terrace. Two trenches, each approximately 3 m wide, were laid out, separated by a 1m baulk (FIG. 4.24, PLATE 28 *c*). These were Trenches 3,1 (PLATE 26 *b*) and 3,2 (PLATE 27 *a*). Each extended some 2.30 m north, until the steep slope of the bedrock was reached. Later the baulk was removed (as Trench 3,3) and Trench 3,4 opened directly to the east of Trench 3,2, along the same E–W line. This extends another 1.40 m east, to the natural rock outcrop, and up to 3 m to the north. In addition, to follow the extension to the south of the important wall running southward beyond the baulk, a trench, Trench 3,5, measuring 2 m E–W, and extending some 90 cm to the south of the baseline was opened.

The principal feature to emerge in Trench 3 was this wall, which runs N–S along the western end of Trench 3,2. This feature, Wall A, thus divides the excavation area in two (PLATE 28 *a* and *c*).

To the west was Room 1, which was unified into a single unit with the later removal of the baulk between Trench 3,1 and Trench 3,2 as Trench 3,3 (see PLATE 28 *c*). To the east was Room 2, including Trench 3,2 and later (following the extension) Trench 3,4 (see PLATE 28 *a*). The southward extension of the Trench (Trench 3,5) allowed this wall to be followed into the terrace walling until its eroded south end could be found. Originally it had extended further to the south.

Wall A is 80 cm in width, well built, of dry-stone slabs. It contains a recess, entered from the west, which is 70 cm wide (N–S) and 50 cm deep.

The east wall of Room 2 (PLATE 27 *b*) is provided by the vertical scarp of the bedrock. In this room the rock floor rises steeply to the north, so that the effective floor space is at the southern side. There is some walling (Wall Θ) 1.20 m to the north of the baseline at the south edge of the trench, and at a higher level, 1.80 cm north of the baseline, Wall Z which closes the space on the north side.

The rock rises steeply from the south to north in the same way in Room 1. The space is delineated at the north by Wall I, some 1.40 m north of the south edge of the trench. There is a pronounced

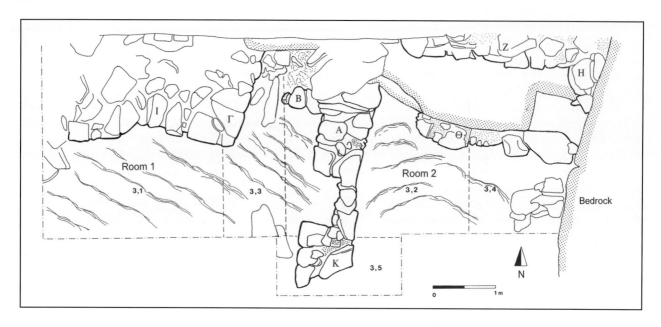

FIG. 4.24. Plan of Trench 3.

corner in Wall I which turns northwards as it approaches the west face of Wall A. Wall I turns north
1.40 m west of the west face of Wall A. The west section of Trench 3,2 is seen in FIG. 4.25, and the
levels diagram in FIG. 4.27.

The elucidation of this area is not easy, but the finds in the lower levels (Trench 3,2 layers 9, 10
and 12) were probably *in situ* since they lay almost immediately upon the bedrock (see FIG. 4.26,
PLATE 27 *a–b*).

The finds in both rooms were numerous, and merit discussion. The pottery throughout formed a
homogeneous assemblage. It was marked by the absence of any really fine ware: all the pottery could
reasonably be described as 'domestic', most of it coarse. From the standpoint of fabric it belonged to

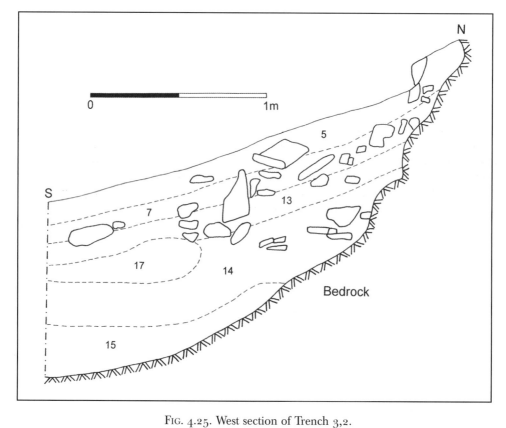

FIG. 4.25. West section of Trench 3,2.

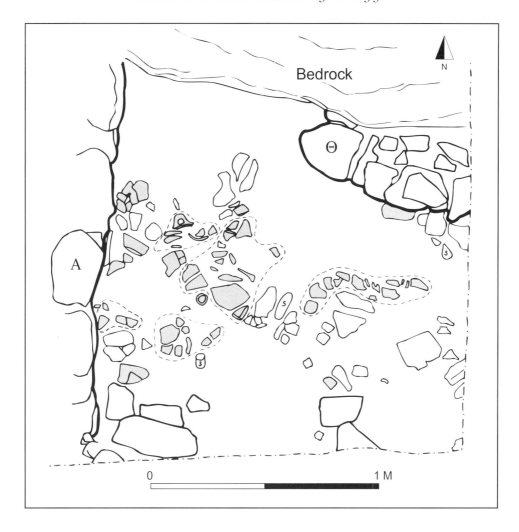

FIG. 4.26. Plan of finds in Trench 3,2, layer 9.

the second of two major ceramic divisions on the site, i.e. Markiani phases I and II versus phases III and IV, the fabric being characteristically tempered with local schist. The surface is in general not specially treated, the shapes are often deep or closed.

There was a complete absence of shapes diagnostic of Ma IV (related to the Kastri Group), such as the tankards, such a conspicuous feature of Space 6 of Terrace 1. Whether this suggests that the finds from Trench 3 were earlier in date than relevant levels of Terrace 1, or were simply a domestic assemblage lacking such (possibly imported) fine wares is a question which was not addressed in detail. At this stage it seems safest to regard the finds as belonging to a late stage of Ma III.

Along with the pottery were other finds, including a series of flat circular stone discs, of diameter from 9 to 34 cm which are here termed 'pot-lids' (*pomata*, see chapter 8B, FIG. 8.14–15 and PLATE 43 *c–d*) although they may have had other functions.

ROOM 2

Room 2 includes the levels of Trench 3,2 situated east of Wall A (see the level diagram, FIG. 4.27), Trench 3,4 and the eastern part of Trench 3,5. During the process of excavation the most obvious concentration of material was the great mass of pottery in the lower levels at the south, specifically in layers Trench 3,2 layers 9, 10 and 12. Particularly notable was the portable oven from Trench 3,2 layer 9 (M104), the function of which appeared to be very clear after restoration. Its reconstruction explained several other, hitherto enigmatic, fragments from elsewhere on the site. It also suggested an explanation for the comparable but smaller objects, one of them (**K 1704**, FIG. 7.13, PLATE 34) Trench 3,2 layer 12) found here. Also particularly abundant in Room 2 were the stone 'pot-lids', and a notable sequence of coarse stone tools.

TABLE 4.2. The stratigraphic context of catalogued finds of Markiani phase I from Trench 6,1.

TRENCH/LAYER	POTTERY				SMALL FINDS				
	Shape	Cat. no.	FIG.	PLATE	Category	Type	Cat. no.	FIG.	PLATE
Trench 6,1 layer 2	Collared jar with concave collar and out-turned rim	K 1459	7.2 : 7						
Trench 6,1 layer 3	Deep bowls with lugs with in-turned walls	K 1457	7.1 : 11						
		K 1458	7.1 : 12						
	Collared jar with concave collar and out-turned rim	K 1082	7.2 : 6						
Trench 6,1 layer 4	Deep bowl with vertical lugs beneath rim	K 1114	7.1 : 9						
	Horizontal cylindrical lug of pithos	K 1113	7.2 : 13	29 c					
Trench 6,1 layer 5	Vessels or braziers with strainer	K 1087	7.2 : 11	29 e	Stone tool	polisher	EE 602		
		K 1088	7.2 : 12	29 e					
Trench 6,1 layer 6	Rolled-rim bowl	K 1481	7.1 : 1	29 a					
	Deep bowls with lugs and in-turned rim	K 1480	7.1 : 6						
	Deep bowl with lugs and in-turned profile	K 1479	7.1 : 10						
	Cooking vessel or part of oven	K 1482	7.2 : 14						
Trench 6,1 layer 7	Deep bowl with horizontal lug near the rim	K 1500	7.1 : 3	29 c					
		K 1501	7.1 : 4	29 c					
	Deep bowl with lugs and in-turned rim	K 1499	7.1 : 5						
Trench 6,1 layer 8	Deep bowl with lugs and inturned rim	K 1503	7.1 : 7						
	Deep bowl with vertical lugs beneath the rim	K 1057	7.1 : 8	29 b					
	Deep bowl with horizontal crescent-shaped lugs	K 1502	7.2 : 1						
	Storage vessel with horizontal handle	K 1052	7.2 : 5	29 d					
	Collared jar with concave collar and out-turned rim	K 1054	7.2 : 8						
	Base of deep bowl	K 1050	7.2 : 9		Mat impression	Radially twined mat rather worn	K 1050		
Trench 6,1 layer 9					Coarse stone	Schist lid	EE 601	8.15	
Trench 6,1 layer 10	Disc/plate	K 1504	7.2 : 15		Obsidian flake				

TABLE 4.3. The stratigraphic context of catalogued finds of Markiani phase II from Trench 1,1 summit and Trench 7.

TRENCH/ LAYER	POTTERY				SMALL FINDS				
	Shape	Cat. no.	FIG.	PLATE	Category	Type	Cat. no.	FIG.	PLATE
Trench 1,1 layer 6	Various bowls of the late rolled-rim type	K 1072	7.6: 10						
	Deep hemispherical bowl with thin walls, 'Kouphonisi' type bowl	K 1123	7.7: 3						
Trench 1,1 layer 7	Frying pan	K 1073	7.3: 2	30 a	Spindle-whorl	Conical	EE 108		
		K 1071	7.3: 5	30 a					
	Deep closed spherical vessel	K 1643	7.4: 2						
	Wide-mouthed vessel with concave collar and out-turned swelling rim	K 1126	7.5: 15						
	Various bowls of the late rolled-rim type	K 1124	7.6: 7						
		K 1125	7.6: 9						
Trench 1,1 layer 8					Spindle-whorl	Flat convex stamped	EE 106	8.20: 1	
						Flat conical	EE 111	8.20: 2	
Trench 1,1 layer 19									
Trench 1,1 layer 20	Mobile hat-shaped hearth	K 1641	7.10: 7	32 c					
Trench 7 layer 2	Footed vessel	K 1589	7.5: 1						
	Various bowls of the late rolled-rim type	K 1590	7.6: 5						
	Deep bowls of various sub-types	K 1596	7.7: 9						
Trench 7 layer 3	Mobile hat-shaped hearth	K 1594	7.1: 3	29 c	Coarse stone	Stone lid type D	EE 701		
		K 1595	7.1: 4	29 c					
	Brazier / 'mask-like' support vessel	K 1174	7.10: 1	32 e					
Trench 7 layer 4	Frying pan	K 1597	7.3: 4	30 a	Terracotta	Boat model	EE 709	8.24	51
	Footed vessel	K 1599	7.5: 4						
		K 1602	7.5: 5						
	Hemispherical bowl	K 1601	7.6: 1						
	Various bowls of the late rolled-rim type	K 1598	7.6: 8						
		K 1600	7.6: 13						
	Fine ware/ decorated sherd	K 1121	7.10: 8						
Trench 7 layer 6	Fine ware/decorated sherd	K 1122	7.10: 9		Spindle-whorl	Flat curved	EE 711		
						Conical with stamped decoration	259/710	8.22: 2	49 a, 50 e
					Perforated pot-sherd	flat	EE 712		

TABLE 4.3 continued.

Trench 7 layer 7	Deep bowl with vertical lugs at the rim	K 1605	7.4: 6	31 *b*					
	Crescent-shaped lug of deep bowl or storage vessel	K 1606	7.8: 14						
Trench 7 layer 8	Footed vessel	K 1608	7.5: 2		Spindle-whorl	Ring-like	262	8.20: 8	
		K 1609	7.5: 3						
	Wide-mouthed vessel with concave collar and out-turned swelling rim	K 1167	7.5: 11						
	Various bowls of the late rolled-rim type	K 1166	7.6: 3						
	Large bowl with rounded flat or swelling in-turned rim	K 1607	7.6: 16						
	Deep hemispherical bowl with thin walls, 'Kouphonisi' type bowl	K 1168	7.7: 2	30 *c*					
	Deep bowl with in-turned rim	K 1170	7.7: 7						
	Deep bowl with thickened out-turned rim and crescent-shaped lugs	K 1169	7.8: 7						
	Crescent-shaped lug of deep bowl or storage vessel	K 1172	7.8: 11						
	Base of household vase	K 1173	7.9: 9						
	Brazier / 'mask-like' support vessel	K 1592 + K 1593	7.10: 1	32 *e*					
Trench 7 layer 9	Deep closed spherical vessel	K 1148	7.4: 1		Base of a vessel	Vine leaf impression	K 1149		
	Deep bowl with vertical lugs at the rim	K 1155	7.4: 5		Spindle-whorl	Flat discoid	EE 716		
	Conical cup	K 1149	7.4: 9	30 *d*					
		K 1151	7.4: 11						
	Closed wide-mouthed vessel with collar and thickened out-turned rim	K 1143	7.5: 6	31 *a*					
	Wide-mouthed vessel with conical collar	K 1160	7.5: 8						
	Wide-mouthed vessel with	K 1162	7.5: 9						
	concave collar and out-turned swelling rim	K 1152	7.5: 14	31 *a*					
	Deep wide-mouthed vessel with flat perforated rim	K 1591	7.5: 16						
	Hemispherical bowl	K 1610	7.6: 2						

TABLE 4.3 continued.

	Various bowls of late rolled-rim type	K 1164	7.6: 11	30 c					
	Large bowl with rounded flat or swelling in-turned rim	K 1150	7.6: 14						
	Deep large bowl with crescent shaped lug	K 1156	7.7: 1	31 b					
	Deep bowl with in-turned rim	K 1157	7.7: 5	30 c					
	Deep bowl with straight or in-turned profile and thickened in-turned rim	K 1161	7.8: 2						
		K 1147	7.8: 3						
		K 1158	7.8: 4						
		K 1163	7.8: 5						
	Deer bowl with thickened out-turned rim with crescent shaped lugs	K 1159	7.8: 6						
	Small deep bowl	K 1144	7.8: 9						
	Crescent-shaped lug of deep bowl or storage vessel	K 1153	7.8: 12						
		K 1142	7.8: 13						
	Small storage vessels	K 1154	7.9: 5						
		K 1611	7.9: 6						
	Base of household vessel	K 1146	7.9: 7						
	Clay spoon	K 1613	7.9: 10						
		K 1612	7.9: 12	32 a					
	Brazier / 'mask-like' support vessel	K 1165	7.10: 2						
Trench 7 layer 10	Frying pan	EE 040	7.3: 1	30 a	Spindle-whorl	Flat discoid	264	8.20: 11	
	Miniature spherical vessel	EE 718	7.3: 6	30 b					
	Deep closed spherical vessel	K 1614	7.4: 3						
	Wide-mouthed vase with concave collar and out-turned swelling rim	K 1138	7.5: 10						
	Various bowls of the late rolled-rim type	K 1139	7.6: 6						
	Large bowl with rounded flat or swelling in-turned rim	K 1140	7.6: 15						
	Deep bowls of various subtypes	K 1141	7.7: 10						
	Baking pan/plate	K 1622	7.9: 3	31 c					
Trench 7 layer 11					Obsidian	Debitage	0588	8.3: 15	
Trench 7 layer 12	Conical cup	K 1629	7.4: 8		Base of a vessel	Mat impression	K 1363		
	Wide-mouthed vase with concave collar and out-turned swelling rim	K 1137	7.5: 12						
	Various bowls of late rolled-rim type	K 1136	7.6: 4						

TABLE 4.3 continued.

	Deep bowl with in-turned rim	**K 1135**	7.7: 6	30 *c*						
	Deep bowls of various subtypes	**K 1627**	7.7: 8							
	Deep bowl with thickened out-turned rim with crescent shaped lugs	**K 1134**	7.8: 8	31 *c*						
	Baking pan/plate	**K 1624**	7.9: 1	31 *c*						
		K 1625	7.9: 2	31 *c*						
	Base of household vessels	**K 1623**	7.9: 8							
	Clay spoon	**K 1628**	7.9: 11							
	Brazier / 'mask-like' support vessel	**K 1626**	7.10: 3							
Trench 7 layer 13										
Trench 7 layer 14	Deep closed spherical vessel	**K 1630**	7.4: 4		Spindle-whorl	Flat discoid with dot impressions	**266**	8.22: 8	50 *d*
	Conical cup	**K 1133**	7.4: 7			2 more examples of flat discoid type			
		K 1631	7.4: 10						
	Closed wide-mouthed vessel with collar and thickened out-turned rim	**K 1129**	7.5: 7	31 *a*					
	Wide-mouthed vessel with concave collar and out-turned swelling rim	**K 1132**	7.5: 13	31 *a*					
	Wide-mouthed vessel with high conical collar	**K 1130**	7.5: 17						
	Various bowls of the late rolled-rim type	**K 1632**	7.6: 12	31 *d*					
	Large bowl with rounded flat or swelling in-turned rim	**K 1127**	7.6: 17						
	Deep hemispherical bowl with thin walls, 'Kouphonisi' type bowl	**K 1633 a+b**	7.7: 4						
	Deep bowl with straight or in-turned profile and thickened in-turned rim	**K 1131**	7.8: 1						
	Crescent-shaped lug of deep bowl or storage vessel	**K 1128**	7.8: 10						
Trench 7 layer 15	Baking pan or plate	**K 1638**	7.9: 4	31 *c*	Base of a vessel	Mat impression	**K 1372**		

TABLE 4.4. The stratigraphic context of catalogued finds of Markiani phase III from the 'Fissure', Trench 1,1 and Trench 9.

TRENCH/ LAYER	POTTERY				SMALL FINDS				
	Shape	Cat. no.	FIG.	PLATE	Category	Type	Cat. no.	FIG.	PLATE
Trench 1,1, layer 43	Conical cup	K 1646			Coarse stone	Stone lid type A	EE 180		
		K 1645							
	Deep handleless open vessel with curved walls	K 1276	7.14: 8		Spindle-whorl	Conical with stamped decoration	321	8.22: 1	
	Base	K 1402	7.15: 7						
	Jar	K 1273	7.15: 2			11 more objects of various types			
	Small spherical narrow collared vessel	K 1277	7.15: 5	33 *f*	Perforated pot-sherd	2 examples			
	Collared jar	K 1275	7.15: 6	33 *f*					
		K 1274							
	Jug	K 1298	7.15: 1	33 *c–d*					
Trench 1,1 layer 44	Conical cup	K 1752-EE 190	7.14: 4		Spindle-whorl	Bell-shaped	220	8.20: 4	
						Flat discoid	216	8.20: 9	
		K 1717-EE 188	7.14: 5			Flat discoid with nail impressions	219	8.22: 6	50 *a*
						Discoid	83		49 *a*
		K 1716-EE 189	7.14: 6			Bell shaped	126		49 *b*
						3 more examples of various types			
	Deep open bowl with lugs	K 1282	7.14: 15		Perforated pot-sherd	4 more examples			
		K 1292	7.14: 17		Seal impression on a pot-sherd	An impressed spiral and a chevron formed of two impressed triangles	EE 197	8.26	52 *e*
	Deep handleless open vessel with curved walls	K 1294	7.14: 11						
		K 1295	7.14: 7						
	Base	K 1278							
		K 1402							
	Jar	K 1616	7.15: 3						
	Jug	K 1298	7.15: 1	33 *c–d*					
	Brazier / 'mask-like' support vessel	K 1280							
	Lid	K 1297	7.15: 9						
Trench 1,1 layer 45	Deep handleless open vessel with curved walls	K 1390	7.14: 12		Spindle-whorl	Flat discoid with nail impressions	208	8.22: 5	50 *a*
		K 1392				4 more examples of various types			
	Base	K 1385			Clay sealing	Meander-like motif	EE 847	8.26	52 *d*
Trench 1,1 layer 46	Bowl with in-turned rim	K 1411	7.14: 2		Base of a vessel	Mat impression	K 1374		
	Baking pan	K 1614			Spindle-whorl	Conical bell-shaped	96/842	8.21: 10	
	Deep open bowl with lugs	K 1409	7.14: 16			11 more examples of various types			
	Deep handleless open vessel with straight walls	K 1410	7.14: 18						
		K 1405	7.14: 19						
		K 1407	7.14: 20						
		K 1413	7.14: 21						
		K 1406							
		K 1408							
	Base	K 1374							

TABLE 4.4 continued.

Trench 9, layer 5	Rolled rim bowl	K 1287	7.14: 1		Spindle-whorl	Discoid biconvex	158	8.20: 5	
	Conical cup	K 1215-EE 904	7.14: 3	33 *e*		Conical	145	8.20: 6	
	Baking pan	K 1285	7.14: 13			Bell-shaped	EE 907		49 *b*
		K 1279	7.14: 14			6 more examples of various types			
	Deep handleless open vessel with curved walls	K 1288	7.14: 9						
		K 1615	7.14: 10						
	Base	K 1286	7.15: 8						
	Jar	EE 905	7.15: 4						

TABLE 4.5. The stratigraphic context of catalogued finds of Markiani phase IV from Terrace 1, Spaces 7, Trench 1,1; Space 3, Trenches 2 and 1,4; Space 6, Trenches 1,3; 1,4; 2.

SPACE	TRENCH/LAYER	POTTERY				SMALL FINDS				
		Shape	Cat. no.	FIG.	PLATE	Category	Type	Cat. no.	FIG.	PLATE
S P A C E 7	Trench 1,1 layer 21	Deep conical bowl	K 1420	7.16: 11						
		Deep hemispherical bowl	K 1421	7.16: 13						
		Deep bowl with lugs	K 1422	7.17: 7						
		Tankard	K 1224	7.19: 6						
		Jar with collar neck	K 1423	7.22: 9	36 d					
	Trench 1,1 layer 22					Spindle-whorl	Flat conical	123		
	Trench 1,1 layer 23	Small hemispherical bowls with incurved walls	K 1724	7.16: 19	35 e	Base of a vessel	Mat impression	EE 126	8.18: 12	
		Large open bowl with straight walls	K 1424	7.18: 1		Spindle-whorl	Flat discoid with dot impressions	151	8.22: 3	50 c
		Deer wide-mouthed vessel	K 1426	7.21: 5			Flat discoid	218		
	Trench 1,1 layer 24	Deep bowl with lugs	K 1434	7.17: 2		Base of a vessel	Vine leaf impression	K 1304		48 f
			K 1435	7.17: 3			Mat impression	K 1355		
								K 1386		
		Large open bowl with straight walls	K 1427	7.18: 3		Spindle-whorl	Conical	129	8.21: 3	
							Flat discoid	87	8.21: 4	49 d
		Tankard	K 1441	7.19: 3			Hemi-spherical	85	8.21: 5	
								163	8.21: 6	49 d
		Baking pan type A	K 1428	7.20: 1			Flat discoid	86		49 d
			K 1429	7.20: 2			Cylindrical convex	214	8.21: 13	
		Baking pan type B	K 1431	7.20: 11			9 more examples of various types			
		Sauceboat and spouted vessel	K 1430	7.20: 14						
			K 1438	7.21: 1						
			K 1439	7.21: 3						
			K 1440	7.21: 2						
			K 1230/ K 1770	7.21: 4	36 e					
		Deep wide-mouthed open vessel	K 1433	7.21: 7						
		Deep wide-mouthed closed vessel	K 1436	7.22: 2						
		Storage vessel/pithos	K 1437	7.23: 3						
		Small pithos	K 1432	7.24: 3	38 c					
		Various bases	K 1355							
			K 1386							
			K 1304							
		Brazier/'mask-like' support vessel	K 1664							
		Sherd with incised linear pattern	K 1488							
			K 1489	7.26: 2						

TABLE 4.5 continued.

		Sherd with incised curvilinear pattern	K 1490	7.26: 16					
		Sherd with incised fish motif	K 1244	7.26: 18					
Trench 1,1 layer 25	Deep conical bowl	K 1442	7.16: 12		Obsidian	Debitage	O361	8.3: 16	49 d
	Large open bowl with straight walls	K 1443	7.18: 2		Base of a vessel	Mat impression	K 1379		
	Depas amphikypellon	K 1723	7.19: 8	35 a	Perforated pot-sherd	Cylindrical	150	8.21: 15	49 f
	Conical cup	K 1446	7.19: 9		Spindle-whorl	Flat discoid	136		
	Jar with collar neck	K 1444	7.22: 3						
	Brazier/'mask-like' support vessel	K 1379	7.25: 5						
	Sherd with incised zigzag pattern	K 1491	7.26: 12	38 b					
	Painted Urfirnis sherd	EE 074							
Trench 1,1 layer 26	Sherd with incised linear pattern	K 1492	7.26: 3		Spindle-whorl	Spherical	90	8.21: 8	
						2 more examples of flat discoid type			
					Perforated pot-sherd	Cylindrical	140	8.21: 14	49 f
							115		49 f
						Non symmetrical	133		49 f
							128		49 f
Trench 1,1 layer 27	Shallow bowl with in-turned rim	K 1448	7.16: 8		Perforated pot-sherd	Non symmetrical	123		49 f
	Small hemispherical bowl with incurved walls	K 1447	7.16: 18		Spindle-whorl	3 more examples of various types			
Trench 1,1 layer 28	Shallow bowl with in-turned rim	K 1450	7.16: 9						
	Collared jar	K 1449	7.22: 6						
	Sherd with incised parallel pattern	K 1493	7.26: 6						
Trench 1,1 layer 29	Shallow bowl	K 1454	7.16: 6		Spindle-whorl		111		
	Deep spouted bowl	K 1451	7.16: 16	36 b					
	Collared jar	K 1453	7.22: 7	38 c					
	Jug	K 1452	7.24: 1	36 b					
	Sherd with incised linear pattern	K 1496	7.26: 4						
	Sherd with deep linear incisions	K 1494	7.26: 8						
	Sherd with curvilinear incisions	K 1495	7.26: 13						
Trench 1,1 layer 30	Sherd with incised curvilinear patterns	K 1227	7.26: 9		Spindle-whorl		306		
		K 1228	7.26: 10						
Trench 1,1 layer 34	Shallow bowl	K 1461	7.16: 1						
	Deep hemispherical bowl	K 1460	7.16: 15						

TABLE 4.5 continued.

		Deep bowl with lugs	K 1464	7.17: 9						
		Large open bowl with curved walls	K 1462	7.18: 4						
			K 1463	7.18: 7						
		Sherd with incised linear pattern	K 1497	7.26: 5						
	Trench 1,1 layer 35	Baking pan type B	K 1465	7.20: 13						
		Sherd incised with curvilinear pattern	K 1498	7.26: 14						
	Trench 1,1 layer 36	Small hemispherical bowl with in-curved walls	K 1466	7.16: 17						
		Deep bowl with lugs	K 1472	7.17: 8						
		Conical cup	K 1470	7.19: 10						
		Storage vessel/pithos	K 1468	7.23: 7						
			K 1471	7.23: 8						
		Various bases	K 1469	7.24: 8						
		Sherd with incised herring-bone pattern	K 1467	7.26: 1	38 d					
SPACE 3	Trench 1,4 layer 4	Deep bowl with lugs and incised decoration of fish motif	K 1212	7.17: 1 see also 7.26: 17	36 e					
		Conical cup	K 1721	7.19: 11						
	Trench 1,4 layer 6	Deep bowl with lugs and incised decoration of fish motif	K 1212	7.17: 1 see also 7.26: 17	36 e	Base of a vessel	Mat impression	K 1366		47 e
						Copper	Blade	EE 089	8.25: 19	52 e
		Large open bowl with curved walls	K 1703	7.18: 9						
		Sherd with incised zigzag pattern	K 1708							
	Trench 1,4 layer 9	Baking pan type A	K 1637	7.20: 6						
	Trench 1,4 layer 11					Coarse stone	Large rubber	EE 1513/ EE 2038	8.9	
	Trench 1,4 layer 12									
	Trench 1,4 layer 22									
SPACE 6	Trench 2 layer 20									
	Trench 2 layer 22	Shallow bowl	K 1196	7.16: 2		Obsidian	Blade	O 433	8.3: 4	39 d
		Horizontal handle	K 1195	7.24: 6		Copper	Blade	EE 233	8.25: 13	
		Sherd with incised linear pattern	K 1635	7.26: 7						
	Trench 2 layer 23	Footed bowl	K 1219	7.17: 10						
		Large open bowl with curved walls	K 1217	7.18: 8						
		Storage vessel/pithos	K 1218	7.23: 2						
			K 1216	7.23: 5						
			K 1221	7.23: 10						

TABLE 4.5 continued.

		Brazier / 'mask-like' vessel	K 1220	7.25: 3					
Trench 2 layer 24		Shallow bowl	K 1186	7.16: 4					
		Deep bowl with lugs	K 1184	7.17: 4					
		Large open bowl with curved walls	K 1185	7.18: 5					
		Tankard	K 1188	7.19: 5					
		Baking pan type B	K 1187	7.20: 12					
Trench 2 layer 25		Shallow bowl	K 1203	7.16: 7					
		Deep bowl with lugs	K 1199	7.17: 6					
		Tankard	K 1115	7.19: 7	35 d				
		Conical cup	K 1205	7.19: 12					
			K 1206	7.19: 14					
		Baking pan type A	K 1201	7.20: 5					
			K 1202	7.20: 7					
			K 1636	7.20: 3	36 a				
		Deep closed wide-mouthed vessel	K 1204	7.21: 8					
		Jar with collar neck	K 1198	7.22: 5					
		Spherical pyxis	K 1200	7.22: 14					
		Storage vessel/pithos	K 1222	7.23: 9					
		Brazier/'mask-like' support vessel	K 1621	7.25: 4					
Trench 2 layer 26		Jar with collar neck	K 1207	7.22: 11		Coarse stone	Pestle and hammer stone	EE 239	8.5: 3	42 c
		Spherical pyxis	K 1209	7.22: 15					
		Storage vessel/pithos	K 1210	7.23: 1					
			K 1208	7.23: 4					
		Horizontal handle	K 1211	7.24: 7					
Trench 2 layer 27		Shallow bowl	K 1176	7.16: 3		Bronze object	pin	EE 241	8.25: 6	52 b
		Deep hemispherical bowl	K 1178	7.16: 14					
		Small hemispherical bowl with incurved walls	K 1177	7.16: 20					
		Large open bowl with curved walls	K 1179	7.18: 6					
		Tankard	K 1182	7.19: 4	35 c				
		Baking pan type A	K 1180						
			K 1181						
			K 1637	7.20: 6					
			K 1640	7.20: 8					
		Spherical pyxis	K 1175	7.22: 13					
Trench 2 layer 28		Baking pan type A	K 1637	7.20: 6		Obsidian	Blade	O457	8.3: 10	
Trench 2 layer 29		Shallow bowl	K 1190	7.16: 5					
		Deep bowl with lugs	K 1191	7.17: 5					
		Jar with collar neck	K 1192	7.22: 4					
			K 1189	7.22: 10	36 d				

TABLE 4.5 continued.

		Horizontal handle	**K 1194**	7.24: 5						
		Various bases	**K 1193**	7.24: 10						
	Trench 2 layer 30									
	Trench 2 layer 31	Tankard	**K 1225**	7.19: 1		Coarse stone	Small grinder	**EE 242**	8.6: 1	42 *e*
	Trench 1,3 layer 3	Shallow bowl	**K 2011**	7.16:10						
		Conical cup	**K 1476**	7.19: 13						
		Collar jar	**K 2010**	7.22: 8						
		Spherical pyxis	**K 1477**	7.22: 12						
	Trench 1,3 layer 4									
	Trench 1,3 layer 5	Brazier / 'mask-like' support vase	**K 1540**	7.25: 2	37 *f*					
		Sherd with incised curvilinear pattern	**K 1226**	7.26: 11	38 *b*					
	Trench 1,3 layer 7									
	Trench 1,4 layer 17									
	Trench 1,4 layer 27	Tankard	**K 1223**	7.19: 2	35 *b*	Base of a vessel	Mat impression	**K 1364**		
		Various bases	**K 1364**							
	Trench 1,4 layer 28									
	Trench 1,4 layer 29	Baking pan type A	**K 1484**	7.20: 8		Base of a vessel	Mat impression	**K 1365**		47 *a*
		Storage vessel/pithos	**K 1483**	7.23: 6						
		Various bases	**K 1365**							
	Trench 1,4 layer 30	Jug	**K 1231**	7.24: 2						
	Trench 1,4 layer 31	Baking pan type A	**K 1485**	7.20: 9		Bone tool	Blunt-ended (polisher?)			
			K 1486	7.20: 10						
		Sauceboat and spouted vase	**K 1230/ 1770**	7.21: 4	36 *e*					
		Jar with collar neck	**K 1232**	7.22: 1						
		Storage vessel/pithos	**K 1487**							
		Sherd with incised double axe motif	**K 1229**	7.26: 15	38 *b*					

TABLE 4.6. The stratigraphic context of catalogued finds of Trench 3, Rooms 1 and 2.

TRENCH/ LAYER	TRENCH 3, ROOM 2 SMALL FINDS					TRENCH/ LAYER	TRENCH 3, ROOM 1 SMALL FINDS				
	Category	Type	Cat. no.	FIG.	PLATE		Category	Type	Cat. no.	FIG.	PLATE
Trench 3,2, layer 1	Fine stone object	Fine pestle	EE 345			Trench 3,1 layer 3	Coarse stone	Socket and pivot	EE 308	8.11	43 b
	Spindle-whorl	2 more examples							EE 310	8.11	43 a
							Lead	Seal	EE 317	8.26	52 a
Trench 3,2 Layer 2	Spindle-whorl	Flay discoid	EE 307	8.20:10							
	Base of vessel	Mat impression	K 1373	8.18: 3							
Trench 3,2 layer 3	Coarse stone	Stone lid type A	EE 314	8.14		Trench 3,1 layer 4	Coarse stone	Stone lid type A	EE 344	8.14	
			EE 320			Trench 3,1 layer 7	Lead	Rivet	EE 377	8.25: 3	52 a
	Copper	Needle/ wire	EE 319	8.25: 9	52 c	Trench 3,3 layer 3	Copper	Blade	EE 384	8.25: 15	
									EE 386	8.25: 18	
							Spindle-whorl		312		
Trench 3,2, layer 4	Fine stone object	Fine pestle	EE 326	8.4: 13	40 b	Trench 3,3, layer 4	Fine stone object	Worked marble	EE 396	8.4: 1	40 g 41 b
	Coarse stone	Waisted weight	EE 324	8.12			Fine stone object	Fine Pestle	EE 395	8.4: 15	40 e-f 41 a
		Stone lid type A	EE 323	8.14			Coarse stone	Small grinder	EE 394	8.6: 2	42 e
			EE 397					Waisted weight	EE 391	8.12	42 d
		Stone lid type B	EE 325	8.15					EE 398	8.12	42 d
	Copper	Blade	EE 327	8.25: 17			Lead	Pendant	EE 399	8.25: 1	
							Spindle-whorl		313		
Trench 3,2 layer 5	Coarse stone	Stone lid type B	EE 656								
	Copper	Blade	EE 329	8.25: 20	52 e						
Trench 3,2 layer 6	Coarse stone	Stone lid type B	EE 331	8.14		Trench 3,3 layer 5	Coarse stone	Grindstone saddle quern type	EE 004	8.7	
Trench 3,2 layer 7	Spindle-whorl		EE 333				Copper	Needle/ wire	EE 389	8.25: 11	52 d
Trench 3,2 layer 8	Coarse stone	Perforated weight	EE 353	8.12		Trench 3,3 layer 6	Coarse stone	Small grinder	EE 633	8.6: 3	42 e-f
Trench 3,2 layer 9	Brazier/ 'mask-like' support vessel		K 1704-EE 351	7.13	34 a-f						
	Coarse stone	Stone lid type A	EE 365	8.14		Trench 3,3 layer 16	Bronze	Blade	EE 639	8.25: 16	52 e
			EE 371	8.14							
		Stone lid type B	EE 364	8.15							
Trench 3,2 layer 10	Coarse stone	Small grinder	EE 372	8.6: 5	42 e	Trench 3,2 layer 14	Fine stone object	Fine Pestle	EE 637	8.4: 16	
		Stone lid type B	EE 373								
Trench 3,2 layer 12	Coarse stone	Stone lid type A	EE 383				Coarse stone	Pestle and hammer stone	EE 638	8.5: 5	
		Stone lid type B	EE 381					Stone lid type C	EE 636		43 c
Trench 3,2 layer 18	Coarse stone	Stone lid type A	EE 645			Trench 3,3 layer 18	Coarse stone	Stone lid type A	EE 644		

TABLE 4.6 continued.

Trench 3,4 layer 3	Coarse stone	Stone lid type A	EE 651			Trench 3,5 layer 19	Spindle-whorl		314		
		Stone lid type B	EE 653								
		Stone lid type D	EE 654								
Trench 3,4 layer 4	Coarse stone	Waisted weight	EE 652	8.12	42 *d*						
Trench 3,5 Layer 1	Spindle-whorl	Flat discoid with incised linear decoration	297	8.22: 10	49 *c*						
Trench 3,5 layer 4	Coarse stone	Stone lid type B	EE 664								
Trench 3,5, layer 5	Fine stone object	Polished stone axe	EE 661	8.5: 2	42 *b*						
	Coarse stone	Stone lid type A	EE 663		43 *d*						
		Stone lid type B	EE 662		43 *c*						
Trench 3,5 Layer 6	Coarse Stone	Stone lid Type A	EE 666		43 *d*						

Chapter 5

The absolute dating of the settlement

Colin Renfrew, Rupert Housley and Sturt Manning

Twelve samples from those selected on stratigraphic grounds and submitted for analysis to the Research Laboratory for Archaeology and the History of Art at Oxford were dated by the accelerator radiocarbon facility. (In addition there were two samples, from Trench 1,1 layer 25 and Trench 6,1 layer 6, which did not have enough collagen in the bones to be dated.)

A. RATIONALE AND CONTEXT
by Colin Renfrew

The stratigraphic and typological rationale for the division of the strata on the site with their accompanying ceramic materials into four phases, Markiani I to IV, was discussed at the beginning of Chapter 4. The stratigraphic and typological basis for the assignment of specific strata to these phases, as defined, was further indicated during the description in Chapter 4 of the excavated areas. The characteristics of the four ceramic phases are described in Chapter 7. The choice of radiocarbon sample was in general determined in order to obtain absolute dates for each phase, with the unfortunate exception of phase I which was represented exclusively in Trench 6,1 where no samples suitable for radiocarbon determination were found.

Only in the case of the Bastion in Trench 8 were radiocarbon samples selected in order to confirm or clarify the stratigraphic context itself: as described in Chapter 4 there were arguments for placing the construction of the Bastion in Ma II or III, with the balance (on the principle of dating by the latest well-stratified sherds in relation to the feature) falling with phase III.

MARKIANI PHASE II

Three samples were selected for Ma II, all coming from the summit area at the top of Rock Cutting 2, specifically from Trench 1,1 layer 6 and Trench 7 layers 8 and 10 (see FIG. 4.14).

MARKIANI PHASE IV

Three samples were chosen from relevant areas of Terrace 1, where well-stratified samples of bone were available from levels which contained characteristic ceramics (notably tankards) characteristic of phase IV. One of these was from Rock Cutting 2 (Trench 1,1 layer 27) and two from a nearby area (Trench 2, layers 29 and 31).

MARKIANI PHASE III

The defining deposit for Ma III, as described in Chapter 7, was that from the fissure adjacent to Wall Λ in Trench 1,1 (Trench 1,1 layers 43 and 44 with Trench 9,1 layer 5). A sample was available from Trench 1,1 layer 44, and a sample was chosen from a layer within Rock Cutting 2 nearby (Trench 1,1 layer 37) which should be of approximately the same date.

In addition two samples were chosen from well-stratified levels in Trench 3 (both from Trench 3,2 layer 6). Trench 3 lay south-east of the main excavated area. The pottery was assigned to a late stage of Ma III: it lacked entirely any of the distinctive forms associated with the Kastri Group which are characteristic of Ma IV.

THE BASTION

Two samples were selected in order to clarify the dating of the Bastion. As noted in Chapter 4 the bulk of the pottery there was assignable to Ma I and II, but Blue Schist Ware sherds (characteristic of phases III and IV) were found well-stratified within the Bastion. None of these had a shape characteristic of Ma IV, so that a date in Ma III was proposed for the construction of this feature. The sample from inside the Bastion (Trench 8,1 layer 8) should give the best indication of the date of its construction, and that from outside (Trench 8,2 layer 7) of its subsequent use.

B. THE RADIOCARBON DETERMINATIONS

by Rupert A. Housley

Radiocarbon accelerator dates based on bone samples from Markiani are listed in TABLE 5.1.

TABLE 5.1. The first series of radiocarbon dates on bone samples from Markiani.

Sample No	Find place	Settlement Phase	Type of Sample	$\delta 13C$	Radiocarbon Date BP
OxA-3291	Trench 1,1 layer 27	Ma IV	bone		3810±80
OxA-3292	Trench 1,1 layer 37	Ma III late	bone		3920±80
OxA-3293	Trench 3,2 layer 6	Ma III late	bone		4090±90
OxA-3294	Trench 3,2 layer 8	Ma III late	bone	$\delta^{13}C = -17.6$ per mil	4060±75
OxA-3295	Trench 8,1 layer 8	Ma II–III?	bone		4105±80
OxA-3296	Trench 8,2 layer 7	Ma II–III?	bone		4080±75
OxA-3297	T1,1 layer 6	Ma II	bone	$\delta^{13}C = -21.9$ per mil	4380±100

These dates are uncalibrated in radiocarbon years BP (Before Present — AD 1950) using the half life of 5568 years and either the $\delta^{13}C$ values quoted (only to within 0.5–1.0 per mil relative to PDB) or an assumed value of –21 per mil for bone collagen.[1] The remaining samples Trench 1,1 layer 25 and Trench 6,1 layer 6, contained insufficient collagen to be dated. Despite this the seven samples which it was possible to date appear to have been very successful since, on a cursory examination, they appear to be in the correct stratigraphic order.

The accelerator radiocarbon dates on the five other bone samples from Markiani are as listed in TABLE 5.2, once again uncalibrated in radiocarbon years BP (Before Present — AD 1950) using the half life of 5568 years. Isotopic fractionation has been corrected for using the measured $\delta^{13}C$ values quoted (to ±0.5–1.0 per mil relative to PDB).

TABLE 5.2. Further radiocarbon dates on bone samples from Markiani.

Sample No	Find Place	Phase	Type of Sample	$\delta^{13}C$	Radiocarbon Date BP
OxA-4003	Trench 7 layer 8	Ma II	bone	$\delta^{13}C = -19.9$ per mil	4390±65
OxA-4004	Trench 7 layer 10	Ma II	bone	$\delta^{13}C = -20.3$ per mil	4160±65
OxA-4005	Trench 1,1 layer 44	Ma III	bone	$\delta^{13}C = -18.9$ per mil	3730±65
OxA-4006	Trench 1,4 layer 29	Ma IV	bone	$\delta^{13}C = -18.7$ per mil	3990±65
OxA-4007	Trench 1,4 layer 31	Ma IV	bone	$\delta^{13}C = -18.8$ per mil	3860±60

---

[1] For details of the chemical pretreatment, target preparation and AMS measurement see Hedges *et al.* 1989, 99–113 and Hedges *et al.* 1992, 306–11.

When calibrated, the age ranges shown in TABLE 5.3 are obtained. Except for OxA-4005, which appears to be too young (possibly an intrusive sample?), the other dates conform to their stratigraphic position and generally agree with the previous dates (OxA-3291 to Ox-3297).

Clare Owen of the Research Laboratory for Archaeology and the History of Art at Oxford on 8 June 2001 kindly supplied the following calibration of these individual dates (see FIG. 5.1), following Stuiver *et al.* 1998 and Bronk Ramsey 2000*a*:[2]

TABLE 5.3. Calibrated radiocarbon dates from Markiani following Stuiver *et al.* 1998 and Bronk Romsey 2000*a*.

Sample No	Uncalibrated Date	Calibrated (68.2% probability)	Calibrated (95.4% probability)
OxA-4005	3730±65BP	2270BC (2.8%) 2250BC 2210BC (64.0%) 2030BC 1990BC (1.3%) 1980BC	2340BC (95.4%) 1930BC
OxA-3291	3810±80BP	2410BC (6.2%) 2370BC 2360BC (62.0%) 2130BP	2470BC (95.4%) 2030BC
OxA-4007	3860±60BP	2460BC (57.4%) 2280BC 2260BC (6.9%) 2230BC 2220BC (3.9%) 2200BC	2480BC (95.4%) 2140BC
OxA-3292	3920±80BP	2560BC (3.8%) 2530BC 2500BC (64.4%) 2280	2630BC (93.4%) 2190BC 2180BC (2.0%) 2140BC
OxA-4006	3990±65BP	2620BC (66.0%) 2400BC 2370BC (2.2%) 2350BC	2900BC (2.9%) 2800BC 2700BC (92.5%) 2250BC
OxA-3294	4060±75BP	2860BC (8.2%) 2810BC 2680BC (60.0%) 2470BC	2880BC (95.4%) 2450BC
OxA-3296	4080±75BP	2860BC (12.9%) 2810BC 2750BC (4.0%) 2720BC 2700BC (41.3%) 2550BC 2540BC (10.0%) 2490BC	2880BC (95.4%) 2460BC
OxA-3293	4090±90BP	2870BC (13.8%) 2800BC 2760BC (46.8%) 2555BC 2540Bc (&.6%) 2490BC	2900BC (95.4%) 2350BC
OxA-4004	4160±65BP	2880BC (13.3%) 2830BC 2820BC (50.5%) 2660BC 2650BC (4.4%) 2620BC	2890BC (95.4%) 2570BC
OxA-3295	4105±80BP	2870BC (15.6%) 2800BC 2780BC (1.1%) 2770BC 2760BC (48.2%) 2570BC 2520BC (3.3%) 2500BC	2880BC (95.4%) 2470BC
OxA-3297	4380±100BP	3310BC (11.8%) 3230BC 3170BC (1.3%) 3160BC 3110BC (55.1%) 2880BC	3400BC (95.4%) 2700BC
OxA-4003	4390±65BP	3260BC (0.8%) 3240BC 3100BC (67.4%) 2910BC	3340BC (17.0%) 3210BC 3190BC (3.7%) 3150BC 3130BC (74.6%) 2880BC

C. CALIBRATION CONSIDERATIONS
by Sturt Manning[3]

All twelve dates were calibrated using the new radiocarbon calibration program (CALMAKER). This program uses the new 1993 calibration data, and uses the same approach as Robinson[4] and Weniger.[5] For Markiani data the bi-decadal calibration curve of Stuiver and Pearson 1993[6] and Pearson and Stuiver

---

[2] Stuiver *et al.* 1998; Bronk Ramsey 2000*a*.
[3] The following note on calibration, written in April 1993, is included in view of the valuable phase-by-phase averaging study conducted by Dr Manning for these determinations.

[4] Robinson 1988.
[5] Weniger 1986.
[6] Stuiver and Pearson 1993.

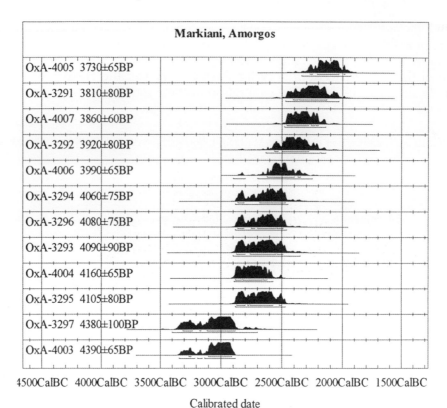

FIG. 5.1. Calibrated radiocarbon dates for Markiani showing probability distributions following the method of Stuiver and colleagues and Bronk Romsey (see text).

1993[7] has been used, since this seems the most appropriate (given sample types, and the usual Oxford AMS standard measurements error).

OxA-4005 has not been used as suggested above by Housley. The results are shown in FIGS. 5.2 to 5.4.

The calibrated calendar probability distributions for these three archaeological groups of dates are shown combined so that the area under each curve is equal to 1.00 (the more dates, the more confidence one has in the respective curve). Some other information, including one-sigma (1σ) calibrated ranges, the central 50% of the distribution,[8] and the weighted averages of the combined calibrated distributions, are given in the figures.

For comparison the one-sigma (1σ) ranges for each date from Stuiver and Reimer 1993[9] are listed below, since these are a 'standard' — although using a slightly illogical approach to statistics and a non-user-friendly output:

TABLE 5.4. Calibrated radiocarbon dates for Markiani using the CALMAKER program.

Sample No	1σ
OxA-3291	2397–2378, 2349–2134, 2071–2060 BC
OxA-3292	2488–2284 BC
OxA-3293	2868–2804, 2770–2718, 2703–2486 BC
OxA-3294	2854–2820, 2662–2635, 2627–2469 BC
OxA-3295	2870–2803, 2773–2716, 2704–2560, 2527–2498 BC
OxA-3296	2861–2813, 2735–2728, 2695–2550, 2549–2491 BC
OxA-3297	3260–3244, 3101–2890 BC
OxA-4003	3093–3052, 3048–2914 BC
OxA-4004	2878–2612 BC
OxA-4005	2198–2028, 1994–1987 BC
OxA-4006	2575–2510, 2509–2456 BC
OxA-4007	2454–2411, 2409–2200 BC

---

[7] Pearson and Stuiver 1993.   [9] Stuiver and Reimer 1993.
[8] Aitchison *et al.* 1991.

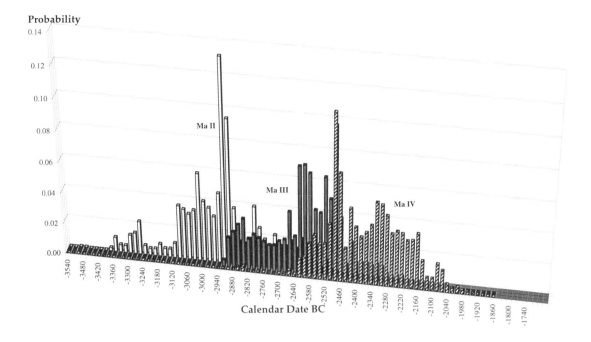

FIG. 5.2. Probability distributions for the dates of Markiani settlement phases II to IV using the radiocarbon determinations discussed.

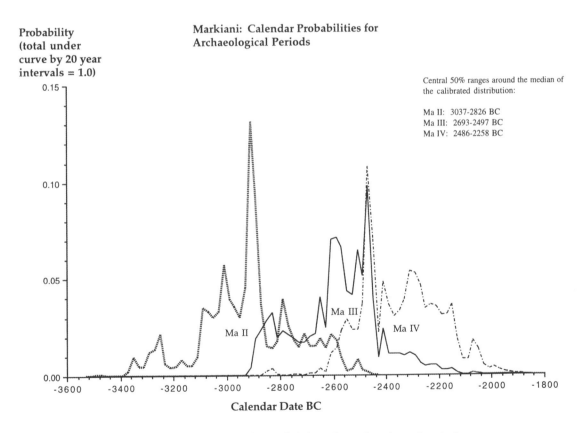

FIG. 5.3. Markiani: calendar probabilities for archaeological periods.

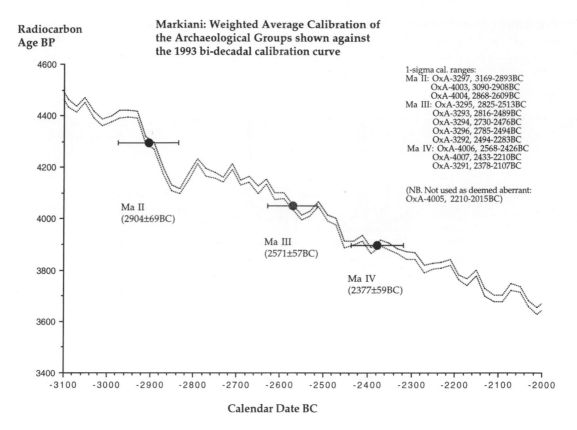

FIG. 5.4. Markiani: weighted average calibration for archaeological groups shows against the 1999 bi-decadal calibration curve.

D. DISCUSSION: SIGNIFICANCE OF THE DETERMINATIONS
by Colin Renfrew

The radiocarbon determinations form a coherent series which conforms very well with the predicted stratigraphic order. Only one determination (OxA-4005) was younger by more than two sigma (2σ), than its predicted place in the order, and this result was excluded from the calculation of averages undertaken by Sturt Manning. (It is possible that the bone utilised was an intrusion from levels of Ma IV into the fissure in the side of Rock Cutting 2 the contents of which were assigned to Ma III.)

MARKIANI PHASE II

The three samples from Ma II form a coherent group (see FIGS. 5.2 to 5.5) with a weighted average calibrated date of 2904 ± 69 BC and a central 50% range around the median of 3037 to 2826 BC. As discussed in Chapter 7, the pottery is closely related to the Kampos Group,[10] which is assigned to the transition between the Grotta-Pelos and Keros-Syros cultures (the EC I/II transition). The date thus conforms well with other estimates for the transition between EB I and II in the Aegean. The samples are not sufficiently numerous to permit estimation of the duration of Ma II, but in round figures we may conclude that it was active over the time range 3000 to 2800 BC.

MARKIANI PHASE I

The dates for Ma II also gives a clear *terminus ante quem* for phase I at Markiani, for which no radiocarbon samples were available. However, the pottery of phase I (from Trench 6,1) may be equated with pottery of the Grotta-Pelos culture, as seen for instance in the Pre-City levels at Phylakopi (phase A).[11] Phase I at Markiani (the Grotta-Pelos culture) can thus be assigned with confidence to the later fourth millennium BC in calendar years, ending somewhere around 3000 BC with the inception of the transitional Kampos phase.

---

[10] Bossert 1960; Renfrew 1972, 527.   [11] Evans and Renfrew 1984; Renfrew and Evans, in press.

The construction of the fortification wall in Trench 6 was assigned to Ma I (although the possibility was examined in Chapter 4 that the rather abraded pottery of phase I found with it might have washed up against it subsequent to its construction in some later phase or indeed been already present at the time of its construction). If the fortification wall belongs to phase I it may well have been constructed within a century or so of 3100 BC, and that is the conclusion offered here. (The alternative possibility could lead to the conclusion that the fortification wall in Trench 6 was constructed only shortly before the Bastion in Trench 8, namely, as suggested below, around 2700 BC).

MARKIANI PHASE IV

The three samples from Ma IV likewise form a coherent group (see FIGS. 5.2 to 5.5) with a weighted average calibrated date of 2377 ± 59 BC and a central 50% range around the median of 2486 to 2258 BC. As discussed in Chapter 7, the pottery is closely related to the Kastri Group, a well-defined ceramic entity.[12] Different authors use different nomenclatures for this phase ('late EC II', 'EC IIIA' etc.), but there is general agreement that it succeeds the *floruit* of the Keros-Syros culture (widely regarded as falling within 'EC II') and is generally earlier than (although may overlap with) the Phylakopi I culture which may, in turn, overlap with the beginning of the MBA. Again we do not have sufficient data to estimate the duration of Ma IV, but in round numbers it should fall within the time range 2500–2200 BC and was certainly active during the century from 2400 to 2300 BC.

MARKIANI PHASE III

The five remaining samples (excluding OxA-4005 from the computation) had been assigned to Ma III, and were used to date this phase, giving a weighted average calibrated date of 2571 ± 55 BC and a central 50% range around the median of 2693 to 2497 BC. It should be noted however that the samples from Trench 3,2 (OxA-3293 and 3294) were from a context considered to be late in phase III, as indeed was the sample from Trench 1,1 layer 37. In the trenches in Terrace 1 the lower levels were not excavated and so no samples were available which could specifically be designated 'early phase III'. This position is borne out very clearly in FIG. 5.3 and by the central 50% ranges around the median for each phase. This suggests that phase III at Markiani was followed by phase IV around 2490 BC without any evident break. The phase III / IV transition can thus be set with some confidence at around 2500 BC in round numbers. Ma III, as represented by these samples, may be regarded as active over the time range 2700 to 2500 BC, which would conform well with the conclusion reached in Chapter 7 that Ma III belongs to the period of the Keros-Syros culture.

It would be consonant with the evidence cited to suggest that the earlier part of this period is not represented among the radiocarbon samples available, and indeed that 'early Markiani III' has not yet been fully excavated or researched. Early Ma III might well fall in the time range 2800–2700 BC.

THE BASTION OF TRENCH 8

Turning specifically to the two radiocarbon samples from contexts relating to the Bastion in Trench 8, it will be recalled that sample OxA-3295 came from a stratified position within the Bastion which should give a date not long after its construction, while Sample OxA-3296 came from Trench 8,2, lying outside the Bastion and dating its subsequent use. This leads to a calibrated date of approximately 2700 ± 150 BC for the construction of the Bastion. As the stratigraphic discussion has already indicated the radiocarbon determinations do not suggest that the Bastion was constructed as early as Ma II. But similarly the radiocarbon determinations support the conclusions based upon the stratigraphic and ceramic evidence that there is no case for suggesting that the Bastion was constructed as late as Ma IV. The radiocarbon samples from the Bastion are clearly earlier than those from levels associated with pottery of Ma IV. As the stratigraphic and ceramic evidence already indicated, the construction and early use of the Bastion is to be assigned to Ma III, that is to say to the period of the Keros-Syros culture (widely designated 'EC II').

COMPARISON WITH DHASKALIO–KAVOS, KEROS

When discussing the chronology of Markiani it is informative to compare the radiocarbon determinations with those obtained by our research group during the investigations undertaken at

---

[12] Renfrew 1972, 533.

Dhaskalio–Kavos on Keros. Much material of the Keros-Syros culture, including fragments of marble figurines and bowls, and of a range of fine wares had been recovered from the site,[13] although it should be noted that there are indications that its use extended into the time of the Kastri Group. The trenches which we cut in the disturbed soil and débris yielded similar material, and a few fragments of human bone. Samples of these were again submitted to the Research Laboratory for Archaeology and the History of Art at Oxford, through the kindness of Rupert Houseley.

The results were as follows:

TABLE 5.5. Radiocarbon dates for Dhaskalio–Kavos on Keros.

Lab. No	Material	Context	δ¹³C	Date BP
OxA 3149	human femur fragment	Trench VIII, 3	18.3 per mil	3920 ± 100
OxA 3150	human phalanx fragment	Trench VIII, 3	18.7 per mil	4150 ± 80
OxA 3151	human skull fragment	Trench VIII, unit 808	19.1 per mil	4000 ± 100

These dates do form a coherent group, although the samples came from a disturbed site and cannot be considered to be well stratified. Sturt Manning assigns to the set of three dates a weighted average calibrated date of 2558 ± 79 BC and a central 50% calibrated calendar age range around the median of the total distribution (of the three data) of 2630 to 2330 BC: 'a date between 2800–2381 BC is a one sigma probability' (see FIG. 5.5).

The average for these three dates, when compared with the Markiani radiocarbon data, is appropriately earlier than that for Ma IV and indeed distinctly later than that for Ma II. The Dhaskalio–

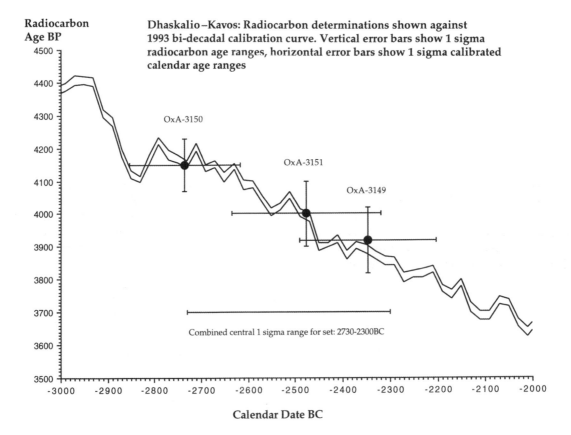

FIG. 5.5. Dhaskalio–Kavos, Keros: radiocarbon determinations shows against 1993 bi-decadal calibration curve. Vertical error bar shows 1 sigma (1?) radiocarbon age range, horizontal bar shows 1 sigma (1?) calibrated calendar age range.

[13] Renfrew 1965, pl. 42; Zapheiropoulou 1968; Broodbank 2000a.

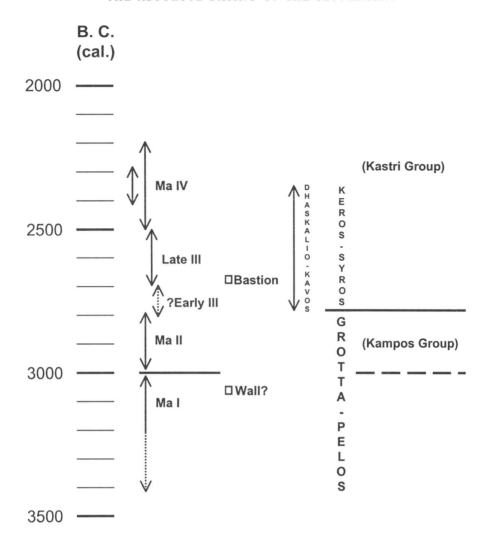

FIG. 5.6. The Early Bronze Age chronology of Amorgos based upon the calibrated radiocarbon dates from Markiani indicating also those from Dhaskalio–Kavos, Keros.

Kavos dates can be seen to overlap substantially with those for Ma III. This is indeed not surprising, since the Dhaskalio–Kavos samples were associated with fine ware ceramics of the Keros-Syros culture, and it has been argued above that Ma III should be set in the time period of the Keros-Syros culture.

This is not the place to discuss the Keros dates in further detail, as we hope to do in the final report for the Dhaskalio–Kavos project. The discussion is relevant, however, in supporting the more general conclusions reached for the Markiani dates, and in particular in confirming the contemporaneity of Ma III with the Keros-Syros culture as represented at Dhaskalio–Kavos.

THE EARLY BRONZE AGE CHRONOLOGY OF AMORGOS

It is pertinent to remark that the chronological observations based upon the Markiani radiocarbon determinations are relevant in the first place to the Cycladic EBA as represented on Amorgos and specifically at Markiani, and that they should not be applied more widely without careful assessment.

The picture may be summarised in FIG. 5.6, although to construct such a diagram risks exaggerating the precision provided by the datings. Each time point or phase division in the diagram might be subject to subsequent adjustment by up to a century in either direction. However one may predict that the transition from phase III to phase IV at *c.* 2500 BC may prove to be secure to within about 50 years. It is the most securely dated single point in the sequence.

It is encouraging to note that these conclusions compare well with those already available in 1972 from a first assessment of the emerging calibrated radiocarbon chronology as available then.[14] The

[14] Renfrew 1972, 221.

time range of the Grotta-Pelos culture was estimated from *c.* 3500 to *c.* 2700 BC, and the Keros-Syros culture from 2700 to *c.* 2400/2300 BC. The Kastri Group was seen as a late continuation of the Keros-Syros culture, situated early in the EB III period[15] and hence from *c.* 2400/2300 to *c.* 2250/2150 BC in calibrated or calendar years. Each of these dates, as proposed in 1972, should be moved earlier by about one century in the light of these new determinations, with the end of EB II and the inception of the Kastri Group now set around 2500 BC. In 1972 it was suggested that the Kampos Group formed a late phase of the Grotta-Pelos culture[16] to be followed by the Keros-Syros culture around 2700 BC: the end of the Kampos Group and the inception of the early Keros-Syros culture is now to be set around 2800 BC. Similarly the chronology for the EC period suggested by Broodbank[17] will need to be set a couple of centuries earlier.[18] It is clear that the Markiani radiocarbon determinations support and indeed refine the developing chronology for the EBA in Amorgos and in the Cyclades.

[15] Renfrew 1972, 201.
[16] Renfrew 1972, 150.

[17] Broodbank 2000*b*, xix.
[18] See also Manning 1995; Warren and Hankey 1989.

Chapter 6

The architecture

Lila Marangou

A. THE FORTIFICATION OF THE EARLY CYCLADIC SETTLEMENT AT MARKIANI ON AMORGOS

Traces of ancient walls visible on the surface[1] among the rocks and wild vegetation (PLATE 8 *a–b*) covering the low, easily accessible, north slope of the hill, led to the opening up of two trial trenches: Trench 6,[2] in the west sector (FIGS. 4.4 and 4.5, PLATE 9 *a–b*), and Trench 8,[3] in the east (FIG. 4.8, PLATE 10 *a–c*), a short distance from Trench 6.

In both trenches the existence of a robust wall (Th. 1.10–1.20 m) was confirmed, while in Trench 8 the 'horseshoe-shaped' projecting structure was identified as a bastion.[4] Remains of the wall encompassing the hilltop and remnants of a second bastion were also identified on the west side of the rocky hill, some distance from Trench 6 (FIG. 6.1, PLATE 12 *a*).

Until 1999 the picture of the superficially visible remains of the fortification was,[5] of necessity, highly circumspect,[6] on account of the limited excavation, the small scale of surface cleaning and removal of vegetation cover and, primarily, the lack of an architect in the team. The new and important evidence that emerged in 1999, after three-days of clearing the bushes,[7] in order to facilitate the preparation of the measured drawings,[8] not only provides additional information and clarification of several obscure points, but also largely confirms the initial observations and hypotheses that had been tentatively proposed in 1985, when the settlement was discovered.[9]

THE FORTIFICATION WALL

As can be seen from the measured drawings (FIGS. 6.1 and 6.2), produced by Antoniou, which give a precise picture of the situation after the recent clearing of vegetation and surface cleaning, the strong wall (PLATE 8 *a–b*) surrounding the north side of the hill, in an E–W direction,[10] has now been exposed for a length of about 70 m.[11]

The course and form of the ancient wall, which was founded directly on the bedrock, can be seen more clearly in the west section which is better preserved, that is from the North Bastion[12] in Trench 8 (PLATE 10 *a–b*) to the North West Bastion[13] (PLATE 12 *a*), as well as from the sizeable crag at the west

---

[1] See Chapter 2.

[2] See Chapter 4, The Fortification: Trenches 6 and 8.

[3] See Chapter 4, Trench 8.

[4] The anachronistic terms tower (*pyrgos*) and bastion (*promachon*) are usually used as synonymous: for their different meaning see Bossert 1967, 58 n. 12, with earlier bibliography. The correct term, bastion, is used by Parlama 1999, 47ff.

[5] See French 1990, 69; Davis 1992, 753, n. 256; Marangou 1994, 470, n. 18, 472ff, pl. 48o, 1 a–b. We discussed here the erroneous comments of Vaia Economidou (1994, 31–2), which are not based upon an understanding of the stratigraphic sequence but follow unsubstantiated 'oral information' (ibid 289, n. 152). See recently Sotirakopoulou 1997, 536 no. 190.

[6] It should be noted that not all the parts of the wall visible on the surface noted since 1985 are indicated in the topographical plan and the rough sketches.

[7] The expensive and laborious task (on account of the fierce winds) was carried out as part of the University of Ioannina research project (no. 232), funded by the Ministry of the Aegean. The clearing of the vegetation and the careful cleaning were carried out between 1 and 5 October with the invaluable assistance of the archaeologist G. Gavalas and the hard work of chief custodian of antiquities S. Giannakos, foreman of the

Ministry of Culture G. D. Gavalas and the workers M. Kovaios, S. Theologitis, A. Despotidis and G. Dedeis.

[8] The measured drawings were made by the architect G. Antoniou with the assistance of the custodian of antiquities G. Vlavianos.

[9] See Chapter 2.

[10] Because the prehistoric settlement at Markiani is not only the subject of research but also one of the island's visitable sites, annual (1991–99) funding from the Ministry of the Aegean, 'For the arrangement and enhancement of archaeological sites', has enabled us to conserve the excavated building remains, to cut down the weeds each year, to renovate the fencing round the site and, in 1999, to lay a road (1.30 m and 2.1 to 1.50 m) and a path (W. 0.40 to 0.60 m) facilitating access to the site, as well as the extensive clearing of vegetation and cleaning along the length of the wall (cf. n. 7 above).

[11] It varies in thickness from 1.10 to 1.35 m. The thickness is only measured in the sections visible on the surface, since these have not yet been excavated.

[12] Henceforth the strong construction excavated in Trench 8 is referred to as the North Bastion.

[13] Henceforth the enceinte-wall in the west section is referred to as the North West Bastion.

end of the terrace on the summit, which was in all probability the north-west limit of the natural fortification of the hill.[14]

In 1999, after the removal of the dilapidated field walls, the ruins lying west of the North Bastion were revealed *in situ*; these are certainly associated with the *enceinte*. Specifically, it was demonstrated that the west wall (L. 2 m), which had been partially revealed in the exploratory Trench 8,6,[15] is indeed part of the fortification and, as was already discernible below the field wall, continues westwards (L. 3.50 m, Th. 1.20 m) to join the section of the fortification wall that had already been located in Trench 6.[16]

Furthermore, it was ascertained that the strong west wall (L. 2.10 m) is the south side of a structure of almost trapezoidal plan with a north opening, slightly curved wall (FIGS. 6.1, 4.8, PLATE 11 *b*). The east wall of this 'trapezoidal' structure (L. max. 2.10 m) abuts the west wall of the North Bastion in the south part (L. 0.80 m) and is very thin (Th. max. 0.25 m), while at the north end it is thicker (Th. max. 1.15 m) and stands to a height of 0.19 m. The south side of the west wall (L. 1.30 m) is also contiguous with the north flank of the fortification wall, while its south end is indistinct because no excavation has taken place here; in contrast, the north end forms an angle with the west end of the slightly curved north wall, in which there is an opening, 0.50 m wide on the outer north side and 0.45 m on the inside, preserved to a height of 0.48 m (FIG. 6.1, PLATE 11 *b*).

The north, external face of the structure is founded on bedrock, which is incorporated into the fortification wall. According to the pottery finds[17] from the first Trench 8,6 and the few surface indications,[18] such as the potsherds[19] visible below the unexplored layer of fallen stones and the manner in which the stones interlock with the west wall of the North Bastion, this is most probably an addition that post-dates the North Bastion. The use of this space remains a matter for speculation, on account of the lack of known parallels.

During the new cleaning of Trench 6 (FIG. 6.1, PLATE 9 *a–b*) sizeable rocks were revealed at a distance of 1.75–1.80 m from its north, external face.[20] It was also ascertained that in the area to the east of Trench 6, the relatively large stones still *in situ*[21] belong to the mighty *enceinte*.

Moreover, 10 m west of Trench 6 a large crag and the north face of the North West Bastion (L. 3 m, H. pres. 1.20–1.35 m) were uncovered and the shape and external limits of the latter were fully clarified[22] (FIG. 6.1, PLATE 12 *a*).

Of importance for completing the picture of both the course of the fortification wall and the manner of its articulation with the natural rocks was the uncovering of a wall oriented E–W and 1.15 m long, which links the North West Bastion with the crags situated to the west and north. Here too the wall follows the natural configuration of the ground and forms an acute angle with the built structure which is 2.70 m long and oriented N–S, and consists of the projections of the natural rock and irregular boulders in the gaps between.

Also noteworthy are the recently exposed but still unexplored building remains and the layer of fallen stones, between which are wedged sherds of vases[23] of various types, found in the space between the west wall of the North West Bastion and the almost triangular projection of the largish rock incorporated in the enclosure wall.

Interesting evidence was revealed during surface cleaning of the hilltop terrace, south of the strong wall and the North West Bastion, and north of the *mandra* (sheepfold): we noted that the slightly sloping bedrock was cut in a stepped arrangement. Preserved on the lowest step is a row of stones belonging to a built structure measuring 1.80 m by 40 cm; this is possibly the tread of a staircase.[24]

---

[14] Prior to clearing the vegetation from the uneven bedrock, which was almost entirely covered by huge wild bushes, mainly of lentisk (*Pistacia lentiscus*), it was impossible to reach secure conclusions.

[15] See Chapter 4 Trench 8,6.

[16] See above Trench 6.

[17] See Chapter 4, Trench 8,6 and Chapter 7C.

[18] It should be stressed that the site has not been excavated fully (see above Trench 8,6).

[19] The sherds collected during the 1999 cleaning have not yet been studied but are assigned to the Blue Schist Ware characteristic of phases Ma III and Ma IV. Also noteworthy is the presence on the surface of the north wall of remains of bones, difficult to identify. Among the few finds are sea pebbles of various sizes, reminiscent of 'sling stones': cf. Tsountas 1899, 120; Doumas 1990, 90, cat. nos. 89–90; Theochari and Parlama 1997, 351 n.16, fig. 6.

[20] During the cleaning (1999) unstratified sherds of EC II date were collected, secure evidence for the continuity of life in the settlement.

[21] The field wall in a north–south direction was founded on

the fortification wall and built with stones from this.

[22] Many badly eroded sherds were collected, assigned to Blue Schist Ware, as well as a pebble-shaped grinder (?) or slingstone (?) (see above n. 19). It is natural that the pottery found on the surface and in the upper levels dates from the horizon of life at and use of the site, in EC III, during which time, for unknown reasons, the settlement was abandoned. In the north-west corner of the bastion, on the inner side, an intact, undecorated, handleless conical cup was found (H. 0.05 m, D. rim 0.072 m, Th. walls 0.005–0.006 m), possibly dated to the Ma III phase (Keros-Syros). Fallen vases, among them a semi-globular, undecorated spouted vase, possibly of the Ma III phase (Keros-Syros), were discovered on the surface, after large lentisk bushes west of the North West Bastion were felled.

[23] It is ascertained, mainly from the fabric and composition of the clay, that most of the sherds belong to Ma III phase.

[24] It is perhaps stepped access from the north-west side of the hill to the area of the settlement on the terraces of the south slope. Cf. similar stepped access at Palamari on Skyros (Theochari and Parlama 1997, 352, fig. 8).

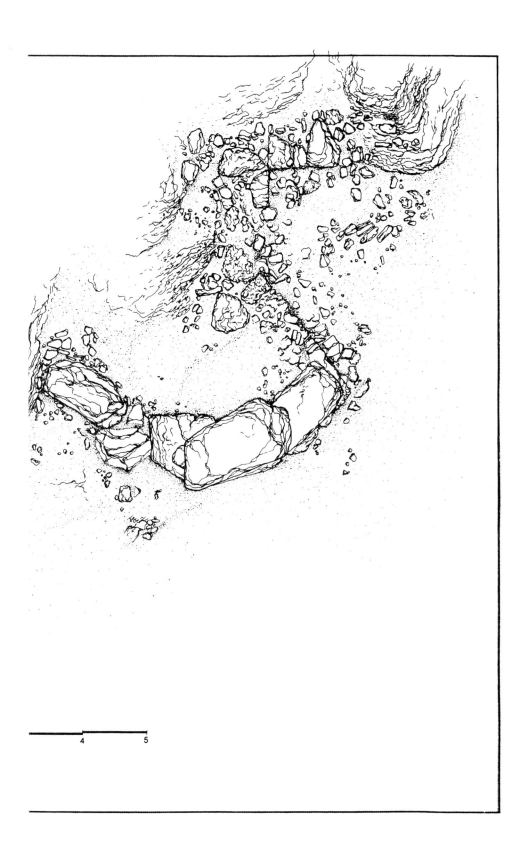

4   5

In its eastern section, at the lowest point of approach from the north side of the hill, the fortification wall has been considerably altered by continuous reconstructions of the high dry-stone field wall that effectively protected from the north wind the once intensively cultivated plot at Markiani, to the south, right at the base of the inside of the wall. The later, high field wall, founded either directly on the bedrock or upon ancient building remains, is built entirely of ancient stones, of irregular shape and different dimensions.

Here too the picture of the remains of the fortification is marred significantly by the wild vegetation that has 'taken over' since the abandonment of cultivation in recent decades and completely obscures the bedrock. Although its eastern limit has not been investigated systematically, I believe that here too, as on the west flank, we should look for the natural fortification formed by the scattered boulders that not only dominate the landscape but also protected and essentially dictated the form of the settlement on the south slope.

During recent clearing of vegetation, a large engraved boulder (1.80 × 0.30 × 0.40 m), set horizontally on the bedrock in a N–S direction, was uncovered 8.20 m from the south-east corner of the North Bastion and 0.75 m from the recent field wall. According to the surface evidence, such as the direct proximity to the dry-stone walling beneath which remains of the ancient fortification wall are clearly visible, it is possibly in its original position and belonged to a third bastion (FIG. 6.2, PLATES 8 *b* and 12 *b*).

Particularly interesting is the discovery, 13.25 m east of the North Bastion (FIG. 6.2, PLATE 12 *c*), of a strong structure which is undoubtedly associated with the fortification wall. It consists of a northwards projecting rock and a large boulder (L. 1.40 m, W. 0.50 m, H. 0.40 m) placed horizontally southwards. The narrow, almost triangular space (W. 0.30–0.58 m) formed between the rock and the boulder is flagged by four horizontally set, roughly worked stone slabs. The dimensions and position of this paved stone structure abutting the remains of the ancient fortification wall visible beneath the field wall, leads us to suggest that it is a narrow passage, communicating with the inside of the fortification.[25]

The surface cleaning and clearing of the vegetation along the inside of the field wall to the south of the passage and over the whole of the terrace revealed remains of sturdy structures as well as large worked stones, most of them displaced from their original position. However, the picture of this important space on the uppermost terrace on the east side (PLATE 12 *b–c*) of the naturally and artificially fortified hill, will only become clear after systematic survey and excavation.

THE BASTIONS

In 1999 it was possible to see clearly the two built structures which project from the fortification wall yet are integral with it: the North and North West Bastions (FIGS. 6.1 and 6.2).

The North Bastion[26] (FIG. 4.8, PLATES 8 *a* and 10 *a–c*) is preserved to a height of 1.04 m and its internal space[27] measures 2.45 × 1.25 m. The side-walls, east and west, are straight, while the north and south ones are slightly curved. The north wall (PLATE 11.1) is 2.65 m long and of maximum width 2.05 m. The east wall is 4.90 m long and 1.40 m thick; the west 3.58 m long and of maximum thickness 1.15 m. The south side, 2.82 m long, comprises the south flank of the fortification wall (Wall A, FIG. 4.10, PLATE 10 *a*). The manner of the interlocking of the stones of the south wall of the bastion with the fortification wall denotes clearly that it is a contemporary construction and not a later addition,[28] as is deduced securely from the pottery evidence[29] found in Trench 8,1, inside[30] the bastion.

The North West Bastion (FIGS. 6.1 and 6.2, PLATE 12 *a*) is located 19.30 m from the North Bastion and reaches a height of 1.20 m. Its outside limits and plan have been fully clarified. Here too the side-walls, east (L. 2.80 m) and west (L. 2.40 m), are straight, while the north (L. 2.85 m) seems to be slightly curved, on account of the relative large boulder on the north-east corner. The thickness of the walls and the limits of the south end can only be determined by excavation.

The bastions in the circumvallation of the Markiani hill, with their almost horseshoe-shape, are essentially no different from the few known examples of man-made fortified settlements in the EBA

---

[25] Compare Kastri on Syros; there is a similar 'opening' (W. 0.58 m) at Palamari, see Parlama 1999, 48, fig. 9. Comparable 'narrow passages for communication' are mentioned for Korfari ton Amygdalion at Panormos on Naxos: Doumas 1990, 90.

[26] Its limits were revealed in Trench 8 but excavation outside the tower has not been completed.

[27] See Chapter 4. Trench 8,1 (inside the bastion).

[28] See Chapter 4. Trench 8,1: 'the Bastion represents an addition to the defences belonging to the subsequent phase of

the occupation'.

[29] See Chapter 4 Trench 8,1 and Chapter 7C.

[30] It should be noted however that although the pottery was found in the deeper, undisturbed level, it indicates the level of use of the Bastion in phase Ma II–III, i.e. EC II (Kampos to Keros-Syros phases), and not the time of construction, since it does not come from excavation control of the foundations. See also Chapters 4 and 5.

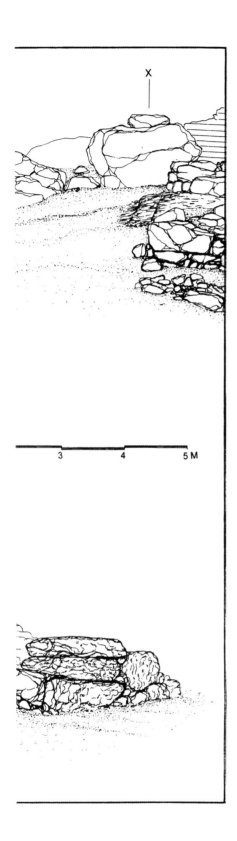

X

3   4   5 M

Aegean: Kastri on Syros,[31] Panormos on Naxos,[32] Palamari on Skyros,[33] as well as the Asia Minor littoral,[34] mainly Liman Tepe[35] and ancient Klazomenai[36] in the Bay of Smyrna.

As far as the eastern origin of fortifications reinforced with horseshoe-shaped bastions is concerned, the view of Höckmann,[37] who on the basis of typological parallels in the geographical region of Syria, Palestine, Lake Tiberias etc. correlated the semicircular shape with the examples in the Cyclades, is nowadays widely accepted.[38]

THE OUTWORK

The small section of the outwork[39] (L. 15 m, Th. 0.51 m, H. max. pres. 0.38 m) is visible 1.18 m north of the north face of the North Bastion (PLATE 10 *b*).[40] Even though there are only scant remains on the surface, it seems that the outwork continued both eastwards, along the length of the uneven natural rock, and westwards. Here too, as in the wall reinforced with bastions, the core consists of rocks dispersed along the entire, slightly sloping north side, which also determined the course of the manmade outwork. The stones from the outwork, like those of the fortification wall and the bastions, have been used in the construction of both recent walls separating the fields and the adjacent threshing floor.

Even though we believe we can trace the course and limits of the outwork, it is not possible to determine these securely without systematic surface cleaning, opening trial trenches and making precise measured drawings.

The site, the nature of the terrain and the scattered boulders *in situ* are definitive factors for both the form of the settlement and the protective fortification wall. The widespread exploitation of boulders *in situ* is a basic feature: not only are the protective wall, the bastions and the outwork founded on the bedrock on the brow of the hillock that rises slightly above the almost flat fields on the north side, the fertile fields, the so-called *platyvolia*, but large boulders *in situ* are also incorporated into the fabric of the north side. As can be seen in the plans (FIGS. 6.1 and 6.2) and photographs (PLATES 8 *a–b* and 10 *b*), it is constructed of irregular stones hewn from the living rock and roughly worked. Small stones are only used to fill the interstices, without mortar.

4. THE DATE OF THE FORTIFICATION[41]

The securest and in many cases the sole criterion for dating fortified settlements of the EBA is pottery. The unstratified pottery from the surface and the stratified material from the two trenches, Trench 6[42] and Trench 8,[43] dates, according to the prevailing system of typological classification, from Ma I to Ma III (EC I–II), that is from the earliest years of the settlement's existence to the level before its abandonment.

Although sparse, the stratigraphical evidence only from Trench 6 inside the fortification wall is nonetheless reliable for the early dating to Ma I (= EC I),[44] contrary to prevailing views[45] on the late appearance of man-made fortifications in the Aegean during the EC III period.

In the case of the North Bastion, the discovery of Ma III pottery (= EC II) in Trench 8,1, which lies within the North Bastion is considered to date its construction to a later phase[46] than the fortification wall. Further support for the later dating of the North Bastion comes from the typological comparison of its architecture with the few examples[47] known so far, Kastri on Syros,[48] Kynthos on Delos[49] and Panormos on Naxos.[50]

[31] Tsountas 1899, 116–30; Bossert 1967, 57–9, plan II.
[32] Doumas 1990, 90–2.
[33] Theochari and Parlama 1997 344–56, Parlama 1999.
[34] Erkanal 1999, 237–42, pls. LII–LIII. On EB II fortified sites in Asia Minor (Joukowski 1986, 446) see also Sotirakopoulou 1997, 537, n. 196.
[35] Erkanal 1997, unpaged pamphlet: topographical plan 2e on the inside cover and plan 3 on the back cover, where four bastions of elliptical plan are indicated. The excavation has been in progress since 1992, under the direction of Professor H. Erkanal; cf. above n. 34; see also Parlama 1999, 50–1, n. 21.
[36] See Akurgal 1950, Erkanal 1999 with earlier bibliography.
[37] Höckmann 1977, 161, 163–4, figs. 161–4, 166, 170.
[38] Sotirakopoulou 1997, 538; Parlama 1999, 51 n. 21, also accepts the view concerning a 'Syro-Palestinian' origin.
[39] During the clearing of the vegetation in 1999 it was ascertained that the small section of wall (H. 0.25 m) uncovered in trial Trench 8,2 (Wall Γ) (see Chapter 4), is part of the outwork.
[40] Its position indicates the 'settlement's vulnerability from the north side', cf. Parlama 1999, 47; cf. also the outwork at Kastri on Syros: Tsountas 1899, 115ff, fig. 32 and Bossert 1967, 53ff.

[41] Here the word fortification includes the fortification wall reinforced with bastions as well as the outwork.
[42] See also, Chapter 7C, pottery of phase I.
[43] See also, Chapter 7C, a note on the pottery from the Bastion.
[44] The fortification of Markiani is related chronologically with the first walls of Poliochni Blue: Marthari 1991, 28; Bernabò Brea 1964, 117–240; 1976, 701–5.
[45] Doumas 1990, 90–2; Theochari and Parlama 1997, 353–5; Parlama 1999. The theory was reformulated, with persuasive arguments based on the archaeological data: Sotirakopoulou 1997, 536–8; 1998, 135ff; 1999, 235–46.
[46] See also Chapters 4 and 5.
[47] On walled settlements see Parlama 1999 and Sotirakopoulou 1999, 245–6, with the earlier bibliography.
[48] Tsountas 1899, 116–30; Bossert 1967, 53ff; Sotirakopoulou 1999.
[49] Plassart 1928, 16, plan III; MacGillivray 1980, 3–45, esp. 4, 7, fig. 1; Sotirakopoulou 1999.
[50] Doumas 1964, 411–12; 1990, 90–2.

However, the similarities between the fortified settlement at Markiani and the 'late' walled sites at Kastri and Panormos are fewer than the differences. All the evidence, surface and stratified moveable finds, indicates that the settlement at Markiani was not short lived — as Kastri[51] and Panormos[52] are considered to be — but of long duration. Early permanent settlement on the narrow terraces of the barren south slope of Markiani hill is, moreover, attested by the stratified small finds, the earliest of which date to the EC I,[53] Markiani phase I. The long duration of occupation, without interruption, until the final period, Ma IV (Kastri phase), when it was abandoned for unknown causes, is indisputable. For this reason, from the outset, I subscribed to the reasonable hypothesis[54] that the construction of the man-made fortification, reinforced with bastions, is contemporary with the founding of the settlement, i.e. it dates back to the time when the first inhabitants occupied the site. Moreover, the position of the man-made fortification on the only side of the settlement that is easily accessible from land and therefore vulnerable,[55] the north, which it should be noted is literally whipped by fierce north winds, and the extensive exploitation of the large boulders *in situ*, belie its purpose of protecting the newly settled inhabitants.

At the present stage of research on fortified EBA settlements,[56] although several theories have been advanced,[57] I believe that it is premature to draw conclusions even of a preliminary nature on the fortified settlement at Markiani, not only because research is still at an early stage, but also because the newly discovered EC citadels on Amorgos[58] have not yet been sufficiently studied.

B. THE BUILDING REMAINS

by Lila Marangou

The building remains at Markiani, although in places subject to erosion and only incompletely excavated in the course of our project, have provided some more insights into the nature of EC domestic architecture. Moreover, they have indicated in a number of ways, for the first time, how early Cycladic craftsmen adapted their techniques to the special conditions of a site where steep hill slopes presented a number of specific constructional problems.

THE SUMMIT AREA

The northern part of the summit of Markiani, south of the fortification wall, has not been investigated, although ancient building remains are visible on the surface (see Chapter 6A). The area is divided by modern dry-stone walls into a number of enclosures and animal pens, associated with the three recent rubble masonry buildings, that is two sheepfolds (*mandres*), Buildings B and C, and a small, one-roomed house, Building A, indicating its use until quite recently (FIGS. 2.2 and 4.1, PLATE 2).

Careful observation of the stones and masonry of Buildings B and C revealed that they are not only constructed of ancient material but also founded on ancient walls, particularly obvious in the east part of Building B where ancient remnants can be seen in the lowest courses (FIG. 2.3, PLATE 7 *a*) and ancient schist slabs have been used for the roof. This situation prevents us from forming a clear picture of the area north of the summit, particularly since no measured drawings have been made of the extant architectural features and the rock outcrops. However, the immediate proximity to the fortification wall, the cuttings in the bedrock south of Building A, as well as the few sherds found in those places where a thin layer of topsoil remains, document the existence of ancient building remains.

Only the south part of the summit has been excavated, specifically the area between Buildings B and C. The earlier form of the site has inevitably been altered by the long duration of occupation, the building and repair of the dry-stone wall delimiting and protecting the small and narrow fertile terraced field to the south (Terrace 1), the wild vegetation and the habitual use — until the excavation began — of part of the west branch of the field wall as a passage (*poros*) for livestock (PLATE 7 *a*).

Investigation of the south part of the summit lying above Rock Cuttings 2 and 3 (FIG. 4.12, PLATE 7 *a–b*; see Chapter 4) revealed considerable erosion. This probably accounts for the fact that there were no clear signs of early structures, other than a few jumbled traces found in clefts in the bedrock

[51] Doumas 1990, 90.
[52] See Sotirakopoulou 1999.
[53] See Chapters 4 and 7C.
[54] Announcement to the Society of Antiquaries of London 1989. As noted above, different conclusions are proposed in Chapter 4, where the initial construction of the wall is ascribed to

Ma I, and the building of the North Bastion assigned to Ma III.
[55] Cf. Parlama 1999, 48.
[56] Parlama 1999; Sotirakopoulou 1999.
[57] Sotirakopoulou 1999.
[58] Marangou 1994, 472–7; 2002, 15.

(Trench 4, PLATE 7 *b*). The finds, notably the pottery, from this area belong to various periods, ranging from EBA to historical times; most were unstratified (see Chapter 4).

However, in the south-west sector of the south part of the summit, very fragmentary traces of what may originally have been important building remains were uncovered in Trench 1,1 and Trench 7, Space 8, and Trench 9 (see Chapter 4). These are dated solely on the basis of the stratified moveable finds, mainly pottery. A principal characteristic of the surviving building remains is the exploitation of the uneven, downward-sloping bedrock, with the natural hollows and sizeable crevices, as well as the adaptation of the built structures to the configuration of the ground (FIG. 4.12, PLATES 14 *a–b* and 15 *a*). They are indisputably related to the building remains on the terrace immediately below (Space 7), but their exact form and purpose or function remain unknown.

The connection between the south part of the summit and the terrace just below (Terrace 1) is certain. The excavated finds and mainly the remains *in situ* between the summit and Terrace 1, i.e. the scarp area of Rock Cutting 2 (Space 7 and the 'fissure'; FIG. 4.18, PLATE 16 *a–c*), prove their organic relationship.

THE BUILDINGS OF TERRACE 1

Terrace 1 can be reached from the east part of the summit (H. max. 2.50 m), south of Building B, where a few steps are still preserved (FIG. 2.3), some cut into the bedrock and others built; from the way in which the steps are cut and from the ancient foundations clearly visible in the lower courses of the south wall of the sheepfold (Building B), it is deduced that there may have been access from the same point in antiquity.

From the photographs (PLATES 18–25) and the plans (FIGS. 6.3 and 6.4) prepared by Clairi Palyvou of the trenches opened in the flat, narrow Terrace 1 (*c.* 40 m E–W and 7.50–8 m N–S), it is clear that the building remains uncovered not only furnish information on the manner and material of construction, but also permit some observations to be made. Of course, the fact that the excavation did not extend over the entire terrace but was restricted to its western part (9.5 × 7.5 m) (see also Chapter 4) prevents us from forming a complete picture as well as from determining the limits of the built space.

The building remains brought to light under the thin layer of topsoil belong, of course, to the final phase of habitation of the site, which was abandoned at the end of Ma IV. This is also confirmed by the datable moveable finds (see Chapter 7 and Chapter 4).

Although the trenches only reached virgin soil or bedrock in a very few places, from the stratification of the finds and the way in which some walls are founded and interlock, the underlying earlier structures can be identified and the earlier use of the site, i.e. the earlier occupation levels in Ma III, can be ascertained. The fact that the walls uncovered stand to a very low height (10–65 cm) makes it difficult to recognise securely the gradual restructuring of space (architectural renovation work) or intermediate building phases, repairs or new constructions or functional alterations, as for example in Space 7, before its final use (Ma IV).

It is equally difficult to reconstruct the architectural morphology of the building complex and to determine the organic relationship between the various areas as well as to understand the function of each space, such as the one in the west part of Terrace 1 and the angular wall (Wall a in Trench 10 and Wall θ in Trench 1,3, FIG. 4.18, PLATE 16 *c*). It was reasonably clear that the walls excavated on Terrace 1 delineated a number of small rooms. However, as already noted, it was not immediately clear which were internal features and which external. For this reason the neutral term *space* is used, to avoid pre-judging the functions of the overall architectural complex.

Outstanding among the building remains are the built curvilinear structure (Space 7, FIG. 6.3, PLATES 5 *a–c* and 15 *b*) and the conduit or drain (FIG. 4.21).

THE CIRCULAR FEATURE

The curvilinear structure (FIG. 4.18, PLATE 16 *c*) undoubtedly forms part of the constructions on the summit. Measuring 2 m E–W × 2.50 m N–S at its upper level and 1.50 m E–W × 1.40 m N–S at its lower, it is set within a natural crevice that has been hewn in the parts where there are walls built of large stone blocks so as to form a rough Rock Cutting.

The relationship between the curvilinear structure and Walls K and Λ in Trench 1,1, which may have been terrace walls following the rock escarpment south of the summit, and the difference in height (2.20 m) between the upper and lower part of the aforementioned structure, suggest that a surface at the top of this space possibly formed a floor associated with the mouth of the cleft (PLATE 16 *a*). If this is the case, then the curvilinear structure may have been roofed by the large schist slabs found in the rubble of the scarp during the first season of excavation.

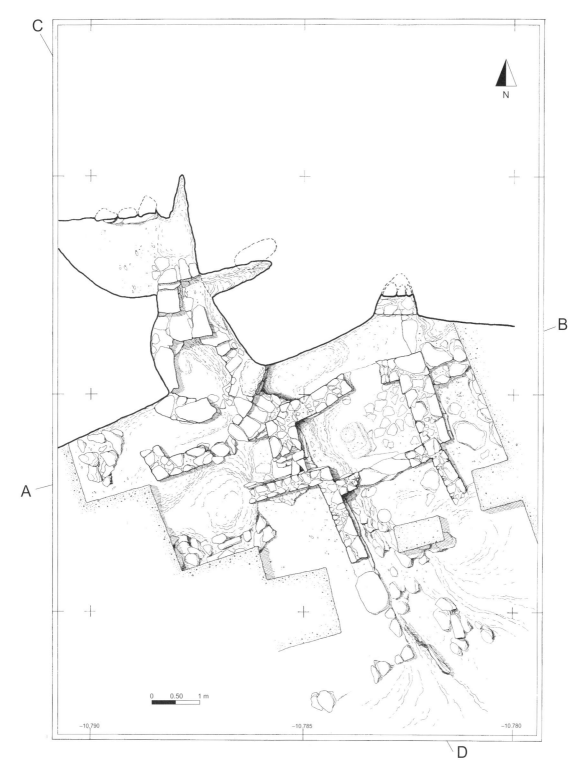

FIG. 6.3. Plan of the building remains of Terrace 1.

The opening in the east side of Rock Cutting 2 is essentially a natural crevice, the 'fissure' (PLATE 16 *a–b*), widened by human intervention. It continues eastwards but narrows to such a degree that excavation proved impossible. Nevertheless, since there were no artefacts in the section of the east part that was excavated, it may be assumed that the functional space of the crevice was the west part, which had been artificially enlarged. It was entered through Space 7. Wall Λ, uncovered in Trench 1, closed off the 'fissure', which belonged functionally to Space 7.

There is no precise parallel from any excavated site in the Aegean which would help us to identify the purpose of this feature. However, its form and the diverse finds recovered from it suggest that it

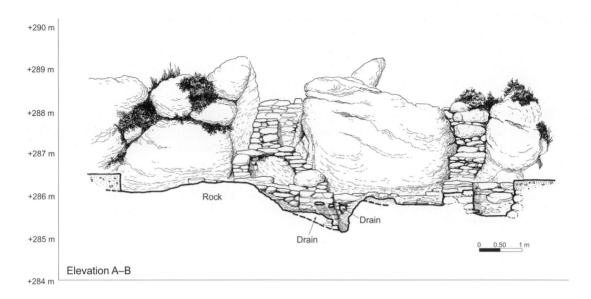

FIG. 6.4. Elevation of the scarp face of Terrace 1 (see FIG. 6.3).

functioned as a storage space where vessels and other artefacts, notably spindle-whorls, were kept. There is no evidence to indicate that it was related to the drainage system.

THE MAIN BUILDING COMPLEX

The architectural complex on Terrace 1, clearly seen in FIG. 6.3, comprises three rectangular spaces (1, 2 and 3), a small passage paved with schist slabs (Space 6), a well-built conduit-drain and, as noted above, a curved structure (Space 7) forming part of an incomplete circle. In addition, there were three probably unroofed spaces (Spaces 4, 5 and 9).

Space 6 (FIGS. 6.3 and 6.4, PLATE 18 *b* and 19 *a*) (4 m E–W × 0.90–1 m N–S), revealed just south of Rock Cutting 3, was used originally for collecting rainwater from the escarpment and channelling this along the surface of the bedrock to the drain. Subsequently, it was laid with small stones (Trench 2, level 48) and covered with beaten earth — possibly to create a floor. This should be related to Floor 'a' in Space 3, since Spaces 6 and 3 communicated via an opening in the wall. Pottery found on this floor dates to the abandonment phase of the settlement (Ma IV). A built structure alongside Rock Cutting 3, continuing to Wall ε-S in Trench 2, may have served as a bench.

Rock Cutting 3 (FIGS. 2.3, 6.4, PLATE 25 *a*) is smaller than Rock Cutting 2 (width of mouth 1.05 m). Its mouth is blocked by a well-built wall of large and small stones (1 × 0.40 × 1.20 m high), founded directly on the bedrock. In the course of cleaning the upper surface of this wall, a second wall was revealed in front of it, preserved to a lower height (0.75 × 0.35 × *c.* 0.40 m high). There was not enough time to investigate these walls further and so date them.

Space 6 may well have been a passage linking Spaces 3 and 2 with Spaces 9 and 4. It was probably not roofed and rainwater was collected there and then channelled to the main drain. This space was later incorporated into Space 3 and functioned as part of it.

Space 3 (FIGS. 4.21, 6.3, PLATE 18 *a–b*) is the most notable construction, and the only one preserved completely. It lies south of Space 6 and therefore of Rock Cutting 3. Roughly rectangular in plan, it measures 2.6 m E–W × 1.75 m N–S. Access was through a large entrance (1.12 × 0.40 m) on the south side, marked by a threshold slab (Threshold 1) from Space 2 and, on the north side, through an opening (0.65 × 0.50 m) from Space 6. Along the west side of Space 3 and under the paved floor runs the main drainage channel (PLATE 20 *a*), carved in the bedrock (L. 1.55, W. 0.35–0.50 m, difference in height between level of floor and bottom of channel, 0.40 m) and covered with stone slabs (PLATE 22 *b*).

Two main building phases could be identified in Space 3. The later phase, which belongs to Ma IV, consists of a floor of beaten earth with paving slabs 'a', the pottery on which was characteristic of the Kastri Group. The earlier phase, identified under Floor 'a', overlies an earlier Floor 'b' (PLATE 24 *a*). Floor 'b' was carefully paved with slabs and may be contemporary with the construction of Walls β-P and ε-S in Trench 2 (PLATE 24 *b*).

The small quantity of potsherds and the almost intact vases found *in situ* gave the impression of a 'tidy' room. However, the function of none of the aforementioned spaces can be determined precisely. This area may have had a domestic use. The last occupation level at the settlement (Ma IV) appears to have been associated with new building activity, after some sort of destruction.

Space 2 (FIGS. 4.21, 6.3, PLATE 18 *a–b*), which lies to the south of Space 3, was probably rectangular; there are now no traces of walls at its south-east corner. It is accessible from Space 3 to the north and Space 1 to the west, and is separated from Space 5 by a wall, which is only partially preserved. Space 2 (4.1 m E–W × 2.35 m N–S) has a floor of bedrock worked to achieve a level surface. A destruction level, in which the debris included large schist roof slabs and compacted earth from a flat roof (*domatochoma*), was found in Space 2. The level seems to be the same as that revealed on Floor 'a' in Space 3 and in Space 6. Along the east side of Wall E-E′ in Space 2 runs the main north–south drainage channel which is carved into the bedrock and was originally covered by slabs, one of which was found *in situ* in front of Threshold 2. The slabs rested on the ledge formed by the cutting of the channel in the rock. This space does not seem to have been roofed and possibly served as an antechamber (*prodomos*) or courtyard of Spaces 1 and 3.

Space 1 (FIG. 6.3, PLATE 19 *b*), which is incompletely preserved (4.35 m N–S × 2 m E–W), lies to the west of Spaces 2 and 3 and south of Space 4. Only its east part has been excavated. It communicates with Space 2 through a doorway, the monolithic threshold slab (Threshold 2; 1 × 0.60 m) of which survives. The south wall of Space 1 is no longer preserved and investigation of this area was only possible after removing part of the modern dry-stone retaining wall on the south side of Terrace 1. The large schist slabs found on top of the floor in Space 1 are thought to have fallen from the roof, which collapsed after abandonment. Beneath this layer was a level of broken vases. At the corner of the north and east walls (Wall A and Wall E respectively), a large stone mortar was found *in situ*; since it was found upright, the level on which it stands is considered to be the floor level of Space 1.

Spaces 1 and 3 appear to have been rooms in regular use. Since the walls of Spaces 2 and 3 abut onto those of Space 1, it would appear that Space 1 was the first 'room' constructed here, followed by Space 2 and then Space 3. Walls A and E in Trench 1,2 may be contemporary with Walls γ-Q and δ-R in Trench 2. Walls β-P and ε-S in Trench 2 are of later date and perhaps contemporary with Walls Γ and Δ in Trench 1,2 (PLATE 23 *a*).[59]

The chronological sequence is proposed based on the criteria of the construction and the width of the walls, since excavation in Space 1 did not continue under Floor 'b' and Wall P. Walls P, S, Γ and Δ are faced with large stones with fill inside, giving a stronger, more stable structure, and are approximately 0.60 m wide. Walls A, E, Q and R are built of two lines of smaller slabs, side by side, and are approximately 0.4 m wide. The thinner walls may be the earlier ones here. All these walls are founded on a socle of smaller stones laid on the bedrock, which is wider than the overlying wall proper.

Space 5 (FIG. 6.3, PLATE 18 *a–b*), lying to the east of Spaces 2 and 3, also rectangular in plan (3 m N–S × 1 m E–W), probably had an access on its south side, from Space 2. In the east part of Space 3 a natural hollow was intentionally filled with successive layers of stones placed horizontally, over which Wall P was built (see PLATE 25 *a*). In this area three large slabs were found lying against Walls P and Q, above which were stones and considerable quantities of limpet shells (*Patella*), all covered by a large slab. The built structure against Wall S on the north side of Space 5 is thought to have served as a bench. It is not clear whether Space 5 was roofed or not. The hundreds of seashells found here, covered by a slab and within a border of small stones, were food residue discarded in middens, remarkably similar to analogous rubbish pits on Amorgos today. The possibility that these makeshift structures served as hearths cannot be precluded.

The area of Terrace 1 was evidently deserted for a long period. In historical times (Late Hellenistic–Roman period), a makeshift retaining wall, Wall α, demarcated by a line of stones, was built at the east of Trench 2 (PLATE 17 *a–b*). Constructed without any special foundations, it stood on a layer of sherds dating from the Geometric to the Hellenistic period, following roughly the line of Wall R of Space 3. In the level above this wall there was material of Late Byzantine date.

THE DRAINAGE SYSTEM

The most striking feature of the architectural complex, and indeed the site, is the well-constructed drainage system (FIG. 6.3 and 4.21, PLATES 20–21). The drain starts from the north side of Terrace 1, at

---

[59] For orthographic convenience the terminology of the walls here differs from that employed during the excavation. Thus, Walls P, Q, R and S in Trench 2 correspond to Walls β, γ, δ and ε (see also Chapter 4).

the foot of the escarpment between Rock Cuttings 1 and 2 (the small area designated Space 6), where there would have been considerable run-off of rainwater. Partly carved in the rock and partly built, and in some places covered with stone slabs, the drain occupies almost the entire width N–S of the terrace (c. 7.50 m). Following the configuration of the bedrock, it runs west from Space 6 and then branches into two channels.

One channel runs south, under the north wall of Space 3 (PLATE 20 a–b), down the west side Space 3, i.e. inside the 'room', under its south wall and then along the west side of Space 2. It was covered by slabs inside Space 3 and also probably in Space 2. The other channel continues westwards from Space 6 into Space 4, then turns south and runs along the east side of Space 4. At the south-east corner of Space 4, it turns east and skirts the north Wall A of Room 1, where thin (W. 0.05 m) orthostats protected the wall from the water (PLATE 22 a). The drain then runs eastwards under Wall Γ, connects with the first branch in Space 3 and then turns south (PLATE 22 b). The covering slabs in this second, western, branch of the channel are still well preserved in the section running eastwards from Space 4 into Space 3. The course of the conduit is marked clearly in FIG. 4.21.

The drain certainly continued onto the lower terrace to the south (PLATE 21 a) but, because investigations were not completed, its further course and destination are not known; possibly it branched on the inhabited lower terrace into other channels which collected the rainwater in an open or closed pit or cistern, in natural or man-made hollows in the rock. The form and primarily the position of the drain in the excavated area, inside and outside the houses, indicate that it collected rainwater both from the roofs of the dwellings and the outdoor spaces, the courtyards and streets. Comparable systems for collecting precious supplies of water are encountered in all the settlements and farms of Amorgos from antiquity to the present day.

TRENCH 3

In the area of Trench 3, to the south-east (FIG. 4.1, PLATE 2), the picture of the remains of the prehistoric settlement is obscured by the maquis vegetation that covers the ancient and modern walls and the bedrock. Indeed, it is difficult to make out how this area was linked to the terraces above. Today there is access along a narrow path beginning from the east part of the terrace on the summit, south of the Bronze Age fortification wall, and continuing westwards and southwards. However, as is deduced from the now roughly blocked entrance (embassa) to the east edge of Terrace 1, in addition to the natural pathways on either side of the hill, there was once a road here, linking the upper terraces with the lower terraces and the flat, fertile fields (platyvolia) near the coast.

In and amongst the dense undergrowth, narrow steps are discernible, some hewn from the bedrock and others built of re-used ancient stones. Moreover, according to reliable information from farmers and shepherds who lived here seasonally until the land was abandoned quite recently, this was the route of one of the paths connecting the narrow strips which they cultivated, with the fertile fields near the shore. It is obvious that until this vegetation is cleared and an accurate topographical plan and measured drawings of the architectural features are made, it is impossible to speak about the precise extent and form of the settlement.

In Trench 3 two spaces (FIG. 4.24, PLATES 26–28) were brought to light, separated by a wall, Wall A, that runs N–S across the entire width of the terrace. To the west is Room 1 (PLATE 28 c) of rectangular plan (4.65 m E–W × 2.04 m N–S), with a solid wall (Wall I, 2.70 m E–W × 1.32 m N–S) built of several courses of stones on its north side. Room 2 (PLATE 28 a–b), to the east, is also rectangular (4.42 m E–W × 3 m N–S) and its east side is delineated by the vertical declivity of the bedrock. The rock forming the floor rises steeply from South to North, in the same way as in Room 1. Wall Θ (PLATE 28 a), on the north side of the room, curves slightly and may have supported the roof. It is not yet clear whether the two rooms communicated. A single course of stones at the south end of Wall A may indicate the position of a doorway (PLATE 28 c) that was subsequently partly blocked.

The walling on the south side of Rooms 1 and 2 is somewhat irregular, possibly because it was constructed to modify the line of the scarp to the north — the natural line of the bedrock essentially defines the north side of the rooms, supplemented with masonry where required.

Examination of the finds from the two rooms reveals a clear distinction in their use. Room 2, to the east, produced a greater quantity of pottery and particularly of 'pot-lids', whereas in Room 1 there was a notable concentration of metal objects, including a lead seal and several fine stone pestles. These objects enhance the impression that Room 1 was associated with special materials and may have been part of or associated with a workshop (see also Chapter 4).

Building Materials

The walls are constructed of flattish stones, of small or medium size and irregular shape, predominantly of dolomitic limestone or schist, depending on the material close at hand. All are carefully built, frequently with a little earth as mortar, and small stones inserted in the interstices. Usually they are founded on the bedrock, which has in some cases been cut specially.

FLOORS

Important information can be drawn from the floors and the two thresholds, for which large single stones were used. The floors are sometimes of bedrock, which is slightly worked to level it, sometimes of beaten earth and sometimes of carefully laid flagstones, particularly in courtyards, passages or corridors.

CEILING

It is deduced from stone slabs found *in situ,* as well as from those found dispersed and incorporated into recent dry-stone walls and roofs of stables, that the spaces were roofed with large schist slabs. It is likely that there were timber beams, perhaps trunks of *pheida,* (ancient Greek akcreuthos, i.e. *Juniperus phoenicea)* or lentisk trees (*Pistacia lentiscus)*. The roofs were rendered waterproof, as in recent times, by spreading a special impervious earth, yellowish or whitish in colour, over the slabs.

It may be concluded that, despite the limited areas excavated and the fact, not all the areas in Terrace 1 have yet been excavated to bedrock, the building remains at Markiani form a significant contribution to our understanding of EC domestic architecture. For hitherto, apart from the rather fragmentary building remains at Pyrgos on Paros and the finds of Tsountas at Kastri on Syros,[60] we have only rather limited documentation for domestic buildings. Publication of those at Ayia Irini on Kea is now imminent,[61] and the complex at Skarkos on Ios,[62] when published in full, will make a significant advance, as will the complex at Panormos on Naxos.[63] But the recent excavations at Phylakopi have added very little to the incomplete information on the architecture of EBA Melos.[64] The soundings undertaken at Akrotiri in Thera have been rich in EBA pottery[65] and EC figurines have been important,[66] but contributions to our knowledge of EC architecture have been few.[67]

Thus interesting features such as the Markiani drainage system offer important new indications which future excavation and study will no doubt amplify.

[60] Tsountas 1899, 116–30; Bossert 1967; Hekman 1994, 47–74.
[61] Wilson-Eliot 1984.
[62] Marthari 1997, 362–77.
[63] Doumas 1965, 41–64.
[64] Atkinson *et al.* 1904.

[65] Sotirakopoulou 1999, 39–65 and 249–64.
[66] Sotirakopoulou 1998, 107–65.
[67] Doumas 1972, 151–70; Marthari 1990, 40–1; Marthari 1997, 362–77.

These observations are helpful, perhaps, in understanding the background to the rather nebulous entity, formerly termed the 'Amorgos Group'.[11] It is characterised principally by the absence of fine or decorated wares, and by a number of shapes, which will be considered in the last section of this chapter after detailed presentation of the Markiani material. Now that we have, as indicated below, a series of stratigraphically excavated, well-associated ceramic assemblages for EBA Amorgos, it is clear that the concept of the 'Amorgos Group' has little substance from a chronological point of view. With the finer chronological structure of the island, which now becomes available, it is a concept best abandoned. We shall return to the chronological positions to be assigned to the various shapes originally felt to constitute the 'Amorgos Group'.

In discussing the Markiani pottery assemblages it is of course necessary to consider first the character of the site. It is constituted now, as it was in the EBA, by a series of terraces leading to the summit. As noted earlier the summit was fortified during the EBA.

The summit of the site is much eroded, and the deposits there (represented principally by Trench 4) are no longer abundant or well stratified, although at the south edge, at the top of our Trench 1,1 and within Trench 7, stratified deposits of early date were recovered. The main deposits investigated by us lie on Terrace 1, to the south and in the scarp between this and the summit (Trench 1,1).

Markiani is not a tell mound like Knossos or Phylakopi, and nowhere is there a continuous stratified sequence of deposits which extends from the earliest to the latest EBA occupation. There are of course, many clear indications of stratigraphic succession, especially in Trench 1,1. But there are other areas, for instance in Trench 6, where a clear and well-associated (and in that sense well-stratified) body of material is found together with architectural remains, and yet cannot be related by direct stratigraphic means to the other well-stratified deposits.

Here, as on most such sites, the appropriate approach is to study, in the first instance and in their entirety, well-associated assemblages of material found together in contexts, which assure their stratigraphic integrity. Once their characteristics have been identified clearly, the chronological relationships between these phases may usually be assumed by direct stratigraphic means. In a few other cases, as for instance for the main deposits of Trench 3, the chronological relationship between the well-associated material found there and other material on the site has to be established by comparative (i.e. typological) means.

As will be made clear in detail below, study of the pottery from the site shows that four principal phases may be identified, each represented by well-associated assemblages. Comparison with other known Cycladic finds allows all four to be assigned unhesitatingly to the Cycladic EBA.

Two assemblages were recognised at an early stage of the excavation as particularly well defined and easy to characterise. One of these (here assigned to the abandonment phase, phase IV) was already evident from the surface survey conducted by Marangou in 1985. Material from Rock Cutting 2 (*Engopi 2*) and nearby areas included tankard fragments in Dark-Faced Burnished Ware and other wares (FIG. 7.19).

The stratigraphic indications here are clear that this represents the last significant phase of occupation of the site in the EBA, and indeed the last substantial occupation of the site. Within the material are shapes which could at once be compared with that of the Kastri Group[12] known from Kastri near Chalandriani on Syros,[13] Ayia Irini III on Kea,[14] Mount Kynthos on Delos,[15] and other Cycladic sites, as well as Lefkandi I on Euboia.[16] Further study of this material as set out below in Chapter 7C, indicates that this comparison is appropriate on numerous grounds.

The other body of material recognised already in an early stage of the excavation comes from the area at the top of Trench 1,1, later excavated as Trench 7. There the occurrence of rolled-rim bowls in heavy burnished ware, along with fragments of frying pans of Kampos type and of a bottle, also of Kampos type, indicated that the body of material might be compared with known finds of the Kampos Group. This material has been designated as phase II of the Markiani sequence.

A further body of material was found in Trench 1,1 and during excavation of Wall Λ, most notably in the cave-like 'fissure' (*rogmi*) in the rock there, which may clearly be differentiated from the two assemblages already mentioned. The shapes are not the same as those of phase II, nor of phase IV. As indicated in Chapter 4, this material is seen stratigraphically as earlier than the material of phase IV and later than that of phase II. It was designated phase III (see Chapter 7D).

[11] Renfrew 1972, 106–9; Doumas 1977, 23; Broodbank 2000b, 209.
[12] Renfrew 1972, 533–4, fig. 11, 2, pl. 9, 1–4; Doumas 1977, 22–3, fig. 11.
[13] Bossert 1967, 69–70.

[14] Caskey 1972, 357–401; Wilson and Elliot 1984, 78–87; Wilson 1999.
[15] MacGillivray 1980, 3–45
[16] Popham and Sackett 1968, 8; Rutter 1979, 4–15.

The trench opened in order to investigate the fortification wall at the north of the site (Trench 6) produced a coherent assemblage of material. With its predominance of thick-walled, burnished bowls of Marble Ware it resembles the material of phase II in a number of ways. However, it completely lacks the frying pan and bottle fragments characteristic of the Kampos Group. In its character it has points of resemblance with the material from Pre-city Phylakopi (phase A1)[17] and other sites of the Grotta-Pelos culture.

Even without this external indication of chronological priority over the material of the Kampos Group, the clear continuity with the material of phase II and the absence of such innovative forms of the Kampos Group as the frying pan and bottle indicate that this precedes the material of phase II. It has been assigned to phase I and may be regarded as representing a developed phase of the Grotta-Pelos culture, prior to the inception of the Kampos Group. Its chronological priority over the material of phase II is not in question. It should be noted that in her discussion in Chapter 7C of the ceramics of Ma I and II, Efi Karantzali is obliged to range rather widely in her search for appropriate parallels. This is, however, inevitable in view of the current lack of well-published pottery from any well-stratified settlement deposits of the Grotta-Pelos culture or of the Kampos Group. Probably the closest parallel to the pottery of Ma I is currently to be found in the pottery from the earliest phase (A1) of Pre-city Phylakopi on Melos.

These four assemblages embrace the entire range of pottery from the EBA found on the near summit of the site (including the material of Terrace 1). The assignment of alpha-numerical designations naturally follows. The most recent material is inevitably designated phase IV, the earliest phase I, and the stratigraphic and typological relationships just discussed assure the succession of assemblages I, II, III and IV in that order, so that these assemblages can properly be taken to represent phases of occupation of the site.

It should be noted that the amount of material recovered from phase III is very limited in extent. Despite this limitation it is clearly different from and earlier than the material of phase IV, and later than that of phase II. These observations are made in first instance on stratigraphic grounds, and can be supported typologically. In general, as the discussion by Kiki Birtacha in Chapter 7D and by Pantelis Eskitzioglou in Chapter 7E establishes, the principal feature which distinguishes the pottery of Ma IV is the presence of the 'Anatolianising' features characteristic of the Kastri Group.

One feature which emerged from the study of the pottery by our three period specialists, and then in particular from the petrographic study by Sarah Vaughan, was the chronological significance of the ceramic fabrics. At a very early stage it was apparent that the pottery (used to define the Ma I ceramic assemblage) from Trench 6,1, the section across the fortification wall, comprised primarily fabrics with a calcareous filler, which were initially described as 'Marble Ware', subsequently divided into sub-categories. The same was essentially true of the pottery from Trenches 7 and 9, which yielded the defining assemblage for what was designated Ma II.

By contrast the pottery of phase III had a high percentage (in excess of 40%) of pottery with a filler apparently of glaucophane schist, which was initially designated Blue Schist Ware (some of which was later assigned by Dr Vaughan to the Red Shale Ware category). The strata assigned to phase IV had an even higher percentage of this fabric, while Marble Ware fell to a frequency of about 30%. The approximate figures for this interesting and diagnostic distinction are as follows:

TABLE 7.1. Frequencies of 'Marble Ware' and 'Blue Schist Ware' at Markiani by phase.

Fabric	Percentage per phase			
	I	II	III	IV
Marble A, B, C	98.5	98.9	42.3	29.1
Blue schist and Red shale	0.0	0.6	41.3	56.0
Other	1.5	0.5	16.4	14.9

This distinction proved a convenient one where chronological interpretation was needed in the course of excavation. In particular, as argued in Chapter 4 above, it was useful in assigning a stratigraphic phase to the Bastion. There a significant frequency of the Blue Schist Ware in the deepest strata inside the Bastion suggested that construction should probably be assigned to Markiani phase III. The pottery most frequently found inside and outside the Bastion could be assigned to phases I, II and III, but the presence near the bedrock inside the Bastion of pottery assignable on the basis of its fabric to phase III, gave the clearest available indication of the relative chronology of the Bastion.

THE TREATMENT OF THE POTTERY

To publish all the pottery from a site in great detail would be a difficult task without first establishing the essentials of the pottery sequence for the site. This we have set out to do here. Moreover, any systematic treatment would need to be based on a competent understanding of the pottery fabrics and their constituent petrology. From a preliminary inspection it was clear that there was no immediately and self-evident division of the material into fabrics. This could only be undertaken using much more careful observation of the pottery, supported by petrographic study. In the section that follows, the fabrics from the site are presented in a systematic overview by Sarah Vaughan.

In dividing up the pottery for publication by various specialists, two principles were followed:
a) the full range of phases (periods) of the EBA from the site would be covered.
b) the procedure would entail the study and publication of entire and well-stratified assemblages.

Following those principles pottery was assigned for study as follows:

Chapter 7C (by Efi Karantzali)
Pottery from Trench 6, the main occurrence of phase I,
Pottery from Trench 7, Trench 1,1 and Trench 9 (selected levels), the main occurrence of pottery from the phase II and
Pottery from Trench 8 (chosen to ensure the accurate dating of the tower in Trench 8).

Chapter 7D (by Kiki Birtacha)
Pottery from the excavation of Wall Λ of Trench 1, and from the rock 'fissure' (Sealed deposit, excepting levels of phase IV studied by Pantelis Eskitzioglou). The pottery in question includes the pottery of phase III.

Chapter 7E (by Pantelis Eskitzioglou)
Pottery of the late phase, phase IV (abandonment phase), specifically from Trench 1,1 and from the area designated Space 3 and Space 6 (from the relevant layers of Trench 2,1, Trench 4, and Trench 1,3).

It should be noted that the material from Trench 3, which is not discussed in detail here, has not been assigned to a specific phase although from the outset it was assumed to be broadly contemporary with (or a little earlier than) phase IV. It clearly belongs to the later part of the EBA. But the lack of tankard fragments and the other points of difference distance it somewhat from the material of phase IV as studied in detail here. It would certainly seem to be later than phase II. Yet it is certainly not identical to the material of phase III seen in Trench 1,1. Since there are no direct stratigraphic links between the material of Trench 3 and other areas the matter must be determined on typological grounds. The conclusion that this material is broadly contemporary with that of phase IV seems plausible. However, we have avoided assigning a numerical phase to this material, preferring to restrict the phase designations to cases where there are strong stratigraphic (and typological) arguments based primarily on a consideration of the Markiani material alone.

TABLE 7.2. The stratigraphic layers at Markiani diagnostic of the successive phases for the site.

Markiani phases	Trenches	Layers	Spaces
Phase I	Trench 6	2–10	Fortification wall
Phase II	Trench 7 Trench 1,1 (summit)	2–4,6–10, 12–15 6–7, 19–20	Space 8
Phase III	Trench 1,1 Trench 9,1	42–46 5	'Fissure'
Phase IV	Trench 1,1 (scarp area) Trench 2 Trench 1,4 Trench 1,3	21–29 , 34–36 , 41 22–29 and 31 4, 6, 9, 12, 17, 19, 22, 27–31 3–5 and 7	Space 7 Space 3 Space 6

It should be noted that the pottery from various other areas is not here presented in detail. This refers in particular to the following: Trench 4 (summit), Trench 5 (eastern end of Terrace 1) and Trench 2 (eastern part of the principal excavated area of Terrace 1, except as indicated above).

The diagnostic material from successive phases is thus found above (TABLE 7.2).

The selection of material presented here assures the full publication of the pottery assemblages required for the dating of the principal architectural features of the site. It also allows the specialists to present the most characteristic assemblages of the principal phases.

B. MACROSCOPIC AND PETROGRAPHIC STUDIES OF POTTERY FROM MARKIANI ON AMORGOS

by Sarah J. Vaughan

INTRODUCTION

This study of the pottery from Markiani was undertaken in conjunction with the excavation and fieldwork at the site of Markiani and represents a component of the author's long-term studies of Cycladic ceramics.[18] The analytical approach correlated technological data from observations of hand specimens with data from microscopic analysis of thin sections of the same samples. The aims of the study included use of the additional data to enhance ceramic description and classification for the site and the comparisons with pottery from contemporary sites in Greece, while reconstructing patterns of use of raw materials on Amorgos by EBA artisans. Systematic geoprospection by the author on Amorgos provided examples of comparative raw materials when prepared as briquettes and thin-sectioned.

In order for it to be most helpful to other excavators, this summary of the material and technological data is set out in relation to the major ware groups as defined by the Markiani excavators using the criteria of vessel shapes and decoration, and minimal fabric information from hand specimens examined in the field. The word 'fabric' in the descriptions below refers to the microscopic data for the fired raw materials as they reflect distinct material patterns of preparation and manufacture by the ancient potters, reinforced by technological traditions of preparation and manufacture observable in fresh and cut breaks. Thus a material tradition may crosscut archaeologically-determined 'ware' groups, but commonly remains associated with technological traditions established over time by potters to ensure successful production. Percentages and inclusion shape were estimated with comparator charts, colours assessed with a Munsell Soil Color Chart in daylight, and hardness estimates determined using a modified version of a Mohs chart on fresh breaks.[19]

The main ceramic fabrics identified in this study are summarised in the table below:

TABLE 7.3. Main ceramic fabrics at Markiani.

Fabric Name (petrographic)	Distinguishing constituents	Samples Studied	Ware name/shapes (archaeological)
Marble Ware	Marble; recrystallised limestone	20	Marble Ware
Phyllite-Quartzite	Finely-foliated phyllite; chlorite, sericite, metamorphic metaquartz	22	Blue Schist Ware
Red Shale	Cross-laminated shale	10	Blue Schist Ware, Light Brown Burnished Ware
Metaquartzite-Schist	Quartzite; plagioclase, K-feldspar, biotite	10	Pale Micaceous Ware; Light Brown Burnished Ware; spindle-whorl, open jars
Volcanic	Basalt; plagioclase phenocrysts, chert, twinned euhedral clinopyroxene.	10	7 brazier fragments 1 rolled rim-bowl
Micritic, shelly Limestone	Micritic limestone with peloids, shell fragments; chert	3	Red Slipped Burnished Ware; Dark Storage Ware
Micaceous	Fine muscovite, biotite, quartz grains, minor plagioclase, rare hornblende and orthopyroxene, detrital meta-quartzites & phyllites	10	Urfirnis Yellow-Mottled Fine Buff Slipped & Burnished Dark Grey Fine Micaceous
Other	Quartz-muscovite schist	1	Pale Micaceous Ware

[18] Vaughan 1989; Vaughan 1990; Vaughan and Wilson 1993; Vaughan *et al.* 1995; Vaughan 2000

[19] Vaughan 2000.

Major Domestic Ceramic Fabrics

There are two main fabric types represented among the major domestic wares of Markiani, clearly reflecting the island's main lithological deposits and raw materials available near the site. Both fabrics have a distinctive appearance making them easily recognisable on Amorgos and at sites elsewhere. The first fabric is a 'marble' tempered fabric distinguishing pottery at Markiani called by excavators Marble Ware. Most of this ware is oxidised, although dark grey examples were also noted. The walls of this ware varied between 1.20–3.00 cm, and vessel shapes included rolled-rim and other bowls, storage vessels and pithoi, collared jars, pyxides and plates. A comprehensive scientific study of this ware elsewhere suggests it may reflect the recycling by local marble artisans of marble debris at workshops on Amorgos and on Naxos.[20]

The second common fabric appears to be pottery tempered by fragments of a glaucophane schist (a high grade metamorphic rock), giving rise to its excavation name, Blue Schist Ware. In fact, however, the abundant tiny purple-blue inclusions distinguishing this product are from an iron-manganese phyllite, a low-grade metamorphic rock. Fragments of this oxidised pottery are also distinguished in hand specimen by a slightly greasy feel, as a result of the dissociation of the soft phyllite fragments. This ware was represented by fragments of rolled-rim and other bowls, pithoi, collared jars, small conical cups, baking pans, a beaked jug and an askos.

A related pottery at Markiani with low-grade metamorphic constituents is a Red Shale fabric, where the inclusions are reddish colour in hand specimen, and distinguished by oxide-stained cross-lamination and foliation visible in thin section. The other main pottery groups at the site include a Metaquartzite-schist fabric characterised by the presence of higher-grade metamorphic constituents, a Volcanic fabric with basalt inclusions, and several examples of micaceous fabrics of varying composition, most of which were identified by excavators as representing imported items (such as sauceboats) to Amorgos.

Analysis and Interpretation

In general the pottery at Markiani reflects the use of locally-available raw materials, the petrographic profile of which encompasses the lithological profile for the island's geological deposits — low-grade to high-grade metamorphic rocks with varying percentages of mica and metaquartz constituents. Even the distinctive Marble Ware fabric exhibits a range of secondary constituents, some examples containing almost exclusively fragments of marble, while others have minor percentages of the phyllitic or quartzitic inclusions that dominate other fabrics at the site. And the fragments of marble reflect problems of descriptive ambiguity inherent in applying strict petrological classifications to a lithological group where the carbonate parent deposits have been metamorphosed to varying grades throughout multiple periods of tectonic activity in the region's geological history. Some of the moderately to well sorted fragments resemble classic marble, with a mosaic texture, while others have a more granoblastic texture. These fragments sometimes co-exist within single samples, and sometimes alongside what would more accurately be described as fragments of limestone or calcareous rocks. Thus, while it is tempting to try to apply strict petrological categories in creating pottery fabric groups at Markiani, it may be more realistic to interpret the lithological continuum exhibited in the petrographic assemblage simply as evidence supporting the use by the ancient potters of the range of local clays and tempering materials.

The phyllitic fabric is consistent with the distinctive, regionally-distributed deposits of ferro-manganese phyllite on Amorgos, called by islanders *patelia*. This material is commonly quarried and crushed for use in waterproofing roofs. The abundant inclusions in the pottery are relatively well sorted, with occasional and minor percentages of micritic calcite and metachert throughout the groundmass. The Metaquartzite-schist fabric is characterised by poorly-sorted fragments of polycrystalline quartz with sutured grain boundaries common, and occasional ribbon texture visible suggestive of deformed quartz veins. Secondary percentages of biotite mica, and rare plagioclase and alkaline feldspars were noted.

The Micritic fabric is characterised by abundant shelly limestone fragments and peloids, with rarer moderately to poorly-sorted metaquartzite and chert fragments and occasional orthopyroxenes. The Volcanic fabric is distinguished by angular-subangular, poor to moderately sorted fragments of basalt, with trachyitic texture visible in some clasts. Plagioclase phenocrysts are common, and twinned clinopyroxenes (some euhedral) occur, with sparse percentages of micritic calcite, quartz grains and orthopyroxene.

When the petrographic data are correlated with specific wares, some useful archaeological associations are revealed. The two most abundant wares, Marble Ware and Blue Schist Ware, reflect the use of

---

[20] Vaughan *et al.* in press.

relatively consistent and distinctive local raw materials. Imported wares such as Urfirnis, Yellow Mottled, and Fine Buff Slipped and Burnished were manufactured from very fine micaceous clays consistent with a source outside Amorgos. Light Brown Burnished Ware was made from both metaquartzite schist materials and clays containing the distinctive local red shale fragments, probably suggesting a local source, as was Pale Micaceous Ware. And it was interesting to note that the fragments of braziers analysed all grouped within the volcanic fabric, a common technological material choice for vessels intended for cooking, but unlikely to be products of local artisans.

CONCLUSIONS

The combined material data suggest that the people utilising the site of Markiani benefited from several strong and distinctive local ceramic traditions, encompassing the range of functional vessels and weaving tools they required. In addition to these abundant local products however, archaeologists recovered significant numbers of vessel fragments representing materials not local to the island (the volcanic and the very fine micaceous fabrics), ample evidence to suggest exchange and contact with settlements and artisans certainly within the Cyclades, and perhaps farther afield.

C. THE POTTERY OF MARKIANI PHASES I AND II
by Efi Karantzali

THE POTTERY OF MARKIANI PHASE I

As mentioned above,[21] the pottery assemblage defined as characteristic of phase I at Markiani was found in closed homogeneous deposits during the investigation of the fortification wall area and specifically in Trenches 6,1 and 6,2, which were opened on the inside and outside respectively of the wall.

In Trench 6,1, body sherds of household wares were found, along with storage and cooking vessels. Because of the poor preservation it is difficult in most cases to distinguish open from closed shapes, especially when dealing with body sherds. From layers 1 to 8 there were 603 sherds in total. They are mainly body sherds (566), 21 rim fragments, 13 bases and a few handles. 21 sherds came from layers 9 and 10, the deepest layers over the bedrock; most of these were very abraded. 18 of them are body sherds, (18%), two flat bases and part of a disc (**K 1504**) all of Marble Ware.

The deposit from Trench 6,2 yielded 163 sherds in total, lacking diagnostic material. The body sherds are predominant (150), while there are 8 rim fragments, few bases and 5 crescent-shaped lugs.

As noted in Chapter 4.2, the well-stratified layers of Trench 6,1 (layers 2 to 8) from the defining deposit for Ma I. There are no well-stratified layers of Ma I in Trench 6,2 which lies outside the wall.

FABRIC/WARE

The predominant fabric is Marble Ware, as seen in TABLE 7.4 (p. 158). Only one sherd from the superficial layer is of Blue Schist Ware and must be dated to a later phase, Ma III or IV. Another sherd with pointillé-incised decoration (**K 1455**, FIG. 7.2: 18) is assigned to the Other Fabrics category and may perhaps be dated to Ma II.

SURFACE TREATMENT

Most of the sherds have a weathered dark surface, well smoothed, but rarely burnished:

- 15 have visible traces of burnish with a dark red (11) to greyish or black (4) burnished surface. The burnish is preserved better on the interior when the sherds are from open vessels.
- 460 body sherds of various vessels have a dark reddish smoothed surface.
- 37 sherds of various vessels have a light smoothed or polished surface.
- 5 are from the body of closed vessels: three with scoring, one with wiping and the fifth with scoring and polish.

Only in the case of one sherd (lug **K 1113**, FIG. 7.2: 13) is the surface treatment more characteristic of the pottery of Trench 7, dated to the period of the Kampos Group (Transitional EC I/II).

---

[21] See Chapter 7A.

DATING

As will be seen from the discussion which follows, the pottery of Trench 6,1 may be dated to the Grotta-Pelos culture (EC I period).

MA I POTTERY SHAPES

1. Deep rolled-rim bowl (phiale) (K 1481 and K 1473, FIG. 7.1: 1 and 2, PLATE 29 *a*)

Sherds **K 1481** and **K 1473** are rather deep bowls with rounded inturned swelling rim, of rolled-rim type. These are known in both the Ma I and Ma II phases of the settlement, with many variants in the degree of the swelling of the rim and in the surface treatment. These bowls often have a horizontal cylindrical lug with horizontal perforation (see also shape 2).

This form of bowl with rolled rim is characteristic of the Grotta-Pelos period (EC I) and also the Kampos phase (EC I/II) and is known as the Kum Tepe bowl type in the Aegean from the end of the Neolithic (Final Neolithic).[22] There are similar typological parallels in marble from Keros and the Kouphonisia.[23]

There are similar bowls from Grotta on Naxos and Phylakopi on Melos,[24] Palati[25] and Ayia Anna[26] on Naxos and other sites. The examples from the Kouphonisia are dated to the transitional Kampos Group (EC I/II) period.[27] There are variants of this shape from Kum Tepe[28] in the Troad and from Emborio on Chios.[29]

At Eutresis in Boiotia this type is known from group II (N section phase, Final Neolithic) and from group III of EH I date.[30] There are also examples from EH sites in Euboia.[31] Variants of this type can be seen in examples from Manika in Euboia.[32]

The slightly thickened, in-turned to rounded rim is characteristic of a variant of this form that can be dated in the Kampos phase. Similar examples come from Palati and Ayia Anna on Naxos, and from Kouphonisi (NM 4828). The earlier (Grotta-Pelos) examples are well burnished (Grotta, Palati and Ayia Anna) while those from the Kouphonisia have a thin slip and a light burnish, e.g. **K 1473**. However, it seems that the degree of rim swelling has no chronological significance, as is clear from the many co-existing variants of this type at Kum Tepe.[33]

On Crete this type appears in EM I and continues with variants during EM IIA, and perhaps later, i.e. bowls from Knossos.[34]

2. Deep bowl (phiale) with horizontally perforated cylindrical lug (**K 1500** and **K 1501**, FIG. 7.1: 3–4, PLATE 29 *c*)

This shape is characteristic of phases Ma I and II and it is common at Grotta, Palati and Ayia Anna on Naxos, in the Grotta-Pelos stratum (A1) of Phylakopi, on Aigina,[35] at Kum Tepe (phase Ib 3),[36] Troy and elsewhere.[37]

3. Various bowls (phiale) and deep bowls with lugs (chytra) with in-turned rim (**K 1499**, **K 1480** and **K 1503**, FIG. 7.1: 5–7)

This shape is seen in the pottery assemblages of Ma I (see **K 1499**, **K 1480** and **K 1503**), Ma II (see below variant **K 1607**, FIG. 7.6: 16) and also Ma III. Although this type continues during all three periods, there are noticeable differences in the quality of the fabric and in the surface treatment techniques. It is obvious that the technical characteristics of the pottery (fabrics, surface treatment etc.) developed more rapidly than the shapes.

This type of bowl, which often has an in-turned swelling rim, is known from EH I[38] and EC I contexts and continues with variants until the end of EC II and EH II, as seen at Panormos on Naxos, Kynthos on

---

[22] Sotirakopoulou 1986, 301–3.
[23] Unpublished material.
[24] Unpublished material of the old and recent excavations on Melos; Renfrew 1972, 155, fig. 10.1; Evans and Renfrew 1984, 63–9; Renfrew and Evans in press.
[25] Unpublished material, Karantzali 1996, 119–20.
[26] Unpublished material.
[27] Zapheiropoulou 1970, 48–51; Zapheiropoulou 1984, 34–6, fig. 2a (= NM 4910).
[28] Sperling 1976, phase IB2, 328, fig. 13: 402, 403, 404, fig. 20: 639, fig. 14, 15, 19: 604.
[29] Hood 1981, 173, fig. 98: 11A, 319, fig. 148: 600–1.
[30] Caskey and Caskey 1960, 137, fig. 4: III.13.

[31] Sampson 1981, 185–7, fig. 132: 8, 133: 44, fig. 142: 178, fig. 145: 246.
[32] Sampson 1985, fig. 6: Π48, fig. 11: 1, fig. 16: A25.
[33] See also Sperling 1976, 328, fig. 13: 334, fig. 14: 335, fig. 15 etc.
[34] Wilson 1985, 297, fig. 8: 339, fig. 33: 325, 333, fig. 29: 259–60.
[35] Walter and Felten 1981, 99, fig. 91.
[36] Sperling 1976, 341, fig. 20: 639, pl. 74: 408, 410, pl. 76: 536.
[37] Belmont and Renfrew 1964, pl. 124: 17–18.
[38] Fossey 1969, 63–5, fig. 3: 3–4, fig. 5: 4–5, 11–12; Sampson 1980, 186–8, fig. 136: 337, fig. 142: 178, fig. 144: 190.

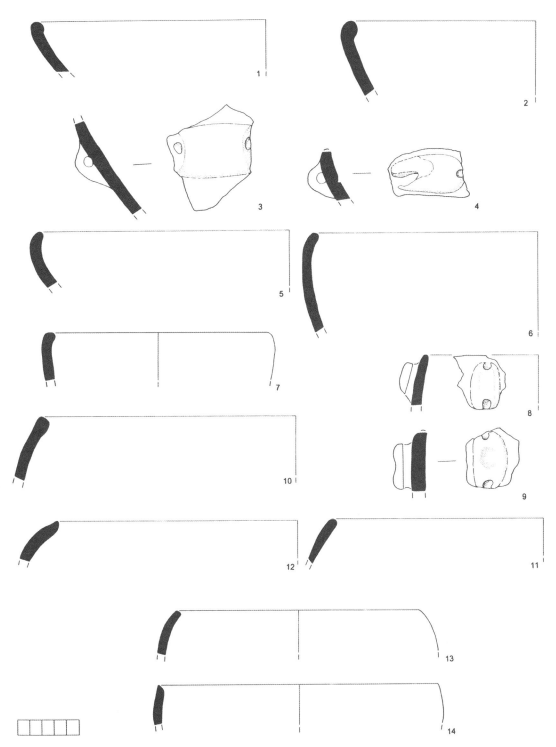

FIG. 7.1. Pottery of Markiani phase I: rolled rim bowls and deep bowls (scale 1:3).

Delos,[39] and Manika on Euboia.[40] Typological parallels are known from Ayios Sostis on Siphnos.[41] In Eutresis group III there are bowls with a swelling rim which is rather flat on the top while in groups IV–V there are many curved wall bowls.[42] On Crete there are parallels from Knossos dated to EM IA.[43]

The three above-mentioned shapes (1, 2 and 3) co-exist within the same pottery group from Trench 6,1.

[39] MacGillivray 1980, 21, fig. 7: 91, 33, fig. 12: 188.
[40] Sampson 1985, 142, fig. 34: 3–4.
[41] Gropengiesser 1987, 38, fig. 3: 9.

[42] Caskey and Caskey 1960, 137, fig. 4: III.4, 144, fig. 7: IV.2, V.1.
[43] Wilson 1985, 297, fig. 8: 1, 2, 5.

Bowl **K 1480** (FIG. 7.1: 6) can be dated to the Kampos Group on the basis of a light thin slip on the exterior surface. The brown-orange thin slip characterises sherds of the early Keros-Syros (EC II) phase, some of which have formerly been classified within the so-called 'Amorgos Group'.[44] Such bowls are a common shape during EB II.[45]

4. Deep bowls with vertical cylindrical lugs near the rim (**K 1057** and **K 1114**, FIG. 7.1: 8–9, PLATE 29 b)

This is a very well known shape from the Kampos Group, i.e. from the Kouphonisia (see below: Ma II bowls) although it is already known in the pottery of the earlier Grotta-Pelos period, as seen in unpublished material from Palati[46] and from Ayia Anna on Naxos. This shape does not continue during phases Ma III and Ma IV.

This bowl type is typical of the pottery from the Kouphonisia. These examples have two pairs of well-shaped vertical cylindrical perforated lugs and dark brown slip or light brown burnish.[47] Examples are known in EM I/II Crete from Pyrgos,[48] and the Ayia Photia cemetery near Siteia.[49] There are also typological parallels from the north-eastern Aegean in Emborio periods VII–VI,[50] contemporary with Kum Tepe Ib.[51]

5. Deep bowls (chytrae) with curved in-turned walls (**K 1479**, **K 1457**, **K 1458** and **K 1475** from Trench 6,1, FIG. 7.1: 10–13 and **K 1509** from Trench 6,2, FIG. 7.1: 14, PLATE 29 f)

This shape has either curved (**K 1479**, FIG. 7.1: 10, **K 1475** and **K 1458**, FIG. 7.1: 12–13) or vertical walls (**K 1457**, FIG. 7.1: 11), while the rim is either slightly rounded or swelling (**K 1479**), or simply rounded (**K 1457**) or relatively vertical (**K 1475**), or pointed (**K 1458**). A base fragment of this type is represented by **K 1474** (FIG. 7.2: 10)

Many variations of bowls with in-turned walls are evident in all four phases of the Markiani settlement. The sherds from the fortification wall have a dark surface, sometimes with slip, while bowl **K 1479** bears the characteristic brown olive-coloured slip observed on some sherds and vases from the Kouphonisia (EC I/II). There are typological parallels from Emborio on Chios, periods VII–VI,[52] and from group III of Eutresis,[53] while variants are known from EH I sites in Euboia[54] and from the EH I settlement on Lake Vouliagmeni at Perachora.[55]

Another sherd of a deep bowl (*chytra*) with markedly in-turned rim, **K 1509**, from Trench 6,2, is paralleled in EH I contexts from Lake Vouliagmeni at Perachora,[56] and Kum Tepe I.[57]

Such deep bowls (*chytrae*) are very common in EB II contexts with many variants, i.e. from Ayia Irini on Kea,[58] Panormos on Naxos,[59] Kynthos on Delos,[60] Manika on Euboia,[61] Lithares,[62] in all the settlement phases, Zygouries[63] and elsewhere. This type of bowl from Lithares has very small triangular non-perforated lugs just below the rim and relief decoration like the equivalent from Panormos.[64]

6. Deep bowl (chytra) with horizontal crescent-shaped non-perforated lugs (**K 1502** and **K 1456** from Trench 6,1, and **K 1506**, **K 1507** from Trench 6,2, FIG. 7.2: 1–4, PLATE 29 d)

This shape is a coarse ware cooking bowl (*chytra*) (see **K 1502**, FIG. 7.2: 1; **K 1456**, FIG. 7.2: 2; **K 1506**, FIG. 7.2: 3; **K 1507**, FIG. 7.2: 4 and PLATE 29 d). It also appears in phases Ma II and Ma III (see also **K 1292**, FIG. 7.13: 17, and **K 1282**, FIG. 7.13: 15) and continues until the last phase, Ma IV.

A few examples of this type have been recognised at Panormos on Naxos. This shape is known from EC I Grotta and Phylakopi,[65] but there are no other published parallels of household pottery from the Cyclades.

---

[44] Doumas 1977, 23–4, see also below pottery of Markiani phase II.

[45] Cosmopoulos 1986, Shape C2, 91, 104, pl. 13.

[46] Karantzali 1996, 20, 118, fig. 2 d

[47] Zapheiropoulou 1984, 33–6, fig. 2 e, f.

[48] Xanthouthidis 1918, 157, fig. 12: 108; a variant of this shape is represented by a deep bowl from Kato Akrotiri on Amorgos (NAM 5353).

[49] Unpublished material. Davaras 1971, 392–7; idem 1972, 648–54; idem 1982.

[50] Hood 1981, 312, fig. 144: 483, 486, fig. 155: 693.

[51] For Anatolian parallels see Mellaart 1963, 217, fig. 9: 6

[52] Hood 1981, 333, fig. 155: 658–9.

[53] Caskey and Caskey 1960, pl. 47: III.8, EH I period.

[54] Sampson 1980, 184–8, fig. 144: 190.

[55] Fossey 1969, 58, fig. 3: 1–3, 18, fig. 5: 7, 22–3.

[56] Fossey 1969, 58, fig. 3: 11.

[57] Contemporary with early Troy I: Sperling 1976, 342, fig. 21: 629.

[58] Caskey 1972, 366, fig. 4: B48–B51, 372, fig. 6: C20–21, C50.

[59] Unpublished material. Karantzali 1996, 24–6.

[60] MacGillivray 1980, 33, fig. 12: 186, 235.

[61] Sampson 1985, 68, fig. 20: K26, 27, 31, 69, fig. 21: K38, K64.

[62] Tzavela-Evjen 1984, 152, pl. 31.

[63] Blegen 1928, fig. 99.

[64] Karantzali 1996, 25, fig. 17: 24, fig. 18: NM5030.

[65] Renfrew 1972, 157, fig. 10.2: 3, 9.

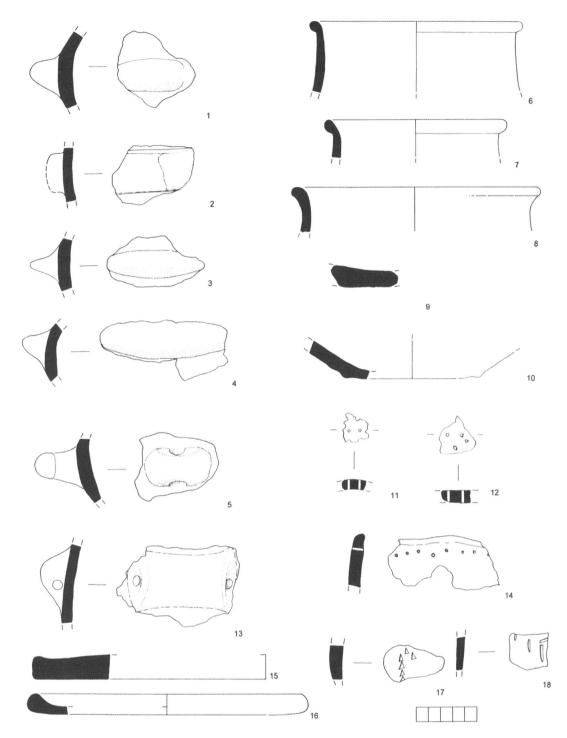

FIG. 7.2. Pottery of Markiani phase I: bowls, collared jars, plates, etc. (scale 1:3).

Variants of this type exist among the EH I material from Lake Vouliagmeni at Perachora,[66] characterised by a different shape in non-perforated lugs; meanwhile EH II parallels have been found at Lithares[67] and Tiryns.[68]

The deep *chytrae* **K 1506** and **K 1507** with the horizontal crescent-shaped non-perforated lugs are also seen in Trench 6,2. This shape is common in all Markiani phases in many variants.

Base **K 1050** (FIG. 7.2: 9) is from a large bowl and has a mat impression. Bases with mat impressions are present at Markiani, mainly in Ma I and Ma III.

[66] Fossey 1969, 63, fig. 5: 15–18.
[67] Tzavela–Evjen 1984, 161, fig. 64.
[68] Weisshaar 1983, 343, fig. 12, 3.

7. Storage vessel with horizontal handle (**K 1052**, FIG. 7.2: 5, PLATE 29 *d*)

Only one sherd of a horizontal handle (**K 1052**) is assigned to this storage (pithoid) type vessel from the fortification wall deposits and has no relevant typological parallels in the following phases of the settlement.

8. Wide-mouthed jar (stamnos) with convex collar and out-turned rim (**K 1082**, **K 1459**, and **K 1054**, FIG. 7.2: 6–8)

This shape is assigned to the category of wide-mouthed closed collared jars (*stamnoi*) characteristic of the EB I and II periods in the Aegean.

K 1054 has clear traces of red slip and recalls the surface treatment techniques on the pottery from the Kouphonisia (e.g. NM 4631). Sherds of similar forms have been identified in Trench 7. Closed wide-mouthed jars with horizontal handles (*stamnoi*) of the well-known Cycladic type with deep oblique incisions on the upper surfaces of the handles have been also recognised in the pottery of Trench 3 and in the material from the Bastion of Trench 8.

This particular shape is known from Emborio periods VII–VI,[69] EH I sites on Euboia,[70] Eutresis[71] and from Lake Vouliagmeni at Perachora.[72] The EC II/EH II examples come from Ayia Irini on Kea[73], Kynthos on Delos,[74] Ayios Sostis on Siphnos,[75] Manika on Euboia,[76] and from Lithares in Boiotia.[77] The EM IIA parallels come from the West Court House at Knossos.[78]

9. Vessels or braziers with strainer (**K 1087** and **K 1088**, FIG. 7.2: 11–12, PLATE 29 *e*)

Two fragments (**K 1087**, **K 1088**) with strainer-like surfaces are too small to be assigned to a known vase shape. They seem to belong to some cooking, household vessel or brazier. Conical shaped braziers with strainer-like inside surface and wide cylindrical stem of the EC III period have been found in Paroikia on Paros. [79]

10. Horizontal cylindrical lug of pithos (**K 1113**, FIG. 7.2: 13, PLATE 29 *c*)

The cylindrical horizontal lugs of this type (**K 1113**) are assigned to pithoi or pithoid vases, like the pithos found at Kynthos on Delos.[80] Similar handles are seen in the unpublished material from Panormos on Naxos relating to the Kastri Group. These examples could be probably dated to the end of the Grotta-Pelos phase (EC I) or to the Kampos Group (ECI/II).

11. Cooking vessel or fragment of oven (ipnos) (**K 1482**, FIG. 7.2: 14)

This shape has thick walls with at least one row of perforations round the rim. The surface is rough, and usually has irregular lines of smoothing or traces of straw or seeds. These vases are known as 'cheese pots' in the literature. This shape is known from the Late and Final Neolithic periods and continues until EC I.[81]

At Markiani it is seen only during Ma I. This shape is known from many EC I contexts, for example from Grotta, Palati[82] and Ayia Anna on Naxos, from Phylakopi on Melos,[83] from Emborio on Chios, from Kolonna on Aigina,[84] and from Ayia Irini on Kea.[85] Hood talks of cooking vases or coarse frying pans at Emborio.[86] In the Cyclades this type is very popular and there have been many suggestions for its possible uses.[87] In the Kouphonisia the type is dated to EC I/II. On Crete similar examples come from trial trenches from Mallia.[88]

[69] Hood 1981, 333, fig. 155: 676, 678, 718, 720.
[70] Sampson 1980, 184–6, fig. 143: 351, fig. 147: 305–7, fig. 136: 73.
[71] Caskey and Caskey 1960, 137, fig. 4: III.10
[72] Fossey 1969, 56, fig. 2: 17, 61, fig. 4: 26–9.
[73] Caskey 1972, 363, fig. 3: B13, fig. 4: B53, fig. 7: C27, 373.
[74] MacGillivray 1980, 29, fig. 11: 43, 225–6, 371.
[75] Gropengiesser 1987, 49, fig. 10: 37.
[76] Sampson 1985, 41, fig. 9 α: 11, 68, fig. 20: K29, 21, fig. 21: K67, 22, fig. 23: K98.
[77] Tzavela-Evjen 1984, fig. 47 α–γ.
[78] Wilson 1985, 339, fig. 29: 255, fig. 33: 330.
[79] Rubenshon 1917, 20, fig. 11 a–b.
[80] MacGillivray 1980, 40–1, fig. 15: 268, fig. 16.

[81] Belmont and Renfrew 1964, 398; Sampson 1987, 88–90, pl. 47, fig. 126, 127; ibid. 1984, 243, fig. 4; Coleman 1977, 17, pl. 37; Vagnetti *et al.* 1989, 63; Cherry *et al.* 1988, 168–9, fig. 8: r, s.
[82] Karantzali 1996, 57–8.
[83] Renfrew 1972, 72, 155, fig. 10.2: 5, 11; Evans and Renfrew 1984, 63–9.
[84] Walter and Felten 1981, pl. 78: 65–71.
[85] Caskey 1972, 360–2, pl. 76: A17–A25.
[86] Hood 1981, 172–3, fig. 98: 3.
[87] Holmberg 1944, 55; Sampson 1988, 96, 261; Heidenreich 1935–36, 139; Karantzali 1996, 124.
[88] Chevallier *et al.* 1975, 64, pl. XIX.

12. Disc/plate (**K 1504** from Trench 6,1 and **K 1505** from Trench 6,2, FIG. 7.2: 15–16)

Only one part of a disc or plate has been found in Trench 6,1 and this is dated to Ma I. It is a very rare shape, a similar example from Tiryns being dated to the EH II period.[89]

Plate **K 1505** comes from Trench 6,2, also dated to phase Ma I, but there are few published parallels.

The simple EC I plates are replaced during the following phases of the settlement by large cooking plates or baking pans. These cooking plates remain almost unchanged typologically during the EBA.

Decorated Sherds from Trench 6 (FIG. 7.2: 17–18)

Two decorated sherds were found within the surface layer of Trench 6,1 layer 1 and Trench 6,2 layer 2 and may be related to the pottery of Ma II.

K 1455 is a small body sherd, which may be assigned to an open vessel and should be dated to Ma II. The surface treatment is simple and the decoration was made by the impression of a pointed tool. The motif is rows of acute angles, a kind of decoration known from Lithares during the EH II period.[90]

K 1508, from Trench 6,2, layer 2, is a body sherd of an open vessel. The surfaces are smoothed and slightly burnished. The decorative motif is a row of impressed triangles.[91]

COMMENT

The pottery of Ma I shows a number of features which may be paralleled in the Grotta-Pelos culture of the Cyclades and during EB I elsewhere in the Aegean. Missing from Ma I pottery are the pouring shapes, which are common in later phases. There are also features that continue into Ma II, which elsewhere are likewise seen in deposits transitional to EB II. It is, however, the absence in Ma I of Kampos Group features, characteristic of Markiani phase II, which led to the conclusion that Ma I represents an earlier phase, assignable to the Grotta-Pelos culture. As noted earlier, it is similar in this respect to the material of phase A1 at Pre-city Phylakopi.

TABLE 7.5 (p. 158) sets out a complete list of the catalogued pottery from Markiani phase I.

THE POTTERY OF MARKIANI PHASE II

The pottery assemblage of Ma II is based on the trenches of the summit area above Rock Cutting 2 where surface survey Unit 222 was designated. As noted in Chapter 4, the stratigraphic observations in Trench 1,1 (summit area) and Trench 7 suggest that the deposit within this area (Space 8) is unified and distinct from the deposit of the fortifications and the Terrace 1 area. The collection studied comes from Trench 1,1 (summit area), layers 6, 7, and 19, 20, and Trench 7, layers 2, 3, 4, 6, 7, 8, 9, 10, 12, 13, 14 and 15. These layers may be a rubble fill placed here to create a terrace to the north of Rock Cutting 2.

The pottery was in a fragmentary condition. The percentage of open vessels is very high. Most of the sherds are body sherds while rim sherds are the second major category.

FABRIC/WARE

There were 1157 sherds in total. Most of them (1145 or 98.9%) are of Marble Ware. Twelve sherds (*c.* 1.0%) belong to other fabric categories, with six body sherds of large vessels in the category Blue Schist Ware (see TABLE 7.6 p. 158).

Most of the sherds may be classed as Coarse Ware (62.4%), from household storage or cooking vessels, generally with thick walls. There are 15 sherds of the same big storage jar. In this assemblage there are significantly few Fine Ware sherds, fewer than ten fragmentary sherds with a light brown or reddish burnished surface. Thirteen bases had leaf impressions and five mat impressions.

SURFACE TREATMENT

Most sherds, *c.* 1000, have a dark to light brown-reddish smoothed or polished surface. The use of a washy black slip on the Coarse Ware is notable (77 sherds). It is similar to the pottery from Kato Akrotiri, now in the Athens National Archaeological Museum. We should mention here the following:

[89] Weisshaar 1982, 461, fig. 77: 18.
[90] Tzavella-Evjen 1984, 165, fig. 19, 21–2, pl. 72–3.
[91] See for parallels: Eutresis, Goldman 1931, 96, fig. 124; Lithares, Tzavella-Evjen 1984, fig. 74: e, pl. 78; Cyclades, Doumas 1977, pl. XXXII j and XXXIII d.

- Six sherds have red or light brown burnished interior surfaces.
- 12 sherds have dark brown or light reddish brown burnished out surfaces.
- 11 have brown, grey or reddish slip outsides, sometimes polished.
- Two have brown slip and traces of wiping.
- Some sherds have washy red or light reddish brown to light brown orange burnished wash on the surfaces, which is similar to the surface treatment of the Kouphonisia pottery assemblage assigned to the Kampos Group (EC I/II).
- Two body sherds have incised crossed lines, like an X, on the interior surface.
- Six body sherds of storage vessels have an incision between the neck and the shoulder.
- One body sherd of a thick walled storage vessel has a non-identifiable incision that resembles a potter's mark.
- Six sherds from the rim of portable hearths have impressed and incised decoration.

MA II POTTERY SHAPES

1. Lids or parts of frying pans with incised decoration (**EE 040, K 1073, K 1071, EE 133** and **K 1597**, FIG. 7.3: 1 to 5, PLATE 30 *a*)

From Trenches 1,1 (summit) and 7 and from layers just above the bedrock come a few (four) small fragments which may be classed as lids or frying pans of the well-known Cycladic type. The exterior surface is dark to black, or has a dark brown or grey-brown slightly burnished slip. All four sherds are of the type with incised spiral decoration on the upper flat surface with vertical parallel lines on the vertical rim of the vessel (**EE 040, K 1073, K 1597**). To this particular type is also assigned a small sherd (**EE 133**) found during the 1985 surface cleaning.

This decoration is characteristic of the frying pan vessels of the Kampos Group[92] (EC I/II), with the Paros frying pan as the closest parallel.[93]

These sherds from Markiani are probably locally produced. Parallels of the same type are known from Pyrgos on Paros,[94] from the Stephanos excavations on Naxos,[95] and from Grotta,[96] also on Naxos. One frying pan sherd found in a grave on the Ano Kouphonisi[97] is decorated with incised running spirals and pointillé dots.

Sherd **K 1071** (**EE 107** (FIG. 7.3: 5, PLATE 30 *a*) bears a simple decoration, consisting of an incised horizontal band with pointillé oval-shaped dots. This particular decoration, rare in the Cyclades, is very common and popular on the Greek mainland and is characteristic of EH II contexts. There are examples from Lithares,[98] Asine[99] and Ithaca.[100]

Many variants of the Kampos Group (EC I/II) frying pan have been found in the Cyclades (e.g. from the Kouphonisia). On the Greek mainland some local EH II variants (e.g. from Ayios Kosmas, Tsepi near Marathon etc.) are very similar to the so called 'Kampos' type.

2. Miniature spherical vessel with wide collar (**EE 718**, FIG. 7.3: 6, PLATE 30 *b*)

This pot is assigned to the miniature vessel type, most of which are from grave contexts. They are usually spherical–biconical or piriform with thick walls and with low cylindrical or high narrow collar. Examples are attested on Naxos in a grave at Louros Athalassou.[101] There is also a double form of this type from Amorgos.[102]

The Markiani vessel is small, spherical–biconical, with thick walls and low and wide collar, which is separated from the body by a deep horizontal incision.

The decoration of this type of miniature vessel usually consists of incised or impressed spirals in various combinations (running or isolated) on a black surface or slip. The Markiani vessel is decorated with rows of thin incised lines at an acute angle (herringbone) on a black surface.

3. Deep closed spherical vessels (pyxides) (**K 1148, K 1614, K 1643** and **K 1630**, FIG. 7.4: 1–4)

These vessels are of various sizes and may be dated to the time of the Kampos Group (EC I/II) or the early Keros-Syros culture (early EC II). They usually have an everted rim or a low collar and a thick

---

[92] Rambach 2000, fig. 75.3: pl. 185,1; Renfrew 1972, 527; Zervos 1957, pl. 224-25; Coleman 1985, 191, pl. 33-37; Tsountas 1898, pl. 9: 16.
[93] Varoucha 1925, 107, fig. 9.
[94] Tsountas 1898, pl. 9.10, 16.
[95] Stephanos 1904, 158 (NAM 4610a); ibid. 1905, 218.
[96] Kontoleon 1949, 120, fig. 10 (NAM 6140).

[97] Zapheiropoulou 1983, 85, fig. 13.
[98] Tzavela-Evjen 1984, 165, pl. 78.
[99] Frödin and Persson 1938, 211, fig. 157, 9.
[100] Dörpfeld 1927, pl. 56d, 83d.
[101] Stephanos 1904, 58; Papathanasopoulos 1962, 132, pl. 66; Doumas 1977, 25.
[102] Marangou 1984, 99-103, fig. 16.

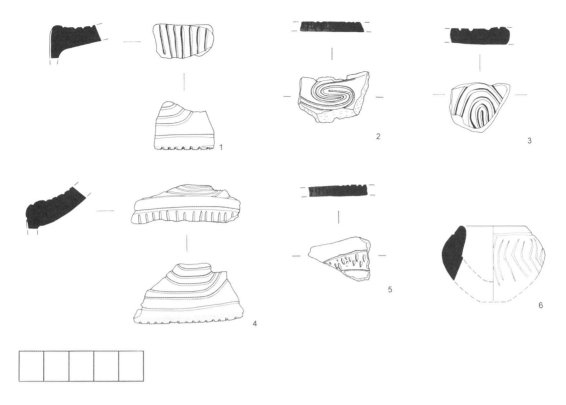

FIG. 7.3. Pottery of Markiani phase II: fragments of frying pans and miniature vessel (scale 2:3).

out-turned rim. They are very common at Greek mainland sites. Among the EH examples are those from Lithares,[103] Manika,[104] Corinth[105] and Tiryns,[106] Eutresis[107] and equivalent EB II levels at Troy.[108] Examples from Knossos,[109] the Mesara[110] and Stavromenos[111] near Rethymnon belong to the EM II (or EM IIA) period. Sherds **K 1614**, **K 1643**, **K 1630** are variants of the same basic type.

Sherd **K 1148** (FIG. 7.4: 1) is a variant of the EC I spherical pyxis, known from Lakkoudes[112] and Melanes[113] on Naxos and from other contexts. On Crete an EM I example of this form comes from Knossos.[114] However, **K 1148** is closer to the biconical pyxis of the Kampos Group (EC I/II). A funerary example comes from Akrotiri on Naxos.[115] An early variant of the pyxis-like vessel was found in Trench 8. This is the closest to **K 1148**.

A deep closed spherical vessel at the Apeiranthos Museum,[116] probably from the Spedos area, seems to be a parallel for **K 1614** (FIG. 7.4: 3). **K 1643** (FIG. 7.4: 2) is assigned to a large deep closed spherical vessel, for purely household use. Parallels are known from Kynthos on Delos[117] and from a grave context from Manika on Euboia.[118] The small deep closed spherical vessel **K 1630** (FIG. 7.4: 4) is similar to an example with miniature non-perforated lugs in the Apeiranthos Museum on Naxos.[119]

The surface treatment of these vessels from Markiani is rather rough. In most cases the exterior surfaces are dark brown or reddish and smoothed. Sherd **K 1643** has traces of smoke, which is firm evidence for household use.

4. *Footed jars (crateriskoi)* (**K 1589**, **K 1608**, **K 1609**, **K 1599** and **K 1602**, FIG. 7.5: 1–5)

Footed/pedestal vessels of Ma II are assigned to the type of vessels with high conical collar and hemispherical body to which a conical stem or foot has been added, often high and with out-turned profile.

[103] Tzavela-Evjen 1984, 155, pl. 40–41.
[104] Papavasileiou 1910, pl. B; Sampson 1985, 87, fig. 24e: G25, 145, fig. 35: 3, 4, 30, 267, fig. 96, 98, 99; idem 1988, 177, fig. 77: 58/5.
[105] Heermance and Lord 1897, 320, fig. I, 11.
[106] Weisshaar 1983, 335–36, fig. 4: 4–5.
[107] Caskey and Caskey 1960, pl. 48: VIII.19, 142–4, 164, group IV; Treuil 1983, 67.
[108] Blegen et al 1950, pl. 223b, C27, C31, C34-variation, pl. 230.
[109] Wilson 1985, no. 173.
[110] Xanthouthides 1924, 11; Walberg 1987, 60.

[111] Kanta 1998, 31–2.
[112] Doumas 1977, 15, 25.
[113] Unpublished material. NM 5110, Karantzali 1996, 22, 96–7.
[114] Hood 1990, 370, fig. 2: 14, 15.
[115] Doumas 1977, 40, 58, 85, pl. XXX: a, NM 1963–4.
[116] Unpublished material. Karantzali 1996, 99, fig. 105 h: Apeiranthos Museum 515.
[117] MacGillivray 1980, 29, fig. 11: 9, 54.
[118] Sampson 1985, 269, fig. 62a: 16.
[119] Karantzali 1996, 99, fig. 14: Apeiranthos Museum 515.

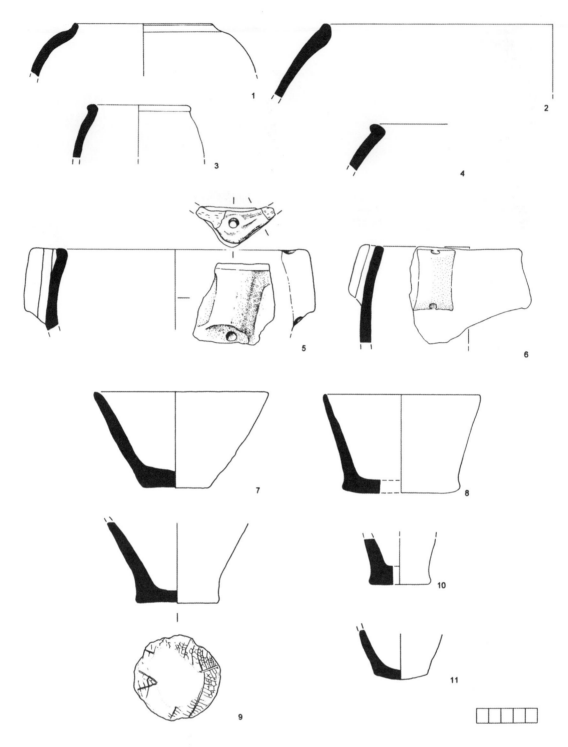

FIG. 7.4. Pottery of Markiani phase II: deep vessels and conical cups (scale 1:3).

The five sherds of footed jars (*crateriskoi*) were originally assigned to the so-called 'Amorgos Group',[120] although the term is widely seen as unsatisfactory. The shape suggests the Keros-Syros culture (EC II) as does the surface treatment; in three of the five examples there is a light red-orange slip; one is burnished (**K 1609**, FIG. 7.5: 3). This slip is characteristic of some shapes, e.g. footed jars, collared vessels with two cylindrical vertical perforated lugs of the developed type just below the rim.[121]

[120] Doumas 1977, 23-4.
[121] Zapheiropoulou 1970, 429, pl. 373 ε–ζ; Doumas 1988, 22–4; Karantzali 1996, 3, 7, 106.

FIG. 7.5. Pottery of Markiani phase II: footed vessels, jars, etc. (scale 1:3).

Sherds **K 1589** (FIG. 7.5: 1) and **K 1608** (FIG. 7.5: 2) have a thin, light brown slip. Sherd **K 1602** (FIG. 7.5: 5) is assigned to a different fabric and there is a possibility that it is an import to Amorgos, perhaps from Naxos.

Two large footed jars of this type from grave 10 at Spedos on Naxos,[122] two from Kato Kouphonisi,[123] which are the same size as those from Markiani, and another from Amorgos[124] all belong to the early

[122] Papathanasopoulos 1961/2, pl. 50 b–c.
[123] Zapheiropoulou 1970, 430, pl. 373, NM 4554–55.
[124] Marangou 1984, 99–103, Amorgos Archaeological collection 130.

Keros-Syros (EC II) type.[125] This type usually has small and narrow non-perforated lugs of triangular section, or miniature perforated cylindrical lugs (like the footed jars from the Kouphonisia).

In general the footed vessel type is characterised by a light yellowish or pale red-orange surface with thin wash and without any polish or with slight burnish. The decorated examples (from Spedos, Kouphonisi and Amorgos) have incised linear patterns (oblique lines, acute angles in a row, herringbone).

5. Closed wide-mouthed collared vessels

This shape has been identified with some variants in the pottery assemblages of Ma I and II. It is very common in the Cyclades, where a great many variants of both EC I and II periods are known.[126] There are, unfortunately, few published examples of household wares.[127]

EC I examples of wide-mouthed collared vessels usually have a burnished red-brown to black surface. This form is seen in the examples from Emborio periods VII–VI,[128] contemporary with Kum Tepe Ib. From EH I there are the examples from Manika on Euboia.[129] Sherds from similar vessels are seen in the EM IIA West Court House at Knossos.[130]

a. Wide-mouthed collared vessels with slightly concave and out-turned swelling rim (**K 1143** and **K 1129**, FIG. 7.5: 6–7, PLATE 31 *a*)

The wide-mouthed vessels of this type (**K 1143**, FIG. 7.5: 6, and **K 1129**, FIG. 7.5: 7) are characteristic of Ma I and II. The shape is simple and continues with many variants from the Grotta-Pelos (EC I) to the Kampos Group (EC I/II) and Keros-Syros (early part of EC II) periods. Sherds of this type are characterised by a relatively dark smoothed surface.

An intact vase of this type from Amorgos and from Kato Akrotiri, now in the Athens National Archaeological Museum,[131] has a spherical–piriform body, wide cylindrical, slightly concave collar, out-turned swelling rim, two horizontal handles and a pale yellow surface.

From the EC I period there are examples from Grotta on Naxos, Phylakopi on Melos,[132] the variants with concave collar and thick out-turned rim, and from Talioti[133] in the Argolid (for **K 1129**), while more distant typological parallels are known from Ayios Sostis on Siphnos.[134]

b. Wide-mouthed vessel with high conical collar (**K 1160**, FIG. 7.5: 8)

Sherd **K 1160** is assigned to the type of wide-mouthed vessel with a simple conical collar. This type is known mainly from EB I contexts in the Aegean and continues with fewer examples until the end of the EB I. The examples from Phylakopi on Melos, with simple conical collar,[135] are similar to **K 1160** from Markiani. Distant parallels are known from EH II contexts, e.g. from Manika on Euboia.[136]

c. Wide-mouthed vessels with concave collar and out-turned wide swelling rim (**K 1162**, **K 1138**, **K 1167**, **K 1137**, **K 1132**, **K 1152**, and **K 1126**, FIG. 7.5: 9–15, PLATE 31 *a*)

This variant of wide-mouthed vase is very common in Ma II, but it is also common in Grotta-Pelos (EC I) contexts and continues through all the Keros–Syros (EC II) phase, like all the other sub-types of the wide-mouthed vessels. An intact vase from Kato Akrotiri (Kampos Group, EC I/II) on Amorgos seems to represent this variant. It has a very well-shaped cylindrical and almost vertical collar, wide out-turned and swelling rim, and reddish-brown, slightly burnished surface.[137]

The Ma II sherds have a dark, reddish or brown, smoothed surface, rarely slightly burnished. **K 1137** (FIG. 7.5: 12) has a washy reddish slip on the exterior: it has two perforations, and recalls EH I examples from Talioti in the Argolid.[138] These may originally have been four or more perforations and they were possibly used to secure a lid. Sherd **K 1152** (FIG. 7.5: 14, PLATE 31 *a*) also has an EH I parallel from Talioti.[139]

[125] Karantzali 1996, 106.
[126] Doumas 1977, 16, fig. 3: b, f, h, i, j; Barber and MacGillivray 1980, 145; Renfrew 1972, 156, fig. 10.2: 1–2, 7–8; Cosmopoulos 1986, 95–6, pl. 16, X–XII.
[127] Cf. Phylakopi on Melos, Karantzali 1996, 38, fig. 51, fig. 52: b–d.
[128] Hood 1981, 335, fig. 156: 732–34.
[129] Sampson 1985, 52, fig. 15: A14, 72, fig. 23: K98, 100, fig. 27: T31, 145, fig. 35.
[130] Wilson 1985, 339, fig. 33: 330.

[131] NAM 4726, Tsountas 1898, pl. 9: 21; Rambach 2000, 185–9.
[132] Renfrew 1972, fig. 10.2: 2, 8.
[133] Weisshaar 1991, fig. 114: 12.
[134] Gropengiesser 1987, 49, fig. 10; 37–8.
[135] Edgar's old excavations, Karantzali 1996, 101, fig. 52: a–d.
[136] Sampson 1985, 145, fig. 35: 31.
[137] NAM 4736; Tsountas 1898, pl. 9: 9.
[138] Weisshaar 1981, fig. 105: 7. See also K 1591.
[139] Weisshaar 1981, fig. 114: 18.

d. Deep wide-mouthed vase with wide flat perforated rim (**K 1591**, FIG. 7.5: 16)

K 1591 is a particular variant of deep wide-mouthed household ware with thick walls, very wide out-turned rim, which is flat on the upper surface and has parallel oblique perforations, which were probably used to secure a lid. Similar examples are known from rim sherds in an EH I context from Talioti in the Argolid.[140] They are usually coarse household wares or pithoid vessels. The sherds from Talioti are remarkably similar to the Markiani ones with respect to the position of the perforations on the rim.

e. Wide-mouthed vessel with high conical collar (**K 1130**, FIG. 7.5: 17)

Vessel **K 1130** is assigned to a vase with a narrow high conical, almost funnel-like, collar. There are no other similar examples in the Ma II pottery group, while a sherd from a similar conical collar within the fine wares of Ma III group has been assigned to the tankard cup type. This type is known in EH I period from Lake Vouliagmeni at Perachora.[141] The parallels from Ayia Irini on Kea,[142] Kynthos on Delos,[143] from Manika,[144] and from Tiryns[145] are datable to EB II.

6. Deep bowls (phiale) with vertical lugs near the rim (**K 1155** and **K 1605**, FIG. 7.4: 5–6, PLATE 31 *b*)

The type of the high deep bowl with two, or two pairs of cylindrical perforated lugs near the rim is known among the Ma I pottery from Trench 6,1 and from Trench 8 (Bastion Area). This type of vessel was first recognised in grave material from Ano Kouphonisi.[146] Bowl **K 1605** (FIG. 7.4: 6, PLATE 31 *b*) is the closest parallel to the canonical type of the Kampos Group (EC I/II) period. Bowl **K 1155** (FIG. 7.4: 5) is similar to the large size examples of the same period from Ano Kouphonisi. The Ma II bowls differ from the Ma I examples mainly in surface treatment

7. Conical cups (**K 1133**, **K 1629**, **K 1149**, **K 1631** and **K 1151**, FIG. 7.4: 7–11, PLATE 30 *d–e*)

This is the simple conical cup type, usually with straight sides. Some examples have a leaf or a mat impression on the base. They may be dated to both the earlier and later phases of EC II.[147] Pot bases with either leaf or mat impressions have been found in Final Neolithic contexts, i.e. the Aspis at Argos,[148] but are also attested in EB I and II. EB I examples are known from Grotta on Naxos,[149] Talioti in the Argolid,[150] Eutresis,[151] and from the EH I and II layers at Lithares.[152] Examples have not been found in Ma I material. The small cup of this form found in the deposits from the Bastion is a variant of the EC II canonical type. Similar examples have been found at Panormos on Naxos.[153] Small cups with very obvious traces of shaping have been found within deposits of Ma III and there also a few among Ma IV pottery.

Cup **K 1133** (FIG. 7.4: 7, PLATE 30 *e*) has a normal conical body and a heavy dark to black burnished surface. Similar examples are known from unpublished grave contexts from Naxos[154] (NM 5173 and NAM 6103.9). Cup **K 1149** (FIG. 7.4: 9, PLATE 30 *d*) has a solid slightly conical base with a leaf impression, while **K 1151** (FIG. 7.4: 11) is a simple conical cup with convex base. The surfaces are simply smoothed.

Cups **K 1629** and **K 1631** are variants of this basic shape: **K 1629** (FIG. 7.4: 8) is open, conical, with projecting base, while **K 1631** (FIG. 7.4: 10) is probably a high conical cup with a high solid and projecting base. These two last sherds have dark brown smoothed surfaces.

This type is very common in EH II and EC II contexts, and continues with some variants until the Kastri Group phase, as seen in examples from Kastri on Syros,[155] and Ayia Irini on Kea.[156] An equivalent type is very common in EB II contexts, e.g. at Ayia Irini[157] and on Syros.[158] Examples occur at Eutresis,[159] Lerna,[160] Zygouries,[161] Ayia Irini,[162] and Kynthos on Delos.[163]

---

[140] Weisshaar 1981, fig. 105: 6.
[141] Fossey 1969, 56, fig. 2: 2.
[142] Caskey 1972, fig. 3: B13, 363.
[143] MacGillivray 1980, 29, fig. 11: 354, 223.
[144] Sampson 1985, 145, fig. 35: 2, 7.
[145] Weisshaar 1981, 242, fig. 85: 5, 8.
[146] Zapheiropoulou 1970, 50, fig. 6; ibid. 1984, 34, fig. 2: e–f.
[147] Tsountas 1899, pl. 9: 17, 28; Caskey 1972, 373; Cosmopoulos 1986, 91, pl. 13.V.
[148] Touchais 1980, 20–1, fig. 8.
[149] Kontoleon 1949, 120, fig. 13.
[150] Weisshaar 1981, fig. 105.
[151] Goldman 1931, 88, fig. 111.

[152] Tzavela-Evjen 1984, pl. 54.
[153] Karantzali 1996, 118, fig. 116 g, h.
[154] Karantzali 1996, 118, fig. 116 g.
[155] Bossert 1967, 70–3, fig. 5, 5.
[156] Caskey 1972, 365–9, fig. 5: C39.
[157] Caskey 1972, 365–9, fig. 5: B29–31, C13, C38.
[158] Tsountas 1899, pl. 9: 28.
[159] Goldman 1931, 98, fig. 125: 3–4, 7–8.
[160] Caskey 1968, 314–15.
[161] Blegen 1928, 88, fig. 75, 90, 106.
[162] Caskey 1972, 365–9, fig. 5: B29–B31.
[163] MacGillivray 1980, 14–15, fig. 4 and 17, fig. 5: 104.

8. Small hemispherical bowls (phiale) (**K 1610** and **K 1601**, FIG. 7.6: 1–2)

These bowls have a simple vertical or in-turned rim, like the example from a grave context at Manika.[164] The small hemispherical bowl **K 1601** (FIG. 7.6: 1) resembles an unpublished example from the Kouphonisia and a small bowl from Akrotiri on Naxos.[165] The large shallow bowl **K 1610** (FIG. 7.6: 2) with rounded rim is a typical shape of the EC II period.[166] There are examples from Kynthos on Delos,[167] Ayia Irini on Kea,[168] and from Manika on Euboia.[169] The examples from Ayios Sostis on Siphnos are more distant variants.[170] The two shallow bowls from Markiani have a smoothed dark, brown or grey-brown, surface. Type and variants of this shape were discussed in the section above on the pottery of Ma I. This shape was replaced during the later EC II period by the large conical or hemispherical bowl.[171]

9. Various (shallow or deep) bowls (phiale) of late rolled-rim type (**K 1166**, **K 1136**, **K 1590**, **K 1139**, **K 1124**, **K 1598**, **K 1125**, **K 1072-EE 105**, **K 1164**, **K 1632**, and **K 1600**, FIG. 7.6: 3–12, PLATE 30 *c* and 31 *d*)

This is a common shape in Ma I and II. Bowls **K 1166** (FIG. 7.6: 3), **K 1590** (FIG. 7.6: 5), **K 1072-EE 105** (7.6: 10) and **K 1632** (FIG. 7.6: 12, PLATE 31 *d*) are very close to the EC I canonical type of rolled-rim bowl, with a smoothly swelling, rounded, in-turned rim. The rest of the sherds have a slightly swelling rim and have been assigned to rather later variants of this type.

Variations in the surface treatment exist in both Ma I and Ma II and reveal the techniques used for this very common and popular shape during the EC I and EC I/II. Most of the sherds dated to Ma II are characterised by a dark, reddish-brown to black, surface. Bowl **K 1072** (FIG. 7.6: 10) is heavily burnished, like the EC I parallels. Bowls **K 1139** (FIG. 7.6: 6), and **K 1164** (FIG. 7.6: 11, PLATE 30 *c*), have a washy dark reddish burnished slip, while **K 1598** (FIG. 7.6: 8) has only a washy dark slip and **K 1590**, **K 1125** (FIG. 7.6: 9), **K 1632**, and **K 1124** (FIG. 7.6: 7) are well burnished. Sherds **K 1124** and **K 1125** have a slightly swelling rim and resemble to the equivalent examples from the Kouphonisia, of EC I/II date, and distant parallels come from Ayios Sostis on Siphnos of EC II date.[172]

10. Various large (shallow and deep) bowls (lopas or lekane) with rounded, flat or slightly swelling in-turned rim (**K 1150**, **K 1140**, **K 1127** and **K 1607**, FIG. 7.6: 14–17)

This shape is characteristic of Ma II and is common in various Cycladic contexts during EC II with some different variants in the Kastri Group. Some of the bowls of this form have a swelling rim.

Most of these sherds have a dark smoothed surface, from red-brown to grey-brown, (**K 1150**, FIG. 7.6: 14, and **K 1140**, FIG. 7.6: 15), which is sometimes burnished. The interior surface of **K 1140** is well burnished. **K 1127** (FIG. 7.6: 17) has a washy black slip on the external surface.

Early examples are known from Kum Tepe Ib,[173] Lake Vouliagmeni at Perachora,[174] and from Eutresis.[175] For **K 1140** (FIG. 7.6: 15) there is a distant parallel at Manika from an EH II funerary context;[176] similar EH I–II examples exist at Lithares.[177] A parallel for **K 1607** (FIG. 7.6: 16) is known from Ayios Sostis on Siphnos.[178]

11. Deep large bowl (lopas or lekane) with crescent-shaped lugs (**K 1156**, FIG. 7.7: 1, PLATE 31 *b*)

The deep large bowl **K 1156** (*lopas* or *lekane*) is very similar to the shape of the deep bowl with the crescent-shaped lugs (*chytra*), which is known from Ma phase I and is also present in Ma III. This is a rather shallower variant of the common type of the EC deep bowl (*chytra*). Parallels are known from EC I Lake Vouliagmeni[179] at Perachora and EH II Ayios Kosmas.[180]

12. Deep hemispherical and conical bowls with thin walls (phiale) (Kouphonisi type bowls) (**K 1168**, **K 1123**, and **K 1633α+β**, FIG. 7.7: 2–4, PLATE 30 *c*)

These bowls, **K 1168** (FIG. 7.7: 2, PLATE 30 *c*), **K 1123** (FIG. 7.7: 3) and **K 1633** (FIG. 7.7: 4), are presented separately because of their different surface treatment, i.e. with a washy or thick red burnished

[164] Sampson 1985, 275, fig. 65: 29.
[165] NM 4113, Doumas 1977, pl. XXXI: e, T16.
[166] Cosmopoulos 1986, 91, pl. 13: II.
[167] MacGillivray 1980, 15, fig. 4: 6.
[168] Caskey 1972, 365, fig. 3: B28.
[169] Sampson 1985, 87, fig. 24 ε: Γ22, Γ41.
[170] Gropengiesser 1987, 37, fig. 2: 1.
[171] Cf. MacGillivray 1980, 23 fig. 7: 91, and 29, fig. 10: 74; Caskey 1972, 370, fig. 6: C4, C6, C34, etc.

[172] Gropengiesser 1987, 37, fig. 1: 3–4.
[173] Sperling 1976, 328, fig. 13: 401.
[174] Fossey 1969, 58, fig. 3: 3–6, 11, 63, fig. 5: 13.
[175] Caskey and Caskey 1960, 144, fig. 7: IV.3.
[176] Sampson 1985, 195, fig. 53 δ: 1.
[177] Tzavela-Evjen 1984, pl. 18–21.
[178] Gropengiesser 1987, 38, fig. 3: 6.
[179] Fossey 1969, 63, fig. 5: 18.
[180] Mylonas 1959, fig. 116: 10–12.

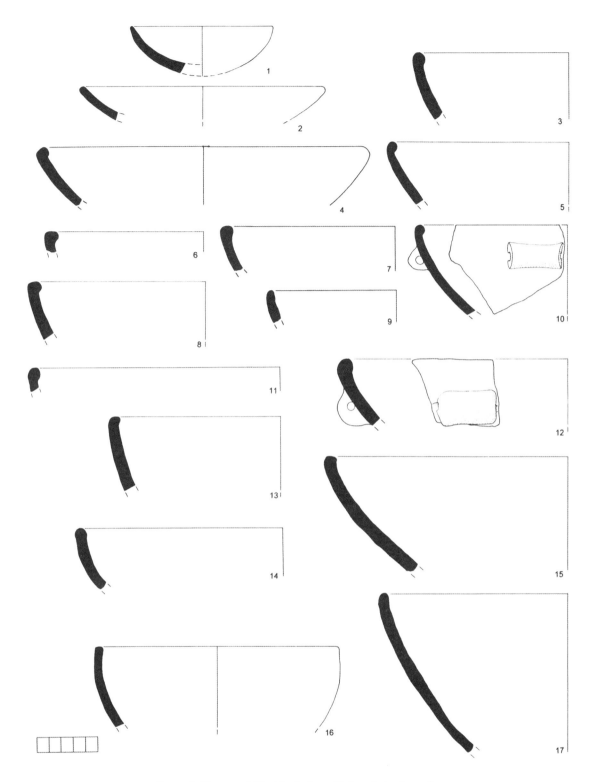

FIG. 7.6. Pottery of Markiani phase II: bowls (scale 1:3).

slip. For this reason they were assigned to a sub-category, the Red Slipped and Burnished Ware of the Marble Ware. This characteristic surface treatment is known from the unpublished material from the Kouphonisia.

These bowls have thin walls, slightly in-turned rounded rim, concave inner base and commonly a horizontal cylindrical perforated lug (see **K 1168** and **K 1633**). Some examples of this type from graves on Ano Kouphonisi also have two pairs of vertical perforated cylindrical lugs,[181] but in most cases, only

---

[181] NM 4607, Karantzali 1996, 119, fig. 117, and 20 fig. 1 f.

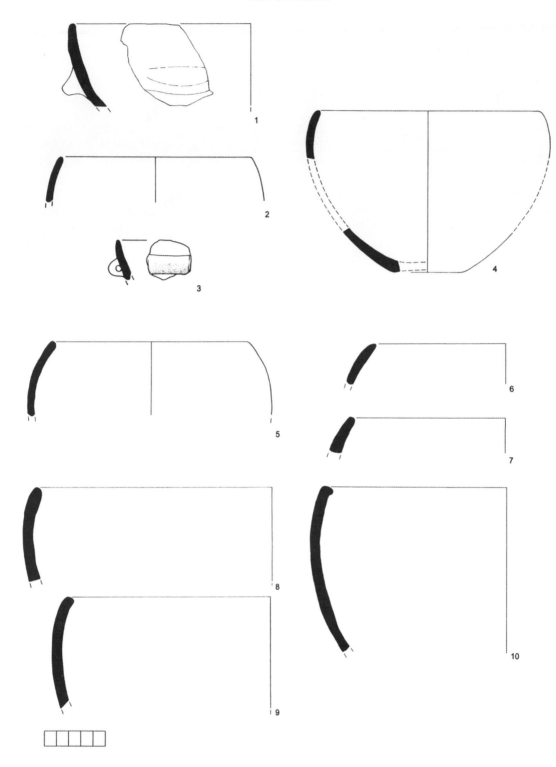

FIG. 7.7. Pottery of Markiani phase II: deep bowls (scale 1:3).

one horizontal cylindrical perforated lug.[182] The two bowls from Markiani have a red burnished slip, like most of the examples from the Kouphonisia where it is sometimes dark (see also NM 4834).

Bowl **K 1123** (FIG. 7.7: 3) is of conical shape, with a horizontal perforated lug and has a washy red slip. Parallels for this variant are known from the Kouphonisia (see also NM 4910 or NM 4828). Other unpublished EC I examples are known from Palati on Naxos,[183] with dark to black burnished surface, and Phylakopi on Melos.[184]

[182] NM 4821, NM 4612.
[183] Karantzali 1996, 119, fig. 52: e, f, and fig. 53: d.

[184] Edgar's old excavations unpublished material.

13. Deep bowls with in-turned profile (chytra-like) (**K 1157**, **K 1135** and **K 1170**, FIG. 7.7: 5–7, PLATE 30 *c*)

This form is known from the assemblage of Ma I with many variants in wall curvature and shape of rim. Two of these Ma II bowls, **K 1157** (FIG. 7.7: 5, PLATE 30 *c*) and **K 1135** (FIG. 7.7: 6, PLATE 30 *c*) have reddish burnished slip on the outside, while **K 1135** has also a washy burnished slip on the inside. These features are similar to the pottery of the equivalent group from the Kouphonisia. By contrast, **K 1170** (FIG. 7.7: 7) has a dark smoothed surface and traces of burning on the rim.

Parallels have been recognised in the unpublished pottery from the Kouphonisia and the Stephanos' excavations on Naxos now held in the Naxos Museum. This shape continues throughout the EBA. Other examples are known from Ayia Irini on Kea,[185] EH II Tiryns,[186] EH II Manika,[187] with EM II parallels attested at Myrtos.[188]

14. Simple deep bowls with lugs (chytra) of various sub-types (**K 1627**, **K 1596** and **K 1141**, FIG. 7.7: 8–10)

This is a very common shape in the pottery assemblages of Ma I, II and III. Many examples are characterised by a thickened in-turned rim (e.g. **K 1141**, FIG. 7.7: 10) of varying thickness.

The surface treatment is simple. Usually the surface is dark (red-brown, grey-brown) smoothed and in many cases carries smoke traces. Sherd **K 1141** has a dark slip on the outside. Deep bowls, typologically close to this shape, are known from Emborio period VII–VI,[189] Ayios Kosmas,[190] and Tiryns.[191]

15. Deep bowls with straight or in-turned profile and thickened in-turned rim (chytra) (**K 1131**, **K 1161**, **K 1145–K 1147**, **K 1158**, and **1163**, FIG. 7.8: 1–5)

This shape has been identified in Ma I, II and III and in the pottery group from the Bastion. Parallels are known from Ayios Kosmas[192] and Manika.[193] The Ma II bowls have many variants differentiated by the inclination of the walls and the degree of the swelling of the rim. The profile is either rather straight (**K 1131**, FIG. 7.8: 1; **K 1145-7**, FIG. 7.8: 3; **K 1163**, FIG. 7.8: 5) or in-turned (**K 1161**, FIG. 7.8: 2; **K 1158**, FIG. 7.8: 4). The rim is either strongly or slightly swelling (**K 1145-7**, FIG. 7.8: 3; **K 1163**, FIG. 7.8: 5), oblique (**K 1131**, FIG. 7.8: 1; **K 1158**, FIG. 7.8: 4) or rounded (**K 1161**, FIG. 7.8: 2). The surface treatment varies from simple washy burnished slip (red-brown or dark brown to black) to dark and smoothed.

16. Deep bowls with thickened out-turned rim with crescent-shaped lugs (chytra) (**K 1159**, **K 1169**, and **K 1134**, FIG. 7.8: 6–8, PLATE 31 *c*)

K 1134 (FIG. 7.8: 8, PLATE 31 *c*) may be considered as a variant of the deep bowl shape with horizontal crescent-shaped non-perforated lugs, identified in Ma I. The typical examples are those from Trench 6 and from Trench 8. This form continues in the Ma III phase. The surface treatment is simple. Usually the surface is dark (reddish or brown) smoothed and only **K 1169** (FIG. 7.8: 7) is slightly burnished inside. While parallels for **K 1159** (FIG. 7.8: 6) are known from Delos,[194] for **K 1169** (FIG. 7.8: 7) there are EH I parallels from Euboia[195] and an EH II variant from Manika.[196] Equivalent shapes in EM IIA come from the West Court House at Knossos.[197]

17. Small deep bowl (lopas or lekane) (**K 1144**, FIG. 7.8: 9)

Sherd **K 1144** is assigned to a small deep open bowl (*lopas* or *lekane*). Similar examples have not been identified in the pottery of other phases of the settlement, while similar parallels are from Manika on Euboia occur during EH II.[198]

18. Crescent-shaped lugs of deep bowls (chytra) or storage vessels (**K 1128**, **K 1172**, **K 1153**, **K 1142**, and **K 1606**, FIG. 7.8: 10–14)

Body sherds with non-perforated crescent-shaped horizontal lugs have been identified in Ma I, II and III (see also **K 1292**, FIG. 7.13: 17; **K 1282**, FIG. 7.13: 15) but not in the last phase of the settlement,

185 Caskey 1972, 366, fig. 4: B48.
186 Weisshaar 1982, 461, fig. 77: 3.
187 Sampson 1985, 38, fig. 7: 66.
188 Warren 1972a, 154, fig. 38: P5.
189 Hood 1981, 312–3, fig. 144: 480–7.
190 Mylonas 1959, fig. 125: 45.
191 Weisshaar 1983, 335–6, fig. 4, 11.
192 Mylonas 1959, fig. 125: 45.
193 Sampson 1985, 39, fig. 8: Π79, and 142, fig. 34: 37.
194 MacGillivray 1980, 33, fig. 12: 194, 201.
195 Sampson 1981, fig. 136: 338.
196 Sampson 1985, 51, fig. 14: A5.
197 Wilson 1985, 333, fig. 29: 266.
198 Sampson 1985, 51, fig. 14: A6, 110, fig. 31 β: Σ10.

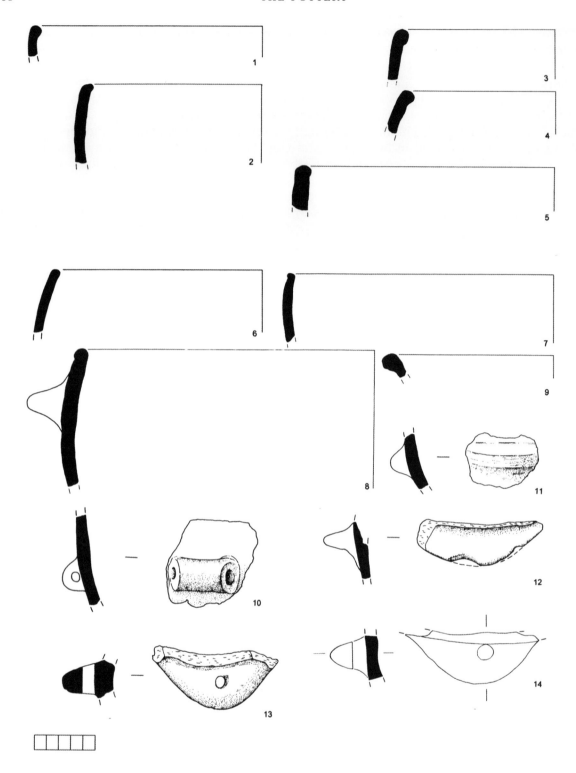

FIG. 7.8. Pottery of Markiani phase II: deep bowls (scale 1:3).

Ma IV. These belong to household cooking vessels, possibly deep bowls (**K 1172**, FIG. 7.8: 11, **K 1153**, FIG. 7.8: 12). There is a relation with the equivalent form of Ma I, but there is a difference in the shape of the lugs. The crescent-shaped lug on **K 1153** (FIG. 7.8: 12) is placed close to the central part of the body while on **K 1172** (FIG. 7.8: 11) it is placed at the lower part of it. Examples of the crescent-shaped non-perforated or perforated lugs with one or two holes come from Lithares.[199]

[199] Tzavela-Evjen 1984, pl. 64.

Sherd **K 1128** (FIG. 7.8: 10) has a different, more developed shape of horizontal cylindrical perforated lug than do EC I equivalent examples. It is cylindrical or spool-shaped, slightly concave on the upper part.

During Ma II, crescent-shaped lugs with one vertical central hole are present (see also **K 1142**, FIG. 7.8: 13; **K 1606**, FIG. 7.8: 14). They continue during Ma III and IV. The last variant is probably characteristic of storage vessels, some with thick walls (see **K 1142**, FIG. 7.8: 13). The surface of all the examples is smoothed dark or light and only **K 1606** bears a washy brown slip.

19. *Baking pans or plates (pinakio)* (**K 1624**, **K 1625**, **K 1622**, and **K 1638**, FIG. 7.9: 1–4, PLATE 31 *c*)

Baking pans or plates are attested from EB I in the early layers of Kum Tepe near Troy.[200] They become more common during the EB II and persist with many variants until the LBA. This type replaced the plain EC I pinakia. At Markiani the baking pans have many variants and are present during Ma II, Ma III and mainly in Ma IV.

The Markiani baking pans are characterised by a dark smoothed surface (red-brown or reddish) that often carries smoke traces, usually on the base. The inside surface is usually well smoothed or slightly burnished.

An EC I parallel of this form has been identified from the Lake Vouliagmeni settlement at Perachora,[201] while many EH II/EC II examples are known from Corinth,[202] Eutresis,[203] Kynthos on Delos,[204] Ayia Irini on Kea,[205] Lithares,[206] Tiryns[207] and elsewhere. Cretan examples are known from EM IIB Myrtos,[208] and from the West Court House at Knossos.[209]

20. *Small storage vessels* (**K 1154**, **K 1611**, FIG. 7.9: 5–6)

Sherds assigned to this type come from different forms: **K 1154** (FIG. 7.9: 5) is probably from a storage pithoid vessel, with high cylindrical or conical collar, which is separated from the rest of the body by a strongly-incised horizontal line. Its external surface is covered by a washy slip in the same colour as the clay.

A similar example is identified in the pottery group of Ma III (see also **K 1616**, FIG. 7.14: 3), with the same incised line at the junction between the collar and the shoulder. Parallel examples come from Kynthos on Delos,[210] Askitario in Attica,[211] and from Panormos on Naxos.[212] There are also early examples at Kum Tepe Ia [213] and distant EH II variations at Lithares (*hydria*).[214]

Sherd **K 1611** (FIG. 7.9: 6) belongs to a somewhat smaller, closed vase of squeezed curvilinear and probably conical shape; the collar from the body is separated by a deep incision. There were no other examples at Markiani. The surface treatment is fine with red-orange coloured burnished slip on the outside.

21. *Spoons (kochliario)* (**K 1613**, **K 1612**, **K 1628**, FIG. 7.9: 10–12, PLATE 32 *a*)

There are very few clay spoons in the EBA Aegean. Ma phase II spoons are fragmentary and are the only ones found in the settlement. The front shallow bowl part of the spoon survives while the long and narrow extension of the handle is lost. The surface treatment is very plain; their surface is mainly dark but also rather lighter.

The clay spoons from Kato Akrotiri on Amorgos are similar to those from Markiani and are dated to the same period.[215] The example from Minoa on Amorgos is dated to the end of the Final Neolithic.[216] There are also parallels from EH I–II Eutresis,[217] Palamari on Skyros.[218]

22. *Bases of various household vessels* (**K 1146**, **K 1623**, and **K 1173**, FIG. 7.9: 7–9)

Sherds **K 1146** (FIG. 7.9: 7), **K 1623** (FIG. 7.9: 8), and **K 1173** (FIG. 7.9: 9) are bases of large household vessels of Ma II date. **K 1623** bears a faint mat impression on the base.

[200] Sperling 1976, 322, pl. 72; 137–8.
[201] Fossey 1969, 59, fig. 3: 1 bottom.
[202] Lavezzi 1979, 343–4, fig. 1: 13393, pl. 87.
[203] Goldman 1931, 108, fig. 142, 107, fig. 141 right.
[204] MacGillivray 1980, 36–8, fig. 13: 386–89, 258–61, fig. 14.
[205] Caskey 1972, 366–7, fig. 4: B65–66.
[206] Tzavela-Evjen 1984
[207] Weisshaar 1983, 345, fig. 14: 1–2.
[208] Warren 1972a, 163, fig. 47: P124.
[209] Wilson 1985, 337, fig. 32: 307–12.
[210] MacGillivray 1980, 39–40, fig. 15: 268.

[211] Theocharis 1953–54, 72, fig. 19 α.
[212] Unpublished material. Karantzali 1996, 68–72.
[213] Sperling 1976, pl. 72: 124, fig. 8, 320.
[214] Tzavela-Evjen 1984, pl. 48.
[215] Tsoundas 1898, now in the NAM; Rambach 2000, fig. 77, 1 and pl. 186, 2.
[216] Marangou 1996, 308.
[217] Goldman 1931, 87, fig. 106; Caskey 1960, 144, fig. 7: IV.8, IV.9.
[218] Parlama 1984, fig. 14.

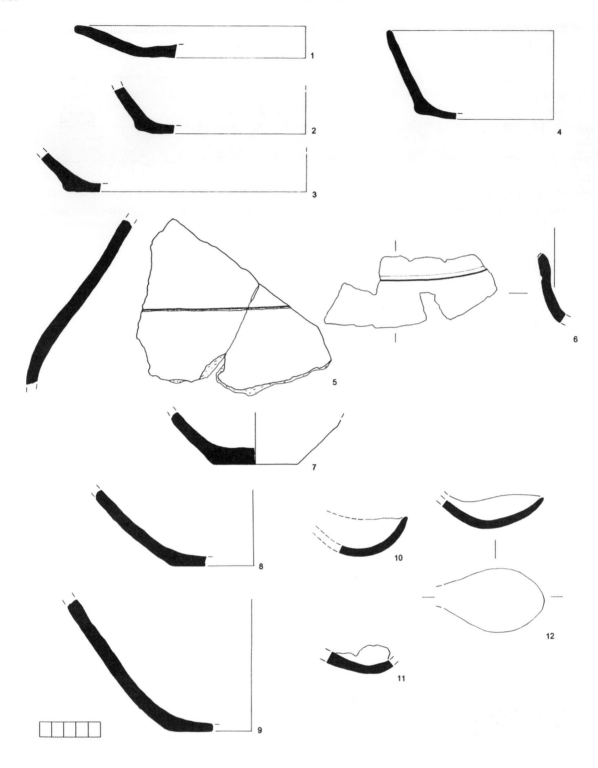

FIG. 7.9. Pottery of Markiani phase II: baking pans, spoons, etc. (scale 1:3).

23. Portable hat-shaped hearths (hestia) (**K 1594**, **K 1595**, **K 1639**, and **K 1641**, FIG. 7.10: 4–7, PLATE 32 *b–d*)

The portable hat-shaped hearths are characterised by a large wide everted rim decorated with rows of stamped triangles in various combinations. The shape is common in Ma II but there are also some distant variants in Ma IV. The surface treatment is simple, usually dark (reddish, brown-red) smoothed, while on one occasion there is a dark brown slip. The decoration consists of rows of antithetically placed triangles (**K 1594**, FIG. 7.10: 4, PLATE 32 *d*; **K 1595**, FIG. 7.10: 5, PLATE 32 *b*), which sometimes

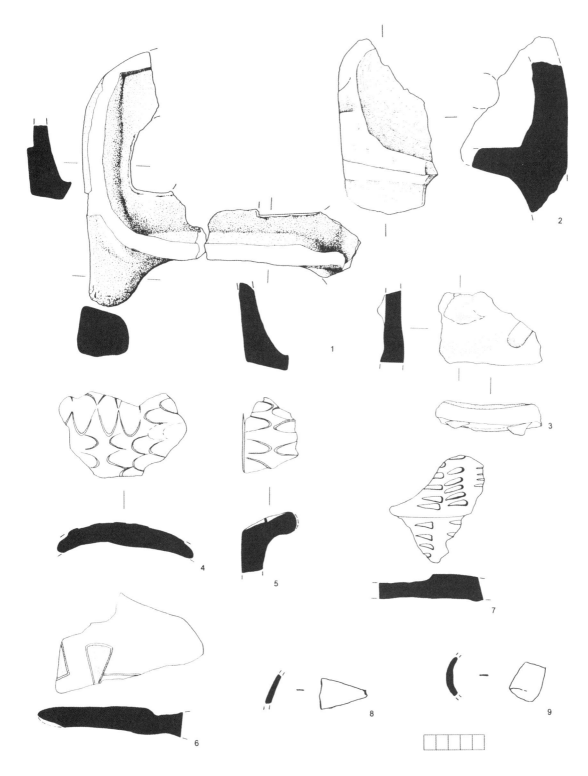

FIG. 7.10. Pottery of Markiani phase II: support vessels, hearths, etc. (scale 1:3).

create an impressed zigzag pattern. These are common in the Cyclades. Published examples come from the cemetery of Ayii Anargyroi on Naxos,[219] Paroikia on Paros,[220] and elsewhere.[221]

Hearth **K 1639** (FIG. 7.10: 6, PLATE 32 *c*) probably belongs to a type, known as Ayia Irini hearths, which are larger in size and could be permanent installations with low vertical walls and wide decorated everted rim.[222] Its decoration is not well preserved and consists of two large stamped triangles and a small double incision.

[219] Doumas 1977, 103, 114–17, fig. 7: c, pl. 38–43a–f.   [221] Metaxa-Muhly 1984, 112, 115.
[220] Rubensohn 1917, 44, fig. 46.   [222] Caskey 1972, 368, pl. 79: B73.

The decoration of **K 1641** (FIG. 7.10: 7, PLATE 32 *c*) is rather sparse. It consists of long and narrow patterns, which must have been produced with a pointed tool, probably a straw. There are no other published examples of this kind of decoration.

Decorated examples of hearths have also been identified on the Greek mainland. There, the large decorated forms are very common, e.g. those from Eutresis,[223] Lerna,[224] and Corinth.[225] Other examples come from Kythera[226] and the Nopegeia Kissamou in western Crete.[227]

24. Braziers or 'mask-like' supports for large household vessels (**K 1174+1592+1593**, **K 1165**, **K 1626**, FIG. 7.10: 1–3, PLATE 32 *e*)

These terracotta objects, of uncertain use, have been interpreted as supports or bases for large household vases (pithoi) or as ceremonial vessels, depending on the context where they were found (e.g. as 'pillows to the dead' in cemeteries).[228] In general they are known as 'mask-like vessels' in the Cyclades and as 'supporting bases' at Lithares.

At Markiani the most complete example of phase Ma II, **K 1174**+ **K 1592**+ **K 1593** (FIG. 7.10: 1, PLATE 32, *a*), has three joining fragments, which allow us to reconstruct the shape of the vessel. The back, which must be rather flat or slightly curved, bears two relatively irregular openings, the first rather oval and the second rectangular. The upper side is hemispherical while the lower is relatively flat. Two thick conical feet, of trapezoid section have been attached to that surface, one of which survives intact. At the front side of the vessel only a few pieces are preserved, a fact which prevents further reconstruction of its shape. The exterior surfaces are well smoothed and covered with a washy red slip.

Fragment **K 1165** (FIG. 7.10: 2) comes from a somewhat smaller vessel of the same shape. Part of the back is preserved along with a section of the wall at right angle and a small part of a round or rectangular opening, part of the wall at right angles and a small part of a foot with a rectangular section. It has a washy red slip on the outside.

The Markiani sherds of these objects are few in number so that it is not possible to distinguish the different variants which may have existed. A similar, but smaller vessel of a different type was found intact among the Ma IV pottery (FIG. 7.24: 1, PLATE 37 *a–e*) while a larger example comes from Trench 3 (FIG. 7.15 and PLATE 34). This suggests either the evolution of the shape from Ma II to Ma IV, or some other use for this particular vessel.

At Lithares, where this type of vessel (mainly the feet and the side-walls) is characteristic for the strata up to the second habitation level, they were named 'supporting vessels' or 'zoomorphic pedestals'.[229] They have plastic or grooved decoration.

Mylonas named these vessels 'zoo-morphic pedestals' or 'supports' and he describes them as coarse clay vessels with four feet, a thick flat or rounded body and a wide flat handle.[230] The objects of this type from Ayios Kosmas were considered relevant to ceremonial activities relating to burial without excluding the possibility of their household use as pedestals or as bases of pithoi or other vessel bases.

The few known fragmentary pieces from Markiani do not allow us to relate them to the above examples, although they are close to those with the rounded body from Ayios Kosmas. The Markiani vessels may have had four coarse feet and red slip.

Similar vessels of various types are known from the Cyclades, and especially from Naxos,[231] Amorgos,[232] Paros and Syros.[233] From the Greek mainland where this type of vase is very common, there are examples from Ayios Kosmas,[234] Eutresis,[235] Askitario, Raphina,[236] Manika,[237] Lithares,[238] and elsewhere. The unpublished vessels from Askitario are smaller than the other examples from the Greek mainland and differ in appearance.

Among the proposals that have been put forward for the use of these vessels, the most persuasive was first proposed by Harland,[239] and subsequently adopted by other scholars, namely that they were used as supports for pithoi or other vessels. But Mylonas notes that if they were used to support deep bowls during the process of cooking then there should have been strong traces of burning and smoke, at least on the feet.[240]

[223] Goldman 1931, 96, fig. 124: 1, 107–8, fig. 141.
[224] Caskey 1990, 17.
[225] Lavezzi 1979, 342–7.
[226] Coldstream and Huxley 1972, pl. 17: 98.
[227] Karantzali 1992, 80, fig. 11.
[228] Mylonas 1959, 146–7.
[229] Tzavela-Evjen 1984, 172.
[230] Mylonas 1959, 146.
[231] Stephanos' excavations.
[232] Tsountas' excavations (Kato Akrotiri).

[233] Zervos 1957, fig. 100.
[234] Mylonas 1959, fig. 172: T21–23, fig. 173.
[235] Goldman 1931, 195; Caskey and Caskey 1960, 145, pl. 47: IV.16–17.
[236] Theocharis 1951, 91, fig. 20.
[237] Sakellaraki 1987, 206, pl. 111ε.
[238] Tzavela-Evjen 1984, pl. 88–89.
[239] Harland 1951, 106–7, pl. 3c–d.
[240] Mylonas 1959, 147.

Sherd **K 1626** (FIG. 7. 10: 3) is assigned to another unidentifiable coarse vessel, with two protuberances on its surface. The sherd is small so it is difficult to reconstruct its shape.

Selected fine ware sherds of Markiani phase II (FIG. 7.10: 8–9)

The two sherds assigned to the fine wares are very small and very eroded. They were found in the main layer of the filling deposit of Trench 7 layers 4 and 6.

Sherd **K 1121** (FIG. 7.10: 8), from Trench 7, layer 4, may be regarded as Urfirnis with well-burnished black surface, red in places. Sherd **K 1122** (FIG. 7.10: 9), from Trench 7, layer 6, has a rather white to yellow slip, easily flaking and belonging to the fine wares of the EC II period. The small size of the sherd does not allow further discussion. However, the surface treatment recalls the fine wares of the Keros-Syros culture (EC II) with a light thick slip that in most cases flakes easily, some with painted decoration others with no decoration at all (see also Keros, Dhaskalio, etc.). These sherds, both of which may be regarded as imports, probably belong to the assemblage of the Kampos Group (EC I/ II) period. It is also possible that they have come into the stratum from the succeeding levels of the more developed EC II period (i.e. of Ma III).

General observations and dating

The pottery of Ma II (Trenches 1,1 (summit) and 7) was found in a fill deposit used for levelling the area. In the main it is made up of coarse household wares (deep bowls, cooking pots, storage vessels etc.). The introduction of new shapes (e.g. frying pans, pyxis, sauceboats, 'mask-like' braziers, large conical cups, footed jars) is significant, as is the development of other shapes like the bowls, both shallow and deep, with various types of lug.

Various shapes identified in Ma I are missing from the Ma II pottery. These include potsherds or fragments of ovens with a row of holes round the rim, the discs or plates, and strainers. The presence of various clay utensils, e.g. clay spoons, the miniature vessel and the clay boat-like model (see Chapter 8), is also notable. The fabric frequencies for the Marble and the Blue Schist-Red Shale Ware suggest a step further from the Ma I phase.

Surface treatment techniques are the main features that help us to determine the sherds belonging to a more developed ceramic phase. It is generally accepted that surface treatment with the application of red slip and with burnishing is characteristic of the EC I and II periods.[241] In the case of the Ma II pottery we note that surface treatment with a washy (dark or light) slip and smoothing is typical for most of the sherds of Trench 7. Such surface treatment has been identified in the unpublished EH II pottery from Eleusis in a context also containing EH II sauceboats. This technique, however, is probably a consequence of the better firing conditions of the vases and could have started as early as the transitional EC I/II or the early EC II periods.

The washy black slip that is known from Kato Akrotiri and the similar red burnished slip known from the Kouphonisia are features of Kampos Group pottery, as is the use of incised and impressed techniques in decoration, which continues in the early phase of EC II.

The dating of each type of pottery was based on both typological criteria and the correlation with relatively well-dated contexts. The special character of this deposit (rubble-fill) supports, the dating of the pottery to the EC I/II and the early EC II periods. The dating of some of the Markiani phase II pottery to the Kampos Group (transitional EC I/II) was based in particular on the frying pan sherds and on the other vessel types which characterise the transitional EC I/II pottery from the Kouphonisia. Moreover, the dating of other ceramic material to the early EC II phase was based on the sherds of characteristic shapes of this phase (like footed vessel, various bowls etc.) with the relevant surface treatment.

TABLE 7.7 (p. 159) sets out a complete list of the catalogued pottery from Trenches 1,1 (summit) and 7.

A NOTE ON THE POTTERY FROM THE BASTION AREA

As noted in Chapter 4, the pottery from inside the Bastion area belongs predominantly to Ma I and II, but with a few sherds which may be assigned to phase III. The material from outside the Bastion has a high proportion (*c.* 38 %) of phase III character.

---

[241] Blegen 1928, class AII.

124 THE POTTERY

THE POTTERY FROM TRENCH 8,1 (INTERIOR OF THE BASTION)

A total of 330 sherds were recovered from Trench 8,1. In the upper layers (1 and 2) Hellenistic sherds were found with abundant EC material. In the south part of the Trench layers 3, 4, 5, 7, 8 and 11 contained pottery of phases I and II.

Nine sherds of Blue Schist Ware, datable to Ma III, were found in layers 6 and 9. The fabric identification was confirmed petrographically. The pottery from inside the Bastion, with the exception of the nine sherds of Blue Schist Ware, showed shapes mainly of Ma I and II character. The examples shown in FIG. 7.11 are of Marble Ware, with the exception of **K 1529** (FIG. 7.11: 2), which is a small deep vase with conical collar and lug; nine others are Pale Micaceous Ware.

Most of the pottery of this area is characterised by a dark (reddish-brown to black) smoothed or slightly burnished surface. Three sherds show a scored decoration, while three base fragments have mat impressions. There are mostly body sherds, some rims (collared jars, deep and shallow bowls) some lugs of various well-known types (crescent type, cylindrical perforated, etc) and parts of discs or plates.

The following shapes are illustrated from Trench 8,1 with notes on comparative material:

1. Spherical pyxis (**K 1517**, FIG. 7.11: 1, PLATE 32 *f*)

Sherd **K 1517** is assigned to a canonical spherical pyxis of the Grotta-Pelos period (EC I), with wide concave everted, nearly flat, rim shaped so as to fit the lid. The fragment is too small for reconstruction of the form.

This particular shape has been recognised among the Ma I assemblage. Similar variations of the transitional Kampos Group have been noted in Ma II. For example, pyxides of similar type are known in Grotta-Pelos assemblages from the Cyclades, notably the pyxis from Akrotiri on Naxos (NM 1972, NM 1971) and Pyrgos on Paros (NAM 4803, NAM 4816). Most examples of this type are decorated, although some are non-decorated,[242] as is **K 1517**.

2. Small deep vases with wide conical collar (**K 1529**, FIG. 7.11: 2, PLATE 32 *f*)

This shape is common on EB I Aegean settlements. Sherd **K 1529** is assigned to the type with a wide conical low neck and compressed egg-shaped body. This shape usually has two vertical cylindrical perforated lugs or two pairs of lugs or, more rarely, two pairs of oblique holes at the upper part of the body. Examples from burials are usually decorated,[243] while undecorated equivalents come from settlements. Among the Ma I material there were no other such examples. There are parallels from other settlement assemblages from the Cyclades, such as those from Palati and Ayia Anna on Naxos,[244] and from Phylakopi on Melos.[245] Sherd **K 1529** could probably be reconstructed with two cylindrical horizontal perforated lugs on the upper part of the body, an equivalent parallel coming from the Pre-city layer of Phylakopi.[246]

3. Shallow bowl (phiale) of the rolled-rim bowl type (**K 1520**, FIG. 7.11: 3)

Bowl **K 1520** is assigned to the shape already identified among Ma I pottery. Most examples have been found in Trench 6,1.

4. Shallow bowl (phiale) with in-turned, slightly thickened rim (**K 1516**, FIG. 7.11: 4)

Sherd **K 1516** belongs to a shallow open bowl, which is common in EBA assemblages. A distant parallel is **K 1481** (FIG. 7.1: 1, PLATE 29 *a*) from Trench 6.

There are also EH I examples from Eutresis.[247] The EC II parallels from Kynthos on Delos are of relevant variants.[248] Examples of EM IIA date are also known from the West Court House at Knossos.[249]

5. Deep bowls (**K 1512** and **K 1519**, FIG. 7.11: 5–6)

This type of bowl is known from many examples in Trench 6,1. The shape of bowl **K 1512** (FIG. 7.11: 5) is common during the two first periods of the EBA and is known from both EH I and II assemblages, e.g. from Eutresis.[250] Distant parallels have been identified at Manika on Euboia. [251]

[242] Doumas 1977, pl. XXXI: b, pl. XXXIII: a.
[243] Doumas 1977, pl. XXVI: d, XXV: f, pl. XXXIII: b.
[244] Unpublished material.
[245] Edgar's excavations, unpublished material.
[246] Edgar's excavations, unpublished material; Karantzali 1996, 38, fig. 51 a–c.

[247] Caskey and Caskey. 1960, 137, fig. 4: III.3.
[248] MacGillivray 1980, 21, fig. 7: 438.
[249] Wilson 1985, 297, fig. 8: 5.
[250] Caskey and Caskey 1960, 144, fig. 7: IV.3.
[251] Sampson 1985, 39, fig. 8: P82.

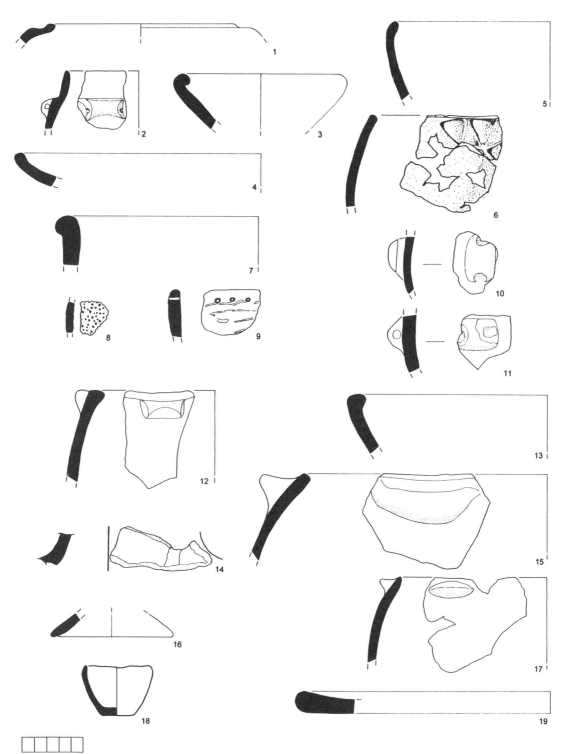

FIG. 7.11. Pottery from the interior of the Bastion (Trench 8).

K 1519 (FIG. 7.11: 6) is a deep bowl with curved in-turned walls. The rim is not even but undulates. On the burnished exterior there are stamped triangles. There are two triangles situated opposite, just visible below the rim, while two others, which probably meet at the apex, are below the others. However, the sherd is too abraded to allow identification of the whole pattern, which is very faint and must have been produced by means of a wide pointed tool. The stamped decoration is usually deeper and stronger. Bowl **K 1519** was found in layer 9 in the pocket of the natural bedrock where most of the sherds are dated to the EC I period.

6. Deep high bowls with lugs below the rim (**K 1514** and **K 1515**, FIG. 7.11: 10 11)

This type of bowl is common in the Ma I assemblage from Trench 6,1 and in Ma II in Trench 7. Bowl **K 1515** (FIG. 7.11: 10) is similar to two sherds of the same shape from Trench 6,1. **K 1514** (FIG. 7.11: 11) however, is very abraded and its attribution to this particular bowl type is not absolutely secure. Parallels have been found in EC I assemblages from the Cyclades.

7. Strainer (**K 1511**, FIG. 7.11: 8)

K 1511 resembles **K 1087** and **K 1088** (FIG. 7.2, 11–12, and PLATE 29 *e*) of Trench 6, which are dated to Ma I.

8. Various household and storage vessels (**K 1518** and **K 1513**, FIG. 7.11: 7)

These vessels are similar to the collared jar (*stamnos*), with high egg-shaped body, narrow cylindrical calyx-shaped collar and two horizontal handles, which are usually incised. This shape has been identified among Ma IV pottery. The horizontal incised handles already appear in Ma III and continue into phase IV. Surface treatment techniques on these vessels are similar to those on the storage vessels from Panormos on Naxos,[252] dated to the late phase of the EC II period.

Sherd **K 1513** (FIG. 7.11: 7) is possibly from a wide-mouthed storage vessel with thick vertical walls and an everted rim. This particular shape has not been identified in either Ma I or Ma II. Very distant parallels occur in some EH I assemblages on Euboia,[253] and from Manika[254] and Lithares[255] of early EH II date.

9. Cooking vessel or fragment of an oven (**K 1510**, FIG. 7.11: 9)

This cooking vessel, of a special form, has already been identified in the Ma I phase assemblage from Trench 6 (**K 1482**, FIG. 7.2: 14). There are parallels from the Ayios Sostis on Siphnos.[256]

TABLE 7.8 (p. 161) sets out a complete list of the catalogued pottery from the interior of the Bastion.

TRENCHES OUTSIDE THE BASTION

The pottery found outside the Bastion was largely of Ma III and IV character. The pottery assemblage from the trenches just outside the Bastion was found in a thin level (near 29 cm thick) down to bedrock. It contained a few EC I sherds and was mainly of EC II character.

The filling from the area between the Bastion and the outwork (Wall Γ), layers 3, 5, 8, 10, 12 yield sherds dated both to the EC I and EC II periods. From the filling north of Wall Γ, layers 2, 4, 6, 7, 11, 13, 14, the ceramic assemblage comprised sherds of EC I, transitional EC I/II or early EC II shapes whose surface treatment recalls pottery of Ma II. However, from the same area (layer 7) near Wall Γ, a collared jar, **K 1524**, was discovered, datable according to close parallels to the Kastri Group. Inside it was found an incised lug and a conical cup.

From the trench west of the Bastion, Trench 8,6, came sherds which range in date from EC I to the Kastri Group, i.e. Ma I to IV. Most belong to storage vessels (*stamnoi* of the Panormos type) and pithos fragments of Blue Schist fabric (76 sherds) usually with a reddish-greyish surface (cf. **K 1530**). There are also body fragments (*c.* 20) of a large storage jar and body sherds of Coarse Ware utensils (cf. **K 1531**, **K 1539**). In addition there are a few sherds of small vases, including a conical cup with parallels ranging from Ma II to IV. The rest of the material is of Marble Ware (80 in total of 176 sherds) and most were very worn.

It should be noted here that the sherds from the area outside the Bastion belong to storage or cooking vases having a similar surface treatment to parallel vessel types from Panormos on Naxos, Kynthos on Delos, Ayia Irini phase III and so are datable to the Kastri Group. As concerns fabric, the majority of sherds (from a total 356) are of Marble Ware. These are mainly body sherds, but also rims of various deep bowls and seven bases, some with mat impressions. In addition there are 67 sherds of different fabrics resembling the corresponding material of EC II ceramic assemblages. Of these 56 are Blue Schist Ware and 11 Pale Micaceous Ware. Their surface has brown light to greyish light slip and in one case a very washy dark to black slip, similar to those applied on some sherds from Panormos on Naxos.[257]

The following forms (and fabrics) are illustrated, with notes on the comparative material:

---

[252] See also NM 5028, Karantzali 1996, 25, fig. 21a.
[253] Sampson 1981, fig. 136: 338.
[254] Sampson 1985, 102, fig. 28: T55, 142, fig. 34: 16, 20.

[255] Tzavela-Evjen 1984, 152, fig. 27: θ.
[256] Gropengiesser 1987, 40, fig. 4: 19.
[257] Karantzali 1996, 24–5.

1. Deep bowl with non-perforated lugs at the rim (phiale) (**K 1535**, FIG. 7.11: 12)

Bowl **K 1535** is assigned to an unusual deep bowl with in-turned walls and in-turned wide, pointed rim. One of the long, non-perforated and narrow lugs is still preserved. This variant of deep bowl is rare in the EC repertoire, and there are no published examples of Cycladic origin. However, parallels have been identified in EB I assemblages from Vouliagmeniat Perachora,[258] from EH I sites in Euboia,[259] and from EH II Manika.[260]

2. Deep bowls (phiale) with thickened in-turned rim (**K 1538**, FIG. 7.11: 13)

Bowl **K 1538** is assigned to a very common form of EB I pottery, like that from Emborio on Chios.[261] Many examples have been identified in the material of Ma I from Trench 6,1.

3. Collar of a closed vessel (prochous?) (**K 1528**, FIG. 7.11: 14)

Sherd **K 1528** is too small and eroded to reconstruct the shape securely. It is a fragment from the collar and the shoulder of some type of jug (prochous). It is notable that sherds of this type of vessel are extremely rare in the pottery assemblage of Ma I and II from the Bastion: **K 1528** is the only well preserved example. It is characterised by thick walls at the collar, which become thinner at the curve towards the shoulder. These technical features have been observed on Keros-Syros (EC II) and Kastri Group forms. Examples are known from Rodinadhes [262] and Panormos[263] on Naxos, and the site 'Nero' on Kato Kouphonisi.[264]

4. Deep bowls with horizontal crescent-shaped non-perforated lugs (chytra) (**K 1527** and **K 1536**, FIG. 7.11: 15–16)

This is a common type of a cooking vessel: **K 1527** and **K 1536** are assigned to a shape seen in the pottery of Ma I which continues into phases Ma II and III and persists until Ma IV. The many parallels from the Cyclades and the Greek mainland have been mentioned above (p. 117).

5. Footed or pedestal jar (crateriskos) (**K 1525**, FIG. 7.11: 17)

Sherd **K 1525** is possibly assigned to a variant of a vessel with a low pedestal. This type of vessel, dated to the Keros-Syros period (EC II), has been identified in the Ma II assemblage from Trench 7. Such vessels are characteristic of the transitional Kampos Group (EC I/II). There are examples from Ayii Anargyroi[265] on Naxos and from the Kouphonisia.[266]

6. Conical cup (**K 1523**, FIG. 7.11: 18, PLATE 33 *b*)

This is a rather common shape in Keros-Syros (EC II) assemblages. Two main variants are known: one with a flat base and another with a low conical base.[267] Parallels for **K 1523**, which was found within the interior of vase **K 1524**, from Markiani have been identified in assemblages of Ma III (see FIG. 7. 14: 3–6, PLATE 33 *e*) and Ma IV (see FIG. 7.19: 9–14).

The Ma II conical cups found in Trench 7 are larger and are assigned to the canonical conical type. One of them has a leaf impression (FIG. 7.4: 7–11, PLATE 30 *d*). The conical cups of Trenches 7 and 8 are assigned to the larger group of conical cups that are evident in the Kampos Group (EC I/II) and are common throughout the Keros-Syros (EC II) culture.

Examples with flat inside base and in-turned rim were found in the Clon Stephanos excavations on Naxos.[268] It seems that this type of conical cup is characteristic of the whole EB II period in the Cyclades. However, it a common, plain and simple cup shape.[269]

7. Plate (pinakio) (**K 1522**, FIG. 7.11: 19)

The shallow plate (**K 1522**) is a common form within the pottery of the Keros-Syros culture (EC II). There are parallels in Ma I (FIG. 7.2: 16), while in the following Ma II, Ma III and mainly Ma IV different and more developed types of pinakia appear.

[258] Fossey 1969, 63, fig. 5: 23.
[259] Sampson 1980/1, fig. 138; 127, fig. 146: 353.
[260] Sampson 1985, 39, fig. 8: P79.
[261] Hood 1981, 318, fig. 148: 575, 581.
[262] Doumas 1977, pl. L: a, NM 3577.
[263] Unpublished material. Karantzali 1996, 25–6, fig. 20: 10.
[264] Zapheiropoulou 1970, 429–30, pl. 373β.
[265] Doumas 1977, 18, fig. 6: f, NM 1915.
[266] Zapheiropoulou 1984, 36, fig. 1e.
[267] Thimme 1977, 112, pl. 409–10.
[268] Unpublished material: NM 5173.
[269] Cosmopoulos 1986, 91, pl. 13.V.

Plate **K 1522** is very low and is assigned to a variant of Keros-Syros type (EC II). At Knossos in the well-stratified EM I Trench FF, sherds of similar shallow plates were found.[270]

8. Collared jar (stamnos) and large storage vessels with narrow collar (**K 1524**, **K 1532**, **K 1526**, and **K 1530**, FIG. 7.12: 1–4, PLATE 33 a)

Jar **K 1524** (FIG. 7.12: 1, PLATE 33 a) is of this type of storage jar with two horizontal slashed handles. Sherds **K 1532** (FIG. 7.12: 2), **K 1526** (FIG. 7.12: 3), and **K 1530** (FIG. 7.12: 4) are fragments from the body and the handles of large storage jars. There are important examples from Panormos on Naxos,[271] belonging to the Kastri Group, a few from Kynthos on Delos,[272] and from elsewhere.

Sherd **K 1524** (FIG. 7.12: 1, PLATE 33 a), with only the lower part preserved, has a spherical to oval or egg-shaped body, a slightly convex base and two horizontal handles. It must have had a high narrow cylindrical collar with concave sides and everted rim. A close parallel to this is NM 5029 from Panormos on Naxos.[273]

Fragments of the same or similar type, but of relatively larger size, have been identified among the pottery of Ma IV and also in the assemblage of Trench 3. An intact vase from Amorgos is assigned to the same type.[274] Distant parallels characterised by the two vertical perforated lugs in place of the handles, are known from Manika in Euboia.[275]

The examples from Panormos do not have a slip or any kind of decoration, and their dark red-brown to greyish surface is smoothed. A body sherd of storage vessel **K 1530** (FIG. 7.12: 4) and the horizontal handles with the incised decoration **K 1526** (FIG. 7.12: 3) and **K 1532** (FIG. 7.12: 2) have been assigned to a variant of this shape.

Two intact collared storage vessels from Panormos on Naxos (NM 5028 and NM 5029) have handles with incisions on the upper surface, like the two above-mentioned handles of the slashed type from Trench 8. But it is possible that the deep incisions of the handles from Trench 8 imply an earlier dating than the equivalent vases from Panormos, which have faint oblique incisions.

Sherd **K 1530** (FIG. 7.12: 4) assigned to a collared jar of this type displays an incised pattern of a 'wheel'. Other examples of incised wheel decoration are unknown from the Cyclades. Two prochoi in the Apeiranthos Museum, from the late phase of EC II, have also incised symbols or patterns. One has a small incised prochous and the other an incised eye.[276] A sherd from Kum Tepe II,[277] possibly part of an anthropomorphic vase, has a stamped wheel pattern.

Storage vessels of this type have been identified at many EC / EH II sites, like the fragmentary examples from Ayia Irini on Kea,[278] Kynthos on Delos,[279] the intact ones from Askitario[280] and Aigina town II,[281] and the variants from Raphina, Orchomenos,[282] Poliochni,[283] and Troy II.[284] A variant of this type is characteristic for period II (EM IIB) at Myrtos.[285]

9. Storage vessel (pithos) (**K 1534**, FIG. 7.12: 5)

Sherd **K 1534**, from the wide out-turned, swelling and wide rim, is assigned to a large storage vase or pithos. Parallels to this have been found in Panormos on Naxos,[286] Kynthos on Delos,[287] as well as on EH sites like Eutresis.[288] This type of pithos must have been in use from EB I onwards, but it is more common during EB II.

10. Baking pan (pinakio) (**K 1533**, FIG. 7.12: 6)

This type of baking pan with markedly out-turned walls, possibly made *in situ* on the ground, is known in EB II. For comments on this type, see above under pottery of Ma II (p. 119).

Sherd **K 1533** is assigned to the baking pan type with asymmetrical undulating rim, which, in some examples, reaches as low the base. It must have had horizontal handles at intervals as is evident from the best-preserved examples from phase IV of the settlement. Some large baking pans of this type

[270] Wilson 1985, 363, fig. 43: 16–18.
[271] Karantzali 1996, 25, 102, fig. 20, 21 a.
[272] MacGillivray 1980, 29, fig. 11:223, 354, 42, 369.
[273] Karantzali 1996, 25, fig. 21a.
[274] Marangou 1984, 101, fig. 15.
[275] Sampson 1988, 65, pl. 16: 2, 3, fig. 101.
[276] Lambrinoudakis 1990, 102, fig. 107–8.
[277] Sperling 1976, 364, fig. 24: 918.
[278] Caskey 1972, 366, B41, 78–9, fig. 7: C17.
[279] MacGillivray 1980, 30, fig. 11: 223, 354.

[280] Theocharis 1953/4, fig. 20, 22–3.
[281] Walter and Felten 1981, pl. 82: 117.
[282] Kunze 1934, pl. III.
[283] Bernabò Brea 1976, pl. CXXX: e.
[284] Blegen et al. 1951, fig. 401: 35.479.
[285] Warren 1972a, fig. 77, 78, pl. 58: P565, 579.
[286] Unpublished material.
[287] MacGillivray 1980, 41–3, fig. 13: 270–1.
[288] Goldman 1931, 89, fig. 108.

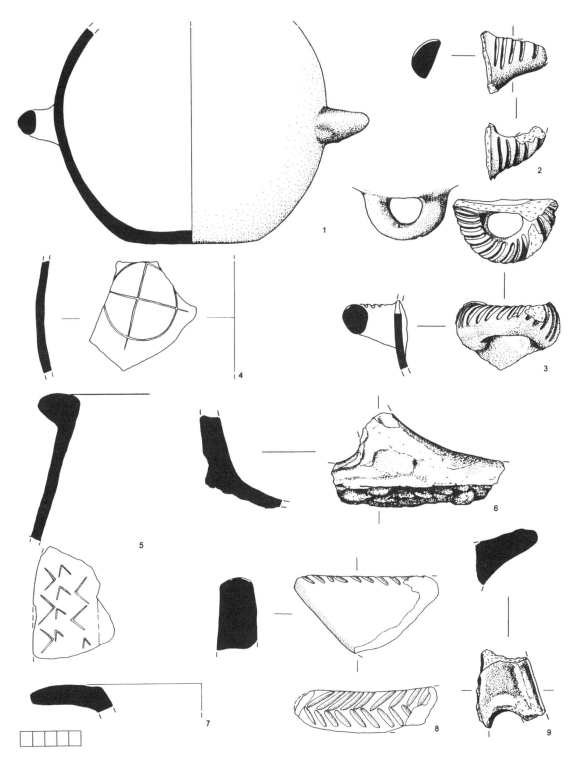

FIG. 7.12. Pottery from outside the Bastion (Trench 8) (scale 1:3).

have traces of fire or smoke inside, a fact which suggests that they were probably used as braziers over which charcoal and the deep cooking vases (*chytra)* could have been placed.

11. Portable hearths (hestiae) (**K 1521, K 1539-EE 821,** (FIG. 7.12: 7–8)

Sherd **K 1521** (FIG. 7.12: 7) comes from a portable hat-shaped hearth. Similar hearths have been found only in Ma II (FIG. 7.10: 4–7, PLATE 32 *b–d*). The Ma IV examples are distant variants. This particular sherd from the Bastion area comes from near the surface.

Sherd **K 1539** (FIG. 7.12: 8) is assigned to a portable hearth or brazier, of rectangular shape, with low everted rim and two nearly triangular handles at its both sides. On the upper surface of these handles there is a deeply incised decoration showing a row of acute angles. An intact example comes from Trench 3. Parallels have been identified in the Ma IV assemblage. Examples of hearths found by Tsountas at Kato Akrotiri, now in the Athens National Archaeological Museum, may possibly be assigned to braziers of this type. There are no other published examples of this type from the Cyclades.

12. Brazier or 'mask-like' support vessel (**K 1531**, FIG. 7.12: 9)

Sherd **K 1531** is too small to allow us to draw definite conclusions. Possibly it can be assigned to a support vessel, pedestal or base for other vessels. Fragments of similar vessels have been found in Trench 7 of Ma II and have been discussed above. Possibly comparable to this are the EM IIB baking pans from Myrtos,[289] where the main vessel is a shallow plate (*pinakio*) supported by high wide feet, solid or with openings. Fragments of this type of vessel have also been identified in Tiryns.[290]

13. Open unidentified vase with scoring or wiping traces (**K 1537**)

Sherd **K 1537** is assigned to an open vessel decorated on the outside by scoring (using a vertical brush). This technique is either hard (scoring) or faint (wiping). Some examples of wiping have been identified in the material of Ma IV. Unfortunately, there are no published examples from the Cyclades. However, among the EC I material from Palati on Naxos,[291] decorated sherds with the scoring technique were identified.

Sherds decorated with the wiping technique (faint non-canonical brush) are characteristic for the pottery from Panormos on Naxos.[292] This technique of scoring or wiping is very common during the EBA in the Aegean and is known from Manika in Euboia,[293] Ayia Irini on Kea,[294] Troy Id–II,[295] Tarsus[296] and elsewhere.

On Crete the technique is attested from the end of the Late Neolithic (Trapeza Cave in Lasithi, west Crete caves) and has been identified in many examples from Knossos and Phaistos. It continues through the EM I period, e.g. at from Debla,[297] and at Knossos (early EM I Well and Trench FF), and persists until the end of the EM IIA period (Knossos West Court House).[298]

TABLE 7.9 (p. 161) sets out a complete list of the catalogued pottery from outside the Bastion.

D. THE POTTERY FROM MARKIANI PHASE III
by Kiki Birtacha

INTRODUCTION

The pottery group of settlement phase III selected for study comprises the material from layers 43 to 46 of Trench 1,1 and layer 5 of Trench 9,1. Although the amount is small it falls stratigraphically in a well-defined phase which follows Ma II and is succeeded by Ma IV.

However, this material does not come from successive layers of a single stratigraphic sequence. As discussed in Chapter 4, it is part of the material excavated as the east half of Wall Λ of Trench 1,1 which was dismantled and from the cave-like 'fissure' located at the eastern side of Rock Cutting 2 (see FIG. 4.18; PLATE 16). This 'fissure' was sealed by the fall of two slabs, which had probably served as its roof. Sherds from the area of Wall Λ joined with sherds from the deepest part of the 'fissure'. The material in question forms a closed deposit, earlier than phase IV. Its character also, is clearly typologically different and seems later than phase Ma II.

GENERAL CHARACTERISTICS OF THE MARKIANI PHASE III POTTERY

This pottery group comprises 563 sherds, many of them (32%) large (>4–5 cm). The largest sherds come from the interior of the fissure. Many can be joined to form recognisable vessel shapes. A large quantity of sherds comes from the fill of Wall Λ, some from the mud between the stones and others

[289] Warren 1972a, 165, fig. 47: P131.
[290] Weisshaar 1981, 232, fig. 79: 8.
[291] Karantzali 1996, 20, fig. 1: e.
[292] Karantzali 1996, 25.
[293] Sampson 1985, 33, fig. 11: P125, 74, fig. 23.
[294] Caskey 1972, pl. 76: A43–A46.

[295] Blegen et al 1950, 39, 45.
[296] Goldman 1956, fig. 243: 125, 137, EBA I, fig. 252: 244, 245a–b, EBA II.
[297] Warren and Tzedakis 1974, 321–31, pl. 52–3.
[298] Wilson 1985, 363, pl. 57, EM I, 333, pl. 41: 273, 276–7, EM IIA.

from the fill. Most are body sherds of large wide-mouthed or closed vessels of Coarse Ware. The only intact vessels are small conical cups. All the vessels may be regarded as of everyday household use.

FABRICS AND WARES

The clays vary in colour from reddish to brown. On the basis of the inclusions the fabrics belong to two principal categories: Blue Schist Ware containing purple *patelia* and Marble Ware.

TABLE 7.10 (p. 162) gives the percentage of fabrics based on microscopic examination conducted by Dr Sarah Vaughan (see also TABLE 7.3). It should be noted that the categories given here are based on preliminary classification in the field. Marble A, B and C are all classified by Vaughan as Marble Ware. Dark Grey Marble is designated by Vaughan as Micritic, Shelly Limestone. Blue Schist A is equivalent to her Phyllite-Quartzite. Overall the Marble Wares and the Blue Schist Wares are almost equally common. The 'Other' categories include Vaughan's Micaceous Wares.

SURFACE TREATMENT

Four main categories of surface treatment may be distinguished: slipped, polished, burnished and plain smoothed. In the best examples the result is a very smooth surface with some polish. Burnish implies the survival of traces of use of a burnishing tool.

On smoothed surfaces there were sometimes traces of brush, cloth or skin, used for smoothing the surface. Very shallow parallel and dense grooves may indicate the use of cloth or skin.[299] Traces of brush use are seen as shallow uneven incisions or parallel grooves. They are usually observed on large Coarse Ware vessels, inside the open ones and on the exterior of the closed vessels.

In most cases of smoothing a very thin layer of clay of the same texture and colour as the core covers the surfaces. It is possible that when the vessel was still wet the hands, or some very soft implement, were used to smooth the surface and to wipe out the original traces of the pottery-making process.[300] The surfaces are still rough to the touch. Only in the case of the small cups was there no attempt at smoothing the surface. The slip is usually achieved by applying a thin layer of clay of the same texture as the core, the slips covering the surfaces uniformly. In TABLE 7.11 (p. 162) percentages of various techniques of surface treatment are indicated as revealed macroscopically by ceramic fabrics.

In the fabrics with marble inclusions the most popular treatment is simply plain surface smoothing, while in the fabrics with blue schist inclusions the most popular is polishing. Slip and burnish are very rare techniques in the surface treatment of Ma III.

POTTERY SHAPES

The typological variety of phase III is rather limited. Deep open vessels with or without lugs, narrow-shaped collared jars (*stamnoi*) storage vessels and baking pans are the most popular forms.

TABLE 7.12 (p. 162) compares shape against fabric. From this we may recognise two main categories of vessel: open and closed. The 'mask-like' ceramic vessels or braziers are considered separately.

OPEN VESSELS

1. Bowls (phiale)

a. Bowl with swelling in-turned rim (**K 1287**, FIG. 7.13: 1)

One very small sherd (**K 1287**) comes from a bowl of rolled-rim type. Its small size precludes reconstruction of rim diameter and its inclination. It should be associated chronologically with the earliest material of the group. The type is very popular in the whole Aegean world from the Neolithic onwards. It is common in the Cyclades with variations in the shape or degree of rim swelling throughout much of the EC period. Sotirakopoulou provides a detailed presentation of the geographical and chronological spread of the type in the publication of pottery from Akrotiri on Thera.[301]

At Markiani it is common in Ma I (**K 1481**, FIG. 7.1:1, PLATE 29 *a*; **K 1473**, FIG. 7.1: 2, PLATE 29 *a*; **K 1500**, FIG. 7.1: 3, PLATE 29 *c*, **K 1501**, FIG. 7.1: 4, PLATE 29 *c*) and Ma II (**K 1164**, FIG. 7.6: 11, PLATE 30 *c*; **K 1166**, FIG. 7.6: 3; **K 1136**, FIG. 7.6: 4; **K 1139**, FIG. 7.6: 6), while it is unknown in phase Ma IV.

[299] Shepard 1982, 188, fig. 13: f.
[300] Shepard 1982, 188.
[301] Sotirakopoulou 1986, 300–3.

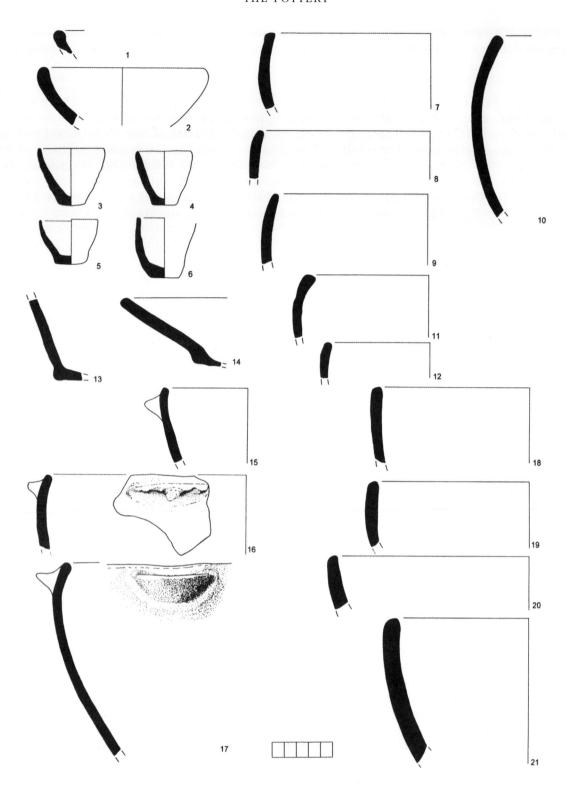

FIG. 7.13. Pottery of Markiani phase III: bowls (scale 1:3).

b. Bowl with in-turned rim (**K 1411**, FIG. 7.13: 2)

There is only one example (**K 1411**) of this shape. This is a type which is very popular in the Cyclades from the first phases of the Keros-Syros (EC II) period and is known from Ano Kouphonisi (Simigdalas plot, grave 7) with handle,[302] and from Ayia Irini III on Kea.[303] In Attica it is attested at Raphina,[304]

[302] Zapheiropoulou 1984, 36 n. 6, fig. 2: e.
[303] Caskey 1972, 370, 373, fig. 6: C6, pl. 81: C31–C33.

[304] Theocharis 1952, 144, fig. 10: 3rd row, first and second from the left; Theocharis 1953, 113, fig. 9: α.

the settlement in Rouf in Athens,[305] and Ayios Kosmas.[306] It occurs in the settlement and cemetery of Manika on Euboia,[307] and at Kolonna (II and III) on Aigina.[308] It is also know at the Heraion[309] on Samos and Poliochni.[310]

2. *Cup (kypello)* (**K 1215, K 1752, K 1717**, and **K 1716** , FIG. 7.13: 3–6, PLATE 33 *e*; **K 1645** and **K 1646**)

These are small, deep, conical cups (Ht max. 5 cm) with flat narrow base and straight walls slightly curved near the rim. They were hastily produced from a spherical ball of clay. In each example marks from the potter's fingers are visible on the exterior, while the interior is more carefully smoothed.

K 1752-EE 190 (FIG. 7.13: 4), **K 1717**-EE 188 (FIG. 7.13: 5), **K 1716**-EE 189 (FIG. 7.13: 6) and **K 1215**-EE 904 (FIG. 7.13: 3, PLATE 33 *e*) were found in the deepest part of the 'fissure' on a schist slab, which constituted the upper surface of Wall Λ of Trench 1,1. Sherds **K 1215** (FIG. 7.13: 3, PLATE 33 *e*) and **K 1646** come from the wall fill. The shape is known from Ma III and continues until Ma IV (**K 1205** FIG. 7.19: 12, **K 1206**, FIG. 7.19: 14). In the few Ma IV examples (**K 1205, K 1206**) there are slight differences in shape: the base is very narrow, the walls are straight and steeper and the cups are more precisely conical in appearance, being made carefully.

In general conical bowls and cups are very popular throughout the Aegean from early in the EBA. The cemetery of Kapsala (grave 9) on Amorgos has a similar small conical cup. [311] On the Greek mainland small conical cups have been found at Gonia in the Argolid,[312] and in the cemetery of Ayios Kosmas in Attica,[313] where the small one-handled cup of Trojan type is most common. Small handleless cups of very open form have been found at Manika.[314] In the north-east Aegean this form occurs at Poliochni Blue phase.[315]

One small cup of the same shape with a roughly shaped ring base, found during the 1985 surface cleaning in Rock Cutting 2 (Trench 1,1, Space 7) may be an indication that these small cups were imitations of the small conical bowls with ring base, which were very popular in EH II settlements and at Ayia Irini, phases II and III. They may be a miniature variety of the conical cups of larger size which often have leaf or mat impressions on the base and are known from all over the Cyclades, where their early presence may be due to a possible Cycladic origin.

3. *Baking pan (hestia)* (**K 1285, K 1279**, FIG. 7.13: 13–14, and **K 1614**)

In this category there are two different vessel types. The first is represented by two fragmentary examples: large, shallow, and roughly shaped vessels of Coarse Ware, with circular or more frequently ellipsoid base with out-turned walls.

The inside of the base is flat (**K 1285**, FIG. 7.13: 13) or slightly concave (**K 1279**, FIG. 7.13: 14). In most examples the base is very thin and, on the outer surface, small stones or traces of grass are evident. One intact example from Korakou in the Argolid,[316] provides further information about the shape: the very open form is circular with both base and circumference slightly concave; the rim is not of the same height around the circumference but slopes down gradually from the highest point to the point opposite.

K 1285, FIG. 7.13: 13, is a large part of a base preserving only a small part of the walls. It is a rather small-sized vessel with an ovoid flat base. On the other hand, **K 1279**, FIG. 7.13: 14 comprises part of the wall as well as a small part of the base. It is assigned to the type in which the inside of the base is concave and has a depression at the centre.

The second type of baking pan is represented by a small fragment of a circular plate. The existing fragment shows that at least at this point there were no sidewalls. There is, instead, a low everted rim. A better-preserved example, **K 1187**, FIG. 7.20: 14, of Ma IV, tells us more about the shape.

The Greek terminology for these vessels frequently found in settlements of the Aegean EBA is τήγανα / *tegana*,[317] οπτήρια / *opteria*, or κεράμια / *keramia*,[318] πινάκια / *pinakia*.[319] These vessels were probably baking plates. It may be that the best-preserved examples, concave in shape and found embedded within floors, were actually permanent hearths or braziers.[320] The smaller examples with traces of fire visible on the outside were possibly put directly onto the fire. The plates of the second

[305] Petrikaki 1980, 157, fig. 24.
[306] Mylonas 1959, 37: n. 36, fig. 131: 36.
[307] Sampson 1985, 29, fig. 7: P68, 124, pl. 10: type 10, fig. 65: 27.
[308] Walter and Felten 1981, fig. 83, pls. 81: 99, 86: 144, IX.
[309] Milojcic 1961, pls. 40: 1, 43: 34, 45: 1–6.
[310] Bernabò Brea 1976, pl. CXXI: 1.
[311] Tsountas 1898, pl. 9, 12.
[312] Blegen 1930, 67, fig. 15.

[313] Mylonas 1959, il. 156: 261.
[314] Sampson 1985, 88, fig. 24 β: Γ2, Γ3.
[315] Bernabò Brea 1964, pl. LXXXIII: v.
[316] Blegen 1921, 13, fig. 15.
[317] Theocharis 1952, 147.
[318] Theocharis 1951, 89.
[319] Tzavela-Evjen 1984, 153.
[320] Theocharis 1953–54, 73.

type were placed on the ground. The fact that traces of fire are seen only on the upper surface, more marked towards the centre, suggests that they are hearths. The associated material, including cooking pots or small storage vessels, suggests their use for cooking or for heating liquids. At Myrtos, as the excavator remarks, plates of this kind were found with cooking vessels and indications of fire.[321]

These vessels are very common at Markiani. They make their appearance in Ma III and were found in all the excavated spaces of the settlement with pottery of Ma IV, in particular the type with a thin concave base. It is very common in the Cyclades, on Crete and the Greek mainland during EB II and EB III. Close parallels for **K 1285** come from Ayia Irini on Kea[322] and Lithares in Boiotia, where one type has at least one handle.[323] In the case of **K 1279** parallels exist from Kynthos on Delos,[324] Akrotiri on Thera,[325] Raphina,[326] Askitario (house Z),[327] the settlement at Rouf in Athens,[328] Eutresis,[329] Korakou,[330] Amarynthos,[331] Manika on Euboia,[332] and Myrtos[333] on Crete. Close parallels for **K 1614** come from Ayia Irini II[334] and Myrtos,[335] as well as from Perachora (EH I), Asea, Lefkandi, and Tiryns.

The ceramic hearth is seen at Beycesultan[336] during the Late Chalcolithic 3 period and also at Aphrodisias[337] in south-west Asia Minor. The baking plate seen from the Chalcolithic continues in use until the end of the EBA.

4. Deep open bowl with lugs (chytra) (**K 1282, K 1409**, and **K 1292**, FIG. 7.13: 15–17)

These are large, deep, open vessels with slightly in-turned walls, a flat base, an in-turned rim and two horizontal crescent-shaped lugs just below the rim. Their shape and size are much the same as those of the next phase of the settlement (Ma IV). Then, however, there are three or four lugs below the rim not of horizontal crescent form but arc-shaped.

The crescent-shaped horizontal lug develops from the Ma I phase. In the earliest examples of Ma I and II, the lugs are larger and are usually placed lower than those of Ma III (see **K 1134**, FIG. 7.8: 8, PLATE 31 c, **K 1156**, FIG. 7.7: 1, PLATE 31 b, and **K 1153**, FIG. 7.8: 12 of Trench 7). The lugs act as real handles since their length (L. max. 5.5–6.5 cm) is large enough to allow the hand a satisfactory grip.

5. Deep handle-less open vessel

These are large, open, deep vessels of Coarse Ware of which there are two sub-types: one with curved walls and the other with straight walls and an almost conical body.

a. With curved walls (**K 1295, K 1276, K 1288, K 1615, K 1294, K 1390**, FIG. 7.13: 7–12, and **K 1392**)

Seven rim sherds are of this type. The rims are slightly in-turned and rounded, of the same thickness as the walls. In **K 1294** (FIG. 7.13: 11) the rim is slightly thickened inwards. The diameter of the mouth varies from 20 to 28 cm, the walls being convex with thickness varying from 0.80 to 1.00 cm. The clay is reddish with mainly marble inclusions. The firing is incomplete and irregular. Smoothing is limited to the outside surfaces and only one example, **K 1288** (FIG. 7.13: 9), is polished.

K 1390 (FIG. 7.13: 12) has a perforation just below the rim made before firing, suggesting that it may have been used to suspend the vessel or attach the lid.

b. With straight walls (**K 1410, K 1405, K 1407, K 1413**, FIG. 7.13: 18–21; **K 1406** and **K 1408**)

Six rim sherds are of this shape. The walls are straight and incline outwards. The rim is rounded and follows the line of the walls or it may be slightly in-turned: thickness between 0.80–1.00 cm. The firing is incomplete and irregular, and in all cases the inner surfaces show a particular surface treatment: either incomplete smoothing or smoothing with a brush or polishing. The shape is simple and the vessels possibly had various uses. It is a very common shape during all Markiani phases (for see phase Ma I, **K 1479**, FIG. 7.1: 10, **K 1457**, FIG. 7.1: 11, **K 1458**, FIG. 7.1: 12, **K 1475**, FIG. 7.1: 13, **K 1509**, FIG. 7.1: 14, PLATE 29 f from Trench 6 and **K 1512**, FIG. 7.11: 5, **K 1519**, FIG. 7.11: 6, from Trench 8,1).

[321] Warren 1972a, 111, fig. 46: P106.
[322] Caskey 1972, 366, fig. 4: B65.
[323] Tzavela-Evjen 1984, 153, pl. 34, 44.
[324] MacGillivray 1980, 23,
[325] Sotirakopoulou 1986, 305, fig. 2: 4182, pl. 20: e.
[326] Theocharis 1951, 89, Theocharis 1952, 147.
[327] Theocharis 1953–4, 65.
[328] Petrikaki 1980, 165, 167, fig. 43–44, pl. 46: ¨, no. 7.
[329] Goldman 1931, fig. 125.

[330] Blegen 1921, 13, fig. 15.
[331] Parlama 1979, 13, fig. 13.
[332] Sampson 1985, 135.
[333] Warren 1972a, 111, fig. 46: P124.
[334] Caskey 1972, 368, fig. 4: B76.
[335] Warren 1972a, 111, fig. 46: P106.
[336] Lloyd and Mellaart 1962, 92, fig. P.9: 15, P.13: 12–17.
[337] Joukowski-Sharp 1986, 316, 330.

In the Cyclades it is known from Ayia Irini periods II and III[338] and Kynthos on Delos (group A/B),[339] as well as Manika on Euboia,[340] and from the settlement at Rouf in Athens.[341]

CLOSED VESSELS

6. Bases (K 1402, K 1286, FIG. 7.14: 7–8, K 1278, K 1385 and K 1374)

The bases published here are flat and belong to large coarse closed vessels. K 1402 (FIG. 7.14: 7) and K 1286 (7.14: 8) are from globular vessels. Two have mat impressions. In general at Markiani in all phases both large and small vessels have flat bases.

7. Jar (pithos) (K 1273, K 1616 and K 1714-EE 905, FIG. 7.14: 2–4)

In this category are two body sherds of large, closed vessels of Coarse Ware. K 1273 (FIG. 7.14: 2) is a sherd from the belly of a large, closed vessel. The body was probably egg-shaped. The brush traces visible on the interior walls suggest that the vessel had a wide mouth. It has a horizontal handle with semi-circular section.

K 1616 (FIG. 7.14: 3) is a sherd from the shoulder and belly of a jar. The body is ovoid and the collar conical. Just below the shoulder at the highest point there are traces of a horizontal handle now broken. An example from Kynthos on Delos has a similar shape and similar horizontal handles.[342]

The horizontal handle K 1714-EE 905 (FIG. 7.14: 4) has deep grooves on its upper surface. Its clay and technical characteristics (lack of inclusions, hardness, and orange/grey in the biscuit colour) are unlike other fabric from the settlement and indicate that this is an imported vessel. This type of handle is very common in EC II and III settlements. At Markiani it first appears in phase Ma III, while in Ma IV this type of handle is also seen most commonly on storage vessels and on collared jars (*stamnoi*). On Amorgos the form is common at sites located by Marangou, i.e. Kastri, Vigla, Vouni, Sellades, Xenotaphia and elsewhere.[343] In the Cyclades the handles are known from Ayia Irini period II,[344] Kynthos on Delos,[345] and on Naxos from Panormos (NM 5028 and 5029), the cemetery of Ayii Anargyroi[346] and Korphi t' Aroniou.[347]

8. Small spherical vessel (pyxis) (K 1277, FIG. 7.14: 5, PLATE 33 f)

There is a small sherd from a relatively small vessel with spherical body, short collar and out-turned rim. The form is quite rare on the settlement and the fabric indicates that it is imported. The type is known from larger vessels from Ayia Irini period II on Kea,[348] Kynthos on Delos,[349] Akrotiri on Thera,[350] Manika on Euboia,[351] and from the settlement of Rouf in Attica.[352]

9. Collared jar (stamnos) (K 1274 and K 1275, FIG. 7.14: 6, PLATE 33 f)

These are closed vessels with a spherical or ovoid body, high cylindrical collar and two horizontal handles at the point of largest diameter. The handles are usually decorated with oblique incisions or grooves on their upper surface. The collared jars (*stamnoi*) are usually large.

Two collar sherds were found in the fill of the Wall Λ of Trench 1,1. The deep parallel oblique incisions at the base of the collar base were probably to assist the join with the body. Many body sherds, some of them refitting, probably belonged to one of the two vessels.

This type appears in phase Ma III and continues with small variations until the abandonment of the settlement (see K 1232, FIG. 7.22: 1).

The collared jar is a very common shape in the Cyclades and on the Greek mainland. It was probably used for storage and possibly transport of liquids. In the Cyclades it is known from Akrotiri on Thera,[353] Christiana,[354] Paroikia on Paros,[355] Ayia Irini period III on Kea,[356] Panormos on Naxos

[338] Caskey 1972, 366, 372, fig. 4: B48, B49, B51, 6: C20, pl. 78: B71; Wilson and Eliot 1984, 81, 87 note 2.
[339] MacGillivray 1979, 19, fig. 13: 188; MacGillivray 1980, 32, fig. 12: 188.
[340] Sampson 1985, 70, fig. 20: K26, fig. 21: K38, 131–134: types 4, 9.
[341] Petrikaki 1980, 162, fig. 31, 168, fig. 49.
[342] MacGillivray 1980, 41, fig. 15: 46.
[343] Marangou 1984, 99–103, fig. 2–4, 7–10.
[344] Caskey 1972, 366, pl. B44.
[345] MacGillivray 1980, 41, fig. 20: 408–410.

[346] Doumas 1977, 102, pl. XLIV: e.
[347] Doumas 1965, 46.
[348] Caskey 1972, 366, fig. 3: B42.
[349] MacGillivray 1980, 31, fig. 11: 43, 371.
[350] Sotirakopoulou 1986, 305, fig. 2: 4192, 5797, 5778, pl. 18: e, f.
[351] Sampson 1985, 126, pl. 10: type 5, 145, fig. 35: 3, 4, 9.
[352] Petrikaki 1980, 170, fig. 56.
[353] Sotirakopoulou 1986, 305, fig. 2: 4188, pl. 19 a.
[354] Doumas 1976, 5, fig. 6, pl. 3.
[355] Rubensohn 1917, 67, fig. 74.
[356] Caskey 1972, 372, fig. 7: C13.

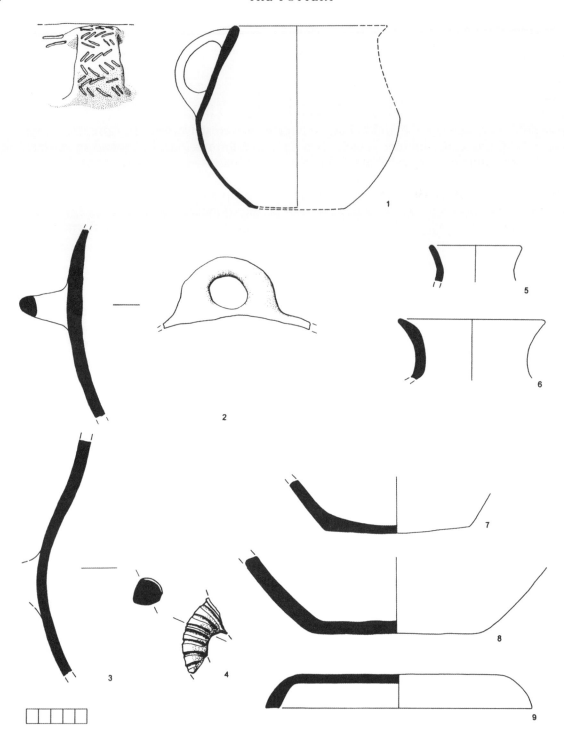

FIG. 7.14. Pottery of Markiani phase III: jug and other shapes (scale 1:3).

(NM 5028, 5029) and Kynthos on Delos (group A/B).[357] On the Greek mainland the form is common in EH II and III settlements: Askitario,[358] Ayios Kosmas,[359] Rouf,[360] Manika,[361] Aigina,[362] Korakou,[363] Asine[364] and Eutresis.[365] Its production continues into the MH period. In Poliochni this type with some variations appears in the Blue period,[366] and it is very common in the Green period.[367]

[357] MacGillivray 1980, 29, fig. 12: 223, 354.
[358] Theocharis 1954, 110, fig. 6; id. 1953–4, 68, fig. 7: first row second, 73, fig. 20, 22.
[359] Mylonas 1959, ill. 117: 14.
[360] Petrikaki 1980, 167, fig. 45–6, pl. 46 2.
[361] Sampson 1985, 145, fig. 20: K23, fig. 35: 1, 2, 7, 70, fig. 22: K70, K80–1.
[362] Walter and Felten 1981, 99, fig. 90, pls. 91, 92: 193, xviiih, pl. 85: 129 ix.
[363] Blegen 1921, 8, fig. 8.
[364] Frödin and Persson 1938, 213–4, fig. 158: 5, 215–6, fig. 159: 4.
[365] Goldman 1931, 118, fig. 153: 3, 157, 159.
[366] Bernabò Brea 1964, pl. LXXVIII: f, g.
[367] Bernabò Brea 1964, pls. CXXIV: a–e, CXXX e.

10. Jug (prochous) (**K 1298**, FIG. 7.14: 1, PLATE 33 c–d)

K 1298 is half of the body of a wide-mouthed jug. The spout has not survived. The vessel is biconical with no differentiation between collar and belly. A wide vertical strap handle with incised decoration rises from the junction between collar and belly and returns just below the rim. This is the only pot of Markiani phase III that we are able to classify as Fine Ware. The fabric has small inclusions of both purple *patelia* and limestone. The firing is good and the surface well polished.

This shape was formerly assigned to the so-called 'Amorgos Group', dated by scholars to the late phase of the EC period.[368] However, it is now recognised that shapes of the 'Amorgos Group' appear at Markiani during both phases III and IV and that this complex has no chronological significance. The closest parallel for this shape comes from Kato Akrotiri on Amorgos.[369] There are two other examples of the same type in the British Museum (London)[370] and another in the Ashmolean Museum (Oxford),[371] the last of supposed Amorgan provenance. Comparable wide-mouthed prochoi have been found in Akrotiri on Thera.[372] Note that the type of jug (*prochous*) with a wide mouth and with a clear differentiation between collar and belly and with an undecorated vertical strap or round handle seems to be less rare.[373]

11. Lid (**K 1297**, FIG. 7.14: 9)

One rim sherd and some body sherds derive from a lid, the upper surface of which is flat while the side walls are convex. The shape is very simple, but there seems to be no exact parallel in the Aegean. This must have served as the lid of a wide-mouthed jar.

During the EBA ceramic lids were common for small vases, in the Cyclades mainly pyxides, usually of quite elaborate form. The lids used for large vessels were usually stone circular slabs (mainly of schist, see also Chapter 8B). Large ceramic lids have been found in the north-east Aegean, at Poliochni, Thermi and Troy.

12. Brazier, 'mask-like' support vessel (**K 1280**)

K 1280 (not illustrated) is a fragmentary sherd of such a brazier or support, 'mask-like' object found in levels of Ma III. It is possible that the sherd **EE 197** with the seal impression (see Chapter 8G, FIG. 8.25: 5, PLATE 53 e) came from another.

The 'mask-like' vessels from Markiani have at least three perforated apertures (two at the sides and one located more centrally opposite the wide mouth between the two protuberances). The walls are thick and the fabric very coarse: the outer surface is not at all smoothed, while the interior is very rough.

These vessels are common in the settlement. An early variant appears in Ma II (**K 1174**+**K 1592**+**K 1593** FIG. 7.10: 1, PLATE 32 e). The sherd **K 1280** belongs to a later form that is also well known in Ma IV. The better preserved examples of the later phase of the settlement help us to identify and reconstruct the type, see **EE 257** (discussed in Chapter 7E, FIG. 7.25: 1, PLATE 36 a–e) and also **K 1704** from Trench 3,2, layer 9 (FIG. 7. 15, PLATE 34 a–f). This is illustrated here for comparative purposes, although the pottery from Trench 3 has not been included in this publication. The sherd discussed here, **K 1280**, may be a fragment of a vessel similar to **EE 257**, FIG. 7.25: 1, PLATE 36 a–e, preserving indications of the 'rim' (with mat impression) and one of the apertures. The complete vessel **K 1704** (FIG. 7.15: PLATE 34 a–f) has a wide mouth, flat lower surface (supported by a pair of protuberances) and a handle above, rather like a terracotta hand-shovel. The grip handle has a circular aperture on each side and one behind so that, seen from the rear, the object has a mask-like appearance. In the case of **K 1704** there are finger impressions around the line of the wide mouth.

Cycladic parallels are attested at Kapros[374] and Kato Akrotiri on Amorgos, from Naxos,[375] and from Phylakopi on Melos. Both the function and the orientation of the vessel are still unclear. The mat impressions seen in all the 'mask-like' vessels on the exterior surface of the mouth may indicate that the vessel actually stood on this surface. The wide distribution of the form in Markiani and its find context with vessels and tools of everyday use, would seem to exclude any possibility of their special ceremonial use.

[368] Doumas 1977, 23; Renfrew 1972, 534–5; ibid. 1984, 12–3.
[369] Tsountas 1898, 167, pl. 9, 20.
[370] Renfrew 1972, 534, pl. 9, 6.
[371] Renfrew 1972, 534; Sherratt 2000, 208, fig. 112, pl. 250, cat. no. III.13.a.10(AE 261; 1896.30).

[372] Sotirakopoulou 1990, 43.
[373] Tsountas 1898, 166, pl. 9, 19; Doumas 1983, 152–3, ctn. 187.
[374] Dümmler 1886, Beil. 2: C, 1.
[375] Zervos 1957, pl. 100; Marangou 1990a, 56, ctn. 22.

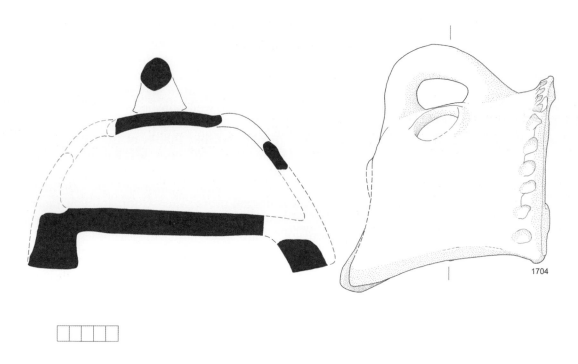

Fig. 7.15. Pottery of Markiani phase III: brazier or 'mask like' support vessel (**K 1704**) from Trench 3 (scale 1:3).

GENERAL REMARKS ON MARKIANI PHASE III POTTERY: RELATIONSHIPS WITH MA II AND MA IV

In order to situate the pottery of Ma III within the general chronological scheme of the settlement it is relevant to examine its relationships with the material of the previous Ma II and succeeding phase Ma IV. In comparison with phase II the rarity of the Marble B Ware is evident. The introduction of local schist fabrics, namely of purple *patelia* (glaucophane), is significant: it characterises the pottery from this period until the abandonment of the settlement.

In Ma II there was more variety in the fabrics than in the succeeding phase. In Ma III the surface treatment is, in general, less careful with a rarity of slip and burnish. But there are some technological improvements, notably in the potting (rather thinner walls), the more complicated forms, with the addition of the horizontal handles to the body, and the addition of collared necks for the collared jars (*stamnoi*).

In Markiani phase III new forms appear: the collared jar (*stamnos*), the small conical cup and the strap handle and the horizontal handle with incised decoration. These new shapes are generally made of fabrics with schist inclusions. Other shapes are seen, such as the deep open vessels with horizontal lugs (*chytrae*), the 'mask-like' vessels and the hearths. Production of some other forms now ceases, such as the portable hat-shaped hearths, the swollen rim bowls (*phialae*) with vertical or horizontal tube-like handles, the strainers and spoons. These observations, although based upon small quantities of material, are nonetheless indicative of the pottery typology of phase III.

Although there are significant differences between the pottery of Ma II and III, this does not indicate discontinuity since both the forms and the fabrics show many continuing elements. Despite the limited quantities of material studied, especially for phase III, it is possible to note the absence from phase IV of certain features seen in phase III. Among the types absent in Ma IV are: the deep bowls (*chytrae*) with horizontal crescent-shaped lugs, and the wide-mouthed jugs (*prochoi*) with strap handle. On the other hand in Ma III several significant forms of Ma IV are not seen: the one-handled cups with conical collar (tankards), the depas amphikypellon, the deep bowls (*chytrae*) with small decorative arc-shaped lugs, the narrow-necked jugs, plus the practice of decoration with figurative or linear incisions on the outer surfaces of the vases.

Meanwhile, some types which appear in Ma III continue with slight variation during Ma IV, such as the collared jars (*stamnos*), baking pans with concave inner bases, braziers or 'mask-like' support vessels, small conical cups and the wide-mouthed deep vessels. In general the household wares are essentially the same in both phases, representing a degree of continuity. So it is mainly the presence of these new forms, most of them typical of the Kastri Group, which characterises Ma IV, and their absence which serves to define the ceramic assemblage of phase III.

Table 7.13 (p. 163) sets out a complete list of the catalogued pottery from Markiani phase III.

E. THE POTTERY OF MARKIANI PHASE IV

by Pantelis Eskitzioglou

INTRODUCTION

The last occupation level of the settlement, designated Ma IV, is associated with new building activities which succeed those of phase III.

In this last phase of occupation at the settlement the greatest concentration of sherds was observed in Spaces 3, 6 and 7 of Trenches 1 and 2 of Terrace 1 and in particular in the following layers:

- Layers 21–30 and 34–36 of Trench 1,1 from the interior of the circular feature of Space 7.
- Layers 20 and 22–31 of Trench 2; layers 3, 4, 5 and 7 of Trench 1,3; layers 17 and 27–31 of Trench 1,4 from the area south of and between the two Rock Cuttings 2 and 3 in Space 6; and
- Layers 4, 6, 9, 12 and 22 of Trench 1,4 above Floor 'a' of Space 3.

It should be noted that this description is based on a rather short study season in the field and that there has been no opportunity to review the classification of the fabrics. The discussion of fabrics should be regarded as provisional. The stratigraphic status of the material may, however, be regarded as secure.

CLAY FABRICS, TECHNICAL CHARACTERISTICS AND SURFACE TREATMENT

The phase IV pottery assemblage under consideration here comprises 2967 sherds, most of them non-diagnostic. Only 7.80% (233 sherds) may be assigned to specific pottery forms (see TABLES 7.16 and 7.17).

The colour of the clay varies between red and brown. We are able to distinguish two main categories: a) clay with schist inclusions, mainly the local purple schist (*patelia*) (Blue Schist Ware A), and b) clay with marble inclusions (Marble Ware A). Both are more frequently used during Ma IV than in phase III. TABLE 7.14 (p. 164) sets out the distribution of pottery fabrics by areal sub-divisions ('spaces') of Trenches 1 and 2. The only the securely identified sherds are placed among the 'Volcanic, Gneissose fabrics' and 'Other' fabric categories.

Four categories of surface treatment can be distinguished (see TABLE 7.15, p. 164): slipped surfaces, burnished (with burnish marks), smoothed (with a quick or hasty smoothing) and polished. In general there was no special treatment of the internal surface of the open vases, even when the external surface bears traces of slip or burnish. In general it is clear that there was some evolution of surface treatment in comparison to earlier phases, although only in a small percentage of pottery do we find the use of slip or burnish. A high percentage of sherds has either very eroded surfaces or surfaces without noticeable traces of any kind of surface treatment.

POTTERY SHAPES

In general it will be seen that the pottery from phase IV at Markiani shows continuity of fabric and form with that of Ma III. Significant new forms are also seen, some characteristic of the Kastri Group, notably the tankard cup (FIG. 7.19: 1–7) and the depas (FIG. 7.19: 8). Forms have been classified into a simple shape repertoire as follows. As seen in TABLES 7.14 and 7.15 the fabrics generally appear to be local, much like those of Ma III.

In TABLE 7.16 (p. 165) the total number of sherds is given according to the frequency of their appearance in each space on the basis of their form and their fabric.

TABLE 7.17 (p. 165) sets out the distribution of the ceramic shapes of phase IV within the building complex spaces revealed in Trenches 1 and 2 on Terrace 1 (see FIG. 4.21).

THE MA IV POTTERY

1. Bowls (phiale)

a. Shallow Bowls (**K 1461, K 1196, K 1203, K 1176, K 1186, K 1190, K 1454, K 1450, K 1448** and **K 2011**, FIG. 7.16: 1–10)

Shallow bowls with curved walls display a considerable degree of variety in the form of the rim. Sometimes the rim thins to an edge (**K 1461**, FIG. 7.16: 1), while some are slightly in-turned (**K 1196**, FIG. 7.16: 2) and others curve upwards to the vertical (**K 1203**, FIG. 7.16: 7; **K 1176**, FIG. 7.16: 3; **K 1186**, FIG. 7.16: 4; **K 1190**, FIG. 7.16: 5; **K 1454**, FIG. 7.16: 6). A number of them are heavily burnished. In other cases, the rim is strongly inturned and slightly thickened (**K 1450**, FIG. 7.16: 9), or it slopes strongly inwards ending at an edge (**K 1448**, FIG. 7.16: 8). Under the rim of **K 1450** (FIG. 7.16: 9) there is a narrow perforated horizontal lug.

Another 28 non-catalogued sherds may be assigned to the same type of bowl. Parallels occur at Ayia Irini period III,[376] on Kynthos,[377] at Manika,[378] Lefkandi period I,[379] Eutresis,[380] Lithares,[381] Troy IV,[382] and Poliochni Yellow period.[383]

K 2011 (FIG. 7.16: 10) is a unique example of a shallow bowl with narrowing in-turned rim and opposing horizontal cylindrical handles just below the rim, which is heavily burnished. This 'skyphos' form does not usually occur in the Kastri Group assemblage, but is seen in contexts of slightly later date (sometimes designated 'MBA') at Ayia Irini, Phylakopi, Paros, and Aigina.

b. Deep bowls

Three sub-types of this shape may be distinguished, with variations in the shape of body and size. There is also a sub-type with a pipe-like spout just below the rim.

i. *Deep bowls, type A* (**K 1420, K 1442**, FIG. 7.16: 11–12)

The upper part of these bowls has an almost cylindrical body with relatively straight walls. Another three non-catalogued sherds are assigned to this type. Parallels exist at Eutresis,[384] Lithares (EH II)[385] and Manika (EH III).[386]

ii. *Deep bowls, type B, with hemispherical body, and spouted bowls* (**K 1421, K 1460 K 1178**, and **K 1451**, FIG. 7.16: 13–16, PLATE 36 *b*)

These bowls have a hemispherical body and curved walls, like **K 1421** (FIG. 7.16: 13) and **K 1460** (FIG. 7.16: 15). In some cases they have a horizontal and flat rim (**K 1178**, FIG. 7.16: 14, which is also burnished). Another nine non-catalogued sherds are of this type. Bowls of this type are known from Ayia Irini period III,[387] Kynthos (group A/B),[388] and Ayios Kosmas;[389] they are generally dated to the beginning of the EC III period.

A sherd of a hemisperical bowl (**K 1451**, FIG. 7.16: 16, PLATE 36 *b*) with a pipe-like spout belongs to this type of deep bowl, based on the evidence of a similar example from Naxos[390] (Spedos, grave 10). This shape is supposed to be characteristic of the Kastri Group.

iii. *Small hemispherical bowls with in-turned walls, type C* (**K 1724, K 1466, K 1177** and **K 1447**, FIG. 7.16: 17–20, PLATE 35 *e*)

These are small bowls, of diameter *c.* 12–14 cm and height *c.* 7–8 cm, which have a hemispherical body with curved walls. Generally speaking they have concave bases, sometimes with mat impressions or in-turned rim like **K 1466**. On occasion there are three arc-shaped lugs below the rim like **K 1724** (FIG. 7.16: 19, PLATE 35 *e*) or a button-like lug under the rim like **K 1177** (FIG. 7.16: 20). **K 1447** (FIG. 7.16: 18) is burnished, while **K 1177** bears traces of wiping. There are another eight non-catalogued sherds of this form. The shape is known in the Cyclades from Kynthos (groups A, B),[391] Naxos (Akrotiri, Avdeli, Lakkoudes)[392] and from Chalandriani on Syros.[393]

2. *Deep bowls with lugs (chytrae)* (**K 1212, K 1434, K 1435, K 1184, K 1191** and **K 1199, K 1422, K 1472, K 1464**, and **K 1219**, FIG. 7.17: 1–10, PLATE 36 *e*)

These bowls are deep, wide-mouthed with relatively thin curved walls, in-turned rims and slightly concave base. Just below the in-turned rim there are arc-shaped lugs, usually two placed opposite each other. On the walls visible traces of fire suggest their use as cooking pots, *chytrae*.

---

[376] Caskey 1972, 370, 372–3, fig. 6: C10, C11, pl. 81: C12, C32, C33.

[377] MacGillivray 1979, 14, fig. 11: 90, 91 / 10, 16, fig. 11: 35, 128, 344; ibid. 1980, 23, fig. 7: 91 / 25–6, fig. 10: 35, 128, 344.

[378] Sampson 1985, 131, 133 types 1–5, type 19, fig. 65: 29; ibid. 1988, 25–6, fig. 79: 102, 110.

[379] Popham and Sackett 1968, 8, fig. 7: 3.

[380] Goldman 1931, 104, fig. 133: 1 / 99–100, fig. 129: 1, fig. 133: 15.

[381] Tzavela-Evjen 1984, 150–1, 153, fig. 1α (first, third and fourth from the left), fig. 6α (1–4 from the left).

[382] Blegen 1951, pl. 43: A 16, 64, 65 / pls. 154a: A16, 156,

157, 176: 32.

[383] Bernabò Brea 1976, pls. CCIV: a–i, CCV: a–c.

[384] Goldman 1931, 104, fig. 133: 2.

[385] Tzavela-Evjen 1984, 152, type ΣΤ fig. 8α.

[386] Sampson 1985, 131, type 9, fig. 23: K 105.

[387] Caskey 1972, 372, fig 6: C18, C22.

[388] MacGillivray 1979, fig 13: 249.

[389] Mylonas 1959, fig. 118: 12, 14, 16, and 17.

[390] Papathanasopoulos 1961, pl. 50: α, Doumas 1977, fig. 11: g.

[391] MacGillivray 1979, fig. 8: 49–50.

[392] Doumas 1977, pls. XXXI: e, XLVII: e, XLIX: e–g–m.

[393] Tsountas 1899, pl. 9: 25.

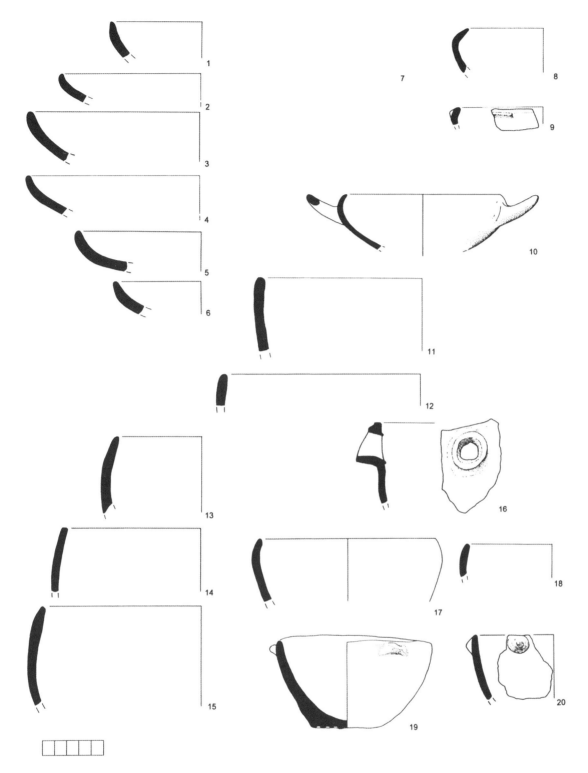

FIG. 7.16. Pottery of Markiani phase IV: shallow bowls (*1–10*) and deep bowls (*11–20*) (scale 1:3).

K 1212 (FIG. 7.17: 1, PLATE 36 *e*) was accompanied by numerous sherds found over the floor of Space 3 and is of H. 21.10 cm, D. max. 81 cm, and D. at rim 23–20 cm. The vessel is slightly elliptical in shape. The rim is strongly in-turned, just below which there are four arc-shaped lugs, two smaller than the other pair, placed diametrically opposite. Between the two lugs there is a figurative decoration of an incised schematic fish (FIG. 7.26: 17). Six other sherds (**K 1434**, FIG. 7.17: 2, **K 1435**, FIG. 7.17: 3, **K 1184**, FIG. 7.17: 4, **K 1191**, FIG. 7.17: 5, and **K 1199**, FIG. 7.17: 6) have arc-shaped lugs. Another eight non-catalogued sherds are of this type.

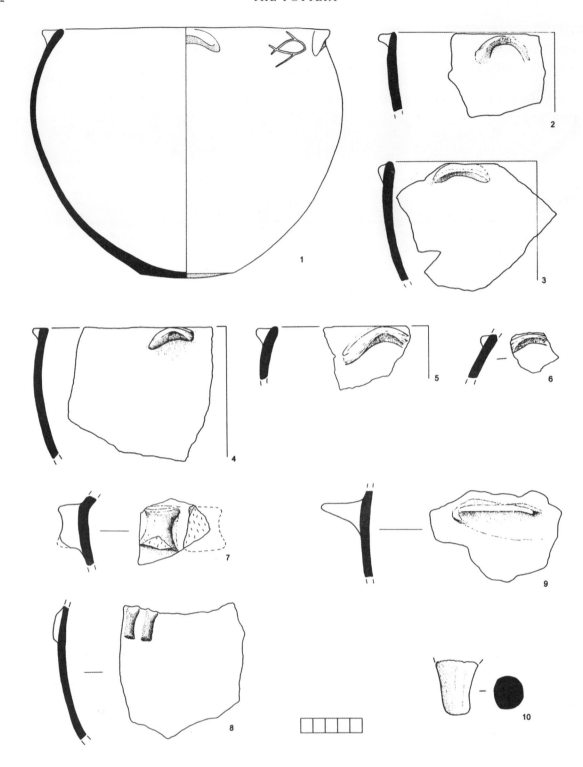

FIG. 7.17. Pottery of Markiani phase IV: deep bowls with lugs (*1–8*) etc. (scale 1:3).

Similar vessels with different type of lugs were found in Ma II and III (see above Chapters 7C and 7D). Typological parallels are known from Panormos on Naxos.[394]

Sherds **K 1422** (FIG. 7.17: 7), **K 1472** (FIG. 7.17: 8) and **K 1464** (FIG. 7.17: 9) have lugs of various shapes: vertical bobbin (FIG. 7.17: 7), two narrow vertical cylinders (FIG. 7.17: 8), or a horizontal flat lug. Due to their small size their designation as cooking vessels is not secure. Meanwhile, **K 1219** (FIG. 7.17: 10) is possibly a sherd of a cylindrical foot of a tripod vessel, probably a cooking vessel.

[394] Unpublished Doumas excavation.

3. *Large deep bowls (lekane)*

The rather thick walls (Th. 0.8–1.2 cm) and the large diameter of the rim (D. 22–42 cm) are the main characteristics which distinguish these vessels from other bowls. There are two different sub-types:

i.   *Large deep bowls with rather straight walls (lekanida)* (**K 1424**, **K 1443** and **K 1427**, FIG. 7.18: 1–3)

The shape of the body is somewhat conical. The rim is either slightly inturned (e.g. **K 1424**, FIG. 7.18: 1, and **K 1427**, FIG. 7.18: 3) or the wall is straight with rounded rim (e.g. **K 1443**, FIG. 7.18: 2). There are parallels with slightly different rim shapes at Manika.[395]

ii. *Large deep bowls with curved walls (lekanida)* (**K 1703**, **K 1462**, **K 1463**, **K 1185**, **K 1217** and **K 1179**, FIG. 7.18: 4–9)

The main characteristic of this sub-type is the horizontal flat rim which is sometimes out-turned, as for example **K 1462** (FIG. 7.18: 4), or in-turned (**K 1217**, FIG. 7.18: 8, and **K 1179**, FIG. 7.18: 6), or rounded like **K 1185** (FIG. 7.18: 5), with a perforation (D. 0.70 cm) on the wall below the rim. Sometimes these large bowls have handles, as in the case of the damaged horizontal handle of circular section in **K 1463** (FIG. 7.18: 7); or horizontal flat lugs as in the semi-preserved lower part of a large bowl, **K 1703** (FIG. 7.18: 9), with flat base, refitted from many sherds and found *in situ* above Floor 'a' of Space 3 (see PLATE 24.2). Another two non-catalogued sherds are of this type. Parallels for this type with incurving walls, sometimes with slightly different rim shape, are known from Kynthos (group A/B),[396] Ayia Irini period II,[397] and Lithares.[398] They seem to be dated to the later part of EC II sequence.

4. *One handled cups, tankards* (**K 1224**, **K 1441**, **K 1188**, **K 1223**, **K 1115**, **K 1182** and **K 1225**, FIG. 7.19: 1–7, PLATE 35 *a–d*)

The fabric used for this form is one of the very few fine wares found in Markiani. The body has a roughly spherical lower part usually with a flat base (e.g. **K 1224**, FIG. 7.19: 6), and a conical wide-mouthed, funnel-like neck (e.g. **K 1225**, FIG. 7.19: 1), joined at an oblique angle at the shoulder; it also has one vertical handle with circular section (**K 1188** (FIG. 7.19: 5), **K 1223** (FIG. 7.19: 2, PLATE 35 *b*), **K 1182** (FIG. 7.19: 4, PLATE 35 *c*). Some, such as **K 1441** (FIG. 7.19: 23) and **K 1223**, are burnished.

K 1115 (FIG. 7.19: 7, PLATE 35 *d*) has an additional feature: at the rim there is a small spout, making this a unique piece. Furthermore, the fabric suggests that this may be an import.

The fabric of the remaining sherds, with the further exception of **K 1225** (Micaceous Ware), is Red Shale, which is regarded as a local product. Another 24 non-catalogued neck or body sherds (of Red Shale or Micaceous Wares) are of tankards. Most of these come from the circular Space 7 and from Space 6; there were also some pieces on the floor of Space 3.

Parallels are known from Chalandriani on Syros[399], Ayia Irini period III,[400] Kynthos (group B),[401] Siphnos,[402] Panormos,[403] Lefkandi phase I,[404] Manika,[405] Orchomenos,[406] Eutresis,[407] Poliochni Red and Yellow periods,[408] Lebena on Crete[409], and from Tarsus in Cilicia.[410]

This shape is generally regarded as typical of the Kastri Group in the Cyclades and the Lefkandi I group on the mainland and is a characteristic shape of EB III. It is sometimes seen as originating in Asia Minor[411] or the north-east Aegean.[412] It has been dated to the end of EC II, to the transitional EC II–III phase and to the beginning of EC III period (EC IIIA).[413]

5. *Depas amphikypellon, two-handled cup* (**K 1723**, FIG. 7.19: 8, PLATE 35 *a*)

The term 'depas amphikypellon', first used by Schliemann,[414] refers to a narrow and deep cylindrical cup with two diametrically placed loop handles and a flat base of thin fine fabric. The Markiani

[395] Sampson 1985, 131 — type 9, 124, pl. 10: 9, fig. 6: P 54, 7: P 59.
[396] MacGillivray 1979, fig. 13: 100, 202, 207/ fig. 14: 253, 383–5.
[397] Caskey 1972, 366, fig. 4: B 58.
[398] Tzavela-Evjen 1984, 151 — type B, fig. 4β (the third and fourth from the left).
[399] Tsountas 1899, pl. 9: 5; Zervos 1957, fig. 184.
[400] Caskey 1972, fig. 6: C45, C46, pl. 80: C1, C9, C42–44.
[401] MacGillivray 1979, fig. 9: 14–16, 58–63, 119, 299–302, 322, 434.
[402] Tsountas 1899, pl. 9: 11; Zervos 1957, fig. 183.
[403] Doumas 1977, fig. 11c; Marangou 1990, 178 [188]
[404] Rutter 1979, 7, table 2, fig. 1: 3–4.

[405] Sampson 1985, fig. 59, 59α: 25, 64α: 58.
[406] Kunze 1934, pl. XXII: 2–4.
[407] Goldman 1931, fig. 138.
[408] Bernabò Brea 1964, pl. CXLIII: a–f; idem 1976, pl. CCVIII: a–i.
[409] Renfrew 1972, fig. 20.4: 2.
[410] Goldman 1956, pl. 266: 467.
[411] Renfrew 1972, 170; Rutter 1979, 6; MacGillivray 1980, 25.
[412] Doumas 1988, 23, 28.
[413] Renfrew 1972, 103, 533; Rutter 1979, 20; Barber and MacGillivray 1980, 143, table 1; Doumas 1988, 23.
[414] Schliemann 1881.

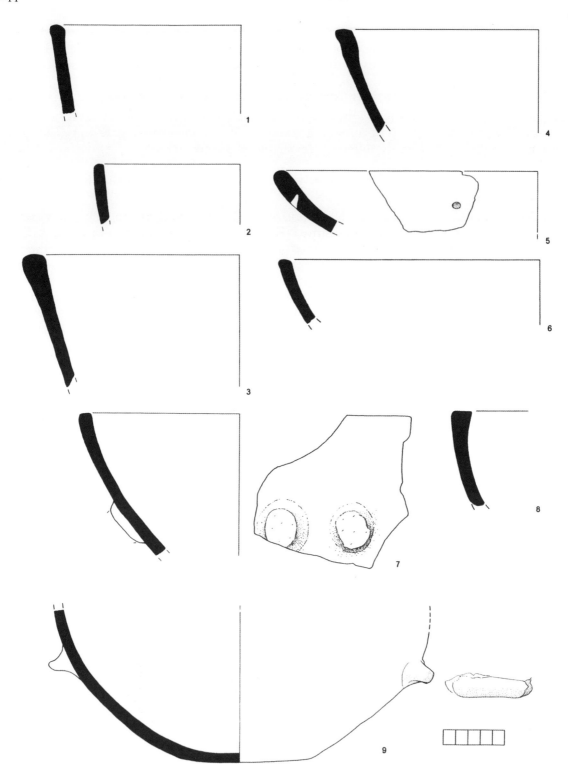

FIG. 7.18. Pottery of Markiani phase IV: deep bowls (scale 1:3).

example, **K 1732**, was not intact. Most of the upper part of body and one of the two handles were missing, while the other is partially preserved. Its dimensions are H. 17.40 cm, D. base 5.80 cm, D. handle 1.70 cm and Th. 0.60 cm. It has a rather high cylindrical body and a slightly concave base. The handle is vertical with circular section, beginning just above the base and ending at the upper body well below the rim, which is not preserved. It is heavily burnished, dark brown in colour. The upper part of the interior is also burnished. It is classified as of the Marble C fabric, which is regarded as local to Markiani. It was found within the circular feature of Space 7 (see also PLATE 15 *b*).

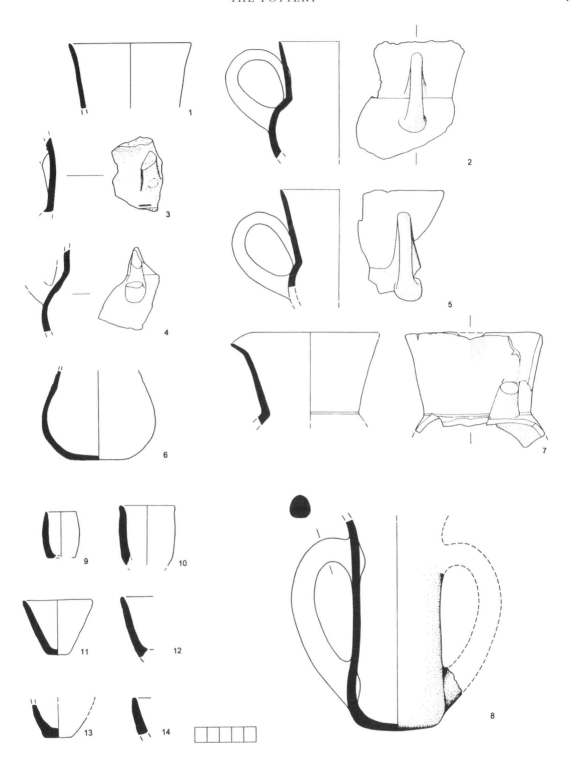

FIG. 7.19. Pottery of Markiani phase IV: tankards (*1–7*), depas (*8*) and cups (*9–14*) (scale 1:3).

According to Blegen this form appears for the first time in Troy IIc and is frequently seen in Troy III. It is also very common in Poliochni Yellow period,[415] at the Tomb of Protesilaos,[416] in Aphrodisias[417] and in Tarsus.[418]

[415] Bernabò Brea 1976, pls. CXCI: a–e, CXCII: a–e.
[416] Demangel 1926, 60, fig. 78.
[417] Joukowski-Sharp 1986, 391, fig. 324.
[418] Goldman 1956, fig. 265.

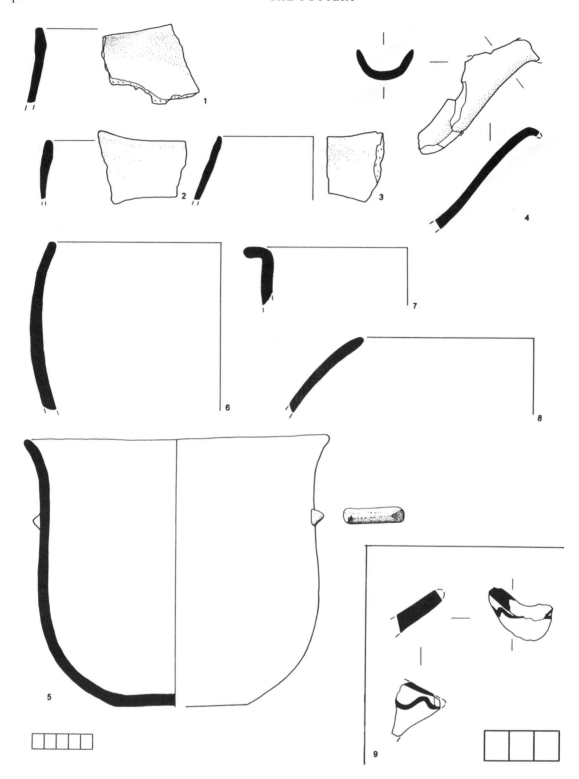

FIG. 7.21. Pottery of Markiani phase IV: sauceboats and other vessels (scale 1:3; no. 9 at scale 2/3).

from the edge of the spout: **K 1230/ K 1770** (FIG. 7.21: 4, PLATE 36 c). This, like the two preceding examples are of Marble Ware and were found in the interior of the circular feature of Space 7.

From the same location, **K 1722** (FIG. 7.21: 9, PLATE 38 g) is also a spout fragment but it is remarkable in having painted decoration of dark brown paint on a pale, whitish well burnished fabric: a band runs along the edge of the spout and there is a thin wavy line below. The thickness of the spout suggests that it is part of a spouted jug. The fabric resembles that of the fine painted wares of Naxos (e.g. Spedos), Syros and Dhaskalio–Kavos on Keros. This, along with the three sherds discussed below, is one of the few sherds of Ma IV firmly regarded as an import.

For this shape there are parallels from other sites on Amorgos,[441] Chalandriani on Syros,[442] Panormos on Naxos,[443] Ayia Irini on Kea (periods II and III),[444] and Kynthos on Delos (group A/B),[445] On the Greek mainland sauceboats are widely known from sites including Ayios Kosmas,[446] Lerna (period III),[447] Zygouries[448] and Eutresis.[449] They are also attested at Poliochni (Green and Red periods),[450] Thermi (period V) on Lesbos,[451] and Troy (period I and II).[452]

9. Deep wide-mouthed vessels (jars) (**K 1426**, **K 1445**, **K 1204** and **K 1433**, FIG. 7.21: 5–8)

The almost half-preserved vase **K 1426** (FIG. 7.21: 5) is assigned to a bell-shaped wide-mouthed vessel. The rim is slightly out-turned. The walls are straight and the base flat. A narrow horizontal lug is attached to the body. On the exterior surface there is red slip. The vessel is heavily burnished and the firing is imperfect. The ware of Gneissose fabric is believed to be an import.

Sherd **K 1445** (FIG. 7.21: 6) is a deep wide-mouthed open vessel with slightly in-turned rounded rim. It is of Micaceous Ware. For this and one more non-catalogued sherd there are parallels from Kynthos (group A/B) differing slightly at the rim,[453] Ayia Irini (periods II and III),[454] the EH II at Rouf in Athens,[455] and Manika (periods II and III).[456] The rim sherd **K 1433** (FIG. 7.21: 7) of a deep cylindrical vessel is of Blue Schist Ware C: the rim is so far out-turned as to project horizontally outwards.

The rim **K 1204** (FIG. 7.21: 8) of a narrow-mouthed, closed vessel is of Marble Ware C. Parallels are known from Kynthos (group A/B)[457] and Ayia Irini (periods II and III).[458]

10. Collared jar with slashed handles (stamnos) (**K 1436**, **K 1232**, **K 1192**, **K 1444**, **K 1423**, **K 1198**, **K 1207** and **K 1189** FIG. 7.22: 1–5 and 9–11, PLATE 36 d)

These vessels have a spherical body, low cylindrical neck and two horizontal slashed handles at the belly, usually decorated with incisions on the upper surface. The rim is usually out-turned and the base flat. The size varies. This shape also occurs in Ma III (see also FIG. 7.14: 6, PLATE 33 f).

Seven cylindrical necks (e.g. **K 1436**, FIG. 7.22: 2; **K 1232**, FIG. 7.22: 1; **K 1192**, FIG. 7.22: 4, and **K 1444**, FIG. 7.22: 3) and two body sherds with horizontal incised handles **K 1423** (FIG. 7.22: 9, PLATE 36 d), **K 1198** (FIG. 7.22: 5) are either of Blue Schist Ware or Marble Ware. The type (with or without incised handles) is known from other EC / EH sites on Amorgos,[459] Akrotiri on Thera,[460] Christiana,[461] Ayia Irini,[462] Kynthos (group A/B) on Delos,[463] Panormos on Naxos,[464] Eutresis,[465] Lerna (IV),[466] Ayios Kosmas,[467] Poliochni[468] and from the Heraion on Samos.[469]

There are fourteen more handles of this type, e.g. **K 1207** (FIG. 7.22: 11) and **K 1189** (FIG. 7.22: 10, PLATE 36 d). These have been found in both settlements and cemeteries and are characteristic of the EC II period.[470] They are also known from Kastri on Syros,[471] Kynthos on Delos (group A/B),[472] Ayia Irini (periods II and III),[473] Ayii Anargyroi on Naxos,[474] from various sites on Amorgos[475] and from Christiana near Thear.[476]

11. Stemmed collared jar (crateriskos) (**K 1449**, **K 1453** and **K 2010**, FIG. 7.22: 6–8, PLATE 38 c)

This shape has quite a high conical neck with out-turned rim (e.g. **K 1449**, FIG. 7.22: 6), joined to a roughly hemispherical body which rests on a conical or bell-shaped pedestal, e.g. **K 2010** (FIG. 7.22: 8). **K 1453** (FIG. 7.22: 7, PLATE 38 c) has a decoration with fish-bone incisions just below the rim. The sherds are of Marble Ware and Blue Schist Ware.

---

[441] Tsountas 1898, pl. 9: 7.
[442] Tsountas 1899, pl. 9: 1, 8.
[443] Renfrew 1972, fig. 20.4: 5.
[444] Caskey 1972, pl. 78: B16.
[445] MacGillivray 1979, fig. 8: 4, 290–2, 412, 432.
[446] Mylonas 1959, drawing 52: S12.
[447] Renfrew 1972, fig. 7.1.
[448] Blegen 1928, fig. 66: 255, 78–81.
[449] Goldman 1931, fig. 117, 118, 127, 129, 130.
[450] Bernabò Brea 1964, pl. CXXIX: c.
[451] Lamb 1936, fig. 32: 251.
[452] Blegen 1950, pl. 252: 5, 12, and 17.
[453] MacGillivray 1979, fig. 8; 55, fig. 13: 188.
[454] Caskey 1972, fig. 4: B48–B52, 6: C19–22.
[455] Petrikaki 1980, fig. 49.
[456] Sampson 1985, types 4, 8, 12, 15, 18, 20, 23.
[457] MacGillivray 1979, fig. 8: 55, fig. 13: 188.
[458] Caskey 1972, fig. 4: B48, B51.
[459] Marangou 1984, fig. 15 a.

[460] Sotirakopoulou 1986, pl. 19 a-4188.
[461] Doumas 1976a, fig. 6 (1829), pl. 3γ.
[462] Caskey 1972, fig. 3: B13, fig. 7: C17.
[463] MacGillivray 1979, fig. 12: 4, 43, 225, 226.
[464] Unpublished, Christos Doumas excavation.
[465] Goldman 1931, fig. 159.
[466] Rutter 1984, fig. 1: b.
[467] Mylonas 1959, il.117: 14.
[468] Bernabò Brea 1976, pl. CCXXIV: d.
[469] Milojcic 1961, pl. 40: 3.
[470] Doumas 1976a, 7, n. 6.
[471] Tsountas 1898, pl. 9, 37; ibid. 1899, 122.
[472] MacGillivray 1980, fig. 15, 392, fig. 20, 408–10, pl. 11, 408–10.
[473] Caskey 1972, pl. 79, B44.
[474] Doumas 1977, pl. XLIV, e.
[475] Marangou 1984, figs. 2, 3, 4, 7, 8.
[476] Doumas 1976a, 7.

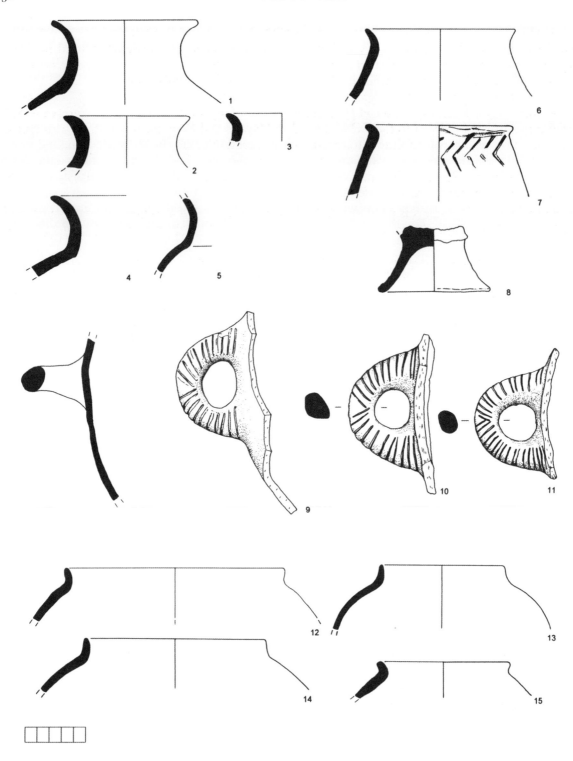

FIG. 7.22. Pottery of Markiani phase IV: collared jars (*1–11*) and spherical pyxides (*12–15*) (scale 1:3).

Similar examples are known from other EC sites on Amorgos,[477] Akrotiri on Thera,[478] Naxos,[479] Kato Kouphonisi,[480] and from the N. P. Goulandris Collection.[481] These stemmed collared jars were formerly assigned to the 'Amorgos Group'.[482]

[477] Marangou 1984, 101, 6, fig. 17.
[478] Sotirakopoulou 1986, fig. 2: 4191, pl. 19: b.
[479] Papathanasopoulos 1961, pl. 50: β–γ.
[480] Zapheiropoulou 1970, pl. 373: α.

[481] Doumas 1978, 141–2, cat. no. 231–2.
[482] Renfrew 1972, 534–5; Doumas 1977, 23, 25–6; Barber and MacGillivray 1980, 143, table 1; Sotirakopoulou 1986, 306, 309.

12. Spherical or lentoid storage vessel (pyxis) (**K 1175**, **K 1200**, **K 1477** and **K 1209**, FIG. 7.22: 12–15)

This shape has a spherical or lentoid body with a low cylindrical neck and straight rounded rim. Four rim sherds **K 1175** (FIG. 7.22: 13), **K 1200** (FIG. 7.22: 14), **K 1477** (FIG. 7.22: 12) and **K 1209** (FIG. 7.22: 15), and part of a body were found in Ma IV. Most are of Blue Schist Ware.

The form is known from Kynthos (group A/B),[483] Ayia Irini (period III),[484] Ano Kouphonisi,[485] Kastri on Syros,[486] Ayios Kosmas,[487] the EH II settlement at Rouf in Athens,[488] Lithares[489] and Knossos.[490] The Cycladic examples are dated to the EC II period.[491] However, their presence in Ayia Irini (period III) is evidence for the survival of the type into the early part of EC III.[492]

13. Pithoi or pithoid vessels (**K 1437**, **K 1218**, **K 1216**, **K 1210**, **K 1483**, **K 1208**, **K 1468**, **K 1471**, **K 1222** and **K 1221** FIG. 7.23: 1–10)

This shape is of Coarse Ware and is a wide-mouthed storage vessel with a somewhat egg-shaped body and a thick, projecting, usually horizontal rim. Sometimes there are wide vertical strap handles on the lower part of the body.

Six sherds of the projecting horizontal rim were found, i.e. **K 1218** (FIG. 7.23: 2), **K 1216** (FIG. 7.23: 5), **K 1483** (FIG. 7.23: 6) and **K 1208** (FIG. 7.23: 4). Sherds **K 1210** (FIG. 7.23: 1) has a flat and wide horizontal projecting rim with incised herringbone decoration on its upper surface and **K 1437** (FIG. 7.23: 3) has a strongly rounded projecting rim, has a relief button-like decoration on the body just below the rim. Eleven more body sherds are of this shape, mostly of Marble Ware. This type of pithoid vessel is known from Kynthos (group A/B) and is dated to EC II to III.[493]

Wide vertical strap handles (**K 1468**, FIG. 7.23: 7, of Blue Schist Ware, **K 1471**, FIG. 7.23: 8, of Dark Grey Marble Ware, and **K 1222**, FIG. 7.23: 9, and **K 1221**, FIG. 7.23: 10, of Marble A Ware) are also of this shape. They are known from Ayia Irini (periods II and III),[494] Akrotiri on Thera,[495] and Manika,[496] and are dated from the late EC II to the early EC III period.

14. Jugs (prochoi) (**K 1452**, **K 1231**, FIG. 7.24: 1–2, PLATE 36 *b*)

This is a wide-mouthed globular jug with a vertically placed cylindrical-sectioned handle which joins at the rim. **K 1452** (FIG. 7.24: 1, PLATE 36 *b*) has a slightly out-turned rim and is of Blue Schist Ware, while **K 1231** (FIG. 7.24: 2) is Marble A Ware. They are known from other sites on Amorgos including Kato Akrotiri.[497] Examples of unknown provenance in the N. P. Goulandris Collection are similar.[498] The shape was formerly assigned to the so-called 'Amorgos Group'.

15. Small pithos (**K 1432**, FIG. 7.24: 3, PLATE 38 *c*)

This is an egg-shaped vessel with a small ring neck and out-turned rim (**K 1432**). It is decorated just below the rim with an incised fish-bone motif. It is of Marble Ware A. Parallels are known from other sites on Amorgos, exhibited in the Amorgos Archaeological Collection.[499] The form is also attested at Kynthos (group A/B),[500] Akrotiri on Thera,[501] the EH II settlement at Rouf in Athens.[502]

16. Horizontal handles (**K 1183**, **K 1194**, **K 1195** and **K 1211** and FIG. 7.24: 4–7)

K 1183 (FIG. 7.24: 4) is a sherd of a spherical body with part of a horizontal handle. **K 1194** (FIG. 7.24: 5), **K 1195** (FIG. 7.24: 6) and **K 1211** (FIG. 7.24: 7) are parts of horizontal handles of circular or ovoid section. Such handles are not easy to assign to a particular closed shape.

17. Bases

There are 35 sherds of usually flat bases.

---

[483] MacGillivray 1979, fig. 8, 9, 13, 54, 114, 297.
[484] Wilson and Eliot 1984, fig. 2, b.
[485] Zapheiropoulou 1984, fig. 1, d.
[486] Bossert 1967, fig. 4, 2.
[487] Mylonas 1959, 26, S19, 71, C19, fig. 131, 51, fig. 147, 205, fig. 150, 209.
[488] Petrikaki 1980, fig. 40.
[489] Tzavela-Evjen 1984, fig. 13, b.
[490] Warren 1972a, fig. 3. Although according to Christos Doumas these sherds are imported from the Cyclades, Doumas 1976b, 71–2.
[491] Barber and MacGillivray 1980, 150; Doumas 1976b, 72, Renfrew 1972, 172.
[492] Wilson and Eliot 1984, 81 and 83.

[493] MacGillivray 1979, fig. 14, 270, 271, 398–400.
[494] Caskey 1972, pl. 81, C53.
[495] Sotirakopoulou 1986, pl. 18, b (3112), c (4187), d (5793).
[496] Sampson 1985, fig. 20, K 25, K61.
[497] Tsountas 1898, pl. 9, 19, 20; Zervos 1957, fig. 68–9; Doumas 1977, fig. 12, a, b, c.
[498] Doumas 1984, 152 (187 — Inv. No 229).
[499] One intact example comes from Giannades near Kolophana Amorgos Archaeological Collection 294, unpublished; Marangou 1984, 101, no. 22, fig. 12.
[500] MacGillivray 1979, fig. 12, 371.
[501] Sotirakopoulou 1986, fig. 2, 5797.
[502] Petrikaki 1980, fig. 56.

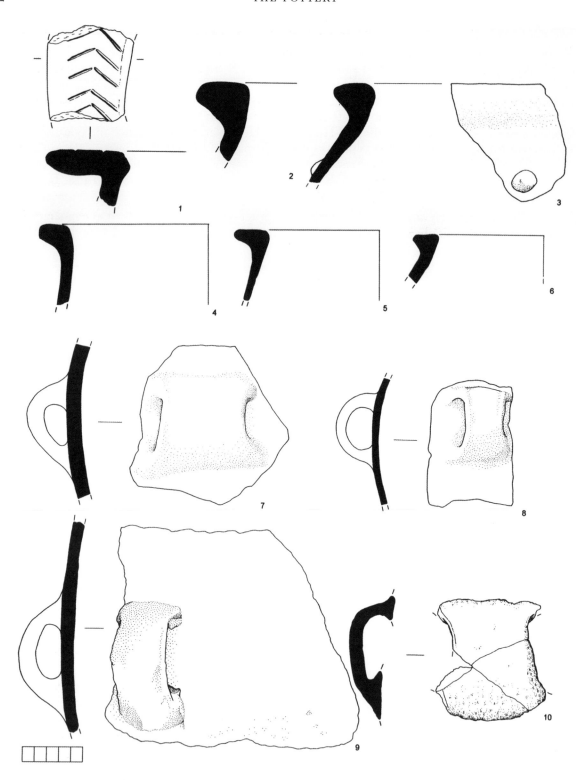

FIG. 7.23. Pottery of Markiani phase IV: pithos and handles (scale 1:3).

i.   *Bases with mat and leaf-impressions* (**K 1355**, **K 1364**, **K 1365**, **K 1386**, **K 1193** and **K 1304** FIG.
     7.24: 10, PLATE 46 *a*)
     All of these are of Coarse Ware and are assigned to Marble Ware A. Mat and leaf impressions on
     pot bases (see Chapter 8C) are very common both in the Cyclades and on the Greek mainland
     during the EBA.[503]

[503] Some such examples include Tsountas 1898, pl. 9; Doumas   fig. 89–91. See also Chapter 8C.
1977, pl. XLIII, f; MacGillivray 1979, pl. 9, 279; Zervos 1957,

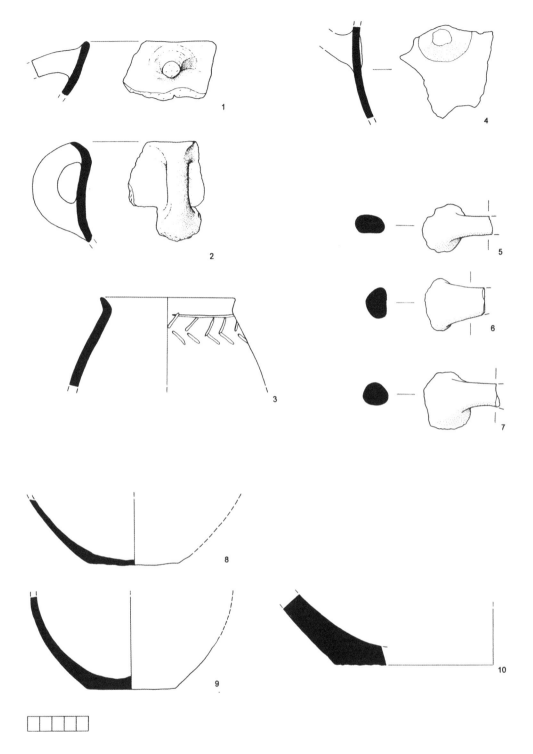

FIG. 7.24. Pottery of Markiani phase IV: jugs etc. (scale 1:3).

ii. *Bases of non-identifiable shapes* (**K 1469** and **K 1478**, FIG. 7.24: 8–9)
     Two sherds are of small vessels of Coarse Ware.

18. Braziers, 'mask-like' support vessels (krateutes) (**EE 251, K 1379, K 1540, K 1220 K 1621**, and **K 1664**, FIG. 7.25: 1–5, PLATE 37 *a–f*)
These are vessels of Coarse Ware with a distinctive form and are probably for household use. Braziers are known from the previous phases Ma II (see FIG. 7.10: 1–3, PLATE 32 *e*) and III (see FIG. 7.15,= new number PLATE 34 *a–f*). There is one a nearly intact brazier, **EE 251** from Space 2 (see also PLATE 19.3) and five sherds from Ma IV.

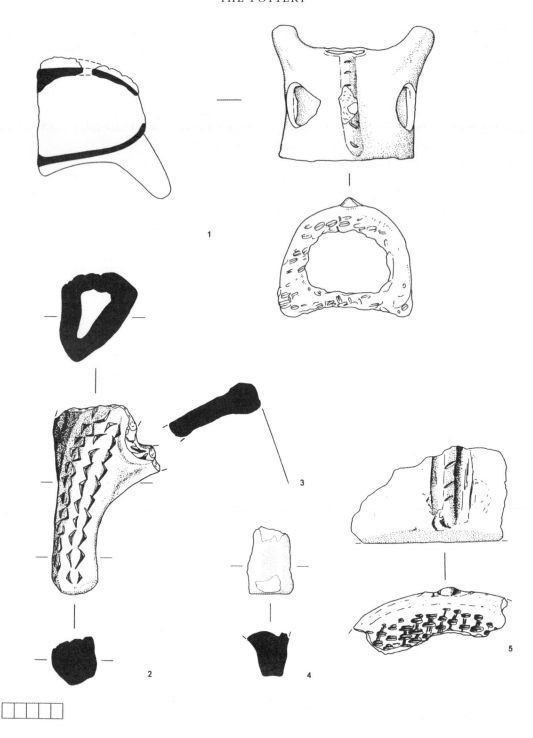

FIG. 7.25. Pottery of Markiani phase IV: braziers or supports (scale 1:3).

The intact brazier **EE 251** (FIG. 7.25: 1, PLATE 37 *a–e*) has a rounded ovoid body with a very wide mouth, and a flat lower surface, with two protuberances or 'feet' at the rear. The function of the object is not clear: in form it resembles **K 1704** of Ma III (FIG. 7.15, PLATE 34 *a–f*), but lacks the handle on the upper surface. It might have been used for carrying hot embers, although the lack of a handle makes this problematic. Another possibility is that such objects were one of a pair, together supporting a metal or wooden spit running between them: in short an andiron.[504] The conclusion as to function determines the orientation in which the object should be viewed. In FIG. 7.25: 1 it is seen in left-facing section, and (to the right) with the aperture facing the viewer. Below it is seen rotated through 90

---

[504] Tzavela-Evjen 1984, 172–3.

degrees, with the aperture at the base and indeed that is the position in which the object was left to dry prior to firing, since there are mat impressions to document this. There is one aperture at the rear, above the legs/protuberances. On the upper surface or 'back' there is an appliqué ridge, on each side of which there is a perforation.

When the object is place mouth-downwards (as in FIG. 7.25: 1 upper row right), the two legs/protuberances project upwards and might be considered as 'ears', while the ridge or the back with flanking apertures could be viewed as nose and eyes, hence the suggestion originally made by Dümmler in relation to a find from Kapros on Amorgos that it was a 'mask-like' object.[505]

Sherd **K 1379** (FIG. 7.25: 5) is part of the upper convex surface of such an object with a narrow relief band with deep oblique incisions on the upper surface and part of the mouth with the mat impressions as in **EE 251. K 1540** (FIG. 7.25: 2, PLATE 37 *f*) is a horn-shaped foot and part of the mouth of a brazier. It is decorated with two rows of impressed triangles. There are similar examples from Lithares.[506]

Sherd **K 1220** (FIG. 7.25: 3), is part of the convex upper surface and the mouth of a brazier. Along the line of the mouth there is a series of finger impressions. **K 1621** (FIG. 7.25: 4) is part of the horn-shaped foot of a smaller brazier. Most of these are of Marble Ware with the exception of **K 1220**, which is of Blue Schist Ware A.

The type is known from other sites on Amorgos[507] and Naxos.[508]

19. Body sherds with linear or other incised decoration

Most of the decorated sherds are body sherds of various vessels. The decoration is usually incised on the outer surface before the firing. Most of the motifs are linear and are assigned to categories on the basis of shape:

i. *Sherds with linear decoration:*

(a) Herringbone incisions along a horizontal axis **K 1467** (FIG. 7.26: 1, PLATE 38 *d*). This sherd may be from a conical pyxis of a form seen in the Phylakopi I culture.
(b) Shallow linear incisions (**K 1488, K 1489**, FIG. 7.26: 2; **K 1492**, FIG. 7.26: 3; **K 1496**, FIG. 7.26: 4; **K 1497**, FIG. 7.26: 5; **K 1635**, FIG. 7.26: 7; and **K 1493**, FIG. 7.26: 6).
(c) Deep incision (**K 1494**, FIG. 7.26: 8).
(d) Incisions intersecting at an acute angle or at right angles (**K 1227**, FIG. 7.26: 9; **K 1228**, FIG. 7.26: 10; and **K 1226**, FIG. 7.26: 11, PLATE 38 *b*).
(e) Zigzag incisions (**K 1491**, FIG. 7.26: 12, PLATE 38 *b*; and **K 1708**).
(f) Curved incisions (**K 1495**, FIG. 7.26: 13; **K 1498**, FIG. 7.26: 14; and **K 1490**, FIG. 7.26: 16).

ii. *Sherds with figurative motifs:*

(a) Probable double axe (**K 1229**, FIG. 7.26: 15, PLATE 38 *b*).
(b) Fish incised decoration (**K 1244**, FIG. 7.26: 18, PLATE 38 *a*; and the almost intact deep bowl **K 1212**, FIGS. 7.17: 1 and 7.26: 17, PLATE 36 *e*).

Similar decorative motifs are known from Phylakopi,[509] Ayia Irini,[510] Lerna,[511] and Zygouries.[512] The repertoire of incised motifs in Ma IV is very limited: the sherds described represent almost the totality of the incised sherds recovered from the strata under consideration.

20. Sherds with painted decoration

Only three sherds with painted decoration were observed from levels of phase Ma IV, and only one of these (**K 1722**, described under sauceboats and spouted vessels, above) was found in the layers chosen for description. It is however worth mentioning for the record that two body sherds with painted decoration, presumed to be imports, were found in other levels of phase IV:

A body sherd **K 1710** (FIG. 7.26: 19, PLATE 38 *e*), from Trench 1,5, layer 60, is of Pale Buff fabric with uniform matt brown painted rectilinear decoration.

Another body sherd **EE 161/K 1711** (PLATE 38 *f*), from Trench 1,2 layer 15, is of Micaceous Brown Biscuit with Buff Slip and two intersecting broad straight lines of brown paint.

---

[505] Dümmler 1876, Beil. 2, 1
[506] Tzavela-Evjen 1984, pl. 89, γ.
[507] Dümmler 1886, Beil. 2, 1.
[508] Marangou 1990*b*, 56 [22]; Zervos 1957, fig. 100.

[509] Atkinson *et al.* 1904, 177–84.
[510] Halepa-Bikaki 1984, pl. 10, VI–1, pl. 16, III–1, pl. 25, VII–5.
[511] Caskey 1956, 168, pl. 45f (second), 46a (first).
[512] Blegen 1928, 107, fig. 92 (right).

FIG. 7.26. Pottery of Markiani phase IV: decorated sherds: incised (*1–18*) and painted (*19*) (scale 1:3).

It is to be noted that in addition to these three painted sherds, only one sherd of apparently imported Urfirnis fabric was noted in phase IV levels. This is **EE 074** (not illustrated), from Trench 1,1 layer 25, a body sherd of dark brown/black Urfirnis fabric. Recognition of these three painted sherds and one Urfirnis sherd emphasises the rarity of imported fine wares in Ma IV.

General remarks
Along with the common shapes which phase IV shares with phase III, new shapes emerge such as the one-handled cup or tankard and the depas amphikypellon, both characteristic of the Kastri Group. In addition there are wide-mouthed jugs, spherical-lentoid pyxides and spouted vessels.

The tankard and the depas, characteristic of the Kastri Group, came into use with spherical–lentoid pyxides, characteristic of the pottery of the Keros–Syros (EC II) period, and also present at Ayia Irini period III on Kea.[513] The same applies to the wide-mouthed jugs and footed jars, *crateriskoi* of the so-called 'Amorgos Group', dated to the late phase of EC II / early EC III[514]

It is generally accepted that the 'Lefkandi I'[515] pottery of the Greek mainland is closely related to the Kastri Group of the Cyclades,[516] as seen at the type site on Syros,[517] Ayia Irini phase III,[518] Mount Kynthos on Delos,[519] Akrotiri on Thera[520] and now in Ma IV.

Much has been written about the chronology of the Kastri Group and we are in agreement with Sotirakopoulou who places it late in the EBA ('EC III'), following on from the Keros-Syros culture, as seen for instance at Ayia Irini II,[521] and probably earlier than but perhaps overlapping with the Phylakopi I phase on Melos.

The Ma IV assemblage supports this view, displaying continuity with the pottery of phase III, along with the introduction of these new forms. The general chronological assessment is confirmed by the radiocarbon determinations for the site.[522] Some scholars have emphasised the parallels between these shapes, notably the tankard and the depas, and those of the north-east Aegean,[523] including Troy. There are remarkable similarities and it seems possible that some of these shapes first appeared in that region. However, there is no evident discontinuity at Markiani and these vessels, with forms of 'Trojan' origin, seem mainly to be of local fabrics and consequently of local production.

TABLE 7.18 (p. 166) sets out a complete list of the catalogued pottery from Markiani phase IV.

---

[513] Caskey 1972, 373–5.

[514] Renfrew 1972, 534–5; Doumas 1977, 23, 25–6; Barber and MacGillivray 1980, 143, table 1; Sotirakopoulou 1986, 306, 309.

[515] Popham and Sacket 1968.

[516] Renfrew 1972.

[517] Bossert 1967.

[518] Wilson 1999.

[519] MacGillivray 1980

[520] Sotirakopoulou 1999

[521] Rutter 1979, 15; Barber and MacGillivray 1980, 147, table II: Sotirakopoulou 1999.

[522] Chapter 5.

[523] Doumas 1988, 24.

TABLE 7.7 continued.

Shape	FIG.	Cat. no.	PLATE	Trench/layer	Fabric
Deep hemispherical or conical bowl with thin walls, 'Kouphonisia' type bowl	7.7: 2	K 1168	30 c	Trench 7 layer 8	Marble Red Slip and Burnished
	7.7: 3	K 1123		Trench 1,1 layer 6	Marble Red Slip and Burnished
	7.7: 4	K 1633 a+b		Trench 7 layer 14	Marble Red Slip and Burnished
Deep bowl with in-turned rim	7.7: 5	K 1157	30 c	Trench 7 layer 9	Marble
	7.7: 6	K 1135	30 c	Trench 7 layer 12	Marble Red Slip and Burnished
	7.7: 7	K 1170		Trench 7 layer 8	Marble
Deep bowls of various sub-types	7.7: 8	K 1627		Trench 7 layer 12	Marble
	7.7: 9	K 1596		Trench 7 layer 2	Marble
	7.7: 10	K 1141		Trench 7 layer 10	Marble
Deep bowl with straight or in-turned profile and thickened in-turned rim	7.8: 1	K 1131		Trench 7 layer 14	Marble
	7.8: 2	K 1161		Trench 7 layer 9	Marble
	7.8: 3	K 1147		Trench 7 layer 9	Marble
	7.8: 4	K 1158		Trench 7 layer 9	Marble
	7.8: 5	K 1163		Trench 7 layer 9	Marble
Deep bowl with thickened out-turned rim and crescent-shaped lugs	7.8: 6	K 1159		Trench 7 layer 9	Marble
	7.8: 7	K 1169		Trench 7 layer 8	Marble
	7.8: 8	K 1134	31 c	Trench 7 layer 12	Marble
Small deep bowl	7.8: 9	K 1144		Trench 7 layer 9	Marble
Crescent-shaped lugs of deep bowls or storage vessels	7.8: 10	K 1128		Trench 7 layer 14	Marble
	7.8: 11	K 1172		Trench 7 layer 8	Marble
	7.8: 12	K 1153		Trench 7 layer 9	Marble
	7.8: 13	K 1142		Trench 7 layer 9	Marble
	7.8: 14	K 1606		Trench 7 layer 7	Marble
Baking pan or plate	7.9: 1	K 1624	31 c	Trench 7 layer 12	Marble
	7.9: 2	K 1625	31 c	Trench 7 layer 12	Marble
	7.9: 3	K 1622	31 c	Trench 7 layer 10	Marble
	7.9: 4	K 1638	31 c	Trench 7 layer 15	Marble
Small storage vessels	7.9: 5	K 1154		Trench 7 layer 9	Marble
	7.9: 6	K 1611		Trench 7 layer 9	Marble
Bases of household vessels	7.9: 7	K 1146		Trench 7 layer 9	Marble
	7.9: 8	K 1623		Trench 7 layer 12	Marble
	7.9: 9	K 1173		Trench 7 layer 8	Marble
Clay spoons	7.9: 10	K 1613		Trench 7 layer 9	Marble
	7.9: 12	K 1612	32 a	Trench 7 layer 9	Marble
	7.9: 11	K 1628		Trench 7 layer 12	Marble
Braziers or 'mask-like' support vessels	7.10: 1	K 1174 + K 1592 + 1593	32 e	Trench 7 layers 3 and 8	Marble and Schist
	7.10: 2	K 1165		Trench 7 layer 9	Marble
	7.10: 3	K 1626		Trench 7 layer 12	Marble
Mobile hat-shaped hearths	7.10: 4	K 1594	32 d	Trench 7 layer 3	Marble
	7.10: 5	K 1595	32 b	Trench 7 layer 3	Marble
	7.10: 6	K 1639	32 c	Trench 7 layer 15	Marble
	7.10: 7	K 1641	32 c	Trench 1,1 layer 20	Marble
Fine ware/decorated sherds	7.10: 8	K 1121		Trench 7 layer 4	Micaceous Urfirnis
	7.10: 9	K 1122		Trench 7 layer 6	Fine Buff Slip and Burnished

TABLE 7.8. The catalogued pottery from the interior of the Bastion.

Shape	FIG.	Cat. no.	PLATE	Trench/layer	Fabric
Spherical vessel (pyxis)	7.11:1	**K 1517**	32 *f*	Trench 8,1 layer 5	Marble
Small bowl with conical collar	7.11:2	**K 1529**	32 *f*	Trench 8,1 layer 1	Blue Schist
Rolled-rim bowl	7.11:3	**K 1520**		Trench 8,1 layer 11	Marble
Shallow bowls with thickened rim	7.11:4	**K 1516**		Trench 8,1 layer 4	Marble
Deep bowls	7.11:5	**K 1512**		Trench 8,1 layer 3	Marble
	7.11:6	**K 1519**		Trench 8,1 layer 9	Marble
Deep bowls with lugs	7.11,:11	**K 1514**		Trench 8,1 layer 3	Marble
	7.11,:10	**K 1515**		Trench 8,1 layer 3	Marble
Strainer	7.11:8	**K 1511**		Trench 8,1 layer 2	Marble
Storage vessel	–	**K 1518**		Trench 8,1 layer 6	Blue Schist
	7.11:7	**K 1513**		Trench 8,1 layer 3	Marble
Cooking vessel or oven	7.11:9	**K 1510**		Trench 8,1 layer 2	Marble

TABLE 7.9. The catalogued pottery from outside the Bastion.

Shape	FIG.	Cat. no.	PLATE	Trench/layer	Fabric
Deep bowl with lugs	7.11:12	**K 1535**		Trench 8,6 layer 3	Blue Schist
Deep bowl with thickened rim	7.11:13	**K 1538**		Trench 8,2 layer 8	Blue schist
Collared jar or jug	7.11:14	**K 1528**		Trench 8,2 layer 14	Blue Schist
Deep bowls with crescent-shaped lugs	7.11:15	**K 1527**		Trench 8,2 layer 11	Marble schist
	7.11:16	**K 1536**		Trench 8,6 layer 4	Marble Schist
Footed jar	7.11:17	**K 1525**		Trench 8,2 layer 7, with **K 1524**	Blue Schist
Conical cup	7.11:18	**K 1523**	33 *b*	Trench 8,2 layer 7 interior of **K 1524**	Marble Schist
Plate	7.11:19	**K 1522**		Trench 8,2 layer 3	Marble
Collared jar (stamnos)	7.12:1	**K 1524**	33 *a*	Trench 8,2 layer 7	Blue Schist
	7.12:2	**K 1532**		Trench 8,3, surface	Blue Schist
	7.12:3	**K 1526**		Trench 8,2 layer 7	Marble
	7.12:4	**K 1530**		Trench 8,6, surface	Blue Schist
Pithos	7.12:5	**K 1534**		Trench 8,6 layer 2	Marble
Baking pan	7.12:6	**K 1533**		Trench 8,6 layer 2	Marble Schist
Portable hearth	7.12:7	**K 1521**		Trench 8,2 layer 1	Blue Schist
	7.12:8	**K 1539**		Trench 8, surface	Marble Schist
Brazier or 'mask-like' support vessel	7.12:9	**K 1531**		Trench 8,3 surface	Marble Schist
Open non-identified vessel	–	**K 1537**		Trench 8,6 layer 5	Marble

TABLE 7.10. The occurrence Markiani phase III pottery by fabric.

Fabric/ware	Total number	Percentage
Marble A, C	221	39.3
Marble B	17	3
Blue Schist A	183	32.6
Red Shale	49	8.7
Dark Grey Marble	20	3.6
Other	72	12.8
Σ	562	100.0

TABLE 7.11. Surface treatment of Markiani phase III pottery.

Fabric/Ware	Eroded %	Smoothed %	Polished %	Burnished %	Slipped %	Slipped & Burnished %	No treatment %
Marble A, C	37.0	44.3	11.3	3.7	3.7		
Marble B	46.0	37.2		16.8			
Blue Schist A	7.6	31.6	57.6				3.2
Red Shale	38.0	29.0	18.2		14.8		
Dark Grey Marble	60.0	31.0			9.0		
Other	35.4	34.8		21.2	4.6	4.0	

TABLE 7.12. The occurrence of shape against fabric for the pottery of Markiani phase III.

Type	Marble A, C	Marble B	Blue Schist A	Red Shale	Other
Shallow open bowl (phiale)	2				
Cup			6		
Deep open bowl with lugs (chytra)	3				
Deep open bowl without lugs	10	2		1	
Hearth, baking pan (hestia)	2	1			
Collared jar (Stamnos)			2		
Jug (Prochous)			1		
Small spherical					1
Brazier, support			1	1	
Base	2	1	1		
Lid			1		

TABLE 7.13. The catalogued pottery of Markiani phase III.

Shape	FIG.	Cat. no.	PLATE	Trench/Layer	Fabric
Rolled-rim bowl	7.13: 1	K 1287		Trench 9,1 layer 5	Marble B
Bowl with in-turned rim	7.13: 2	K 1411		Trench 1,1 layer 46	Marble A, C
Conical cups	7.13: 3	K 1215-EE 904	33 e	Trench 9,1 layer 5	Blue Schist A
	7.13: 4	K 1752-EE 190		Trench 1,1 layer 44	Blue Schist A
	7.13: 5	K 1717-EE 188		Trench 1,1 layer 44	Blue Schist A
	7.13: 6	K 1716-EE 189		Trench 1,1 layer 44	Blue Schist A
	–	K 1646		Trench 1,1 layer 43	Blue Schist A
	–	K 1645		Trench 1,1 layer 43	Blue Schist A
Baking pans	7.13: 13	K 1285		Trench 9,1 layer 5	Marble A, C
	7.13: 14	K 1279		Trench 9,1 layer 5	Marble C
	–	K 1614		Trench 1,1 layer 46	Marble A
Deep open bowls with lugs	7.13: 15	K 1282		Trench 1,1 layer 44	Marble B, C
	7.13: 16	K 1409		Trench 1,1 layer 46	Marble A
	7.13: 17	K 1292		Trench 1,1 layer 44	Marble B, C
Deep handleless open vessels with curved walls	7.13: 7	K 1295		Trench 1,1 layer 44	Marble C
	7.13: 8	K 1276		Trench 1,1 layer 43	Marble
	7.13: 9	K 1288		Trench 9,1 layer 5	Marble A, C
	7.13: 10	K 1615		Trench 9,1 layer 5	Marble A, C
	7.13: 11	K 1294		Trench 1,1 layer 44	Marble A
	7.13: 12	K 1390		Trench 1,1 layer 45	Marble A, C
	–	K 1392		Trench 1,1 layer 45	Marble C
Deep handleless open vessels with straight walls	7.13: 18	K 1410		Trench 1,1 layer 46	Marble C
	7.13: 19	K 1405		Trench 1,1 layer 46	Marble B
	7.13: 20	K 1407		Trench 1,1 layer 46	Marble A, C
	7.13: 21	K 1413		Trench 1,1 layer 46	Marble A
	–	K 1406		Trench 1,1 layer 46	Marble C
	–	K 1408		Trench 1,1 layer 46	Marble A, C
Bases	7.14: 7	K 1402		Trench 1,1 layers 43 & 44	Marble B
	7.14: 8	K 1286		Trench 9,1 layer 5	Marble A, C
	–	K 1278		Trench 1,1 layer 44	Blue Schist A
	–	K 1385		Trench 1,1 layer 45	Marble A, C
	–	K 1374		Trench 1,1 layer 46	Marble B
Jars	7.14: 2	K 1273		Trench 1,1 layer 43	Marble A, C
	7.14: 3	K 1616		Trench 1,1 layer 44	Blue schist A, C
	7.14: 4	EE 905		Trench 9,1 layer 5	–
Small spherical narrow collared vessel	7.14: 5	K 1277	33 f	Trench 1,1 layer 43	–
Collared jars	7.14: 6	K 1275	33 f	Trench 1,1 layer 43	Blue Schist A
	–	K 1274		Trench 1,1 layer 43	Blue Schist A
Jug	7.14: 1	K 1298	33 c–d	Trench 1,1 layers 43 & 44	Blue Schist A
Brazier or 'mask-like' support vessel	–	K 1280		Trench 1,1 layer 44	Blue Schist A
	7.15	K 1704-EE 351	34 a–f	Trench 3,2, layer 9	–
Lid	7.13: 9	K 1297		Trench 1,1 layer 44	Blue Schist A

TABLE 7.14. The distribution of pottery fabrics by areal sub-divisions ('spaces') of Trenches 1 and 2.

Fabric/ ware	Space 7 Σ	%	Space 6 Σ	%	Space 3 Σ	%	Total	%
Blue Schist A	826	53.42	725	59.52	89	43.84	1640	55.27
Marble A	326	21.08	369	30.29	52	25.61	747	25.61
Marble C	86	5.56	7	0.57	12	5.91	105	3.53
Dark Grey Marble	242	15.65	19	1.55	27	13.30	288	9.70
Light Brown Burnished	2	0.12	5	0.41	2	0.98	9	0.30
Micaceous	57	3.68	80	6.56	12	5.91	149	5.02
Red Shale			12	0.98	8	3.94	20	0.67
Volcanic					1	0.98	1	0.03
Gneissose	7	0.45						
Other			1	0.08			1	0.03
Total	1546		1218		203		2967	

TABLE 7.15. The surface treatment of Markiani phase IV sherds according to fabric.

Fabric/Ware	Slipped Σ	%	Burnished Σ	%	Smoothed Σ	%	Polished Σ	%	Eroded/ no treatment Σ	%	Total
Blue Schist A	335	20.42	271	16.52	645	39.32	183	11.15	206	12.56	1640
Marble A	89	11.91	14	1.87	240	32.12	18	2.40	386	51.67	747
Marble C	23	21.90	10	9.52	31	29.52	9	8.57	32	30.47	105
Dark Grey Marble	4	1.38	–	–	85	29.51	29	10.06	170	59.02	288
Light Brown Burnished	2	22.22	7	77.77	–	–	–	–	–	–	9
Micaceous	9	6.04	3	2.01	62	41.61	–	–	75	50.33	149
Red Shale	3	15.0	2	10.0	12	60.0	–	–	3	15.0	20
Volcanic	–	–	–	–	1	100.0	–	–	–	–	1
Gneissose	–	–	4	57.14	1	14.28	–	–	2	28.57	7
Other	1	100.0	–	–	–	–	–	–	–	–	1
Total	466	15.70	311	10.48	1077	36.29	239	8.05	874	29.45	2967

TABLE 7.16. The distribution of Markiani phase IV ceramic forms according to fabric.

Forms	Fabrics-wares										Total
	Blue Schist A	Marble A	Marble C	Dark Grey	Light Brown Burnished	Micaceous	Red Shale	Volcanic	Gneissose	Other	
Bowl	36	16	7	–	9	–	–	–	–	–	68
Deep bowl with lugs	2	4	3	–	–	4	–	1	–	–	14
Large open bowl	4	5	1	–	–	–	1	–	–	–	11
Tankard	–	–	–	–	–	4	26	–	–	1	31
Depas cup	–	–	1	–	–	–	–	–	–	–	1
Conical cup	7	2	–	–	–	–	–	–	–	–	9
Baking pan	10	6	–	–	–	10	11	–	–	–	37
Spouted bowl	–	1	4	–	–	–	–	–	–	–	5
Deep wide mouthed vessel	1	1	1	–	–	1	–	1	–	–	5
Collared jar	9	2	3	3	–	–	–	–	–	–	17
Stemmed collared jar	3	3	–	–	–	–	–	–	–	–	6
Small pithos	–	1	–	–	–	–	–	–	–	–	1
Pithos	4	13	–	–	–	–	–	–	–	–	17
Jug	1	1	–	–	–	–	–	–	–	–	2
Spherical Pyxis	3	1	–	–	–	–	–	–	–	–	4
Brazier	1	2	2	–	–	–	–	–	–	–	5
Total	81	58	22	3	9	19	38	1	1	1	233

TABLE 7.17. The distribution of Markiani phase IV ceramic shapes by find location ('space') in Trenches 1 and 2.

Form	Space 7	Space 6	Space 3	Total
Bowl (phiale)	35	24	9	68
Deep bowl with lugs (chytra)	5	8	1	14
Large open bowl (lekane)	5	4	2	11
Tankard	6	24	1	31
Two handled cup(depas)	1	–	–	1
Conical cup	5	3	1	9
Baking Pan	12	22	3	37
Spouted bowl	4	1	–	5
Deep wide-mouthed vessel	3	1	1	5
Collared jar (stamnos)	8	6	3	17
Stemmed collared jar (crateriskos)	3	2	1	6
Small pithos	1	–	–	1
Pithos	8	8	1	17
Jug (prochous)	1	1	–	2
Spherical pyxis	–	4	–	4
Brazier	2	3	–	5
Total	99	111	23	233

TABLE 7.18. The catalogued pottery of Markiani phase IV.

Shape	FIG.	Cat. no.	PLATE	Trench/layer	Fabric
Shallow bowls	7.16: 1	K 1461		Trench 1,1 layer 34	Blue Schist A
	7.16: 2	K 1196		Trench 2 layer 22	Marble A
	7.16: 7	K 1203		Trench 2 layer 25	Marble A
	7.16: 3	K 1176		Trench 2 layer 27	Blue Schist A
	7.16: 4	K 1186		Trench 2 layer 24	Blue Schist A
	7.16: 5	K 1190		Trench 2 layer 29	Marble C
	7.16: 6	K 1454		Trench 1,1 layer 29	Blue Schist A
	7.16: 10	K 2011		Trench 1,3 layer 3	Light Brown Burnished
Shallow bowls with in-turned rim	7.16: 9	K 1450		Trench 1,1 layer 28	Marble A
	7.16: 8	K 1448		Trench 1,1 layer 27	Marble C
Deep bowls conical	7.16: 11	K 1420		Trench 1,1 layer 21	Blue Schist A
	7.16: 12	K 1442		Trench 1,1 layer 25	Marble C
Deep bowls hemispherical	7.16: 13	K 1421		Trench 1,1 layer 21	Marble C
	7.16: 15	K 1460		Trench 1,1 layer 34	Marble C
	7.16: 14	K 1178		Trench 2 layer 27	Marble C
Deep bowls spouted	7.16: 16	K 1451	36 b	Trench 1,1 layer 29	Marble C
Small hemispherical bowls with in-curved walls	7.16: 19	K 1724	35 e	Trench 1,1 layer 23	Marble C
	7.16: 17	K 1466		Trench 1,1 layer 36	Blue Schist A
	7.16: 20	K 1177		Trench 2 layer 27	Marble A
	7.16: 18	K 1447		Trench 1,1 layer 27	Light brown Burnished
Deep bowls with lugs(chytra)	7.17: 1 see also 7.26: 17	K 1212	36 e	Trench 1,4 layers 4 and 6	Volcanic
	7.17: 2	K 1434		Trench 1,1 layer 24	Marble C
	7.17: 3	K 1435		Trench 1,1 layer 24	Marble C
	7.17: 4	K 1184		Trench 2 layer 24	Marble A
	7.17: 5	K 1191		Trench 2 layer 29	Micaceous
	7.17: 6	K 1199		Trench 2 layer 25	Marble A
	7.17: 7	K 1422		Trench 1,1 layer 21	Marble A
	7.17: 8	K 1472		Trench 1,1 layer 36	Dark Grey Marble
	7.17: 9	K 1464		Trench 1,1 layer 34	Marble A
Foot of footed bowl	7.17: 10	K 1219		Trench 2 layer 23	Blue Schist A
Large open bowls with straight walls: (lekane)	7.18: 1	K 1424		Trench 1,1 layer 23	Blue Schist A
	7.18: 2	K 1443		Trench 1,1 layer 25	Blue Schist A
	7.18: 3	K 1427		Trench 1,1 layer 24	Marble A
Large open bowls with curved walls: (lekanida)	7.18: 9	K 1703		Trench 1,4 layer 6	Red Shale
	7.18: 4	K 1462		Trench 1,1 layer 34	Marble A
	7.18: 7	K 1463		Trench 1,1 layer 34	Blue Schist A
	7.18: 5	K 1185		Trench 2 layer 24	Marble A
	7.18: 8	K 1217		Trench 2 layer 23	Marble A
	7.18: 6	K 1179		Trench 2 layer 27	Marble C
Tankards	7.19: 6	K 1224		Trench 1,1 layer 21	Red Shale
	7.19: 3	K 1441		Trench 1,1 layer 24	Red Shale
	7.19: 5	K 1188		Trench 2 layer 24	Red Shale
	7.19: 2	K 1223	35 b	Trench 1,4 layer 27	Red Shale
	7.19: 7	K 1115	35 d	Trench 2 layer 25	Individual sample Grey-brown
	7.19: 4	K 1182	35 c	Trench 2 layer 27	Red Shale
	7.19: 1	K 1225		Trench 2 layer 31	Micaceous
Depas amphikypellon	7.19: 8	K 1723	35 a	Trench 1,1 layer 25	Marble C
Conical cups	7.19: 9	K 1446		Trench 1,1 layer 25	Marble A
	7.19: 10	K 1470		Trench 1,1 layer 36	Blue Schist A
	7.19: 11	K 1721		Trench 1,4 layer 4	Blue Schist A
	7.19: 12	K 1205		Trench 2 layer 25	Blue Schist A
	7.19: 14	K 1206		Trench 2 layer 25	Blue Schist A
	7.19: 13	K 1476		Trench 1,3 layer 3	Blue Schist A

TABLE 7.18 continued.

Shape	FIG.	Cat. no.	PLATE	Trench/layer	Fabric
Baking pans type A	7.20: 1	K 1428		Trench 1,1 layer 24	Micaceous
	7.20: 2	K 1429		Trench 1,1 layer 24	Micaceous
		K 1180		Trench 2 layer 27	Red Shale
		K 1181		Trench 2 layer 27	Red Shale
	7.20: 8	K 1484		Trench 1,4 layer 29	Blue Schist A
	7.20: 9	K 1485		Trench 1,4 layer 31	Micaceous
	7.20: 10	K 1486		Trench 1,4 layer 31	Micaceous
	7.20: 5	K 1201		Trench 2 layer 25	Blue Schist A
	7.20: 7	K 1202		Trench 2 layer 25	Blue Schist A
	7.20: 3	K 1636	36 a	Trench 2 layer 25	Blue Schist A
	7.20: 6	K 1637		Trench 2,26 layers 27 and 28 and Trench 1,4 layer 9	Red Shale
	7.20: 8	K 1640		Trench 2 layer 27	Red Shale
Baking pans type B	7.20: 13	K 1465		Trench 1,1 layer 35	Marble A
	7.20: 11	K 1431		Trench 1,1 layer 24	Marble A
	7.20: 14	K 1430		Trench 1,1 layer 24	Marble A
	7.20: 12	K 1187		Trench 2 layer 24	Marble A
Sauceboats and spouted vessels	7.21: 1	K 1438		Trench 1,1 layer 24	Marble C
	7.21: 3	K 1439		Trench 1,1 layer 24	Marble C
	7.21: 2	K 1440		Trench 1,1 layer 24	Marble C
	7.21: 4	K 1230 / K 1770	36 e	Trench 1,4 layer 31	Marble C
	7.21: 9	K 1722	38 g	Trench 1,1 layer 24	Marble A
Deep wide mouthed vessels open	7.21:5	K 1426		Trench 1,1 layer 23	Gneissose
	7.21: 6	K 1445		Trench 1,1 layer 25	Micaceous
	7.21: 7	K 1433		Trench 1,1 layer 24	Blue Schist A
Deep wide mouthed vessels closed	7.21: 8	K 1204		Trench 2 layer 25	Marble C
Jars with collar neck (stamnoi)	7.22: 2	K 1436		Trench 1,1 layer 24	Blue Schist A
	7.22: 1	K 1232		Trench 1,4 layer 31	Marble C
	7.22: 4	K 1192		Trench 2 layer 29	Blue Schist A
	7.22: 3	K 1444		Trench 1,1 layer 25	Marble C
	7.22: 5	K 1198		Trench 2 layer 25	Blue Schist A
	7.22: 9	K 1423	36 d	Trench 1,1 layer 21	Marble A
	7.22: 11	K 1207		Trench 2 layer 26	Marble A
	7.22: 10	K 1189	36 d	Trench 2 layer 29	Blue Schist A
Collared jars (crateriskoi)	7.22: 6	K 1449		Trench 1,1 layer 28	Marble A
	7.22: 7	K 1453	38 c	Trench 1,1 layer 29	Marble A
	7.22: 8	K 2010		Trench 1,3 layer 3	Blue Schist A
Spherical pyxis	7.22: 13	K 1175		Trench 2 layer 27	Marble A
	7.22: 14	K 1200		Trench 2 layer 25	Blue Schist A
	7.22: 12	K 1477		Trench 1,3 layer 3	Blue Schist A
	7.22: 15	K 1209		Trench 2 layer 26	Blue Schist A
Storage vessels (pithoi and pithoid)	7.23: 3	K 1437		Trench 1,1 layer 24	Marble A
	7.23: 2	K 1218		Trench 2 layer 23	Marble A
	7.23: 5	K 1216		Trench 2 layer 23	Marble A
	7.23: 1	K 1210		Trench 2 layer 26	Marble A
	7.23: 6	K 1483		Trench 1,4 layer 29	Blue Schist A
	7.23: 4	K 1208		Trench 2 layer 26	Marble A
	7.23: 7	K 1468		Trench 1,1 layer 36	Blue Schist A
	7.23: 8	K 1471		Trench 1,1 layer 36	Dark grey marble
	7.23: 9	K 1222		Trench 2 layer 25	Marble A
	7.23: 10	K 1221		Trench 2 layer 23	Marble A
	–	K 1487		Trench 1,4 layer 31	Blue Schist A
Jugs	7.24: 1	K 1452	36 b	Trench 1,1 layer 29	Blue Schist A
	7.24: 2	K 1231		Trench 1,4 layer 30	Marble A
Horizontal handles	7.24: 5	K 1194		Trench 2 layer 29	Marble A
	7.24: 6	K 1195		Trench 2 layer 22	Blue Schist A
	7.24: 7	K 1211		Trench 2 layer 26	Blue Schist A
	7.24: 4	K 1183		Trench 2 layer 27	Blue Schist A

TABLE 7.18 continued.

Shape	FIG.	Cat. no.	PLATE	Trench/layer	Fabric
Small pithos	7.24: 3	**K 1432**	38 *c*	Trench 1,1 layer 24	Marble A
Bases		**K 1355**		Trench 1,1 layer 24	Marble A
	7.24: 10	**K 1193**		Trench 2 layer 29	Marble A
	7.24: 8	**K 1469**		Trench 1,1 layer 36	Marble A
	–	**K 1364**		Trench 1,4 layer 27	Marble A
	–	**K 1365**		Trench 1,4 layer 29	Marble A
	7.24: 9	**K 1478**			
	–	**K 1386**		Trench 1,1 layer 24	–
	–	**K 1304**		Trench 1,1 layer 24	Marble A
Braziers, 'mask like' support vessels	7.25: 1	**EE 251**	37 *a–e*	Trench 2p, layer 57	
	7.25: 5	**K 1379**		Trench 1,1 layer 25	Marble C
	–	**K 1664**		Trench 1,1 layer 24	Marble C
	7.25: 2	**K 1540**	37 *f*	Trench 1,3 layer 5	Marble A
	7.25: 3	**K 1220**		Trench 2 layer 23	Blue Schist A
	7.25: 4	**K 1621**		Trench 2 layer 25	Marble A
Sherds with incised decoration (herringbone)	7.26: 1	**K 1467**	38 *d*	Trench 1,1 layer 36	–
Linear incisions	–	**K 1488**		Trench 1,1 layer 24	–
	7.26: 2	**K 1489**		Trench 1,1 layer 24	–
	7.26: 3	**K 1492**		Trench 1,1 layer 26	–
	7.26: 4	**K 1496**		Trench 1,1 layer 29	–
	7.26: 5	**K 1497**		Trench 1,1 layer 34	–
	7.26: 7	**K 1635**		Trench 2 layer 22	–
Deep incisions	7.26: 8	**K 1494**		Trench 1,1 layer 29	–
Linear or curvilinear incisions	7.26: 16	**K 1490**		Trench 1,1 layer 24	–
Zigzag incisions	7.26: 12	**K 1491**	38 *b*	Trench 1,1 layer 25	–
	–	**K 1708**		Trench 1,4 layer 6	–
Parallel incisions	7.26: 6	**K 1493**		Trench 1,1 layer 28	–
Curvilinear incisions	7.26: 13	**K 1495**		Trench 1,1 layer 29	–
	7.26: 14	**K 1498**		Trench 1,1 layer 35	–
	7.26: 9	**K 1227**		Trench 1,1 layer 30	–
	7.26: 10	**K 1228**		Trench 1,1 layer 30	–
	7.26: 11	**K 1226**	38 *b*	Trench 1,3 layer 5	–
Incised fish motif	7.26: 18	**K 1244**	38 *a*	Trench 1,1 layer 24	–
	7.26: 17, see also 7.17. 1	**K 1212**	36 *e*	Trench 1,4 layers 4 and 6	–
Incised double axe motif	7.26: 15	**K 1229**	38 *b*	Trench 1,4 layer 31	–
Painted sherds	7.26: 19	**K 1710**	38 *e*	Trench 1,5, layer 60	Pale buff
	–	**K 1711 / EE 161**	38 *f*	Trench 1,5, layer 15	Micaceous Brown
	–	**EE 074**	–	Trench 1,1, layer 25	Dark brown/ black Urfirnis

Chapter 8

The small objects

A. THE CHIPPED STONE

by Anastasia Angelopoulou

The chipped stone, almost exclusively obsidian, recovered from the settlement at Markiani gives the first clear impression of the lithic industry from a settlement of the Cycladic EBA. The material recovered comes from the surface survey, 291 pieces, and from the excavation, 348 finds. Together they give a clear impression of what, as we shall see, was primarily a blade industry.

RECOVERY

The recovery process for the surface finds is described in Chapter 3. In most cases it involved the collection by the survey worker of all cultural materials, mainly pottery but also stone, bone etc. from a circle of radius 1 m. The recovery process from the excavation was naturally very different. It involved both recovery in the excavation trench in the course of the actual digging, and recovery during the screening process. As noted in Chapter 4, sieving was undertaken at a central point using a 1 cm aperture mesh. Such a large mesh would not in practice retain the smaller pieces of obsidian, but the procedure at least offered a second phase of scrutiny during the recovery process.

It should be recognised, however, that smaller pieces of obsidian including small blade and débitage fragments would not routinely be recovered during this process, and the account which follows should be read in that light.

RAW MATERIAL

Most of the chipped stone material recovered is of obsidian. Out of the total of 639 pieces recovered only three were of other materials: two of grey flint, **Ma 21** and **O 350**, one of white stone, **Ma 11**, possibly flint (plus an unworked fragment of schist).

SOURCE

Although no trace-element analysis was undertaken, it seems clear that most or all of the obsidian was imported from Melos. Certainly no pieces were observed with the greater transparency and white flecking characteristic of the obsidian of Giali, Nisyros. All the pieces recovered had the grey, slightly milky texture characteristic of both the Melian sources at Adhamas and Dhemenegaki.

No unworked lumps of obsidian were found, and no cores with cortex. Among the débitage 45 pieces were found with traces of cortex on one surface (7.1% of the total industry), and in nine of these, mostly small pieces, cortex covered the entire outer surface. In addition, five blades or blade fragments of the 395 recovered (1.3%, of the blades) had indications of cortex ('primary débitage').

TABLE 8.1. Cortex. The presence of cortex ('primary débitage') in the débitage.

Category	Surface	%	Excavation	%	Total	%
Primary Débitage	31 (6)	23.3	14 (3)	15.7	45	20.3
Secondary Débitage	102	78.7	75	84.3	177	79.7
Total	133	100.0	89	100.0	222	100.0

(Cases with cortex over one entire surface are given in brackets)

The paucity of cores and the general nature of the industry indicate that obsidian was not wasted and was probably in relatively short supply. It is likely that the material was imported in roughly worked cores.

LITHIC INDUSTRY

The lithic industry, as we shall see, may certainly be classified as a blade industry. The finds have been divided into the categories: cores, blades, flakes and débitage.

TABLE 8.2. The Markiani obsidian industry, as recovered.

Category	Surface find	% Surface collection	Excavation find	% Excavation recovered	Overall	% of total finds
Blade cores	0	0	2	0.6	2	0.3
Blades	144	49.8	251	72.5	395	62.2
Flakes	12	4.2	4	1.2	16	2.5
Débitage	133	46.0	89	25.7	222	35.0
Total	289	100.0	346	100.0	635	100.0

The finds from the surface collection and from the excavation are here separated.

The proportions do not vary very markedly but, as noted above, there was no fine-mesh sieving of the excavation spoil which would certainly have produced greater quantities of very small fragments. The mesh size, 1 × 1 cm, did not yield obsidian in notable quantities.

CORES

Only two cores were recovered. The first (**O 395**), from Trench 2, layer 48, (FIG. 8.3: 1, PLATE 39 *a*, measuring 3.40 × 1.90 × 0.80 cm), is a worked-out tabular blade core, now only 3.40 cm in length. On one side it bears the scars where short parallel-sided blades have been detached.

The second (**O 490**) from surface levels of Room 2 in Trench 3; (FIG. 8.3: 2, PLATE 39 *b*, measuring 1.90 cm × 1.70 cm × 1.40 cm, is a truncated conical core, again used for the production of regular, parallel-sided blades.

The tabular core (**O 395**) shows preparation of the striking platform, a common feature in the EBA[1] It is a characteristic feature of the technique introduced during the Late Neolithic for the production of blades.[2] It facilitates the production of regular, parallel-sided blades.[3] As van Horn has noted,[4] the use of such cores produces mainly blades of considerable regularity.

The fact that only two such cores were found and their very small size indicate clearly that obsidian was not in abundant supply at Markiani. It would be interesting to compare the quantities and small sizes at Markiani with those from some contemporary site on the west coast of Amorgos with better access to a harbour where, one may predict, greater quantities might be available.

BLADES

The blades recovered were divided into three categories: A, very regular, parallel-sided blades; B, less regular parallel sided blades; and C, other blades.

The blades of category A in general, had either a dorsal surface with a single ridge or 'spine' (making them triangular in section: here type II); or a dorsal surface with two ridges separating a horizontal surface running parallel to the ventral surface (and thus with a trapezoidal section: here type I : **O 408** (FIG. 8.3: 3) and **O 433** (FIG. 8.3: 4, PLATE 39 *d*).

Most of the blades were trapezoidal, of type I (**O 408**, FIG. 8.3: 3), representing 85.6% of the excavated blades and 81.3% of the blades from the surface. Most of the remainder were triangular in section, of type II (14% of the excavated blades and 17% of the blades from the surface).

Two of the largest preserved blades are illustrated **O 433** (FIG. 8.3: 4, PLATE 39 *d*, L. 8.40 cm) and **O 408**, (FIG. 8.3: 3, L. 6.20 cm). The dimensions of the complete blades recovered (of categories A and B) are seen in FIG. 8.1. The frequency distributions for the width of all the blades and blade fragments recovered (of categories A and B) are seen in FIG. 8.2.

While the principal products are the highly regular parallel sided blades (Category A) or reasonably regular parallel sided blades (Category B), there are other less regular parallel sided blades (Category C: **O 453**, FIG. 8.3: 5; **O 396+397+398**, FIG. 8.3: 6; **O 409**, FIG. 8.3: 7, PLATE 39 *b*).

---

[1] Torrence 1979, 71.
[2] Cherry and Torrence 1984, 18.
[3] Moundrea-Agrafioti 1990, 399.
[4] Van Horn 1980, 490–1, fig. 5d,

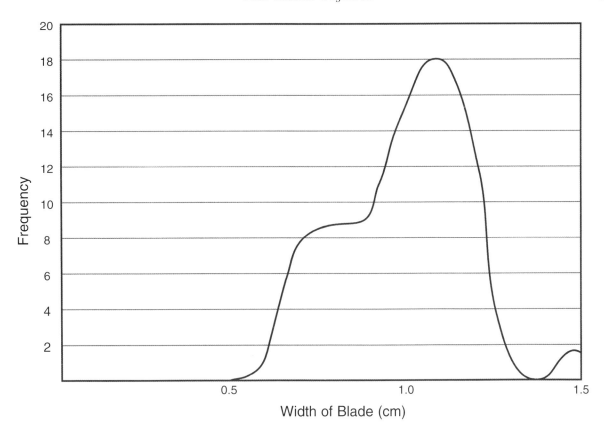

FIG. 8.1. Frequency distribution of obsidian blade widths.

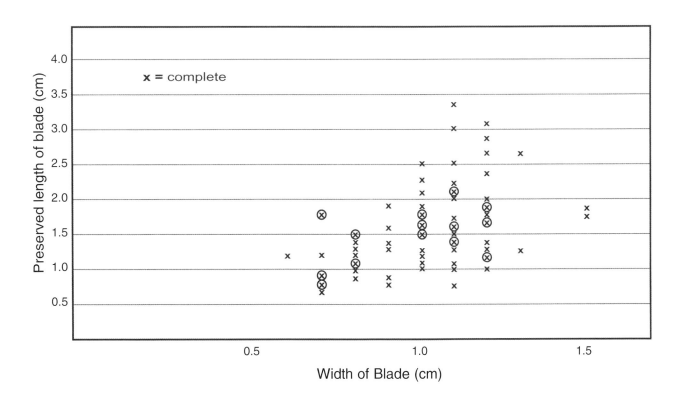

FIG. 8.2. Plot of length against width for complete blades.

TABLE 8.3. The obsidian blades from Markiani.

Category	Cross-section type	Surface find	% Surface collection	Excavation find	% Excavation recovery	Σ	% total of finds
Blade category A+B	trapezoid	91	81.3	190	85.6	281	84.1
	triangular	19	17.0	31	14.0	50	15.0
	other	2	1.7	1	0.4	3	0.9
	Σ	112	100.0	222	100.0	334	100.0
Blade category C	trapezoid	18	56.2	15	51.7	33	54.1
	triangular	14	44.0	12	41.4	26	42.6
	other			2	6.9	2	3.3
	Σ	32	100.0	29	100.0	61	100.0
	Total	144		251		381	

Most of the blades of Category C are core rejuvenation blades, produced in the process of restoring the regular form of the core. This was achieved first by detaching very small flakes from the core by striking it transversely along its length in the protruding area. When regularity had been approximately restored, this scarred region was itself detached by a blow to the striking platform, removing a blade. This blade shows surface traces of this lateral flaking on its dorsal, frequently in alternating directions: the so-called dog tooth rejuvenation blade.

As noted in TABLE 8.3, 112 blades and blade fragments of categories A or B were found on the surface, and 222 from the excavation. It should be noted that about 4.5% of the excavated blades were found intact, but only 1.8% of the surface finds. Furthermore 32 of the surface blades and 29 of the excavated blades were of Category C.

The distribution of blade and débitage finds in the principal excavation areas is seen in TABLE 8.4.

TABLE 8.4. Finds of blades and débitage in the principal excavation areas.

	Space 8	Space 7	Space 1	Space 2	Space 3	Space 4	Space 5	Space 6	drain	Trench 3,1	Trench 3,2	Σ
Blades	12	11	3	15	3		2	6	8	20	20	100
Débitage	3	4	4	6	1	1		1		10	3	33
Σ	15	15	7	21	4	1	2	7	8	30	23	133

In general the blades were not modified by retouch, although in some there are indications of use wear (**O 651**, FIG. 8.3: 8; **O 201**, FIG. 8.3: 9, PLATE 39 *d*), and in a few, rare cases (e.g. **O 457**, FIG. 8.3: 10) there might have been some retouch at the edges.

Potential artefacts were recognised in just a few cases rather than the usual blades. Two roughly circular discs were difficult to interpret as simple débitage (e.g. **O 505/15**, FIG. 8.3: 11). The dorsal surface showed small secondary scars which did not at once appear to be the consequences of fortuitous abrasion. One flake (**O 501/16**, FIG. 8.3: 12) has a concave edge with probable 'backing' by retouch. This was singled out during study because of the regularity and steepness of the small secondary percussion scars which suggested that there might be the result of débitage retouch.

These few exceptions serve to reinforce the conclusion this was primarily a blade industry.

THE DÉBITAGE

The débitage recovered all seems to be the by-product of blade production. It includes a number of irregular flakes (e.g. 20, FIG. 8.3: 13; **O 518**, FIG. 8.3: 14; and **O 588**, FIG. 8.3: 15) and less regular blades (e.g. **O 651**, FIG. 8.3: 8) which may result from the preparation process. Some of these have scars on the ventral surface indicating the prior detachment of blades (FIG. **O 524**, FIG. 8.3: 17; and **O 361**, FIG. 8.3: 16, PLATE 39 *d*). The quantities of débitage with indications of cortex (i.e. 'primary débitage') are seen in TABLE 8.1. The proportions compare with those from Akrotiri on

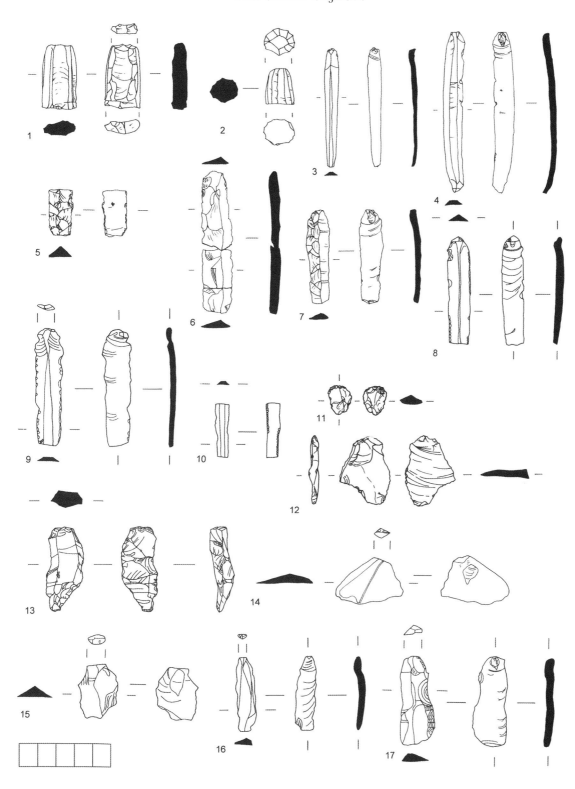

FIG. 8.3. Obsidian cores (*1–2*), blades (*3–10*) and débitage (scale 1:2).

Thera,[5] Ayia Irini on Kea, and Lerna in the Argolid.[6] The relatively modest quantities of débitage suggest the importation of rough macrocores from Melos, as has been proposed for Akrotiri on Thera[7] and Ayia Irini on Kea.[8]

[5] Moundrea-Agrafioti 1990, 394, table 2.2–3, 396.
[6] Torrence 1986, table 7, 128.
[7] Moundrea-Agrafioti 1990, 397.
[8] Torrence 1986, 127.

DISTRIBUTION

The distribution of obsidian finds in the principal excavated areas is seen in TABLE 8.4.

There is no notable concentration of finds which might suggest the intensive use (or breakage) of obsidian. Nor are there any special concentrations of débitage suggesting the production (or repair or refurbishment) of blades on the spot.

It is of interest however that *c.* 50% of the regular blades recovered during surface survey came from the walled field to the west of the site (survey unit 301 to 324). No concentration of cortex débitage was recognised on the site, and only a few thin spread of the larger débitage flakes.

The widespread presence of débitage (albeit in small quantities) does seem to indicate that obsidian blades were made on site and not imported ready-made to Markiani.

TABLE 8.5. The illustrated obsidian objects.

Category	FIG.	Cat. no.	PLATE	Find location	Phase
Blade cores	8.3: 1	O 395/EE260	39 *a*	Trench 2 layer 48	Ma IV
	8.3: 2	O 490	39 *b*	Trench 3,2 layer 1 (room 2)	Ma III
Blades	8.3: 3	O 408		Trench 2π, layer 57	Ma IV
	8.3: 4	O 433	39 *d*	Trench 2, layer 22	Ma IV
	8.3: 5	O 453	39 *c*	Trench 2,4, layer 1	Ma IV
	8.3: 6	O 396+397+398		Trench 2π, layer 59	Ma IV
	8.3: 7	O 409		Trench 2π, layer 59	Ma IV
	8.3: 8	O 651		Trench 2,1 layer 45	Ma IV
	8.3: 9	O 201	39 *d*	Rock Cutting 2 1985 surface cleaning	Ma IV
	8.3: 10	O 457		Trench 2, layer 28	Ma IV
	8.3: 11	O 505		Surface survey 1987	
	8.3: 12	O 501		Surface survey 1987	
Débitage	8.3: 13	20		Surface survey 1987	
	8.3: 14	O 518		Trench 3,2 layer 14	Ma III
	8.3: 15	O 588		Trench 7 layer 11	Ma II
	8.3: 17	O 524		Trench 3,2 layer 18	Ma III
	8.3: 16	O 361	39 *d*	Trench 1,1 layer 25	Ma IV

B. STONE VESSELS AND IMPLEMENTS

by Chris Scarre

INTRODUCTION

The particular objective of the excavations at Markiani was to investigate an EC domestic site and its assemblage, in order to redress the balance of research on this period which has hitherto focused largely on cemetery material. The island of Amorgos is rich in sources of hard stone, and for many domestic and agricultural operations the early prehistoric populations will have relied heavily on stone tools. This is amply documented by the excavations at Markiani, which have revealed an extensive assemblage of shaped and/or utilised stone, ranging from large coarse saddle querns and rubbers to fine marble vessels. This assemblage provides important evidence of the nature of the site and the activities carried out there.

The present study began with the recording of all items of stone from the excavations (other than obsidian, treated separately) which showed traces either of intentional shaping or of wear or damage that could be attributed to human activity. The latter was often difficult to establish with certainty since human and natural agency may leave similar marks. In many cases, however, the identification was assisted by the regularity in the shape of the stone, which strongly suggested that it had been brought to the site from elsewhere. Few regularly rounded stones can be picked up on Amorgos today and it is likely that many of those found in the settlement layers were especially collected from the beach and were smoothed by wave action.

A full list of stone implements and utilised pieces from the excavated layers is given below. The less diagnostic pieces are indicated by the simple classification 'rubber' or 'possible rubber'; in most cases these are merely utilised natural stones showing signs of wear or abrasion.

Objects of Finely-Worked Stone

It is convenient first to deal with those artefacts and vessels which may be regarded as of finely worked (usually polished) stone, as opposed to the tools and other artifacts of coarse (i.e. not polished) stone.

It should be noted that apart from the possible instance of **EE 396**, no figurines or figurine fragments were found at Markiani. Other stone artefacts, which feature in the well-known assemblages from the Cycladic cemeteries, were rare. Four fragments of marble vessels may represent forms found in Cycladic graves. The six finely-worked stone pestles are also of a type known in Cycladic cemetery contexts. Otherwise there are at Markiani very few finds which usually are at home in the Cycladic cemeteries of which of course several (e.g. Dokathismata, Kapsala etc.) are known.

RINGS AND BEADS

Two small perforated beads and part of a small finger ring, all of chlorite schist have been found.

The small irregular bead **EE 096** (FIG. 8.4: 2, PLATE 40 *a*) is of dark grey chlorite schist, (L. 1.62, W. 1.34, Th. 0.65 cm) and has a biconically-drilled perforation. The small pendant bead **EE 1001** (FIG. 8.4: 3, PLATE 40 *a*) is of polished green chlorite schist (steatite) (L. 1.14, W. 0.81, Th. 0.73 cm), and has also a biconically drilled hole for suspension. It was probably part of a necklace.

Only a fragment of small ring **EE 218** (FIG. 8.4: 4, PLATE 40 *a*) of greenish chlorite schist (steatite) has been found. It is circular internally, and probably hexagonal or seven-sided externally (L. 1.75, W. 1.00, Th. 0.43 cm). The external facets are sawn. The surviving fragment represents approximately one-third of the ring, with two complete external facets and parts of two more. The estimated internal diameter of *c.* 0.90 cm makes it too small to be a finger ring for a modern adult, though it would be a suitable size for a child.

OTHER WORKED MARBLE

Greater interest attaches to **EE 396** (FIG. 8.4: 1, PLATE 40 *g* and 41 *b*), which could represent a very schematic kind of marble figurine. This is a small rounded piece of marble (L. 3.90, W. 1.60, Th. 0.90 cm) with a central groove 0.20 cm wide × 0.075 cm deep dividing it into two unequal parts, 'head' and 'body'. The groove does not extend around the back, which is relatively flat though in a twisted plane; the front of the 'body' is also flat, but the 'head' is rounded. The piece may have been sawn, and then ground to give rounded edges. Purpose uncertain: it may have been a bead or pendant, or even a small weight, with the groove designed to take a string for suspension. Alternatively, it may have been a simple figurine, though this is less likely. The piece is intact save for some damage to the back of the 'head'.

It may be compared broadly to a piece from Thermi, also of marble, which Lamb suggested could have been a figurine.[9] Lamb was not sure of this interpretation, however, and the Thermi 'idol' is less schematic and more convincing than this piece from Markiani. The same may be said of a figurine from Troy I (no. 37-525)[10] where the neck is divided from the body by a shallow groove. But the overall 'violin' shape of the Troy piece makes identification as a figurine more confident than either the Markiani or Thermi examples. On balance, the interpretation of **EE 396** as a pendant or amulet is probably to be preferred, with the central groove designed to allow the tying of a cord for suspension.

A marble object, **EE 822/099** (FIG. 8.4: 5), comes from the area outside the bastion within the large two-handled vessel **K 1524** (FIG. 7.12: 1, PLATE 33 *a*). It is a rounded marble object, three-quarter spherical with flat base (L. 5.80, W. 4.90, Th. 4.30 cm). It may have been a rubber or a pounder, but with no clear traces of wear or use. The shape is probably natural, although human agency cannot be excluded. If it is a rubber, the working surface may have been the flat base, though this has hollows and irregularities. It is perhaps most probable that the flat base is the result of breakage along a natural line of cleavage or imperfection in the marble.

MARBLE VESSEL FRAGMENTS

Two rim and two body fragments of marble bowls were recovered from the site. As far as can be ascertained the forms are of EC type, but only one of the pieces (**EE 068**) came from a sealed context of Ma IV.

EE 068 (FIG. 8.4: 7, PLATE 40 *c–d*) is a rim fragment (L. 6.40, W. 3.70, Th. 0.90 cm) of a deep bowl with slightly inturned flattened rim of white/cream, heavily patinated, marble. Its original external

---

[9] Lamb 1936, 177; no. 31.98.   [10] Blegen *et al.* 1950, fig. 216.

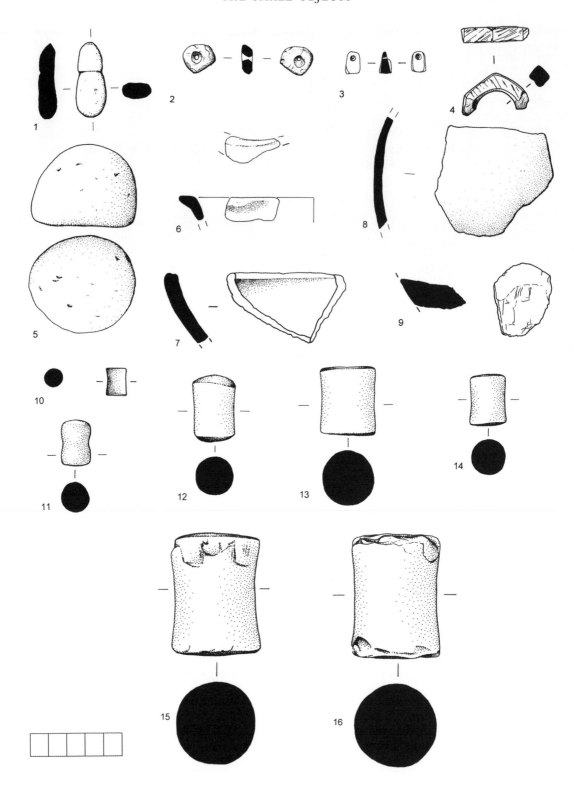

FIG. 8.4. Fine stone objects (scale 1:2).

diameter is *c.* 13 cm. All the breaks are ancient. This vessel form is of broadly EC II type, similar to the complete example no. 65 in the N. P. Goulandris collection.[11] Another rim fragment (L. 2.86, W. 1.25, Th. 0.50 cm) of a marble vessel with the greater part of a projecting lip or 'ear' is **EE 1019** (FIG. 8.4: 6, PLATE 40 *c–d*). Its material is white/cream marble, heavily patinated. The lower break seems

[11] Doumas 1983, 86.

fresh, while all the others are ancient. Possible parallels of the Keros-Syros (EC II) phase are illustrated by Thimme.[12] This fragment could equally well be from a footed bowl of the kind illustrated by Warren from Myrtos.[13] Its estimated original external diameter is *c.* 12 cm.

EE 097 (FIG. 8.4: 8, PLATE 40 *c–d*) is a marble vessel body fragment (L. 6.60, W. 5.80, Th. 0.50 cm), which is gently curved and an even 5 cm in thickness. This comes from a relatively large and thin-walled vessel. The material is a grey marble. The break along the lower edge of it seems to coincide with an imperfection in the material betrayed by a grey band. Another body fragment of a marble vessel is **EE 1026** (FIG. 8.4: 9).

THE FINE PESTLES

The fine pestles of stone are among the most notable finds. They belong to a well-defined class of object known in many EH II and Keros-Syros culture (EC II) contexts. These are generally of well-worked and polished stone, although examples carved from *Spondylus* shell are known. The form is approximately cylindrical, although the sides are lightly concave, not vertical, and the two ends of the cylinder are slightly convex rather than flat. Their occasional occurrence in Cycladic graves in association with pigment has led to the suggestion that they were used in some cases as grinders, but it has recently plausibly been argued that they served as weights.[14]

Catalogue

EE 395 (FIG. 8.4: 15, PLATES 40 *e–f* and 41 *a*) is a particularly striking example, made of a very special stone, a fine yellow limestone with small fossils of rosette or star-shaped form and of diameter *c.* 0.50 cm which are clearly seen at both ends (H. 6.30 cm, D. 4.80 cm, Wt. 261 g). Traces of abrasion are seen at the centre of the convex surfaces at both ends. There is also some damage at both ends. The unusual choice of material makes this an especially interesting piece.

EE 637 (FIG. 8.4: 16, PLATE 40 *b*) is of similar form and made of the reddish yellow limestone sometimes termed 'Kouphonisi' limestone (H. 6.50 cm, D. 4.60 cm, Wt. 283 g). The surfaces are smooth but not highly polished; there is some flaking at the surface. There is also surface damage, mainly on the edges at the two ends, and there is encrustation at the ends. This and the preceding are of similar size and shape. They are the largest and heaviest pestles found in EC contexts, with the notable exception of one much larger and heavier pestle found at Ayia Irini on Kea.[15]

EE 345 (FIG. 8.4: 12) is of grey limestone with pale yellow flecks. (H. 3.60 cm, D. 2.10–2.30 cm, Wt. 32 g). One of the ends has a more oval section. The surfaces are rather rough and a whitish encrustation covers part of one end.

EE 1612 (FIG. 8.4: 14, PLATE 40 *b*) is again of reddish 'Kouphonisi' limestone. (H. 2.50 cm, D. 1.90–2.00 cm, Wt. 19.8 g). The surfaces are smooth; white encrustation covers part of one end.

EE 326 (FIG. 8.4: 13, PLATE 40 *b*) is similar, of orange 'Kouphonisi' limestone. (H. 3.60 cm, D. 2.90–3.00 cm, Wt. 60 g). The surfaces are smooth.

EE 258 (FIG. 8.4: 10) is a miniature version, of pale buff limestone. (H. 1.50 cm, D. 1.10 cm, Wt. 3 g). There are minor breakages at both ends.

EE 1008 (FIG. 8.4: 11) is of pale quartz and of less regular shape, with markedly concave sides. (H. 2.40 cm, D. 1.50–1.60 cm, Wt. 11 g). Traces of working are visible on the surfaces. It has been broken: the two pieces were joined during conservation work.

Given the modesty of the other finds of finely-worked stone, this is an impressive collection. As will be seen from TABLE 8.6, five of the pestles come from Trench 3, where they are assigned to the Markiani III period, which conforms with chronological expectations. The last two listed are assigned to Ma IV, contemporary with the Kastri Group, in the later part of the Keros-Syros culture.

POLISHED STONE AXES

One complete polished greenstone axe, one fragment of a polished emery axe and one miniature emery axe were found at Markiani.

EE 054 (PLATE 42 *a*) is a fragment of polished emery axe. A small area of the original convex polished surface is preserved (L. 3.70, W. 3.60, Th. 1.80 cm). **EE 1018** (FIG. 8.5: 1, PLATE 42 *a*) is a miniature polished stone emery axe (L. 3.70, W. 3.10, Th. 1.10 cm), asymmetrical in shape but carefully smoothed and finished. The surfaces are slightly damaged and it resembles the small axe from Poliochni illustrated by Bernabò Brea; Thermi also has yielded emery axes, but none of miniature size.[16]

Only **EE 661** (FIG. 8.5: 2, PLATE 42 *b*) is a nearly intact polished stone axe with rounded butt (L. 9.30, W. 5.20, Th. 3.00 cm). The working edge is very worn and damaged at one corner. Material is a hard greenish stone, possibly serpentinite or jadeite. The greenstone axe may be paralleled by the

---

[12] Thimme 1977, fig. 85, nos. 2 and 4.
[13] Warren 1972*a*, 237 and fig. 104, no. 210.
[14] Rahmstorf 2003.

[15] Wilson 1999, SF 115, pl. 38 and 96.
[16] Bernabò Brea 1964, vol. I.2, pl. clxxxvii, no. 9 (Poliochni); Lamb 1936, 187, nos. 31.64 and 29.3 (Thermi).

178

FIG. 8.5. Polished stone axes (*1* and *2*) and hammerstones (scale 1:2).

slightly smaller example from Myrtos.[17] Greenstone or serpentine axes are also known from Thermi, the largest of these (no. 30.56: L. 9.30 cm) being of similar size to Markiani **EE 661**.

It should be noted that the excavations at Markiani did not recover any fragments of the perforated hammer-axes or battle axes common in the eastern Aegean at this time.

[17] Warren 1972a, 232.

TABLE 8.6. The catalogued finely-worked stone objects from Markiani.

	FIG.	Cat. no.	PLATE	Find place	Space	Phase
Rings and beads	8.4: 2	**EE 096**	40 *a*	Unit 513, 1987 Surface Survey		
	8.4: 4	**EE 218**	40 *a*	Trench 2,2 layer 10	Space 3	Ma IV
	8.4: 3	**EE 1001**	40 *a*	Terrace 1, Rock Cutting 2 (cleaning 1985)	Space 7	Ma IV
Worked marble	8.4: 1	**EE 396**	40 *g*, 41 *b*	Trench 3,3 layer 4	Room 1	Ma III
	8.4: 5	EE 822/099		Trench 8,2, layer 2	bastion	Ma III
Marble vessels	8.4: 6	**EE 068**	40 *c–d*	Trench 2 layer 16	Space 3	Ma IV
	8.4: 8	**EE 097**	40 *c–d*	Terrace 1, Rock Cuttings 2–1 (1985, cleaning)	Space 9	Ma IV
	8.4: 7	**EE 1019**	40 *c–d*	Terrace 3, (surface)		
	8.4: 9	**EE 1026**	–	Terrace 1, Rock Cuttings 2–3 (1985, cleaning)	Space 6	Ma IV
Fine pestles	8.4: 15	**EE 395**	40 *e–f*, 41 *a*	Trench 3,3 layer 4	Room 1	Ma III
	8.4: 16	**EE 637**	40 *b*	Trench 3,2 layer 14	Room 2	Ma III
	8.4: 12	**EE 345**	–	Trench 3,2 layer 1	Room 2	Ma III
	8.4: 14	**EE 1612**	40 *b*	Trench 1,6 layer 6	Space 1	Ma III
	8.4: 13	**EE 326**	40 *b*	Trench 3,2 layer 4	Room 2	Ma III
	8.4: 10	**EE 258**	–	Trench 2 layer 44	Space 3	Ma IV
	8.4: 11	**EE 1008**	–	Terrace 1 Rock Cutting 2 (1985, cleaning)	Space 7	Ma IV
Polished stone axes	–	**EE 054**	42 *a*	Unit 301, 1987 Surface Survey		
	8.5: 1	**EE 1018**	42 *a*	Terrace 3, surface		
	8.5: 2	**EE 661**	42 *b*	Trench 3,5 layer 5	Room 2	Ma III

THE COARSE STONE ARTIFACTS

Most of the categories of worked stone found at Markiani are common to other EBA sites of the Cyclades and Greece. Worked stone has, however, been the poor relation in many Aegean prehistoric studies, with the result that documentation of this kind of material is much less abundant than one might expect. The intention here has been to describe and illustrate the worked stone from Markiani to help determine the range and character of a typical EC domestic assemblage. Wherever possible, comparisons have been drawn between the Markiani coarse stone and material described from other sites of the Aegean EBA.

PESTLES AND HAMMERSTONES

These are not a well defined form and although some of the Markiani examples resemble the pestles illustrated from Myrtos (e.g. 176) the parallel is not close. **EE 013** (FIG. 8.5: 4, PLATE 42 *c*) and **EE 638** (FIG. 8.5: 5) resemble no. 30.55 from Thermi, in Lesbos, while **EE 239** (FIG. 8.5: 4, PLATE 42 *c*) can be paralleled in no. 31.27a from the same site.[18] A strict typological series should not however be expected for such rough and ready tools.

Catalogue

EE 013 (FIG. 8.5: 4, PLATE 42 *c*): Unit 201. Surface (L. 13.70, W. 10.60, Th. 7.30 cm). Stone pestle, tapering from rounded butt to convex working surface. Carefully shaped (probably ground smooth), although the stone is coarse grained and the surface texture rough. The working surface has been worn smoother still through use, but asymmetrically, more at one side than the other.

EE 239 (FIG. 8.5: 3, PLATE 42 *c*): Trench 2,26 (L. 9.00, W. 4.30, Th. 3.90 cm). Small stone pestle, regularly shaped,

with working surface worn smooth through use. Material is a relatively fine-grained stone, though with veins of quartz.

EE 638 (FIG. 8.5: 5): Trench 3,2 layer 14 (L. 14.10, W. 8.80, Th. 5.80 cm). Pestle or hammer-stone of tapering oblong form. One of the lateral faces is smooth, possibly through use as a rubber, though its evenness is broken by veins of quartz. Both ends are rounded and battered, and either could have been used for hammering or pounding.

---

[18] Lamb 1936, 189, fig. 56.

stone saddle quern, broken along two edges. Concave grinding surface heavily worn.

EE 834 (FIG. 8.8): Trench 1,1 layer 45 ('fissure') (L. 23.50 W. 21.50, Th. 5.70 cm) is a fragment of one corner of coarse conglomerate quernstone, roughly chipped and broken. Grinding surface worn and concave.

EE 1024 (FIG. 8.8), from Terrace 1, Rock Cutting 2 (1985) (L. 19.70, W. 19.40, Th. 6.30 cm). This fragment of two-sided quernstone is perhaps one-third of the original, with both upper and lower surfaces concave and worn through use. Material is a conglomerate, though finer than the stone of 004 or 834. The profile shows the 'upper' surface to be more undercut than the 'lower', although it is difficult to say which is the original grinding surface. The 'lower' surface is however the more worn of the two, and may have been considered worn out.

EE 1511 (FIG. 8.8): Trench 2π, 56 (L. 43.10, W. 23.80, Th. 6.90 cm) is a finely shaped quernstone of the so-called 'Ios' type, with straight and smoothed long sides and under-surface. Both ends are chipped and damaged, but appear to have been less regular in shape than the long sides. The grinding surface is edged by a slightly raised rounded lip, but is not entirely regular in shape: the long sides are not quite straight, and the short sides are curved and irregular. The proximal end of the quernstone is thicker and higher than the other. The centre of the grinding surface is slightly concave, probably through wear. The material is marble or fine limestone.

LARGE RUBBERS

These are elongated loaf-shaped pieces of coarse stone with flattened concave under-surface and roughly rounded back. In size and shape they would have been suitable for use with any of the saddle querns described above. Only one complete example was found: **EE 1513/2038** (FIG. 8.9), reassembled from two halves found in adjacent trenches on Terrace 1.

Stone rubbers of various types were found at Myrtos, including 35 elongated quern rubbers similar to those from Markiani. The largest Myrtos example measured 35.30 × 13.50 × 6.20 cm, which compares fairly well with the intact rubber **EE 1513/2038** (FIG. 8.9) from Markiani (39.20 × 13.03 × 4.10 cm). This size of rubber would have been suitable for saddle querns such as **EE 004** and **EE 027** (see FIG. 8.7). The largest Markiani rubber (**EE 1703**, FIG. 8.9) would have been significantly larger than this when complete, and may in fact have been a small saddle quern.

Catalogue

EE 024 (FIG. 8.8): Unit 316, surface (L. 17.90, W. 11.30, Th. 3.80 cm). Fragment of rubber with up-turned end and rounded under-surface. Coarse textured abrasive stone (devitrified ash).

EE 1513/2038 (FIG. 8.9): Trench 2π, layer 56/Trench 1,4 layer 11 (L. 22.70, W. 13.10, Th. 3.90 cm; L. 22.80, W. 13.30, Th. 4.10 cm; total joined length 39.20 cm). This complete rubber is in two halves, found in adjacent trenches in successive years. Level grinding surface is up-curved at one end. The under-side is encrusted but smooth and level and may also have been used. The material is a coarse conglomerate.

EE 1521 (FIG. 8.9): Trench 2π, layer 59 (L. 18.60, W. 16.50, Th. 4.90 cm). This fragment of the one end of a rubber with rounded under side, was probably chipped into shape.

The grinding surface is heavily encrusted. Raw material is a high grade schist or gneiss.

EE 1703 (FIG. 8.9): Trench 10, layer 5 (L. 36.8, W. 18.2, Th. 6.2 cm). Greater part of large rubber or small quern, with concave grinding surface and smooth under-surface, worked to a fairly regular shape. Material is a rough conglomerate.

EE 2019 (FIG. 8.10): Trench 1,2, layer 24 (L. 25.60, W. 11.20, Th. 6.70 cm). Fragment of one corner of rubber with concave grinding surface and under-side chipped to semi-smooth shape. Material is a relatively fine-grained stone.

EE 403 (FIG. 8.10): Trench 4, layer 1 (L. 23.80, W. 13.50, Th. 6.20 cm). Broken rubber with regular convex working surface, roughly chipped to shape along one edge; rough under-surface. Material is a coarse-grained stone.

MORTARS

Two heavy coarse stone objects with surface hollows are interpreted as mortars (**EE 002** and **EE 072**, FIG. 8.10). To these could be added **EE 253** (FIG. 8.13), which is here classified as a shallow stone vessel or tray, but which closely resembles the more complete example from Poliochni which Bernabò Brea interpreted as a mortar.[29]

Catalogue

EE 002 (FIG. 8.10): Test Trench 3, surface (L. 18.70, W. 13.80, Th. 5.00 cm). Fragment of coarse conglomerate mortar in shape of a shallow thick walled dish or saucer with thick flattened/rolled rim. There is no clear evidence of wear on the interior, though the rim and interior are smoother than the exterior or under-surface.

EE 072 (FIG. 8.10): surface (location unrecorded). Broken mortar with shallow oval hollow and curved rim. Under surface rough and either broken or unworked. The grinding surface is small in relation to the massive size of the piece of conglomerate in which it has been made.

---

[29] Bernabò Brea 1976, 310, pl. CCLXIII, no. 3.

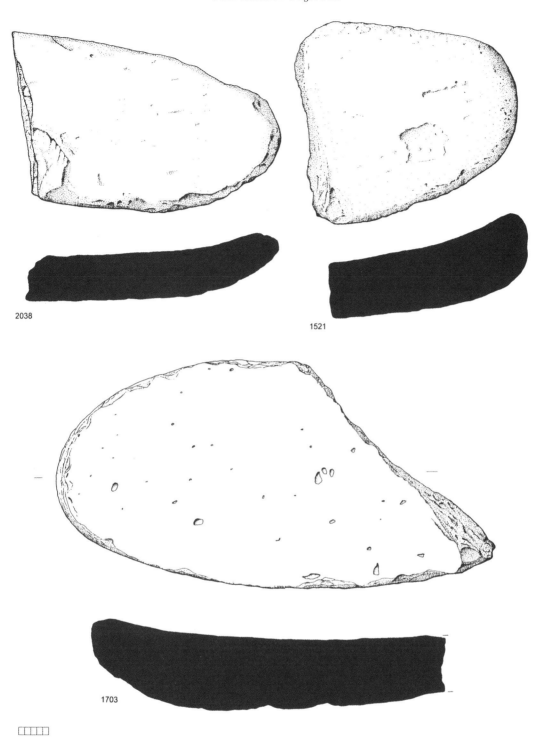

FIG. 8.9. Large rubbers (scale 1:6).

STONE SOCKETS AND PIVOTS

Three objects found at Markiani may be identified as door sockets with varying degrees of confidence. Two were found in Trench 3 and were presumably from buildings discovered there, though neither was *in situ*. **EE 308** (FIG. 8.11, PLATE 43 *b*) may indeed have been a stone vessel rather than a pivot or socket. **EE 310** (FIG. 8.11, PLATE 43 *a*), on the other hand, has concentric scratches caused by a rotating post and the identification is hence secure. **EE 028** (FIG. 8.11) was found in the fill within the rock fissure of Trench 1,1 and must have fallen to this position from the surface of the plateau above.

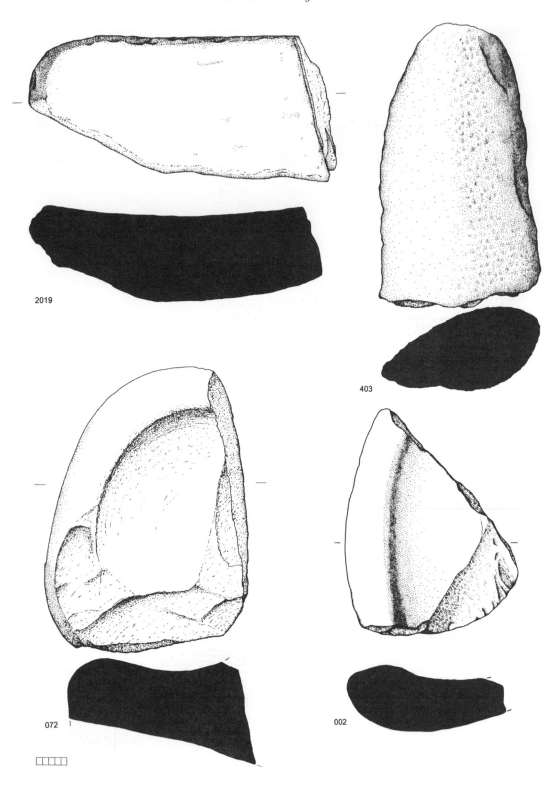

FIG. 8.10. Large rubbers and mortars (scale 1:6).

Seventeen door sockets were discovered at Myrtos, one still *in situ* at the main south-east Entrance 64, another two *in situ* on top of each other in the entrance to Room 78. Door sockets were also recovered at prehistoric Emborio[30] and there were a number of *in situ* examples at Thermi on Lesbos,[31] and at Troy, e.g. Troy I, Houses 102, 103 and 118; Troy II Room 200 and Square F5–6.[32]

[30] Hood 1981, 647.   [32] Blegen *et al.* 1950.
[31] Lamb 1936, 52–4.

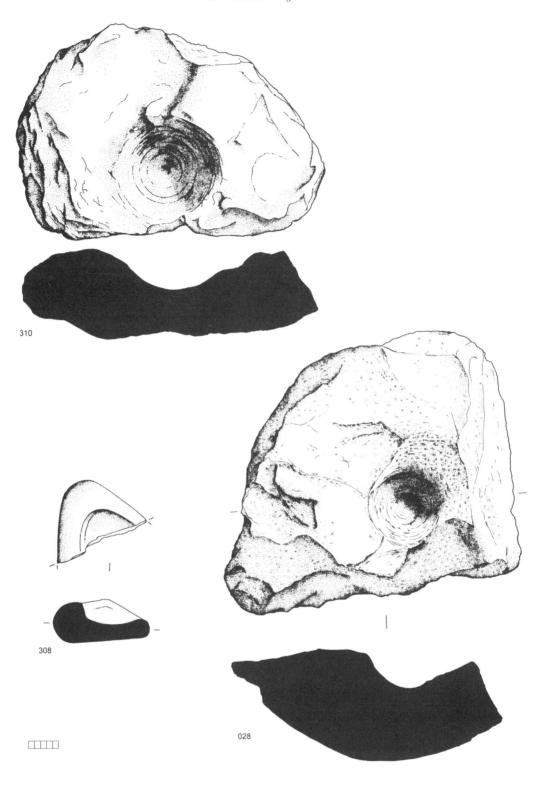

FIG. 8.11. Stone sockets (scale 1:6).

Catalogue

EE 028 (FIG. 8.11): Trench 1,1 layer 14 (L. 24.00, W. 20.00, Th. 9.20 cm). Irregular and broken block of coarse sandstone in the shape of a quarter-circle with a circular concavity near one corner. Though not so well worn nor so regular as **EE 310**, this is most likely to have been a socket, though the alternative interpretation as a small mortar cannot be ruled out.

EE 308 (FIG. 8.11, PLATE 43 *b*): Trench 3,1 layer 2 (L. 7.10, W. 6.90, Th. 3.30 cm). Finely finished fragment of stone, of pointed/semi-circular shape with part of a deep roughly

circular hollow. The purpose of the piece is unclear. The hallow is 2.10 cm deep, but asymmetrical in cross-section. The fine working of the under surface suggests it may have been from a shallow stone vessel, but the irregularity of shape argues in favour of a socket or pivot.
EE 310 (FIG. 8.11, PLATE 43 *a*): Trench 3,1 layer 3 (L. 25.60,

W. 18.10, Th. 6.60 cm). Irregular block of coarse conglomerate with circular hollow near one (broken) edge. The hollow shows traces of heavy wear including a number of deeply scratched concentric grooves, indicating its use as a door socket.

WAISTED WEIGHTS ETC.

The majority of the weights from Markiani are of the waisted type. The identity of these objects as weights is not beyond doubt, but it seems to provide the best explanation for the central groove or narrowing, around which we may imagine a cord was attached.

Not all of these are 'waisted' but they are all likely to have been attached to a cord hanging vertically to hold down or secure some feature or object. They are not seen as 'weights' for use in metrication: they are not balance weights.

A stone object from Naxos tentatively described as a tool or sling stone may fall in the same category.[33] At least four of the waisted weights from Markiani show signs of re-use, three as rubbers (**EE 324**, **EE 1908**, FIG. 8.12; **EE 398**, FIG. 8.12, PLATE 42 *d*), the fourth as a hammerstone (**EE 652**, FIG. 8.12, PLATE 42 *d*).

Only a single perforated weight was found at Markiani **EE 353** (FIG. 8.12). This may be contrasted with almost 80 from Myrtos, generally a regular circular or ovoid shape, plus 19 irregular weights made by boring a hole through a pebble. None of the illustrated examples from Myrtos approaches, in terms of roughness and shape, the perforated sub-rectangular weight from Markiani (**EE 353**). This unfortunately indicates a difference in activities at the two sites — or in those parts of the two sites which have been excavated. Warren suggests the Myrtos weights may have been associated with textile production, tied to cloth to hold it down when drying after washing or dyeing.

Catalogue

a. Waisted weights

EE 324 (FIG. 8.12): Trench 3,2 layer 4 (L. 11.80, W. 8.00, Th. 6.20 cm). Waisted stone object with rounded ends and wide shallow groove around middle, *c.* 2.50 cm wide and 0.30 cm deep. One face is smoothed so that the groove has been partly worn away. This may suggest re-use as a rubber, though it is a feature of two other waisted weights from Markiani (398 and 1908). One of the ends shows signs of damage, perhaps from secondary use as a hammerstone or pounder. The central groove argues however that this object was originally shaped for suspension as a weight.
EE 391 (FIG. 8.12, PLATE 42 *d*): Trench 3,3 layer 4 (L. 9.10, W. 4.40, Th. 4.00 cm). Small stone with rounded ends and concave sides, possibly a weight.
EE 398 (FIG. 8.12, PLATE 42 *d*): Trench 3,3 layer 4 (L. 17.80, W. 12.10, Th. 9.10 cm). This is a large waisted stone, with carefully pecked central groove 3.50 cm wide, *c.* 1 cm deep. The object tapers towards both ends, with a gently curving profile. The ends themselves have been pecked into a roughly flattened form. In cross-section the piece is rounded

except for one facet which has been worn flat and smooth, almost wearing away the central groove. This appears to be secondary to the cutting of the groove, and most likely represents the re-use of the grooved weights as a grindstone or rubber. The ends also show traces of battering, probably from secondary use as a hammer or pounder. Weight **EE 324** is similar in both these respects.
EE 652 (FIG. 8.12, PLATE 42 *d*): Trench 3,4 layer 4 (L. 12.60, W. 7.20, Th. 6.10 cm). Waisted stone of irregular form with shallow central groove *c.* 2 cm wide, 0.30 cm deep. The piece is roughly rounded and was probably pecked into shape. One end shows traces of battering, suggesting re-use as a hammer or pounder.
EE 1908 (FIG. 8.12); Unit 705, surface (L. 13.20, W. 7.60, Th. 5.60 cm). Waisted stone with shallow depression across one (rounded) face deepening into groove *c.* 0.40 cm deep at sides. The other face has been worn flat and smooth, probably through re-use as a rubber. Damage to its ends may be recent.

b. Perforated weights

EE 353 (FIG. 8.12): Trench 3,2 layer 8 (L. 13.00, W. 9.10, Th. 6.00 cm, Wt. 660 g). Sub-rectangular perforated sandstone weight, now reddish in colour possibly as a result of burning. The perforation is off centre and is of hour-glass section. It appears to have been formed by chipping a conical depression in both faces of the stone, then drilling

or breaking out the remaining stone, and finished by rotary grinding. The weight may have been broken along one edge close to the perforation, although the irregularity and roughness of the piece are such that is impossible to be certain which surfaces are original and which the result of breakage.

---

[33] Marangou 1990*a*, 80, no. 74.

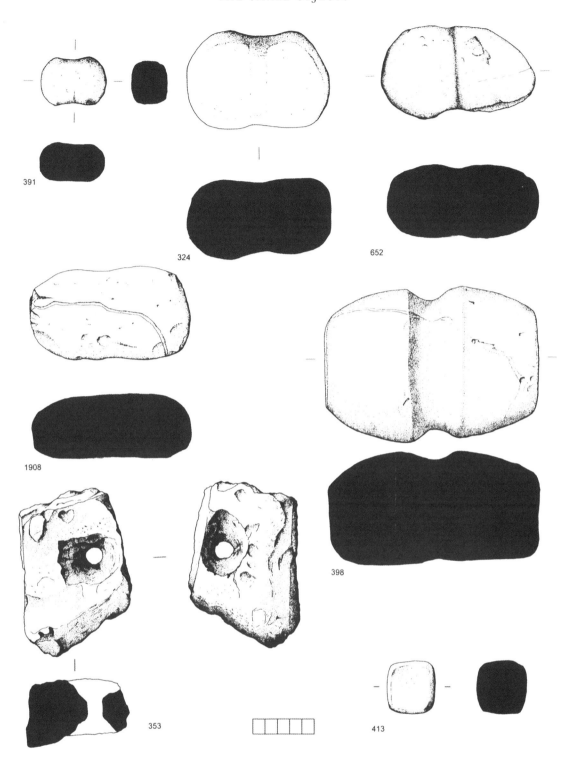

FIG. 8.12. Stone weights waisted, perforated and cuboid (scale 1:3).

c. Cuboid weights

EE 413 (FIG. 8.12): Trench 4,6 layer 1 (L. 4.30, W. 4.10, Th. 4.20 cm, Wt. 140 g). Cuboid stone of relatively fine-grained material with convex faces. The piece is carefully shaped but bears no trace of use; it may have been a weight but could also belong in the category of small grinders which are of approximately this size but mostly in emery and less regularly shaped.

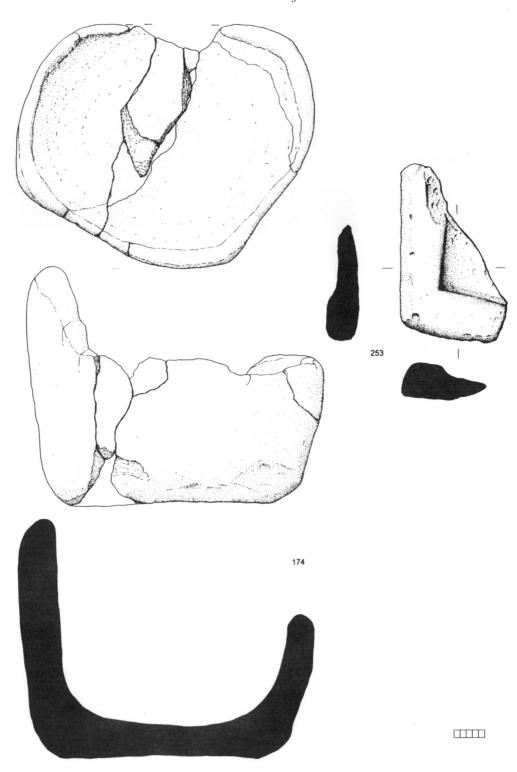

FIG. 8.13. Coarse stone vessels (scale 1:6).

OTHER STONE VESSELS

Stone vessels of materials other than marble are known from several Aegean EBA sites. Myrtos yielded fragments of two serpentine vessels,[34] and shallow stone vessels of various shapes were found at Poliochni — triangular, lozangic, rectangular. **EE 253** (FIG. 8.13) could well be from a vessel such as one illustrated from Poliochni.[35] However, the excavator interprets this as a mortar. The large porous stone vessel from Markiani (**EE 174**, FIG. 8.13, PLATE 43 *e*) has no close parallels.

[34] Warren 1972*a*, 236–7, nos. 208 and 209.   [35] Bernabò Brea 1976, vol II.2, pl. cclxiii, no. 3.

Catalogue

EE 174 (FIG. 8.13, PLATE 43 *e*): Trench 1,2 layer 27 (Max. D. 48.40, Ht *c.* 31.00 cm). This large stone vessel of soft and fragile yellow/brown porous stone is probably of poor quality limestone. The shape is simple with thick rounded base and straight slightly flaring walls, thinning towards the top. The working and shaping are uneven, so that the vessel is irregular, higher at the ends, lowest in the middle of the longer sides; this may in part be due to breakage, and subsequent erosion of the breaks in this soft stone to produce a rounded rim-like form. A few separate fragments of the same material found with this vessel do not appear to fit and may be from part of the vessel wall which has broken away. The purpose of such a vessel is uncertain; it could

never have held liquids and, in its present state, would be considerably more fragile than pottery, though how far this is the result of centuries of chemical action in the soil it is difficult to say.

EE 253 (FIG. 8.13): Trench 2,3 layer 4 (L. 13.10, W. 8.60, Th. 2.80 cm). Fragment of regularly-worked shallow stone vessel or tray with flat raised rim. Material is a coarse crystalline rock. The surviving fragment is a vessel corner with straight sides meeting at an obtuse angle (*c.* 100 degrees). The complete vessel may have been hexagonal. The raised rim is *c.* 3.50 cm wide and stands *c.* 1.10 cm above the inner surface.

TABLE 8.7. The catalogued coarse stone artifacts from Markiani.

Coarse stone	FIG.	Cat. no.	PLATE	Find place	Space	Phase
Pestles and	8.5, 4	EE 013	42 *c*	Unit 201, Surface survey 1987		
hammerstones	8.5, 3	EE 239	42 *c*	Trench 2 layer 26	Space 3	Ma IV
	8.5, 5	EE 638		Trench 3,2 layer 14	Trench 3 Room 2	Ma III
Small grinders	8.6, 1	EE 242	42 *e*	Trench 2 layer 31	Space 3	Ma IV
	8.6, 4	EE 254	42 *e*	Trench 2 layer 45	Space 3	Ma IV
	8.6, 5	EE 372	42 *e*	Trench 3,2 layer 10	Trench 3 Room 2	Ma III
	8.6, 2	EE 394	42 *e*	Trench 3,3 layer 4	Trench 3 Room 1	Ma III
	8.6, 3	EE 633	42 *e–f*	Trench 3,3 layer 6	Trench 3 Room 1	Ma III
	8.6, 6	EE 1900	42 *f*	Surface find 1985		
	8.6, 7	EE 1902	42 *f*	Terrace 4 surface find		
	8.6, 8	EE 1903	42 *f*	Terrace 4 surface find		
	8.6: 9	EE 1904	42 *f*	Trench 1,2 layer 32	Space 1	Ma III
Grindstones	8.7	EE 004		Trench 3 layer 5	Trench 3 Room 1	Ma III
Saddle quern	8.7	EE 027		Terrace wall of Terrace 1		
type	8.7	EE 250		Trench 2, layer 40	Space 3	Ma IV
Shallow	8.8	EE 834		Trench 1,1, layer 45	'fissure'	Ma III
rectangular	8.8	EE 1024		Terrace 1 Rock Cutting 2, (1985 cleaning)	Space 7	Ma IV
palette	8.8	EE 1511		Trench 2π layer 56	Drain	Ma IV
Large rubbers	8.8	EE 024		Unit 316, Surface survey 1987		
	8.9	EE 1513 / 2038		Trench 2π layer 56/ Trench 1,4 layer 11	Drain	Ma IV
	8.9	EE 1521		Trench 2π layer 59	Drain	Ma IV
	8.9	EE 1703		Trench 10,5	Space 9	Ma IV
	8.10	EE 2019		Trench 1,2 layer 24	Space 1	Ma III
	8.10	EE 403		Trench 4 layer 1		
Mortars	8.10	EE 002		Test trench 3. surface		
	8.10	EE 072		Surfce find 1987		
Sockets and	8.11	EE 028		Trench 1,1 layer 14	Space 7	Ma IV
pivots	8.11	EE 308	43 *b*	Trench 3,1 layer 3	Trench 3 Room 1	Ma III
	8.11	EE 310	43 *a*	Trench 3,1 layer 3	Trench 3 Room 1	Ma III
a. waisted	8.12	EE 324		Trench 3,2 layer 4	Trench 3 Room 2	Ma III
weights	8.12	EE 391	42 *d*	Trench 3,3 layer 4	Trench 3 Room 1	Ma III
	8.12	EE 398	42 *d*	Trench 3,3 layer 4	Trench 3 Room 1	Ma III
	8.12	EE 652	42 *d*	Trench 3,4 layer 4	Trench 3 Room 2	Ma III
	8.12	EE 1908		Unit 705, surface survey 1987		
b. perforated	8.12	EE 353		Trench 3,2 layer 8	Trench 3 Room 2	Ma III
c. cuboid	8.12	EE 413		Trench 4,6 layer 1		
Other stone	8.13	EE 174	43 *e*	Trench 1,2 layer 27	Space 1	Ma III
vessels	8.13	EE 253		Trench 2,3 layer 4	Space 3	Ma IV

The Stone Discs/Lids

by Anastasia Angelopoulou

Among the stone objects of Markiani there are 45 disc-shaped objects (see TABLE 8.10) of diameter between a little less than 20 cm and a little more than 35 cm. Their common feature is the circular outline and the planar form.

CLASSIFICATION

The basic criterion for the classification (see TABLES 8.8 and 8.10) is the nature of the surfaces. There are four different forms of disc-shaped stone object: type A with two smooth flat surfaces (FIG. 8.14), and a diameter between 9 and 20 cm. Only three examples have diameters over 25 cm; type B, with one smooth flat surface (FIG. 8.15), and a diameter between 8 and 17 cm. Only one example has a diameter over 35 cm; type C with curved lower surface (FIG. 8.15); and, type D with irregular surfaces (FIG. 8.15) and diameter between 8 to 11 cm.

RAW MATERIAL

The stone discs of forms A and B are mainly of schist. 20% of form D is also of schist. Only disc **EE 636/84** (FIG. 8.15, PLATE 43 *c*) of type C and another one of type D (**EE 25**, FIG. 8.15) are made of marble. Some of these lids have a round groove on the under surface for the better fitting on the rim, equivalent to the groove on type C.

Stone lids **EE 331/54** (FIG. 8.15) and **EE 2041/76** are made of a grey coarse stone; based on texture and hardness they do not seem to be schist. **EE 701** and **EE 18** are made of a dark brown and a grey rock, difficult to identify without petrographic examination.

TABLE 8.8. The material of the stone lids according to type.

Stone lids	Schist		Marble		Other		Total	%
	Total	%	Total	%	Total	%		
Type A	22	100					22	48.9
Type B	15	88.2	1	5.9	1	5.9	17	37.8
Type C			1	100			1	2.2
Type D	1	20	1	20	3	60	5	11.1
Total	38	84.4	3	6.6	4	8.8	45	100

TECHNIQUE

In 41 or 73.2% of cases the difference between the maximum and minimum diameter is less than 1 cm, which gives the impression that the intention was to make a perfectly round object. This would not be possible without the use of a geometrical instrument such as a compass. The curve on the under surface of the lid of type C was also made by a compass.

In the 26.8% of the material the difference between the maximum and the minimum diameter is more than 1 cm. In the case of **EE 1611/80** it reaches 3.90 cm.

Most of the material is dated to Ma III and IV. Similar objects have been found in Ayia Irini.[36]

DISTRIBUTION

The largest assemblage of disc-like stone objects come from the area of Trench 3, assignable to Ma III.

Two disc-like stone lids come from the area of Room 1 of Trench 3 (**EE 313/81** and **EE 344/68**, FIG. 8.14). **EE 313/81** is assigned to type B and **EE 344/68** (FIG. 8.14) to type A. From the same room come another two objects (**EE 378/69** and **EE 644/59**) which did not come from closed EC deposits.

In Room 2 of Trench 3, seventeen stone lids were found, seven of which are assigned to type B and eight to type A, while one belongs to type C (**EE 636/84**, FIG. 8.15, PLATE 43 *c*) and one to type D (**EE 654/56**). Another two examples come from the same area (**EE 645/51** and **EE 656/57**) but not from well-stratified levels. Additionally four disc-like stone lids come from Trench 3,5. Two of them are

---

[36] Wilson 1999, 148, pl. 94.

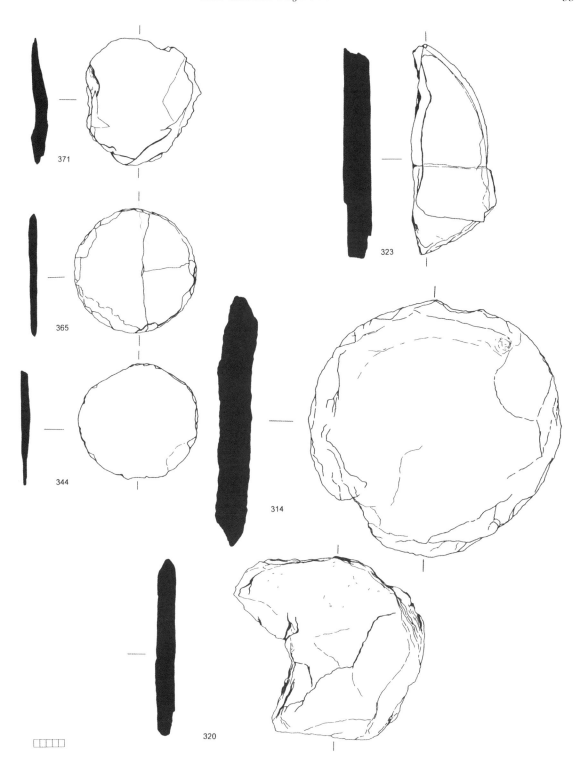

FIG. 8.14. Stone lids type A (scale 1:6).

assigned to type B (**EE 662/64**, PLATE 43 *d*, and **EE 664/66**), while one to type A (**EE 663/77**, PLATE 43 *d*). One (**EE 666/67**, PLATE 43 *d*) does not come from a well-stratified level.

Three disc-like stone lids come from the main channel of the drain in Space 2 (**EE 1510/49**, **EE 1518/83**, **EE 1519**). These are assigned to type A and are probably dated to Ma IV.

There are other examples similar to the surface finds **EE 18**, **EE 25** (FIG. 8, 15). **EE 78/79** and **EE 77/71** come from the area of the 'grave' and **EE 2041/76** from Terrace 1. **EE 404** was found in Trench 4, within not well stratified levels and may not dated securely.

TABLE 8.9. Distribution of the stone lids in the Markiani excavated areas.

| Shape | Fortification | | Summit | | | Terrace 1 | | | Trench 3 | | Surface |
	T6	T8	S 8	T4	S 7	drain	S 3	S 1	T3 R1	T3 R2	
A		2			1	3	1	1	1	8	1
B	1			1					1	7	2
C										1	
D			1							1	2
Total	1	2	1		1	3	1	1	2	17	5

TABLE 8.10. The catalogued stone lids from Markiani.

Form	Cat. no.	FIG.	PLATE	Find location	Max. D	Min. D	T	Phase
Type A	EE 818/65			Trench 8, cleaning	12.0 cm	11.6 cm	1.0 cm	Ma II–III
	EE 80/72			Trench 8,2 layer 7	11.4	11.2	1.9	Ma II–III
	EE 180/73			Trench 1,1 layer 43	11.7	10.9	1.7	Ma III
	EE 2032/70			Trench 1,4 layer 6	15.0	14.3	1.3	Ma IV
	EE 1510/49			Trench 2π layer 56	11.8	11.4	0.9	Ma IV
	EE 1518/83			Trench 1,5, layer 60	27.5	26.7	1.5	Ma IV
	EE 1519			Trench 1,5, layer 60	17.5	17.0	2.0	Ma IV
	EE 1611/80			Trench 1,6, layer 6	18.4	14.5	2.0	Ma III?
	EE 344	8.14		Trench 3,1, layer 4	9.5	9.1	1.1	Ma III
	EE 644/59			Trench 3,3, layer 18	10.0	8.3	0.7	Ma III
	EE 645/51			Trench 3,2, layer 18	16.7	16.5	0.4	Ma III
	EE 382/55			Trench 3,2, layer 12	13.8		1.0	Ma III
	EE 365/50	8.14		Trench 3,2, layer 9	9.8	9.7	0.5	Ma III
	EE 314/52	8.14		Trench 3,2, layer 3	20.6	20.5	2.6	Ma III
	EE 371/75	8.14		Trench 3,2, layer 9	10.4	9.4	0.8	Ma III
	EE 320			Trench 3,2, layer 3	32.3	29.3	3.6	Ma III
	EE 323	8.14		Trench 3,2, layer 4	17.4		2.2	Ma III
	EE 397/82			Trench 3,2, layer 4	29.0	26.0	2.0	Ma III
	EE 651/62			Trench 3,4, layer 3	10.0	9.8	0.8	Ma III
	EE 663/77		43 d	Trench 3,5, layer 5	10.8	10.7	0.4	Ma III
	EE 666/67		43 d	Trench 3,5, layer 6	13.8	11.9	1.0	Ma III
	EE 77/78			Surface, 'grave'	16.5	14.5	0.4	
Type B	EE 601/48	8.15		Trench 6,1, layer 9	12.3	10.4	2.6	Ma I
	EE 404			Trench 4,1, layer 2	11.4		0.6	Ma II?
	EE 225	8.15		Trench 2, layer 14	9.9	7.4	0.4	Ma IV
	EE 313/81			Trench 3,1, layer 4	35.8	34.3	5.2	Ma III
	EE 378/69			Trench 3,1, layer 13	13.9	13.4	0.8	Ma III
	EE 373/74			Trench 3,2, layer 10	14.2	13.5	2.3	Ma III
	EE 381/58			Trench 3,2, layer 12	10.9	9.3	1.3	Ma III
	EE 325/53	8.15		Trench 3,2, layer 4	10.2	9.9	1.1	Ma III
	EE 364/60	8.15		Trench 3,2, layer 9	11.6	10.9	1.2	Ma III
	EE 331/54	8.15		Trench 3,2, layer 6	9.5	9.0	0.7	Ma III
	EE 649/61			Trench 3,4, layer 2	10.7	10.6	1.0	Ma III
	EE 653/63			Trench 3,4, layer 3	9.6	8.2	1.9	Ma III
	EE 656/57			Trench 3,4, layer 5	16.0	15.0	0.6	Ma III
	EE 662/64		43 c	Trench 3,5, layer 5	14.9	14.6	1.9	Ma III
	EE 664/66			Trench 3,5, layer 4	16.6	16.1	0.7	Ma III
	EE 78/79			Surface, 'grave'	14.0	12.4	0.4	Ma III
	EE 79/71			Surface, 'grave'	12.8	12.7	2.0	Ma III
Type C	EE 636/84	8.15	43 c	Trench 3,2, layer 14	34.5 / 28,7	34.0 / 28,4		Ma III
Type D	EE 701			Trench 7, layer 3	9.1	8.9	3.0	Ma II
	EE 2041/76			Trench 1,4, layer 15	9.9	9.3	1.9	Ma IV
	EE 654/56			Trench 3,4, layer 3	10.7	10.6	0.6	Ma III
	EE 18			Unit 503	19.6	18.6	3.5	
	EE 25	8.15		Unit 116	15.3	14.8	3.3	

FIG. 8.15. Stone lids types B, C, and D (scale 1:6).

C. THE LEAF, MAT AND CLOTH IMPRESSIONS
by Jane M. Renfrew

Accidental but clear impressions of leaves, mats and fragments of cloth were found on 72 sherds of pottery, mainly pottery bases, from Markiani. The pots were handmade, and they were probably being made, and certainly air-dried to the leather hard stage, resting on these items, which may well have acted as a sort of precursor to the potters' wheel. It is not surprising that they should have been found here, since some of the earliest reports of such evidence of impressions on prehistoric pottery from the Cyclades come from Amorgos: mat impressions are recorded by Dümmler,[37] Myres[38] and Tsountas.[39] Tsountas also records a leaf impression.[40]

From the excavations at Markiani reported in this volume there were a total of 10 sherds with leaf impressions (six are from well-stratified contexts), 59 sherds had mat impressions of which 35 are well dated, and there are three cloth impressions.

In order to study the impressions, plaster of Paris casts were taken of the clearest of them using the following method. The surface of the sherd was cleaned and thoroughly dried. Then, using a toothbrush, the surface was covered with concentrated washing-up liquid. A plasticine collar was then placed round the impression. The plaster of Paris was mixed to a thick, pourable consistency, and poured onto the impression. It was then left for approximately 30 minutes, until it had set thoroughly and felt warm to the touch. The cast was then removed easily, giving positive impressions of the leaves, matting and cloth, and the sherds were cleaned straight away with water and a soft brush to remove any traces of washing-up liquid or plaster of Paris.

VINE LEAF IMPRESSIONS

Impressions of vine leaves were found on 10 base sherds. Of those which come from stratified contexts one belongs to phase Ma II, two to phases Ma II/III, one to phase Ma III, one to phase Ma III/IV and one to phase Ma IV; the remaining four are not from well-dated contexts. The use of vine leaves to stand handmade pots on to dry was quite widespread during the EBA in the Aegean: vine leaf impressions are known from Chalandriani on Syros,[41] Paros,[42] Naxos,[43] Siphnos,[44] Myrtos on Crete,[45] EH Corinth,[46] Zygouries,[47] and Synoro in trhe Argolid[48] and they often provide the only evidence at these sites for the cultivation of vines during this period, as they do at Markiani. Leaves of other species were also used. Tsountas reports that leaf impressions of the white poplar, *Populus alba*, were found on the base of a jar from Dokathismata, Amorgos.[49]

The most notable of these impressions is that of two vine leaves on the base of a large Coarse Ware pot (**K 1302**); all the others are of single leaves on the pots with small bases. Some of them are rather worn through constant use of the pot, the impressions of the ribs of the leaves only left to show how the pot had been dried during its manufacture. In some cases it seems that the pot was stood deliberately on the middle part of the leaf so that it left a more or less symmetrical impression on the base. In all cases the leaves were used with the flat side down, the ribs and veins leaving clear impressions on the pottery bases. Once the pot was dry they could easily be peeled off.

TABLE 8.11 provides a catalogue of vine leaf impressions from Markiani.

TABLE 8.11. Vine leaf impressions from Markiani.

Cat. no.	PLATE	Trench/level	Space	Phase	Description
K 1149		Trench 7 layer 9	Space 8	Ma II	A clear vine leaf impression
M1061	48 c	Trench 4,10 layer 3	Summit	Ma II/III	A clear impression, the pot being placed centrally on the vine leaf
K 1301		Trench 4 layer 10	Summit	Ma II/III	A large vine leaf with pronounced central rib
K 1302	48 d	Trench 1,6 layer 6	Terrace 1 Space 1	Ma III	Base of a large Coarse-Ware pot with impressions of two vine leaves
K 1300		Trench 10 layer 1	Terrace 1 Space 4	Ma IV	A clear impression with the pot being positioned centrally on the leaf
K 1304	48 f	Trench 1,1 layer 24	Terrace 1 Space 7	Ma IV	A large leaf impression, rather worn, with ribs only showing on base of a coarse, straight-sided vessel
M1068	48 e	Surface collection	Surface	Unstratified	Worn impression of a large leaf
K 1303		Surface collection	Surface	Unstratified	Very worn impression of a small fragment of vine leaf
M850		Unit 507, K 2 and 3	Surface	Unstratified impression	A small base fragment with clear vine leaf
M200		Unit 117, K 1 and 2	Surface	Unstratified	Very worn vine leaf impression

[37] Dümmler 1886, 38.
[38] Myres 1897, 178f.
[39] Tsountas 1898, 167, pl. 9, no. 24.
[40] Tsountas 1898, 155, 167, 182, pl. 9, no. 11a.
[41] Renfrew 1969: at Chalandriani no fewer than 49 vine leaf impressions have been found on the bases of small bowls (Sherratt 2000, 355, no. 15).
[42] Tsountas 1898, 174.

[43] Zervos 1957, pls 89, 91.
[44] Gropengiesser 1987, 29, 52 no. 60, pl. 4.11.
[45] Renfrew in Warren 1972; 31b.
[46] Kosmopoulos 1948, fig. 45.
[47] Blengen 1928, fig. 91, 2.
[48] Willerding 1973.
[49] Tsountas 1898, 155, 184.

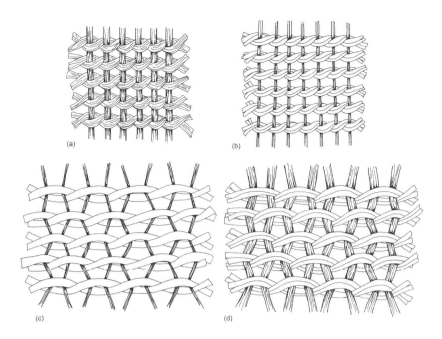

FIG. 8.16. Diagram of twining technique for matting: simple twining on parallel warp with single (*a*) or double (*b*) weft strands and on split/combined warp with single (*c*) or double (*d*) weft strands.

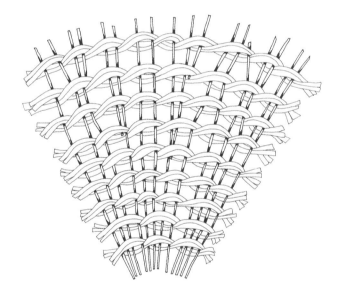

FIG. 8.17. Diagram: circular mat made by twining, a 'star-shaped' radial warp (with double weft strands).

2. MAT IMPRESSIONS

The bulk of the impressions on the pottery bases were of matting of three different types. All were made using the twining technique: there was simple twining on a parallel warp using either single or double weft strands (see schematic diagrams, FIG. 8.16 *a–b*); split twining where the warp strands were alternately split or combined by the weft strands on alternate rows, the weft strands again being single or double (see schematic diagrams, FIG. 8.16 *c–d*); and finally circular mats made by radial twining over a 'star-shaped' warp, and again the weft strands being either single or double (see schematic diagrams, FIG. 8.17). There is an impression on a large EC pottery base from 'tzi Viglais', Amorgos, in the Ashmolean Museum, Oxford (AE 248),[50] which is made in a similar way with radial twinning over a star shaped warp. There are no impressions of coiled mats here.

[50] Evely 1999, 244, pl. LIVb and pl. LVb; Sherratt 2000 356–7, pls. 607–8, fig. 262, no. III.13.c.1

TABLE 8.12. Mat impressions from Markiani.

	FIG.	Cat. no.	PLATE	Trench/Layer	Space	Phase	Description
126		**K 1050**		Trench 6, 1 layer 8	Fortification wall	Ma I	Radially twined mat rather worn
114		**K 1363**		Trench 7 layer 12	Space 8	Ma II	Radially twined mat
124		**K 1372**		Trench 7 layer 15	Space 8	Ma II	Radially twined mat
100		**K 1350**	44 *a–b*, 45 *a*	Trench 1,6 layer 6	Space 1	Ma III	Complete base parallel warp
116		**M1037**		Trench 1,2 layer 5	Space 1	Ma III	Radially twined mat
131	8.18: 4	**K 1377**		Trench 1,1 layer 38	Space 7	Ma III	Wide spaced
125	8.18: 3	**K 1373**		Trench 3, layer 2	Trench 3	Ma III	Radially twined mat loose weave
138		**K 1381**		Trench 8, cleaning	bastion	Ma III	Wide spaced
151		**K 1383**		Trench 8,2 layer 7	bastion	Ma III	
152		**K 1384**		Trench 8,2 layer 13	bastion	Ma III	
157		**K 1387**		Trench 8,2 layer 14	bastion	Ma III	worn
158		**K 1388**		Trench 8,2 layer 14	bastion	Ma III	worn
133		**K 1378**		Trench 10 layer 2	Space 9	Ma III?	
105		**K 1193**		Trench 2 layer 29	Space 6	Ma IV	Split twining
111	8.18: 10	**K 1360**	46 *c*	Trench 1,5 layer 6	Space 1	Ma IV	
113		**K 1362**	47 *b*	Trench 2π layer 60	Drain	Ma IV	
115		**K 1364**		Trench 1,4 layer 27	Space 6	Ma IV	
117		**K 1365**	47 *a*	Trench 1,4 layer 29	Space 6	Ma IV	Parallel warp very clear
106		**K 1355**		Trench 1,1 layer 24	Space 7	Ma IV	
119		**K 1367**		Trench 1,1 layer 33	Space 7	Ma IV	Loose weave
123		**K 1371**		Trench 1,1 layer 33	Space 7	Ma IV	Neat radial
127		**K 1374**		Trench 1,1 layer 46	'Fissure'	Ma III	Wide spaced
135		**K 1379**		Trench 1,1 layer 25	Space 7	Ma IV	Loose weave
149		**K 1382**	47 *f*	Trench 1,1 layer 33	Space 7	Ma IV	Pot inside basket
150	8.18: 12	**EE 126**		Trench 1,1 layer 23	Space 7	Ma IV	Double weft
153		**K 1385**		Trench 1,1 layer 45	Space 7	Ma IV	Wide spaced
156		**K 1386**		Trench 1,1 layer 24	Space 7	Ma IV	Loose weave rubbed impression
107		**K 1356**		Rock Cutting 2	Space 7	Ma IV	Wide spaced
120	8.18: 9	**K 1368**	48 *a–b*	Rock Cutting 2	Space 7	Ma IV	Radially twined mat inside pedestal
121	8.18: 6	**K 1369**	46 *d*	Rock Cutting 2	Space 7	Ma IV	Split twining
122		**K 1370**	47 *c*	Rock Cutting 2	Space 7	Ma IV	Tightly woven mat
128		**K 1375**		Rock Cutting 2	Space 7	Ma IV	
129		**K 1376**	47 *d*	Rock Cutting 2	Space 7	Ma IV	Split twining
118		**K 1366**	47 *e*	Trench 1,4, layer 6	Space 3	Ma IV	
136		**K 1380**		Trench 2, 35	Space 3	Ma IV	
130		**K 1047**		Trench 1,3, layer 1	Space 4	Ma IV	
101	8.18: 1	**K 1351**	46 *f*		surface	unstratified	Worn mat
102		**K 1352**			surface	unstratified	Worn impression
103		**1353**			surface	unstratified	Worn impression
104		**K 1354**		Rock Cutting 2–4	surface	unstratified	
108		**K 1357**		Rock Cutting 4	surface	unstratified	
109		**K 1358**			surface	unstratified	
110		**242/ K 1359**	46 *e*		surface	unstratified	
112		**K 1361**			surface	unstratified	
134		**Ma87**		Unit 507, K 2+3	surface	unstratified	
137		**M161**		Unit 133, E	surface	unstratified	
139		**M455**		Unit 216, E	surface	unstratified	
140		**M126**		Unit 113, E	surface	unstratified	
141		**M148**		Unit 108, E	surface	unstratified	
142		**M359**		Unit 202, E	surface	unstratified	
143		**M304**	46 *a*	Unit 208, K 1,2,3	surface	unstratified	
144		**Ma87/**		Unit 208, K 1,2,3	surface	unstratified	
145		**M845**	46 *b*	Unit 507, K 1	surface	unstratified	
146		**M841**		Unit 507, K 1	surface	unstratified	
147		**M842**		Unit 507, K 1	surface	unstratified	
148		**M843**		Unit 507, K 1	surface	unstratified	
154		**M805**		Unit 509, K 1,2,3	surface	unstratified	
155		**M820**		Unit 509, K 1,2,3	surface	unstratified	
159		**K 1389**		Unit 507, K 2+3	surface	unstratified	

In addition the weave of the mats was either tight, with the weft strands packed closely together, or loose when the warp strands were clearly visible between each row of weft strands. In most cases the warp strands were composite bundles of finer material than the weft.

The question arises as to what materials were being used, and it is not easy to be sure. The largest weave seems to have been of reed, perhaps *Phragmites*; some was possibly straw, other of a harder material may have been the bases of *Phragmites* stems or of fine willow branches. It is possible that the finer warp strands may have been made from grass stems.

What is clear is that many of the mats show signs of being worn out. Some are frayed and others have holes in them; they look as though this function in manufacturing pottery was their final rather than their primary use. None of those pots placed on circular mats appears to have been placed in the centre of the mat.

The position of the impressions can sometimes throw interesting light on the processes of manufacture of some of the pot forms. For example it appears that the impression 149 (**K 1382**, PLATE 46 *f*) shows that a small pot was actually moulded within a basket. This technique was used for a series of small basket-moulded pots from MM II levels at Mallia on Crete,[51] and was also used in the EBA of eastern Anatolia and Transcaucasia.[52]

Impression 120 (**K 1368**, FIG. 8.18: 9, PLATE 48 *a–b*) is of a radially twined mat on the bottom of a bowl, which was dried on the mat prior to being set on its pedestalled base. Impression 118 (**K 1366**, PLATE 47 *e*) occurs on the top of a coarse-ware lid of a collared jar, suggesting that this was dried upside down to the leather-hard stage.

These impressions do indicate that this community was well used to weaving mats of a wide range of qualities, and that they had the abilities to make mats and baskets to meet all their everyday needs.

The largest mat impression **K 1350** (PLATES 44 *a–b* and 45 *a*), of a simple twined mat on a parallel warp comes from, Trench 1,6, layer 6, within Space 1, dated to Ma III phase: it shows 62 rows of simple twinning in 7 1/4 inches, (i.e. *c.* 9 rows to the inch) and 32 weft strands in 7 1/4 inches *c.* 4 strands to the inch) (see PLATE 44 *a* or *b*).

TABLE 8.12 lists the mat impressions from Markiani; 36 come from well dated contexts: There is one from phase Ma I, two from phase Ma II, ten from phase Ma III and 23 from Ma IV. In addition 22 were surface finds.

THE CLOTH IMPRESSIONS

There were just three cloth impressions found at Markiani. They are all small fragments and show a simple tabby weave where the weft passes under and over alternate warp threads. They are not very distinct so it is not possible to ascertain whether it was linen or woollen cloth. They are notably coarser than the fabric found at Kephala on Kea and probably represent some sort of sacking-type cloth. They were found at the following locations:

Impression **K 1557** (FIG. 8.18: 13) from Trench 3,3, layer 4, dated to Ma III, is a fragment of cloth with 7 rows of weft threads to the inch, it is rather loosely woven with double weft, the warp showing between each row of weft threads (see FIG. 8.18: 3)

Impression **K 1341** (PLATE 45 *b*) from Trench 2, level 27, Space 6, dated to Ma IV, shows 11 weft threads to the inch, and is the finest fabric represented. The impression is on the outer surface of a fine ware pot.

Impression **K 1340/M1046** (PLATE 45 *c*), shows a small are of a tabby weave with about ten weft threads to the inch.

D. THE SPINDLE-WHORLS AND RELATED OBJECTS

by Giorgos Gavalas

The significant assemblage of 171 spindle-whorls, most of which were recovered inside the circular feature of space in successive layers in the area of Rock Cutting 2, provides us with new information concerning spinning during the third millennium BC in the Cyclades. It is the first time since the excavation of Troy that such a considerable quantity of this kind of material from closed, well-dated deposits is available for study, but here only a representative sample is presented. It spans the period

[51] Poursat 1980.   [52] van Loon 1978, 68, 120, pl. 141–4.

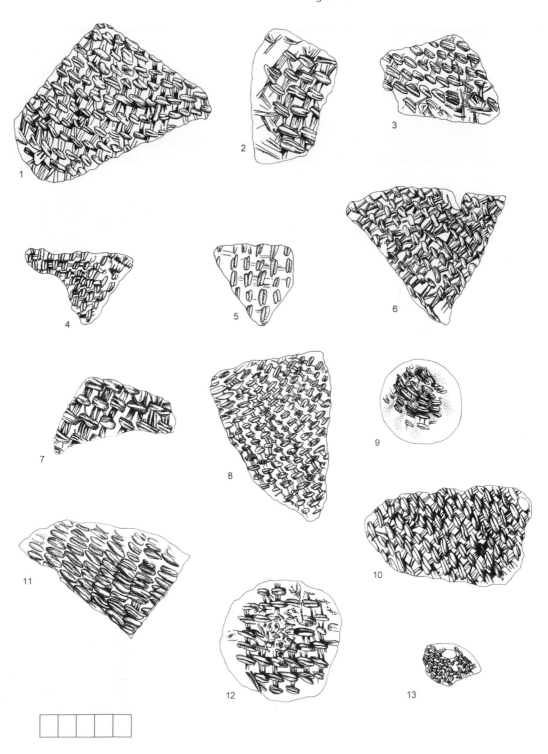

FIG. 8.18. Mat impressions (*1–12*) and cloth impression (*13*) on pot bases (scale 1:3).

from Ma II to IV. Within the same deposits 31 clay discs made from cut and perforated potsherds were found in association with the spindle-whorls and thus these are examined together.

In addition, one cuboid rectangular object with two perforated holes in the long sides, initially thought to be a loom-weight, and is also presented in this section.

THE SPINDLE-WHORLS

The surface surveys of 1985 and 1987 and the excavation (1988–1990) revealed 203 objects which relate to spinning and weaving activities, specifically 171 spindle-whorls, 31 perforated clay discs and one object initially identified as a loom-weight. The surface survey of 1987 produced only two spindle-whorls from units 129 and 303 respectively, from the selective collection outside circles, at the north and west of the excavation site

The spindle-whorls and perforated discs, found during the surface survey of 1985 (31 spindle-whorls and five discs) come from the surface cleaning in the area of Rock Cutting 2 in Spaces 6 and 7 which were later excavated. For that reason they are considered together with the material from the same spaces. One comes from Terrace 3 and two from the south-west area.

The excavation produced 128 spindle-whorls, 26 perforated discs and the putative loom-weight. Of the 171 spindle-whorls, 81 are preserved intact. Most of them (109, i.e. more than 55% of the total, see TABLE 8.13) were found concentrated in successive layers, covering the area of the circular feature, namely Space 7, along with perforated potsherds and pottery characteristic of the Kastri Group (see Chapter 4). A small assemblage of 14 spindle-whorls and perforated sherds was found north from Wall K in Space 8 on the summit. Finally, seven spindle-whorls were from the two-roomed building of Trench 3, which has been interpreted as a house.

TABLE 8.13. The occurrence of spindle-whorls and potsherds by find location.

	Space 8 Trenches 1,1 and 7	The 'fissure' Trenches 1,1 and 9,1	Space 7 Trench 1,1	Trench 3	Total
Spindle-whorls	12	45	43	7	107
Perforated potsherds	2	11	10		23
Total	14	56	53	7	130

Of the 171 whorls 165 are of clay while only six are stone. For the clay spindle-whorls, fabrics similar to those employed for pottery were used. As it has been noted in Chapter 7 the two main categories Marble Ware and Blue Schist Ware are the most frequent. Most of them, which come from layers dated to Ma IV, are of Blue Schist fabric (*c.* 60%). The surface treatment is the same as for the pottery, mainly smoothing.

Various stones, including schist, limestone and at least one volcanic rock, probably imported from Thera, were used in their manufacture. These are small flat stones, shaped into discs by using harder stone or metal tools, and then smoothed and polished (**EE 297**, **EE 1006** and **EE 306** PLATE 49 *c*).

TYPOLOGY

The Markiani spindle-whorls were classified using the following criteria: shape of section,[53] ratio of diameter to thickness[54] and weight.[55] This study produced the following types (see FIG. 8.19 and TABLE 8.14):

1. The *discoid* is the most common type. Their weight varies between 14 and 27 g. There are three main variants:
   (a) the flat discoid, which are very similar to the perforated discs with the shape of a flat cylinder (e.g. **EE 420**, FIG. 8.20: 6; **216**, FIG. 8.20: 9; **175**, FIG. 8.21: 1; **208**, FIG. 8.22: 5, PLATE 50 *a*).
   (b) the flat convex discoid[56] which is characterised by both large diameter and small height, and (e.g. **158**, FIG. 8.20: 5).
   (c) the biconvex (**EE 106**, FIG. 8.20: 1; **220**, FIG. 8.20: 4).
   These are known from Tsountas' excavations at Kato Akrotiri,[57] as well as from the later layers at Myrtos on Crete,[58] but are more rare in the north-east Aegean, occurring in the Yellow period at Poliochni, at Troy and at Thermi.[59]

[53] Carington Smith 1975, 196–217.
[54] Banks 1967, 485.
[55] Carington Smith 1975, 196ff and Barber 1991, 52.
[56] Carington Smith 1975, 199 but they are not considered as a particular variation.
[57] Tsountas 1898, pl. 8,4.
[58] Warren 1972a, 222.
[59] Bernabò Brea 1964, pl. CLXIX; Blegen *et al.* 1951, pl. 5; Lamb 1936, 163, fig. 47, 30.

Spindle-whorls

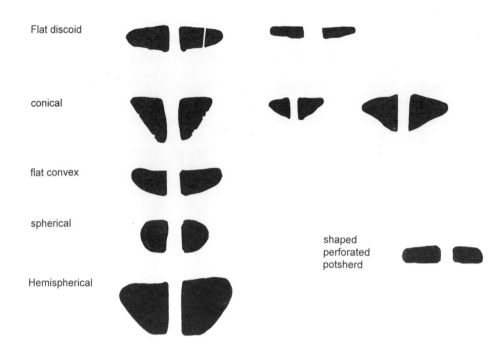

Flat discoid

conical

flat convex

spherical

shaped
perforated
potsherd

Hemispherical

FIG. 8.19. Spindle-whorl typology.

2. The *conical* type (e.g. **EE 062**, FIG. 8.20: 3; **EE 307**, FIG. 8.20: 10; **85**, FIG. 8.21: 5 and **259**, FIG.
    8.22: 2, PLATE 49 *a*), classified on the basis of the ratio of diameter against thickness, into three
    categories:
    (a) low cones; (b) high cones; and (c) those with curved walls. The last have sub-categories with (i)
    acute edges; (ii) rounded/blunt edges; (iii) concave walls (**100**, FIG. 8.21: 9); (iv) truncated cones
    (**85**, FIG. 8.21: 5);[60] (v) a flat upper surface or bell shaped (**96**, FIG. 8.21: 10). This type is very
    common all over the Aegean,[61] especially on the Greek mainland. Smaller quantities were found
    in the north-east Aegean and on Crete. In the Cyclades, a few conical spindle-whorls come from
    the earlier excavations in the cemeteries.[62]
3. *Flat convex* whorls constitute a special type (e.g. **111**, FIG. 8.20: 2; **145**, FIG. 8.20: 7; **240**, FIG. 8.21:
    7). They may be divided into big and small, according to the ratio of diameter to thickness, and
    those with curved wall.
4. *Spherical* spindle-whorls, i.e. in the shape of a flattened sphere or ellipsoid (e.g. **90**, FIG. 8.21: 8
    and **284**, FIG. 8.21: 11), constitute another type, which appears very rarely, mainly in the north-
    east Aegean, namely at Poliochni,[63] and Thermi on Lesbos.[64]
5. The *hemispherical* spindle-whorl with a flat, or slightly concave lower surface[65] appears at Markiani
    in small quantities (see **277**, FIG. 8.21: 2; **87**, FIG. 8.21: 4; **163**, FIG. 8.21: 6 and **86** PLATE 49 *d*).
    The spindle-whorls of this type are the heaviest. It was believed until recently that these spindle-
    whorls appeared exclusively in the north-east Aegean. This may be an indication that these
    particular spindle-whorls were used for flax spinning.

There are also individual forms which appear only once, such as the cylindrical (**141**, FIG. 8.21: 12)
with a concave lower surface and curved surfaces, the flat discoid with a slightly curved surface (**244**),
the biconcave discoid (**214**, FIG. 8.21: 13).
    It should be noted that by far the most common forms are the flat discoid and the conical both seen
in phases II, III and IV.

[60] Carington Smith 1977, 199.
[61] Cosmopoulos 1991, 87.
[62] Tsountas 1898, pl. 8,5 and Doumas 1977, pl. XLVI, h.
[63] Bernabò Brea 1976, 280.
[64] Lamb 1936, 163, fig. 47, 1, 14.
[65] Cosmopoulos 1991, 88.

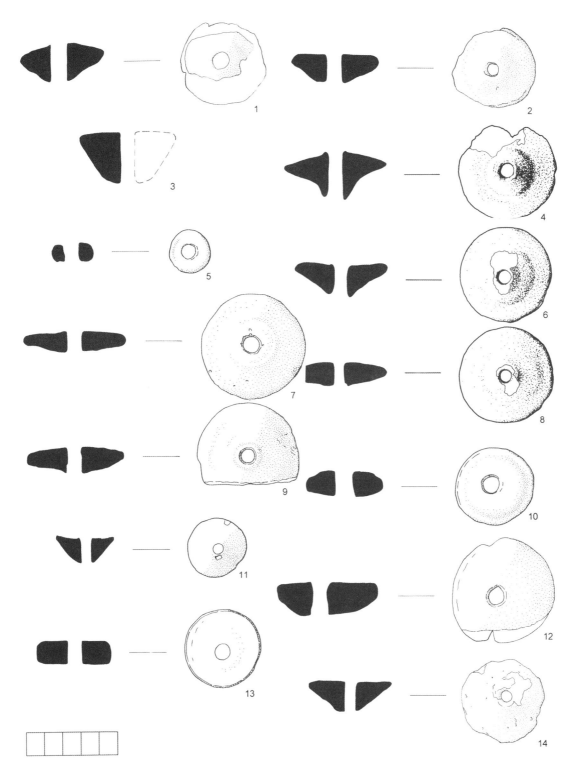

FIG. 8.20. Spindle-whorls and shaped perforated potsherds of phase II–III (scale 1:2).

DECORATION

Only ten whorls out of 171 (see TABLE 8.14) are decorated with incisions or impressions. A semi-circular linear decoration (probably made by a fingernail) forms a simple circular arrangement (e.g. **219**, FIG. 8.22: 6, PLATE 50 *a* or **208**, FIG. 8.22: 5, PLATE 50 *a*) or radiating curvilinear rows (e.g. **250**, FIG. 8.22: 4, PLATE 50 *a*). This technique and the decorative motifs, which appear mainly in Ma III and IV, are known both from Troy I,[66] and Poliochni Yelow.[67]

[66] Blegen *et al.*, 1950, pl. 222, no. 35–103.   [67] Bernabò Brea 1976, pl. CCXXX e.

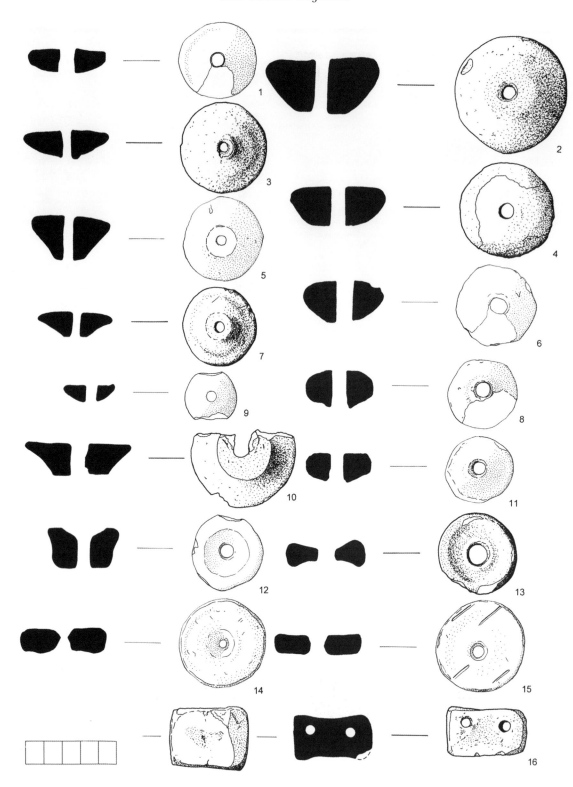

FIG. 8.21. Spindle-whorls and shaped perforated potsherds of phase IV (scale 1:2).

One spindle-whorl (**EE 310**, broken in half FIG. 8.22: 9, PLATE 50 *g*) bears a unique figurative depiction. There are at least two incised quadruped animals, the first with horns and the second, larger one, with a longer tail. These animals are aligned one behind the other. A parallel for this depiction is known from the Heraion in Samos.[68]

---

[68] Isler, 1973, 173.

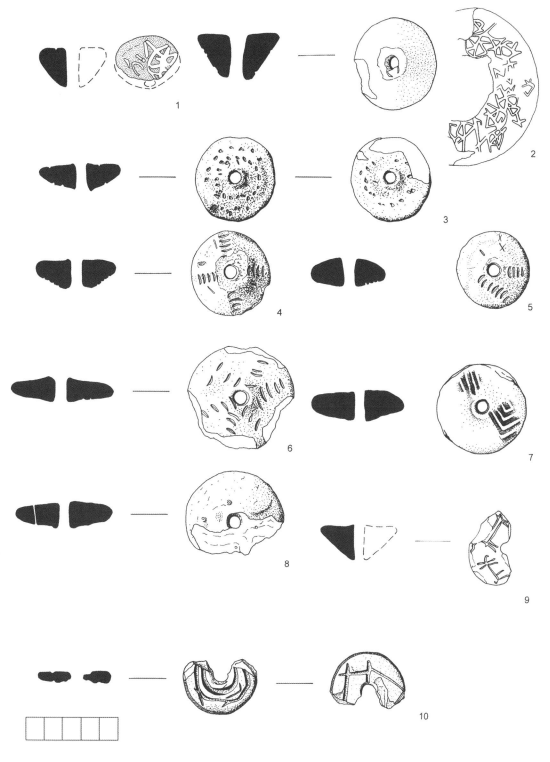

FIG. 8.22. Decorated spindle-whorls (scale 1:2).

Another spindle-whorl (**320**, FIG. 8.22: 7, PLATE 50 *f*) bears a seal impression with a row of acute angles. A seal-impressed weight from Lerna provides a parallel of sorts, as do the newly discovered examples from Skarkos on Ios.[69] However, there is no published parallel for a spindle-whorl with a seal impression. Two more examples, **321** (FIG. 8.22: 1) and **259** (FIG. 8.22: 2, PLATE 50 *e*) have a very slight impressed or stamped motif of acute angles and triangles in a non-symmetrical alignment.

[69] Wiencke, 1969, 500, 508, pl. 129 no. 191; *CMS* V no. 51. Cf. also now the seal-impressed 'weights' from Skarkos: *CMS* V Suppl. 3 nos. 169–174.

Another decorative type shows impressed dots in cyclical (like **151**, FIG. 8.22: 3, PLATE 50 *c*) or cross-like arrangement (like **266**, FIG. 8.22: 8, PLATE 50 *d*), known from similar examples at Troy I[70] or Poliochni Yellow.[71]

The only decorated spindle-whorl of stone, **297** (FIG. 8.22: 9, PLATE 49 *c*) has incisions in both sides: curvilinear-spiral and linear motives, probably by the means of a metal tool.

DISCUSSION

The spindle-whorls come from sealed contexts over a long period within the third millennium. More specifically, they date from the second phase of the settlement, Ma II, to the abandonment of the settlement in Ma IV. Considerable variety is seen in each phase. This fact may reveal an intentional division of spindle-whorl types for the different stages of spinning in relation to the production of various types of threads or different fabrics.

The small number of decorated whorls may be an indication of their possible use for specialised work rather embellishment. That some particular spindle-whorl types continue without interruption during the entire third millennium BC suggests that there was a strong tradition and an attachment to traditional techniques.

This spindle-whorl material constitutes a unique assemblage in the Cyclades in both quantity and variety. During the early excavations of Tsountas, on Amorgos, in Kato Akrotiri,[72] and in Syros, both in the cemeteries and the settlements of Chalandriani,[73] only a small number of whorls was discovered. A few whorls were also found during excavations by both Clon Stefanos[74] and Doumas[75] on Naxos.

Close similarities in both shape and decoration are seen in the north-east Aegean, and especially at Troy, where 8,000–10,000 are recorded from Troy II.[76] Parallels are also attested from Poliochni on Lemnos,[77] Thermi on Lesbos, Emborio on Chios,[78] and Aphrodisias in Asia Minor.[79]

In the Cyclades, and especially at Markiani, we see a clear preference for flat discoid and conical spindle-whorls. On the other hand, in Asia Minor and in the islands of the north-east Aegean biconical and the spherical spindle-whorls are more common.[80] Meanwhile, on the Greek mainland, and especially on the coast, at Lefkandi on Euboia, Ayios Kosmas in Attica, but also at Lithares in Boiotia, there is a clear preference for conical whorls, cylindrical spindle-whorls[81] of larger size, and for other varieties, which are not very common in the rest of the Aegean.

2. SHAPED PERFORATED POTSHERDS

Along with the spindle-whorls, 31 perforated discs of shaped rounded potsherds (like **118**, FIG. 8.21: 13; **140**, FIG. 8.21: 14; **150**, FIG. 8.21: 15, PLATE 49 *f*) were found in similar contexts. Seventeen of these are intact, and fourteen fragmentary. They fall into two categories dependant on shape (see also FIG. 8.19).

The first category is the rounded cylindrical disc (e.g. **140**, **150**, **115**, **251**, **176**, PLATE 49 *f*). These are present from Ma II to Ma IV. The second category is the ellipsoid disc, in which the hole is not placed symmetrically in the centre (e.g. **256**, **123**, **133**, **128**, **206** and **239**, PLATE 49 *f*). They appear mainly during the later periods, Ma III and Ma IV.

These sherds come from large, mainly open vessels, with a few from closed vessel shapes; their fabric and the surface treatment is similar to the pottery as described in Chapter 7C, D and E. The perforation is made by the parallel trimming of both sides as seen in **288** and **256** (PLATE 49 *g*).

Shaped perforated potsherds were also found at Lerna,[82] Lithares,[83] Ayios Kosmas,[84] Eutresis,[85] Asine,[86] and Thermi[87] in the same period.

The exact use of the perforated discs constitutes a more general problem. It is possible that they were used in place of spindle-whorls for specialised work,[88] such as the production of coarser threads, in the first stage of the spinning of the thread, which would than be subjected to further processing.

[70] Blegen *et al.*, 1950, pl. 222, no. 36–277.
[71] Bernabò Brea 1976, pl. CCXXVII, f, I, j.
[72] Tsountas 1898, 166, 168, pl. 8, 4–7.
[73] Tsountas 1899, 105, pl. 10, 6–7
[74] Papathanasopoulos, 1961/2, 127, pl. 57d.
[75] Doumas 1977, pl. XLVI, f, g, h.
[76] Blegen, 1963, 88.
[77] La Rossa, 1997, 126–9.
[78] Hood, 1981/82, 637.
[79] Joukowski *et al.*, 1986, 373.

[80] Carington Smith 1975, 211.
[81] Carington Smith 1975, 209.
[82] Carington Smith 1975, 217.
[83] Tzavela-Evjen 1984, 174, fig 92, δ, θ, ι, κ.
[84] Mylonas 1959, 146.
[85] Goldman, 1931, 295, fig. 120.
[86] Frödin and Persson, 1938, 251, 177.
[87] Lamb 1936, pl. XXVI 31–53a.
[88] See also Joukowski *et al.* 1986, 381.

3. THE RECTANGULAR PARALLELEPIPED OBJECT WITH TWO PERFORATED HOLES IN THE LONG SIDES

From Markiani there is only one rectangular parallelepiped object **257** (FIG. 8.21: 16, PLATE 49 *e*) with two perforated holes in the long sides (from Trench 1,3, layer 2, H. 3.3, W. 4.25, Th. 2.42, D. perforations 0.55–0.60 cm, Wt. 52 g). On one of its narrow sides there is an impression from barley seed (see below Chapter 9C, PLATE 54 *c*). It is similar to the clay object from Lerna,[89] which Carington Smith[90] considered (although with reservations) to be a loom-weight on account of its similarity in shape with the cubic loom-weights of the same period in Crete.

However, nobody has yet clearly explained the attachment of the warps in such a use and the proposal of Carington Smith appears to be purely hypothetical.[91] A different use for this object seems more likely.

Somewhat similar objects but with seal impressions have been found at Skarkos,[92] and reference has also been made in this context to the sealings from the Zas Cave on Naxos.[93]

SPINNING AND WEAVING IN THE CYCLADES IN THIRD MILLENNIUM

With regard to the raw materials used in EC textiles, we are certain about the use of flax (*Linum usitatissimum*). However, the study of the bone material from Markiani on Amorgos, suggested that sheep and goat were also bred for fibre.[94] Wool gradually became the most commonly used raw material for textiles during the third millennium BC.

Spinning has been well studied by Carington Smith. She first established a typological series for the spindle-whorls from all excavations in the Aegean for each period. However, in many cases, the chronological position of the objects she refers to is not clear.

The frequent presence of spindle-whorls and clay discs in particular spaces of the settlement, like Spaces 7 and 8 (FIG. 4.21) and also in the entire summit area (Trench 4) is a clear indication that this was possibly the area where spinning and weaving took place or, at least, the place where the tools for this work were stored. The large quantity of finds is an indication of extensive use, and of craft specialisation. However, there are insufficient indications to presume a centralised organisation for textile production, or that this was the particular place where an organised textile workshop with many craftsmen operated. A broadly similar picture was observed at Asomatos on Rhodes, particularly in Room D, where many small size spindle-whorls were found.[95] At Myrtos on Crete, in specific areas of the building complex, many loom-weights were found with a few spindle-whorls, many perforated stone disks, as well as stone rubbers and mortars — presumably for the first processing of raw materials.[96] And at Sitagroi near Drama in eastern Macedonia, especially during phase V, in several excavated areas, many spindle-whorls, loom-weights and bone tools were revealed.[97]

In Asia Minor there is much evidence for the use of the warp-weighted loom. At Troy IIg, in Room 206, about 40 pyramidal loom-weights were found in successive layers over the floor, as well as two post-holes through the floor near the wall which, as the excavators have suggested, were used to position the wooden beams of a vertical warp-weighted loom.[98] Similar finds have been made in Aphrodisias,[99] in Alishar,[100] and in Mersin in period XIIb where many conical loom-weights were found in what is believed to have been a textile workshop.[101] On the islands of the north-east Aegean discoid loom-weights have been found, for example at Thermi on Lesbos, towns II[102] and IV.[103] At Myrtos on Crete,[104] discoid loom-weights were also found, which suggests the use of the warp-weighted loom in these areas.

On the Greek mainland, perforated objects were found, which the excavators regarded as loom-weights of warp-weighted looms. More specifically, at Lithares,[105] some cylindrical or cubical objects with two vertical perforations are mentioned as possible loom-weights and also at Kolonna on Aigina,[106] towns II and III, cylindrical objects with perforated holes have been found.

[89] Caskey 1955, 45; Wiencke 1969, 500. 508 pl. 129 no. 19; *CMS* V no. 51

[90] Carington Smith 1975, 215.

[91] Carington Smith 1975, 219.

[92] Marthari 1997, 375, fig. 15, n. See now *CMS* V Suppl. 3 nos. 169–173.

[93] Marthari 1997, 382. *CMS* V Suppl. 1A nos. 106–109 and summary report by Dousougli-Zachos, ibid. pp. 103–5.

[94] See also Chapter 9A.

[95] Marketou 1997, 402.

[96] Warren 1972*a*, 200–3.

[97] Elster, 1992, 36.

[98] Blegen *et al.* 1950, 350–3, fig. 369, 461.

[99] Joukowski *et al.* 1986, 379–81.

[100] Von der Osten 1937, 42, 93, 214, fig. 44, 99, 224, 279.

[101] Garstang 1953, 173, fig. 110–12, pl. 26.

[102] Lamb 1936, 163, fig. 43.

[103] Kouka 1997, 472.

[104] Warren 1972*a*, 52–4, fig. 21 and 220–2, fig. 96.

[105] Tzavela-Evjen 1984, 173 fig. 24 δ, ε, θ, fig. 25 ι, κ, λ, pl. 91, ζ, θ, λ.

[106] Walter and Felten 1981, 142, 178, pl. 126.

In the Cyclades, at Ayia Irini on Kea, sixteen flat ellipsoid, perforated objects were found which, according to Carington Smith,[107] show typological similarities with loom-weights from Aphrodisias, Thermi on Lesbos and the Heraion on Samos during the EBA. However, most of this material still remains unpublished and is, unfortunately, not safely dated to this period.

We cannot entirely exclude the possibility that the discoid spindle-whorls or the shaped perforated potsherds were used as loom-weights. The absence of loom-weights in relation to the great numbers of spindle-whorls found in excavations of EC settlements, such as Markiani and Skarkos, poses a number of questions. Tzachili has attempted to answer some of them.[108] It is possible, however, that another type of loom was used, such as the vertical two-beam loom or the horizontal ground loom,[109] which appears in a model from Middle Kingdom Egypt.

There are many indications of different spinning and weaving techniques used in the same period in the south-east Mediterranean. It seams that each cultural group followed a different convention. However, by the end of the EBA, there is a tendency towards a similar development of products of spinning and weaving, which is echoed in the similarity in the tools utilised, especially in the north-east Aegean and the Cyclades. This may indicate a *koiné*, a phenomenon that has been also claimed on the basis of common or similar shapes of pottery, metallurgy and indeed in the architecture and burial customs.

The co-existence of these objects in the same part of the site indicates special working areas for spinning and weaving. The great issues of organisation of production, existence of centrally-organised workshops, craft specialisation, trading of surplus raw materials and textiles in the neighbouring areas and their role in the economy and society cannot be developed in detail here since very little is known about the organisation of production at this time, in contrast to the better-documented picture available for the LBA.

TABLE 8.14. The illustrated spindle-whorls and perforated potsherds from Markiani.

	FIG.	Cat. no.	PLATE	Trench/Layer	Space	Phase	Fabric	Description
Spindle-whorls	8.20, 1	**EE 106**		Trench 1,1 layer 8	Space 8	Ma II	Blue schist	Flat convex, stamped
	8.20, 2	**EE 111**		Trench 1,1 layer 8	Space 8	Ma II	Blue schist	Flat conical
	8.20, 3	**EE 062**		Trench 4,1 layer 2		Ma II	Marble	Flat discoid
	8.20, 5	**158**		Trench 9,1 layer 5	'fissure'	Ma III	Blue schist	Discoid biconvex
	8.20: 4	**220**		Trench 1,1 layer 44	'fissure'	Ma III	Micaseous	Bell shaped
	8.20: 7	**420**		Trench 4,10 layer 4		Ma II	Marble	Flat discoid
	8.20: 6	**145**		Trench 9,1 layer 5	'fissure'	Ma III	Blue schist	Conical
	8.20: 8	**262**		Trench 7 layer 8	Space 8	Ma II	Marble	Ring like
	8.20: 9	**216**		Trench 1,1 layer 44	'fissure'	Ma III	Marble	Flat discoid
	8.20: 10	**EE 307**		Trench 3,2, layer 2	Room 2	Ma III	Marble	Flat discoid
	8.20: 11	**264**		Trench 7 layer 10	Space 8	Ma II	Marble	Flat discoid
	8.20: 12	**EE 064**		Trench 4,10 layer 2		Ma II	Marble	Flat convex
	8.21: 1	**175**		Rock Cutting 2 1985	Space 7	Ma IV	Marble	Flat discoid
	8.21: 2	**277**	49 *d*	Trench 1,4 layer 21	Drain	Ma IV	Blue schist	Hemispherical
	8.21: 3	**129**		Trench 1,1 layer 24	Space 7	Ma IV	Marble	Conical
	8.21: 4	**87**	49 *d*	Trench 1,1 layer 24	Space 7	Ma IV	Blue schist	Flat discoid
	8.21: 5	**85**		Trench 1,1 layer 24	Space 7	Ma IV	Blue schist	Hemispherical
	8.21: 6	**163**	49 *d*	Trench 1,1 layer 24	Space 7	Ma IV	Blue schist	Hemispherical
	8.21: 7	**240**		Rock Cutting 2 1985	Space 6	Ma IV	Marble	Discoid, bell-shaped
	8.21: 8	**90**		Trench 1,1 layer 26	Space 7	Ma IV	Blue Schist	Spherical
	8.21: 9	**100**		Trench 1,1 layer 33	Space 7	Ma IV	Blue schist	Conical
	8.21: 10	**96/842**		Trench 1,1 layer 46	'fissure'	Ma III	Marble	Conical, bell-shaped
	8.21: 11	**284**		Trench 1,3 layer 1	Space 4	Ma IV	Marble	Spherical

[107] Carington Smith 1975, 233–4.
[108] Tzachili 1997, 125–9.

[109] See Barber 1991, 84–5.

	FIG.	Cat. no.	PLATE	Trench/Layer	Space	Phase	Fabric	Description
Potsherd	8.21: 12	118		Trench 1,1 layer 36	Space 7	Ma IV?	Blue schist	Cylindrical
	8.21: 13	214		Trench 1,1 layer 24	Space 7	Ma IV	Blue schist	Cylindrical convex
	8.22: 1	321		Trench 1,1 layer 43	'fissure'	Ma III	Marble	Conical with stamped decoration
	8.22: 2	259/710	49 a, 50 e	Trench 7 layer 6	Space 8	Ma II	Marble	Conical, with stamped decoration
	8.22: 3	151	50 c	Trench 1,1 layer 23	Space 7	Ma IV	Blue schist	Flat discoid, impressed dots
	8.22: 4	250	50 a	Rock Cutting 1985	Space 6	Ma IV	Micaceous	Bi-convex, nail impressions
	8.22: 5	208	50 a	Trench 1,1 layer 45	'fissure'	Ma III	Marble	Flat discoid, nail impressions
	8.22: 6	219	50 a	Trench 1,1 layer 44	'fissure'	Ma III	Marble	Flat discoid, nail impressions
	8.22: 7	320	50 f	Rock Cutting 1985	Space 6	Ma IV	Marble	Flat discoid, stamped decoration
	8.22: 8	266	50 d	Trench 7 layer 14	Space 8	Ma II	Marble	Flat discoid with dot impressions
	8.22: 9	310	50 g	Rock Cutting 2	Space 6	Ma IV	Blue schist	Conical, incised figurative decoration
	8.22: 10	297	49 c	Trench 3,5 layer 1	Trench 3 Room 2	Ma III	Stone	Flat discoid, incised linear decoration
		83	49 a	Trench 1,1 layer 44	'fissure'	Ma III	Micaceous	Discoid
		EE 1003	49 a	Rock Cutting 2 1985	Space 6	Ma IV	Marble	Conical
		EE 1512	49 a	Trench 2p layer 56	Drain	Ma IV	Marble	Flat discoid
		EE 907	49 b	Trench 9,1 layer 5	'fissure'	Ma III	Marble	Bell shaped
		126	49 b	Trench 1,1 layer 44	'fissure'	Ma III	Marble	Bell shaped
		EE 1006	49 c	Rock Cutting 2 1985	Space 6	Ma IV	Stone	Flat discoid
		EE 306	49 c	Trench 3,2 layer 1	Room 2	Ma III	Stone	Flat discoid
		86	49 d	Trench 1,1 layer 24	Space 7	Ma IV	Blue schist	Flat discoid
Potsherds	8.21: 14	140	49 f	Trench 1,1 layer 26	Space 7	Ma IV	Marble	Cylindrical
	8.21: 15	150	49 f	Trench 1,1 layer 25	Space 7	Ma IV	Blue schist	Cylindrical
		123	49 f	Trench 1,1 layer 27	Space 7	Ma IV	Blue schist	Non symmetrical
		133	49 f	Trench 1,1 layer 26	Space 7	Ma IV	Blue schist	Non symmetrical
		115	49 f	Trench 1,1 layer 26	Space 7	Ma IV	Blue schist	Cylindrical
		128	49 f	Trench 1,1 layer 26	Space 7	Ma IV	Blue schist	Non symmetrical
		251	49 f	Trench 1,1 layer 14	Space 7	Ma IV	Marble	Cylindrical
		206	49 f	Trench 10 layer 1	Space 9	Ma IV	Blue schist	Non symmetrical
		176	49 f	Rock Cutting 2 1985	Space 7	Ma IV	Marble	Cylindrical
		239	49 f	Rock Cutting 2 1985	Space 6	Ma IV	Marble	Non Symmetrical
		288	49 g	Trench 4,1 layer 5		Ma II	Marble	Non symmetrical
		256	49 g	Trench 1,2 layer 6	Space 1	Ma III	Marble	Non symmetrical
	8.21: 16	257	49 e, 54 c	Trench 1,3, layer 2	Space 6	Ma IV	Marble	Parallelepiped object with barley impression

E. THE TERRACOTTA BOAT MODEL
by Neil Brodie

A small terracotta model (**EE 709** FIG. 8.23, PLATE 51) of what might be a boat was found in layer 4 of Trench 7 (Ma II). It is roughly oval in shape, with maximum dimensions of L. 6.40 cm, Ht. 1.80 cm, upper W. 3.20 cm, and lower W. 2.30 cm. Small pieces have been broken off each of the two ends and from the centre of one of the sides. Finger impressions are still clearly visible on its inner and outer surfaces and the model appears to have been made from a single lump of clay with the sides pinched up and the base pressed down against a flat surface. The upper parts of the side-walls have been pinched out thinner. It has a marble fabric with a variable black to red surface, which is probably the result of uneven firing.

This piece joins a small corpus of boat models known from Aegean EBA contexts which have recently been listed and discussed by Davaras.[110] First are the four lead models bought by R. M. Dawkins in Athens and said to be from a cist grave on Naxos. Three are in the Ashmolean Museum Oxford,[111] while the fourth is probably the one currently in the National Museum and Galleries on Merseyside.[112] Their maximum preserved lengths are within the range 34–40 cm and their widths 3–4 cm. The authenticity of these pieces has been questioned,[113] and although lead isotope analysis has confirmed that they are made of Siphnian lead,[114] this does not settle the matter with any degree of certainty. More secure in its provenance and authenticity is the clay model discovered in an EM II burial at Palaikastro.[115] The Palaikastro and lead models appear to be three dimensional representations of the longboats shown on EC II 'frying pans', which are thought to have been crewed by 25 rowers or more and used for long-distance sea voyages.[116]

In shape, however, the Markiani piece is shorter and rounder than the longboats and resembles more closely the clay model found in an EM II/III house deposit at Mochlos,[117] which has positions for four rowers and is considered to represent a vessel distinct from the longboats, perhaps used for inshore fishing.[118] The Mochlos model also has a flat base which appears to be splayed out at the waterline so as to depict the vessel afloat, not as it would appear out of water. If a similar convention was followed by the maker of the Markiani piece it increases the security of its interpretation as a boat.

EC II longboats were probably built in whole or in part of wooden planks,[119] and Marangou has documented the existence of probable dugout log boats on the Greek mainland and Balkans through a series of Late Neolithic and Copper Age models.[120] Thus the Markiani boat would have been built in an area with an evolving tradition of wooden boat construction, and may itself have been so constructed. Marangou[121] illustrates two clay boat models from EBA Troy, both about 9 cm long, which closely resemble the Markiani piece, and which she interprets as basic dugouts used as inland craft.[122] However, the thinned upper parts of the Markiani vessel's walls suggest wash strakes added to increase the freeboard of a dugout after its beam had been expanded by the application of heat. Marangou has pointed to a small terracotta model from Tsangli with a central cross-member or thwart which she interprets as an expanded log boat;[123] although it is different in shape to the Markiani piece, with a flat stern and pointed prow, it has similar proportions (length:width ratio of 1.5:1, compared to the Markiani 2.3:1, and the estimated longboat ratio of something in the region of 11:1). Marangou considers that the boat would have been eminently seaworthy.[124] Another possible clay model of an expanded log boat, albeit narrower, is from Middle Neolithic Knossos.[125]

If the Markiani piece is indeed a representation of an expanded log boat, it presupposes that there was a supply of suitable timber on Amorgos. This has not been demonstrated archaeologically but there was, on the eastern end of Amorgos until 1835, a mixed forest of cedar, oak and prickly oak which produced timber for shipbuilding.[126] Presumably, then, this timber may also have been available during the EBA. Cedar, which is a soft wood, would have been suitable for the construction of an expanded dugout if logs of sufficient diameter were available.

[110] Davaras 1984.
[111] Renfrew 1967.
[112] Mee and Doole 1993, 48.
[113] Sherratt 2000, 102, 106.
[114] Gale and Stos-Gale 1981, 213.
[115] Dawkins 1904, 197.
[116] Broodbank 1989, 329.
[117] Seager 1909, 290.
[118] Basch 1991, 50; Hutchinson 1960, 91.
[119] Marinatos 1933, 173; Basch 1991, 47, 51; Broodbank

1989, 329.
[120] Tzachili 1997, 125–9.
[121] Marangou 2001, 751.
[122] Marangou 2001, 742.
[123] Marangou 1991, 27.
[124] Marangou 1991, 40, 41.
[125] Theocharis 1973, 316.
[126] Meliariakis 1928, 9; I am grateful to Giorgos Gavalas for drawing my attention to the Meliariakis publication.

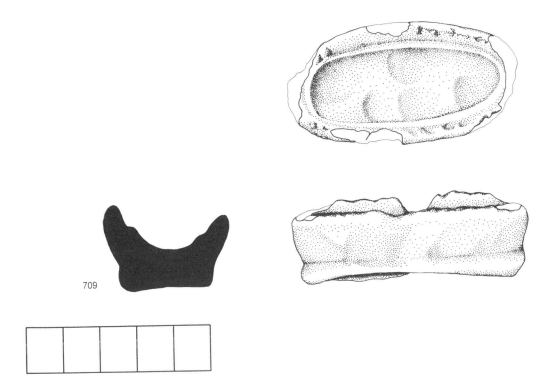

FIG. 8.23. Terracotta boat model (**EE 709**) (scale 1:1).

Unfortunately, the identification of the Markiani piece as an expanded log boat is not without its problems. The model does not have the raised prow and stern which are characteristic of such boats, nor does it have any indication of load bearing thwarts which are necessary for the boat to retain its shape. An alternative hypothesis would be that it represents a small skin boat, analogous to a coracle. The best Aegean evidence for a skin boat is in the form of a clay model (of Mycenaean date), found at Phylakopi,[127] whose painted vertical stripes have suggested to some a wooden frame pressing against a skin hull. Johnstone[128] and Marinatos[129] are both sceptical of a skin boat building tradition in the prehistoric Mediterranean but, for the Markiani piece, it cannot be ruled out.

In sum, the Markiani model may represent a small boat used for inshore fishing or coastal navigation. It was probably an expanded dugout but could have been skin-built.

F. THE METAL OBJECTS
by Kiki Birtacha

Amorgos, along with Syros and Naxos, has yielded the richest known finds of EC metal objects. The majority of metal objects from Amorgos, whether from excavations or from illicit activities of *archaiokapiloi*, are weapons (daggers and spearheads) found either in isolated graves or in cemeteries.

There are some 22 objects altogether from Markiani, from both the surface survey and the excavation. Apart from the lead seal,[130] there are tools for everyday use or ornaments, which are mainly simple in form. Eighteen of these come from the 1988–90 excavations and the remaining four from the surface cleaning of 1985 and the 1987 survey. Given that this assemblage comes from a settlement of which only a small part has been investigated through excavation, the total number of the metal objects is significantly large. The types and the number of finds recovered within a settlement are of course related to the causes and the nature of its abandonment or destruction.

[127] Bosanquet and Welch 1904, 206.
[128] Johnstone 1988, 57.

[129] Marinatos 1933, 217.
[130] See also Chapter 8G.

In the Cyclades (apart from Kastri on Syros) and on the Greek mainland very few metal objects have been found in settlements, whereas many occur in the settlements of the north-east Aegean.

The objects are of lead, copper or bronze and are dated to EBA. The excavated material belongs to the final phase of the settlement, Ma IV, or to late in the preceding phase, Ma III.

LEAD OBJECTS

Lead was widely used for mending broken objects because of its low melting point and because of its great plasticity. Stone objects (vessels and figurines), clay vessels, large storage pithos jars and also bowls were all mended with during the Aegean EBA.

TABLE 8.15. The lead objects from Markiani.

Lead Objects	FIG.	PLATE	Cat. no.	Find place	Space	Phase	Dimensions in cm		
							length	width	thickness
Rivets	8.24: 2	52 a	EE 214	Trench 2,1N layer 7	Space 3	Ma IV	3	0.93	0.7
	8.24: 3	52 a	EE 377	Trench 3,1 layer 7	Trench 3 Room 1	Ma III	6	2.5	0.76
Pendant	8.24: 1	–	EE 399	Trench 3, 3 layer 4	Trench 3 Room 1	Ma III	1.85	1.40	0.26–0.07
Unidentified	8.24: 5	–	EE 021	1987 SurveyUnit 504 C			3.7	2.75	1.3
	8.24: 4	52 a	EE 204	Trench 2/2 layer 2.		Ma IV	3.72	2.76	0.93

LEAD RIVETS (EE 214 AND EE 377, FIG. 8.24: 2 AND 3, PLATE 52 *a*)

Two fragments of lead rivets **EE 377** and **EE 214** provide us with evidence for the use of lead in mending broken objects. These two fragments come from rivets on the outside of the vessels or objects. **EE 214** (FIG. 8.24: 2) is elongated; one surface is rough, and the other is smooth, with a nearly semi-circular section. **EE 377** (FIG. 8.24: 3) preserves one of the plugs (D. 0.60 cm) for its connection to the object in question.

The form of these rivets attached to a convex exterior surface and the shallow grooves preserved along the edges provide information about their manufacture. After perforation of the object to be repaired, a semi-tubular mould was applied (half of a bone or reed, connecting the two perforations). Lead was then poured in through the open end (the other being closed). After casting, the mould was removed.

The lead rivets were not further worked beyond the removal of excess lead after casting. The experimental production of such rivets for mending a broken clay vessel has documented the procedure.

Fragment **EE 214** was found in Space 3, in an undisturbed layer over the later floor, Floor 'a', where pottery of Ma IV was found. **EE 377** was found in Room 1 of Trench 3, within the destruction layer. In this room pottery dated to Ma III, i.e. a mature phase of the EC II period, was also found.

The discovery of rivets within these spaces does not necessarily indicate that repairs were actually made there, i.e. they may have been leftovers or derive from old mended objects subsequently discarded.

The use of lead as material for repairs is very common in the Cyclades during the EC period. Examples of such joins come from Ayia Irini on Kea,[131] Kynthos on Delos,[132] Naxos,[133] Kastri on Syros,[134] and Phylakopi,[135] as well as various sites on the Greek mainland,[136] such as Asea, Asine, Zygouries, Ayios Kosmas, Raphina,[137] Askitario[138] and Aigina.[139] Such repairs are not found in Crete, perhaps because access to raw material was limited. The rivets from these sites, either Cycladic or Helladic, are not the same form as those found at Markiani, being usually of rectangular section.

[131] Caskey 1971, 371; Wilson 1999, 111, 117 and 144–5.
[132] Macgillivray 1980, 42, fig. 22.
[133] Stephanos 1905, 224; Stephanos 1904, 61; Doumas 1990, 162, cat. no. 166–170.
[134] Tsountas 1899, 126, Bossert 1967, pl. 42 c, d.
[135] Atkinson 1904, 192, pl. XL: 20–21.
[136] Renfrew 1967, 4; Renfrew 1972, 318.
[137] Theocharis 1952, 139, 148.
[138] Theocharis 1954, 75.
[139] Renfrew 1967, pl. 2 b.

LEAD PENDANT (**EE 399**, FIG. 8.24: 1)

EE 399 is a very small flat pear-shaped piece of lead foil with a perforation (D. perforation 0.30 cm at the upper edge). This pendant comes from the destruction layer of Room 1 in Trench 3 and is dated on the basis of the pottery to late Ma III. We may regard this object as a pendant, since lead pendants from the EBA have been found in Crete as burial offerings: one from Krasi Pediados,[140] dated EM II–III, and two from Mochlos in the shape of a double axe.[141] Another lead pendant in the Museum of Archaeology and Ethnology in Cambridge (no. 27.1154B) has a probable Aegean origin.

UNIDENTIFIED LEAD OBJECTS (**EE 204** AND **EE 021**, FIG. 8.24: 4 AND 5, PLATE 52 A)

EE 021 is the irregular corner of a flat piece of lead, thinning gradually away from the edges. This is a surface find from the 1987 surface survey, probably a fragment of a rivet. **EE 204** is a small irregular lump of lead, rather flat and round with shallow curves on the one surface, four near the edge and one larger at the centre. It was found in a disturbed surface level of Trench 2.

Such irregular lead fragments have been found at many EBA sites.[142] Their use is not clear.

COPPER AND BRONZE OBJECTS

ORNAMENTS (**EE 241** AND **EE 246**, FIG. 8.24: 6 AND 8, PLATE 52 B AND C)

Two objects could be assigned to this category: a pin of bronze (**EE 241**, FIG. 8.24: 6, PLATE 52 *b*) and the wire (**EE 246**, FIG. 8.24: 8, PLATE 52 *c*). Pin **EE 241** has a hemispherical head (D. 0.77 cm). The stem is long and ends in a point. It is made of a wire of circular section (D. 0.33–0.35 cm), shaped to end in a point (D. 0.14 cm) by hammering the edge while at the other end the head was added. It is assigned to the Branigan pin type IV.[143] It was found on the later floor, Floor 'a', of Space 3 along with pottery of the last phase of occupation, Ma IV.

This type of pin is very common in the north-east Aegean during the EBA. It is known from the period of Troy I,[144] Poliochni Blue,[145] and Thermi I,[146] and its production continues throughout the EBA in Poliochni Red, Green[147] and Yellow periods,[148] Emborio,[149] Troy II[150] and III.[151] In the Cyclades it is known from Syros,[152] and on the Greek mainland from Zygouries[153] and Manika.[154] It is also well known in Anatolia, from Beycesultan and Alishar Hüyük.[155]

EE 246 is a wire of circular section (D. 0.20 cm). One end has a point (D. 0.12 cm), while the other is bent creating a kind of loop. It is now no more than 3.50 cm long. Initially the wire was longer but is now broken. Probably after the breakage one end was bent so as to create a loop. This object could possibly have been used as a pin, although it is very small. It would be difficult to use it as a needle. It was found on the later floor, Floor 'a', of Space 3, dated to Ma IV. A similar pin of this form and size comes from Poliochni Green and Red period.[156]

HOUSEHOLD TOOLS

To this category may be assigned the needles, the awl, the small blade fragments and fragments of bronze wires.

1. Needles (**EE 319**, FIG. 8.24: 9, PLATE 52 *c*, **EE 1600, EE 389, EE 086**, FIG. 8.24: 10, 11, 12, PLATE 52 *d*)

The only intact object of this type is needle **EE 319** (FIG. 8.24: 9, PLATE 52 *c*). This is a small wire of rectangular section, which comes to a point at one end (D. 0.10 cm) and is hammered flat at the other end (D. 0.54 cm) and then perforated near the centre (D. of perforation 0.30 cm).

This is assigned to Branigan's[157] needle type III but it has some special features, namely the rectangular section (with rounded corners) and the width at the head. It resembles the modern bodkin or packing

[140] Marinatos 1929, fig. 14: 38.
[141] Branigan 1974, 35.
[142] Renfrew 1972, 318.
[143] Branigan 1974, 35.
[144] Blegen *et al.* 1950, 215, 34–502.
[145] Bernabò Brea 1964, 265, 593, fig. 322: g, pl. LXXXVII: 7.
[146] Lamb 1936, 166, fig. 48a: 31.53.
[147] Bernabò Brea 1964, 664, pl. CLXXVI: 5, 8, 13.
[148] Bernabò Brea 1976, 294, pl. CCXXXVII: 1, 7, 29.
[149] Hood 1980, 658, fig. 295: 1, pl. 138: 1.

[150] Blegen *at al.* 1950, 22, 26–7, pl. 125: 1, pl. 358: 35–549.
[151] Blegen *et al.* 1952, II, pl. 47: 33–208, 34–421.
[152] Zervos 1957, pl. 260.
[153] Blegen 1928, pl. XX.8.
[154] Sampson 1985, 107, fig. 98a, pl. 93.
[155] Lloyd and Mellaart 1962, 289, fig. F.11: 3, pl. XXXV: 3, from Beycesultan level XII; Schmidt 1932, fig. 67, 69; 1930–31, 198.
[156] Bernabò Brea 1976, pl. CLXXVI: 17.
[157] Branigan 1974, 30.

needle (*sakorapha*). Its use was probably more specialised, perhaps for sewing of rather hard materials, such as leather. The transition from the stem to the point is not smooth: the wire has been cut obliquely to create a point. It may originally have been longer with the production of a fresh pointed end after accidental breakage. It was found within an undisturbed EC layer in Room 2 of Trench 3. It is dated by the pottery to the abandonment phase of this part of the settlement assigned to Ma III, but may be close in date to Ma IV. The type may be related to the bone needles known as early as the Poliochni Blue period.[158] In the Cyclades the type is known from the cemeteries of Chalandriani on Syros.[159]

In addition, the fragments **EE 1600** (FIG. 8.24: 10, PLATE 52 *d*, D. at the ends 0.07–0.13 cm), **EE 389** (FIG. 8.24: 11, PLATE 52 *d*, and **EE 086** (FIG. 8.24: 10, PLATE 52 *d*, D. 0.13 cm) are fragments of wires with circular or oval sections may be regarded as needles or pins.

EE 1600 was found within the filling of the drain in Space 3 and is dated to the last phase of occupation, Ma IV. It is a long thin wire of circular section, which gradually gets thinner towards its point, and is now bent into a curve. Meanwhile, **EE 389** is a simple needle of ellipsoid section and preserves the point. It is also now bent into a curve. It was found within the destruction layer of Room 1 in Trench 3. **EE 086** is a small fragment of a wire of circular section, which preserves none of its ends and is surface find from the summit area.

2. *Copper and Bronze Sheets and Foils*

This is a group of eight pieces, five of which are sufficiently well preserved to give us enough evidence for the shape of the tools. There are two main categories.

(a) Blades/Knives (**EE 089, EE 1606, EE 384, EE 639, EE 327, EE 386** and **EE 233**, FIG. 8.24: 13–20, PLATE 52 *e*)

EE 089 (FIG. 8.24: 19, PLATE 52 *e*), **EE 1606** (FIG. 8.24: 13, PLATE 52 *e*) and **EE 386** (FIG. 8.24: 15) are blades (L. pres. 4.50–7.50, Th. 0.10–0.15 cm), each preserving a point. The point is produced by cutting the sheet obliquely at one (**EE 089**) or both sides (**EE 1606**).

The process of manufacture by cutting from a sheet is clear in the case of **EE 386** where the point is straight at one side continuing the line of the blade and oblique on the other. The presence of wear on the oblique side suggests that this edge was made for cutting. For knife **EE 386** there is a parallel at from Troy IIg.[160]

EE 639 (FIG. 8.24: 16) of bronze was produced in a simple way. The wear pattern suggests its use as a one-edged blade or knife. A similar knife comes from Kastri on Syros.[161] These simple objects served as multiple-use household tools: they could be used as knives, razors, awls or cutting tools. There is no evidence for the handle. However the fold at the top of **EE 384** suggests that there may have been some kind of handle there. These tools may in part have replaced the obsidian blades so common earlier on. Made of metal they were more effective and durable.

Fragments **EE 327** (FIG. 8.24: 17), **EE 384** (FIG. 8.25: 18) and **EE 233** (FIG. 8.24: 14) may have come from similar blades or knives.

EE 386 and **EE 639** come from the destruction layer of Room 1 in Trench 3, while **EE 327** comes from Room 2 of Trench 3. **EE 1606** comes from the destruction layer above the floor of Space 1. The associated pottery suggests a late Ma III date. Meanwhile, **EE 233** comes from Space 6, and **EE 089** comes from the destruction layer of Space 3. The associated pottery is dated to Ma IV.

(b) Sheet with blunt end (**EE 329**, FIG. 8.24: 20, PLATE 52 *e*)

EE 329 has parallel sides and terminates in a rounded blunt end. It is a blade and resembles a chisel but it may have been spatula or scraper. It comes from the destruction layer (fallen stones) of Room 2 in Trench 3.

(c) Awl (**EE 087**, FIG. 8.24: 7, PLATE 52 *b*)

Awl **EE 087** is intact (L. 11 cm) and comes from the surface cleaning of 1985 from Terrace 1. It is a wire of rectangular section, which changes gradually over the lower third of its length, becoming a blunted end of rounded section. It is thicker at the transition between the two sections and is assigned

---

[158] Bernabò Brea 1976, pl. LXXXIX: 17, 18, 24.
[159] Tsountas 1899, pl. 9: 22; Zervos 1957, pl. 261 upper row, left.

[160] Branigan 1974, cat. no. 699, pl. 14: 699; Schliemann 1881, 967.
[161] Tsountas 1899, pl. 10: 43.

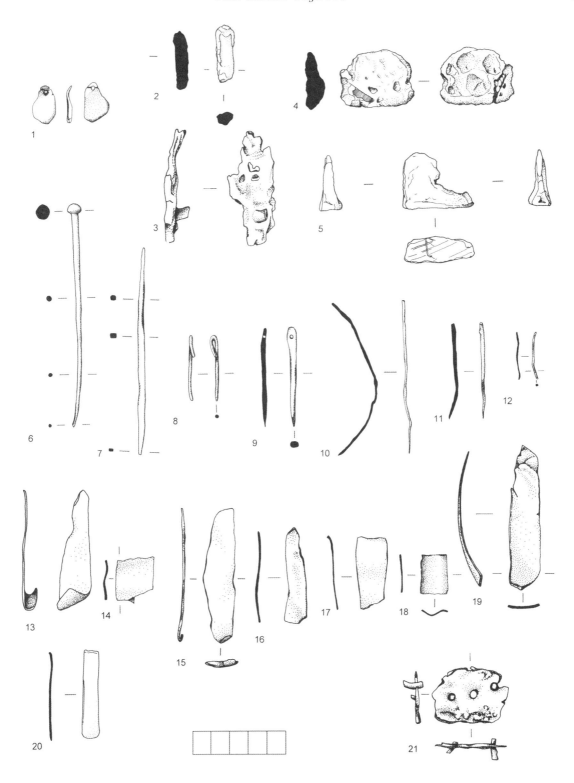

FIG. 8.24. Metal objects of lead (*1–5*), copper (*7–14* and *16–22*) and bronze (*6* and *15*) (scale 1:2).

to the Deshayes' awl type A2.[162] This is one of the most common metal tools all over the Aegean, the Balkans, Asia Minor and Egypt during the EBA.

An exact parallel for this type comes from Thermi II.[163] Awls of this form are known through all the phases at Poliochni.[164] Similar awls with blunted end have been found in Louros Athalassou cemetery, grave 26.[165]

[162] Deshayes 1960, 40, II, 2–3.
[163] Lamb 1936, 168–9, fig. 49: 30, 38.
[164] Bernabò Brea 1964, 593, 595, fig. 322b, 665, pl. CLXXVI:

18–30, pl. LXXXVIII: 1–18.
[165] Papathanasopoulos 1962, 134, pl. 68 γ.

WEAPONS

Heel of a Dagger (**EE 039**, FIG. 8.24: 21, PLATE 52 *f*)
EE 039 is a heel of a dagger. It is rounded and preserves three holes and fragments of two nails in the holes to attach the handle. It was probably a long dagger with flat blade, although the absence of the blade makes its precise attribution and the identification of parallels difficult. From the shape of the heel and the arrangement of the nails it could possibly be assigned to Branigan's dagger types I or II.[166] The dagger was broken where the blade was inserted into the handle. The maximum preserved length of the nails (1.10 cm) suggests that the handle was reasonably thick and probably of wood.

   This is a surface find from Terrace 1. Its date in the EC period may be regarded as secure, since even in the disturbed layer of the terrace very little modern or Late Hellenistic material was found. In Terrace 1 the building complex is assigned to the EC period and the upper levels of the spaces investigated are dated to Ma IV.

   It is not yet clear which techniques were used for the manufacture of this dagger, i.e. if it was cast in a mould or shaped by hammering a bronze sheet. The heel towards the upper convex side was rendered thinner by hammering.

TABLE 8.16. The copper/bronze objects from Markiani.

Bronze or Copper objects		FIG.	PLATE	Cat. no.	Find place	Space	Phase	Dimensions in cm		
								length	width	thickness
Ornaments		8.24: 6	52 *b*	EE 241 bronze	Trench 2	Space 6 layer 27	Ma IV	11.8		
		8.24, 8	52 *c*	EE 246	Trench 2 layer 34	Space 5	Ma IV	3.50		
Tools	Needles / wires	8.24: 9	52 *c*	EE 319	Trench 3,2 layer 3	Trench 3	Ma III	5.32	0.37	0.28
		8.24: 10	52 *d*	EE 1600	Trench 1,4 layer 21	Space 3	Ma IV	9.7		
		8.24: 11	52 *d*	EE 389	Trench 3,3 layer 5	Trench 3, Room 1	Ma III	5.08		
		8.24: 12	52 *d*	EE 086	Surface find from the entrance of building A	Summit		2.57		
	Blades / wires	8.24: 13		EE 233	Trench 2, layer 22	Space 6	Ma IV	2.1	2.36	0.10
		8.24: 14	52 *e*	EE 1606	Trench 1,6 layer 5	Space 1	Ma III	6.53	1.80–0.40	0.15
		8.24: 15		EE 386	Trench 3,3 layer 3	Trench 3, Room 1	Ma III	7.03	1.75	0.13
		8.24: 16	52 *e*	EE 639 bronze	Trench 3,3 layer 16	Trench 3, Room 1	Ma III	4.97	1.15	0.10
		8.24: 17		EE 327	Trench 3,2 layer 4	Trench 3, Room 2	Ma III	3.74	1.87–1.43	
		8.24: 18		EE 386 bronze	Trench 3,3 layer 3	Trench 3, Room 1	Ma III	2.03	1.40	0.10
		8.24: 19	52 *e*	EE 089	Trench 1,4 layer 6	Space 3	Ma IV	7.55	1.88	0.13
		8.24: 20	52 *e*	EE 329	Trench 3,2 layer 5	Trench 3, Room 2	Ma IV	4.55	0.94–0.80	0.20–0.08
	Awl	8.24: 7	52 *b*	EE 087	Terrace 1 1985 surface cleaning			10.93	0.38–	0.16
	Nail			EE 205	Trench 2,2 layer 2	Space 3				
Weapons		8.24: 21	52 *f*	EE 039	Terrace 1, surface find			2.9	4.3	1.02–2.07

[166] Braningan 1974.

3. General Observations

TECHNIQUES

The technique of producing sheets and wires may be securely documented from these metal objects. The wires (needles and pins) were probably made by twisting narrow sheets and then spinning or rotating them between flat stone slabs. Heating to the temperature of re-crystallisation produced the final form. Finally, the edges or the point were achieved by cold hammering.[167] The small knives were cut from sheets and then hammered to harden and sharpen the edges.

For the heel of dagger **EE 039** a mould was probably used. On the other hand, hammering is the presumed technique of manufacture for the blades and knives, which are relatively thin (0.1–0.80 cm).

Slag fragment **EE 690** comes from the surface survey and so does not constitute a secure indication for the extraction of copper within the settlement.

All the metal objects from Markiani are simple tools and do not suggest a high level of craft specialisation. The techniques used can already be seen in the earliest phases of the Aegean EBA.

DISTRIBUTION

The distribution of the material as seen in TABLE 8.17 may be significant for the discussion of how the excavated spaces at Markiani were used.

TABLE 8.17. Distribution of metal objects in the Markiani excavated areas.

Type	Trench 3, Room1	Trench 3, Room 2	Space 1	Space 3	Space 6	Space 5	Surface	Disturbed	Σ
Needle		1							1
Pin					1	1			2
Wire	1			1			1		3
Blades/knives	3	2	1	1	1				8
Awl							1		1
Dagger							1		1
Seal								1	1
Lead rivets	1			1					2
Pendant	1								1
Unidentified lead objects							1	1	2
	6	3	1	3	2	1	4	2	22

Rooms 1 and 2 of Trench 3, assigned to the same house unit, yielded most of the metal objects found at Markiani. Their presence with a large number of stone tools[168] possibly suggests some sort of industrial space or workshop.

DATING

As noted, all the metal objects from the excavation are dated either to Ma III or Ma IV. Ma IV is associated with pottery characteristic of the Kastri Group. Some scholars have associated the Kastri Group with particular metallurgical features,[169] especially the introduction of new techniques, notably the use of tin rich alloys for the production of bronze objects.

Typological analysis shows that the network of Markiani's trading relationships was oriented towards the north-east Aegean, as may be seen from the parallels of pin **EE 241**, wire **EE 246**, needle **EE 319** and knife **EE 386**. The chemical analysis of the Markiani metal finds which follows gives a number of insights into the metallurgy of the Markiani finds. It should be noted that only two of the pieces analysed are of tin-bronze: **EE 241**, a pin assigned to Ma IV and **EE 639** a blade with a parallel from Kastri on Syros, which may be from a late stage of Ma III. These analyses serve to confirm the view that the use of tin-bronze was not widely practised until late in the EBA.

[167] Tylecote 1976, 141.
[168] See Chapter 8B.

[169] Doumas 1988, 26–8.

NOTE ON THE CHEMICAL ANALYSIS OF THE MARKIANI METAL OBJECTS

by Heleni Andreopoulou-Mangou

Sampling and chemical analysis was possible for 12 copper-based objects and three lead items. Sampling was achieved by extraction of a very small quantity of material by drill or of a small fragment, *c.* 10 mg in the case of the very small objects and of 45 mg in the case of the larger objects.

The experimental method followed for the analysis of these samples has been described by Mangou and Ioannou for the copper-based objects and by Hughes *et al.* for the lead objects.[170] The measured percentage of the elements is given in TABLE 8.18 and does not total to 100% because of the severe corrosion of the objects and the unavoidable contamination of the sample by erosion products. The chemical analysis was undertaken in the Chemical Laboratory of the National Archaeological Museum in Athens by the atomic absorption technique.

RESULTS

1. The following results came from the chemical analysis of the copper-based artefacts:

a. Two copper objects, the needle **EE 319** and the nail **EE 205,** have a chemical composition of relatively pure copper (Cu) with less than 1% of arsenic (As), antimony (Sb) and iron (Fe), and less than 0.10% for the other elements identified. The use of relatively pure copper in the Late Neolithic and EBA in the Aegean is well attested.[171]

b. Eight objects: the blade **EE 233**, the needle **EE 1600**, blade (spatula) **EE 329**, blade **EE 1606**, the heel of a dagger **EE 039**, blades **EE 327** and **EE 386**, and the awl **EE 087**, have a chemical composition of arsenic rich copper, or an alloy of copper-arsenic (Cu-As) with percentages of arsenic respectively (As%): 2.51%, 2.77%, 1.78%, 3.90%, 3.48%, 3.42%, 2.65 and 1.58%.

    The percentage of arsenic in these cases is more than 1% and this natural alloy may be characterised as arsenic-rich copper,[172] with a possible provenance of the arsenic through the mineral/ore rather than by deliberate addition.

    The presence of lead (Pb) is less than 3% and it may be assumed that it comes from the ore and was not an intended enrichment.

c. The presence of antimony,[173] 1.09% in the awl **EE 087**, and the presence of both antimony and bismuth (Bi), in blade **EE 233** (1.08% Sb and 1.51% Bi), must follow the type of ore used, and suggests the use of a different source of ore for these pieces than that used for the other artefacts of this category, of the arsenic-rich copper.

d. Two bronze objects, the blade **EE 639** and the pin **EE 241**, have a composition of bronze, a copper-tin alloy (Cu-Sn). In this copper tin alloy the tin percentages are 7.66% and 7.48% while lead is present with 2.20% and 2.70% respectively. The copper/tin ratios are 10.1 and 11.1 respectively.

    The presence of tin in copper in these quantities may be supposed to be an indication of the deliberate alloying of the copper and consequently as a deliberate use of bronze during the EBA in the Aegean. Local production of bronze has not as yet been documented *in situ* in the Aegean. Many of the bronze objects of the EBA have typological parallels with artefacts found in the north-east Aegean (Lemnos, Lesbos and, in Asia Minor, in the Troad), where there is some evidence that bronze was produced. One of the tin-bronze objects at Markiani was found in a context with pottery of the Kastri Group. Lead is present in concentrations of less than 3% and this is probably a feature the original ore rather than a deliberate enrichment, although it should be noted that a concentration of more than 2% of lead promotes more effective casting of copper and its alloys.

Thus the chemical composition of the copper-based artefacts at Markiani offers a range of variation of chemical compositions (copper, arsenic-rich copper with lead <3%, and bronze with lead <3%) which is characteristic for the copper-based artefacts found in the rest of the Aegean during the EBA[174] and on the Greek mainland and Crete.[175]

[170] Mangou and Ioannou 1997; Hughes *et al.* 1982.
[171] Nakou 1995; Mangou and Ioannou 1993; Renfrew and Slater 2003.
[172] See Charles 1967; Renfrew 1967.

[173] For the presence of antimony see Mangou and Ioannou 1997, 70.
[174] Nakou 1995; Mangou and Ioannou 1997
[175] Mangou and Ioannou 1998, 1999

2. The results of the chemical analysis of the three lead artefacts are as follows:

All three, namely, the unidentified object **EE 204**, the rivet **EE 214** and the lead seal **EE 317** are of lead with antimony present as 0.89%, 1.70% and 0.96% respectively and silver (Ag) as 0.09%, 0.06% and 0.14%. Both those elements will have been present in the original lead ore.

TABLE 8.18. Percentage (%) chemical composition of the EBA copper-based and lead artefacts from Markiani, Amorgos.

Cat. No.	Description	Cu	Sn	As	Sb	Pb	Fe	Zn	Bi	Ag	Au	Ni	Co
EE 087	Awl	81.62	–	1.58	1.09	2.13	0.18	0.01	0.38	0.02	–	0.11	–
EE 233	Blade	79.38	–	2.51	1.08	0.8	0.08	0.01	1.51	0.13	–	0.51	–
EE 319	Needle	95.48	–	0.46	0.22	0.06	0.11	0.01	0.28	0.02	–	0.05	0.04
EE 639	Blade	77.09	7.66	0.27	0.13	2.21	0.09	0.01	0.28	0.004	–	0.04	–
EE 1600	Needle	77.4	–	2.77	0.41	0.73	0.05	0.01	0.19	0.93	–	0.05	–
EE 329	Blade	86.52	–	1.78	0.25	0.65	0.08	0.01	0.09	0.01	–	0.06	–
EE 386	Blade	79.8	–	2.65	0.43	1.27	0.04		0.09	0.01	–	0.08	–
EE 205	Nail	85.98	–	0.1	0.28	0.51	0.05	0.05	0.09	0.05	–	0.09	–
EE 1606	Blade	82.9	–	3.9	0.48	0.3	0.05	–	–	0.02	–	0.07	–
EE 039	Heel of a dagger	80.4	–	3.48	0.48	0.96	0.06	–	–	0.02	–	0.08	–
EE 241	Pin	82.96	7.48	0.52	0.56	2.69	0.14	–	0.19	0.11	–	0.07	–
EE 327	Blade	83.6		3.42	0.27	0.28	0.06	–	0.28	0.1	–	0.02	–
EE 204	Lead object	0.07	–	0.004	0.89	90.72	0.02	–	0.04	0.09	–	–	–
EE 214	Lead rivet	0.17	–	0.003	1.7	94.54	0.01	–	0.05	0.06	–	0.01	–
EE 317	Lead seal	0.08	–	0.001	0.96	94.2	0.02	–	0.03	0.14	–	0.01	–

(–) = below limit of detection

G. THE LEAD SEAL AND THE CLAY SEALINGS
by Anastasia Angelopoulou

INTRODUCTION

The lead seal and the clay sealings are significant sources of information for the social structure and the economic relationships within a Cycladic settlement in the EBA. The fact that the excavated part of the settlement is relatively limited offers hope for further finds of this kind in the future.

2. THE LEAD SEAL

The lead seal **EE 317** (FIG. 8.25, PLATE 52 *a*) (D. max. 1.80, D. min. 1.60, H. max. 1.10 cm) comes from the disturbed layers of Room 2 of Trench 3 in Unit 508, Terrace 3. This does not allow us to place it with certainty in one particular phase of the settlement, but the stratified material from this area may all be assigned to Ma III. Both the material and the motif upon it suggest an EBA date. The Markiani seal thus should be added to the small catalogue of metal seals from the Cyclades and from the Aegean generally datable to the EBA.[176]

The seal has the form of a disc with one flat circular surface upon which is the seal design itself. The reverse surface is slightly convex and had a semi-circular loop of circular section 3 mm in diameter. This loop has been broken in antiquity at one side, leaving there a short protruding stub, while the free end has been bent down to the convex surface. This again creates a small aperture of *c.* 0.3 cm by means of which the seal may have been suspended.

The decorated surface has the motif of a rectilinear, angle-filled cross. It was probably cast from a circular mould of clay in which four pairs of lines were incised, meeting at right-angles near the

---

[176] Branigan 1974, 198–9. [Ed. note: see now Pini 2005 for a thorough discussion of Aegean metal seals. The lead seal from Markiani now appears in *CMS* V Suppl. 3 no. 43. A second seal or stamp (ibid. no. 44) made of hard-baked clay (a surface find from 1990; **EE 667**) does not appear in the present report since its date is uncertain. It is rather crude conoid without piercing; the seal-face is decorated with an irregular network of short lines].

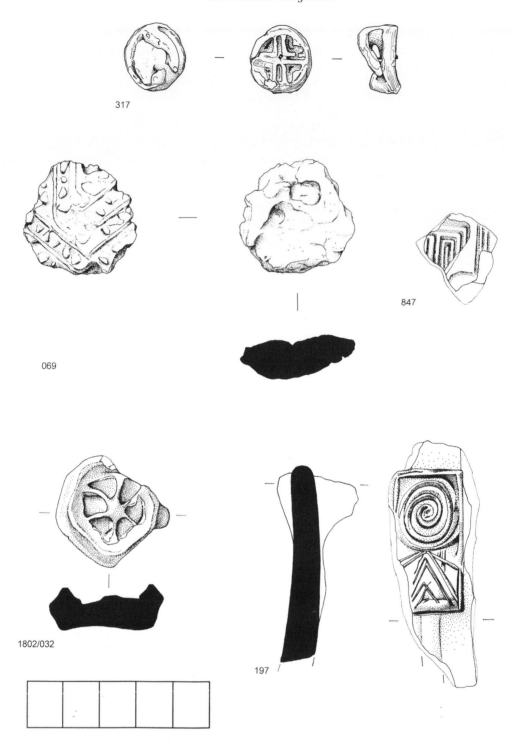

317

847

069

1802/032

197

FIG. 8.25. Lead seal (*1*), sealings (*2–4*) and seal impression (*5*) (scale 1:1).

centre: this in turn will be the impression left by the seal. The surface of the seal itself thus shows these lines in relief, so that what we see looks like an incised Greek cross with four equal segments removed from each of the four quadrants which it defines.

The seal finds a fairly close parallel for the motif if not for the form, in the lead seal from Tsoungiza, Ancient Nemea, which likewise shows an angle-filled cross.[177] The motif is common in the Aegean and further east.[178] It consists of two lines at right angles which divide a circular or rectangular surface into four parts, each of which is filled with various motifs. One of the earliest examples of such a motif

[177] Pullen 1994. *CMS* V Suppl. 1B no. 128.   [178] See *CMS* passim; French 1968, 421ff.

is from Sesklo[179] from the earliest Neolithic period. A parallel comes from Markiani itself. A potsherd **K 1530** (FIG. 7.12: 4) a surface find (Trench 8,5, layer 1), possibly of Ma III or IV, has an incised circle which a cross divides into four parts. Similar cross motifs are known from various sites in Asia Minor and the Near East, on sealings, such as those from Tarsus,[180] Karahöyük[181] and Mersin,[182] and also on seals such as those from Tepe Hissar[183] and Byblos.[184] The closest parallels in date are the EH II seal from Tsoungiza and two seals from Crete, one from Ayios Onouphrios[185] and the other from Mallia,[186] dated to the beginning of the MM period.

The motif of the cross with quadrants infilled by lines at right angles is widely seen on seals, sealings, and seal impressions notably in the Cyclades, the seals from Kapros on Amorgos[187] and Ayia Irini on Kea,[188] and the seal impressions on vases from Ayia Irini[189] and Chalandriani on Syros.[190] On Crete this motif appears on seals from Ayia Triada,[191] the Trapeza Cave,[192] Kaminaki[193] and Kaloi Limiones,[194] and on a sealing from Phaistos.[195] In the north-east Aegean the same motif appears on the bronze seal from Poliochni,[196] while on the Greek mainland it appears on a vase from Lerna.[197] The catalogue is completed by seals in private collections[198] and museums, the origins of which are not known.

Lead is one of the most commonly used metals in the Cyclades from the earlier phases of the EBA because of its relatively low melting point.[199] It was used mainly for lead clamps for mending broken objects. The use of lead for the manufacture of a seal is highly uncommon. The seal here has its only Cycladic parallel in the large seal of the EC II period found in Grave I of the Aplomata cemetery on Naxos.[200] On Crete early lead seals are rare: the earliest attested is a stamp-cylinder from an MM I context at Archanes–Phourni.[201]

CLAY SEALINGS

Two of the three sealings come from Space 7. They derive from undisturbed layers that may be dated to the last two phases of the settlement, i.e. Ma III and Ma IV. The third sealing (**EE 1802**) comes from the disturbed layer of Space 4 (filling of the drain) and cannot be securely dated to the EBA, although such a date is likely.[202]

The motifs of the sealings are very simple and do not compare with the complex motifs of the Lerna sealings.[203] The lumps of clay bearing the sealings **EE 069** and **EE 1802** have traces of smoothing on their back surface which may suggest that they have been stuck onto something, but the object in question cannot now be identified.

Similar observations may apply to **EE 847** but its condition makes this unclear.

Sealing **EE 069** (FIG. 8.26, PLATE 52 *b*) from Trench 1,1 layer 14 (Max. W. 3.05 cm Clay/fabric: Pale Brown Schist Ware) shows on its convex surface an impression of parallel lines with infilled dots and triangles intersecting at an acute angle with similar parallel lines with infilled dots and triangles. The acute angle is probably the result of two or more successive impressions upon the clay of the sealing applied by the same seal. If this is the case, the seal had a simple motif of infilled parallel lines. The closest parallel for this is the motif of a seal from Aphrodisias.[204]

EE 847 (FIG. 8.26, PLATE 52 *d*, from Trench 1,1 layer 45 (Max. W. 1.80 cm. Clay: Brown-Red Clay) is a very worn fragment of a sealing where the motif is hardly discernible, probably a meander-like motif. This is a very common motif on seals in the Aegean from the Neolithic period.[205]

[179] Tsountas 1908, 339, 341, fig. 272.
[180] Goldman 1956, 240, pl. 396, 1.
[181] Alp 1968, Sts no. 156, 206, pl. 99/277, Sts no. 162, 207, pl. 69/180, Sts no. 163, 207, pl. 171/523, fig. 141, Sts no. 164, 207, pl. 171/524, Sts no. 165, 207, pl. 171/525, Sts no. 171, 209, pl. 173/529.
[182] Garstang 1953, fig. 54, 11.
[183] Schmidt 1937, 56, no. H.4534, pl. XV.
[184] Dynand 1973, 327, fig. 202, no. (T.1823) 33808.
[185] CMS II.1 no. 116.
[186] CMS IV no. 56.
[187] Thimme 1977, 545, no. 453. Sherratt 2000 38-42, pls. 13–14; no. 1.a.6.
[188] CMS V, no. 486; Wilson 1999, pl. 14 and pl. 59.
[189] CMS V nos. 470–471.
[190] CMS I Suppl. no. 171, CMS XI no. 121; Bossert 1967, 74, fig. 5.10.
[191] CMS II.1 no. 96.
[192] CMS II.1 nos. 428 and 435.

[193] CMS II.1, no. 463.
[194] CMS IV nos. 28 and 106.
[195] CMS II.5 no. 75.
[196] Bernabò Brea 1964, 376, 663, pl. clxxv 5, clxx 4.
[197] Wiencke 1969, 508, S85, no. 192, pl. 129; CMS V no. 52.
[198] CMS VIII no. 15b, CMS X nos. 19 and 26. CMS XII no. 6, CMS XI nos. 87, 138, 139.
[199] Renfrew 1967, 4; see also Chapter 8F.
[200] Kontoleon 1972, 151, pl. 195 β-γ; CMS V Suppl. 1B no. 105.
[201] PAE 1972, 325 pl. 274δ.
[202] Ed. note: two sealings from Markiani now appear in CMS V Suppl. 3 nos. 46 (EE 069) and 47 (EE 1802). EE 847 is not included.
[203] Heath 1958; Wienke 1969; Weingarten 1997; CMS V nos. 44-50; 53-119.
[204] Joukowski 1986, 383, fig. 318, no. 4.
[205] Theocharis 1981, 66-7.

Finally, on sealing **EE 1802/032** (FIG. 8.26, PLATE 52 *c*), from Trench 10, layer 4 (Max. W. 1.80 cm. Clay/fabric: Brown-Red Schist ware) there is a rosette motif which is common in the Aegean.[206]

Renfrew suggests that the sealings imply a differentiation between property ownership and the immediate possession.[207] The idea is that the objects that bear the sealing were still the property of the owner of the seal even if not in his immediate possession. This of course does not exclude the suggestion that the sealings give indications of the origin, destination or even content of the object, which they accompanied. Similar suggestions have been also put forward for potter's marks (see also Chapter 7D). The seals and the sealings seem to be elements of a communication system.

4. SEAL IMPRESSION ON POTTERY

We can refer also here to a seal-impressed pottery fragment **EE 197** (FIG. 8.26, PLATE 52 *e*), which comes from the 'Fissure' area of Rock Cutting 2, Trench 1,1, layer 44 (L. 3.75 cm, W. 1.80 cm) datable to phase Ma III.[208] Within an impressed rectangle (of proportion 2 by 1) two motifs are seen: an impressed spiral and a chevron formed of two impressed triangles (one inside the other) the pointed end of which abuts the spiral. There do not appear to be precise parallels for this example, but the combination of curvilinear and rectangular motifs is well known from the cylinder seal of Kapros on Amorgos,[209] where concentric circles are combined with acute angles. Similar decorative motifs are known on the cylinder impressions from the Argolid used to decorate pithoi or hearths, during the EH II period.[210]

EE 197 is a rim of a vessel probably of a brazier or 'mask-like' support vessel. Although the function of the mask-like brazier vessels is still uncertain they are quite common at Markiani. Some of those on the rim preserve mat-impressions. Seal impressions are quite common on pots, like those from Chalandriani[211] on Syros and from Ayia Irini both on pots and hearths.[212]

---

[206] See also *CMS* passim.
[207] Renfrew 1972, 388; see also Pullen 1994; Weingarten 1997.
[208] Ed. note: *CMS* V Suppl. 3 no. 45.
[209] Thimme 1977, 545, no. 453; Sherratt 2000, 38–42, pls. 13–14; no. 1.a.6.
[210] E.g. Lerna: Wiencke 1970, 94–110, esp. 104; *CMS* V nos. 120–149.
[211] Bossert 1960, 12–3, fig. 11a–b, 12; *CMS* I Suppl. nos. 171–172.
[212] Caskey 1972, 368, pl. 79: B73, 368, fig. 4: B67, pl. 79: B68, 366, pl. 78, 79: B41a–c; *CMS* V nos. 451–478, 480–482.

Chapter 9

The organic materials

A. THE BONES AND BONE TOOLS

by Katerina Trantalidou

The study of the bones and bone tools from Markiani offers the opportunity to analyse an assemblage from an EBA settlement in the Cyclades. Both the bones and the bone tools may contribute to our interpretation of the use of the various architectural spaces and the organisation of the economy of the settlement.

THE BONES

The animal bones from Markiani total 3817. Some 3496 come from the settlement itself and about 316 are anatomical parts of recent fauna collected during the demolition of modern dry-stone walls. They have been studied in detail, searching for comparisons and patterning in breakage, cut-marks and evidence of animal gnawing.

PRESERVATION

The bones are badly weathered and very fragmented (see TABLE 9.1), so that complete bones (isolated teeth, carpals, tarsals and phalanges) represent only 9.80% of the total number.

TABLE 9.1. Preservation and frequency of the bones by settlement phase.
The percentages relate to the total of bones of each phase.

Phase	Total	Intact		Identifiable		Vertebral segments		Rib segments		Unidentifiable long bone fragments		Modification: Heavily abraded					
												Burned		Traces of roots		Tooth marks	
		No.	%	No.	%	No.	%	No.	%	No.	%	No.	%	No	%	No	%
Ma I	17	1	5.8	10	52.8	1	5.8	1	5.8	5	29.4						
Ma II	667	139	20.8	86	12.8	57	8.5	44	6.6	341	51.1	134	20	10	1.5	5	0.7
Ma II–III	23			6	26.0			2	8.6	15	65.2						
Ma III	48	7	14.5	18	37.5	2	4.1	17	35.4	4	57.1	8	16.6				
Ma IV	1420	147	10.3	585	41.1	145	10.9	125	8.8	418	29.4	61	4.2	7	0.5	17	1.2
Disturbed	1321	51	3.8	430	32.5	124	9.3	113	8.5	603	45.6	174	13.1	6	0.5	20	1.5
Total ancient	3496	345	9.8	1135	32.4	329	9.4	302	8.6	1386	39.9	377	10.7	23	0.6	42	1.2
Total modern	316	12	3.7	218	68.9	8	2.5	2	0.6	76	24.0	104	32.9			7	2.2
Total	3812	357	9.3	1353	35.5	337	8.8	304	7.9	1462	38.3	481	12.6	23	0.6	49	1.2

Most of the material is in the form of long bone fragments, flakes (size of splinters 0.10–0.30 m, rarely longer), of broken vertebrae (none intact) and segments of ribs. These are mainly assigned to the sub-family of caprinae (sheep and goats). It is not possible to determine whether the bone fragments were produced through deliberate smashing for marrow extraction or, for example by trampling,[1] through

---

[1] Binford 1981; Brain 1981; Gifford *et al.* 1985; Behrensmeyer *et al.* 1986; Nicholson 1992; Noe-Nyggard 1997.

continuing use of the settlement until recently for penning animals. Both the ancient and the most recent bone material show similar breakage patterns. Only in one case could as many as six bones be assigned to the same animal.

The abrasion factors, including the nature of the soil[2] (which in the Cyclades is acid, and thus poor in calcium carbonate) and the activity of carnivores and rodents, which may damage bone remains are complicated (PLATE 55 *a–b*). The macroscopically-examined marks left by roots[3] appear on about 0.60% of the total, while tooth-marks are seen on 1.20% of the material. The majority of the burnt bones are splinters (20–23% of the total) and were found with charcoal and seashells; it is therefore likely that they were not only food remains but were probably used as fuel.

DISTRIBUTION

The greatest frequency of bone was observed in Space 6 in Terrace 1 and Space 8 in the summit area, in fill deposits. From the study of the material of the final phase, Markiani phase IV which is the most abundant, there is a clear distinction between the interior (Spaces 3 and 1) and the exterior spaces (Spaces 2 and 5). It seems that the non-roofed areas yield more garbage.

TABLE 9.2. Distribution of the bone material in the principal excavated areas.

Phase	T6	T8	S8	T9	T4	S1	S2	S3	S4	S5	S6	S7	T5	T3	Varia	Σ
Ma I	12	5														17
Ma II			617									50				667
Ma III				14						23		34		220		291
Ma IV		105				67	220	128	5	137	446	92				1200
Disturbed				42	263	102	117	77	68	18	116	71	142	105	205	1326
Modern				27	72	2	13		2	1			132		67	316
Σ		122		1035					2063					325	272	3817

TABLE 9.3. Comparative species frequencies.

Species	Ma I	Ma II	Ma III–IV	Mixed	Total	%
Bos taurus	1	2	2	4	9	0.6
Ovicaprids	10	202	635	407	1254	84.7
Sus scrofa dom.	–	19	114	40	173	11.6
					1436	
Leporidae		2		20	22	1.4
Canidae			1	2	3	0.2
Mustelidae				1	1	0.1
Pisces		2	9	3	14	0.9
Aves				4	4	0.2
	11	227	761	481	1478	100.0

ARTIODACTYLA

1. Suidae, Pigs

173 bone fragments are assignable to pigs (see also TABLE 9.3) which represent 11.6% of the total of the domestic animals from Markiani.

2. Bovidae — Bovinae, Cattle

Cattle are rare at Markiani. There are only nine fragments, all from adult individuals.

---

[2] Poplin 1973, 347.
[3] Wood and Johnson 1978; the presence of roots and bulbs was evident in the superficial layer of the excavated areas.

3. Bovidae — Caprinae, Goat and Sheep

For sheep and goat the data are also relatively limited. The bones are extensively fragmented. Even the phalanges and the astragali are usually broken, bones that are generally preserved in good condition from sites of the Holocene, whereas during the Palaeolithic breakage of all bones, sometimes even including the third phalanx, is usually the rule.[4]

This fact complicates any observation on the definition of species and sex. Even if known morphological criteria are used,[5] the results are limited because of the small quantity of the assemblage. It is significant that horn cores are preserved nearly intact only among the modern material. The cranium fragments are too small and the frontal bone, the parietal and the occipital bones were not preserved in large enough pieces to allow clear conclusions. A similar problem occurs with the examination of the cervical vertebrae and the pelvis (usually only the articular acetabulum is preserved). The long and short bones in most cases are not intact. Among long bones, breakage for marrow extraction is possible. It is also possible that the wear on the phalanges is due to rodent activity (PLATE 55 b). It should be noted that the long bones of the modern material, which are better preserved, display similar breakage patterns.

For the above reasons the sheep and goat bones are considered as a single assemblage with regard to both species and sex. Application of diagnostic criteria,[6] such as the examination of the proximal part of the radius, the distal metacarpal, the second phalanx, etc., suggests that goats are more numerous than sheep.

This observation is based on material from Ma III and IV, which is the larger sample, although there remain reservations since sample size is small.

In general body parts are equally represented (see TABLE 9.4) because caprines were butchered within or close to the settlement. Estimation of age at the time of death of the animals, based on dental attrition, had limited results since only isolated teeth were found. The most secure criterion used for estimation of age is the appearance and growth of the teeth.[7]

It is notable that for Ma IV the Minimum Number of Individuals (MNI) total for sheep and goat, calculated on the basis of the mandible, is only nine. No further observations can be put forward as to the number of animals consumed in each architectural space or during each Markiani phase, since the assemblage is too small for secure conclusions.

Age estimation was based on epiphyseal fusion.[8] 260 bone fragments from caprinae sub-species and 43 from pigs were used. On the basis of these criteria and the conventions mentioned above it was concluded that half of the stock was slaughtered by the age of two–three years. The slaughtering of the animals at an age less than two years has been assured to be characteristic for a meat-production oriented economy.[9] At Markiani, as at other Aegean sites (see TABLE 9.5), we can see, from the ovicaprid data, an economy which becomes oriented towards secondary products such as wool production (see also TABLE 9.7).

TABLE 9.4. Age of slaughter *Ovis* sp. and *Capra* sp. according to skeletal development.

Age in months	Bones	Ma I f	Ma I N/f	Ma II f	Ma II N/f	Ma III–IV f	Ma III–IV N/f	Mixed f	Mixed N/f	Total f	Total N/f
0–6			1		3		8		9		21
6–10	Scapula			2	1	4				6	1
	Humerus d.			4		3	5	4	5	11	10
	Radius p.			4				2		6	
18–28	Metacarpal d.			1		2	7	3	1	6	8
	Metatarsal d.				3	1	3		7	1	13
	Tibia d.			3	3	4	4	1	2	8	9
30–42	Humerus					1	3	3	2	4	5
	Radius d.	1		2		2	2		2	5	4
	Ulna p.			3	1	3	1		2	6	4
	Femur p., d.		1		5	5	10	4	8	9	24
	Tibia p.			1	4	1	2	1	2	3	8
	Calcaneum				2		1		2	1	4

[4] Leroi-Gourhan 1984; Binford 1984; Davis 1987, 150.

[5] Boessneck *et al.* 1964; Payne 1985a; Noddle 1974; Prunnel and Frisch 1986; Becker 1986.

[6] Coy 1973, 241; Bökönyi 1976, 326; Klippel and Snyder 1991, 181.

[7] Payne 1985b, 230.

[8] Silver 1973.

[9] Payne 1973, 281-5.

Table 9.5. Sheep/goat mortality (epiphyseal fusion data and tooth eruption stage) in Early Bronze Age Aegean sites.

Age	Pentapolis, Macedonia	Pefkakia, Thessaly	Magoula Zarkou, Thessaly	Skala Sotiros, Thasos	Kaloyerovrisi, Euboea	Markiani, Amorgos
0–6 m				22.15		16.10
<1 year	40.0	40.0	36.17	48.73	37.50	23.02
<2 years	60.0	45.0	61.70	58.22	68.70	44.60
<3 years	70.0	72.25	72.34	68.35	81.25	84.09
4–10 years	100.0	100.0	100.0	100.0	100.0	100.0

In the case of pigs the available data show that they were kept for their meat as at most Aegean sites (see also TABLE 9.7). The average age at the time of slaughter was two years, as indicated by the study of epiphyseal fusion of 40 long bones (see also Appendix) and the dental attrition of five teeth.

Table 9.6. Age of the slaughter of *Sus* sp. according to skeletal development.

Age in months	Bones	Ma I f	Ma I N/f	Ma II f	Ma II N/f	Ma III–IV f	Ma III–IV N/f	Mixed f	Mixed N/f	Total f	Total N/f
0–12							3		1		4
12	Scapula	1				1				2	
	Humerus d						2				2
	Radius p	2								2	
	Phalanx II					1	5	1	1	2	6
24–30	Metapodia					2	5		2	2	7
	Phalanx I			2			2	1	1	1	5
36–42	Humerus p			1			2				3
	Radius p					1	1		1	1	2
	Ulna d								1		1
	Femur p, d			1			2				3
	Tibia p			1							1

Table 9.7. Suid mortality at Aegean Early Bronze Age sites.

Age	Pentapolis, Macedonia	Magoula Zarkou, Thessaly	A. Dimitrios, Peloponnese	Skala Sotiros, Thasos	Markiani, Amorgos
0–12 m	11.00	32.00	81.25	46.55	57.10
12–30 m	62.96	59.09	87.50	85.63	80.00
30–42 m	92.56	70.96	97.91	97.12	90.00
42+ m	100.00	100.00	100.0	100.000	100.00

BUTCHERY MARKS[10]

Butchery marks were noted on 38 bones assigned to Ma I—IV (PLATE 55 *c* and *d*). One cut-mark was found on a cattle scapula (Ma IV) and two were found on pig humerus bones (Ma IV). Most of the cut-marks were on the bones of caprini; 42 were observed which mainly result from dismemberment of the animal (78.50%).[11] The bones which exhibit most cut marks are the ribs, astragali and vertebrae. It appears that the skull was separated from the body between the occipital bone and atlas, while the limbs (front and rear) were separated from the vertebral column. The mandible was separated from the skull at a later stage, as were the humerus from the scapula, and the radius from the humerus and

---

[10] Von den Driesch and Boessneck 1975; Binford 1981. [11] Gamble 1978, 749.

the carpals-metacarpals. At the same time, or later, the femur was separated from the pelvis, and the tibia from the femur and from the tarsals, and the metatarsals from the phalanges. During dismemberment of the vertebral column, the axis was separated from the other cervical vertebrae, the ribs from the thoracic vertebrae, and the thoracic from the lumbar vertebrae. The thoracic vertebrae were usually chopped into two parts and the spines cut off.

Similar observations have been made on bone material from LBA Akrotiri on Thera.

TABLE 9.8. Position of butchery marks.

Bones	Ma II	Ma IV	Mixed	Modern
Horns				X
Mandible			X	X
Atlas				X
Axis				X
Vertebrae		X	X	X
Ribs	X	X	X	X
Scapula	X	X	X	
Humerus		X		
Radius	X	X		X
Ulna			X	
Pelvis	X			X
Femur			X	
Tibia	X			
Carpals		X		
Astragalus		X	X	
Calcaneum	X	X		
Metapodials		X		X
Phalanx I	X			

PATHOLOGY

In only three cases was it possible to trace some pathological conditions at Markiani, notably on caprine long bones (PLATE 55 f). These observations are based simply on macroscopic examination of the bones.

General observations

With all the reservations that the limited size of the assemblage suggest the following observations on the size of animals are put forward (see also Appendix):

– for the caprinae sub-family some increase in size takes place over Ma II to IV. It seems that in Amorgos we can trace a development of this sub-family during the third millennium. Estimation of wither height from sheep metapodial lengths in Macedonia,[12] Thessaly[13] or the Peloponnese[14] and Euboia,[15] indicates a similar situation associated with the appearance of a new, larger and woolly variety of sheep. On the other hand the wither height from goats varies from site to site and reaches 51.75 cm (specimen) at Skarkos on Ios[16] to 72.82 cm (male animal) at Tiryns.[17]

– For the pigs the available data show an opposite development, i.e. a reduction in size, a phenomenon not attested in mainland Greece.

– In general, the animal bones from Markiani, in comparison to the bone material from EBA sites in Macedonia, Thessaly, the Peloponnese and the Aegean islands (Rhodos, Ios, Skyros),[18] are either smaller in size or similar to the minimum dimensions given.

[12] Yannouli 1994, 191.
[13] Boessneck 1962, 42; Hinz 1979, 67.
[14] Gejvall 1969, 75.
[15] Kotzabopoulou and Trantalidou 1993, 395.
[16] Trantalidou, material under study.

[17] Von den Driesch and Boessneck 1990.
[18] Becker 1986; Boessneck 1962; Jordan 1975; Amberger 1979; Gejvall 1969; von der Driesch and Boessneck 1990; Trantalidou 2000; Trantalidou material uder study (Skarkos on Ios and Palamari on Skyros).

Animal husbandry seems to have been one of the main economic activities at Markiani. It is possible that the composition of the herds was equivalent to that of the other Cycladic settlements of the EBA.[19] It may be compared with other settlements of the south Aegean, e.g. Crete,[20] where the geological characteristics are very similar.

TABLE 9.9. Taxonomic abundance (percentages and total Number of Identifiable Specimens) reported from the Aegean islands.

Species	Skala Sotiros, Thasos I	II	mixed	Kaloyero-vrisi, Euboia	Phylakopi, Melos o	1	Markiani, Amorgos I	II	II–III	III	IV	mixed	Skarkos, Ios	Myrto, Crete	Asomatos, Rhodos BA IIb	BA III	Poliochni, Lemnos
Domestic mammals																	
Bos taurus	5.86	5.86	6.53	23.18	2.50	5.10	1.00	0.80			0.20	0.80	1.63	1.50	61.11	49.47	7.21
Ovis aries / Capra hircus	53.26	51.00	54.67	52.17	89.80	80.00	90.90	89.70	10.00	76.00	83.30	84.60	83.00	90.30	36.72	48.03	60.80
Sus scrofa dom.	26.12	30.86	29.04	23.18	7.70	14.00		8.40		4.00	15.40	8.30	14.83	8.20	1.23	2.49	14.81
Canis familiaris	1.71	1.69	1.46							0.10	0.10	0.40					1.16
Wild mammals																	
Cervus elaphus.	0.33	0.64	0.38	5.79													
Dama dama	0.83	1.09	0.29												0.92		
Capreolus capreolus	0.37	0.27	0.19	2.89													3.56
Lepus europeus	0.14	0.27								4.00	0.10	4.10	0.35				
Felis silvestris	0.14																
Vulpes vulpes																	0.33
Mustela sp												0.20					
Erinaceus europeus	0.20																
Rodentia			0.38														
Testudo sp	5.42	3.66	6.04														2.33
Aves	0.43	1.19										0.80	0.35				9.46
Pisces	5.11	3.47	0.97					0.80		16.00	0.60	0.60	1.63				
NISP	4789	1092	1026	69	365	214	17	225	6	25	732	481	835	301	324	762	1796
Unidentifiable fragments	2969	913	46	4			17	667	23	48	1420	1321					

Data after: Yannouli 1994, 407 (Skala Sotiros); Trantalidou 1993, 165 (Kaloyerovrisi), Gamble 1982a, 166 (Phylakopi); Trantalidou under study (Skarkos); Jarman 1972, 318 (Myrtos); Trantalidou 2000 (Asomatos); Sorrentino 1997, 158 (Poliochni).

[19] Gamble 1982a.   [20] Jarman 1972.

TABLE 9.10. Taxonomic abundance of fauna (percentages and NISP) reported from mainland Greece.

	Sitagroi		Pentapolis			Kastanas	Servia	Magoula Zarkou	Pefkakia		Tiryns		Lerna		A. Dimitrios	
	IV	V	I	II							EH II	EH III	EHI II	EH III	EH II	FN/ EBA
Domestic mammals																
Bos taurus	12.86	16.14	14.00	14.28	31.08	31.87	10.00	21.53	26.93	23.23	22.53	23.79	20.04	29.09	23.00	24.40
Ovis aries / Capra hircus.	29.40	39.81	32.68	29.54	28.99	17.83	50.00	47.69	22.71	37.05	39.91	33.53	40.33	33.01	42.20	31.10
Sus sp.	38.20	35.68	44.35	42.46	30.56	26.60	35.00	19.97	22.11	23.89	23.14	20.51	27.99	28.89	26.30	36.10
Canis sp.	1.80	1.85	1.16	3.71		0.58		1.15	1.33	1.96	0.91	1.12	2.96	3.38	1.30	0.80
Equus sp.					0.51	0.87						0.12	0.23	0.22		
Wild mammals																
Bos primigenius	1.41	0.13						0.07	0.60	0.25			0.83	0.07		
Rupicapra rupicapra		0.01														
Cervus elaphus	6.60	1.55	2.72	2.54	1.32	3.21	5.00	6.42	22.84	11.03	0.27	8.60	2.37	1.90	7.20	5.90
Dama dama	2.19	1.63	3.50	4.69		16.95					0.03					0.80
Capreolus capreolus	0.95	0.28	0.77	0.97		0.29		2.21	0.08	0.03				0.10		
Sus scofa dom.	2.31	1.78				4.67		0.85	2.58	0.70	0.30	0.51		1.09		
Felis silvestris		0.02						0.07		0.01			2.13			
Martes sp.	0.04									0.01				0.27		
Meles meles	0.02							0.05		0.01						
Ursus arctos	0.42	0.05							0.08	0.04						
Canis lupus	0.11	0.14							0.08	0.03			0.11			
Vulpes vulpes	0.11	0.14						0.27	0.08	0.18	0.16	0.08	0.47	0.10		
Castor fiber europeus	0.11	0.12														
Lepus	0.02	0.11	0.38	0.39				0.22	0.21	0.43	0.30	0.08	0.94	1.06		0.80
Erinaceus europeus		0.01											0.23	0.02		
Rodentia	0.06	0.01		0.19												
Testudo sp	2.17	0.31	0.38	1.17				0.40	0.04	0.30	0.13	0.34				
Aves	0.09	0.06						0.37	0.17	0.23	0.37					
Pisces	1.01	0.11							0.08	0.53	0.10					
NISP	4330	9119	257	511		342		3969	2320	8207	2951	2311	843	3929	152	119
Unidenti-fiable fragments			355	645				2795								

Data after: Bökönyi 1986, 68 (Sitagroi); Yannouli 1994, 396–7 and Koufos 1981, 113–5 (Pentapolis); Decker 1986, 333 (Kastanas); Watson 1979, 228 (Servia); Becker 1991, 18 (Magoula Zarkou); Jordan 1975, 7–10 and Amberger 1979, 16–7 (Pefkakia); von den Driesch and Boessneck 1990, 89 (Tiryns); Gejvall 1969, 10 (Lerna); Rusche and Halstead 1987 (Ayios Dimitrios). Note the relative importance of wild fauna, notably of red deer and hare, in comparison with the faunal remains in the Cyclades.

In more recent times, both in descriptions of fauna[21] and in the statistical census dealing with animal husbandry of the nineteenth and the twentieth centuries,[22] Amorgos is quoted as a part of the eparchia of Thera or as a part of the central Aegean islands. Therefore, it is difficult to understand if any similarities existed in the enviroment and the subsistence economy. Only in the 1911 census is there a separate reference to Amorgos and particularly to the regions of Chora (Amorgos), Vroutsi, Katapola and Kato Meria. By contrast, nineteenth century travellers, the statistical tables, and the early twentieth century census illuminate the diet of the inhabitants of the island during modern times and their preference for the meat of lamb and goat.

Albenhoven states that for a population of 2800 people on Amorgos in the middle of nineteenth century there were 7000 sheep and goats, 3000 cattle, 2000 equidae and some smaller animals.[23] Meliarakes is more specific.[24] He notes that the main diet of the inhabitants is legumes and especially fava, and that the Amorginians do not eat much meat and the salted meat is mainly lamb and goat. Their diet was supplemented with wine, olive oil, cereals, various crops, cheese and sardines.

The census of 1911 has further interesting data: 1205 cattle, 114 sheep, 2727 goats, 243 pigs, 562 equidae, 1188 domestic birds (chicken, geese, pigeons) and 33 rabbits are listed.[25] These data are similar to the modern material found at the site (see TABLE 9.1).

OTHER VERTEBRATES

There are few bibliographical references for the wild fauna of Amorgos. Small sized deer (of the *Cervus cretensis* type) and other micromammals which lived during the Lower and Middle Pleistocene[26] have been noted. The evidence from Markiani adds further information. Apart from the domestic animals, (cattle, sheep and goat, pigs and rabbits) other species have been found, as follows:

– The *Mustelidae*. A fragment from the lower jaw mandible of a weasel (*Mustela nivalis*), 'atsidha' in the local Amorginan dialect. This small carnivorous mammal has been recorded in a few excavated sites of the Aegean area[27] (PLATE 55 *e*).

– Rodents. There are 27 fragments or intact bones assignable to the *Myridae* family, mainly the genus *Rattus*. Not uncommonly, most of those bones have been found together (e.g. LB I *Murinae* material from Akrotiri, Thera) and they were burnt. Judging from their state of preservation and their texture it is assumed that these should be assigned to the modern material. Yet, it should be noted that the species *Rattus rattus*, the black rat, has been recorded as early as the LM IIIC period.[28]

– Birds. The bones, found in disturbed levels, are as follows: a lower part of tarsometetarsus (lower breadth of metatarsus 22.00mm), two intact phalanges, and a fragment of illium, assigned to a bird of the class of the falconiformes (*Aquila sp.*?). Falcon, buzzard, owl and crow[29] were regularly migratory, some of them wintering in the Aegean.

Among the modern material there are a fragment of a carpometacarpus, a fragment of a distal femur and one fragment of a tarsometatarsus. These may be ascribed to bird species that resemble, in size and morphology, the duck or goose family, *Anatidae*. Finally, a fragment of scapula is possibly to be assigned to partridge.

FISH BONES AND FISHING

Nine vertebrae and five skull fragments (PLATE 56 *b*) are assigned to various fish species found in spaces at the summit and on Terrace 1.

The skull fragments are assigned to the species *Scarus cretensis*, the parrot fish. The breath of the two pharyngeal bones is 15.00 and 16.80 mm. The height of the vertebrae is between 5.70 and 21.70 mm and the diameter between 6.60 to 21.40 mm. The two vertrebrae (with the larger height and diameter) should be assigned to the species of the family of *Serranidae*.[30] The vertebrae of the *Serranidae* family

[21] Heldreich 1978; Ondrias 1965.
[22] Apographi Georgiki 1911–60.
[23] Albenhoven 1854.
[24] Melirakis 1884, 31–2.
[25] Apographi Georgiki. 1911–60.
[26] Kotsakis and Petronio and Sirma 1980, 36.
[27] Thermi: Bate 1936, 216; Kastanas: Becker 1986, 153; Crete: Reese 1995, 193, Nyder and Klippel 1999, 68. For the present distribution see also Erhard 1858; Heldereich 1878, 9;

Ondrias 1965, 11, 63; Masseti 1998, 5.
[28] Klippel and Snyder 1991, 180.
[29] Von der Muehle 1844; Erhard 1858; Heldereich 1878; Vikelas 1879; Ondrias 1965; Dimitropoulos 1989a, and 1989b; ibid. 1993.
[30] Dr J. Desse (Sophia-Antipolis C.N.R.S. France) contributed essentially to the identification of the species. I acknowledge my warmest thanks for that.

usually have dimensions between 21.70 by 20.00 and 21.40 by 20.00 mm. Both those species are known in the Aegean.[31] *Scarus* and *Ceris* (*Epinephelus* sp.) are referred by Atheneus.[32] The first has been identified in the material from Eleutherna[33] and Kommos[34] in Crete. The second is known from the Neolithic and Bronze Age settlements of Khirokitia[35] in Cyprus, Kalythies on Rhodes,[36] Pseira on Crete,[37] Saliagos in the Cyclades,[38] Ayios Petros[39] and Youra[40] in the Sporades, and Pefkakia in Thessaly.[41] The above species and the large quantity of limpets and the other seashells[42] found within the same areas live in such rocky environments as the southern coastline of Amorgos.

We have no information about fishing techniques.[43] Desse's theory that the fishing tackle was kept near the seashore, thereby accounting for its absence from settlements, seems acceptable.[44]

Fishing seems to contribute to the diet of the inhabitants of Markiani only to a limited extent. Controversial theories have at times been put forward to account for the small quantities of fish-bones often preserved in the settlements.[45] Bronze Age Kommos and Akrotiri are until now the only exceptions. It seems that after the Mesolithic collecting seashells and fishing became less important activities than animal husbandry and agriculture.[46]

HUMAN BONES

There are five fragments of human skull (PLATE 56 *a*). The remaining human bones were found within Spaces 2, 3, and 7. One surface find was made west of the excavated area (D. Kovaios field), possibly outside the settlement area, and one joined from three fragments and assigned to a baby, were found in the area of the Rock Cutting 3

All the human bones come from superficial, disturbed layers except the skull fragment from Space 7, which was found with material of Ma phase IV. Therefore, we cannot draw positive conclusions about the period, the burial type, the death ritual, the place of inhumation (inside the habitation area?), the sex and age (four adults and one baby?) and palaeodemography of EBA Markiani.

WORKED BONE TOOLS

Only 10 worked bones were found at Markiani.[47] They are preserved in very fragmentary condition and in most cases their external surface, the periosteum was very decayed. Only two were preserved nearly intact (FIG. 9.1; PLATE 54).

POINTED TOOLS

1.1 (PLATE 53 *a*): from Trench 2,3 layer 5, phase Ma IV. This is an awl belonging to the type for which the metapodial of the sheep or goat was used as the basis for worked article.[48] It is a goat metacarpal. Its distal epiphysis (22.20 mm) was used as a handle. Its diaphysis was sliced along the medullar cavity to the middle of the long bone at the point were the 4th joins to the 3rd metacarpal (44.10 mm). The rest was thrown away along with the proximal epiphysis. The cut surfaces were then smoothed to give the tool a circular cross section very close to the point. This tool was probably used as an awl. Its total length is 86.30 mm.

1.2 (PLATE 53 *a*): from Trench 2 layer 32, Space 6, phase Ma IV. The point of an awl with flat section (preserved length 31.07 mm). Similarly worked bone (metapodial or tibia).

1.3 (FIG. 9.1, PLATE 53 *a*): EE 422 (Trench 4,10 layer 5). A fragment of an awl, decorated (FIG. 9.1 *a–d*). This was made

from a long bone fragment. The exterior may have been shaped and made more regular by abrasion using a whetstone with a central groove[49] (55.80 mm × 6 mm × 5 mm). It has an ellipsoid section, circular at the point. A net of incisions is visible. Beneath these incisions there are five parallel grooves, which may be related to the use of the tool. There is evidence of perforation. It resembles modern steel needles in form, using for stitching clothing and footwear, and such was probably its function. Awls and needles could have clearly been used to pierce hides.[50]

1.4 (FIG. 9.1, PLATE 53 *a*): EE 228, Trench 2 layer 18 phase Ma IV. An intact tool (88.30 mm × 18.10 mm × 4.00 mm) made from a cattle rib, pointed end. The base of the tool is rounded and the section at the end ellipsoid. The spongy substance inside the rib is visible for 3/5 of its length towards the base. It is worn at the middle which suggests wear occasioned by intensive use. It is possible that this tool was used for scraping relatively soft materials.[51]

[31] Heldrereich 1878, 80–93; Vikelas 1879, 21; Powell 1996, 26 and 28.
[32] Gulick 1930 (ed.), 355; Dumont 1988, 105.
[33] Trantallidou, unpublished material.
[34] Rose 1995, 206
[35] Desse 1984, 167–8; Desse and Desse-Berset 1989, 223–33.
[36] Halstead 1987, 138.
[37] Rose 1996, 136; ibid. 1998, 148.
[38] Renfrew *et al.* 1968, 118–21; Stratouli 1996, 7.
[39] Schwartz 1985, 152; Stratouli 1996, 7.
[40] Powell in press, Mylona in press.
[41] Hinz 1979; Stratouli 1996, 7.

[42] See Chapter 9b.
[43] Desse 1984, 168; Brewer and Friedman 1989, 21–46
[44] Desse and Desse-Berset 1989, 230.
[45] Cambitoglou 1991, 81–3; Trantalidou 1991.
[46] Powell in press.
[47] Here I would like to acknowledge my warmest thanks to Dr Georgia Stratouli, specialist on bone tools, for her help.
[48] Poplin 1975, 179–92; Stordeur-Yedid 1976, 39–42; Camps-Fabrer and D'Anna 1977, 311–23; Murray 1979, 27–35.
[49] Moundrea-Agraphioti 1980*b*, 494; Stratouli 1987*b*, 159.
[50] LeMoine 1997, 33, 51, 60.
[51] Stratouli 1987, 159.

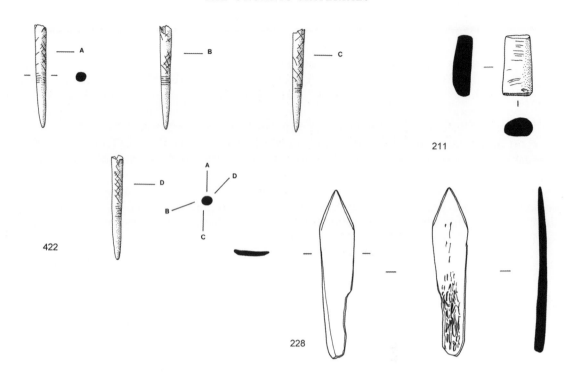

FIG. 9.1. Worked shell (2) and bone tools (scale 1:2).

BLUNT-ENDED (?POLISHER)

Trench 1,4 layer 31, Space 6, Ma IV. Made from a long bone (tibia?), the base is not preserved. It was probably used for polishing or burnishing (preserved length 92.20 mm; flat and curved section).

FRAGMENT OF A HANDLE

Rock Cutting 2, Space 7. This comes from the diaphysis of a long bone and is very badly preserved. It was reconstructed from small flakes, cylindrical section (Max. L. 70.8 mm). Tubular tools made on a femur or humerus of sheep or goat have been found in several places in the Aegean (e.g. Akrotiri, Thera).

BASES OF TOOLS (PLATE 53 *a*)

These are made from a sliced radius (of a sheep or goat). The working end, pointed or blunt, is not preserved.

4.1 (PLATE 53 *a*): from Trench 1,5, Level 6, Space 2. The surface of the proximal epiphysis of the long bone has been roughly worked (Max. W. 22.40 mm). The edges have been worn flat. The section is flat and curved. (Max. preserved L 66.90 mm).
4.2 (PLATE 53 *a*): from Trench 3,3, phase Ma III. Probably a handle, the surface of the proximal epiphysis of the long bone without any smoothing (Max. breath of the basis 27.90 mm, Max. preserved L. 55.10 mm). Very similar to 4.1.
4.3 Trench 2,3 layer 5, Space 2, phase Ma IV. Fragment from the diaphysis of a radius, with ends missing (Max. L. 92.10 mm). The preparation of the tool is the same as in the above mentioned tools.

PERFORATED

5.1 (PLATES 53 *a* and 56 *f*): Trench 3,1 layer 3. Intact astragalus (Max. L. 27.30 mm) of a small sheep or goat. The perforation (*c.* 2 mm) on the groove at the tarsal articulation is small, possibly to permit suspension from a thread. The bone shows no other working traces apart from some cut marks from the dismembering process. The use of the astragalus during antiquity as a pendant, toy or amulet is well known over the east Mediterranean region.[52] We should note here that this was found in Trench 3 where a lead pendant[53] was also found.

---

[52] See Amandry 1984, 347–80, with earlier bibliography.

[53] See Chapter 8F.

GENERAL OBSERVATIONS

The pattern of use of bone tools in the Neolithic settlements of Kephala[54] on Kea and Saliagos[55] was similar. The bone tools from EBA Phylakopi on Melos were few in number.[56] A small but varied collection of bone tools, pins and other items was recovered from EBA levels at Ayia Irini on Kea; worked antler and shell was also found.[57] So far from the Cyclades there is nothing to match the substantial number of bone tools known from EBA sites in the north-east Aegean, including Poliochni, Thermi and Troy. On the Greek mainland a few bone tools are attested from Ayios Kosmas in Attica,[58] and at Lerna and Asine in the Argolid.[59]

The tools recovered may be dated to phases Ma III and IV with some from the superficial disturbed layer. Most of them come from Terrace 1, within Spaces 2 and 6; one was found at Trench 4 on the summit and three in Trench 3.

The import of organic raw materials, such as deer antler or wild boar's tusk, seen at Ayia Irini on Kea,[60] was not observed. In general it seems that the use of such imported materials was rare in the Cyclades.

The worked bone assemblage from Markiani was too small for statistical analysis of typology, and the abrasion was too heavy to allow the secure identification of use. In general the data from other settlements of the same period in Macedonia,[61] Boiotia,[62] Lesbos,[63] Chios[64] and Lakonia[65] suggest that pointed tools were common. Their main functions were for leather processing and food production.

APPENDIX: MEASUREMENTS OF THE OVICAPRID AND SUID BONES

NOTES ON PLATES 55 AND 56

PLATE 55

a. Typical pattern of breakage and rodent gnawing on a goat metacarpal (posterior / caudal view). Proximal phalanges (posterior view) of ovicaprids modified by non-human taphonomic agents such as teeth of rodents and sedimentary abrasion.

b. Position of cut-marks on lateral and anterior (cranial) part of ovicaprid humerus. These butchery marks relate to disarticulation.

c. Disjointing procedures on the medium-size animals: proximal anterior part of a metatarsus of the main stock species, the ovicaprids. These cut-marks refer to the disarticulation of the humerus from the radio-cubitus (front limb) and of the tarsals from the metatarsus (rear limb).

d. Mandible fragment of *Mustela nivalis*. Although the palaeontological record is incomplete, this anthropophilous wild animal can be considered as a man-made introduction designated as a murid predator.

f. Pathological lesion of a joint: combined radius-ulna of an ovicaprid (anterior view). The pathogenesis of the condition is unknown. New supporting tissue has formed but the limb was not functional. The final diagnosis should therefore be determined by X-ray photography.

PLATE 56

a. Human skull bones of found in a disarticulated and fragmentary state.

b. Fish bone (head and vertebrae) assemblage. The most informative remains are the two pharyngeal bones, the premaxilla and the fragment of neurocranium from the *Scaridae* family (first and second row) and the two larger vertebrae from the *Serranidae* family. They belong to the Perciformes order; they live in shallow seas, and are relatively easy to catch.

c–d. Miscellaneous bone tools from Markiani: Right radius, distal epiphysis unfused, from a young sheep (posterior –c- and anterior –d- view). Bone tool from the same anatomical element. The tool was held in the right hand. The proximal epiphysis was its handle (similar tools on Ios).

[54] Coleman 1977, 8, 90–5.
[55] Evans and Renfrew 1968, 66–8.
[56] Atkinson *et al.* 1904, 192.
[57] Krzyszkowska 1999, 157–9, pl. 99; cf. Krzyszkowska 1984, 43–5, pl. 32.
[58] Mylonas 1959, 147.
[59] Lerna: Banks 1967, 263–453; Asine: Frodin and Persson 1938, 253–7.

[60] Caskey 1966, 374–5; Krzyszkowska 1999, 157–9 (worked antler and boar's tusk in EBA levels).
[61] Heurtley 1939, 87, 202.
[62] Goldman 1931, 211–15.
[63] Lamb 1936.
[64] Hood 1981, 70–2.
[65] Renard 1989, 91.

e.   Proximal part of two bone tools manufactured from split ovicaprid radii.
f.   Perforated right talus (dorsal surface). The butchery marks indicate the cutting of the tendons of
        two muscles which cross from the lower leg to the metatarsal. The pierced astragalus may have
        been used as an amulet as it has been found in isolation.

THE MEASUREMENTS

CAPRA HIRCUS

Horn-core

1. Diameter of the base

Phase	Number	Min.–max. dimension	Average dimension
Ma IV	1		47.0
Mixed	2	20.2–31.5	25.8
Modern	4	23.0–42.2	32.3

Scapula

1. Length of angulus articularis

Phase	Number	Min.–max. dimension	Average dimension
Ma II	1		28.8
Ma IV	2	30.0–32.3	31.1
Mixed	1		29.6
Modern	2	27.6–31.4	29.5

2. Length of facies articularis

Phase	Number	Min.–max. dimension	Average dimension
Ma II	2	22.5–23.4	22.9
Ma IV	3	22.0–27.3	24.6
Mixed	1		21.7
Modern	2	24.3–24.6	24.4

3. Breadth of facies articularis

Phase	Number	Min.–max. dimension	Average dimension
Ma II	2	17.8–19.3	18.5
Ma IV	3	19.2–20.6	19.5
Mixed	1		20.7
Modern	2	17.6–22.6	20.1

Humerus

1. Max. proximal breadth

Phase	Number	Min.–max. dimension	Average dimension
Ma II	1		30.1
Ma IV	9	25.4–29.6	27.2
Mixed	5	25.4–35.4	28.6
Modern	1		27.8

2. Max. distal breadth

Phase	Number	Min.–max. dimension	Average dimension
Ma II	2	15.0–16.9	15.9
Ma IV	9	15.0–20.7	19.4
Mixed	3	15.7–17.9	16.9
Modern	1		18.9

1st Phalanx

1. Max. length

Phase	Number	Min.–max. dimension	Average dimension
Ma II	1		32.0
Ma III–IV	14	30.1–36.4	33.6
Mixed	13	30.1–40.5	39.9
Modern	2	35.4–35.9	35.6

2. Max. proximal breadth

Phase	Number	Min.–max. dimension	Average dimension
Ma II	1		11.0
Ma III–IV	14	10.5–12.7	11.3
Mixed	13	9.2–16.8	15.7
Modern	2	11.8–12.9	12.3

3. Smallest breadth

Phase	Number	Min.–max. dimension	Average dimension
Ma II	3	7.9–10.2	9.3
Ma III–IV	15	7.9–10.9	9.4
Mixed	13	6.4–13.4	9.0
Modern	2	10.1–10.6	10.3

4. Max. distal breadth

Phase	Number	Min.–max. dimension	Average dimension
Ma II	3	10.4–14.1	11.6
Ma III–IV	12	8.9–14.8	11.8
Mixed	13	9.8–14.2	12.4
Modern	2	10.9–12.2	11.5

5. Max. proximal breadth

Phase	Number	Min.–max. dimension	Average dimension
Mixed	1		43.0

Radius

1. Max. proximal breadth

Phase	Number	Min.–max. dimension	Average dimension
Ma II	3	25.8–32.1	28.8
Ma IV	3	24.9–28.5	27.2
Mixed	3	25.3–35.1	29.2
Modern	1		26.8

2. Max. distal breadth

Phase	Number	Min.–max. dimension	Average dimension
Mixed	1		26.3

Ulna

1. Max. breadth of oleacranon

Phase	Number	Min.–max. dimension	Average dimension
Ma IV	2	37.6–22.9	30.2

Metacarpal

1. Max. proximal breadth

Phase	Number	Min.–max. dimension	Average dimension
Ma II	3	20.2–22.3	21.3
Ma IV	4	20.7–22.3	21.6
Mixed	1		24.2
Modern	1		24.1

2. Max. distal breadth

Phase	Number	Min.–max. dimension	Average dimension
Ma II	1		23.2
Ma IV	2	22.5–24.7	23.6
Mixed	2	26.4–28.2	27.3

Pelvis

1. Max. breadth of acetabulum

Phase	Number	Min.–max. dimension	Average dimension
Mixed	1		20.7

Femur

1. Max. proximal breadth

Phase	Number	Min.–max. dimension	Average dimension
Ma IV	1		44·5

2. Max. distal breadth

Phase	Number	Min.–max. dimension	Average dimension
Ma IV	1		37.8

Tibia

1. Greatest length

Phase	Number	Min.–max. dimension	Average dimension
Ma II	1		174·5

2. Max. proximal breadth

Phase	Number	Min.–max. dimension	Average dimension
Ma II	1		34·9

3. Smallest breadth

Phase	Number	Min.–max. dimension	Average dimension
Ma II	2	12.1–14.5	13·3

4. Max. distal breadth

Phase	Number	Min.–max. dimension	Average dimension
Ma II	2	22.1–23.5	22.8
Ma IV	4	22.9–24.9	24.0
Mixed	1		23.8

Metatarsal

1. Max. proximal breadth

Phase	Number	Min.–max. dimension	Average dimension
Ma II	1		17.8
Ma IV	4	17.6–21.1	19.1
Modern	1		23·3

Calcaneum

1. Greatest length

Phase	Number	Min.–max. dimension	Average dimension
Ma II	1		52.3
Ma III–IV	5	44.3–55.1	49.7
Mixed	2	49.5–51.6	50.5
Modern	1		51.7

2. Max. breadth

Phase	Number	Min.–max. dimension	Average dimension
Ma II	1		28.8
Ma IV	2	30.0–32.3	31.1
Mixed	1		29.6

Astragalus

1. Greatest external length

Phase	Number	Min.–max. dimension	Average dimension
Ma II	2	24.6–26.4	25.5
Ma IV	10	24.3–29.1	27.7
Mixed	5	26.2–28.8	27.8
Modern	1		28.2

2. Greatest internal length

Phase	Number	Min.–max. dimension	Average dimension
Ma II	2	22.2–24.6	23.4
Ma III–IV	9	22.4–27.1	25.5
Mixed	5	24.7–26.7	25.5
Modern	1		27.1

3. Lateral diameter

Phase	Number	Min.–max. dimension	Average dimension
Ma II	2	13.6–14.0	13.8
Ma IV	10	11.1–16.4	14.3
Mixed	3	13.4–16.8	15.3
Modern	1		15.0

4. Medial diameter

Phase	Number	Min.–max. dimension	Average dimension
Ma II	2	13.6–14.7	14.5
Ma III–IV	11	12.8–17.2	14.2

2nd Phalanx

1. Greatest length

Phase	Number	Min.–max. dimension	Average dimension
Ma II	5	19.6–24.4	21.8
Ma III–IV	12	19.5–26.6	20.3
Mixed	8	19.9–27.3	23.1
Modern	3	20.4–22.7	21.5

2. Max. proximal breadth

Phase	Number	Min.–max. dimension	Average dimension
Ma II	5	9.7–12.4	10.9
Ma IV	12	9.4–14.2	10.9
Mixed	8	9.6–14.4	12.3
Modern	3	9.6–12.3	11.0

3. Smallest breadth

Phase	Number	Min.–max. dimension	Average dimension
Ma II	5	7.2–7.9	7.8
Ma III–IV	12	6.9–9.6	8.2
Mixed	8	7.0–11.4	9.2
Modern	3	7.3–9.4	8.6

4. Distal breadth

Phase	Number	Min.–max. dimension	Average dimension
Ma II	5	6.9–8.8	8.0
Ma III–IV	12	7.6–12.8	9.1
Mixed	7	8.0–11.8	9.8
Modern	3	8.1–10.5	9.4

3rd Phalanx

1. Plantar diagonal length of the foot

Phase	Number	Min.–max. dimension	Average dimension
Ma II	2	27.9–28.5	28.5
Ma IV	3	26.9–32.6	29.7
Mixed	2	24.6–31.0	27.8

2. Volar length

Phase	Number	Min.–max. dimension	Average dimension
Ma II	2	21.5–22.5	22.0
Ma IV	3	23.5–26.7	24.9
Mixed	2	19.5–25.9	22.7

3. Min. breadth of plantar

Phase	Number	Min.–max. dimension	Average dimension
Ma II	2	5.5–6.3	5.9
Ma IV	3	4.9–5.0	4.9
Mixed	2	4.8–5.1	4.9

SUS SCROFA DOM

Length of lower M3

Phase	Number	Min.–max. dimension	Average dimension
Mixed	2	28.5–37.3	32.9

Scapula

1. Breadth of facies articularis

Phase	Number	Min.–max. dimension	Average dimension
Ma II	1		27.3
Ma IV	1		26.3

2. Diameter of facies articularis

Phase	Number	Min.–max. dimension	Average dimension
Ma II	1		22.5
Ma IV	1		18.6

Astragalus

1. Greatest external length

Phase	Number	Min.–max. dimension	Average dimension
Ma II	1		40.8
Modern	1		34.7

2. Greatest internal length

Phase	Number	Min.–max. dimension	Average dimension
Ma II	1		37.1

1st Phalanx

1. Greatest length

Phase	Number	Min.–max. dimension	Average dimension
Ma IV	1		34.6
Mixed	1		34.6

2. Max. proximal breadth

Phase	Number	Min.–max. dimension	Average dimension
Ma IV	1		16.7
Mixed	1		16.4

3. Smallest breadth

Phase	Number	Min.–max. dimension	Average dimension
Ma IV	1		14.4
Mixed	1		12.1

4. Max. distal breadth

Phase	Number	Min.–max. dimension	Average dimension
Ma IV	1		15.6
Mixed	1		15.6

2nd Phalanx

1. Greatest length

Phase	Number	Min.–max. dimension	Average dimension
Ma IV	2	11.9–16.1	22.8
Mixed	5	20.7–25.0	23.7

2. Max. proximal breadth

Phase	Number	Min.–max. dimension	Average dimension
Ma IV	2	11.9–16.1	14.0
Mixed	5	14.7–15.8	14.6

3. Smallest breadth

Phase	Number	Min.–max. dimension	Average dimension
Ma IV	2	8.7–12.9	10.8
Mixed	5	9.9–14.1	11.8

4. Distal breadth

Phase	Number	Min.–max. dimension	Average dimension
Ma IV	2	9.3–14.0	11.6
Mixed	5	10.6–13.9	12.1

3rd phalanx

1. Diagonal plantar length

Phase	Number	Min.–max. dimension	Average dimension
Ma IV	1		25.9

2. Volar length

Phase	Number	Min.–max. dimension	Average dimension
Ma IV	1		26.2

3. Min. plantar breadth

Phase	Number	Min.–max. dimension	Average dimension
Ma IV	1		16.6

B. THE MOLLUSCS

by Lilian Karali-Giannakopoulou

The study of the molluscan material from Markiani may contribute to our knowledge of the natural environment and the economy of the settlement, especially when considered in association with the studies of the animal bones and the seeds.

Molluscs are organisms which live in particular ecosystems. They are not able to move long distances. Their presence in a region is indicative of the climate, the temperature conditions and the nature of the coastline.

At Markiani molluscs played a significant role in the diet of the inhabitants. The species identified are common in the Aegean; no imported or rare species were found in the assemblage. The species noted are not very different from the modern ones and their presence implies a similar ecological environment to the present one.

THE MOLLUSCS

Most of the shells were found in a fragmentary condition. Their natural colour and lustre are not usually preserved. Special effort was made to join the fragments for the identification of the species either to gastropod or bivalve species. The bivalves identified preserved in most of the cases only one constituent shell, since the other is usually broken or missing.

The identified species from Markiani are presented in the following catalogue according to the frequency of their appearance in the settlement.

MARITIME SPECIES (6790 MARINE MOLLUSCS IN TOTAL)

Patella: 5917 examples, 87.10%; two different species of patella were identified: *Patella coerulea* Linné and *Patella lusitanica* Gmelin. Most of the shells are fragmentary or broken. These species are usually found along rocky coasts. A large number of them were found along with burnt animal bones and potsherds in Space 5 (Trench 2,1 layer 20). The limpets probably came from the nearby seashore which is very rocky. Most of them bear traces of an implement/utensil (stone or a bladed tool) used to detach the limpet from the rock.

Monodonta turbinata Born: about 690 shells, 10.20%, most of which are in a fragmentary condition. This species also lives on rocky coastlines. A large quantity was found in Space 5 (Trench 2,1 layer 20).

Gibbula divaricata Linné: 94 shells, 1.40%, most of which are fragmentary. The species lives in muddy or sandy conditions among seaweed, but it is also common on stony coasts.

Murex: 31 shells, 0.50%, of two different species have been identified: *Murex trunculus* Linné and *Murex brandaris* Linné. Most of them were in fragmentary condition. These species are usually found on rocky coasts among seaweed. In view of their small number and their occurrence among food remains, it is unlikely that the presence of this species suggests their use for the production of purple at such an early period.

Tritonium nodiferum Lamarck: 25 fragmentary shells. This carnivorous species of the Triton family lives in sandy ground, mainly in deep waters. It is one of the most powerful of the molluscs of the European seas. Its surface is white, yellow or light brown and resembles marble. It has radial brown grooves.

Cerithium vulgatum Bruguière: seven shells. This is a gastropod with pointed end. It is common in the Mediterranean on coastlines with seaweed.

Glycimeris glycimeris Linné: five shells. This lives in muddy or stony ground

Pinna nobilis Linné: five shells. This species lives with its pointed internal side in the sand. It is common in the Mediterranean region and is supposed to be one of the most delicious molluscs. Often its thick mother of pearl is used for decorative purposes.

Euthria cornea Linné: three shells. This species usually lives in sandy ground, mainly in deep waters.

Nassa neritea Linné: three shells of this species. This lives in sandy ground and in shallow waters.

Chama gryphoides Linné: two shells. This species lives in rocky ground.

Columbella rustica Lamarck: two shells. This species lives on rocky coasts just under the surface.

Cassidaria cassidaria Lamarck: two shells. This lives on coral and on rocks from the coastline to deeper waters.

Pisania maculosa Lamarck: one shell of this gastropod was found. It is associated with rocky coasts.

Spondylus gaederopus Linné: one shell was found. It is a rocky environment species, the presence of which may be significant since it was commonly used to produce ornaments in prehistoric societies in the Aegean.

Conus ventricosus Gmelin: one shell of this gastropod was found. This is usually very common along the rocky coastlines of the Mediterranean.

Astralium rugosum Linné: one shell was found. This species lives in rocky environments.

Echinus melo Lamarck: seven shells of sea urchin. Although this species is not a mollusc it is usually presented along with them. It belongs to the *Echinoderma* and is regarded as a delicious food. It is rarely found in archaeological contexts since its shell has to be broken in order to eat the contents, and is rarely preserved.

TERRESTRIAL SPECIES

Helix figulina Rossmaller: 228 shells, mostly fragmentary. This is a terrestrial snail species very common in the Aegean islands.

Chilostoma cyclolabris Deshayes: 78 shells. This is another snail species common in Greece and many other regions of the Mediterranean.

Thus 93% of the shells recovered are marine species from rocky environments with 4% terrestrial species and 2% from sandy environments. The principal species represented are: *Patella* (80%) and *Monodonta* (9%).

USES

The main use of the molluscs was for food. The shell residues then had multiple uses either as tools or ornaments. The identification of those uses is difficult.

Thus the uses of the molluscs from Markiani include: (a) diet — food or bait; (b) raw material for tools; and (c) possible symbolic use of the species *Triton*.

(a) From Space 5, Trench 2,1 layer 20, comes the most significant evidence of food use. Numerous, about 2146, limpets were found along with burnt animal bones and burnt sherds within rough slab-covered structures. These molluscs were probably consumed *in situ* and the shell residues buried within the structures which may have functioned as hearths.

(b) One worked object of *Spondylus gaederopus* Linné was found at Markiani during the surface cleaning of 1985. It is trapezoidal and resembles a small axe. Its dimensions are 0.33 cm × 0.14–0.16 cm (**EE 211**, FIG. 9.1, PLATE 54). The workmanship is excellent but its use is difficult to determine. There are no traces of fastening or perforation. It may have been used as a rubber. Shell tools have been identified in settlements of the Neolithic period.[66] They were used for polishing pottery. Similar objects but spool-shaped (i.e. pestles) have been found at both Kephala and Ayia Irini on Kea.[67]

---

[66] Shackleton 1968.
[67] Kephala: Coleman 1977. Ayia Irini (Period III): Krzyszkowska 1999, 157–9, pl. 99 (nos. 235–237) with references; also noteworthy are the bivalves (chiefly glycymeris) which evidently served as containers, some displaying traces of pigment (ibid nos. 240–247).

(c) The presence of *Triton* shell residues in Markiani may be significant. Residue of one intact Triton shell was found on the floor of Space 1 in Trench 1,6. There were also 21 fragmentary finds.

Intact *Triton* shells residues have been found in EC cemeteries, such as Chalandriani[68] on Syros and the Panagia[69] cemetery in Paros. Their presence in graves has been interpreted as a symbolic offering to the dead.[70] The Triton shell can produce a loud and clear sound and for that reason it was commonly used as a conch from early times. Because of its large size it may also have been used as a utensil for the transfer of liquids.

The presence of *Triton* shells within Bronze Age settlements has often been related to cult practice,[71] either as an offering/libation implement or as a conch. However, in most cases this interpretation is uncertain. In the EM settlement of Myrtos there was a similar number (27) of occurrences of *Triton*.[72] Their interpretation as cult objects has been doubted, since only in one case was the pointed end cut to produce the possible mouthpiece.

3. GENERAL OBSERVATIONS

The molluscan material from Markiani is characteristic of the Cyclades as known from the EC cemeteries of Syros, Paros, Naxos[73] and Amorgos.[74] Most of the shells come from rocky environments. A similar picture is provided by the molluscs from Neolithic Saliagos,[75] where most of the shells also come from rocky environments.

They are present at Markiani from the first phase of the occupation (Ma I) to the last (Ma IV) and they are usually found in association with animal and fish bones[76] in non–roofed areas. The greatest frequency of molluscs was observed in the summit area of Space 8, in Trenches 1,1 layers 7 and 9, and at Space 5 of Terrace 1, in Trench 2 as seen at TABLE 9.11.

The small quantities of the molluscan material from Markiani and the absence of other similar published material for the same period from the Cyclades prevent general observations on the uses of this material.

TABLE 9.11. The occurrence of mollusc species at Markiani by trench.

Mollusc Species	Trench 6	Trench 8	Trench 4	Trench 7	Trench 9	Trench 1	Trench 2	Trench 10	Trench 5	Trench 3	Surface	Σ
Patella sp.	25	36	60	180	190	2146	1999	8	61	274	938	5917
Monodonta turbinata B.		20	14	4	11	170	286	2	61	65	57	690
Echinus melo L.						4	3					7
Murex brandaris L.				1	2	6	6			2		18
Murex trunculus L.				1	1	4	4			3		13
Gibbula divaricata L		2		20	1	67	1		1	2		94
Glycimeris glycimeris L.				1		2	1				1	5
Tritonium nodiferum L.	1			2	2	8	6		1	1	4	25
Pinna nobilis L.						2	2			4		8
Cerithium vulgatum B.		2				2				2	1	7
Euthria cornea L.							2		1			3
Helix figulina R.		2		24		141	20			48	13	228
Chilostoma cyclolabris D.				3		58	1			16		78
Astralium rugosum L.							1					1
Columbella rustica L				1			1					2
Pisania maculata L											1	1
Spondylus gaederopus L.											1	1
Cassidaria cassidaria L.									1	1		2
Chama gryphoides L.										2		2
Conus ventricosus G.						1						1
Total	26	62	74	274	210	2697	2376	10	126	445	1070	7370

[68] Tsountas 1899, 105.
[69] Tsountas 1898, 156–7.
[70] Tsountas 1899, 105.
[71] The rock crystal lentoid from the Idaean Cave: *CMS* II.3 no. 7; Åström and Reese 1990.

[72] Jarman 1972, 324.
[73] Doumas 1977; Demakopoulou 1990, 70–1.
[74] Tsountas 1898, 166; Marangou 1990a, 171.
[75] Shackleton 1968.
[76] See also Chapter 9A.

C. THE CARBONISED SEEDS
by Jane M. Renfrew

Although 34 soil samples were floated for carbonised seeds, disappointingly only three of them yielded any identifiable material. Traces of burnt straw were found in two other samples and fragments of charcoal occurred in 11 samples, large quantities being found in a Hellenistic pithos from Trench 5,1, Δ 504. Details of these finds are given below.

CARBONISED SEEDS

EE 386, Trench 3,3, layer 3: Two fragments of half a carbonised olive stone, *Olea europoea*, were discovered here (see PLATE 54 *f*). They measured a combined length of 10.00 mm and breadth of 6.50 mm well within the range for cultivated olives.

Δ800, Trench 8,2 west section, contents of the pot **K 1524** (FIG. 7.12). This pot contained 39 seeds of small pulse cf. *Lathyrus clymenum*. They were circular in outline, more or less spherical in shape, some being slightly flattened at the top of the base (see PLATE 54 *d*). The following measurements were obtained for 31 of them: Diameter 2.20–3.70 mm, average 2.90 mm.

Δ305, Trench 3,2 layer 12. A single seed of bitter vetch, *Vicia ervilia*, of characteristic triangular shape (see PLATE 54 *e*). It measured: length 3.00 mm, breadth 2.90 mm and width 2.50 mm.

In addition to these carbonised seeds a single impression of a barley grain was recovered from Trench 1,3 layer 2 on the rectangular object, 257, with the two holes initially identified as a possible loom-weight (see Chapter 8D, FIG. 8. 21, PLATE 49 and PLATE 54 *c*).

CARBONISED STRAW

Two samples contained fragments of carbonised straw: Δ 247 from Ma 89, Trench 2, layer 32, and Δ 259 from Ma 89, Trench 2, layer 43. This was too fragmentary for proper identification and it is not clear what it was being used for, although farming communities do find it an extremely useful commodity. Some of it may well have been used to make the mats discussed in Chapter 8C.

CHARCOAL

Fragments of charcoal were found in soil samples from the following contexts:

Ma 88, Trench 2, layer 15, 'burnt soil'.
Δ229, Ma 89, Trench 2, layer 22.
Δ236, Ma 89, Trench 2, layer 24.
Δ237, Ma 89, Trench 2, layer 25.
Δ242, Ma 89, Trench 2, layer 27, charcoal mixed with shells.
Δ258, Ma 89, Trench 2, layer 43.
Δ259, Ma 89, Trench 2, layer 43, mixed with burnt straw.

Δ504, Ma 88, Trench 5,1, **EE 505**, large quantity of charcoal in a Hellenistic pithos.
Δ112, Ma 89, Trench 1,1, layer 24.
Δ106, Ma 89, Trench 1,1, layer 9.
Δ115, Ma 89, Trench 1,1, layer 16.

None of the charcoal has been identified; much of it was very fragmentary.

There were two soil samples which had a very curious consistency best described as burnt granules of compacted earth. They came from the following contexts:

Δ103, Ma 88, Trench 1, layer 5.
Δ125, Ma 89, Trench 1,4, layer 14.

CONCLUSIONS

Markiani was not rich in carbonised plant remains, but those that survived were fairly typical of the EBA in the Aegean area. The only cereal present was barley, *Hordeum vulgare*. Barley was already being grown in the Cyclades in the Late Neolithic: it was found at Saliagos[77] and Kephala,[78] and even today barley is the chief cereal crop cultivated in the Cyclades. The carbonised straw was probably barley straw.

Of the pulse crops *Vicia ervilia*, bitter vetch, is native in Anatolia and the Levant and is grown mainly as a minor fodder crop in the eastern Mediterranean and the Near East today. Its seeds are toxic to humans and to some animals, especially pigs and horses due to the presence in the seeds of the toxic amino acid, canavanine. Cattle and sheep can eat the seeds without becoming unwell and it is said to encourage and sustain milk production. It is possible to make the seeds palatable for humans

[77] Renfrew 1968. [78] Renfrew 1977.

by soaking them in water for up to 36 hours, then rubbing off the seed coat by hand, drying the cotyledons either in an oven or in the sun. Human consumption of the seeds is only as a last resort in cases of cereal crop failure when the seeds treated as above can be ground to flour. Human consumption of the bread made with this flour leads to drowsiness and fatigue. Finds of bitter vetch seeds are fairly common on Late Neolithic and EBA sites in Greece and Bulgaria.[79]

Lathyrus clymenum, the Spanish vetchling, is a rare local crop still growing today in the Aegean islands of Thera, Anafi and Karpathos.[80] It grows wild in the Mediterranean basin from Turkey to Spain. Storage jars containing large quantities of its seeds were discovered in the Bronze Age settlement of Akrotiri on Thera. It is also known from Late Minoan Knossos and from Phylakopi.

The two fragments of half an olive stone indicate that olives were exploited here. They join the small number of finds of EBA olives from the Aegean:[81] the stones recovered from EM levels at Myrtos,[82] Knossos,[83] and Lebena,[84] and the oil found in an EC jug in a grave on Naxos.[85] Wild olives were extensively exploited in the east Mediterranean area in the Mesolithic and the Neolithic especially in Cyprus and Israel,[86] and they do not appear to have been cultivated before 3700 BC when they appear at the site of Tuleitat Ghassul north of the Dead Sea. In the EBA of Israel and Jordan they are quite common, elsewhere there are rather few finds from Syria, Cyprus and Greece. It was not until the LBA that olive oil production was established on an industrial level in Crete and the Aegean.[87]

Thus although the finds of carbonised seeds from Markiani are rather sparse they do fit into the overall picture which is emerging of the development of agriculture in the Aegean in the EBA.

[79] Renfrew 1979, 248, 259, 260; Kroll 1984, 243–6.
[80] Sarpaki and Jones 1990.
[81] Runnels and Hansen 1986, 299–308.
[82] Renfrew 1972, 315–17.
[83] Evans 1928, 135.
[84] Alexiou 1960, 225–7.
[85] Vickery 1936, 51.
[86] Zohary and Hopf 2000, 149–51.
[87] Renfrew 1982, 156–60.

Chapter 10

General remarks

A. MARKIANI IN PERSPECTIVE
by Colin Renfrew

The work at Markiani so far has been limited to the surface surveys of 1985 and 1987 and the two excavation seasons of 1988–90, followed by brief supplementary work in later seasons. Only limited parts of the site have been examined, nor have excavations been taken to bedrock in the excavated areas of Terrace 1. Moreover only a representative selection of the pottery is considered in detail here. In particular the pottery of Trench 3 awaits comprehensive study, and the ceramic assemblage of Markiani phase III has not yet been fully described.

Yet despite these limitations certain features of the site have emerged very clearly. Its principal occupation was limited to the EBA, despite later episodes of occupation or use. And the extent of settlement, despite the rather limited areas excavated, has been closely studied through the exceptionally thorough and methodologically innovative surface survey organised by Todd Whitelaw (see Chapter 3).

Indeed, despite the considerable range of material now available from the prehistoric Cyclades and the various works of synthesis devoted mainly or partly to the Cycladic EBA, it is a remarkable circumstance that Markiani is the first settlement whose occupation was primarily during the Cycladic EBA to attain systematic and representative publication. To say this is not, of course, to question the importance of the publications of the great sites of the later Bronze Age Cyclades which have also yielded highly informative EBA finds, notably Phylakopi on Melos, Ayia Irini on Kea and Akrotiri on Thera, while those of Paroikia on Paros and Grotta on Naxos have been less comprehensively reported. Indeed the situation is already changing, with the impact of the two recent and major syntheses devoted to the cemeteries and to the special implications of insularity and with the publication of the settlement of Panormos on Naxos, and in particular that of the important recent excavations at Skarkos on Ios.[1] Nor should the interest of the earlier excavations of Tsountas at Pyrgos on Paros and at Kastri on Syros be overlooked.

Already it is possible to draw a number of conclusions about Markiani, some of which are likely to prove of wider relevance for the Cycladic EBA in general. Conclusions may be advanced, in some cases tentatively, about the character of the site, its sequence and chronology, its extent, and its nature.

THE CHARACTER OF THE SITE

Markiani was a fortified settlement located in inland Amorgos, overlooking the steep slopes of 'Notina', which characterise the south-eastern side of the island, but communicating by land with the more gentle slope to the west. As we have seen it was not the home of a community marked by particular wealth. Nor has its cemetery been located, at least not by us, so that while other finds from Amorgos, notably by Dümmler and Tsountas, may allow us to guess its character, nothing definitive is known.

Already, however, we may say that there are features in the domestic assemblage at Markiani which make it very different from the materials which have hitherto been used to characterise the Grotta-Pelos culture of the EC I period, or the Keros-Syros culture of EC II. Already we can begin to see, and the material so-far published from Skarkos confirms[2] that when these and other settlements of the Cycladic EBA are published, a much more appropriate series of characterisations and definitions will be possible. In the future they will be based primarily upon the domestic assemblages, rather than upon the special ceramic fine wares and the special stone ritual and funerary objects which characterise the Cycladic cemeteries and the funerary (and perhaps ritual) deposits from Dhaskalio–Kavos on Keros.

---

[1] Rambach 2001; Broodbank 2000b; Marthari 1999.
[2] We are grateful to Dr Marisa Marthari for the opportunity

of inspecting in the apotheke the finds from her important excavations at Skarkos.

The character of Markiani as a straightforward village settlement is clear, We regard its excavation and publication, along with that of Skarkos, as a significant step towards the investigation of the domestic reality of the EBA Cyclades. It should bring the rectification of an imbalance which more than a century of concentration almost exclusively upon the cemetery finds from the Cyclades[3] has created.

Sequence and Chronology

The exposed, hilltop position of Markiani has allowed erosion of the deposits at the summit. The configuration of stratified deposits is thus very different from such deeply-stratified sites as the Bronze Age town on Naxos, or Phylakopi on Melos or Ayia Irini on Kea. As discussed earlier, the oldest assemblage of material was found in the course of excavating the fortification wall at the north side of the site, while the best stratified materials from what we have defined as the second phase of occupation, Ma II, came from the south side of the summit area in Trench 1. On the other hand the most conspicuous finds from the last phase of EBA occupation of Ma IV were from the terrace below, Terrace 1.

The sequence of occupation is clear. The site was first occupied during phase I, characterised by domestic pottery of the Grotta-Pelos culture of EC I. This pottery, with its many parallels discussed in Chapter 7C, belong to the period frequently designated EC I. Unfortunately no radiocarbon samples were available from this phase, but that it is earlier than the well-documented phase II is clear. It may be that other deposits of exclusively phase I material will be found in further excavations at the site, but at present it is documented in a stratified context only in the area to the north of the summit, from Trench 6. The fortification wall was investigated by means of Trench 6. The excavated area is not large, and the possibility was discussed that the ceramic material found inside the wall might have washed in subsequent to its construction from adjacent and possibly earlier deposits or being cut through by the construction of the wall (which would make a later date for the wall itself a possibility). It was concluded however that this part of the defensive wall should indeed probably be dated to Ma I. Phase I is dated to the centuries immediately prior to 3000 BC.

Deposits of a chronologically more developed character were found on the south side of the summit of the site, in Trenches 1,1 and 7, in the area above Rock Cutting 2. They were well stratified. They showed continuity in the ceramic tradition with the materials of phase I, along with new forms relating to those of the Kampos Group first defined in Paros and known now from various islands, including the Ano Kouphonisi. It is generally accepted that this represents a transitional phase between the Grotta-Pelos culture (or EC I) and the Keros-Syros culture (or EC II). These deposits were taken to define Ma II. The radiocarbon determinations suggest a time range from 3000 BC to 2800 BC. Comparable material was found in the region of the fortification wall in Trench 8.

The structures most intensively investigated during our excavations lay on Terrace 1. The uppermost levels there contained ceramic forms which could be recognised as related to those of the Kastri Group, known from the site of Kastri on Syros, from Mount Kynthos on Delos, from Panormos on Naxos, from Ayia Irini on Kea and from other Cycladic sites. The levels beneath lacked these conspicuous forms and contained material which in some cases could be related to the Keros-Syros culture of EC II. The ceramic material from these lower levels on Terrace I was taken as defining Ma III. The overlying material, including forms recognisably of the Kastri Group defines Ma IV.

Material recognisably of Ma III was found in association with the fortification wall in Trench 8 and specifically with the Bastion there. As discussed in Chapter 4, the stratigraphic context clearly suggested that the Bastion of Trench 8 should be assigned to the Ma III period. Although the pottery from Rooms 1 and 2 of Trench 3, lying downhill and to the south-east of the main Terrace 1 area, has not been studied in detail, it too has been assigned to Ma III. The radiocarbon dates when calibrated suggest a time range of 2700 to 2500 BC for Ma III.

Ma IV represents the latest phase of EBA occupation on the site. The most abundant finds came from the uppermost levels of Terrace 1. It is clear that the ceramic tradition of Ma IV follows from that of Ma III, although with the introduction of such new forms as the tankard and the two-handled ('depas') cup. The radiocarbon dates when calibrated suggest that Markiani phase IV falls within the time range 2500 to 2200 BC, and that the site was certainly occupied over the century from 2400 to 2300 BC during phase IV.

---

[3] From Dümmler 1886 to Sherratt 2001.

It is possible, but not certain, that Markiani was occupied throughout the period from *c.* 3200 to 2200 BC. Certainly the indications are that the material found there from the Cycladic EBA spans a thousand years. Nothing found in the course of excavation indicates a hiatus or abandonment of the site during the EBA. But equally there are no indications which would demonstrate unbroken occupation. It is however suggested in Chapter 3 that the occupation of Markiani was sporadic rather than continuous, and nothing from the excavation contradicts that view.

Settlement and Population

A principal objective of the 1987 surface survey was to determine the extent of the site, building upon the earlier observations made during the initial survey of 1985.

As discussed in Chapter 3, sherds were found distributed in fairly high density over an area of about 0.3 hectare (i.e. 3000 sq. m). Sherds are found over a very much wider area, of the order of 20 ha, at lesser densities, but this is likely to be due mainly to downslope erosion. The occupied area was probably less than this during phases I and II, and the site underwent expansion in phase III. The discussion in Chapter 3 suggests that a single household, presumed to be a nuclear family, might occupy between 40 and 80 sq. m, and leads to the conclusion that in phases III and IV there may have been a maximum of 12 to 15 households, the equivalent of perhaps 60 to 75 individuals. It is concluded that the figure would be markedly less during phases I and II.

The Subsistence Base

The agrarian economy must in part be a matter of inference since carbonised material was rare and no cereal grains were recovered. This must, however, be seen as the result of taphonomic (and recovery) processes. Only a single barley grain impression was noted on the pottery. However the consistent use of cereals at the site, presumably mainly barley, can safely be inferred. The saddle querns from the site are likely to have been used for the grinding of cereals to produce flour. Two complete querns and three fragments were found at the site. One large rubber and five fragments were also found, and it is likely that these were used as grinders in conjunction with the saddle querns.

Carbonised seeds of a pulse were found, and these were certainly systematically collected, although it is not clear that this was a domesticated crop. Parts of a single olive stone were recovered, and as argued in Chapter 9C this is in harmony with the view that the olive was by then a domesticated plant, although this cannot be demonstrated by the Markiani finds alone. Similarly the find of ten impressions of vine leaves on the pottery, along with 59 mat impressions (Chapter 8C), extending other such finds from the EBA Cyclades, accords with the view that the vine was domesticated by this time, although vine leaf impressions alone are not a complete documentation. In this context it is pertinent to note that drinking cups first become numerous during Ma IV (specifically the tankards). The sauceboats so commonly seen elsewhere during the EB II period are not a prominent feature at Markiani, although chronologically they would fall within the time of Ma III.

The faunal remains give a useful further insight into the farming economy. The great majority of the animal bones found — 87.3% — were of sheep and goat (with the possibility that goat were in the majority). Not surprisingly, therefore, the herding of sheep and goat was a major feature of the rural economy at Markiani, as it is today. The bones represent in part butchery for meat, but the production of milk and cheese is also likely. The age profile, it is proposed in Chapter 9A, suggests that the sheep were reared to produce wool. Cattle represent a very small proportion (0.6%) of the bones recovered, and this small figure may reflect the use of cattle for ploughing. These figures are broadly in line with those quoted for Phylakopi on Melos and for EBA Myrtos on Crete. It is interesting to note, however, that pig bones were found in significant quantities, representing 12.0% of the assemblage, a proportion comparable with that from Myrtos, but much greater than the Phylakopi figure.

The overall picture does not differ markedly from the traditional exploitation of Amorgos and other Cycladic islands in recent times, although it should be noted that equids were not yet available. The presence of dog was noted. Wild animals did not make a significant contribution to the diet: deer were not recovered, although hare was present.

The sieving procedure used (a mesh of 1 cm) was not conducive to the recovery of fish bones. It may be significant that only nine fish vertebrae were in fact recovered and five skull fragments, and it is not possible to suggest that fishing played a significant role in the economy. Molluscs on the other hand were recovered in significant quantities, the most frequent being limpets (87%). The other common genus was *Monodonta*, again from the coast. So there is here no evidence of seafaring, simply of the use of the rocky foreshore.

CRAFTS

The finds from Markiani document a wide range of rural crafts in addition to the subsistence activities discussed above, namely the assumed cultivation of barley, the putative viticulture and olive production, and the practice of animal husbandry.

OBSIDIAN

The obsidian industry, with the skilled production of parallel sided blades, is discussed in Chapter 8A. It was indeed a blade industry, and as at other EC sites there is very little evidence of retouch and little indication of the use of flakes. Moreover the blade production was conducted in a manner that was economical of the raw material which does not seem to have been available in abundant quantities.

GROUND STONE

In addition there were ground stone tools of the kind familiar already in the Aegean from the Neolithic, notably the saddle querns and rubbers familiar already from Neolithic Saliagos and from EBA Skarkos on Ios. The collection of 'pot lids' (or flat stands for pots) is a notable one. Most of these are made from the local schist which fractures readily to produce flat laminar fragments which are easily worked to a circular shape.

LAPIDARY WORK

Objects, or fragments of objects, of finely worked stone were few in number, notably fragments of four marble bowls and three small objects of chlorite schist. It may be that most of these were imported pieces. However several small grinders of emery were found, three of them from Trench 3, along with other lithic material. It seems perfectly plausible to suggest that some modest lapidary work was undertaken in this area. The evidence does not go so far as to suggest craft specialisation, but a modest working area could certainly be suggested.

Mention should be made also of the five finely made 'pestles' of ground and polished stone. Such objects, occasionally found in graves, have sometimes been considered as grinders for pigments, used for cosmetic purposes. The recent discovery by Rahmstorf[4] that these belong to a system of standardised weights, centred in EH II Greece and the Cyclades opens interesting new perspectives, suggesting a role in metallurgical practice (see below). It is notable that several were found with metal objects in Room 1 of Trench 3.

BONE WORK, AND LEATHER WORKING

The bone tools recovered were few in number and comparable to those found on prehistoric sites through much of Greece. Many of them were pointed tools, which may have been used in the processing of leather. Direct evidence of leather has not been found from the Aegean Neolithic or EBA. But a site such as Markiani, used for the herding of sheep and goat, was almost certainly a location for leather working.

CARPENTRY

The practice of carpentry is never easy to document on a site where wood is not preserved. However the polished greenstone axe (**EE 661**), of length 9.3 cm, was almost certainly used for woodworking. Moreover the three stone objects identified in Chapter 8F as door sockets naturally indicates the use of upright wooden pivots for doors, and reminds us that although the houses may have been of stone, wood will undoubtedly have been used as a constructional material also.

TEXTILE PRODUCTION

Certainly the production of textiles is suggested by the abundant evidence for spinning, seen in Chapter 8D, although only a single terracotta object was found which might be specifically identified as a loom-weight. Several waisted weights of stone were found which may have served this purpose. The spindle-whorls represent an exceptionally rich assemblage, however, and the suggestion is made that they may in some cases have been tied to the ends of the warp to serve as weights for the warp-weighted loom. This might explain the large quantities found. No fewer than 109 (more than 50% of the total) came from the area of the circular feature of Space 7, which strongly supports this interesting

---

[4] Rahmstorf 2003.

suggestion. Certainly it is difficult to imagine that the spinning process alone would require so many. It is concluded therefore that textile production is likely to have been one of the crafts practised at the site. It may be that wool was first used in the Aegean during the EBA, supplementing or replacing the use of flax. The three cloth impressions support the evidence for textile use, whether linen or wool. It should of course be noted that the cloth impressions document the use of cloth at the location where the pottery was dried prior to firing, but by implication the use of the cloth and indeed its production can be applied to the Markiani community itself.

MAT AND BASKETRY PRODUCTION

The mat impressions give a striking documentation of the importance of basketry and matting throughout the occupation of the settlement. As noted in Chapter 8C, there is abundant evidence for matting from impressions on the bases of EC pots, and one imagines this as a household craft along with weaving.

POTTERY PRODUCTION

Pottery is of course the most abundant craft product at any Aegean prehistoric site. No kilns have been discovered from the prehistoric Cyclades and very little has yet been written about the craft production of EC ceramics. It may probably be inferred that the pottery was made either at household or at village level. There is nothing in the relatively unsophisticated ceramics found at Markiani to suggest any highly skilled specialist production, whether or not that might be argued for some of the painted fine wares seen in the EC cemetery assemblages of Syros and Naxos or for the 'Urfirnis' fabric seen in Phase A2 at Phylakopi on Melos and at Ayia Irini on Kea.

The petrological analysis of Chapter 7B suggests that nearly all of the pottery was made on Amorgos, and at present it may be appropriate to assume that it was made and fired locally, at or near Markiani, although this has certainly not yet been demonstrated.

METALLURGY

The metal objects found at Markiani certainly imply a knowledge of metallurgy. There is, however, no direct on-site indication of melting and smelting: there are no slags and no crucible fragments, such, for instance as are found at prehistoric Sitagroi in Macedonia.

The on-site use of lead does, however, seem to be implied by the use at Markiani of lead clamps or rivets used in the repair of small objects, usually pottery. Certainly when lead rivets are used to repair pots, the inference must be that this was undertaken on site, since it would be a strange procedure to repair a pot and then transport it by land over some distance to another location. Pack animals were not available at this time, and it is suggested below that Markiani was not normally reached by sea.

Of course the melting point of lead is low, but it is possible that if lead was melted and cast at Markiani, the same may have been true for copper or bronze. Certainly the repertoire of metal objects from Markiani is modest. There are eight fragments from the blades of knives and one fragment (the heel) of a dagger. Otherwise most objects are simply needles or fragments of wire. It may be reasonable to see these as the result of local production, as the presence of weights ('pestles') suggests, but whether these objects were obtained by trade with other settlements on Amorgos cannot at present be established.

TRADE AND INTERACTION (SEE FIG. 10.1)

The site of Markiani gives very little indication of inter-island trade. The principal imported material was obsidian. But this was never in generous supply at the site, as the scarcity and small size of blade cores indicates. Indeed this circumstance and the very limited data for fish and molluscs suggests that there may have been no direct access to sea travel for Markiani itself. Certainly there is no good harbour on the rocky coast of Notina which would make it possible to moor a ship over the seasons of the year.

There were just a few ceramic imports which can be recognised by their fabric as originating outside Amorgos. Most of the pottery seems to have been of local Amorgian fabrics. This is certainly true of the Blue Schist Ware discussed in Chapter 7B. In particular the pots of phase IV with forms relateable to those of the Kastri Group were in many (perhaps all) cases of the local schist wares, and there need be no suggestion that these vessels at Markiani were imports from outside Amorgos.

It is possible that the metal objects were made from ores which were not local to Amorgos, and it may be that isotopic analysis might throw some light on this point. Until such analysis has been

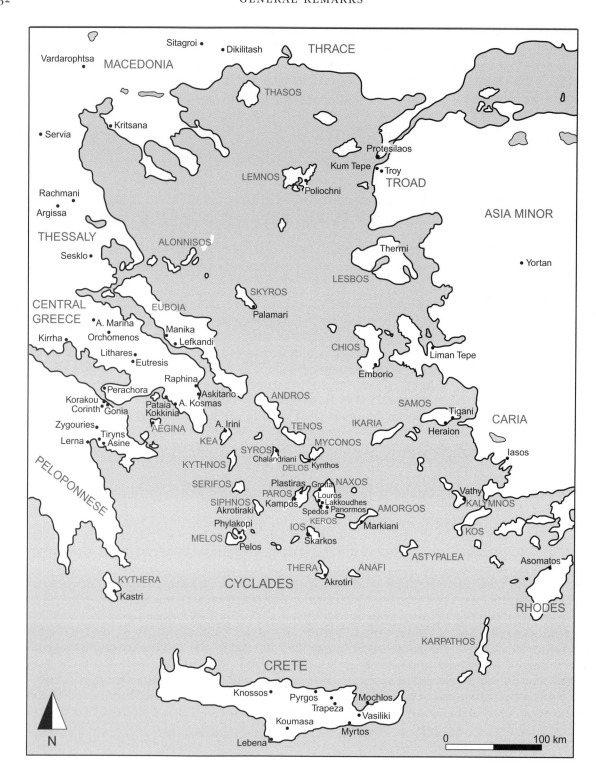

FIG. 10.1. Selected settlements and cemeteries of the Aegean Early Bronze Age.

carried out on a systematic basis with respect to Amorgos, it cannot however be excluded that there may have been copper or lead resources on the island.

On the other hand it is clear that the site of Markiani was not entirely self sufficient. No doubt its inhabitants had various links and ties with other communities on the island. We have already concluded that their obsidian supply is likely to have been procured by exchange within Amorgos, and the same may be true for the metal objects. This may well be the case also for the material of the eight emery grinders (Chapter 8F) which was imported to Amorgos from Naxos.

At the same time the site may have been able to produce supplies beyond its own requirements and available for external exchange of barley, of sheep and goat, and perhaps of textiles. The range and variety of basketry indicated in the pot impressions suggest that this too may have been a material for exchange with other communities on the island.

SOCIAL ASPECTS

When we come to consider the social aspects of the Markiani community, it must at once be observed that the eroded nature of the site presents many difficulties. In the first place the summit area is so much eroded at the very top, and then disturbed by subsequent occupation episodes, that this prime position in the settlement is virtually a blank archaeologically. That is was the natural prime site is suggested by the location of the two modern huts at its summit today. These break the strong winds very effectively, and in summer this is a very pleasant location, although it may be that in winter a more sheltered spot would be desirable. At the southernmost edge of the summit area, above Rock Cutting 2 we were fortunate to find well-stratified deposits of Ma II. But they were not accompanied by intelligible structures.

Secondly it must be conceded that we were able to excavate only rather few deposits which were both in place stratigraphically — which was not so rare — and also in a coherent relationship with an intelligible structure. This was indeed the case for Rooms 1 and 2 of Terrace 1, and again for Rooms 1 and 2 of Trench 3 (below and to the south-east of the summit area), and again for some of the deposits associated with the Bastion of Trench 8. But it must be conceded that we did not have an abundance of well-stratified deposits found secure in a coherent architectural position.

Furthermore we do not have the benefit of a cemetery associated with the settlement. The discovery of undisturbed graves might give some insight into social rankings in terms of the accompanying grave goods.

At the same time, however, we do have a number of interpretive advantages. In the first place, the scale of the site is readily intelligible. It is a location primarily of the EBA, and its disposition, as systematically examined in the surface survey, is much more intelligible than are the surviving EBA levels at Phylakopi on Melos, Ayia Irini on Kea or Akrotiri on Thera. Relevant inferences from the site survey are briefly considered in the section above on settlement and population.

Our understanding of Markiani as a community is greatly enhanced by the defining role of the fortifications. Their careful consideration in Chapter 6A reminds us that the eastern part of the site, within the line of the fortifications, remains to be effectively explored. The discussion in Chapter 4, while acknowledging that there were some arguments for a possible later construction date for the initial fortification wall, nonetheless concluded that it was constructed during Ma I. Clearly any community which has undertaken systematic defensive works will already show the impact upon it of the socially significant activity undertaken by those involved in the organisation and in the labour input required for the construction of these public works. Markiani emerges, on this basis, as a defended community already from the time of its inception, and in social terms will have developed a level of internal organisation commensurate with that achievement. At that time, occupation may well have been restricted to the summit area.

The fortifications were strengthened in Ma III by the construction of the Bastion of Trench 8 (and possibly by other works not yet examined). This is the period when, as the survey of Chapter 3 suggests, there was a significant increase in size and population. It is of course contemporary with the Keros-Syros culture or EC II, which was a period of marked development in the Cyclades as a whole.

The next line of argument which we may develop is that of the range of the craft activities, already discussed in the previous section. Moreover it is striking how many of these are documented in the finds from the very restricted spaces of Rooms 1 and 2 in Trench 3. Some relevant objects were found stratified in the deepest part, and had probably been lying on the floor level. Other finds were stratified rather higher, among the fallen debris. Some may have been carried in to these spaces from rooms further up the slope. But it is possible also that some material may originally have been utilised at roof level, and that it fell into the room below with the collapse of the roof.

Among metal objects, a lead rivet (**EE 377**) and a lead pendant (**EE 399**) came from Room 1 of Trench 3, and of copper or bronze, two needles or wire objects came from Trench 3 and no fewer than five of the eight knife blades recovered at the site. Of the 100 obsidian blades recovered 40 (i.e. 40%) likewise came from the same area, and were accompanied by approximately the same proportion of débitage. Five of the waisted weights came from this area, and three of the nine emery grinders. These in particular seem indicative of some workshop activity. In addition, seven spindle-whorls came from this area, and this represents 5.4% in relation to the total from the site as a whole. This however is eclipsed by the finding of 78% of the site total from the circular area of Space 7 on Terrace 1.

The most important specific finds from the standpoint of social organisation must however be the lead seal and the three clay sealings discussed in Chapter 8G. The seal (**EE 317**) once again came from Room 2 of Trench 3, and hence, like the other objects from the same area discussed above, from Markiani phase III. Two of the three sealings came from Space 7 (as did the 100 spindle-whorls) and these are assigned to Markiani phase III or IV. A seal-impressed pottery fragment (**EE 197**) comes from nearby, from Markiani III levels in the fissure area of Rock Cutting 2.

The notion that sealings (and therefore seals) are at home in the EB II period of the Aegean is a familiar one, in view of the abundant finds from the House of the Tiles at Lerna, and certain other mainland sites. A structure such as the House of the Tiles or the Rundbau at Tiryns of course represents the summit of architectural achievement of the highly developed EH II culture of the mainland. Such structures were not surpassed in mainland Greece until the emergence of the megaron complex of the developed palace period of LH III. But while the find of clay sealings might, by analogy, be unsurprising in the central building of some imposing EBA settlement (in one of the principal structures in the acropolis of Troy IIg for instance), they certainly prompt a pause for reflection at rural Markiani. For the emergent centralised administration which one may infer for Lerna would seem out of place at this smaller Cycladic site which lacks any indications of central administrative structures. Yet there is no specific reason to regard these sealings as imports to Markiani from outside, although this remains possible. On the contrary the lead seal itself clearly suggests that there was some role for sealing procedures on the site. In this context it is relevant to recall the find of sealings of this date from the Cave of Zas on Naxos,[5] although in that specific case they may be importations to the cave rather than the product of a stamping or sealing procedure carried out on the spot there. These finds raise new questions about the organisation of production and exchange at smaller, rural sites in the Cyclades, such as Markiani. For while it may be possible to suggest that sites like Lerna and Tiryns had the status of proto-urban centres during the EB II,[6] such an argument can hardly be sustained for Markiani, where the more modest finds might appropriately be compared with those from such EM sites as Myrtos–*Fournou Korifi*.

Of course it would be wrong to build too much of a theoretical superstructure upon the basis of the discovery of one small lead seal and three clay sealings (one of which was unstratified). Markiani contained no House of the Tiles, it was no Troy, nor even a Myrtos. But it is of very real interest that some recording or registering procedures were already in use at this early time in the EC II period. The discovery is heralded already by occasional finds of sealstones, such as the celebrated find from Kapros in Amorgos, which has of course an uncertain context[7] or indeed the lead seal from the cemetery of Aplomata on Naxos,[8] one of the sites which Broodbank[9] has identified as crucial nodes in his network analysis. It is clear that such sites as Markiani and Skarkos, despite their modest size show interesting indications of organisation, related probably to ownership, indications which remain to be better understood. As Pullen remarks with reference to the comparable find from EH II Tsoungiza near Nemea: 'seals and sealings appear at numerous EH II sites, including smaller, non-coastal sites such as Tsoungiza, which might suggest greater social and economic integration.'[10]

It would of course be a mistake automatically to equate a modest degree of information structuring, which these finds seem to indicate, with the suggestion that they are the insignia of persons of high rank. But stamped sealings are often indicative of a clear sense of property, and of the likelihood that we are dealing with a context in which the ownership or custody of property is being transferred from one persona to another.

These considerations lead us on to another interesting social question, which is for the moment a rather speculative one. Was Markiani, this small fortified village settlement, an autonomous political entity? Or was it perhaps part of some loose association of peer polities? Or was it possibly subordinate in status to one of the larger settlements on this part of the island of Amorgos? Of course these questions which can only be considered effectively within the context of an understanding of the settlement pattern of Amorgos as a whole during the EBA.[11] During the Classical period, as is well known, Amorgos was a tripolis (indeed Keos was a tetrapolis), and this gives us a clue that there is

---

[5] *CMS* V Suppl. 1B nos. 106–109; Dousougli-Zachos 1999, 103–9

[6] See Weingarten 1997.

[7] Renfrew 1967, 6 and cat. 19; Marangou in Fitton 1984, 54; Sherratt 2000, 38–42, pls. 13–14; no. 1.a.6.

[8] *CMS* V Suppl. 1B no. 105; Marangou 1991, no 83.

[9] Broodbank 2000*b*, 261.

[10] Pullen 1994, 52. For further seals / sealings of EB II date see now *CMS* V Suppl. 1A–B and V Suppl. 3.

[11] Marangou 1994.

thus perhaps no reason to suggest that the island was under a single administrative jurisdiction already in the EBA. But one can readily imagine that Markiani may have been situated within the territory and region of influence of some larger site, probably located on the more accessible coast at the west of the island. We have already seen that maritime access to Markiani was likely to have been difficult, and that it may have acquired necessary imports originating outside the island (such as obsidian or emery) by exchange with some suitable neighbouring settlement with better maritime access. Questions such as these have been addressed for the island of Melos[12] where there appears to have been, from the EB II period, a prime site with a dominating influence over the island as a whole, namely Phylakopi. Broodbank[13] has usefully discussed the notion of significant sub-regional centres within the Cyclades, which were notable for their maritime, inter-island role. It is pertinent to remark that such centres are likely to have held also a primacy of place within their own island. Chalandriani on Syros is another such centre. But it is not yet clear whether there was such a primate site for Amorgos at this time, or indeed for one portion of the island of Amorgos.

So the position of Markiani, whether as a small, autonomous unit, or as a subordinate unit in a larger territorial entity within Amorgos, is unclear. This is the sort of question which we can expect to emerge and perhaps ultimately to see resolved as the study of the settlement archaeology of the Cyclades, initiated by such excavations as that of Skarkos or Markiani, develops.

SYMBOLIC ASPECTS

At first sight, the repertoire of finds of symbolic significance at Markiani seems restricted. But the case has been made long ago[14] for attempting to consider all the relevant subsystems of the overall cultural system, and it is pertinent to consider also the negative evidence: what is so far lacking as well as what has already been found. There were no figurine finds which could be related to the well-known series of marble sculptures so familiar from the Cycladic cemeteries. The most notable representational discovery was the small terracotta boat found in levels of Ma II on the south side of the summit area. In view of the already significant evidence available for Cycladic seafaring, this find is of considerable interest: the significance of maritime access for Markiani was discussed above and is further considered in Chapter 10B below. Of course this find does not represent one of the Cycladic longships so familiar from the 'frying pans' of Chalandriani on Syros. This is a more modest vessel which could be controlled by a single oarsman. Why a model boat of terracotta should be found here is far from clear. There are no further contextual indications which might be suggestive of a 'ritual deposit', but as discussed in Chapter 8, other boat models are known from the EBA Cyclades. Further discoveries may yet clarify the contexts of their production and use.

We have no clear indications for cult practice or other ritual activities at Markiani, although the presence of conch shell fragments (Triton) could suggest some symbolic use. At the same time we should not overlook the general observation that most artefacts have their own symbolic significance. This may indeed be true for those artefacts where the form is largely dictated by functional constraints such, for instance, as the saddle querns used for grinding barley into flour. But when we turn to other artefact forms we inevitably find that the shapes are governed as much by convention or by the exercise of choice as they are by functional constraints. This observation would hold for most of the ceramic types found at the site. Indeed the exercise of conventions or choices of style form the basis for our ceramic classifications upon which the basic chronological understanding of the site is based, at least until the radiocarbon determinations are brought into play.

To take one example, the levels which we have assigned to Ma II are so ascribed because of the presence of such characteristic forms (albeit in fragmentary condition) as the well-known 'frying pan' of Kampos type. The shape and the decoration are already well known from other sites of this period within the Cyclades. Indeed it is on the basis of such comparisons that the idea of such Cycladic 'cultures' as the Grotta-Pelos culture and the Keros-Syros culture is based, along with the 'groups' — such as the Kampos Group or the Kastri Group, which are conceived by some scholars as classificatory units which are more restricted in their temporal scale. That is to say they are used sometimes as chronological subdivisions within the larger cultural entities (and they have also their spatial or regional aspect). This is not the place for a prolonged discussion upon these matters. But it is interesting that some of these symbolic (and typological) forms and assemblages have a widespread distribution in the Cyclades and indeed in the Aegean. The EH II and EC II 'sauceboat' form for instance is widely

[12] Renfrew and Wagstaff 1982.
[13] Broodbank 2000b.

[14] Renfrew 1972, Chapter 19.

distributed in the Aegean. Others, like some features of the Markiani ceramics of phase III and IV are more restricted in extent — and initially gave rise to discussion of an 'Amorgos Group',[15] although that term is generally now agreed to be so vague as to be of little value.

Thus, it may well be the case that Markiani has so far yielded few objects, which we may regard as dedicated to specialised symbolic uses: there are no horns of consecration or double axes here. Yet at the same time the forms of most of the artefacts, and especially the pottery forms, do have a symbolic dimension. The decorated spindle-whorl with two incised animals, one with horns and another with long tail is a case in point. They are the product of choices and conventions which are only in part functionally determined. Today it is fashionable to ascribe such factors to 'agency'. But these have long been familiar issues in the prehistory of the Aegean and indeed more widely. With the distinction which is now emerging between the repertoire of artefact forms seen in the Cycladic settlements and those seen in the cemeteries, new insights into these processes are now becoming possible.

B. THE SETTLEMENT ARCHAEOLOGY OF AMORGOS
by Lila Marangou

My decision to invite Colin Renfrew to collaborate on the Markiani project was based not only on his ground-breaking studies on the nature and particularities of EC culture[16] but also on his long, close and lively relationship with the Cycladic islanders, from 1961 onwards; his knowledge of vernacular Greek and of the daily life, customs, music and dances, even modern poetry and songs, ensure his interaction with the local people, *conditio sine qua non*[17] for the better understanding of and approach to the Cycladic islanders' habitat during the third millennium BC.

On Amorgos, even now remote and rather difficult to reach, changes in the old way of life have come only recently; with the supply of electricity to the main villages and the construction of roads linking these, the fields and particularly the farmsteads (*katoikies*), the self-sufficient agricultural-cum-stock-raising units which have existed since ancient times, have been abandoned. Only the place remains virtually unaltered by more recent human interventions, as at the fortified settlement of Markiani and other EC sites.[18] Thus it is possible to make some correlations, albeit anachronistic, which help us in our partial reconstitution of the picture of life in the past. Lacunae or gaps in our knowledge gained from the limited excavation and surface survey research can sometimes be filled by drawing parallels, always tentative, with data from typologically-akin rural installations of Classical Antiquity and later times.

The lack of basic evidence, such as systematic maps and topographical plans of all the settlement units, and examination of their location in conjunction with the geology, the routes of communication by land and sea, the configuration of the coastline and the bays and coves suitable for anchorages, as well as the winds and sea currents,[19] not only makes it difficult to approach and to understand the EC topography and settlement archaeology, but also leads to conclusions of theoretical character, often erroneous and continuously changing.

Therefore, I wish to stress that the observations that follow are not categorical generalisations. Nevertheless, it should be noted that they are not based solely on the findings of interdisciplinary research at Markiani, but take into account surface evidence from other — still unexplored — Cycladic sites on Amorgos.[20] Moreover, some assertions made prior to excavation are supported significantly by the present, preliminary synthesis of the interdisciplinary data from Markiani.

Concerning the criteria for choice of sites for permanent or seasonal habitation and the distribution of solitary dwellings-farmsteads (*katoikies*) or clusters thereof in the EBA, we have already ascertained[21] that remains of *katoikies* exist in inland locations, on rocky eminences, mountainous or low hills and barren slopes protected from the winds, but always in visual contact with the sea and with access to it. Coastal settlements have not been identified so far on Amorgos, nor have traces of occupation been found at the foot of crags or knolls, where the cultivable fields lie. Obviously, in the small infertile islands of the Cyclades, as in Classical Antiquity and later times, the islanders exploited all available soil for growing cereals and pulses, and built small dwellings on stony ground. The Amorgians' deeply-

[15] Renfrew 1972, 534–5; Doumas 1977, 23; Broodbank 2000b, 209.

[16] Renfrew 1969, 1973, etc.

[17] Koumanoudes 1871, Romaios 1903. Cherry *et al.* 1991, Marangou 1994.

[18] Marangou 1994; 2002; Marangou in press.

[19] Agouridis 1997; Papageorgiou 1997.

[20] Marangou 1994; ead. in press.

[21] Marangou 1994; 1999a; 2002; Marangou in press.

rooted faith — until recently — in 'a small house, but a large field', 'a house just big enough to live in, and a field as far as you can see', and the apposite phrase in Isocrates (*Panegyric*, 132) ... τοὺς νησιώτας, οὕς ἄξιον ἐλεεῖν, ὁρῶντας τούτους διὰ τὴν σπανιότητα τῆς γῆς ὄρη γεωργεῖν ἀναγκαζομένους (... the islanders, who are deserving of their pity, seeing that because of the scarcity of land they are compelled to till mountains ...),[22] are telling clues to the criteria of selection and the pressing reasons for settlement in non-cultivable locations.

Building remains, as was confirmed at Markiani, are visible on the surface, usually below later farmsteads,[23] sheep-pens and retaining walls between terraces, frequently built of ancient stones. An important comparandum for Markiani is the natural acropolis at Kastellas or Kastellia, in the district of Kato Meria, south of the village of Arkesine;[24] here too there are sizeable buildings on the flat summit, while preserved on the rocky south slope are dwellings of small dimensions with rectilinear walls, adapted to the terrain of the narrow terraces which are frequently supported by man-made structures, that is makeshift dry-stone walls, just like the half-excavated one at Markiani, below the later dry-stone wall at the southern edge of Terrace 1 (FIG. 2.2, PLATE 3.1–2).

The natural rock was usually exploited for constructing the dwellings and the fortification walls (see Chapter 6A), the foundations or even the lowest part of the side walls being cut in the bedrock, as in later times. The building material is always stone, dolomite or schist, depending on the kind of rocks in the region;[25] both types are encountered frequently in the walls, while cornerstones, thresholds and roof-beams are of hard limestone. The flat roofs were laid with schist slabs covered with impervious earth, mainly glaucophane (see Chapter 7B). The floor was sometimes the bedrock, roughly worked or in its natural state, as at Kastelli and on the natural acropolis at Biounas, Aigiali,[26] and sometimes of beaten earth (see Chapter 6B).

Man-made fortification is only encountered on those hillsides accessible from inland, and never on the seaward side which is usually precipitous and difficult of access from the shore, as at Biounas, Aigiale.[27] The indications are that the man-made fortification was intended primarily to protect the settlement and the few arable fields from neighbours, rather than from external threat from the sea. In any case, on long narrow Amorgos, regardless of the distance, all EC settlements, large or small, had access to the sea. As the moveable finds (ship, seals etc., see Chapters 8E and G) and, primarily, the organic remains (countless limpet shells, see Chapter 9B) from Markiani indicate, the sea was an important factor in the inhabitants' life and economy, which was not based exclusively on agriculture and animal husbandry. It should also be stressed that Markiani, like the other EC settlement sites, seasonal or permanent, was closely involved with the sea and in contact with the nearby islands, as in later times. Roads and paths, most of them now in ruinous state due to desertion, linked all the highland EC settlement units and the later farmsteads with the small coves/anchorages on the coasts, both on the south side of the island with its steep cliffs and on the less rugged north side.[28] The coast below and at the south side of the acropolis at Kapsala,[29] however sheer and inhospitable it seems today, was, because of its privileged position in the open sea, always a bridge with Crete and the East,[30] the islands of the East Aegean, the Dodecanese and the Asia Minor littoral, as well as with the North Aegean. The small sheltered indentations and numerous coves on the south coast even today provide safe anchorage for the caiques of Kalymnian fishermen. The coves of Diotrachili and the neighbouring promontories certainly facilitated communication of the inhabitants of Markiani with both Astypalaia and Santorini (Thera), as well as with other, nowadays uninhabited, islets, such as Anydros, to the south of Amorgos, or Kinaros and Levintha which are literally littered with EC sherds. Thus, the possibility that the first inhabitants of Markiani arrived by sea cannot be excluded.

The crucial geographical position of Amorgos at a nodal point on the sea route linking the south and the east[31] was undoubtedly the paramount determinant factor for the density of habitation and the cultural *floruit* on the island in the EBA.

I believe that the most important gain from our short-term investigation of the EC settlement at Markiani and the preliminary presentation of the material evidence, will emerge from the awareness of the gaps in our knowledge about EC topography and settlement archaeology, as well as about other issues still open to question.

[22] Norlin (ed.) 1928, 203.
[23] Meliarakes 1928; Marangou 1994.
[24] Marangou 1994.
[25] Philippson 1959; Weinmann 1967; Dürr 1985; Dürr 1986.
[26] Marangou 1994.
[27] Marangou 1994.
[28] Dürr 1985; Marangou 2002; Marangou in press.
[29] Marangou in press.
[30] Agouridis 1997
[31] Agouridis 1997; Sherratt 2000; Marangou 2005.

Μαρκιανὴ Ἀμοργοῦ: ἕνας ὀχυρωμένος οἰκισμός τῆς Πρώιμης Ἐποχῆς τοῦ Χαλκοῦ

Ἐπισκόπηση τῶν ἐρευνῶν 1985–1991

Περίληψη

ΚΕΦΑΛΑΙΟ 1. ΕΙΣΑΓΩΓΗ

Οἱ ὀλιγοήμερες ἀνασκαφές στὴν Μαρκιανὴ Ἀμοργοῦ, στὸ νοτιότερο νησί τῶν Κυκλάδων (ΕΙΚ. 2.1, ΠΙΝ. 1 *a* καὶ 1 *b*) διεξήχθησαν ἀπὸ τὸ 1988 ἕως τὸ 1990 μετὰ ἀπὸ μία περίοδο συστηματικῆς ἐπιφανειακῆς ἔρευνας τὸ 1987. Ἡ θέση ἐντοπίστηκε τὸ 1985 ἀπὸ τὴν Καθηγήτρια Λίλα Μαραγκοῦ, ἡ ὁποία τότε διεξήγαγε καὶ μικρᾶς ἐκτάσεως ἐπιφανειακὸ καθαρισμό. Ἡ πρώτη ἔρευνα τοῦ 1985 στάθηκε ἀφορμὴ γιὰ τὴν ἔναρξη εὐρύτερης ἐρευνητικῆς συνεργασίας στὴν Ἀμοργὸ καὶ στὴν Κέρο τῶν Πανεπιστημίων Ἰωαννίνων, Ἀθηνῶν καὶ Cambridge ὑπὸ τὴν διεύθυνση τῶν καθηγητῶν Λίλας Μαραγκοῦ, Χρίστου Ντούμα καὶ Colin Renfrew (Διαπανεπιστημιακὸ Ἐρευνητικὸ Πρόγραμμα Ἀμοργοῦ – Κέρου).

Ἡ παροῦσα δημοσίευση ἀποβλέπει στὴν παρουσίαση ἑνὸς συνοπτικοῦ ἀπολογισμοῦ τῆς ἀνασκαφικῆς ἔρευνας καὶ τῶν κυριωτέρων κινητῶν εὑρημάτων, συμπεριλαμβανομένης τῆς κεραμικῆς.

Οἱ ἀνασκαφεῖς ἐπιθυμοῦν νὰ εὐχαριστήσουν τὴν Ἑλληνικὴ Ἀρχαιολογικὴ Ὑπηρεσία καὶ ἰδιαιτέρως τὸν Ἰωάννη Παπαχριστοδούλου, Δρ. Φιλ. Ἔφορο τῶν Ἀρχαιοτήτων, Προϊστάμενο τῆς ΚΒ' Ἐφορείας Προϊστορικῶν καὶ Κλασσικῶν Ἀρχαιοτήτων γιὰ τὴν ἄδεια διενέργειας τῶν ἐρευνῶν στὴν Μαρκιανή, καθὼς καὶ τοὺς χορηγοὺς (τὰ τρία Πανεπιστήμια, τὴν British Academy, τὸ McDonald Institute for Archaeological Research καὶ τὸ Ὑπουργεῖο Αἰγαίου) γιὰ τὴν οἰκονομική τους βοήθεια, καθὼς καὶ τὴν Βρεταννικὴ Ἀρχαιολογικὴ Σχολὴ Ἀθηνῶν. Θερμὲς εὐχαριστίες ἐκφράζονται στοὺς κυρίους Σίμο Γιαννακὸ καὶ Μανόλη Δεσποτίδη, φύλακες τῶν Ἀρχαιοτήτων Ἀμοργοῦ γιὰ τὴν πολύτιμη συνεργασία καὶ βοήθειά τους.

Εἰλικρινῶς εὐχαριστοῦν γιὰ τὴν συμβολή τους, τοὺς ἀρχαιολόγους καὶ φοιτητές, καθὼς καὶ τοὺς συνεργάτες καὶ μελετητές, τὰ ὀνόματα τῶν ὁποίων ἀναφέρονται στὸν ἐπίλογο τῆς Εἰσαγωγῆς.

ΚΕΦΑΛΑΙΟ 2. Η ΑΝΑΚΑΛΥΨΗ ΤΟΥ ΟΙΚΙΣΜΟΥ ΚΑΙ Η ΕΡΕΥΝΑ ΤΟΥ 1985

Ἡ ἀνακάλυψη τοῦ προϊστορικοῦ οἰκισμοῦ τῆς Μαρκιανῆς ἐντάσσεται στὸ πλαίσιο τῆς συστηματικῆς καταγραφῆς καὶ ἔρευνας τῶν ἀρχαίων θέσεων τῆς Ἀμοργοῦ, κυρίως τῶν *ἱστορικῶν χρόνων*, ἡ ὁποία ἄρχισε τὴν δεκαετία τοῦ 1970 ἀπὸ τὴν Λίλα Μαραγκοῦ. Τὸν Ἰούλιο τοῦ 1985, στὴν διάρκεια μίας πολύωρης περιοδείας στὴν περιφέρεια τοῦ Σταυροῦ τῆς Καθηγήτριας Λίλας Μαραγκοῦ μὲ τὸν φύλακα Σίμο Γιαννακὸ καὶ ὁμάδα φοιτητῶν τοῦ Παν/μίου Ἰωαννίνων, πρὸς ἀναζήτησιν μίας ἀρχαίας ἑλληνικῆς ἐπιγραφῆς, γνωστῆς ἀπὸ τὸν 19ο αἰῶνα στὴν θέση μὲ τὸ χαρακτηριστικὸ τοπωνύμιο 'Στά Γράμματα', ὁ Μάρκος Ν. Μενδρινός, τότε μόνιμος κάτοικος στὸν Σταυρό, παρατηρῶντας τὸ ἰδιαίτερο ἐνδιαφέρον μας γιὰ ἐπιφανειακῶς ὁρατὰ ὄστρακα καὶ ὀψιανοὺς ὑπέδειξε τὴν τοποθεσία *Μαρτσανάδες-Μαρκιανάδες* ἢ *Μαρκιανή*, στὴν κορυφὴ ἑνὸς παρακείμενου λόφου, «*γεμάτη κατάκολα* (=ὄστρακα) *καὶ μαῦρα γυαλιστερὰ πετραδάκια* (=ὀψιανούς)».

Ἡ θέση τῆς Μαρκιανῆς (ΠΙΝ. 1 *a* καὶ 1 *b*), στὸ μεσόστρατο τοῦ ἀμαξιτοῦ δρόμου ποὺ συνδέει τὴν *Χώρα*, τὴν πρωτεύουσα τοῦ νησιοῦ, μὲ τὴν *Κάτω Μεριά*, τὴν περιφέρεια τῆς ἀρχαίας πόλεως τῆς *Ἀρκεσίνης*, βρίσκεται στὴν περιοχή *Νοτινὰ* σὲ ἀπόσταση 1500 περίπου μέτρων ΝΔ ἀπὸ τὸ ξωκκλῆσι τοῦ Σταυροῦ. Ἂν καὶ παντελῶς ἄγνωστη στὴν ἀρχαιολογικὴ βιβλιογραφία, ἦταν γνωστὴ στοὺς βοσκοὺς καὶ στοὺς ὀλίγους κατοίκους τῆς περιφερείας τοῦ Σταυροῦ γιὰ σπουδαῖα τυχαῖα εὑρήματα, «*βρεσίματα ἀρχαίων, ὅπως κουκλάκια* (=εἰδώλια) *καὶ ὅπλα*»

Ὁ Μ. Μενδρινὸς βαθὺς γνώστης τῆς περιοχῆς, μᾶς ὁδήγησε στὶς μάντρες ἰδιοκτησίας Νικολάου Συνοδινοῦ στὴν βραχώδη κορυφὴ τοῦ λόφου (ὕψος 265 μέτρα ἀπὸ τὴν ἐπιφάνεια τῆς θάλασσας ΠΙΝ. 1.1–2 καὶ 6 *a*), νότια ἀπὸ ἕναν ὑψηλὸ προστατευτικὸ χωραφότοιχο. Στὸ ἄνδηρο τῆς κορυφῆς τῆς

Μαρκιανῆς, ὅπου βρίσκονται ἕνα μονόχωρο σπιτάκι (Κτίσμα A) καὶ δύο στεγασμένοι σταῦλοι αἰγοπροβάτων (Κτίσματα B καὶ C) (ΕΙΚ. 2.2 καὶ 4.1, ΠΙΝ. 2), συνυπῆρχαν ὄστρακα ἀρχαίων πήλινων ἀγγείων, διαφόρων ἐποχῶν μὲ σπασμένες νεώτερες στάμνες, γυάλινες φιάλες καὶ λιγοστὰ κομμάτια ἀπὸ πλαστικὰ ντεπόσιτα νεροῦ καὶ σκεύη γιὰ τὴν μεταφορὰ τοῦ γάλακτος. Πάμπολλα ὄστρακα ἦταν ὁρατὰ καὶ στὸ δωματόχωμα τῆς στέγης τῶν σταύλων. Χαμηλότερα καὶ νοτίως τῆς κορυφῆς στὸ Ἄνδηρο 1, σὲ μία στενή, ἐπίπεδη λωρίδα καλλιεργήσιμης γῆς, προσπελάσιμη μὲ σκαλάκια λαξευμένα στὸν βράχο, τὰ ὄστρακα ἦταν περισσότερα ἀπὸ τὸ χῶμα: θραύσματα ἀπὸ μικρὰ καὶ μεγάλα ἀγγεῖα, πήλινα σφονδύλια, ὀψιανοί, θαλάσσια ὄστρεα, πλάκες σχιστολίθου, λίθινα ἐργαλεῖα καὶ ἄλλα ἀντικείμενα προϊστορικῆς ἐποχῆς· πολλὰ ἦταν συγκεντρωμένα στὶς παρυφὲς τῶν ἀναλημματικῶν χωραφότοιχων, ἀρκετά, κυρίως μεγάλα κομμάτια, ἦταν κτισμένα στὶς ξερολιθιές, ἄλλα ἦταν τοποθετημένα στὴν ἐπιφάνεια τῶν χωραφότοιχων. Ἀνάλογη εἰκόνα μὲ χρονολογικὰ καὶ εἰδολογικὰ συγγενῆ ἀντικείμενα, ἐπιφανειακῶς ὁρατὰ συναντήσαμε καὶ στὰ χαμηλότερα ἄνδηρα τῆς βραχώδους πλαγιᾶς, ἐξαιρετικὰ δύσβατης ἢ ἀπροσπέλαστης ἀπὸ τὴν αὐτοφυὴ βλάστηση.

Μὲ τὴν ἄδεια τῆς ΚΒ' Ἐφορείας Προϊστορικῶν καὶ Κλασσικῶν Ἀρχαιοτήτων πραγματοποιήσαμε ὀλιγοήμερη ἐπιφανειακὴ ἔρευνα καὶ καθαρισμὸ στὸ Ἄνδηρο 1, σὲ ἐγκοπές (ΕΙΚ. 2.3 καὶ 6.4, ΠΙΝ. 3 a, 4 a καὶ 5 a) στὰ ριζὰ τοῦ διαχωριστικοῦ ἀναλημματικοῦ χωραφότοιχου, καθὼς καὶ περισυλλογὴ ὀστράκων καὶ διαφόρων ἀντικειμένων στὰ παρακείμενα καὶ ὑποκείμενα ἄνδηρα. Ἀπὸ τὸν καθαρισμὸ νοτίως τῶν Ἐγκοπῶν 2 καὶ 3 προῆλθαν πάμπολλα ὄστρακα διαφόρων σχημάτων ἀγγείων καθὼς καὶ σφονδύλια, θραύσματα μετάλλινων ἀντικειμένων, ὀψιανοί, λίθινοι τριπτῆρες καὶ ὄστρεα. Μολονότι ἀνάμεσα στὰ περισυλλεγέντα ὄστρακα , κυρίως ἀπὸ τὸ Ἄνδηρο 1, ὁρισμένα ὑποδήλωναν τὴν χρήση τοῦ χώρου καὶ σὲ μεταγενέστερες ἐποχές, στὴν Γεωμετρική, Ἑλληνιστική, Ρωμαϊκὴ καὶ Βυζαντινὴ περίοδο, καθὼς καὶ στοὺς Νεώτερους χρόνους, τὸ εἶδος τῆς πλειονότητας τῶν ἀντικειμένων, ἡ φύσει ὀχυρὰ θέση καὶ τὰ ἐπιφανειακῶς εὐδιάκριτα κατάλοιπα τεχνητῆς ὀχύρωσης στὴν Β. πλευρά, στὸ φρύδι τοῦ λόφου, ὁδήγησαν στὴν ὑπόθεση περὶ πρωτοκυκλαδικοῦ οἰκισμοῦ. Γιὰ τὴν ἐπιβεβαίωση αὐτῆς τῆς ὑπόθεσης ἦταν ἀναγκαία συστηματικὴ ἀνασκαφικὴ ἔρευνα, ἀφοῦ, γιὰ πρώτη φορὰ μετὰ ἀπὸ τὶς ἔρευνες τοῦ Χρίστου Τσούντα τὸ 1894, ἐντοπίστηκε προϊστορικὸς οἰκισμὸς στὴν Ἀμοργό. Γι' αὐτὸ ἡ καθηγήτρια Λίλα Μαραγκοῦ ἀποφάσισε νὰ καλέσει σὲ συνεργασία τοὺς καθηγητὲς Colin Renfrew καὶ Χρίστο Ντούμα. Τὸ 1986 ἐπισκέφθηκαν τὴν θέση συνοδευόμενοι ἀπὸ τὸν Dr Todd Whitelaw, τότε στὸ Πανεπιστήμιο τοῦ Cambridge, ὁ ὁποῖος καὶ ἀνέλαβε τὴν ὀργάνωση τῆς συστηματικῆς ἐπιφανειακῆς ἔρευνας στὴν Μαρκιανή.

ΚΕΦΑΛΑΙΟ 3. Η ΕΠΙΦΑΝΕΙΑΚΗ ΕΡΕΥΝΑ ΚΑΙ Η ΔΙΑΒΡΩΣΗ ΤΟΥ ΕΔΑΦΟΥΣ

3A. Η ΕΠΙΦΑΝΕΙΑΚΗ ΕΡΕΥΝΑ ΤΟΥ 1987

Τὸ 1987 πραγματοποιήθηκε συστηματικὴ ἐπιφανειακὴ ἔρευνα διάρκειας δύο ἑβδομάδων σὲ ὅλην τὴν ἔκταση ποὺ εἶχε διαπιστωθεῖ ὅτι ὑπῆρχαν ἀρχαιολογικὰ εὑρήματα. Ἡ περισυλλογὴ διεκόπτετο ὅπου ἡ πυκνότητα τοῦ ἐπιφανειακοῦ ὑλικοῦ ἔπεφτε στὸ σύνηθες ἐπίπεδο διασπορᾶς τῶν ἀντικειμένων σὲ παρακείμενες περιοχές. Ἀπὸ τὴν συνολικὴ ἔκταση τῆς βαθμιδωτῆς κλιτύος, ποὺ κατὰ προσέγγισιν ξεπερνάει τὰ 200 στρέμματα, ἐρευνήθηκαν περίπου τὰ 140. Ἄς σημειωθεῖ ὅτι στὰ πιὸ ἀπότομα σημεῖα τῆς κλιτύος, μόνον ὀλίγα, μεμονωμένα μικρὰ χτιά (=ἄνδηρα) ἦταν προσπελάσιμα. Σὲ κάθε ἑνότητα τοῦ ἐρευνούμενου χώρου ἕνας ἕως τέσσερεις δειγματοληπτικοὶ κύκλοι διαμέτρου ἑνὸς μέτρου ὑλοποιοῦνταν ἐπὶ τοῦ ἐδάφους ἐντὸς τῶν ὁποίων ἔγινε συστηματικὴ περισυλλογὴ ὅλων τῶν ἀντικειμένων, καθὼς καὶ τῶν ὀστράκων ποὺ ἦταν μεγαλύτερα τοῦ 1 ἑκατοστοῦ τοῦ μέτρου (ΠΙΝ. 4 b). Κατ' αὐτὸν τὸν τρόπο συστηματικὴ περισυλλογὴ ἔγινε σὲ 707 κύκλους ἀπὸ 271 διαφορετικὲς ἑνότητες, ποὺ ἀναλογοῦν στὸ 1,6% τῆς συνολικῆς ἐπιφάνειας τοῦ ἐρευνηθέντος χώρου. Ὁ ὑπόλοιπος χῶρος τῶν πρὸς ἔρευναν ἑνοτήτων ἐξετάστηκε γιὰ τὴν ἐνδεχόμενη ὕπαρξη διαγνωστικῶν ἀντικειμένων, τὰ ὁποῖα καὶ περισυνελέγησαν ὡς ἐπιλεγμένα δείγματα. Τὸ ὑλικὸ ἀπὸ τοὺς κύκλους περιελάμβανε περίπου 5000 ὄστρακα τῆς Πρώιμης Ἐποχῆς τοῦ Χαλκοῦ, ἐνῶ μερικὲς ἀκόμα χιλιάδες ὀστράκων περισυνελέγησαν ὡς ἐπιλεγμένα δείγματα. Τὰ ὄστρακα αὐτὰ καταμετρήθηκαν, ζυγίστηκαν, πλύθηκαν καὶ ἀποθηκεύθηκαν γιὰ μελέτη καὶ ἀνάλυση.

Τὰ ἀποτελέσματα τῆς ἐπιφανειακῆς περισυλλογῆς ἀποτυπώνονται στὶς ΕΙΚ. 3.3 ἕως 3.14. Ἡ ΕΙΚ. 3.3 παρουσιάζει τὴν ἀνεπεξέργαστη πυκνότητα τοῦ ὑλικοῦ (ἀριθμὸ ὀστράκων ἀνὰ τετραγωνικὸ μέτρο) τῶν ὀστράκων τῆς Πρώιμης Ἐποχῆς τοῦ Χαλκοῦ ποὺ περισυνελέγησαν. Ὅσο ἀπομακρυνόμαστε ἀπὸ τὴν περιοχὴ τῆς κορυφῆς τοῦ λόφου παρατηρεῖται μία ἀπότομη μείωση τῆς πυκνότητας τοῦ ἀριθμοῦ τῶν ὀστράκων. Αὐτὸ εἶναι ἐμφανέστερο ὅταν οἱ πυκνότητες συγκρίνονται μὲ τὸ βάρος (ΕΙΚ. 3.4, βάρος σὲ γραμμάρια ἀνὰ τετραγωνικὸ μέτρο) καὶ εἰδικότερα στὸν πίνακα μέσου ὅρου διακύμανσης τοῦ βάρους τῶν ὀστράκων (ΕΙΚ. 3.5). Παρόμοια εἰκόνα παρατηρεῖται στὴν κορυφὴ τοῦ λόφου ὅσον ἀφορᾶ στὸ ὑλικὸ ποὺ ἀνάγεται σὲ μεταγενέστερες περιόδους μετὰ ἀπὸ τὴν Ἐποχὴ τοῦ

Χαλκοῦ (ΕΙΚ. 3.7). Τὸ σύνολο τῶν ἀντικειμένων ἀπὸ ὀψιδιανὸ ποὺ περισυνελέγησαν ἀποτυπώνεται στὴν ΕΙΚ. 3.8. Ἂς σημειωθεῖ ὅτι δὲν ἀποτελεῖ ἀπολύτως ἀντιπροσωπευτικὸ δεῖγμα καθώς, λόγῳ τῆς διαφορετικῆς ἐμπειρίας τῶν ἐρευνητῶν, ἡ ἱκανότητα ἐντοπισμοῦ καὶ ἀναγνώρισης ἀπολεπισμένων ἐργαλείων ποικίλλει.

3Β. Η Μελετη της Διαβρωσης του Εδαφους και της Μετατροπης των Ανδηρων σε Καλλιεργησιμα στην Μαρκιανη με την Χρηση Μικρομορφολογικων Τεχνικων

Ἡ μελέτη τῶν διαδικασιῶν ποὺ ἀκολούθησαν τὴν ἐγκατάλειψη τοῦ χώρου, μέσῳ ἐδαφικῶν ἀποθέσεων καὶ ἀνάλυσης ἱζημάτων, ἐξετάζεται στὸ ὑποκεφάλαιο 3(b). Ἡ ἐξέταση τῆς ἔκθεσης τῶν ἀνδήρων σὲ διάβρωση καὶ ἡ μικρομορφολογικὴ ἀνάλυση ἐπιλεγμένων ἱζηματικῶν δειγμάτων χώματος τεκμηριώνουν ἀρκετὲς φάσεις μεταβολῶν στὴν κλιτύ, οἱ ὁποῖες μποροῦν νὰ συσχετισθοῦν μὲ τὰ ἀρχαιολογικὰ δεδομένα γιὰ τὴν χρήση τοῦ χώρου. Ἡ ἀνάλυση ὑποδεικνύει ὅτι οἱ ἀρχαιολογικὲς ἀποθέσεις στὴν Μαρκιανὴ ὅτι ἀντὶ νὰ ὑπόκεινται σὲ 4.500 χρόνια διαρκοῦς διάβρωσης, ἐξετέθησαν σὲ σχετικὰ σύντομες φάσεις διαταραχῆς τῆς διαβρωτικῆς διαδικασίας: κατὰ τὴν ἴδια τὴν φάση κατοίκησης στὴν Πρώιμη Ἐποχὴ τοῦ Χαλκοῦ, κατὰ τὴν ἐπανεγκατάσταση στὴν Ἑλληνιστικὴ περίοδο, καθὼς καὶ σχετικὰ πιὸ πρόσφατα, μὲ τὴν μετατροπὴ τῶν χτιῶν (=ἀνδήρων) σὲ καλλιεργήσιμα, σήμερα ἐγκαταλελειμμένα χωραφάκια. Τὸ συγκλῖνον συμπέρασμα τῶν διαφορετικῶν προσεγγίσεων εἶναι ὅτι τὸ διασπαρμένο σὲ κατὰ προσέγγισιν 200 στρέμματα ἀρχαιολογικὸ ὑλικό, σήμερα ὁρατὸ στὴν Μαρκιανή, προέρχεται ἀπὸ τὴν διάβρωση μίας περιοχῆς, ἡ ἔκταση τῆς ὁποίας εἶναι ἀπίθανο νὰ ὑπερέβαινε τὰ 30 στρέμματα κατὰ τὴν Πρωτοκυκλαδικὴ περίοδο.

Ἡ συστηματικὴ μελέτη ἑνὸς ἀριθμοῦ ἐπιλεγμένων δειγμάτων ἀποθέσεων, λαμβανομένης ὑπ᾽ ὄψιν τῆς διάγνωσης ἀπὸ τοὺς ἀνασκαφεῖς τεσσάρων χρονικῶν φάσεων κατοίκησης τοῦ οἰκισμοῦ κατὰ τὴν Πρώιμη Ἐποχὴ τοῦ Χαλκοῦ, καθὼς καὶ τοὺς χρονικοὺς προσδιορισμοὺς τῶν ραδιοχρονολογήσεων, ὑποδηλώνει ὅτι ἡ ἐγκατάσταση στὸν χῶρο εἶχε διάρκεια περίπου 10 αἰώνων: τὸ πολύ, δύο αἰώνων γιὰ τὴν φάση Ι, δύο ἢ τριῶν γιὰ τὴν φάση ΙΙ, δύο ἢ τριῶν γιὰ τὴν φάση ΙΙΙ, καὶ τριῶν γιὰ τὴν φάση ΙV. Οἱ ἐνδείξεις μαρτυροῦν μία πολὺ μικρὴ κοινότητα κατὰ τὶς φάσεις Ι καὶ ΙΙ, ἡ ὁποία μεγαλώνει σημαντικὰ κατὰ τὶς φάσεις ΙΙΙ καὶ ΙV, μὲ μᾶλλον διακεκομμένη, ἐπεισοδιακή, παρὰ συνεχὴ χρήση τοῦ χώρου.

Βασιζόμενοι στὶς οἰκιακὲς ἐνότητες ὅπως διακρίθηκαν στὸν σύχρονο οἰκισμὸ *Φούρνου Κορυφὴ* στὴν Μύρτο τῆς Κρήτης, καθὼς καὶ σὲ παρατηρήσεις γιὰ τὴν ὀργάνωση τῶν χώρων στὴν ἀκρόπολη τοῦ *Καστριοῦ*, στὴν Χαλανδριανὴ τῆς Σύρου, εἶναι δυνατὸν νὰ προτείνεται περίπου μία ἔκταση 40 ἔως 80 τετραγωνικῶν μέτρων γιὰ κάθε ᾽νοικοκυριὸ᾽ (*οἶκον*). Χρησιμοποιώντας αὐτὸ τὸ στοιχεῖο ὡς μέτρον εἶναι δυνατὸν νὰ ὑπολογίσομε κατὰ προσέγγισιν, ὅτι ἡ συνολικὴ ἔκταση τῶν ἀρχαιολογικῶν ἀποθέσεων στὴν Μαρκιανὴ ὑποδηλώνει ἕνα μέγιστον περίπου 12 ἕως 15 ᾽νοικοκυριῶν᾽ (*οἶκων*) ἢ ἕναν πληθυσμὸ τῆς τάξεως τῶν 60 ἕως 75 ἀτόμων κατὰ τὶς φάσεις ΙΙΙ καὶ ΙV. Ἡ ἐφαρμογὴ ὑπολογισμῶν γιὰ τὴν πυκνότητα τῶν οἰκισμῶν ἀπὸ τὴν συστηματικὴ ἐπιφανειακὴ ἔρευνα τῆς Μήλου ὑποδηλώνει στὴν περίπτωση τῆς Ἀμοργοῦ τὴν ὕπαρξη μόνον 4 ἢ 5 οἰκισμῶν σὲ κάθε χρονικὸ σημεῖο κατὰ τὴν διάρκεια τῆς Πρώιμης Ἐποχῆς τοῦ Χαλκοῦ καὶ ἕναν συνολικὸ πληθυσμὸ τοῦ νησιοῦ λιγότερου τῶν 300 κατοίκων.

ΚΕΦΑΛΑΙΟ 4. ΣΥΝΟΠΤΙΚΗ ΠΕΡΙΓΡΑΦΗ ΤΗΣ ΑΝΑΣΚΑΦΙΚΗΣ ΕΡΕΥΝΑΣ 1988–1990

Ἡ μορφὴ καὶ ὁ χαρακτήρας τοῦ λόφου τῆς Μαρκιανῆς ἀποτυπώνονται στὶς τομὲς τῆς ΕΙΚ. 4.2, ὅπου διακρίνονται καθαρὰ ἡ περιοχὴ τῆς κορυφῆς καὶ ἡ ἀνασκαφὴ στὴν Ἐγκοπὴ 2 τοῦ Ἀνδήρου 1.

Ἡ θέση τῶν ἀνασκαφικῶν τομῶν σημειώνεται στὴν ΕΙΚ. 4.1, καὶ ἡ γενικὴ εἰκόνα τοῦ τόπου παρέχεται στὴν ἀεροφωτογραφία (ΠΙΝ. 2). Ἡ περιοχὴ τῆς κορυφῆς, μὲ τὶς σύγχρονες μάντρες καὶ τὰ κτίσματα (Α, Β, καὶ C) δὲν εἶχε καλὰ στρωματογραφημένη ἐπίχωση (ΠΙΝ. 7 a καὶ 7 b). Μεγαλύτερες καὶ καλύτερα διατηρημένες ἐπιχώσεις διαπιστώθηκαν στὴν περιοχὴ τῆς ὀχύρωσης βορειότερα (Τομὲς 6 καὶ 8), καθὼς καὶ στὸ Ἄνδηρο 1 νότια. Ἐπιπροσθέτως, μία τομὴ (Τομὴ 1,1) ἐρευνήθηκε ἀπὸ τὸ ἐπίπεδο τοῦ ἀνδήρου τῆς κορυφῆς (ὅπου καὶ ἐπεξετάθη πρὸς βορρᾶν ὡς Τομὴ 7) ἕως τὶς χαμηλότερες ἀποθέσεις στὸ ἐπίπεδο τοῦ Ἀνδήρου 1.

Ἡ Τομὴ 1,1 ἐπέτρεψε τὴν μελέτη τῶν στρωματογραφικῶν συσχετισμῶν μεταξὺ τοῦ ἀνδήρου τῆς κορυφῆς καὶ τοῦ Ἀνδήρου 1· σημειώνομε ὡστόσο, ὅτι δὲν διεπιστώθη ἄλλη στρωματογραφικὴ σύνδεση μεταξὺ τῆς περιοχῆς τῆς ὀχύρωσης (Τομὲς 6 καὶ 8) καὶ τοῦ Ἀνδήρου 1 νότια. Αὐτό, ὅμως, δὲν ἀποτελεῖ πρόβλημα, καθὼς ἡ πρώιμη κεραμική, ἡ ὁποία συνδέεται μὲ τὸν πρώιμο ὀχυρωτικὸ τοῖχο (στὴν Τομὴ 6), ἔχει χαρακτηριστικὰ πολὺ γνωστὰ στὶς Κυκλάδες κατὰ τὴν πρωιμότερη φάση τῆς Πρωτοκυκλαδικῆς περιόδου, συγκρίσιμα μὲ τὰ εὑρήματα ἀπὸ τὰ παλαιότερα στρώματα στὴν Φυλακωπὴ τῆς Μήλου (Πρὸ τῆς Πόλεως, Ἐπίπεδο Α1). Αὐτὴ ἡ κεραμικὴ ἀντιπροσωπεύει τὴν φάση

I στὴν Μαρκιανή. Ἐξίσου ἀσφαλὴς ἦταν ἡ διαπίστωση ὅτι τὰ ἀνώτερα στρώματα στὸ Ἄνδηρο 1 ἀντιπροσωπεύουν τὴν τελευταία φάση συστηματικῆς κατοίκησης στὸν χῶρο στὸ τέλος τῆς Πρώιμης Ἐποχῆς τοῦ Χαλκοῦ. Ἡ κεραμικὴ ἀπὸ τὰ ἀνώτερα στρώματα τοῦ Ἀνδήρου 1 παρουσιάζει πολλὲς ὁμοιότητες μὲ τὴν λεγομένη ‘Ὁμάδα Καστριοῦ’, ἡ ὁποία ἀπαντᾶται καὶ σὲ ἄλλα νησιά, συμπεριλαμβανομένης τῆς Σύρου, τῆς Δήλου καὶ τῆς Κέας, καὶ στὴν Μαρκιανὴ ἀντιστοιχεῖ στὴν φάση IV.

Ὑλικὸ χαρακτηριστικὸ τῆς παλαιότερης φάσεως I στὴν Μαρκιανὴ βρέθηκε ἐπίσης στὸ ἀνώτερο τμῆμα τῆς Τομῆς 1, καθὼς καὶ στὰ κατώτερα στρώματα τῆς παρακείμενης Τομῆς 7. Ἀπὸ τὰ ἀνώτερα στρώματα τῆς Τομῆς 7 προῆλθε κεραμικὴ παρόμοια μὲ τὴν ‘Ὁμάδα Κάμπου’, ἡ ὁποία γενικῶς χρονολογεῖται κατὰ τὴν μεταβατικὴ περίοδο μεταξὺ τοῦ πολιτισμοῦ Γρόττας-Πηλοῦ καὶ Κέρου-Σύρου (μεταβατικὴ περίοδος Πρωτοκυκλαδικὴ I/II). Στὴν Μαρκιανὴ αὐτὴ ἡ κεραμικὴ προσδιορίζει τὴν φάση II.

Κεραμικὴ ἀπὸ τὴν φάση τὴν ὁποία χαρακτηρίσαμε φάση III στὴν Μαρκιανὴ προέρχεται ἀπὸ δύο θέσεις: ἀπὸ τὸ κλειστὸ σύνολο ἐντὸς τῆς σπηλαιώδους ρωγμῆς μέσα στὸ βραχῶδες πρανές, στὴν ἀνατολικὴ παρειὰ τῆς Τομῆς 1, 1, καθὼς καὶ ἀπὸ ἄλλα, διάφορα εὑρήματα στὸ Ἄνδηρο 1 στὶς Τομὲς 1 καὶ 2, σὲ στρώματα παλαιότερα τῆς φάσεως IV.

Στὸν ὀχυρωτικὸ τοῖχο, στὸ βόρειο τμῆμα τοῦ οἰκισμοῦ (ΕΙΚ. 6.1, ΠΙΝ. 8 a καὶ 8 b) ἐρευνήθηκε ἀνασκαφικὰ ἕνα μικρὸ τμῆμα του στὴν Τομὴ 6 (ΕΙΚ. 4.4 καὶ 4.5 ΠΙΝ. 9 a καὶ 9 b). Ἡ κεραμικὴ ἀπὸ τὴν διερευνητικὴ Τομὴ 6, 1, στὴν ἐσωτερικὴ παρειὰ τοῦ τείχους ἦταν ὁμοιογενής, ἀλλὰ πολὺ ἀποσπασματικὰ διατηρημένη (ἀναλύεται στὸ κεφάλαιο 7C). Πρόκειται γιὰ τὴν πρωιμότερη κεραμικὴ ἀπὸ τὸν χῶρο καὶ αὐτὴ χρησιμοποιήθηκε ὡς σημεῖο ἀναφορᾶς γιὰ τὴν διάγνωση τῆς φάσης I. Ὑποστηρίχθηκε βέβαια καὶ ἡ δυνατότητα, τὸ διαβεβρωμένο αὐτὸ κεραμικὸ σύνολο νὰ ἔχει παρασυρθεῖ ὡς ἐκεῖ μὲ τὰ νερὰ ἀπὸ γειτονικὲς πρωιμότερες ἀποθέσεις καὶ ὡς ἐκ τούτου δὲν θὰ πρέπει νὰ θεωρηθεῖ ὡς καθοριστικὸς παράγων γιὰ τὴν χρονολόγηση τοῦ τείχους. Ἂς σημειωθεῖ ὅμως, ὅτι σὲ κανένα ἀπὸ τὰ στρώματα ποὺ ἐρευνήθηκαν στὴν ἐσωτερικὴ παρειὰ τοῦ τείχους δὲν βρέθηκε ὄστρακο κεραμικῆς μὲ ἐγκλείσματα γαλάζιου σχιστολίθου (=πατελιᾶς) (Blue schist fabric), κατ’ ἐξοχὴν χαρακτηριστικὸ τῆς κεραμικῆς τῶν ὑστερότερων φάσεων στὸν οἰκισμό. Γι’αὐτὸ καὶ ἐπὶ τῇ βάσει τῆς ἀνευρεθείσας κεραμικῆς φαίνεται πιθανότερη ἡ χρονολόγηση τῆς κατασκευῆς τοῦ τείχους στὴν φάση I.

Ὁ Βόρειος Προμαχών, ὁ ὁποῖος εἶναι ὁρατὸς ἀνατολικότερα, ἐρευνήθηκε ἀνασκαφικὰ στὴν Τομὴ 8 (ΕΙΚ. 4.8, ΠΙΝ. 10 a, 2, 3 καὶ 11 a). Τὰ εὑρήματα ἀπὸ τὴν Τομὴ 8,1, στὸ ἐσωτερικὸ τοῦ προμαχῶνος, ὁδήγησαν στὴν κατὰ προσέγγισιν χρονολόγησή του: στὰ κατώτερα στρώματα, ἀνάμεσα στὰ ὄστρακα ποὺ ἀνήκουν στὶς φάσεις I καὶ II, ὑπῆρχαν ἀρκετὰ μὲ ἐγκλείσματα γαλάζιου σχιστολίθου (=πατελιᾶς) (Blue schist fabric), τὸ ὁποῖο εἶναι χαρακτηριστικὸ τῶν μεταγενέστρων φάσεων III καὶ IV. Ἐπὶ τῇ βάσει αὐτῆς τῆς μαρτυρίας θεωρήθηκε ὅτι ἡ κατασκευὴ τοῦ προμαχῶνος ἀνάγεται στὴν φάση III κατοίκησης τοῦ οἰκισμοῦ.

Ἀνασκαφὴ στὴν περιοχὴ τῆς κορυφῆς διενεργήθηκε στὶς Τομὲς 1,1, 7, 9 καὶ 4. Ἀπὸ τὶς Τομὲς 1,1 καὶ 7 (ΕΙΚ. 4.12, ΠΙΝ. 7 a, 13 a καὶ b, 14 a καὶ b καὶ 15 a) προῆλθε κεραμικὴ τῆς φάσεως II. Παρὰ τὸ ὅτι ἡ στρωματογραφία στὴν Τομὴ 1,1 ἦταν περίπλοκη λόγω τῆς φύσεως τοῦ ἀπότομου βραχώδους πρανοῦς, στὸ ἀνώτερο τμῆμα σὲ ἀδιατάρακτα στρώματα, ἦταν ἀπολύτως σαφὴς ἡ ὕπαρξη κλειστῶν συνόλων τῶν πρωιμότερων φάσεων. Οἱ Τομὲς 1,1, 7 καὶ 9 ἀπέδωσαν σημαντικὸ ὑλικὸ τῆς φάσεως II, ἐνῶ στὴν Τομὴ 4 (ΕΙΚ. 4.15, ΠΙΝ. 7 a) ἡ ὁποία βρίσκεται ἀνατολικότερα, στὶς λεπτὲς διαταραγμένες στρώσεις ποὺ εἶχαν ἀπομείνει ἐπάνω στὸν φυσικὸ βράχο βρέθηκαν ὄστρακα διαφόρων φάσεων.

Ἰδιαίτερη μνεία πρέπει νὰ γίνει στὴν σπηλαιώδη ρωγμὴ (ΠΙΝ. 16 a καὶ b), ἡ ὁποία ἀποκαλύφθηκε μετὰ ἀπὸ τὴν διάλυση τοῦ ἀνατολικοῦ τμήματος τοῦ Τοίχου Λ, στὴν Τομὴ 1,1 στὴν ἀνατολικὴ παρειὰ τοῦ βραχώδους πρανοῦς: ἐδῶ βρέθηκε κλειστὸ σύνολο κεραμικῆς τῆς φάσεως III, καθὼς καὶ πολλὰ πήλινα σφονδύλια. Στὸ κατώτερο τμῆμα τῆς Τομῆς 1,1 καὶ στὸ ἐσωτερικὸ μίας περίπου κυκλικῆς κατασκευῆς (ΕΙΚ. 4.18, ΠΙΝ. 5 b καὶ 3, 15 b, 16 c), κάτω ἀπὸ ἐπάλληλες στρώσεις πεσμένων λίθων, ἀποκαλύφθηκε σύνολο κεραμικῆς χαρακτηριστικὸ τῆς φάσεως IV, συγγενὲς μὲ τὴν ‘Ὁμάδα Καστριοῦ’, μαζὶ μὲ πολλὰ πήλινα σφονδύλια καὶ ἕνα σφράγισμα.

Ὁ κυρίως τομέας κατοίκησης στὴν Μαρκιανὴ ἀποκαλύφθηκε στὸ Ἄνδηρο 1, στὶς τομὲς 1,2–1,7 καὶ 2,1 ἕως 2,4. Τὸ ἀποκαλυφθὲν τμῆμα οἰκοδομικοῦ συγκροτήματος ἀποτελεῖται ἀπὸ μία σειρὰ δωματίων, ὁρισμένα ἀπὸ τὰ ὁποῖα εἶναι μεταξύ τους συνδεδεμένα (ΕΙΚ. 4.21, 6.3, ΠΙΝ. 17 a–b, 18 a–b, 19 a–b). Τὸ κυριώτερο χαρακτηριστικὸ τοῦ συγκροτήματος εἶναι ὁ ἐν μέρει λαξευμένος καὶ ἐν μέρει κτιστός, καὶ πλακοσκεπὴς ἀγωγὸς (ΠΙΝ. 20 a–b, 21 a–b καὶ 22 a–b) ποὺ διατρέχει ὅλον τὸν χῶρο ἀπὸ τὸ μέτωπο τοῦ βραχώδους πρανοῦς κατὰ μῆκος τῶν τοίχων τοῦ συγκροτήματος καὶ διέρχεται κάτω ἀπὸ τὸ δάπεδο τοῦ ἑνὸς ἀπὸ τὰ δωμάτια. Ἡ ἀνασκαφικὴ ἔρευνα στὸ Ἄνδηρο 1 δὲν ἔφθασε σὲ ὅλες τὶς τομὲς ἕως τὸν φυσικὸ βράχο. Γι’ αὐτὸ καὶ μολονότι βρέθηκε κεραμικὴ τῆς φάσεως ΙΙΙ στὶς περισσότερες τομὲς σὲ στρώματα ὑποκείμενα τῆς φάσεως IV, τὰ κατώτερα στρώματα στὸ Ἄνδηρο 1 δὲν ἐρευνήθηκαν.

Στὴν πλαγιὰ τοῦ λόφου καὶ σὲ ἄνδηρο χαμηλότερα ἀπὸ τὸ Ἄνδηρο 1, στὰ νοτιοανατολικά, διερευνήθηκε ἀκόμη μία τομή, ἡ Τομὴ 3 (ΕΙΚ. 4.24, ΠΙΝ. 26, 27, 28), στὴν ὁποία ἀποκαλύφθηκε ἕνα δίχωρο κτίσμα. Μολονότι ἦταν περιορισμένος ὁ χῶρος ποὺ ἐρευνήθηκε καὶ τὰ οἰκοδομικὰ λείψανα δὲν ἀποκαλύφθηκαν πλήρως, ἀπὸ τὴν Τομὴ 3, προῆλθαν σημαντικὰ εὑρήματα, μεταξὺ τῶν ὁποίων μετάλλινα ἀντικείμενα, καὶ μία μολύβδινη σφραγίδα, καθὼς καὶ πολλὰ λίθινα ἐργαλεῖα.

Οἱ στρωματογραφικὲς τομὲς (ΕΙΚ. 4.6, 4.9, 4.16, 4.19, 4.22 καὶ 4.25) ἀπὸ τὶς διάφορες περιοχές, καθὼς καὶ τὰ διαγράμματα τῶν ἀνασκαφικῶν στρώσεων (ΕΙΚ. 4.7, 4.11, 4.14, 4.17, 4.20, 4.23, 4.27) ποὺ ἀποτυπώνουν τὴν διαδοχὴ τῶν ἀρχαιολογικῶν στρωμάτων δίνουν μία σαφῆ εἰκόνα τῆς στρωματογραφικῆς ἀλληλουχίας στὸν οἰκισμό.

ΚΕΦΑΛΑΙΟ 5. Η ΑΠΟΛΥΤΗ ΧΡΟΝΟΛΟΓΗΣΗ

Ἡ στρωματογραφικὴ ἀκολουθία, καθὼς καὶ ἡ μελέτη τῆς κεραμικῆς (βλ. παρακάτω κεφάλαιο 7) ἐπιτρέπουν τὴν διάγνωση τεσσάρων ἐπαλλήλων διαδοχικῶν φάσεων καὶ τὴν πρόταση μίας σχετικῆς χρονολόγησης : ἡ παλαιότερη φάση Ι τῆς Μαρκιανῆς εἶναι σύγχρονη μὲ τὸν πολιτισμὸ Γρόττας–Πηλοῦ (Πρωτοκυκλαδικὴ Ι), ὅπως εἶναι γνωστὸς ἀπὸ τὰ κατώτερα στρώματα τῆς Φυλακωπῆς στὴν Μῆλο. Ἡ φάση ΙΙ στὴν Μαρκιανὴ εἶναι σύγχρονη μὲ τὴν 'Ὁμάδα Κάμπου', ἡ ὁποία θεωρεῖται μεταβατικὴ μεταξὺ τῶν πολιτισμῶν Γρόττας-Πηλοῦ καὶ Κέρου-Σύρου (δηλαδὴ Πρωτοκυκλαδικὴ Ι/ ΙΙ). Ἡ φάση ΙΙΙ στὴν Μαρκιανὴ συσχετίζεται μὲ τὸν πολιτισμὸ Κέρου-Σύρου ἢ τὴν Πρωτοκυκλαδικὴ ΙΙ. Τὸ ὑλικὸ τῆς φάσεως IV στὴν Μαρκιανὴ παρουσιάζει πολλὲς συγγένειες μὲ τὴν Ὁμάδα Καστριοῦ, ἡ ὁποία γενικῶς τοποθετεῖται στὴν ὑστερότερη φάση ἢ στὸ τέλος τοῦ πολιτισμοῦ Κέρου–Σύρου (στὴν ὁρολογία ὁρισμένων χρονολογικῶν συστημάτων στὴν Πρωτοκυκλαδικὴ ΙΙΙ).

Δώδεκα δείγματα ἐπιλέγησαν γιὰ ραδιοχρονολόγηση σύμφωνα μὲ τὴν στρωματογραφικὴ ἀλληλουχία, τὰ ὁποῖα ἐπιτρέπουν τὸν περαιτέρω προσδιορισμὸ αὐτῆς τῆς χρονολόγησης σὲ ἀπόλυτα ἔτη. Τὰ δείγματα ἐπεξεργάστηκε ἐπιταχυντὴς μάζας γιὰ τὴν ραδιοχρονολόγηση στὸ Ἐρευνητικὸ Ἐργαστήριο γιὰ τὴν Ἀρχαιολογία καὶ τὴν Ἱστορία τῆς Τέχνης στὴν Ὀξφόρδη. Οἱ συνάφειες τῶν δειγμάτων καὶ προσδιορισμοὶ τῆς ραδιοχρονολόγησης δίνονται στοὺς ΠΙΝ. 5 a καὶ 5 b. Σὲ διορθωμένη μορφή, μετὰ ἀπὸ τὴν ἀναγωγή, δίνονται στὸν ΠΙΝ. 5 c.

Οἱ προσαρμοσμένες στὴν ἀποδεκτὴ κλίμακα ραδιοχρονολογήσεις παρατίθενται στὶς ΕΙΚ. 5.1 ἕως 5.3, μαζί με μία σειρὰ ραδιοχρονολογήσεων ἀπὸ τὴν θέση Κάβος Δασκαλιοῦ στὴν Κέρο, ὅπου τὰ εὑρήματα χρονολογοῦνται κυρίως στὸν πολιτισμὸ Κέρου-Σύρου (Πρωτοκυκλαδικὴ ΙΙ) μὲ τὴν παρουσία μερικῶν ὀστράκων τῆς Ὁμάδας Καστριοῦ. Ἡ συνεξέταση αὐτῶν τῶν χρονολογήσεων ἀπὸ τὸν Κάβο Δασκαλιοῦ συμβάλλει στὴν ἐπιβεβαίωση τῆς διαπίστωσης ὅτι ἡ φάση Μαρκιανὴ ΙΙΙ εἶναι σύγχρονη μὲ τὸν πολιτισμὸ Κέρου-Σύρου, ὅπως ἀντιπροσωπεύεται στὸν Κάβο Δασκαλιοῦ.

Ἡ χρήση τῶν στρωματογραφικῶν δεδομένων καὶ τῶν προσαρμοσμένων στὴν κλίμακα ραδιοχρονολογήσεων ἐπιτρέπει νὰ προτείνομε μὲ σχετικὴ βεβαιότητα μία ἀπόλυτη χρονολόγηση γιὰ τὴν Πρώιμη Ἐποχὴ τοῦ Χαλκοῦ στὴν Ἀμοργὸ (ΕΙΚ. 5.4). Ἔτσι, τὸ τέλος τῆς φάσεως Μαρκιανὴ Ι, βάσει τῶν νέων δεδομένων, μπορεῖ νὰ τοποθετηθεῖ περίπου στὸ 3000 π.Χ., ἐνῶ ἡ διάρκεια τῆς φάσεως Μαρκιανὴ ΙΙ μεταξὺ τοῦ 3000, περίπου, καὶ τοῦ 2800 π.Χ. Τὰ χρονικὰ ὅρια τῆς φάσεως Μαρκιανὴ ΙΙΙ (καὶ κατὰ συσχετισμὸν τοῦ πολιτισμοῦ Κέρου-Σύρου) εἶναι δυνατὸν νὰ προσδιοριστοῦν ἀπὸ περίπου τὸ 2800 ἕως τὸ 2500 ἢ τὸ 2400 π.Χ. Ἡ διάρκεια τῆς φάσεως Μαρκιανὴ IV τοποθετεῖται ἀνάμεσα στὸ 2500 καὶ τὸ 2200 π.Χ περίπου (ἔτσι συνάγονται μὲ περισσότερη βεβαιότητα καὶ τὰ χρονικὰ ὅρια τῆς Ὁμάδας Καστριοῦ').

Ἡ ἐπεξεργασμένη χρονολόγηση ἐναρμονίζεται μὲ τὴν γενικῶς ἀποδεκτὴ χρονολόγηση τῆς Πρωτοκυκλαδικῆς περιόδου, ποὺ ἔχει καθιερωθεῖ, ἤδη ἀπὸ τὸ 1972, καὶ ἐντάσσεται πλέον στὴν σταθερὴ βάση τῶν διορθωμένων προσδιορισμῶν τῆς ραδιοχρονολόγησης.

ΚΕΦΑΛΑΙΟ 6. ΑΡΧΙΤΕΚΤΟΝΙΚΗ

6Α. Τὸ Τεῖχος

Τὸ ὀχυρωτικὸ τεῖχος προστατεύει τὴν βόρεια πλευρὰ τοῦ λόφου τῆς Μαρκιανῆς, καὶ ὅπως ἐμφαίνεται σὲ κάτοψη καὶ σὲ ὄψη στὶς ΕΙΚ. 6.1 καὶ 6.2, καθὼς καὶ στὸν ΠΙΝ. 8, ἔχει ἀποκαλυφθεῖ σὲ μῆκος περίπου 7ομ. Ἡ πορεία καὶ ἡ μορφὴ τοῦ ὀχυρωτικοῦ τοίχου εἶναι εὐδιάκριτες στὸ καλύτερα σωζόμενο δυτικὸ τμῆμα, δηλαδὴ ἀπὸ τὸν *Βόρειο Προμαχῶνα* (Τομὴ 8), ἕως τὸν *Βορειοδυτικὸ Προμαχῶνα* (ΠΙΝ. 12 a), ὁ ὁποῖος ἐρευνήθηκε ἐν μέρει τὸ 1999, κατὰ τὸν καθαρισμὸ γιὰ τὴν ἀρχιτεκτονικὴ ἀποτύπωση.

Στὴν βόρεια, ἐξωτερικὴ ὄψη τοῦ ὀχυρωτικοῦ τοίχου διακρίνεται ἡ θεμελίωση στὸν φυσικὸ βράχο, τμήματα τοῦ ὁποίου ἔχουν ἐνσωματωθεῖ στὸ τεῖχος. Στὸ Ἀνατολικὸ τμῆμα του, ὁ ὀχυρωτικὸς τοῖχος ἔχει ὑποστεῖ σημαντικὲς ἀλλοιώσεις ἀπὸ τὶς συνεχεῖς μετασκευὲς τοῦ ὑψηλοῦ διαχωριστικοῦ χωραφότοιχου (ΠΙΝ.12 b-c), ὁ ὁποῖος προστατεύει ἀπὸ τοὺς ἰσχυροὺς βόρειους ἀνέμους τὸ ἄνδηρο τῆς κορυφῆς μὲ τὶς μάντρες τῶν αἰγοπροβάτων. Καὶ ἐδῶ, ὅπως καὶ ἀλλοῦ, ἐξ αἰτίας τῆς ἐγκατάλειψης τῆς καλλιέργειας κατὰ τὶς τελευταῖες δεκαετίες, τὰ λείψανα τῆς ἀρχαίας ὀχύρωσης εἶναι δυσδιάκριτα λόγω τῆς ἄγριας βλάστησης ποὺ ἔχει καλύψει ἀκόμα καὶ τοὺς ριζιμιοὺς βράχους. Μολονότι τὸ ἀνατολικὸ πέρας τῆς ὀχύρωσης δὲν ἔχει ἐρευνηθεῖ συστηματικά, εἶναι πιθανόν, ὅτι, καὶ ἐδῶ, ὅπως στὸ δυτικὸ τμῆμα, τὴν φυσικὴ ὀχύρωση ἀποτελοῦσαν οἱ διάσπαρτοι βραχόλιθοι, τοὺς ὁποίους παντοιοτρόπως ἐκμεταλλεύθηκαν ἢ ἐνσωμάτωσαν στὴν τεχνητὴ ὀχύρωση.

Οἱ δύο προμαχῶνες, Βόρειος καὶ Βορειοδυτικός, εἶναι ἰδιαιτέρως σημαντικοί. Ὁ Βόρειος (ΕΙΚ. 4.8, 6.1 καὶ 6.2, ΠΙΝ. 10 a-c καὶ 11 a), σωζ. ὕψ. 1,1μ., ἐρευνήθηκε στὴν Τομὴ 8. Ὁ τρόπος τῆς ἐμπλοκῆς τῶν λίθων τοῦ νοτίου τοίχου τοῦ Προμαχῶνος μὲ τὸν ὀχυρωτικὸ τοῖχο δείχνει ὅτι πρόκειται γιὰ σύγχρονες κατασκευὲς καὶ ὅτι ὁ Βόρειος Προμαχών δὲν φαίνεται νὰ ἀποτελεῖ μεταγενέστερη προσθήκη. Ὁ Βορειοδυτικὸς Προμαχών βρίσκεται περίπου 19,3μ. Δυτικὰ τοῦ Βορείου καὶ διατηρεῖται σὲ ὕψος 1,2μ. Ἐπειδὴ δὲν ἔχει ἐρευνηθεῖ, τὸ πάχος τῶν τοίχων του, καθὼς καὶ τὸ νότιο πέρας του εἶναι δυνατὸν νὰ προσδιορισθοῦν μόνον μετὰ ἀπὸ ἀνασκαφικὴ ἔρευνα.

Οἱ προμαχῶνες τῆς ὀχύρωσης τοῦ λόφου τῆς Μαρκιανῆς μὲ τὴν σχεδὸν πεταλόσχημη μορφὴ τους, δὲν διαφέρουν οὐσιαστικὰ ἀπὸ τοὺς ἀντίστοιχους στὶς λίγες γνωστὲς ὀχυρωμένες θέσεις τῆς Πρώιμης Ἐποχῆς τοῦ Χαλκοῦ στὸ Αἰγαῖο: στὸ Καστρὶ τῆς Σύρου, στὸν Πάνορμο τῆς Νάξου, στὴν Λέρνα Ἀργολίδος, στὸ Παλαμάρι τῆς Σκύρου, καθὼς στὸ Liman Tepe στὸν κόλπο τῆς Σμύρνης.

Τὸ προτείχισμα (ΕΙΚ. 6.1, ΠΙΝ. 20 b), μέρος τοῦ ὁποίου ἀποκαλύφθηκε στὴν Τομὴ 8,2, βρίσκεται Βορείως τοῦ Βορείου Προμαχῶνος, σὲ ἀπόσταση 1,18μ. Τὸ ἀκριβὲς μῆκος του καὶ ἡ μορφή του δὲν εἶναι δυνατὸν νὰ προσδιορισθεῖ χωρὶς συστηματικὸ ἐπιφανειακὸ καθαρισμὸ καὶ τὴν διάνοιξη δοκιμαστικῶν τομῶν.

Γιὰ τὴν χρονολόγηση τοῦ ὀχυρωτικοῦ τοίχου σημαντικὴ εἶναι ἡ μαρτυρία τῶν στρωματογραφημένων ἀνασκαφικῶν εὑρημάτων ἀπὸ τὴν μοναδικὴ ἐντὸς τοῦ ὀχυρωτικοῦ τοίχου Τομὴ 6 : οἱ ἐνδείξεις, μολονότι βέβαια λιγοστές, εἶναι δεσμευτικὲς γιὰ τὴν πρώιμη χρονολόγηση τῆς κατασκευῆς τοῦ τοίχου στὴν φάση Μαρκιανὴ I (Πρωτοκυκλαδικὴ I), ἀντιθέτως δηλαδὴ, μὲ τὴν ἐπικρατέστερη ἄποψη περὶ τῆς ὄψιμης παρουσίας τεχνητῶν ὀχυρώσεων στὸν χῶρο τοῦ Αἰγαίου, καὶ ἰδιαίτερα κατὰ τὴν Πρωτοκυκλαδικὴ III περίοδο. Ἡ ἀνεύρεση στὸ ἐσωτερικὸ τοῦ Βορείου Προμαχῶνος (Τομὴ 8,1) κεραμικῆς χρονολογούμενης στὴν φάση Μαρκιανὴ III, ἐθεωρήθη ὅτι ἀποτελεῖ κριτήριο γιὰ τὴν χρονολόγηση τῆς κατασκευῆς του σὲ φάση ὑστερότερη ἀπὸ τὴν ἵδρυση τοῦ ὀχυρωτικοῦ τοίχου. Πρόσθετο ἔρεισμα γιὰ τὴν ὑστερότερη χρονολόγηση τοῦ Βορείου Προμαχῶνος ἀποτέλεσε ἡ τυπολογικὴ σύγκριση τῆς ἀρχιτεκτονικῆς του μορφῆς μὲ τὰ ὀλίγα γνωστὰ παραδείγματα, ὅπως, στὸ Καστρὶ τῆς Σύρου, στὸν Κύνθο τῆς Δήλου καὶ στὸν Πάνορμο τῆς Νάξου. Ὡστόσο, ὁρισμένες κατασκευαστικὲς λεπτομέρειες, καθὼς καὶ ἄλλες παρατηρήσεις, ἐπιτρέπουν τὴν διατύπωση τῆς ὑπόθεσης περὶ τῆς κατασκευῆς τοῦ ὀχυρωτικοῦ τοίχου μὲ τοὺς προμαχῶνες συγχρόνως μὲ τὴν ἵδρυση τοῦ οἰκισμοῦ.

Στὸ παρὸν στάδιο τῆς ἔρευνας γιὰ τοὺς ὀχυρωμένους οἰκισμοὺς κατὰ τὴν Πρώιμη Ἐποχὴ τοῦ Χαλκοῦ, εἶναι ἀκόμη πρόωρη ἡ συναγωγὴ συμπερασμάτων, ἔστω καὶ προσωρινοῦ χαρακτήρα, ἐφόσον οἱ νεοαποκαλυφθεῖσες Πρωτοκυκλαδικὲς ἀκροπόλεις στὴν Ἀμοργὸ δὲν ἔχουν ἀκόμα ἐρευνηθεῖ.

6Β. Τα Οικοδομικα Λειψανα

Στὸ ἄνδηρο τῆς κορυφῆς τὰ σωζόμενα, ὁρατὰ οἰκοδομικὰ λείψανα εἶναι λιγοστὰ καὶ ἀλλοιωμένα ἀπὸ τὶς μεταγενέστερες κατασκευές. Ἐλάχιστα πολὺ ἐφθαρμένα λείψανα μίας πιθανῶς σημαντικῆς κατασκευῆς ἀποκαλύφθηκαν στὶς Τομὲς 1,1, 7 καὶ 9 (ΕΙΚ. 4.12, ΠΙΝ. 13 a-b, 14 a-b καὶ 15 a) στὸν Νοτιοδυτικὸ τμῆμα τοῦ ἀνδήρου τῆς κορυφῆς.

Τὸ Ἄνδηρο 1, ὅπως καὶ στοὺς ἀρχαίους χρόνους εἶναι προσπελάσιμο ἀπὸ τὸ ὑπερκείμενο στὴν κορυφὴ μὲ μερικὲς βαθμίδες λαξευμένες στὸν βράχο στὸ ἀνατολικό της τμῆμα νοτίως τοῦ στεγασμένου σταύλου (Κτίσμα Β). Ἀπὸ τὴν ἀνασκαφὴ στὸ δυτικὸ τμῆμα (διαστ. 9,50μ. ἐπὶ 7,50μ.) τοῦ ἐπίπεδου καὶ ἐπιμήκους Ἀνδήρου 1 (διαστ. 40μ. Α>Δ καὶ 7,50–8,0μ. Β>Ν) κάτω ἀπὸ τὴν ἐλάχιστη ἐπίχωση τῆς φτενῆς στρώσης καλλιέργειας, ἀποκαλύφθηκε μέρος οἰκοδομικοῦ συγκροτήματος (ΕΙΚ. 6.3, καὶ 4.21, ΠΙΝ. 18–23) ἀποτελούμενο ἀπὸ τρεῖς τουλάχιστον ὀρθογωνίους χώρους, (1, 2 καὶ 3, ΕΙΚ. 4.21) ἕναν μικρὸ διάδρομο μὲ σχιστόπλακες (χῶρος 6, ΕΙΚ. 4.21), ἕναν καλοκτισμένο ἀγωγὸ (ΕΙΚ. 4.21, ΠΙΝ. 20–22) μία κτιστὴ καμπυλόγραμμη κατασκευὴ (χῶρος 7, ΕΙΚ. 4.18, ΠΙΝ. 15, 16) καὶ δύο πιθανότατα ἄστεγους (ὑπαίθριους;) χώρους (4 καὶ 5, ΕΙΚ. 6.3, ΠΙΝ. 18, 19). Ἡ ἀκριβὴς μορφὴ καὶ ἡ ὀργανικὴ σχέση τῶν διαφόρων δωματίων, καθὼς καὶ ἡ χρήση ἑκάστου χώρου δὲν ἔχουν ἀκόμη ἀποσαφηνισθεῖ πλήρως. Ἐξίσου δυσχερὴς εἶναι ἡ ἀνασύνθεση τῆς εἰκόνας, καθὼς καὶ τῶν ὁρίων τοῦ οἰκοδομημένου χώρου, ἀφοῦ δὲν ἐρευνήθηκε ἀνασκαφικὰ ὁλόκληρο τὸ ἄνδηρο.

Ἀνάμεσα στὰ ἀποκαλυφθέντα οἰκοδομικὰ κατάλοιπα ἰδιαίτερη σημασία ἔχουν ἡ κτιστὴ καμπυλόγραμμη κατασκευὴ (χῶρος 7, ΕΙΚ. 6.3 καὶ 4.18) καὶ ὁ ἀγωγὸς (ΕΙΚ. 4.21).

Ἡ κτιστὴ καμπυλόγραμμη κατασκευὴ (ΕΙΚ. 6.3), τὸ κατώτερο τμῆμα τῆς ὁποίας εἶναι ὁρατὸ στὸ χαμηλότερο νότιο τμῆμα τῆς Τομῆς 1,1 (ἐπίπεδο Ἄνδήρου 1), πρέπει ἀρχικῶς νὰ στήριζε ἕνα ὑπερυψωμένο κτίσμα, ποὺ ἔφτανε ἕως τὸ ὑπερκείμενο ἄνδηρο τῆς κορυφῆς καὶ ἀσφαλῶς συνδέεται μὲ τὴν ἐν μέρει λαξευμένη στὸν φυσικὸ βράχο σπηλαιώδη ρωγμὴ (ΠΙΝ. 16 a–b) στὸ ἀνατολικὸ τμῆμα τῆς Ἐγκοπῆς 2. Ἡ σπηλαιώδης ρωγμή, χωρὶς κανένα ἀκριβὲς παράλληλο στὸν χῶρο τοῦ Αἰγαίου, πιθανότατα χρησίμευε ὡς ἀποθηκευτικὸς χῶρος, ἀφοῦ περιεῖχε ἀγγεῖα καὶ ἄλλα ἀντικείμενα, κυρίως σφονδύλια.

Ἰδιαίτερο ἐνδιαφέρον παρουσιάζουν τὰ ἀποκαλυφθέντα τμήματα ὑδροσυλλεκτηρίου ἀγωγοῦ (ΠΙΝ. 20, 21, 22) : ξεκινᾶ ἀπὸ τὴν βόρεια πλευρὰ τοῦ Ἄνδήρου 1 καὶ εἶναι ἐν μέρει λαξευμένος στὸν φυσικὸ βράχο, καταλαμβάνει ὅλο σχεδὸν τὸ πλάτος τοῦ ἀνδήρου ἀπὸ Βορρᾶ πρὸς Νότον, ἐνῶ διακλαδίζεται ἐντὸς τοῦ οἰκοδομημένου χώρου καὶ ἀσφαλῶς συνεχίζεται πρὸς Νότον στὰ κατοικημένα χαμηλότερα ἄνδηρα. Τὸ δυτικὸ τμῆμα του ἦταν κτιστὸ μὲ πλάκες καλῶς προσαρμοσμένες στὸ δάπεδο καὶ στὸ νότιο τμῆμα του κατὰ μῆκος τῆς Βόρειας ὄψης τοῦ τοίχου Α. Τὰ δύο τμήματα τοῦ ἀγωγοῦ ἑνώνονται σὲ ἕνα ποὺ διέτρεχε κατὰ μῆκος τοῦ δυτικοῦ τμήματος τοῦ χώρου 2 καὶ ἦταν πλακοσκεπὲς κατὰ τόπους. Ἡ μορφὴ καὶ κυρίως ἡ θέση του στὸν ἀνεσκαμμένο χῶρο ἐντὸς καὶ ἐκτὸς τῶν δωματίων, δείχνουν ὅτι παροχέτευε τὰ ὄμβρια ὕδατα ποὺ προέρχονταν ἀπὸ τὶς στέγες τῶν κατοικιῶν, καθὼς καὶ ἀπὸ τοὺς ὑπαίθριους χώρους, τὶς αὐλές καὶ τοὺς δρόμους. Πρὸς τὸ παρὸν ὅμως, δὲν γνωρίζομε τὴν πορεία καὶ τὴν κατάληξή του.

Ἀπὸ τοὺς ἀνασκαφέντας χώρους ὁ καλύτερα διατηρημένος εἶναι τὸ περίπου ὀρθογώνιο δωμάτιο 3 (ΠΙΝ. 18 a–b καὶ 24 a–b) : ἐδῶ, ἐκτὸς ἀπὸ τὸ μονόλιθο κατώφλι στὴν νότια πλευρὰ καὶ τὸν λαξευμένο καὶ πλακοσκεπῆ ἀγωγό, (ΠΙΝ. 22 b), κατὰ μῆκος τῆς δυτικῆς πλευρᾶς καὶ κάτω ἀπὸ τὸ στρωμένο μὲ σχιστόπλακες δάπεδο, τὰ κατὰ χώραν λείψανα καὶ ἡ διαστρωμάτωση τῶν κινητῶν εὑρημάτων ἐπιτρέπουν τὴν διάκριση δύο οἰκοδομικῶν φάσεων. Γενικῶς, παρατηρήθηκε ὅτι ἡ κατασκευαστικὴ διαφορὰ στὴν τοιχοποιία τῶν τοίχων τοῦ χώρου 1 καὶ ὁρισμένων τοῦ χώρου 3, οἱ ὁποῖοι ἔχουν μικρότερο πάχος ἀπὸ τοὺς ὑπολοίπους (ΠΙΝ. 23 a) πιθανότατα χρονολογοῦνται σὲ παλαιότερη φάση ἀπὸ τὴν τελευταία φάση ζωῆς τοῦ οἰκισμοῦ. Ἡ διαπίστωση αὐτὴ εἶναι σημαντικὴ γιατὶ τὸ σχετικὰ μικρὸ ὕψος τῶν τοίχων (ἐλάχιστο 0,10 μ. καὶ μέγ. 0,65μ.) δυσχεραίνει τὴν ἀσφαλῆ διάγνωση ἐνδιάμεσων οἰκοδομικῶν φάσεων, ἐπισκευῶν ἢ νέων κατασκευῶν.

Στὴν Τομὴ 3 (ΕΙΚ. 4.24, ΠΙΝ. 26, 27, 28) ποὺ βρίσκεται χαμηλότερα καὶ νοτιοανατολικὰ τοῦ Ἄνδήρου 1, ἀποκαλύφθηκαν δύο δωμάτια ποὺ χωρίζονταν ἀπὸ ἕναν τοῖχο. Ἐκτὸς ἀπὸ τα σημαντικὰ κινητὰ εὑρήματα, ὅπως ἡ μεγάλη ποσότητα κεραμικῆς καὶ τὰ λίθινα πώματα (δωμάτιο 2) στὰ ἀνατολικὰ καὶ ὁ συγκεντρωμένος μεγάλος ἀριθμὸς μετάλλινων ἀντικειμένων (δωμάτιο 1), διεπιστώθη ὅτι, καὶ ἐδῶ, ἡ ἀρχιτεκτονικὴ μορφὴ τῶν οἰκοδομῶν ὑπαγορεύθηκε ἀπὸ τὴν μορφολογία τοῦ ἐδάφους καὶ ἀπὸ τὴν δυνατότητα ἐκμετάλλευσης τοῦ φυσικοῦ βράχου.

ΚΕΦΑΛΑΙΟ 7. Η ΚΕΡΑΜΙΚΗ

7Α. ΕΙΣΑΓΩΓΗ

Ἡ κεραμικὴ ἀπὸ τὴν Μαρκιανὴ χρονολογεῖται κυρίως στὴν Πρώιμη Ἐποχὴ τοῦ Χαλκοῦ. Ὅπως ἔχει σημειωθεῖ παραπάνω εἶναι δυνατόν, ἐπὶ τῇ βάσει στρωματογραφικῶν παρατηρήσεων, νὰ χωρισθεῖ σὲ τέσσερα διαδοχικὰ χρονικὰ διαστήματα ἢ φάσεις.

Χαρακτηριστικὴ εἶναι ἡ ἀπουσία ἱκανοῦ ἀριθμοῦ διακοσμημένων ὀστράκων, καθὼς καὶ ἐντόπιας γραπτῆς κεραμικῆς. Πολὺ ὀλίγα δείγματα εἶναι καὶ τὰ δείγματα εἰσηγμένης γραπτῆς κεραμικῆς. Ἐπιπλέον, διαπιστώθηκε ἐντόπια κεραμική, ἡ ὁποία μπορεῖ νὰ χαρακτηρισθεῖ ὡς ἐγχάρακτη. Ἡ χάραξη χρησιμοποιεῖται σὲ περιορισμένη κλίμακα, ὅπως ἐπὶ παραδείγματι σὲ μερικοὺς τύπους λαβῶν, ἐνῶ ἐμπίεστη ἢ ἔντυπη διακόσμηση ἀπαντᾶται στὴν κεραμικὴ τῆς φάσεως Μαρκιανὴ ΙΙ. Ἀξιοσημείωτη εἶναι ἡ σποραδικὴ παρουσία ἐγχάρακτων διακοσμητικῶν στοιχείων στὴν φάση IV καὶ ἡ σπανιότητα σχημάτων λεπτῆς κεραμικῆς.

7Β. ΤΑ ΜΙΓΜΑΤΑ ΤΩΝ ΠΗΛΩΝ

Ἀπὸ τὴν πετρογραφικὴ μελέτη εἶναι φανερὸ ὅτι στὶς φάσεις Ι καὶ ΙΙ περισσότερο ἀπὸ τὸ 98% τῆς κεραμικῆς ἀποτελεῖται ἀπὸ πηλούς οἱ ὁποῖοι ἐντάσσονται στὴν κατηγορία μὲ ἐγκλείσματα Μαρμάρου (Marble Ware)· στὴν φάση ΙΙΙ ὁ Γαλάζιος Σχιστόλιθος(=πατελιά, στὴν τοπικὴ διάλεκτο)

(Blue Schist) καὶ οἱ συναφεῖς πηλοὶ (ποὺ περιέχουν γλαυκοφάνη) ἀποτελοῦν τὸ 41% τοῦ συνόλου, τὸ ὁποῖο αὐξάνεται στὸ 56% στὴν φάση IV. Ἡ διαπίστωση αὐτὴ εἶναι ἕνα χρήσιμο διαγνωστικὸ κριτήριο γιὰ τὴν χρονολόγηση, τὸ ὁποῖο, τώρα ποὺ ἔχει καθορισθεῖ ἡ στρωματογραφική του ἀκολουθία εἶναι δυνατὸν νὰ χρησιμοποιηθεῖ γιὰ τὴν χρονικὴ ἔνταξη, τόσον χαρακτηριστικῶν, ὅσον καὶ μὴ διαγνωστικῶν ὀστράκων ἀπὸ τὸ σῶμα ἀγγείων ἢ διαβεβρωμένων, ὅπως τῶν ὀστράκων ποὺ προῆλθαν ἀπὸ τὴν ἐπιφανειακὴ ἔρευνα.

7C. Η ΚΕΡΑΜΙΚΗ ΤΩΝ ΦΑΣΕΩΝ I ΚΑΙ II ΚΑΙ ΣΥΝΟΠΤΙΚΗ ΠΑΡΟΥΣΙΑΣΗ ΤΗΣ ΚΕΡΑΜΙΚΗΣ ΑΠΟ ΤΗΝ ΠΕΡΙΟΧΗ ΤΟΥ ΠΡΟΜΑΧΩΝΟΣ

Ἡ κεραμικὴ τῆς φάσεως Μα I (ΕΙΚ 7.1–7.2, ΠΙΝ. 29 a–e) περιλαμβάνει σχήματα τὰ ὁποῖα οὐσιαστικὰ δὲν διαφέρουν ἀπὸ αὐτά τῆς φάσεως Γρόττας-Πηλοῦ (ΠΚ I). Τὰ κύρια σχήματα εἶναι οἱ βαθιὲς φιάλες μὲ τὸ ἀναδιπλωμένο ἢ διογκωμένο ἐσωστρεφὲς χεῖλος (rolled-rim bowls), οἱ βαθιὲς φιάλες μὲ ὁριζόντιες διάτρητες κυλινδρικὲς ἀποφύσεις (deep bowls with horizontally perforated cylindrical lugs), βαθιὲς φιάλες μὲ ἀποφύσεις ἢ χύτρες (deep bowls with lugs), διάφορες ἄλλες βαθιὲς χύτρες, κλειστὲς εὐρύστομες στάμνους (closed wide-mouthed jars) καὶ μερικὰ σπανιότερα σχήματα. Τὰ τυπολογικὰ παράλληλα αὐτῶν τῶν ἀγγείων ἐμπίπτουν ἐντὸς τῆς φάσεως Γρόττας–Πηλοῦ στὶς Κυκλάδες, ἐνῶ ἄλλα παρόμοια εἶναι γνωστὰ ἀπὸ τὴν Πρωτοελλαδικὴ I περίοδο στὴν Ἠπειρωτικὴ Ἑλλάδα καὶ ἀπὸ τὸ Kum Tepe Ib καὶ τὴν Τροία I στὸ Βορειοανατολικὸ Αἰγαῖο.

Ἡ κεραμικὴ τῆς φάσεως Μα II (ΕΙΚ. 7.3–7.10, ΠΙΝ. 29 f, 30 a–e) ἐμφανίζει μία ἀξιοσημείωτη συνέχεια μὲ αὐτὴν τῆς φάσεως Μα I, μὲ τὴν διαφορὰ ὅτι παρουσιάζονται γιὰ πρώτη φορὰ μερικὰ σχήματα τὰ ὁποῖα εἶναι δυνατὸν νὰ συσχετισθοῦν μὲ αὐτὰ τῆς 'Ομάδας Κάμπου'. Ἀνάμεσα στὰ νέα σχήματα συγκαταλέγονται πώματα ἢ τηγανόσχημα σκεύη (frying pans) μὲ ἐγχάρακτη διακόσμηση (ΕΙΚ. 7.3, ΠΙΝ. 30 a), χαρακτηριστικὸ γνώρισμα τῆς 'Ομάδος Κάμπου', τὸ μικύλλο σφαιρικὸ ἀγγεῖο μὲ τὸ εὐρὺ χεῖλος (miniature spherical vessel with wide collar)(ΠΙΝ. 30 b), οἱ βαθιὲς σφαιρικὲς πυξίδες (deep spherical vessels), οἱ κρατηρίσκοι μὲ στέλεχος (footed jars) (ΠΙΝ. 31 a) καὶ μία σειρὰ κλειστῶν εὐρυστόμων ἀγγείων μὲ ὑψηλὸ λαιμό. Ὑπάρχουν, ἐπίσης, κωνικὰ κύπελλα (conical cups) (ΠΙΝ. 30 e) καὶ μιὰ μεγάλη σειρὰ ἀπὸ τύπους φιαλῶν (bowls). Ἀπαντῶνται, ἐπίσης, ἑστίες ἢ τηγανοειδῆ ρηχὰ σκεύη (baking plates) καὶ πήλινα κοχλιάρια (clay spoons)(ΕΙΚ. 7.9, ΠΙΝ. 32 a), καθὼς καὶ οἱ φορητὲς καπελλόσχημες ἑστίες (portable hat-shaped hearths) μὲ διακόσμηση ἐμπίεστων σειρῶν ἀντιθετικῶν τριγώνων (ΕΙΚ. 7.10, ΠΙΝ. 32 b–d). Πύραυνα ἢ κρατευτὲς σὲ σχῆμα προσωπείων (mask-like braziers or supports) καὶ ἄλλα οἰκιακὰ σκεύη (ΕΙΚ. 7.10, ΠΙΝ. 32 e) ἐμφανίζονται γιὰ πρώτη φορά. Ἡ ἀντιβολὴ αὐτῶν τῶν κεραμικῶν τύπων μὲ τὰ ἕως τώρα γνωστὰ παραδείγματα τῆς ἰδίας ἐποχῆς στὶς Κυκλάδες ἐπιβεβαιώνει τὴν ἔνταξή τους στὴν 'Ομάδα Κάμπου', ἐνῶ, οἱ συγκρίσεις μὲ παράλληλα κυρίως ἀπὸ τὴν Ἠπειρωτικὴ Ἑλλάδα στηρίζουν τὴν χρονολογικὴ τοποθέτησή τους στὸ τέλος τῆς Πρωτοκυκλαδικῆς I καὶ στὴν ἀρχὴ τῆς Πρωτοκυκλαδικῆς II περιόδου.

7D. Η ΚΕΡΑΜΙΚΗ ΤΗΣ ΦΑΣΕΩΣ III

Ἡ κεραμικὴ τῆς φάσεως Μα III (ΕΙΚ. 7.13–7.15, ΠΙΝ. 33 c, d, e) προέρχεται ἀπὸ ἕνα κλειστὸ καλὰ χρονολογημένο σύνολο ἀπὸ τὸ ἐσωτερικὸ τῆς σπηλαιώδους ρωγμῆς στὸ ἀνατολικὸ τμῆμα τῆς Ἐγκοπῆς 2 ποὺ ἀνασκάφηκε στὴν Τομὴ 1, 1 καὶ 9, καὶ ἀντιπροσωπεύει μόνον ἕναν περιορισμένο ἀριθμὸ ἀγγείων. Πρόκειται γιὰ μία σειρὰ φιαλῶν (bowls) διαφόρων τύπων, μικύλλα κωνικὰ κύπελλα (conical cups), ἑστίες ἢ τηγανοειδῆ σκεύη (baking pans), βαθιὰ ἀνοικτὰ ἄωτα ἀγγεῖα (deep handless open vessels), στάμνους (jars), κρατηρίσκους (collared jars), μία πρόχου (jug) καὶ πύραυνα ἢ κρατευτὲς σὲ σχῆμα προσωπείων (mask-like braziers or supports) (ΕΙΚ. 7.13, ΠΙΝ. 34 a–f). Τώρα ἐμφανίζονται ὅλα τὰ τυπικὰ χαρακτηριστικὰ αὐτοῦ τοῦ κεραμικοῦ συνόλου : ὁ πηλὸς μὲ ἐγκλείσματα Γαλάζιου Σχιστολίθου (=πατελιᾶς) (Blue Schist ware), καὶ νέα σχήματα, ὅπως ὁ κρατηρίσκος, τὸ μικρὸ κωνικὸ κύπελλο, ἢ ἡ ταινιωτὴ κάθετη λαβὴ καὶ ἡ ὁριζόντια κυλινδρικὴ λαβὴ μὲ τὶς ἐγχαράξεις. Δὲν συναντοῦμε ὅμως, πλέον σχήματα, ὅπως, τὴν φορητὴ καπελλόσχημη ἑστία, τὶς φιάλες μὲ τὸ ἀναδιπλωμένο ἢ διογκωμένο χεῖλος οὔτε φιάλες μὲ τὶς κυλινδρικὲς ἀποφύσεις. Μολονότι ὀλίγα μόνον στοιχεῖα εἶναι συγκρίσιμα μὲ τὴν γνωστὴ διακοσμημένη λεπτὴ κεραμικὴ τῆς φάσεως Κέρου-Σύρου, ὑπάρχουν πολλὰ τυπολογικὰ παράλληλα στὸ ἀπόθεμα τῆς ἀδιακόσμητης κεραμικῆς αὐτῆς τῆς περιόδου καὶ ἡ χρονολογικὴ ἔνταξή της στὴν Πρωτοκυκλαδικὴ II περίοδο εἶναι σαφής.

7E. Η ΚΕΡΑΜΙΚΗ ΤΗΣ ΦΑΣΕΩΣ IV

Ἡ κεραμικὴ τῆς φάσεως IV (ΕΙΚ. 7.16–7.26, ΠΙΝ. 35–38) δείχνει μία ἀδιάκοπη συνέχεια μὲ αὐτὴν τῆς φάσεως Μα III, καὶ πολὺ μεγαλύτερη χρήση τῶν πηλῶν μὲ ἐγκλείσματα Γαλάζιου Σχιστόλιθου (=πατελιᾶς) (Blue Schist), καθὼς καὶ μὲ τὴν εἰσαγωγὴ νέων χαρακτηριστικῶν σχημάτων.

Στὰ νέα σχήματα αὐτῆς τῆς κεραμικῆς συγκαταλέγονται τὸ μόνωτο κύπελλο (tankard) (ΕΙΚ. 7.19, ΠΙΝ. 35 b-d) καὶ τὸ δίωτο κύπελλο, γνωστὸ ὡς *δέπας ἀμφικύπελλον* (ΕΙΚ. 7.19, ΠΙΝ. 35 a). Τὰ σχήματα τῆς κεραμικῆς αὐτῆς περιλαμβάνουν, βαθιὲς φιάλες μὲ ἢ χωρὶς ἀποφύσεις, χύτρες (ΕΙΚ. 7.17), μεγάλες ἀνοικτὲς φιάλες ἢ λεκάνες (ΕΙΚ. 7.18), μόνωτα κύπελλα (tankard), *δέπας ἀμφικύπελλον*, κωνικὰ κύπελλα (ΕΙΚ. 7.19), ἑστίες ἢ τηγανοειδῆ, (baking pans), προχυτικὰ σκεύη (spouted vessels) μεταξὺ τῶν ὁποίων *κύμβες* (sauceboats) (ΕΙΚ. 7.21), βαθιὰ εὐρύστομα ἀγγεῖα (deep wide-mouthed vessels), στάμνοι μὲ τὶς χαρακτηριστικὲς ὁριζόντιες κυλινδρικὲς λαβὲς μὲ ἐγχαράξεις (collared jars with slashed handles), κρατηρίσκοι (stemmed conical jars) (ΕΙΚ. 7.22), πίθοι, πρόχοι (jugs), σφαιρικὲς πυξίδες (deep spherical vessels), καθὼς καὶ πύραυνα ἢ κρατευτὲς σὲ σχῆμα προσωπείων (mask-like braziers or supports) (ΕΙΚ. 7.25, ΠΙΝ. 37 a-f).

Ἀξιοσημείωτη αὐτὴν τὴν περίοδο εἶναι καὶ ἡ παρουσία ἐγχάρακτων διακοσμητικῶν στοιχείων (ΕΙΚ. 7.26, ΠΙΝ. 36 f, 38 a-g). Μεταξὺ τῶν νέων σχημάτων εἶναι οἱ εὐρύστομες πρόχοι, οἱ σφαιρικὲς ἢ φακοειδεῖς πυξίδες καὶ τὰ προχυτικὰ ἀγγεῖα. Τὰ σχήματα αὐτὰ συσχετίζονται μὲ τὴν 'Ομάδα Καστριοῦ', ὅπως τὰ γνωστὰ δείγματα ἀπὸ τὴν Σύρο καὶ τὴν φάση ΙΙΙ τῆς Ἁγίας Εἰρήνης στὴν Κέα, καθὼς καὶ ἀπὸ τὴν φάση Ι στὸ Λευκαντὶ τῆς Εὔβοιας καὶ χρονολογοῦνται στὸ τέλος τῆς φάσεως Κέρου-Σύρου, στὴν ΠΚ ΙΙΙ περίοδο.

Ἡ κεραμικὴ ἀπὸ τὴν Μαρκιανὴ καλύπτει ὅλην τὴν διάρκεια τῆς Πρώιμης Ἐποχῆς τοῦ Χαλκοῦ στὴν Ἀμοργό. Ἡ ὁμοιογένεια τῶν συνόλων, ἡ ἀσφαλὴς θέση τους στὴν στρωματογραφικὴ ἀκολουθία, καθὼς καὶ ἡ ἀπόλυτη χρονολόγηση, ὅπως προσδιορίστηκε ἀπὸ τὴν ραδιοχρονολόγηση, παρέχουν νέα ἀσφαλέστερη βάση γιὰ τὴν ἀκριβέστερη χρονολόγηση στὴν Πρωτοκυκλαδικὴ περίοδο. Ἡ μελέτη αὐτὴ δίνει ἔμφαση στὴν ἰδιαιτερότητα τῆς κεραμικῆς ἀπὸ τὴν Ἀμοργὸ (μολονότι ὁ ἁπλουστευτικὸς ὅρος 'Ομάδα Ἀμοργοῦ' θὰ πρέπει πλέον νὰ ἐγκαταλειφθεῖ) καὶ παράλληλα ὑπογραμμίζει τὴν ἀνάγκη τῆς συστηματικῆς μελέτης τῆς πρωτοκυκλαδικῆς κεραμικῆς γιὰ κάθε νησί.

ΚΕΦΑΛΑΙΟ 8. ΤΑ ΜΙΚΡΑ ΕΥΡΗΜΑΤΑ

Τὰ μικροαντικείμενα, μολονότι κρύβουν καὶ μερικὲς ἐκπλήξεις, παρέχουν μία χρήσιμη εἰκόνα γιὰ τὴν μικροτεχνικὴ παραγωγὴ καὶ τὴν οἰκοτεχνία σὲ ἕναν ἀγροτικοῦ χαρακτῆρα πρωτοκυκλαδικὸ οἰκισμό. Γι' αὐτὸν τὸν λόγο παρουσιάζονται ἀρκετὰ λεπομερῶς, εἰδολογικὰ καὶ κατὰ ὑλικό.

8A. ΤΑ ΑΠΟΛΕΠΙΣΜΕΝΑ ΕΡΓΑΛΕΙΑ

Ἡ πρώτη ὕλη γιὰ τὴν κατασκευὴ ἀπολεπισμένων ἐργαλείων ἦταν σχεδὸν ἀποκλειστικὰ ὁ ὀψιδιανὸς (ΕΙΚ. 8.3, ΠΙΝ. 39 a-d). Ἡ ἐργαλειοτεχνία ἦταν κυρίως προσανατολισμένη στὴν κατασκευὴ λεπίδων. Βρέθηκαν ὀλίγα ἐργαλεῖα καὶ μόνον δύο πυρῆνες (ΠΙΝ. 39 a-b), ὁ μεγαλύτερος μήκους 3,4 ἑκατοστῶν. Οἱ λεπίδες εἶναι τοῦ γνωστοῦ τύπου μὲ παράλληλες ἀκμές, ἀπὸ τὶς ὁποῖες τὸ 85% ἔχει τριγωνικὴ τομὴ (ΠΙΝ. 39 c-d). Οἱ μεγαλύτερες λεπίδες ἔχουν μῆκος 8,4 ἑκατοστά. Δὲν βρέθηκαν θραύσματα μὲ ἰδιαίτερη προσπάθεια δευτερογενοῦς ἐπεξεργασίας ἢ δευτερογενοῦς ἀπολέπισης μὲ τὴν μέθοδο τῆς πίεσης. Ἀντιθέτως, βρέθηκαν ἀρκετὲς λεπίδες προερχόμενες ἀπὸ τὴν δευτερογενὴ ἐπεξεργασία πυρήνων καὶ τὰ ἀπολεπίσματα ἦταν ἀπορρίματα προερχόμενα ἀπὸ τὴν παραγωγὴ λεπίδων. Ὁ μικρὸς ἀριθμὸς θραυσμάτων μὲ φλοιὸ ὑποδηλώνει ὅτι τὸ ὑλικὸ εἰσαγόταν ἀπὸ τὴν Μῆλο ὑπὸ μορφὴν προχείρως διαμορφωμένων πυρήνων.

8B. ΤΑ ΛΙΘΙΝΑ ΑΓΓΕΙΑ ΚΑΙ ΑΛΛΑ ΑΝΤΙΚΕΙΜΕΝΑ

Στὰ ἀντικείμενα ἀπὸ ἐπιμελῶς λειασμένο λίθο συγκαταλέγονται οἱ πελέκεις, δακτύλιοι καὶ ψῆφοι, θραύσματα μαρμαρίνων ἀγγείων καὶ τριπτῆρες (ΕΙΚ. 8.4, ΠΙΝ. 40 a-g). Συνολικὰ βρέθηκαν ἕνας ἀκέραιος πέλεκυς ἀπὸ πρασινωπὸ λίθο, θραῦσμα καὶ ἕνας ἀκέραιος πέλεκυς ἀπὸ σμύριδα (ΠΙΝ. 42 a-b)· δύο μικρὲς διάτρητες ψῆφοι καὶ θραῦσμα ἑνὸς δακτυλίου ἀπὸ χλωρίτη λίθο (ΠΙΝ. 40 a), δύο θραύσματα ἀπὸ τὸ χεῖλος καὶ δύο ἀπὸ τὸ σῶμα μαρμαρίνων φιαλῶν (ΠΙΝ. 40 c-d), καθὼς καὶ ἕνα μαρμάρινο ἀποστρογγυλευμένο ἀντικείμενο μὲ κεντρικὴ αὐλάκωση, πιθανῶς σχηματικὸ εἰδώλιο (ΠΙΝ. 40 g, 41 c-e). Μεταξὺ τῶν λεπτότεχνων λίθινων εὑρημάτων ξεχωρίζουν ἑπτὰ κυλινδρικὰ ἢ πηνιόσχημα ἀντικείμενα ἀπὸ διαφόρους λίθους, πιθανότατα τριπτῆρες εἰδικῆς χρήσης (ΠΙΝ. 40 b, e, f, 41 a).

Στὰ χονδροειδῆ λίθινα ἀντικείμενα συμπεριλαμβάνονται τριβέες (ΕΙΚ. 8.4-8.6) καὶ μεγάλοι τριπτῆρες (ΕΙΚ. 8.7), ἰγδία (ΕΙΚ. 8.7, ΠΙΝ. 43 e), τριπτῆρες (ΕΙΚ. 8.11, ΠΙΝ. 42 e-f) καὶ σφῦρες (ΕΙΚ. 8.12, ΠΙΝ. 42 c), στροφεῖς γιὰ τὴν ὑποδοχὴ ξύλινων στηριγμάτων θύρας (ΕΙΚ. 8.8, ΠΙΝ. 43 a-b), λίθινα βάρη διαφόρων τύπων (ΕΙΚ. 8.9, ΠΙΝ. 42 d) καὶ λίθινα πώματα (ΕΙΚ. 8.13-14, ΠΙΝ. 43 c-d). Ὅλα περιγράφονται λεπτομερῶς, ἐπειδὴ συνήθως, παρόμοια βαριὰ καὶ δυσμετακίνητα ὡς ἐπὶ τὸ πλεῖστον, ἀντικείμενα παραβλέπονται σὲ ἀνασκαφικὲς ἐκθέσεις. Καὶ οἱ πέντε τριβέες κατατάσσονται στὸν τύπο τῶν σαμαρωτῶν (saddle quern type). Βρέθηκαν ἐπίσης, ἕξι μεγάλοι τριπτῆρες καὶ δύο μεγάλα καὶ βαριὰ ἰγδία καὶ τέσσερεις τριπτῆρες ἢ σφύρες. Τρία λίθινα ἀντικείμενα μὲ κοιλότητα ἑρμηνεύτηκαν ὡς στροφεῖς γιὰ τὴν στήριξη ξύλινων ἀξόνων θύρας. Ἡ πλειονότητα τῶν βαρῶν ἐντάσσεται στὸν τύπο τῶν *ἀνηρτημένων* βαρῶν. Βρέθηκαν, ἐπίσης, ἐννέα μικροὶ τριπτῆρες. Ἀξιοσημείωτα εἶναι καὶ 45 λίθινα δισκόμορφα ἀντικείμενα, τὰ περισσότερα ἀπὸ σχιστόλιθο διαμέτρου περίπου 20–35 ἑκ., τὰ ὁποῖα πιθανῶς χρησίμευαν ὡς πώματα μεγάλων πίθων.

8C. Τα Αποτυπωματα Φυλλων, Ψαθας και Υφασματος

Σημαντικά εἶναι καὶ τὰ διάφορα ἀποτυπώματα σὲ ἀρκετὲς βάσεις ἀλλὰ καὶ σὲ θραύσματα ἀπὸ τὸ σῶμα ἀγγείων, περίπου ἑβδομῆντα δύο : πολὺ καθαρὰ ἀποτυπώματα ἀπὸ φύλλα (ΠΙΝ. 48 *c–f*), πλέγματα ψάθας (ΕΙΚ. 8.17, ΠΙΝ. 44, 45 *a*, 46, 47, 48 *a–b*) καὶ ὑφασμάτων (ΕΙΚ. 8.17, ΠΙΝ. 45 *b–c*).

Σὲ δέκα περίπου βάσεις ἀναγνωρίστηκαν ἀποτυπώματα φύλλων ἀμπέλου. Τὰ ἀποτυπώματα ψάθας ἀνήκουν σὲ τρεῖς διαφορετικοὺς τύπους, οἱ ὁποῖοι ἔχουν ὡς κοινὸ χαρακτηριστικὸ τὴν τεχνικὴ τῆς συστροφῆς μὲ τὴν προσθήκη νέων στελεχῶν στὶς περισσότερες περιπτώσεις (ΕΙΚ. 8.15 καὶ 16). Βρέθηκαν, ἐπίσης, τρία ἀποτυπώματα ὑφασμάτων, τὰ ὁποῖα παρουσιάζουν ἁπλὴ παράλληλη ὕφανση, ὅπου τὰ ὑφάδια συμπλέκονται ἐναλλὰξ μὲ τὰ στημόνια.

8D. Τα Σφονδυλια και Αλλα Σχετικα Αντικειμενα

Τὰ πολυάριθμα σφονδύλια, συνολικὰ ἑκατὸν ἑβδομῆντα ἕνα (ΕΙΚ. 8.19–21, ΠΙΝ. 49 *a–b*, 50 *a–g*) καὶ τὰ τριάντα ἕνα διάτρητα ἀποστρογγυλευμένα ὄστρακα (ΕΙΚ. 8.19–21, ΠΙΝ. 49 *d–e*) παρέχουν σημαντικὴ δυνατότητα γιὰ τὴν μελέτη τῆς νηματουργίας καὶ τῆς ὑφαντικῆς τέχνης. Ἡ ἀξιοσημείωτη ἀνεύρεση τῆς πλειονότητας αὐτῶν τῶν εὑρημάτων ἐντὸς καὶ πλησίον τοῦ καμπυλόσχημου χώρου 7 στὴν Τομὴ 1,1 στὸ κατώτερο τμῆμα τῆς Ἐγκοπῆς 2, καθὼς καὶ στὸ ὑπερκείμενο ἄνδηρο τῆς κορυφῆς, πιθανῶς ὑποδεικνύει τὸν χῶρο ὅπου συντελοῦνταν οἱ σχετικὲς μὲ τὴν ὑφαντικὴ δραστηριότητες ἢ ἀποθήκη γιὰ τὴν φύλαξη αὐτῶν τῶν ἐργαλείων.

Ἡ τυπολογικὴ ποικιλία τῶν σφονδυλίων θέτει τὸ ἐρώτημα ἐὰν χρησιμοποιήθηκαν εἰδικὰ σφονδύλια γιὰ τὴν παραγωγὴ διαφορετικῶν νημάτων. Διατυπώνεται ἡ ὑπόθεση ὅτι, ἡ χρήση τοῦ λινοῦ, μολονότι ἦταν εὐρύτατα γνωστή, ἀντικαθίσταται σταδιακὰ ἀπὸ τὸ μαλλί, ἡ χρήση τοῦ ὁποίου ὡς πρώτης ὕλης φαίνεται ὅτι διαρκῶς γενικεύεται κατὰ τὴν 3ῃ π.Χ. χιλιετία. Ἡ ἀπουσία ὑφαντικῶν βαρῶν δίνει τὴν δυνατότητα διατύπωσης ὑποθέσεων γιὰ τὴν χρήση διαφορετικοῦ τύπου ἀργαλειῶν ἀντίθετα ἀπὸ τὴν ἕως τώρα ἐπικρατοῦσα ἄποψη.

Τέλος, ἕνα παραλληλεπίπεδο σχεδὸν κυβικὸ ἀντικείμενο μὲ δύο διαμπερεῖς σχεδὸν παράλληλες ὀπὲς (ΕΙΚ. 8.21, ΠΙΝ. 49 *f–h*), τὸ ὁποῖο εἶχε ἀρχικῶς θεωρηθεῖ ὑφαντικὸ βάρος, ἀποσυνδέεται ἀπὸ αὐτὴν τὴν δραστηριότητα καὶ συσχετίζεται μὲ παρόμοια ἀντικείμενα ποὺ βρέθηκαν πρόσφατα στὸν Σκάρκο τῆς Ἴου.

8E. Το Πηλινο Νηοσχημο Ομοιωμα

Ξεχωριστὸ ἐνδιαφέρον ἔχει ἕνα μοναδικὸ εὕρημα, ἕνα πήλινο νηόσχημο ἀντικείμενο ποὺ θυμίζει τὰ ὁμοιώματα πλοίων τῆς Πρώιμης Ἐποχῆς τοῦ Χαλκοῦ ἀπὸ τὸ Αἰγαῖο (ΕΙΚ. 8.22 ΠΙΝ. 51 *a–c*), διαφέρει ὅμως στὴν μορφὴ ἀπὸ τὰ μακρὰ πλοῖα, τὰ ὁποῖα ἀπεικονίζονται στὰ τηγανόσχημα σκεύη ἀπὸ τὴν Σύρο καὶ τὰ τυπολογικὰ συγγενῆ μολύβδινα ὁμοιώματα πλοίων. Ἀποτελεῖ ἕνα ἀπὸ τὰ ὀλίγα ὁμοιώματα ἢ ἀπεικονίσεις τὰ ὁποῖα βρέθηκαν στὸ οἰκισμὸ καὶ γι' αὐτὸ ἐνδεχομένως μπορεῖ νὰ τοῦ ἀποδοθεῖ συμβολικὸς χαρακτῆρας.

8F. Τα Μεταλλινα Αντικειμενα

Τὰ δεκαεπτὰ μετάλλινα ἀντικείμενα ποὺ βρέθηκαν στὴν Μαρκιανὴ ἀποτελοῦν μεγάλο ἀριθμὸ σὲ σχέση μὲ τὴν μικρὴ ἔκταση τοῦ οἰκισμοῦ ποὺ ἐρευνήθηκε. Ἀπὸ μόλυβδο εἶναι ἕνα περίαπτο, δύο σύνδεσμοι γιὰ τὴν ἐπισκευὴ πήλινων ἀγγείων καὶ δύο ἀντικείμενα ἀδιάγνωστης χρήσης (ΕΙΚ. 8.23, ΠΙΝ. 52 *a*). Οἱ μολύβδινοι σύνδεσμοι ἀποδεικνύουν ὅτι ὁ μόλυβδος μεταποιοῦνταν *κατὰ χώραν* (δηλαδὴ τὸν ἔλιωναν καὶ τὸν διαμόρφωναν).

Στὰ μπρούντζινα ἢ χάλκινα ἀντικείμενα συγκαταλέγονται ἕνα προσωπικὸ ἀντικείμενο, ἡ περόνη (ΠΙΝ. 52 *b*), διάφορα ἐργαλεῖα οἰκιακῆς χρήσεως μεταξὺ τῶν ὁποίων τρεῖς βελόνες καὶ ἕνας ὀπέας-σουβλὶ, καθὼς καὶ πέντε λεπιδόμορφα ἐλάσματα (ΕΙΚ. 8.23, ΠΙΝ. 52 *e*). Σημαντικὴ εἶναι καὶ ἡ ἀνεύρεση μίας πτέρνας ἐγχειριδίου (ΠΙΝ. 52 *f*).

Ἡ χημικὴ ἀνάλυση μὲ τὴν μέθοδο τῆς χημικῆς ἀπορρόφησης ποὺ ἔγινε στὰ ἐργαστήρια τοῦ Ἐθνικοῦ Ἀρχαιολογικοῦ Μουσείου Ἀθηνῶν ἀποδεικνύει τὴν χρήση χαλκοῦ καὶ μίγματος χαλκοῦ ἐμπλουτισμένου μὲ ἀρσενικό, καθὼς καὶ μπρούντζου γιὰ τὴν κατασκευὴ αὐτῶν τῶν ἀντικειμένων.

8G. Η Μολυβδινη Σφραγιδα και τα Πηλινα Σφραγισματα

Τὸ σημαντικότερο μετάλλινο ἀντικείμενο ἀπὸ τὴν Μαρκιανὴ εἶναι ἡ μοναδικὴ μολύβδινη σφραγίδα (ΕΙΚ. 8.24, ΠΙΝ. 53 a) ποὺ βρέθηκε στὸ δωμάτιο 2 τῆς Τομῆς 3. Εἶναι δισκόμορφη καὶ στὴν μία πλευρὰ φέρει μία ἡμικυκλικὴ θηλιὰ γιὰ ἀνάρτηση. Τὸ διακοσμητικὸ θέμα ἀποτελεῖται ἀπὸ σταυρόσχημο κόσμημα μὲ ἐνάλληλες ὀρθὲς γωνίες, καὶ εἶναι εὐρύτατα γνωστὸ στὸν χῶρο τοῦ Αἰγαίου. Ἡ χρήση ὡστόσο τοῦ μολύβδου γιὰ τὴν κατασκευὴ σφραγίδας ἀπαντᾶται στὶς Κυκλάδες μόνον στὸ νεκροταφεῖο τῶν Ἀπλωμάτων στὴν Νάξο.

Εἰδολογικὰ συγγενῆ εἶναι καὶ τὰ πήλινα σφραγίσματα (ΕΙΚ. 8.24, ΠΙΝ. 53 b–d). Βρέθηκαν τρία σφραγίσματα ἐπὶ πήλινων ἀντικειμένων, καθὼς καὶ ἕνα ὄστρακο μὲ ἐμπίεστο κόσμημα (ΠΙΝ. 53 e) προερχόμενο ἀπὸ σφραγίδα πρὶν ἀπὸ τὴν ὄπτηση.

ΚΕΦΑΛΑΙΟ 9. ΤΑ ΟΡΓΑΝΙΚΑ ΚΑΤΑΛΟΙΠΑ

9Α. Τα Οστα και τα Οστεινα Εργαλεια

Τὰ ὀστὰ (ΠΙΝ. 55–56) δὲν διατηροῦνται σὲ πολὺ καλὴ κατάσταση. Περίπου τὸ 87% εἶναι αἰγοπρόβατα καὶ πιθανότατα οἱ αἶγες ἦταν πολυπληθέστερες τῶν προβάτων, 12% χοῖροι καὶ μόνον 0.6% βοοειδῆ. Διατυπώνεται ἡ ὑπόθεση ὅτι ἡ οἰκονομία πιθανότατα εἶχε ἤδη προσανατολισθεῖ στὴν ἐκτροφὴ ζώων γιὰ τὴν παραγωγὴ μαλλιοῦ. Οἱ ἀναλυτικοὶ πίνακες μὲ τὶς μετρήσεις τῶν ὀστῶν θὰ εἶναι χρήσιμοι γιὰ συγκρίσεις, ὅταν ἀντίστοιχα σύνολα ἀπὸ τὶς Κυκλάδες μελετηθοῦν καὶ δημοσιευθοῦν.

Ἕνδεκα ὀστέινα ἀντικείμενα (ΕΙΚ. 9.1, ΠΙΝ. 54 a) βρέθηκαν μὲ ἴχνη κατεργασίας, τρία ἀπὸ τὰ ὁποῖα εἶναι ὀπεῖς-σουβλιά.

9Β. Τα Μαλακια

Ἀπὸ τὸ ἐξετασθὲν μαλακολογικὸ ὑλικὸ εἶναι φανερὸ ὅτι τὸ 93% τῶν εἰδῶν εἶναι θαλάσσα ἀπὸ βραχῶδες περιβάλλον. Πολυπληθέστερο ὅλων εἶναι οἱ πατελίδες (Patella, 87%), ἐνῶ τὰ Μονόδοντα καλύπτουν τὸ 10%. Τὸ μοναδικὸ κατεργασμένο ὄστρεο σπονδύλου, Spondylus gaederopous, ποὺ βρέθηκε (ΕΙΚ. 9.1, ΠΙΝ. 54 b), καὶ τὰ θραύσματα ὀστρέων τρίτωνος εἶναι δυνατὸν νὰ ὑποδηλώνουν συμβολικὴ χρήση.

9C. Οι Απανθρακωμενοι Σποροι

Οἱ ἀπανθρακωμένοι σπόροι (ΠΙΝ. 54 c–e) ποὺ βρέθηκαν εἶναι ὀλίγοι σὲ ἀριθμὸ καὶ μολονότι ὅτι ἔγινε ὑδροκοσκίνισμα σὲ ἱκανὸ ἀριθμὸ δειγμάτων, μόνον τρία περιεῖχαν σπόρους. Μεταξὺ αὐτῶν ἀπαντῶνται ἡ ἐλαία, Olea europea, ὁ πικρὸς βίκος, Vicia ervilia καὶ ὁ μικρὸς ἀρακὰς (=κατσούνι;), Lathyrus clymenum μαρτυρεῖται σὲ αὐτά. Σὲ πήλινο ἀντικείμενο βρέθηκε ἕνα μόνον ἀποτύπωμα σπόρου κριθαριοῦ.

ΚΕΦΑΛΑΙΟ 10. ΓΕΝΙΚΕΣ ΠΑΡΑΤΗΡΗΣΕΙΣ

10Α. Η Μαρκιανη και οι Κυκλαδες

Παρὰ τὴν περιορισμένης κλίμακος ἀνασκαφικὴ ἔρευνα συνάγονται εὐάριθμα σημαντικὰ συμπεράσματα. Ἄλλωστε, η Μαρκιανὴ εἶναι ὁ πρῶτος οἰκισμὸς τῆς Πρώιμης Ἐποχῆς τοῦ Χαλκοῦ στὶς Κυκλάδες ὁ ὁποῖος δημοσιεύεται συστηματικά. Ἐκτὸς ἀπὸ τὴν διαπίστωση ὅτι ὁ οἰκισμὸς ἦταν ἐξ ἀρχῆς τεχνητὰ ὀχυρωμένος, τὰ κινητὰ εὑρήματα, ὅπως καὶ ἀπὸ τὸν σημαντικὸ οἰκισμὸ τοῦ Σκάρκου στὴν Ἴο, δίδουν μία εἰκόνα τοῦ ὑλικοῦ πολιτισμοῦ τελείως διαφορετικὴ ἀπὸ ἐκείνη ποὺ παρέχουν τὰ ἕως τώρα γνωστὰ σύνολα τῶν πολιτισμῶν Γρόττας-Πηλοῦ καὶ Κέρου-Σύρου, τὰ ὁποῖα προέρχονται ἀπὸ τάφους.

Ἡ ἀκολουθία τῶν φάσεων κατοίκησης στὴν Μαρκιανὴ εἶναι σαφής. Ἡ παλαιότερη ἐγκατάσταση κατὰ τὴν διάρκεια τοῦ πολιτισμοῦ Γρόττας-Πηλοῦ (Πρωτοκυκλαδικὴ Ι) ἦταν ἕνας ταπεινός, περιορισμένης ἔκτασης οἰκισμὸς προστατευόμενος ἐξ ἀρχῆς ἀπὸ ὀχυρωτικὸ τοῖχο. Κατὰ τὴν δεύτερη φάση τῆς κατοίκησης, Μαρκιανὴ ΙΙ, σύγχρονη μὲ τὴν 'Ομάδα Κάμπου' διαπιστώθηκε μικρὴ ἐπέκταση τοῦ οἰκιστικοῦ πυρήνα. Στὴν διάρκεια τῆς φάσεως ΙΙΙ, στὰ χρόνια τοῦ πολιτισμοῦ Κέρου-Σύρου (Πρωτοκυκλαδικὴ ΙΙ) σημειώνεται σημαντικὴ ἐπέκταση, καὶ σύμφωνα μὲ τὴν μαρτυρία τῆς κεραμικῆς ἀπὸ τὸν Βόρειο Προμαχώνα, πιθανότατα ἐνισχύεται ὁ ὀχυρωτικὸς τοῖχος μὲ τὴν προσθήκη τοῦ προμαχῶνος. Σὲ αὐτὴν τὴν περίοδο ἀνάγεται καὶ ἡ κατασκευὴ τῶν οἰκοδομημάτων ποὺ ἀποκαλύφθηκαν στὸ Ἄνδηρο 1, καθὼς καὶ τοῦ διμεροῦς κτίσματος στὰ νοτιοανατολικά, στὴν Τομὴ 3. Ἡ φάση ΙV στὴν Μαρκιανὴ ἀποτελεῖ τὴν τελευταία φάση ζωῆς καὶ ἐγκατάλειψης τοῦ οἰκισμοῦ κατὰ τὴν Πρώιμη Ἐποχὴ τοῦ Χαλκοῦ καὶ κύριο χαρακτηριστικὸ της εἶναι ἡ παρουσία κεραμικῆς τῆς Ὁμάδας Καστριοῦ'. Μὲ τὴν βοήθεια τῶν προσδιορισμῶν τῆς ραδιοχρονολόγησης οἱ ἀρχαιολογικὰ διαπιστωθεῖσες φάσεις χρονολογοῦνται πλέον ἀσφαλῶς καὶ καλύπτουν μία χρονικὴ περίοδο ἀπὸ τὸ 3200 π.Χ. ἕως περίπου τὸ 2200 π.Χ.

Βασικὸ προϊὸν γιὰ τὴν ἐπιβίωση τῶν κατοίκων ἦταν πιθανότατα τὰ δημητριακά, κυρίως ἡ καλλιέργεια κριθαριοῦ (κριθῆς), ἡ ὁποία ἐνισχυόταν συμπληρωματικὰ ἀπὸ τὴν καλλιέργεια τῆς ἐλιᾶς καὶ τῆς ἀμπέλου, καθὼς καὶ ἡ ἐκτροφὴ ζώων, κυρίως αἰγοπροβάτων καὶ χοίρων. Τὰ αἰγοπρόβατα ὑπερτεροῦν μεταξὺ τῶν ἄλλων ζώων, ἐνῶ ὁ μέσος ὅρος τῆς ἡλικίας τῶν αἰγοπροβάτων ὑποδηλώνει ὅτι τὰ ἐξέτρεφαν γιὰ νὰ προσπορίζονται μαλλί.

Σημαντικὲς ἐνδείξεις γιὰ τὴν ποικιλία τῶν δραστηριοτήτων τῶν κατοίκων τοῦ ἀγροτικοῦ οἰκισμοῦ παρέχουν τὰ διάφορα τέχνεργα, ὅπως τὰ ἀπολεπισμένα λίθινα ἐργαλεῖα ἀπὸ ὀψιανό, τὰ λειασμένα ἐργαλεῖα, γιὰ τὴν κατεργασία τοῦ λίθου, τὰ ὀστέινα καὶ τὰ μετάλλινα ἐργαλεῖα, γιὰ τὴν κατεργασία τῶν ὀστῶν καὶ τοῦ ξύλου καὶ τὴν ἐπεξεργασία τῶν δερμάτων, καθὼς καὶ τὰ δείγματα πολυάριθμων σφονδυλίων γιὰ τὴν νηματουργία καὶ τὴν ὑφαντικὴ παραγωγή. Ἱκανὲς εἶναι καὶ οἱ μαρτυρίες γιὰ τὴν κατασκευὴ ψάθας καὶ γιὰ τὴν καλαθοπλεκτική, καθὼς καὶ γιὰ τὴν ἐντόπια παραγωγὴ κεραμικῆς καὶ τὴν γνώση τῆς μεταλλοτεχνίας, μολονότι μόνον ἡ ἐπιτόπου κατεργασία τοῦ μολύβδου διαπιστώθηκε ἄμεσα στὸν οἰκισμό.

Τὸ ἐμπόριο μὲ τὰ νησιὰ πιστοποιεῖται ποικιλοτρόπως, κυρίως μὲ τὴν εἰσαγωγὴ ὀψιανοῦ ἀπὸ τὴν Μῆλο, καὶ ἀπὸ τὰ ὀλίγα εἰσηγμένα πήλινα ἀντικείμενα, καὶ σαφῶς ὑπονοεῖται ἀπὸ τὸ εὕρημα τοῦ πήλινου νηόσχημου ἀντικειμένου. Ἐρωτήματα σχετικὰ μὲ τὴν κοινωνικὴ ὀργάνωση μποροῦν νὰ προσεγγισθοῦν ἐπὶ τῇ βάσει ὁρισμένων ἐνδείξεων καὶ συγκεκριμένων μαρτυριῶν, ὅπως ἡ μολύβδινη σφραγίδα καὶ τὰ πήλινα σφραγίσματα. Παρόμοια ἀντικείμενα θὰ περίμενε κανεὶς νὰ βρεθοῦν σὲ μεγαλύτερο οἰκισμό, ποὺ θὰ μποροῦσε νὰ ἦταν ἕνα εἶδος οἰκονομικοῦ κέντρου· γι'αὐτὸ καὶ ἡ παρουσία τους σὲ ἕναν σχετικὰ μικρότερο οἰκισμό, ποὺ πιθανῶς δὲν εἶχε ἀνάλογο ρόλο, ἔχει ἰδιαίτερο ἐνδιαφέρον.

10Β. Η Αρχαιολογια των Οικισμων στην Αμοργο

Ἡ ἔρευνα στὴν Μαρκιανὴ συμβάλλει ἐν μέρει καὶ στὴν ἀνασύνθεση τῆς ἄγνωστης εἰκόνας τῆς *ἀρχαιολογίας τῶν οἰκισμῶν* στὴν Ἀμοργό. Ἔτσι, ἐπειδὴ οἱ πανάρχαιες συνθῆκες ζωῆς καὶ ὁ πατροπαράδοτος τρόπος καλλιέργειας μόλις πρόσφατα ἄρχισαν νὰ ἀλλάζουν στὴν Ἀμοργό, ὁρισμένοι συσχετισμοί, ἂν καὶ ἀναχρονιστικοὶ παρέχουν ἔμμεσες, ἀλλὰ πολύμορφες πληροφορίες. Εἶναι ἀξιοσημείωτο ὅτι στὸ νησὶ διατηροῦνται ἀκόμα κατὰ τόπους ζωντανὲς οἱ *κατοικιές*, αὐτόνομες ἀγροτοποιμενικὲς μονάδες, συνήθως σὲ μεσόγειες βραχώδεις θέσεις, προστατευμένες ἀπὸ τοὺς ἀνέμους, πάντοτε πλησίον ἀγρῶν καὶ βοσκοτόπων, καὶ μὲ πρόσβαση καὶ ὀπτικὴ ἐπαφὴ μὲ τὴν θάλασσα. Ἡ λαϊκὴ ρήση: «*σπίτιν ὅσον νὰ χωρεῖς, χωράφιν ὅσον νὰ θωρεῖς*», ἀντικατοπτρίζει τὴν μόνιμη ἔγνοια τῶν νησιωτῶν ἀπὸ τὰ ἀρχαῖα ἕως τὰ νεώτερα χρόνια, γιὰ ἐξοικονόμιση σπόριμης γῆς, καὶ αἰτιολογεῖ τὶς μικρῶν διαστάσεων κατοικιές. Τῷ ὄντι, ὁ πρωτοκυκλαδικὸς οἰκισμὸς τῆς Μαρκιανῆς ἔχει συγγενὲς παράλληλο στὴν φυσικὴ ἀκρόπολη τοῦ *Κάστελλα* στὴν περιφέρεια τῆς Κάτω Μεριᾶς· ἐδῶ, εἶναι ἐπιφανειακῶς ὁρατὰ οἰκοδομικὰ λείψανα τῆς Πρώιμης Ἐποχῆς τοῦ Χαλκοῦ, τόσον στὸ ἐπίπεδο ἄνδηρο τῆς κορυφῆς, κάτω καὶ γύρω ἀπὸ τὴν νεώτερη κατοικιὰ καὶ τὶς μάντρες, ὅσον καὶ στὴν βραχώδη νότια κλιτύ.

Τυπικὸ χαρακτηριστικὸ τῶν ΠΚ οἰκισμῶν εἶναι ἡ προσαρμογὴ τῶν κτιστῶν κατασκευῶν στὸ ἀνάγλυφο τοῦ ἐδάφους, καθὼς καὶ ἡ ἐκμετάλλευση τοῦ ριζιμιοῦ βράχου. Στοὺς τοίχους χρησιμοποιοῦν λίθους πλακοειδεῖς, μικροῦ ἢ μεσαίου μεγέθους, ἀκανόνιστου σχήματος, ἀπὸ δολομίτη (ἀσβεστόλιθο) ἢ σχίστη, ἀνάλογα μὲ τὸ εἶδος τῶν πετρωμάτων ποὺ βρίσκονται σὲ ἄμεση γειτνίαση· εἶναι προσεκτικὰ κτισμένοι, συχνὰ μὲ λιγοστὸ χῶμα ὡς συνδετικὸ ὑλικό, καὶ λίθους μικρῶν διαστάσεων στὰ κενά. Συνήθως ὁ φυσικὸς βράχος ἀποτελεῖ τὸ σταθερὸ θεμέλιο τῶν τοίχων, ἀλλὰ χρησιμοποιεῖται καὶ ὡς δομικὸ ὑλικό, ἄλλοτε ἁπλῶς ἐνσωματωμένος καὶ ἄλλοτε ἐπιμελῶς λαξευμένος. Λίθους σκληρούς, μεγάλων διαστάσεων χρησιμοποιοῦν στὶς γωνίες, στὰ κατώφλια καὶ στὰ ἀνώφλια. Στὰ δάπεδα, ἐκτὸς ἀπὸ τὸν ἐξομαλυνμένο, ἐλαφρὰ λαξευμένο ριζιμιὸ βράχο, μεταχειρίζονται καὶ πατημένο χῶμα, καθὼς καὶ πλάκες προσεκτικὰ τοποθετημένες ὅπως σὲ αὐλὲς καὶ διαδρόμους. Γιὰ τὶς στέγες χρησιμοποιοῦν ἐπιμήκεις λίθους σὰν πετροδόκαρα ἢ ξύλινα δοκάρια, πλάκες λεπτὲς ἀπὸ σχίστη καὶ στεγανὸ *δωματόχωμα*. Τεχνητοὶ ὀχυρωτικοὶ τοῖχοι κατασκευάζονται μόνο στὶς πλαγιὲς τῶν λόφων, προσπελάσιμες ἀπὸ τὴν ἐνδοχώρα, καὶ σύμφωνα μὲ πολλὲς ἐνδείξεις ἀπέβλεπαν κυρίως στὴν προστασία τοῦ οἰκισμοῦ καὶ τῶν λιγοστῶν καλλιεργήσιμων ἀγρῶν ἀπὸ τοὺς γείτονες, καὶ ὄχι ἀπὸ πιθανοὺς ἐξωτερικούς, ἀπὸ θαλάσσης ἐχθρούς.

Ἡ ἔλλειψη βασικῶν στοιχείων, ὅπως ἡ χαρτογράφηση καὶ ἡ τοπογράφηση ὅλων τῶν οἰκιστικῶν μονάδων, ἡ συνεξέταση τῶν γεωλογικῶν δεδομένων, τῶν χερσαίων καὶ θαλασσίων δρόμων ἐπικοινωνίας, τῆς ἀκτογραμμῆς καὶ τῶν εὐλίμενων ὅρμων, καθὼς καὶ τῶν ἀνέμων καὶ τῶν θαλασσίων ρευμάτων, ὄχι μόνον δυσχεραίνει σημαντικὰ τὴν προσέγγιση ἤ τὴν ὀρθότερη κατανόηση τῆς Πρωτοκυκλαδικῆς τοπογραφίας καὶ τῆς ἀρχαιολογίας τῶν οἰκισμῶν, ἀλλὰ ὁδηγεῖ καὶ σὲ θεωρητικοῦ χαρακτῆρα συμπεράσματα, συχνὰ ἐπισφαλῆ καὶ συνεχῶς μεταβαλλόμενα. Ἡ παροῦσα πρώτη δημοσίευση τῶν ἀποτελεσμάτων τῆς βραχυχρόνιας καὶ περιορισμένης ἐκτάσεως διεπιστημονικῆς ἔρευνας στὸν Πρωτοκυκλαδικὸ οἰκισμὸ τῆς Μαρκιανῆς, ἐλπίζεται ὅτι θὰ συμβάλει στὴν ἐν μέρει *ἀναπλήρωση πολλῶν ἐλλειπόντων.* Ἀπομένει, φυσικά, ἀκόμα πολλὰ νὰ μάθομε καὶ κυρίως ἀπαιτεῖται μακροχρόνια συστηματικὴ ἔρευνα.

Bibliography

ABBREVIATIONS

AA	*Archäologischer Anzeiger*
AAA	*Athens Annals of Archaeology / Αρχαιολογικά Ανάλεκτα εξ Αθηνών*
Aegeaum	Annales d'archéologies égéenne de l'Université de Liège et University of Texas Program in Aegean Scripts and Prehistory (PASP)
AJA	*American Journal of Archaeology*
AM	*Mitteilungen des Deutschen Archäologischen Instituts (Athenische Abteilung)*
AR	*Archaeological Reports*
ArchDelt	*Αρχαιολογικόν Δελτίον*
ArchEph	*Αρχαιολογική Εφημερίς*
BAR-IS	British Archaeological Reports — International Series
BCH	*Bulletin de correspondance hellénique*
BICS	*Bulletin of the Institute of Classical Studies*
BSA	*Annual of the British School at Athens*
CMS	*Corpus der minoischen und mykenischen Siegel.* Berlin 1964–2000; Mainz 2002–
JHS	*Journal of Hellenic Studies*
OJA	*Oxford Journal of Archaeology*
PAE	*Πρακτικά της εν Αθήναις Αρχαιολογικής Εταιρείας*
SIMA	Studies in Mediterranean Archaeology

SHORT TITLES

Apographi Georgiki, 1911–1960. (Recensement agricole) Γεωργική Απογραφή 1911, Ετήσια γεωργική στατιστική της Ελλάδος 1926–1930, Γεωργική και Κτηνοτροφική απογραφή της Ελλάδος 1931–1936, Γεωργική και Κτηνοτροφική στατιστική της Ελλάδος 1937–1938, Γεωργική παραγωγή της Ελλάδος 1950–1960. Athens, Ministry of National Economy.

CMS I	A. Sakellariou, *Die minoischen und mykenischen Siegel des Nationalmuseums in Athen.* Berlin 1964.
CMS I Suppl.	J. A. Sakellarakis, *Athen. Nationalmuseum.* Berlin 1982.
CMS II.1	N. Platon, *Iraklion Archäologisches Museum. Die Siegel der Vorpalastzeit.* Berlin 1969.
CMS II.3	N. Platon and I. Pini, *Iraklion Archäologisches Museum. Die Siegel der Neupalastzeit.* Berlin 1984.
CMS II.5	I. Pini, *Iraklion Archäologisches Museum. Die Siegelabdrücke von Phaistos.* Berlin 1970.
CMS IV	J. A. Sakellarakis and V. E. G. Kenna, 1969. *Iraklion Archäologisches Museum. Sammlung Metaxas.* Berlin 1969.
CMS V	I. Pini *et al., Kleinere griechische Sammlungen.* Berlin 1975.
CMS V Suppl. 1B	I. Pini *et al., Kleinere griechische Sammlungen. Lamia — Zakynthos und weitere Länder des Ostmittelmeerraums.* Berlin 1993.
CMS V Suppl. 3	I. Pini *et al., Neufunde aus Griechenland und der westliche Turkei.* Mainz 2004.
CMS VIII	V. E. G. Kenna, *Die englischen Privatsammlungen.* Berlin 1966.
CMS X	J. H. Betts, *Die schweizer Sammlungen.* Berlin 1980.
CMS XI	I Pini *et al., Kleinere europäische Sammlungen.* Berlin 1988.
CMS XII	V. E. G. Kenna, *Nordamerika* I. *New York: The Metropolitan Museum of Art.* Berlin 1972.

REFERENCES

Agouridis, C., 1997. 'Sea routes and navigation in the third millennium Aegean', *OJA* 16: 1–24.

Aitchison, T., B. Ottaway and A. S. Al-Ruzaiza, 1991. 'Summarizing a group of ^{14}C dates on the historical time scale: with a worked example from the late Neolithic of Bavaria', *Antiquity* 65: 108–16.

Akurgal, E., 1950. Bayrakli Kasizi ön Rapor: Bayrakli, erster vorlaeufiger Bericht über die Ausgrabungen in Alt-Smyrna. Sonderabdruck aus der *Zeitschrift der Philosophischen Facultaet der Universitaet Ankara*, Band VIII Nr. 1. März 1950. Ankara.

Albenhoven, F., 1854. *Itinéraire descriptif de l'Attique et du Peloponnèse.* Athens.

Alexiou, S., 1960. 'New light on Minoan dating: early Minoan tombs at Lebena', *Illustrated London News*, August 6th: 225–7.

Alp, S., 1968. *Zylinder- und Stempelsiegel aus Karahöyük bei Konya.* Ankara.

Amandry, P., 1984. 'Os et coquilles', in *L'Antre Corycien II. BCH* Suppl. 9: 347–80. Athens.

Amberger, K.-P., 1979. 'Neue Tierknochenfunde aus der Magula Pevkakia in Thessalien, II. Die Wierderkäuer' (unpublished PhD thesis, University of Munich).

Åström, P. and D. S. Reese, 1990. 'Triton shells in East Mediterranean cults', *Journal of Prehistoric Religion* 3–4: 5–14.

Atkinson, T. D., R. C. Bosanquet, C. C. Edgar, A. J. Evans, D. G. Hogarth, D. Mackenzie, C. Smith and F. B. Welch, 1904. *Excavations at Phylakopi in Melos.* Society for the Promotion of Hellenic Studies, Supplementary Paper 4. London.

Banks, E. C., 1967. 'The Early and Middle Helladic small objects from Lerna' (unpublished PhD thesis, University of Cincinnati).

Barber, E. J. W., 1991. *Prehistoric Textiles. The Development of Cloth in the Neolithic and Bronze Ages.* Princeton.

Barber, R. L. N. and J. A. MacGillivray, 1980. 'The Early Cycladic period: matters of definition and terminology', *AJA* 84: 141–57.

Basch, L., 1991, 'Carènnes égéennes à l' âge du Bronze', in R. Laffineur and L. Basch (eds.), *Thalassa. L'Égée préhistorique et la mer.* Aegaeum 7: 43–54. Liège.

Bate, D. M. A., 1936. 'Animal remains, fish etc.', in W. Lamb, *Excavations at Thermi in Lesbos*: 216. Cambridge.

Becker, C., 1986. *Kastanas. Ausgrabungen in einem Siedlungshügel der Bronze- und Eisenzeit Makedoniens 1975–1979. Die Tierknochenfunde.* Prähistorische Archäologie in Südosteuropa 5. Berlin.

——, 1991. 'Die Tierknochenfunde von der Platia Magoula Zarkou. Neue Untersuchungen zu Haustierhaltung, Jagd und Rohstoffverwendung im neolithisch-bronzezeitlichen Thessalien', *Prähistorische Zeitschrift* 66: 14–78.

Behrensmeyer, A. K., K. D. Gordon and G. T Yanagi, 1986. 'Trampling as cause of bone surface damage and pseudo-cutmarks', *Nature* 319: 768–70.

Belmont, J. S. and C. Renfrew, 1964. 'Two prehistoric sites on Mykonos', *AJA* 68: 395–400.

Bent, J. T., 1884. 'Researches among the Cyclades', *JHS* 5: 42–58.

Bernabò Brea, L., 1964. *Poliochni: Città preistorica nell'insola di Lemnos*, vol. I. Rome.

——, 1976. *Poliochni: Città preistorica nell'insola di Lemnos*, vol. II. Rome.

Binford, L. R., 1981. *Bones: Ancient Men and Modern Myths.* London and New York.

——, 1984. *Faunal Remains from Klasies River Mouth.* London and New York.

Blegen, C. W., 1921. *Korakou: A Prehistoric Settlement near Corinth.* Boston and New York.

——, 1928. *Zygouries: A Prehistoric Settlement in the Valley of Cleonae.* Cambridge, MA.

——, 1931. 'Gonia', *Metropolitan Museum Studies* 3: 55–80.

——, J. L. Caskey, M. Rawson and J. Sperling, 1950. *Troy I. General Introduction. The First and Second Settlements.* Princeton.

——, J. L. Caskey, M. Rawson and J. Sperling, 1951. *Troy II. The Third, Fourth and Fifth Settlements.* Princeton.

Boessneck, J., 1962. 'Die Tierreste aus der Argissa-Magula vom präkeramischen Neolithikum bis zur mittleren Bronzezeit', in V. Milojčić, J. Boessneck and M. Hopf, *Die deutschen Ausgrabungen auf der Argissa-Magula in Thessalien I, Das präkeramische Neolithikum sowie die Tier- und Pflanzenreste.* Beiträge zur ur-und frühgeschichtlichen Archäologie des Mittelmeer-Kulturraumes 2: 27–99. Bonn.

——, H. H. Muller and T. M. Teichert, 1964. 'Osteologische Unterscheidungsmerkmale zwischen Schaf (*Ovies aries Linné*) und Ziege (*Capra hircus*)', *Kühn-Archiv* 78: 1–129.

Bökönyi, S., 1976. 'The vertebrate fauna from Anza', in M. Gimbutas, *Neolithic Macedonia as reflected by Excavation at Anza, Southeast Yugoslavia*: 313–63. Los Angeles.

Bosanquet, R. C. and F. B. Welsh, 1904. 'The obsidian trade', in T. D. Atkinson, R. C. Bosanquet, C. C. Edgar, A. J. Evans, D. G. Hogarth, D. Mackenzie, C. Smith and F. B. Welch, 1904. *Excavations at Phylakopi in Melos.* Society for the Promotion of Hellenic Studies, Supplementary Paper 4: 216–33. London.

Bossert, E. M., 1954. 'Zur Datierung der Gräber von Arkesine auf Amorgos', in W. Kimming (ed.), *Festschrift für Peter Goessler*: 23–34. Stuttgart.

——, 1960. 'Die gestempelten Verzierungen auf frühbrozezeitlichen Gefässen der Ägäis', *Jahrbuch des Deutschen Archäologischen Instituts* 75: 1–16.

——, 1967. 'Kastri auf Syros. Vorbericht ueber eine Untersuchung der praehistorischen Siedlung', *ArchDelt* 22 (Meletai): 53–76.

Brain, C. K., 1981. *The Hunters or the Hunted? An Introduction to African Cave Taphonomy.* Chicago.

Branigan, K., 1974. *Aegean Metalwork of the Early and Middle Bronze Ages.* Oxford.

Brewer, D. J. and R. F. Friedman, 1989. *Fish and Fishing in Ancient Egypt, The Natural History of Egypt II*: 30–46. Warminster.

Bronk Ramsey, C., 1995. 'Radiocarbon calibration and analysis of stratigraphy: the OxCal Program', in G. T. Cook, D. D. Harkness, B. F. Miles and E. M. Scott (eds.), *Proceedings of the 15th International 14C Conference, Radiocarbon* 37.2: 425–30.

——, P. B. Pettitt, R. E. M. Hedges, G. W. L. Hodgins and D. C. Owen, 2000a. 'Radiocarbon dates from the Oxford AMS system: *Archaeometry* datelist 29', *Archaeometry* 42: 243–54.

——, P. B. Pettitt, R. E. M. Hedges, G. W. L. Hodgins and D. C. Owen, 2000b. 'Radiocarbon dates from the Oxford AMS system: *Archaeometry* datelist 30', *Archaeometry* 42: 459–79.

Broodbank, C., 1989. 'The longboat and society in the Cyclades in the Keros-Syros culture', *AJA* 93: 319–37.

——, 2000a. 'Perspectives on an Early Bronze Age island centre: an analysis of pottery from Daskaleio-Kavos (Keros) in the Cyclades', *OJA* 19: 323–42.

——, 2000b. *An Island Archaeology of the Early Cyclades*. Cambridge.

Cambitoglou, A., 1991. *Ζαγορά Άνδρου. Αρχαιολογικός οδηγός.*

Camps-Fabrer, H., 1979. 'Principes d'une classification de l'industrie osseuse Néolithique et l'âge des Métaux dans le Midi Mediterranéen', in H. Camps-Fabrer (ed.), *L'industrie en os et bois de cervidé durant le Néolithique et l'âge des Métaux*:17–26. Paris.

—— and D. Stordeur, 1979. 'Orientation et définition des differentes parties d'un objet en os', in H. Camps-Fabrer (ed.), *L'industrie en os et bois de cervidé durant le Néolithique et l'âge des Métaux*: 9–15. Paris.

Carington Smith, J., 1975. 'Spinning, weaving and textile manufacture in prehistoric Greece from the Neolithic to the Late Bronze Age (Unpublished PhD thesis, University of Tasmania).

——, 1977, 'Appendix 2: cloth and mat impressions', in J. E. Coleman, *Keos I. Kephala. A Late Neolithic Settlement and Cemetery*: 114–27. Princeton.

Caskey, J. L., 1956. 'Excavations at Lerna, 1955', *Hesperia* 25: 147–73.

——, 1966. 'Excavations in Keos, 1964–1965', *Hesperia* 35, 363–376.

——, 1968. 'Lerna in the Early Bronze Age', *AJA* 72: 313–16.

——, 1971. 'Investigations in Keos. Part I: excavations and explorations, 1966–1970', *Hesperia* 40: 359–96.

——, 1972. 'Investigations in Keos. Part II: a conspectus of the pottery', *Hesperia* 41: 357–401.

—— and E. G. Caskey, 1960. 'The earliest settlements at Eutresis: supplementary excavations, 1958', *Hesperia* 29: 126–67.

Caskey, M., 1990. 'Thoughts on Early Bronze Age hearths', in R. Hägg and G. C. Nordquist (eds.), *Celebrations of Death and Divinity in the Bronze Age Argolid*: 13–21. Stockholm.

Catling, H. W., 1987. 'Archaeology in Greece, 1986–87', *AR* 33: 3–61.

——, 1988. 'Archaeology in Greece, 1987–88', *AR* 34: 3–85.

——, 1989. 'Archaeology in Greece, 1988–89', *AR* 35: 3–116.

Cherry, J. F., J. L. Davis, A. Demitrack, E. Mantzourani, T. F. Strasser and L. E. Talalay, 1988. 'Archaeological survey in an artifact rich landscape: a Middle Neolithic example from Nemea, Greece', *AJA* 92: 159–76.

——, J. L Davis and E. Mantzourani, 1991. *Landscape Archaeology as Long-Term History: Northern Keos in the Cycladic Islands, from the Earliest Settlement until Modern Times*. Monumenta Archaeologica 16. Los Angeles.

—— and R. Torrence, 1984. 'The typology and chronology of chipped stone assemblages in the prehistoric Cyclades', in J. A. MacGillivray and R. L. N. Barber (eds.), *The Prehistoric Cyclades. Contributions to a Workshop on Cycladic Chronology*: 12–25. Edinburgh.

Chevallier, H., B. Detournay, S. Dupré, R. Jullien, J.-P. Olivier, M. Séfériadès and R. Treuil, 1975. *Fouilles exécutés à Mallia: sondages au Sud-Ouest du Palais (1968)*. Études Crétoises 20. Paris.

Coldstream, J. N. and G. L. Huxley (eds.), 1972. *Kythera. Excavations and Studies*. London.

Coleman, J. E., 1977. *Keos I. Kephala. A Late Neolithic Settlement and Cemetery*. Princeton.

——, 1985. '"Frying pans" of the Early Bronze Age Aegean', *AJA* 89: 191–219.

Cosmopoulos, M., 1986. 'The Early Bronze Age II period in the Aegean: metallurgy, pottery, foreign connections' (MA thesis, Washington University in St. Louis).

——, 1991. *The Early Bronze 2 in the Aegean*. SIMA 97. Jonsered.

Coy, J. P., 1973. 'Bronze Age domestic animals from Keos, Greece', in J. Matolcsi, *Domestikationsforschung und Geschichte der Hausetiere*: 239–243. Budapest.

Cummer, W. W. and E. Schofield, 1984. *Keos III: Ayia Irini: House A*. Mainz.

Dalongeville, R. and J. Renault-Miskovsky, 1993. 'Paysages passés et actuels de l'île de Naxos', in R. Dalongeville and G. Rougemont (eds.), *Recherches dans les Cyclades: Résultats des travaux de la RCP 583*. Collection de la Maison de l' Orient Méditerranéen 23: 9–57. Lyons.

Davaras, C., 1971. 'Πρωτομινωικόν νεκροταφείον Αγίας Φωτιάς Σητείας', *AAA* 4: 392–7.

——, 1972. 'Κρήτη: Αγία Φωτιά Σητείας', *ArchDelt* 27, B2 (Chronika): 648–50.

——, 1982. *Haghios Nikolaos Museum*. Athens.

——, 1984. 'Μινωικό κηριοφόρο πλοιάριο της Συλλογής Μητσοτάκη', *ArchEph* 123: 55–95.

Davis, J. L., 1992. 'Review of Aegean prehistory I: the islands of the Aegean', *AJA* 96: 699–756.

Davis, S. J. M., 1987. *The Archaeology of Animals*. London.

Dawkins, R. M., 1904. 'Excavations at Palaikastro III', *BSA* 10: 192–226.

De Heldreich, T., 1878. *La faune de la Grèce*. Paris.

Delamarre, J., 1908. 'Inscriptiones Amorgi et insularum vicinarum', *Inscriptiones Graecae XII.7*. Berlin.

Demakopoulou, E., 1991. 'Diet', in L. Marangou (ed.), *Κυκλαδικός Πολιτισμός. Η Νάξος στην 3η π.Χ. χιλιετία*: 70. Athens.

Demangel R., 1926. *Le Tumulus dit de Protesilas*. Paris.

Demetropoulos, A., 1989a. 'Κατάλογος των πουλιών της Σύρας', *Syriana Grammata* 7: 185–92.

——, 1989b. 'Αρπακτικά πουλιά στη Σύρα', *Syriana Grammata* 7: 193–6.

——, 1993. 'Τα θαλασσοπούλια στις Κυκλάδες', *Syriana Grammata* 23–24: 147–86.

Deshayes, J., 1960. *Les outils de bronze de l'Indus au Danube (IVe–II Millénaire)*. Institut Français d'Archéologie de Beyrouth, Bibliothèque Archéologique et Historique LXXI. Paris.

Desse, J., 1984. 'L' ichthyofaune du site néolithique de Khirokitia (Chypre)', in A. Le Brun (ed.), *Fouilles récentes à Khirokitia (Chypre) 1977–1981*: 167–8, 182. Paris.

——, and N. Desse-Berset, 1989. 'Les poissons de Khirokitia (campagnes 1983, 1984 et 1986)', in A. Le Brun (ed.), *Fouilles récentes à Khirokitia (Chypre) 1983–1986*: 223–33. Paris.

Dörpfeld, W., 1927. *Alt-Ithaka. Ein Beitrag zur Homer-Frage. Studien und Ausgrabungen aus der Insel Leukas-Ithaka.* Munich.

Doumas, C., 1965. 'Κορφή τ' Αρωνιού', *ArchDelt* 20 (Meletai): 41–64.

——, 1972. 'Notes on Cycladic architecture', *AA* 87: 151–70.

——, 1976*a*. 'Πρωτοκυκλαδική κεραμεική από τα Χριστιανά Θήρας', *ArchEph*: 1–11.

——, 1976*b*. 'Προϊστορικοί Κυκλαδίτες στην Κρήτη', *AAA* 9: 69–80.

——, 1977. *Early Bronze Age Burial Habits in the Cyclades*. SIMA 48. Göteborg.

——, 1984. *Κυκλαδική Τέχνη*. Athens.

——, 1988. 'Early Bronze Age in the Cyclades: continuity or discontinuity?', in E. B French and K. A. Wardle (eds.), *Problems in Greek Prehistory*: 21–9. Bristol.

——, 1990. 'Όπλα και οχυρώσεις', in L. Marangou (ed.), *Κυκλαδικός Πολιτισμός. Η Νάξος στην 3η π.Χ. χιλιετία*: 90–2. Athens.

—— and V. La Rosa (eds.), 1997. *Η Πολιόχνη και η Πρώιμη Εποχή του Χαλκού στο Βόρειο Αιγαίο / Poliochni e l'Antica Età del Bronzo nell' Egeo Settentrionale*. Athens.

—— and L. Marangou, 1978. *Έκθεση Αρχαίας Ελληνικής Τέχνης: Κυκλαδικός Πολιτισμός — Ιστορικοί Χρόνοι, Συλλογή Ν. Π. Γουλανδρή*. Catalogue of the Exhibition at Benaki Museum, Athens.

Dousougli-Zachos, A., 1993. 'Zas Höhle', in *CMS* V Suppl.1B: 103–9.

Dümmler, F., 1886. 'Mitteilungen von den griechischen Inseln', *AM* 2: 15–46.

Dürr, S. *et al.*, 1985. *Amorgos. Geologische Karte* (1:50.000).

——, 1986. 'Das Attisch-kykladische Kristallin, Ostägäische Inseln und Gebirgsverbindungen im Ägäis-Bereich', in V. Jacobshagen (ed.), *Geologie von Griechenland*: 145–6. Berlin.

Dumont, J. 1988. 'Les critères culturels du choix des poissons dans l'alimentation grecque antique. Le cas d'Athènèe de Naucratis', in L. Bodson (ed.), *L'Animal dans l'alimentation humaine. Les critères de choix: actes du colloque international de Liège 26–29 novembre 1986, Antropozoologica no sp.* 2: 99–113.

Dunand, M., 1973. *Fouilles de Byblos* V. Paris.

Economidou, V., 1994. 'Cycladic settlements in the Early Bronze Age and their Aegean context' (Unpublished PhD thesis, University of London).

Elster, E. S., 1992. 'An archaeologist's perspective on prehistoric textile production: the case of Sitagroi', in *Η Δράμα και η περιοχή της. Πρακτικά Επιστημονικής Συνάντησης, Δήμος Δράμας.*

Erhard, D., 1858. *Fauna der Kykladen. Die Wirbelthiere der Kykladen.* Leipzig.

Erkanal, H., 1997. *Archaeological Researches at Liman Tepe.* Urla.

——, 1999. 'Early Bronze Age fortification systems in Ismir region', in P. P Betancourt, V. Karageorghis, R. Laffineur and W.-D. Niemeier (eds.), *Meletemata. Studies in Aegean Archaeology presented to Malcom H. Wiener as he enters his 65th year.* Aegaeum 20: 237–42. Liège and Austin.

Evans, A. J., 1928. *The Palace of Minos at Knossos* II. London.

Evans, J. D. and C. Renfrew, 1968. *Excavations at Saliagos near Antiparos.* BSA Suppl. 5. London.

Evans, R. K and C. Renfrew, 1984. 'The earlier Bronze Age at Phylakopi', in J. A. MacGillivray and R. L. N. Barber (eds.), *The Prehistoric Cyclades. Contributions to a Workshop on Cycladic Chronology*: 63–9. Edinburgh.

Evely, D., 1999. 'Mats and baskets: some observations on their study', in P. P. Betancourt, V. Karageorghis, R. Laffineur and W. D. Niemeier (eds.), *Meletemata. Studies in Aegean Archaeology Presented to Malcom H. Wiener as he enters his 65th year.* Aegeum 20: 243–5. Liège and Austin.

Fitton, J. L., 1984. *Cycladica: Studies in Memory of N. P. Goulandris.* London.

Fossey, J., 1969. 'The prehistoric settlement by Lake Vouliagmeni, Perachora', *BSA* 64: 53–70.

French, C. A. I. and T. M. Whitelaw, 1999. 'Soil erosion, agricultural terracing and site formation processes at Markiani, Amorgos, Greece: the micromorphological perspective', *Geoarchaeology* 14: 151–89.

French, D., 1968. 'Anatolia and the Aegean in the third millennium B.C.' (unpublished PhD thesis, University of Cambridge).

French, E. B., 1990, 'Archaeology in Greece, 1989–90', *AR* 36: 3–82.

—— and K. A. Wardle (eds.), 1988. *Problems in Greek Prehistory.* Bristol.

Frödin, O. and A. W. Persson, 1938. *Asine. Results of the Swedish Excavations 1922–1930.* Stockholm.

Gale, N. H and Z. A. Stos-Gale, 1981. 'Cycladic lead and silver metallurgy', *BSA* 76: 169–224.

Gamble, C. S., 1978. 'The Bronze Age animal economy from Akrotiri: a preliminary analysis', in C. Doumas (ed.), *Thera and the Aegean World I.* Papers presented at the Second International Scientific Congress, Santorini, Greece, August 1978: 745–53. London.

——, 1982*a*. 'Animal husbandry, population and urbanisation', in C. Renfrew and M. Wagstaff (eds.), *An Island Polity: The Archaeology of Exploitation in Melos*: 161–71. Cambridge.

——, 1982*b*. 'Leadership and "surplus" production', in C. Renfrew and S. Shennan (eds.), *Ranking Resource and Exchange: Aspects of the Archaeology of Early European Society*: 100–5. Cambridge.

Garstang, J., 1953. *Prehistoric Mersin: Yümük Tepe in Southern Turkey.* Oxford.

Gejvall, N. G., 1969. *Lerna: A Preclassical Site in the Argolid, I: the Fauna.* Princeton.

Gifford-Gondalez, D. P., D. R. Damrosch, D. B. Damrosch, P. John and R. L. Thumen, 1985. 'The third dimension in site structure: an experiment in trampling and a vertical dispersal', *American Antiquity* 50: 803–18.

Goldman, H., 1931. *Excavations at Eutresis in Boeotia*. Cambridge, MA.

——, 1956. *Excavations at Gözlü Kule, Tarsus II: From the Neolithic through to Bronze Age*. Princeton.

Goodison, L., 1989. *Death, Women and the Sun. Symbolism of Regeneration in Early Aegean Religion*. *BICS* Suppl. 53. London.

Gropengiesser, H., 1987. 'Siphnos, Kap Agios Sostis. Keramische Prähistorische zeugnisse aus dem Gruben und Hüttenrevier II', *AM* 102: 32–53.

Gulick, C. B., 1930. *Athenaeus. The Deipnosophists IV: Book VIII*. London.

Halepa-Bikaki, A., 1984. *Keos IV. Ayia Irini: The Potters' Marks*. Mainz.

Halstead, P. and G. Jones, 1980. 'Early neolithic economy in Thessaly — some evidence from excavations at Prodromos', *Anthropologika* 1: 93–117.

—— and G. Jones, 1987. 'Bioarchaeological remains from Kalythies Cave, Rhodes', in A. Sampson, *Η Νεολιθική περίοδος στα Δωδεκάνησα. Δημοσιεύματα του Αρχαιολογικού Δελτίου* 35: 135–52. Athens.

Harland, J. P., 1951. 'An Early Helladic kitchen utensil', in G. E. Mylonas (ed.), *Studies Presented to David Moore Robinson on his Seventieth Birthday*: 106–7. Saint Louis, Missouri.

Heath, M. C., 1958. 'Early Helladic clay sealings from the House of the Tiles at Lerna', *Hesperia* 27: 81–121.

Hedges, R. E. M., M. J. Humm, J. Foreman, G. J. van Klinken and C. R. Bronk, 1992. 'Developments in sample combustion to carbon dioxide and in the Oxford AMS carbon dioxide ion source system', *Radiocarbon* 34.3: 306–11.

——, I. A. Law, C. R. Bronk and R. Housley, 1989. 'The Oxford accelerator mass spectrometry facility: technical developments in routine dating', *Archaeometry* 31.2: 99–113.

Heermance, T. W. and G. D. Lord, 1897. 'Pre-mycenaean graves in Corinth', *AJA* 1: 313–32.

Heidenreich, R., 1936. 'Vorgeschichtliches in der Stadt Samos. Die Funde', *AM* 60/61: 125–83.

Hekman, J. J., 1994. 'Chalandriani on Syros: an Early Bronze Age cemetery in the Cyclades', *ArchEph* 133: 47–74.

Heurtley, W. A., 1939. *Prehistoric Macedonia: An Archaeological Reconnaisance of Greek Macedonia (west of the Struma) in the Neolithic, Bronze and Early Iron Ages*. Cambridge.

Hinz, G., 1979. 'Neue Tierknochenfunde aus der Magula Pevkakia in Thessalien. I. Die Nichtwiederkäuer', (unpublished PhD thesis, University of Munich).

Höckmann, O., 1977. 'The Cyclades and their Eastern neighbours', in J. Thimme (ed.), *Art and Culture of the Cyclades*: 155–62. Karlsruhe.

Holmberg, E. J., 1944. *The Swedish Excavations at Asea in Arcadia*. Lund.

Hood, S., 1981. *Excavations in Chios 1938–55. Prehistoric Emporio and Ayio Gala*. *BSA* Suppl. 15. London.

——, 1990. 'Autochthons or settlers? Evidence for immigration at the beginning of the Early Bronze Age in Crete', in *Πεπραγμένα του ΣΤ΄ Διεθνούς Κρητολογικού Συνεδρίου*: 367–75. Chania.

Hughes, M. J., J. P. Northover and B. E. P. Staniaszek, 1982. 'Problems in the analysis of leaded bronze alloys in ancient artifacts', *OJA* 1: 359–63.

Hutchinson, R. W., 1962. *Prehistoric Crete*. London.

Isler, H. P., 1973. 'An Early Bronze Age settlement on Samos', *Archaeology* 26: 173–5.

Jarman, M. R., 1972. 'The fauna', in P. M. Warren, *Myrtos: An Early Bronze Age Settlement in Crete. BSA* Suppl. 7: 318–20. London.

Johnstone, P., 1988. *The Sea-craft of Prehistory*. London.

Jordan, B., 1975. 'Tierknochenfunde aus der Magula Pevkakia in Thessalien' (unpublished PhD thesis, University of Munich).

Joukowski-Sharp, M., 1986. *Prehistoric Aphrodisias*. Louvain.

Karantzali, E., 1993. 'Στοιχεία Πρωτομινωικής κατοίκησης στα Νοπήγεια Κισάμου', *ArchDelt* 47–48, A (Meletes): 65–82.

——, 1996. *Le Bronze Ancien dans les Cyclades et en Crète. Les rélations entre les deux régions. Influence de la Grèce Continentale*. BAR-IS 631. Oxford.

Klippel, W. E. and L. M. Snyder, 1991. 'Dark-Age fauna from Kavousi, Crete: the vertebrates from the 1987 and 1988 excavations', *Hesperia* 60: 179–86.

Kontoleon, N. M., 1949. 'Ανασκαφαί εν Νάξω', *PAE*: 112–22.

——, 1970. 'Ανασκαφαί εν Νάξω', *PAE*: 146–55.

Kotsakis, T., C. Petronio and G. Sirna, 1979. 'The quaternary vetrebrates of the Aegean islands: paleogeographical implications', *Annales geologiques du pays Hellénique* 30: 31–64.

Kotjabopoulou, E. and K. Trantalidou, 1993, 'Faunal analysis of the Skoteino Cave', in A. Sampson, *Skoteini Tharrounia Cave: The Settlement and Cemetery*: 392–434. Athens.

Kosmopoulos, L. W., 1948. *The Prehistoric Habitation of Corinth*. Munich.

Koufos, G., 'Το οστεολογικό υλικό' in D. Grammenos, 'Ανασκαφή σε οικισμό της εποχής Χαλκού (Πρώιμης) στην Πεντάπολη του νομού Σερρών', *ArchEph*: 113–15.

Kouka, O., 1997. 'Οργάνωση και χρήση του χώρου στην Θερμή της Λέσβου κατά την πρώιμη Εποχή του Χαλκού', in C. Doumas and V. La Rosa (eds.), *Η Πολιόχνη και η Πρώιμη Εποχή του Χαλκού στο Βόρειο Αιγαίο / Poliochni e l'Antica Età del Bronzo nell' Egeo Settentrionale*: 467–97. Athens.

Koumanoudes, S. A., 1871. *Αττικής Επιγραφαί Επιτύμβιοι*. Athens (reprint 1993).

Kroll, H., 1984. 'Bronze and Iron Age agriculture in Kastanas, Macedonia', in W. Van Zeist and W. A. Casparie (eds.), *Plants and Ancient Man*: 243–6. Rotterdam.

Kunze, E., 1934. *Orchomenos III. Die Keramik der frühen Bronzezeit*. Munich.

Lamb, W., 1936. *Excavations at Thermi in Lesbos*. Cambridge.

Lambrinoudakis, V., 1990. 'Θρησκεία', in L. Marangou (ed.), *Κυκλαδικός Πολιτισμός. Η Νάξος στην 3η π.Χ. χιλιετία*: 99–112. Athens.

Lavezzi, J., 1979. 'Early Helladic hearth rims at Corinth', *Hesperia* 48: 342–7.

LeMoine, G., 1997. *Use Wear Analysis on Bone and Antler Tools of the Mackenzie Inuit*. BAR-IS 679. Oxford.

Leroi-Gourhan, A., 1984. *Pincevent: Campement magdalènien de chasseurs de rennes*. Paris.

Lloyd, S. and J. Mellaart, 1962. *Beycesoultan I*. London.

MacGillivray, J. A., 1979. 'Early Cycladic Pottery from Mt. Kynthos in Delos', Edinburgh (privately circulated catalogue).

——, 1980. 'Mount Kynthos in Delos. The Early Cycladic settlement', *BCH* 104: 3–45.

——, 1984. 'The relative chronology of Early Cycladic III', in J. A. MacGillivray and R. L. N. Barber (eds.), *Prehistoric Cyclades. Contributions to a Workshop on Cycladic Chronology*: 70–7. Edinburgh.

Mangou, H. and P. V. Ioannou, 1997. 'On the chemical composition of prehistoric Greek copper-based artifacts from the Aegean region', *BSA* 92: 59–72.

—— and P. V. Ioannou, 1998. 'On the chemical composition of prehistoric Greek copper-based artifacts from Crete', *BSA* 93: 91–102.

—— and P. V. Ioannou, 1999. 'On the chemical composition of prehistoric Greek copper-based artifacts from the Mainland Greece', *BSA* 94: 81–100.

—— and P. V. Ioannou, 2002. 'Trends in the making of copper-based artifacts during the prehistoric period (4000–1050 BC)', *Opuscula Atheniensis*: 105–18.

Manning, S. W., 1995. *The Absolute Chronology of the Aegean Early Bronze Age: Archaeology, History and Radiocarbon*. Monographs in Mediterranean Archaeology 1. Sheffield.

Marangou, C., 1991. 'Maquettes d'embarcation: les débuts', in R. Laffineur and L. Basch (eds.), *Thalassa. L'Égée préhistorique et la mer*. Aegaeum 7: 21–42. Liège.

——, 2001. 'Neolithic craft: evidence about boat types and uses', in Y. Bassiakos, E. Aloupi and Y. Fakorellis (eds.), *Archaeometry Issues in Greek Prehistory and Antiquity*: 737–44. Athens.

Marangou, L., 1984. 'Evidence for the Early Cycladic period on Amorgos', in J. L. Fitton (ed.), *Cycladica. Studies in Memory of N. P. Goulandris*: 99–115. London.

——, 1985. 'Μινώα Αμοργού', *PAE*: 177–200.

——, (ed.) 1990*a*. *Κυκλαδικός Πολιτισμός. Η Νάξος στην 3η π.Χ. χιλιετία*. Athens.

——, 1990*b*. 'Κυκλαδικό ειδώλιο από την Μινώα της Αμοργού', *ArchEph* 129: 159–76.

——, 1994. 'Νέες μαρτυρίες για τον Κυκλαδικό πολιτισμό στην Αμοργό' in Ch.Tzouvara–Souli, A.Vlachopoulou-Oikonomou and C. Gravani-Katsiki (eds.), *Φηγός, Τιμητικός τόμος για τον καθηγητή Σωτήρη Δάκαρη*: 467–88. Ioannina.

——, 1995. 'Amorgo', in *Enciclopedia dell'Arte Antica*, sec. Suppl. I (1971–1994): 195–8.

——, 1996. 'Νέες μαρτυρίες για την ιστορία της αρχαίας Αμοργού', in *Επετηρίς Εταιρείας Κυκλαδικών Μελετών* 15 (Πρακτικά του Α2 Κυκλαδολογικού Συνεδρίου. Μνήμη Στυλιανού Γ. Κορρέ, Andros 5–9 September 1991): Β307–32.

——, 1999*a*. 'Μαρμάρινο κυκλαδικό αγαλμάτιο μουσικού από την Αμοργό', in N. C. Stampolidis (ed.), *Φώς Κυκλαδικόν. Τιμητικός τόμος στην μνήμη του Νίκου Ζαφειρόπουλου*: 20–9. Athens.

——, 1999*b*. *Archaeological Collection of Amorgos: I. Marble Sculpture*. Athens.

——, 2002. *Αμοργός I. Η Μινώα. Η πόλις, ο λιμήν και η μείζων περιφέρια*. Βιβλιοθήκη της εν Αθήναις Αρχαιολογικής Εταιρείας 228. Athens.

——, 2005. *Αμοργός II. Οι αρχαίοι πύργοι*. Βιβλιοθήκη της εν Αθήναις Αρχαιολογικής Εταιρείας 239. Athens.

——, in press. in M. E. Marthari (ed.), *The Early Bronze Age in the Cyclades in the Light of Recent Research at Settlement Sites, Proceedings of a 1 day colloquium, Hermoupolis, Syros, 1st November 1998*: 111–28. Athens.

Marinatos S., 1929. 'Πρωτομινωικός θολωτός τάφος στο Κράσι Πεδιάδος', *ArchDelt* 12: 103–41.

——, 1933. 'La marine créto-mycénienne', *BCH* 57: 170–235.

Marketou, T., 1997. 'Ασώματος Ρόδου. Τα μεγαρόσχημα κτίρια και οι σχέσεις τους με το βορειοανατολικό Αιγαίο', in C. Doumas and V. La Rosa (eds.), *Η Πολιόχνη και η Πρώιμη Εποχή του Χαλκού στο Βόρειο Αιγαίο / Poliochni e l'Antica Età del Bronzo nell' Egeo Settentrionale*: 395–413. Athens.

Marthari, M., 1997. 'Από τον Σκάρκο στην Πολιόχνη. Παρατηρήσεις για την κοινωνικο-οικονομική ανάπτυξη των οικισμών της Πρώιμης Εποχής του Χαλκού στις Κυκλάδες και στα νησιά του βορειοανατολικού Αιγαίου', in C. Doumas and V. La Rosa (eds.), *Η Πολιόχνη και η Πρώιμη Εποχή του Χαλκού στο Βόρειο Αιγαίο / Poliochni e l'Antica Età del Bronzo nell' Egeo Settentrionale*: 362–82. Athens.

Masseti, M., 1998. 'Holocene endemic and anthropochorous wild mammals of the Mediterranean islands', *Antropozoologica* 28: 3–20.

Mee, C. and J. Doole, 1993. *Aegean Antiquities on Merseyside*. Liverpool.

Meliarakes, A., 1928 (1884). *Υπομνήματα περιγραφικά των Κυκλάδων Νήσων, Αμοργός*. Chicago.

Mellaart, 1963. 'Early cultures of the South Anatolian plateau II: the Late Chalcolithic and Early Bronze Age in the Konyan plain', *Anatolian Studies* 13: 199–235.

Metaxa-Muhly, P., 1984. 'Minoan hearths', *AJA* 88: 107–22.

Mitchaud, J. P., 1973. 'Chronique des fouilles en 1972', *BCH* 97: 330–4.

Milojcic, V., 1961. *Samos I. Die prähistorische Siedlung unter dem Heraion. Grabung 1953 und 1955.* Bonn.

Mosso, A., 1910. *The Dawn of Mediterranean Civilisation.* London.

Moundrea-Agrafioti, A., 1980. 'Παλαιοεθνολογικά συμπεράσματα από την μελέτη των λίθινων και οστέινων εργαλείων του νεολιθκού οικισμού Προδρομού Καρδίτσας', *1το Συνεδρίο Θεσσαλικών Σπουδών. Thessalika Chronika* 1981: 489–97.

——, 1990. 'Akrotiri, the chipped stone industry: reduction techniques and tools of the LC I phase', in D. A. Hardy, C. G. Doumas, J. A. Sakellarakis, and P. M. Warren (eds.), *Thera and the Aegean World III, 1: Archaeology*: 390–406. London.

Murray, C., 1979. 'Les techniques de débitage des métapodes des petits ruminants à Auvernier-Port', in H. Camps-Fabrer (ed.), *L' industrie en os et bois de cervidé durant le Néolithique et l âge des Métaux*: 27–35. Paris.

Mylona, D., forthcoming. 'The cave of Cyclope. Fish vertebrae analysis', in A. Sampson (ed.), *The Cave of Cyclope, Youra, Alonnessos.*

Mylonas, G. E., 1959. *Agios Kosmas. An Early Bronze Age Settlement and Cemetery in Attica.* Princeton.

Myres, J. L., 1898. 'Textile impressions on an early clay vessel from Amorgos', *Journal of the Anthropological Institute of Great Britain and Ireland* 27: 178–80.

Nicholson, R. A., 1992. 'Bone survival: the effects of sedimentary abrasion and trampling on fresh and cooked bone', *International Journal of Osteoarchaeology* 2: 79–90.

Noddle, B., 1974. 'Ages of epiphyseal closure in feral and domestic goats and ages of dental eruption', *Journal of Anthropological Studies* 1: 195–204.

Noe-Nygaard, N., 1997. 'Butchering and marrow fracturing as a taphonomic factor in archaeological deposits', *Paleobiology* 3: 218–37.

Norlin, G. (ed.), 1928. *Isocrates: Panygyricus* (Loeb Classical Library). London.

Ondrias, J. C., 1965. 'Die Saugetiere Griechenlands', *Saugetierkundliche Mitteilungen* 13, 3: 109–27.

Papavasileiou, G., 1910. *Περί των εν Ευβοία αρχαίων τάφων.* Athens.

Papageorgiou, D. K., 1997. 'Ρεύματα και άνεμοι στο Βόρειο Αιγαίο', in C. Doumas and V. La Rosa (eds.), *Η Πολιόχνη και η Πρώιμη Εποχή του Χαλκού στο Βόρειο Αιγαίο / Poliochni e l'Antica Età del Bronzo nell' Egeo Settentrionale*: 424–39. Athens.

Papathanasopoulos, G. A., 1962. 'Κυκλαδικά Νάξου', *ArchDelt* 17 A (Meletai): 104–51.

Pariente, A., 1992. 'Chronique des fouilles et découvertes archéologiques en Gréce en 1991', *BCH* 116: 833–954.

Parlama, L., 1984. 'Η προϊστορική εποχή στην Σκύρο,' (unpublished PhD thesis, University of Ioannina).

——, 1999. 'Σκύρος, Cycladum te Sporadum extima', in N. C. Stampolidis (ed.), *Φώς Κυκλαδικόν. Τιμητικός τόμος στην μνήμη του Νίκου Ζαφειρόπουλου*: 43–53. Athens.

Payne, S., 1973. 'Kill-off patterns in sheep and goats: the mandibles from Asvan Kale', *Anatolian Studies* 23: 281–303.

——, 1985*a*. 'Morphological distinctions between the mandibular teeth of young sheep, *Ovis*, and goats, *Capra*', *Journal of Archaeozoological Studies* 12: 139–47.

——, 1985*b*. 'Zoo-archaeology in Greece: a reader's guide', in N. Wilkie and W. Coulson (eds.), *Contributions to Aegean Archaeology: Studies in Honor of W. A. McDonald*: 211–44. Dubuque, Iowa.

Pearson, G. W. and M. Stuiver, 1993. 'High-precision bidecadal calibration of the radiocarbon time-scale, 500–2500 BC', *Radiocarbon* 35: 1, 215–30.

Petrikaki, M., 1980. 'Λείψανα πρωτοελλαδικού οικισμού στο Ρούφ', *ArchDelt* 35 (Meletes): 147–85.

Philippson, A., 1959. *Die griechischen Landschaften. Das Aegaeische Meer und seine Inseln*, IV. Frankfurt.

Pini, I., 2005. 'Minoische und helladische Metallsiegel und –stempel', *Creta Antica* 6: 59–87.

Plassart, A., 1928. *Les sanctuaires et les cultes du Mont Cynthe.* Exploration Archéologique de Délos par l'École Française d'Athènes XI. Paris.

Popham, M. R. and L. H. Sackett, 1968. *Excavations at Lefkandi, Euboea 1964–1966: A Preliminary Report.* London.

Poplin, F., 1975. 'La faune danubienne d'Armeau (Yonne, France): ses donnes sur l'activité humaine', in A. T. Clason (ed.), *Archaeozoological Studies. Papers of the Archaeozoological Conference 1974, held at the Biologisch-Archaelogisch Instituut of the State University of Groningen*: 179–92. Amsterdam.

Powell, J., 1996. *Fishing in the Prehistoric Aegean.* SIMA Pocket-book 137. Jonsered.

——, forthcoming. 'The fish bone assemblage from the cave of Cyclops, Youra, Part 1: The identified bones', in A. Sampson (ed.), *The Cave of Cyclops, Youra, Alonnessos.*

Poursat, J.-C., 1980. 'Vannerie', in B. Detournay, J.-C. Poursat and F. Vandenabeele (eds.), *Fouilles exécutées à Mallia: Le Quartier Mu II. Vases de pierre et de métal, vannerie, figurines et reliefs d'applique, éléments de parure et de décoration, armes, sceaux et empreintes.* Études Crétoises 26: 91–8. Paris.

Prummel, W. and H. J. Frisch, 1986. 'A guide for the distinction of species, sex and body side in bones of sheep and goat', *Journal of Archaeozoological Studies* 13: 567–77.

Rahmstorf, L., 2003. 'The identification of Early Helladic weights and their wider implications', in K. P. Foster and R. Laffineur (eds.), *Metron. Measuring the Aegean Bronze Age*. Aegaeum 24: 292–303. Liège and Austin.

Rambach, J., 2000. *Kykladen. Die Frühe Bronzezeit*. Beiträge zur ur- und frühgeschichtlichen Archäologie des Mittelmeer-Kulturraumes 33. Bonn.

Renard, J., 1989. *Le site néolithique et hélladique ancien de Kouphovouno (Laconie): fouilles de O.-W. von Vacano (1941*. Aegaeum 4. Liège.

Renfrew, C., 1965. 'The Neolithic and Early Bronze Age cultures of the Cyclades and their external relations' (unpublished PhD thesis, University of Cambridge).

——, 1967. 'Cycladic metallurgy and the Aegean Early Bronze Age', *AJA* 71: 1–20.

——, 1972. *The Emergence of Civilization. The Cyclades and the Aegean in the Third Millennium B.C.* London.

——, 1990. 'Introductory remarks', in D. A. Hardy and C. Renfrew (eds.), *Thera and the Aegean World III, 3: Chronology. Proceedings of the Third International Congress, Santorini, Greece, 3–9 September 1989*: 11–12. London.

——, 1991. *The Cycladic Spirit: Masterpieces from the Nicholas P. Goulandris Collection*. London and New York.

—— and R. K. Evans, in press. 'The Early Bronze Age pottery', in C. Renfrew (ed.), *Excavations at Phylakopi on Melos 1974–1976. BSA* Suppl. London.

Renfrew, J. M., 1968. 'Appendix X: the cereal remains', in J. D. Evans and C. Renfrew, *Excavations at Saliagos near Antiparos. BSA* Suppl. 5: 139–41. London.

——, 1969. 'Palaeoethnobotany and the Neolithic cultures of Greece and Boulgaria' (unpublished PhD thesis, University of Cambridge).

——, 1972. 'Appendix 5: the plant remains', in P. M. Warren, *Myrtos: An Early Bronze Age Settlement in Crete. BSA* Suppl. 7: 315–18. London.

——, 1977. 'Appendix 3: seeds from Area K', in J. E. Coleman, 1977, *Keos I. Kephala. A Late Neolithic Settlement and Cemetery*: 127–8. Princeton N.J.

——, 1979. 'The first farmers in south east Europe', in U. Korber-Grohne (ed.), *Festschrift Maria Hopf, Archaeo-Physika* 8: 243–65. Koln.

——, 1982. 'Early agriculture on Melos', in C. Renfrew and J. M. Wagstaff (eds.), *An Island Polity: The Archaeology of Exploitation in Melos*: 156–60. Cambridge.

——, 1995. 'Palaeothnobotanical finds of *Vitis* from Greece', in P. E. McGovern, S. Fleming and S. H. Katz (eds.), *The Origins and Ancient History of Wine*. Luxembourg.

——, P. H. Greenwood and P. J Whitehead, 1968. 'Appendix VIII: The fish bones', in J. D. Evans and C. Renfrew, *Excavations at Saliagos near Antiparos. BSA* Suppl. 5: 118–21. London.

Reese, D. S., 1995. 'The larger mammals', in J. W. Shaw and M. C. Shaw (eds.), *Kommos I. The Kommos Region and Houses of the Minoan Town, Part 1. The Kommos Region, Ecology and Minoan Industries*: 165–94. Princeton.

Robinson, S. W., 1986. 'A computational procedure for the utilization of high-precision radiocarbon calibration curves' (unpublished manuscript).

——, 1988. CALSTS5 (Computer Calibration program demonstrated at the 12th International Radiocarbon Conference, Trondheim).

——, n.d. 'Further improvements in probabilistic radiocarbon calibration' (unpublished manuscript).

Romaios, K. A., 1903. 'Μικρά συμβολή εις την αρχαίαν γεωγραφίαν', *Athena* 14: 3–36.

Rose, M. J., 1995. 'The fish remains', in J. W. Shaw and M. C. Shaw (eds.), *Kommos I. The Kommos Region and Houses of the Minoan town, Part 1. The Kommos Region, Ecology and Minoan Industries*: 204–39. Princeton.

——, 1996. 'Fishing at Minoan Pseira: formation of a Bronze Age fish assemblage from Crete', *Archaeofauna* 5: 135–40.

——, 1998. 'The fish bones', in C. R. Floyd, *Pseira III. The Plateia Building*: 146–8. Philadelphia.

Rubensohn, O., 1917. 'Die prähistorischen und frühgeschichtlichen Fünde auf dem Burghügel von Paros', *AM* 42: 1–96.

Runnels, C. N. and J. Hansen, 1986. 'The olive in the prehistoric Aegean: the evidence for domestication in the Early Bronze Age', *OJA* 5: 299–308.

Rusche, C. and P. Halstead, 1987. 'The animal bones from Ayios Dimitrios', in C. L. Zachos, 'Ayios Dimitrios, a prehistoric settlement in the southwestern Peloponnesos: the Neolithic and Early Helladic periods' (unpublished PhD thesis, University of Boston).

Rutter, J., 1984. 'The EC III gap: what it is and how to go about filling it without making it go away', in J. A. MacGillivray and R. L. N. Barber (eds.), *Prehistoric Cyclades. Contributions to a Workshop on Cycladic Chronology*: 95–107. Edinburgh.

Sampson, A., 1981. *Η Νεολιθική και η Πρωτοελλαδική Ι στην Εύβοια*. Athens.

——, 1985. *Μάνικα Ι. Μία Πρωτοελλαδική πόλη στην Χαλκίδα*. Athens.

——, 1988. *Μάνικα ΙΙ. Ο Πρωτοελλαδικός οικισμός και το Νεκροταφείο*. Athens.

Sapouna-Sakellaraki, E., 1987. 'New evidence from the Early Bronze Age cemetery at Manika, Chalkis', *BSA* 82: 233–62.

Sarpaki, A. and G. Jones, 1990. 'Ancient and modern cultivation of *Lathyrus Clymenum* L. in the Greek islands', *BSA* 85: 363–8.

Schliemann, H., 1881. *Ilios: The City and Country of the Trojans*. London.

Schmidt, E. F., 1932. *The Alishar Hüyük, Seasons of 1928–29, part I.* Chicago.

——, 1937. *Excavations at Tepe Hissar, Damghan.* Philadelphia.

Schofield, E., 1990. 'Evidence for household industries on Thera and Kea', in D. A. Hardy, C. G. Doumas, J. A. Sakellarakis, and P. M. Warren (eds.), *Thera and the Aegean World III, 1: Archaeology. Proceedings of the Third International Congress, Santorini, Greece, 3–9 September 1989*: 201–11. London.

Schwartz, C. A., 1985. 'Agios Petros. The vertebrate and molluscan fauna; final report', in N. Efstratiou, *Agios Petros. A Neolithic Site in the Northern Sporades: Aegean Relationships during the Neolithic of the 5th Millennium.* BAR-IS 241: 151–60. Oxford.

Seager, R. B., 1909. 'Excavations on the island of Mochlos, Crete, in 1908', *AJA* 13: 273–303.

Shackleton, N., 1968. 'The mollusca, the crustacea, the echinoderma', in J. D. Evans and C. Renfrew, *Excavations at Saliagos near Antiparos. BSA* Suppl. 5: 122–38. London.

Shepard, A. O., 1980. *Ceramics for the Archaeologist.* Washington D.C.

Sherratt, S., 2000. *Catalogue of Cycladic Antiquities in the Ashmolean Museum. The Captive Spirit,* I–II. Oxford.

Silver, I. A., 1970. 'The ageing of domestic animals', in D. R. Brothwell and E. S. Higgs (eds.), *Science in Archaeology: A Survey of Progress and Research* (second edition). New York.

Snyder, L. M. and W. E. Klippel, 1999. 'Dark Age subsistence at the Kastro site, East Crete: exploring subsistence change and continuity during the Late Bronze Age–early Iron Age transition', in S. J. Vaughan and W. D. E. Coulson, *Palaeodiet in the Aegean.* Oxbow Monographs 96: 65–83. Oxford.

Sorrentino, C. 1997. 'Poliochni: il materiale faunistico', in C. Doumas and V. La Rosa (eds.), *Η Πολιόχνη και η Πρώιμη Εποχή του Χαλκού στο Βόρειο Αιγαίο / Poliochni e l'Antica Età del Bronzo nell' Egeo Settentrionale*: 157–67. Athens.

Sotirakopoulou, P., 1986. 'Early Cycladic pottery from Akrotiri on Thera and its chronological implications', *BSA* 81: 297–312.

——, 1993. 'The chronology of the "Kastri Group" reconsidered', *BSA* 88: 5–20.

——, 1997. 'Κυκλάδες και Βόρειο Αιγαίο οι σχέσεις τους κατά το δεύτερο ήμισυ της 3ης χιλιετίας π.Χ.', in C. Doumas and V. La Rosa (eds.), *Η Πολιόχνη και η Πρώιμη Εποχή του Χαλκού στο Βόρειο Αιγαίο / Poliochni e l'Antica Età del Bronzo nell' Egeo Settentrionale*: 522–42. Athens.

——, 1998. 'The Early Bronze Age stone figurines from Akrotiri on Thera and their significance for the Early Cycladic settlement', *BSA* 93: 107–65.

——, 1999. *Ακρωτήρι Θήρας Η Νεολιθική και η Πρώιμη Εποχή του Χαλκού επί τη βάσει της Κεραμικής.* Βιβλιοθήκη της εν Αθήναις Αρχαιολογικής Εταιρείας 191. Athens.

Sperling, J. W., 1976. 'Kum-Tepe in the Troad: trial excavation, 1934', *Hesperia* 45: 305–64.

Stephanos, C., 1904. 'Ανασκαφαί εν Νάξω', *PAE*: 57–61.

——, 1905. 'Les tombeaux prémycéniens de Naxos', in *Comptes Rendus du Congrès International d'Archéologie, Ire session*: 216–25. Athens.

Stratouli, G., 1987. 'Τα οστέινα εργαλεία του σπηλαίου Άγιος Γεώργιος στης Καλυθίες Ρόδου', in A. Sampson, *Η νεολιθική περίοδος στα Δωδεκάνησα. Δημοσιεύματα του Αρχαιολογικού Δελτίου* 35: 156–63. Athens.

——, 1996. 'Die Fischerei in der Ägäis während des Neolithikums. Zur Technik und zum potentiellen Ertrag', *Prähistorische Zeitschrift* 71: 1–27.

Stordeur-Yedid, D., 1976. 'Les poinçons d'os a poulie articulaire: observations techniques d'après quelques examples syriens', *Bulletin Societé Préhistorique Française* 73: 39–42.

Stuiver, M. and G. W. Pearson, 1993. 'High-precision bidecadal calibration of the radiocarbon time-scale, AD 1950–500 BC and 2500–6000 BC', *Radiocarbon* 35, 1: 1–23.

—— and P. J. Reimer, 1993. 'Extended ^{14}C data base and revised CALIB 3.0 14C Age Calibration Program', *Radiocarbon* 35, 1: 215–.

——, P. J. Reimer, E. Bard, J. Warren Beck, G. S. Burr, K. A. Hughen, B. Kromer, G. McCormac, J. van der Plicht and M. Spurk, 1998. 'INTCAL98 radiocarbon age calibration, 24,000–0 cal BP', *Radiocarbon* 40, 3: 1041–83.

Theocharis, D. R., 1951. 'Ανασκαφαί εν Αραφήνι', *PAE*: 77–92.

——, 1952. 'Ανασκαφή εν Αραφήνι', *PAE*: 129–51.

——, 1954. 'Ασκηταριό. Πρωτοελλαδική ακρόπολις παρά την Ραφήναν', *ArchEph*: 59–76.

——, 1973. *Neolithic Greece.* Athens.

Theochari, M. D. and L. Parlama, 1997. 'Παλαμάρι Σκύρου η οχυρωμένη πόλη της Πρώιμης Χαλκοκρατίας', in C. Doumas and V. La Rosa (eds.), *Η Πολιόχνη και η Πρώιμη Εποχή του Χαλκού στο Βόρειο Αιγαίο / Poliochni e l'Antica Età del Bronzo nell' Egeo Settentrionale*: 344–56. Athens.

Thimme, J. (ed.), 1977. *Art and Culture of the Cyclades.* Karlsruhe.

Torrence, R., 1979. 'A technological approach to Cycladic blade industries', in J. L. Davis and J. F. Cherry (eds.), *Papers in Cycladic Prehistory.* UCLA Institute of Archaeology Monograph 14: 66–86. Los Angeles.

——, 1986. *Production and Exchange of Stone Tools: Prehistoric Obsidian in the Aegean.* Cambridge.

Touchais, G., 1980. 'La céramique néolithique de l' Aspis', in *Études argiennes. BCH* Supp. 6: 1–40.

Trantalidou, C., 1990. 'Animals and human diet in the prehistoric Aegean', in D. A. Hardy, J. Keller, V. P. Galanopoulos, N. C. Flemming and T. H. Druitt (eds.), *Thera and the Aegean World III, 3: Earth Sciences. Proceedings of the Third International Congress, Santorini, Greece, 3–9 September 1989*: 392–405. London.

——, 2000. Ἀσώματος Ρόδου, μία θέση της πρώιμης εποχής του χαλκού στην περιοχή της αρχαίας Ιαλυσίας. Τα ζωοαρχαιολογικά κατάλοιπα (Ανασκαφικές περίοδοι 1986, 1989, 1991)', *AAA* 29–31: 113–24.

—— and I. Kavoura, forthcoming. 'The astragaloi from the cave of the Nymph Koroneia on Mount Helikon in Boeotia: A contribution to the ethnology of everyday life in the ancient Greek world', *BSA*.

Tsountas, C., 1898. 'Κυκλαδικά Ι', *ArchEph*: 137–212.

——, 1899. 'Κυκλαδικά ΙΙ', *Arch Eph*: 73–134.

Tylecote, R. F., 1976. *A History of Metallurgy*. London.

Tzachili, I., 1997. *Υφαντική και Υφάντρες στο προϊστορικό Αιγαίο, 2000-1000 π.Χ.* Herakleion.

Tzavela-Evjen, C., 1984. *Λιθαρές*. Athens.

Vagnetti, L., A. Christopoulou and Y. Tzedakis, 1989. 'Saggi negli strati neolitici', in *Scavi a Nerokourou, Kydonias* I. Incunabula Graeca 91: 11–97. Rome.

van Horn, D., 1980. 'Observations relating to Bronze Age blade core production in the Argolid of Greece', *Journal of Field Archaeology* 7: 487–92.

van Loon, M. N. (ed.), 1978. *Korucutepe. Final Report on the Excavations of the Universities of Chicago, California (Los Angeles) and Amsterdam in the Keban Reservoir, Eastern Anatolia, 1968-1970*, II. Amsterdam.

Varoucha, E. A., 1926. 'Κυκλαδικοί τάφοι της Πάρου', *ArchEph*: 98–114.

Vaughan, S. J., 1989. 'Petrographic analysis of Mikre Vigla wares', in R. L. N Barber and O. Hadjianastasiou, 'Mikre Vigla: a Bronze Age settlement on Naxos', *BSA* 84: 150–9.

——, 1990. 'Petrographic analysis of Early Cycladic wares from Akrotiri, Thera', in D. A. Hardy, C. G. Doumas, J. A. Sakellarakis, and P. M. Warren (eds.), *Thera and the Aegean World III, 1: Archaeology. Proceedings of the Third International Congress, Santorini, Greece, 3-9 September 1989*: 470–87. London.

——, 2000. 'Contributions of petrography to the study of archaeological ceramics and man-made building materials in the Aegean and Eastern Mediterranean', in *The Practical Impact of Science on Aegean and Near Eastern Archaeology*: 60–8. London.

——, V. Kilikoglou and A. Papagiannopoulou, 1995. 'An interdisciplinary study of Middle Cycladic White wares from Akrotiri on Thera', in P. B. Vandiver, J. R. Druzik, J. L. G Madrid, I. C Freestone and G. S. Wheeler (eds.), *Material Issues in Art and Archaeology* 4. Material Research Society 352: 445–52.

—— and D. Wilson, 1993. 'Interregional contacts in the Aegean in Early Bronze II: the Talc Ware connection', in C. W. Zerner, P. Zerner and J. Winder (eds.), *Wace and Blegen. Pottery as Evidence for Trade in the Aegean Bronze Age, 1939-1989*: 169–86. Amsterdam.

——, in press. 'The technology and materials of the Early Bronze Age pottery from Phylakopi on Melos', in C. Renfrew (ed.), *Excavations at Phylakopi on Melos 1974-1976. BSA* Suppl. London.

——, N. Herz and S. H. Pikem, forthcoming. 'Stable Isotope Analysis as a ceramic provenancing technique: applications to Early Cycladic Marble-Tempered wares', in R. P. Evershed (ed.), *American Chemical Society Symposium on Geochemistry and Archaeology, Journal of Archaeological Science*.

Vickery, K. F., 1936. *Food in Early Greece*. Illinois Studies in Social Sciences 20.3. Urbana, Illinois.

Vikelas, M. D., 1879. *Sur la nomenclature de la faune grecque*. Paris.

von den Driesch, A. and J. Boessneck, 1975. 'Schnittspuren an neolithischen Tierknochen. Ein Beitrag zur Schlachttierzelegung in vorgeschichtlicher Zeit', *Germania* 53: 1–23.

—— and J. Boessneck, 1990. 'Die Tierreste von der mykenischen Burg Tiryns bei Nauplion/Peloponnes', in *Tiryns. Forschungen und Berichte* XI: 87–164. Mainz.

von der Mühle, H. G., 1844. *Beiträge zur Ornithologie Griechenlands*. Leipzig.

von der Osten, 1937. *The Alishar Hüyük, Seasons 1930-32, Part II*. Chicago.

Walberg, G., 1987. 'Early Cretan tombs: the pottery', in R. Laffineur (ed.), *Thanatos. Les coutumes funéraires en Égée à l'âge du Bronze*. Aegaeum 1: 53–60. Liège.

Walter, H. and F. Felten, 1981. *Alt-Ägina III, 1. Die vorgeschichtliche Stadt. Befestigungen, Häuser, Funde*. Bayerische Akademie der Wissenschaften, Institut für klassische Archäologie der Universität Salzburg. Mainz.

Warren, P. M., 1972a. *Myrtos: An Early Bronze Age Settlement in Crete. BSA* Suppl. 7. London.

—— 1972b. 'Knossos and the Greek mainland in the third millennium B.C.', *AAA* 5: 392–8.

——, and V. Hankey, 1989. *Aegean Bronze Age Chronology*. Bristol.

Warren, P. and Y. Tzedakis, 1976. 'Debla: an Early Minoan settlement in western Crete', *BSA* 69: 299–342.

Watson, J. P. N., 1997. 'Appendix 3: faunal remains', in C. Ridley and K. A. Wardle, 'Rescue excavations at Servia 1971-1973: a preliminary report', *BSA* 92: 401–34.

Weil, R., 1876. 'Von der griechischen Inseln', *AM* 1: 235–52.

Weinmann B., 1967, *Der Boden der Kykladeninsel Amorgos und ihre landwirtschaftliche Nützung*. Wiesbaden.

Weisshaar, H.-J., 1981. 'Ausgrabungen in Tiryns 1978–79', *AA* 96: 185–251.

——, 1982. 'Ausgrabungen in Tiryns 1980', *AA* 97: 420–66.

——, 1983. 'Ausgrabungen in Tiryns 1981 — Bericht zur frühhelladischen Keramik', *AA* 98: 310–57.

——, 1990. 'Die Keramik von Talioti', in *Tiryns. Forschungen und Berichte* XI: 1–34. Mainz.

Weniger, B., 1986. 'High-precision calibration of archaeological radiocarbon dates', in *Acta Interdisciplinaria Archaeologica* IV: 11–53. Nitra, AIA.

Whitelaw, T. M., 1983. 'The settlement at Fournou Korifi, Myrtos and aspects of Early Minoan social organisation', in O. Krzyszkowska and L. Nixon (eds.), *Minoan Society*: 323–45. Bristol.

——, 2000. 'Settlement instability and landscape degradation in the southern Aegean in the third millenium BC', in P. Halstead and C. Frederic (eds.), *Landscape and Landuse in Postglacial Greece*. Sheffield Studies in Aegean Archaeology, 3: 135–161. Sheffield.

——, 2001. 'From sites to communities: defining the human dimensions of Minoan urbanism', in K. Branigan (ed.), *Urbanism in the Aegean Bronze Age*. Sheffield Studies in Archaeology 4: 15–37. Sheffield.

Wiencke, M. H., 1969. 'Further seals and sealings from Lerna', *Hesperia* 38: 500–21.

——, 1970. 'Banded pithoi from Lerna III', *Hesperia* 39: 94–110.

Willerding, U., 1973. 'Bronzezeitliche Pflanzenreste aus Iria und Synoro', in *Tiryns. Forschungen und Berichte* VI: 221–40. Mainz.

Wilson, D. E., 1985. 'The pottery and architecture of the EM IIA West Court House at Knossos', *BSA* 80: 281–364.

——, 1999. *Keos IX. Ayia Irini Periods I–III. The Neolithic and Early Bronze Age Settlements. Part 1: The Pottery and Small Finds*. Mainz.

—— and M. Eliot, 1984. 'Ayia Irini, Period III: the last phase of occupation at the EBA settlement', in J. A. MacGillivray and R. L. N. Barber (eds.), *Prehistoric Cyclades. Contributions to a Workshop on Cycladic Chronology*: 78–87. Edinburgh.

Wood, R. W. and D. L. Jonson, 1978. 'A survey of disturbance processes in archaeological site formation', in M. E. Schiffer (ed.), *Advances in Archaeological Method and Theory* 1: 539–94.

Xanthouthides, S. A., 1918. 'Μέγας Πρωτομινωικός Τάφος Πύργου', *ArchDelt* 4: 136.

Yannouli, E., 1994. 'Aspects of animal use in prehistoric Macedonia, Northern Greece, examples from the Neolithic and Early Bronze Age' (unpublished PhD thesis, University of Cambridge).

Yule, P., 1981. *Early Cretan Seals: A Study of Chronology*. Marburger Studien zur Vor- und Frühgeschichte 4. Mainz.

Zapheiropoulou, P., 1968. 'Κυκλάδες: ανασκαφικαί έρευναι-περιοδείαι, Κέρος', *ArchDelt* 22 (Chronika): 381.

——, 1970*a*. 'Πρωτοκυκλαδικά ευρήματα εξ άνω Κουφονησίου', *AAA* 3: 48–51.

——, 1970*b*. 'Αρχαιότητες και Μνημεία των Κυκλάδων. Κουφονήσι', *ArchDelt* 25, B2 (Chronika): 428–30.

——, 1984. 'The chronology of the Kampos Group', in J. A. MacGillivray and R. L. N. Barber (eds.), *Prehistoric Cyclades. Contributions to a Workshop on Cycladic Chronology*: 31–40. Edinburgh.

Zervos, C., 1957. *L'Art des Cyclades. Du début à la fin de l'âge du Bronze, 2500–1100 avant notre ère*. Paris.

Zohary, D. and M. Hopf, 2000. *Domestication of Plants in the Old World. The Origin and Spread of Cultivated Plants in West Asia, Europe and the Nile Valley* (3rd edition). Oxford.

Index

Plates

PLATE 1

(a)

(b)

(a) The small hill top of Markiani (from the north-west). (b) The slopes below Markiani and the southern part of Amorgos seen from the north-east (note the modern Building C on the right).

Aerial photograph of Markiani seen from the north-east showing the summit (with Buildings A, B and C) and Terrace 1 to the left.

PLATE 3

(*a*)

(*b*)

(*a*) Terrace 1, seen from the east before excavation, showing the rock clefts (right). (*b*) Terrace walls and vegetation below Terrace 1.

PLATE 4

(a)

(b)

(a) Rock Cuttings 2 (*left*) and 3 (*centre*) on Terrace 1 before clearance of vegetation, seen from the south-west.
(b) Survey in progress on terraces below Terrace 1, seen from the north.

PLATE 5

(a)

(b)   (c)

(a) Rock Cutting 2 (with measuring rod in the same position as in PLATE 4 a) prior to the excavation of Trench 1.
(b) The beginning of the excavation of Trench 1, seen from the south in 1988. (c) Trench 1 showing Wall Λ and
the Circular Feature (Wall B), seen from the south in 1989.

P<small>LATE</small> 6

(*a*)

(*b*)

(*a*) Entrance to animal fold (*embassa*): looking up from Terrace 1 towards the summit area and the modern Building C, seen from the south-west. (*b*) Excavation in progress on Terrace 1 seen from the north-east.

PLATE 7

(*a*)

(*b*)

(*a*) View of Cape Diotrachili seen from the site, from the north-west. (*b*) Excavation on the summit area, showing Trench 4, seen from the north-east.

PLATE 8

(a)

(b)

(a) The site from the north, with recent walls set upon the line of defences, and the modern Building A. (b) The area of the Bastion and the continuation of the defensive wall to the east, seen from north-west.

PLATE 9

(*a*)

(*b*)

(*a*) The area of Trench 6 seen from the north-west, with recent Building A in the background. (*b*) Trench 6, seen from the west.

PLATE 10

(*a*)

(*b*)

(*c*)

(*a*) Trench 8 from the north looking up towards the Bastion and the recent Building A. (*b*) Trench 8,2 from the north with Wall Γ in the foreground. (*c*) Trench 8,1 from the north.

PLATE 11

(a)

(b)

(a) The Bastion from the north-west. (b) The room west of the Bastion (Trench 8,6), seen from the north.

PLATE 12

(a)

(b)   (c)

(a) North-west Bastion (unexcavated) seen from the north. (b) Features at the north-east of the site seen from the east. (c) Features at the north-east of the site seen from the north-east.

PLATE 13

(a)

(b)

(a) The summit area, prior to the removal of modern walling at the top of Trench 1, looking south. (b) View at the top of Trench 1,1 looking down from the summit area (after removal of modern walling) down to Terrace 1 and Trench 1,3 (note same rock outcrops at left in both plates).

PLATE 14

(a)

(b)

(a) Trench 1,1 and Trench 7, seen from the south at an early stage of excavation. (b) Trench 7 seen from the south during excavation showing irregular stone layer.

PLATE 15

(*a*)

(*b*)

(*a*) Trench 7 seen from the north at an early stage of excavation. (*b*) Trench 1,1 from the south showing Wall Λ above and the depas cup *in situ* within space 7.

PLATE 16

(*a*)

(*b*)

(*c*)

(*a*) Trench 1,1 from the south with Wall Λ partly removed to reveal Wall K and the mouth of the 'fissure' at the right.
(*b*) The 'fissure' of Trench 1,1, seen from the south-west. (*c*) The circular structure (Space 7) at the foot of Trench 1,1
seen from the south with Structure Z (of Trench 1,3) at the bottom right, below which one branch of the draining
channel of Space 4 passes.

PLATE 17

(*a*)

(*b*)

(*a*) Trench 2, seen from the west at an early stage (prior to the removal of the west baulk), showing the Roman Wall 'a' running from west to east. (*b*) Trench 2, seen from the north showing the Roman Wall 'a' (prior to its removal) running east–west over the Early Bronze Age Wall P (later seen as the east wall of Space 3).

PLATE 18

(a)

(b)

(a) Terrace 1: general view seen from the summit area to the north: Space 3 in the foreground. (b) Terrace 1: general view seen from the west: Space 3 in the centre.

PLATE 19

(a)

(b)

(c)

(a) The terrace area seen from the north-west: Space 1 is on the right; Space 4 in the foreground. (b) Space 1 (of Trench 1,2) seen from the west during excavation. (c) 'Mask-like' object (**EE 251**) in the north-east corner of Space 2 seen from the west.

PLATE 20

(*a*)

(*b*)

(*a*) The main channel of the drain, seen from the north running beneath Wall Γ of Space 3. (*b*) The main channel of the drain seen from the south, running beneath Wall R (below) and Wall Γ (above).

PLATE 21

(a)

(b)

(a) The run-off of the drain from Terrace 1, seen from the south-east. (b) Detail of the drain of Terrace 1: the outer face of Wall A seen from the north.

PLATE 22

(a)

(b)

(a) The drain of Terrace 1 from the west in Space 4, running eastwards along the north of Wall A and of Space 1.
(b) Space 3 seen from above (from the north) showing the line of the drain running southwards.

PLATE 23

(*a*)

(*b*)

(*a*) North-east corner of Space 2 and south-east corner of Space 3 showing wall construction, seen from the south.
(*b*) The east face of Wall P in Space 5, seen from the east.

(*a*)

(*b*)

(*a*) Successive floor surfaces in Space 3, seen from the north (Wall P on the left). (*b*) Floor surface in Space 3, seen from the south against Wall Δ.

PLATE 25

(*a*)

(*b*)

(*a*) Rock Cutting 3 with the north end of Wall P in Space 3 seen from the south at an early stage of excavation.
(*b*) Trench 5 of Terrace 1 seen from the west.

PLATE 26

(a)

(b)

(a) The area of Trench 3 seen from the west prior to excavation. (b) View of Trench 3,1 seen from the north during excavation.

PLATE 27

(*a*)

(*b*)

(*a*) Trench 3,2 from the south-east in the course of excavation. (*b*) Room 2 of Trench 3 seen from west during excavation.

PLATE 28

(*a*)

(*b*)   (*c*)

(*a*) View of Room 2 seen from the north at the end of excavation. (*b*) Trench 3 seen from the east in the course of excavation. (*c*) Trench 3 seen from the west at the conclusion of the excavation (baulk removed).

PLATE 29

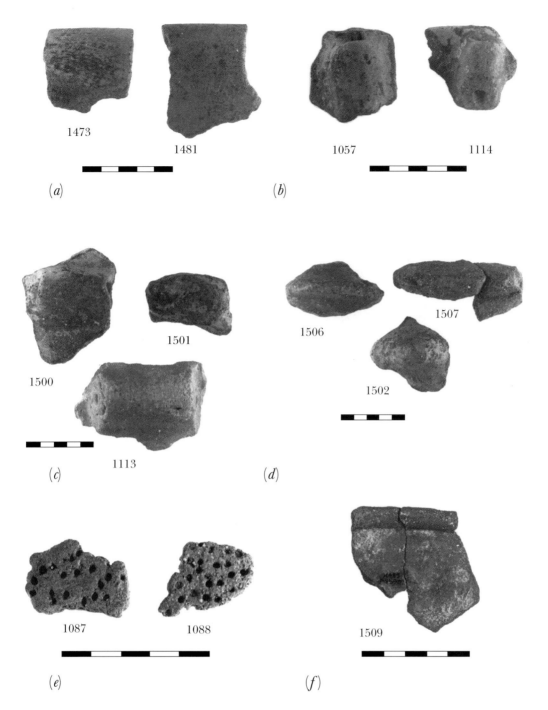

1473

1481

1057

1114

(a)

(b)

1500

1501

1113

1506

1507

1502

(c)

(d)

1087

1088

1509

(e)

(f)

Marble Ware Pottery of (a–e) Markiani phase I and (f) Markiani phase II.

PLATE 30

1597 1073

718

(b)

040 1071

1133

(a)

(c)

1149

1157

1164

1168 1135

(d)

(e)

Pottery of Markiani phase II: (a) incised sherds, (b) miniature vessel fragment, (c) and (d) conical cups, and (e) sherds of Kouphonisi Red Slipped and Burnished Ware.

PLATE 33

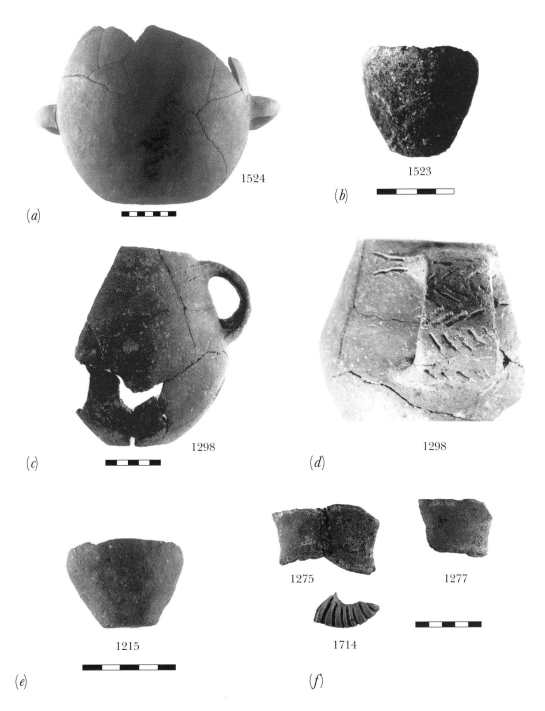

(*a–b*) Vessels from Trench 8, and jug (*c–d*), conical cup (*e*) and sherds (*f*) from Markiani phase III.

PLATE 34

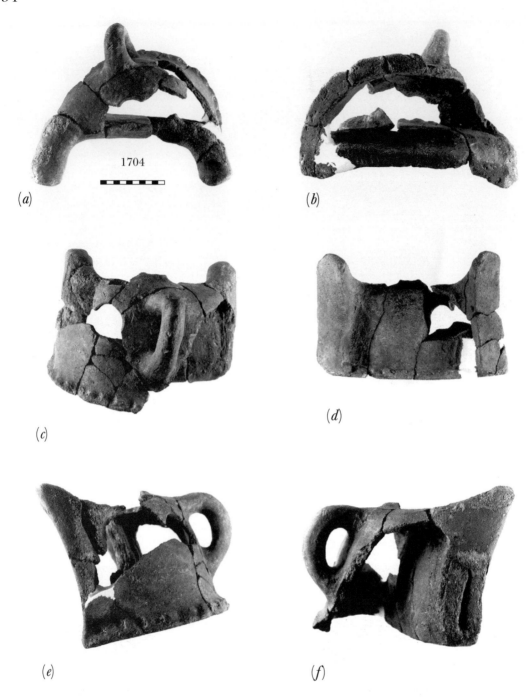

'Mask-like' support or brazier (**K 1704**) of Markiani phase III.

PLATE 35

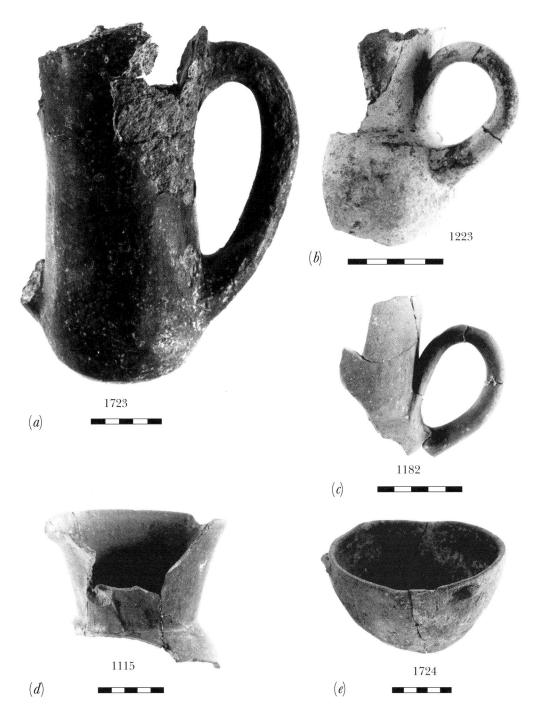

1723

(a)

1223

(b)

1182

(c)

1115

(d)

1724

(e)

Ceramic vessels of Phase IV.

PLATE 36

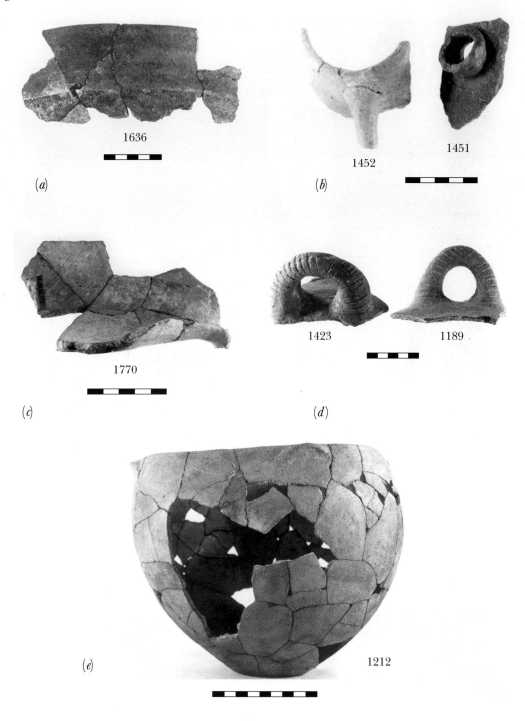

1636

(a)

1452

1451

(b)

1770

(c)

1423

1189

(d)

(e)

1212

Pottery of phase IV including *(b)* sauceboat, *(c)* baking plate and *(e)* bowl with incised fish.

PLATE 37

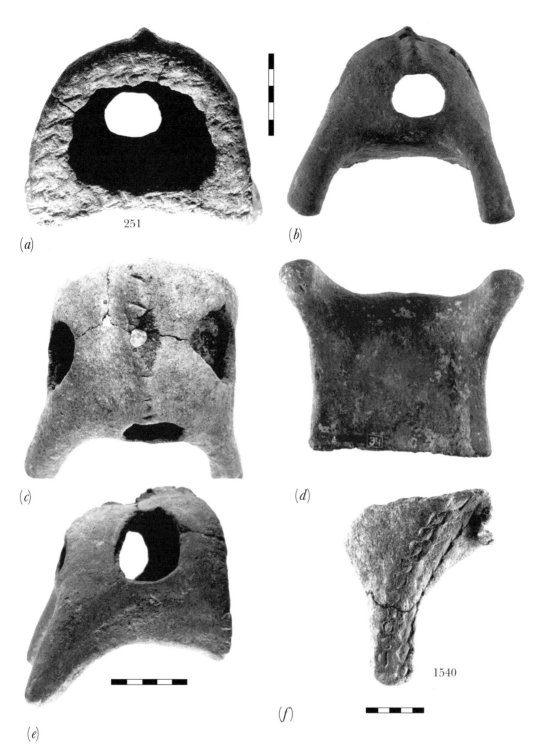

251

(a)

(b)

(c)

(d)

(e)

(f)

1540

Braziers of phase IV: (a–e) **EE 251**; (f) **K 1540**.

PLATE 38

1244

(a)

1229

(b)

1226

1491

1432

1453

(c)

1467

(d)

1710

(e)

1711

(f)

1722

(g)

Incised and painted sherds of phase IV.

PLATE 39

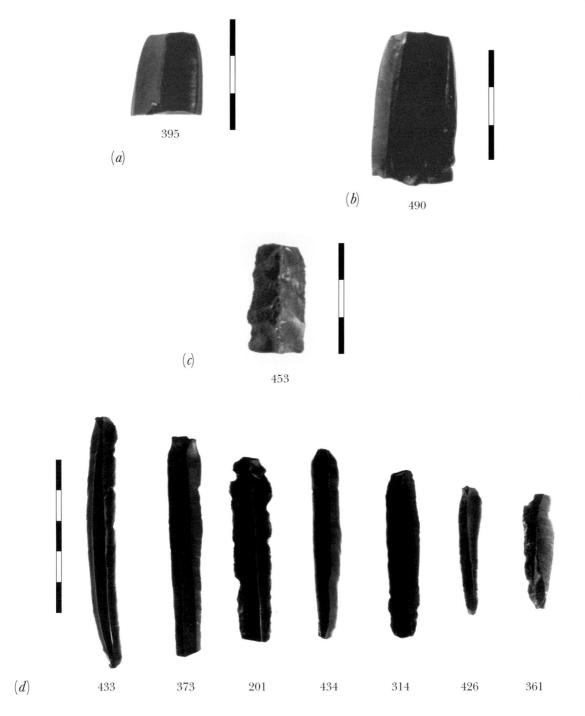

395

(a)

(b)

490

(c)

453

(d)   433   373   201   434   314   426   361

Obsidian tools: (a–b) cores, (c–d) blades.

PLATE 40

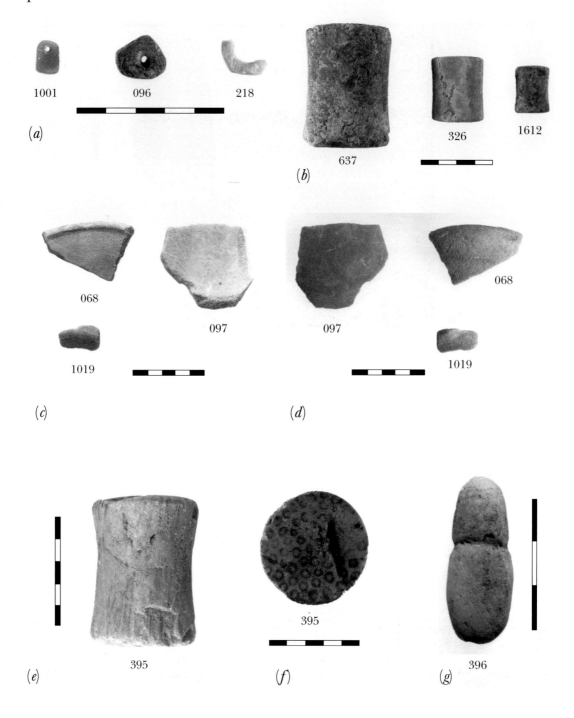

Fine stone objects: (*a*) beads, (*c–d*) marble bowls, (*b*), (*e*) and (*f*) fine pestles and (*g*) figurine.

PLATE 41

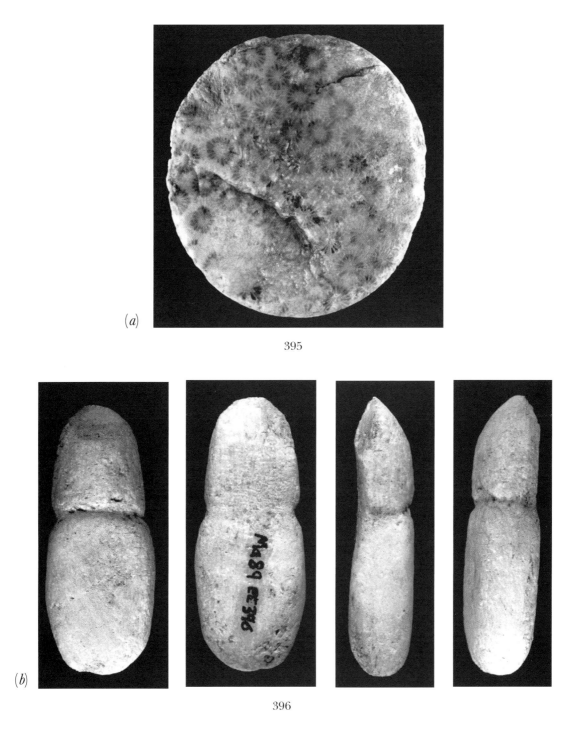

(a)

395

(b)

396

Fine stone objects (see PLATE 40): (a) pestle (**EE 395**), (b–e) figurine (**EE 396**).

PLATE 42

Stone axes (*a–b*), (*c*) hammerstones, (*d*) waisted weights, (*e–f*) small grinders.

PLATE 43

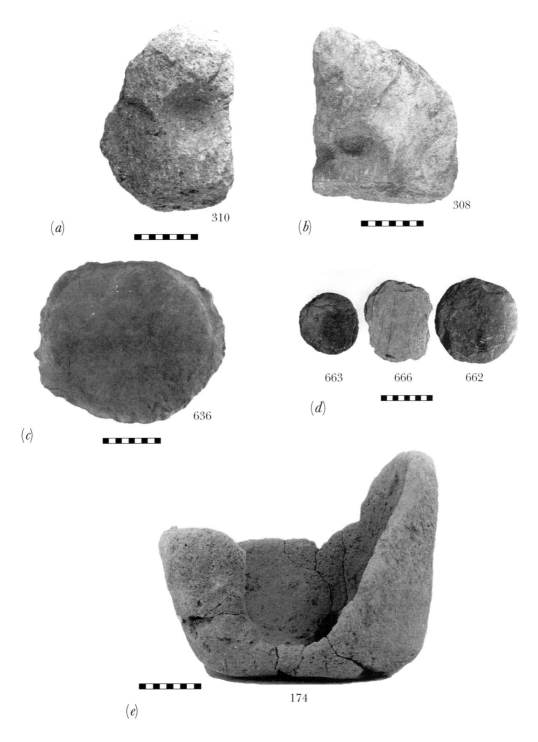

(a) 310

(b) 308

(c) 636

(d) 663 666 662

(e) 174

Coarse stone objects: *(a–b)* sockets, *(c–d)* stone lids, *(e)* large stone vessel.

PLATE 44

(*a*) Mat impression (**K 1350**), and (*b*) plaster cast.

PLATE 45

(*a*)

1350

1341

1340

(*b*)   (*c*)

(*a*) Mat impression (detail of **K 1350**), (*b–c*) cloth impressions.

PLATE 46

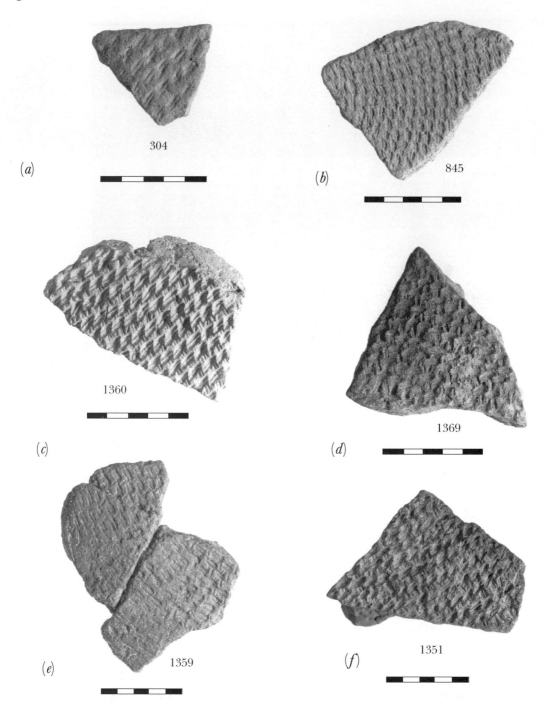

304

(a)

845

(b)

1360

(c)

1369

(d)

1359

(e)

1351

(f)

Mat impressions.

PLATE 47

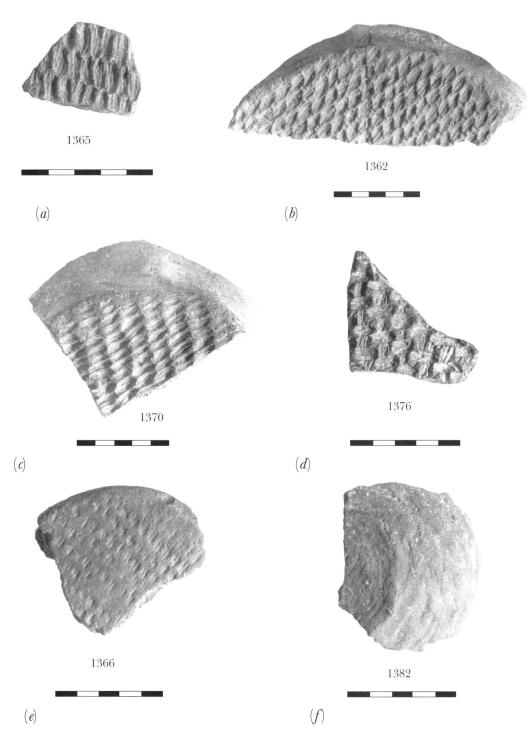

1365

(a)

1362

(b)

1370

(c)

1376

(d)

1366

(e)

1382

(f)

Mat impressions.

PLATE 48

1368

(a)

1368

(b)

1061

(c)

1302

(d)

1068

(e)

1304

(f)

(a) and (b, detail) Mat impressions, (c–f) vine leaf impressions.

PLATE 49

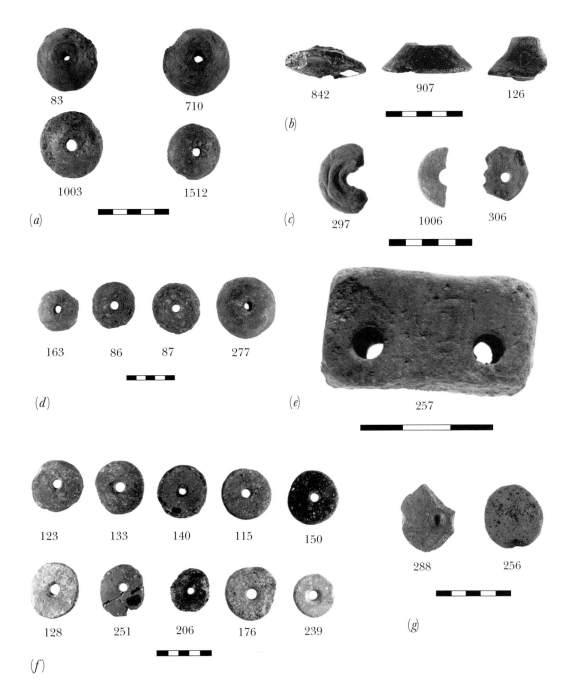

Spindle-whorls: (*a*) and (*b*) conical, (*c*) stone whorls, (*d*) hemispherical whorls, (*e*) perforated parallelpiped object, (*f*) group of perforated sherds and (*g*) partly perforated shaped potsherds.

PLATE 50

219

250

208

178

(a)

(b)

151

266

259

(c)

(d)

(e)

320

310

(f)

(g)

Decorated spindle-whorls.

PLATE 51

709

The terracotta boat model (**EE 709**) seen from above, below and from the side.

PLATE 52

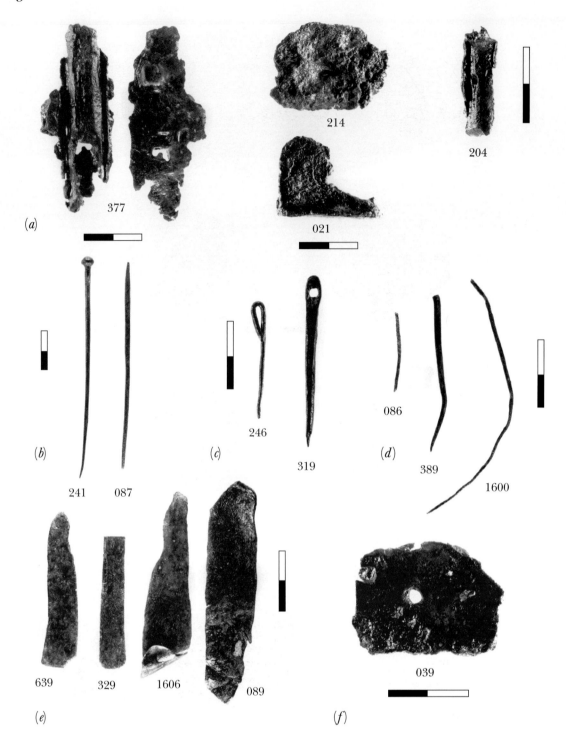

Metal objects: (*a*) of lead, (*b–f*) copper or bronze (note **EE 039**, heel of a dagger with two rivets remaining).

PLATE 53

(a) Lead seal, (b–d) sealings, and (e) seal impression.

PLATE 54

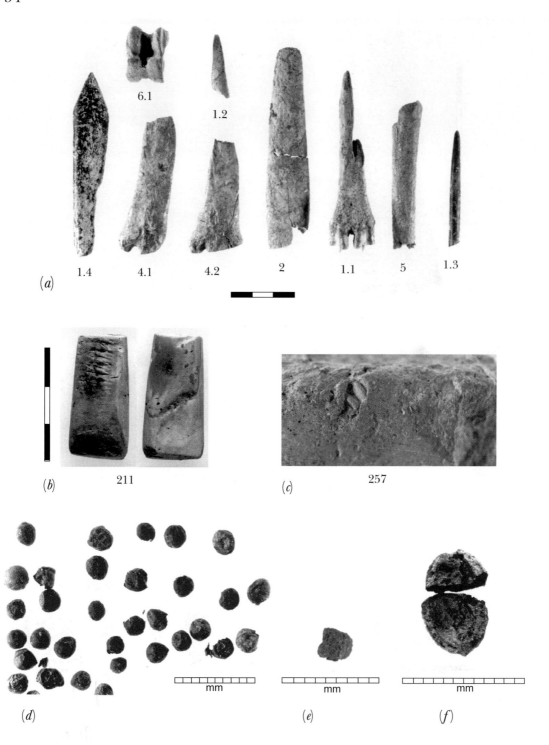

(*a*) Bone artefacts, (*b*) worked shell object, (*c*) barley impression on **EE 257** and carbonised plant remains, (*d*) pulse seeds (*Lathyrus clymenum*), (*e*) bitter vetch (*Vicia ervilia*) and (*f*) olive stone (*Olea europea*).

PLATE 55

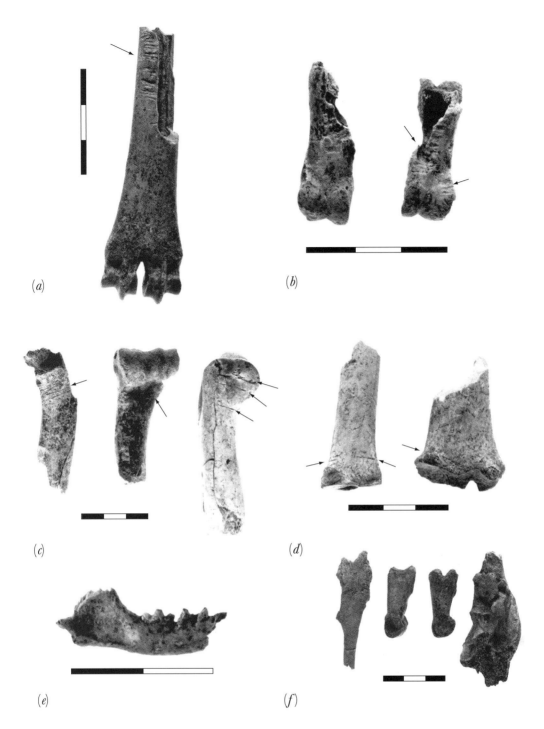

The animal bones (see Appendix to Chapter 9A): (*a*) pattern of breakage, (*b*) modification of proximal phalanges, (*c*) cut marks, (*d*) disjoining, (*e*) mandible fragment of *Mustela*, (*f*) pathological lesion.

PLATE 56

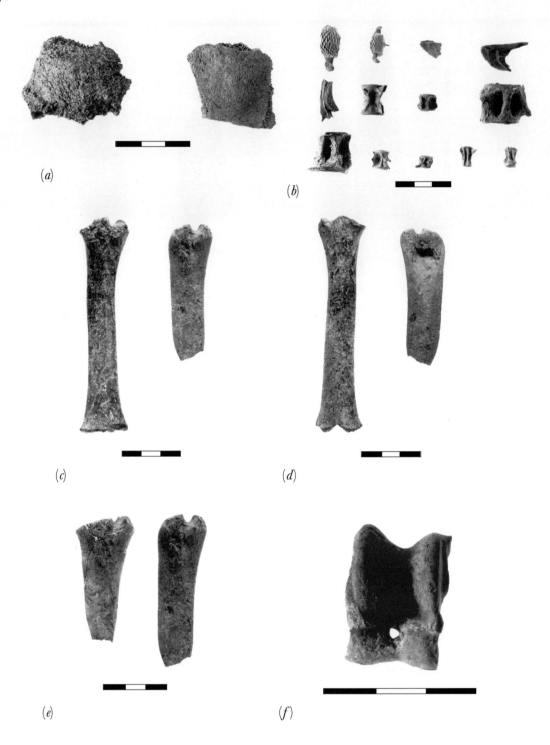

(*a*) Human skull bones, (*b*) fish bones, (*c–e*) bone tools, (*f*) pierced astragalus (see Appendix to Chapter 9A).